SIXTH EDITION

Market-Based Management

Strategies for Growing Customer Value and Profitability

Roger J. Best

Emeritus Professor of Marketing
University of Oregon

PEARSON

Boston   Columbus   Indianapolis   New York   San Francisco   Upper Saddle River
Amsterdam   Cape Town   Dubai   London   Madrid   Milan   Munich   Paris   Montreal   Toronto
Delhi   Mexico City   São Paulo   Sydney   Hong Kong   Seoul   Singapore   Taipei   Tokyo

Editorial Director: Sally Yagan
Acquisitions Editor: Erin Gardner
Director of Product Development: Ashley Santora
Director of Marketing: Maggie Moylan
Executive Marketing Manager: Anne Fahlgren
Senior Managing Editor: Judy Leale
Senior Editorial Project Manager: Kierra Bloom
Editorial Assistant: Anastasia Greene
Production Project Manager: Clara Bartunek
Creative Art Director: Jayne Conte
Cover Designer: Bruce Kenselaar
Manager, Visual Research: Beth Brenzel
Manager, Rights and Permissions: Zina Arabia
Manager, Cover Visual Research & Permissions: Karen Sanatar
Lead Media Project Manager: Lisa Rinaldi
Full-Service Project Management: Kailash Jadli/Aptara®, Inc.
Composition: Aptara®, Inc.
Printer/Binder: Edwards Brothers
Cover Printer: Lehigh-Phoenix Color/Hagerstown
Text Font: Times

Credits and acknowledgments borrowed from other sources and reproduced, with permission, in this textbook appear on appropriate page within text.

Library of Congress Cataloging-in-Publication Data

Best, Roger J.
  Market-based management : strategies for growing customer value and profitability/
Roger J. Best.—6th ed.
    p. cm.
  Includes index.
  ISBN-13: 978-0-13-038775-2
  ISBN-10: 0-13-038775-4
  1. Marketing--Management. I. Title.
HF5415.13.B46 2013
658.8—dc23

                                                        2011037795

10 9 8 7 6 5 4 3 2 1

PEARSON

ISBN 10:   0-13-038775-4
ISBN 13: 978-0-13-038775-2

To Robin, Oliver, Mary, Mike, and Mitchell

CONTENTS

PART II ■ MARKET ANALYSIS   79

CHAPTER 4   THE CUSTOMER EXPERIENCE AND VALUE CREATION   115

CHAPTER 6   COMPETITIVE POSITION AND SOURCES OF ADVANTAGE   191

CHAPTER 9   MARKETING CHANNELS AND CHANNEL MAPPING   305

CHAPTER 10   MARKETING COMMUNICATIONS, SOCIAL MEDIA, AND CUSTOMER RESPONSE   337

PART IV ■ STRATEGIC MARKETING 373

CHAPTER 11 PORTFOLIO ANALYSIS AND STRATEGIC MARKET PLANNING 375

CHAPTER 12 OFFENSIVE STRATEGIES 405

CHAPTER 15   MARKETING METRICS, PERFORMANCE, AND STRATEGY IMPLEMENTATION   493

CHAPTER 16   MARKET-BASED MANAGEMENT AND FINANCIAL PERFORMANCE   517

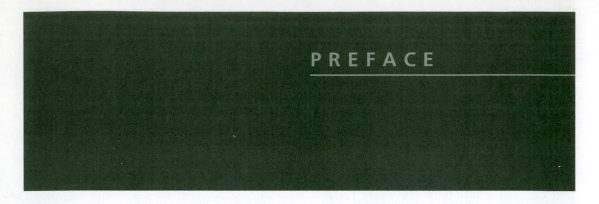

PREFACE

■ **Gains in marketing knowledge without application are missed learning opportunities.**

Dr. Roger J. Best

On the basis of positive feedback from students, professors, and those working in the field of marketing, I was encouraged to continue to build on the philosophy of learning through the application of knowledge with this sixth edition of *Market-Based Management.* The book's strength lies in its focus on processes and tools for building marketing strategies that deliver superior levels of customer satisfaction, value, and profitability. The main differentiating feature of the book is its emphasis on marketing performance and on the role that marketing strategies play in building the profits of a business. The central theme is that the best way to improve profitability is with market-driven strategies that attract, satisfy, and retain target customers with a value that is superior to that of competing products or services.

Changes in the sixth edition underscore this theme in several ways. Special efforts were made to include meaningful coverage of marketing profitability, branding strategies, product line strategies, customer value, value pricing, social media marketing, and the influence of technology on market potential. This edition's discussions of marketing communications and customer response have also been extensively revised, mostly in response to developments in digital media. Other changes include new strategic marketing examples, a new 3-year Stericycle Sample Marketing Plan, and a revised presentation on how to get started using marketing metrics. The online Marketing Performance Tools and Application Exercises continue to be an important part of the book. They give students and others a degree of practical experience by engaging them in performance-based marketing simulations.

Market-based management is seemingly difficult but intuitively easy. The reason marketing students and marketing professionals like this book is because it is readable and it presents the tools and processes needed to actually build a market-driven strategy. The concepts, by themselves, are important and are the backbone of market-based management. However, they are of limited value if they cannot be applied in a way that delivers superior customer value and profitability. Those in marketing need to take a greater level of responsibility for managing profits and the external performance metrics of a business. It is my hope that this new edition of *Market-Based Management* will help achieve that goal, and I hope that it will also help you in your understanding of, commitment to, and practice of market-based management.

Roger J. Best
Emeritus Professor of Marketing
University of Oregon

What's new in the sixth edition of *Market-Based Management: Strategies for Growing Customer Value and Profitability*:

MODIFICATIONS, ADDITIONS, AND IMPROVEMENTS

Part I: Market Orientation and Marketing Performance

Chapter 1: Customer Focus, Customer Performance, and Profit Impact

- "American Customer Satisfaction Index" is a new section, and new Figures 1-2 and 1-4 have been added. The section demonstrates how companies with higher levels of customer satisfaction achieve higher stock price appreciation.
- "Building a Strong Customer Focus" is a new section, and new Figure 1-3 is added, with three major categories for building a stronger customer focus, each category with three actionable areas of marketing management.
- A discussion of dissatisfied customer revenge and the use of social media is a new addition. It includes ways that customers and companies use social media.
- The section "Customer Loyalty" (see especially Figures 1-13 to 1-17) is revised and presents a much simpler method of managing customer loyalty and profitability.

Chapter 2: Marketing Metrics and Marketing Profitability

- A new section, "Marketing Metrics," which demonstrates why marketing analytics and marketing metrics are important, has been added, along with new Figures 2-3, 2-5, and 2-8. This section also has a new discussion on forward-looking and backward-looking performance metrics and their role in market-based performance management.
- Figure 2-12 is new. The data it shows for seven major companies provide a way to estimate marketing and sales expenses for companies that do not report these expenses separately.
- The section entitled "Benchmarking Marketing Profitability" is revised. New Figure 2-22 benchmarks Apple's marketing profitability to operating income, and new Figure 2-23 illustrates the benchmarking of Apple with its major competitors on the basis of marketing ROS, marketing ROI, and operating income (as a percentage of sales).
- A new section, "Benchmarking Company Marketing Profitability Metrics," is added. New Figure 2-24 plots the relationship between marketing ROS and operating income, and between marketing ROI and operating income, for a sampling of major companies.

Part II: Market Analysis

Chapter 3: Market Potential, Market Demand, and Market Share

- A section entitled "How Innovation Changes Market Potential" was added, with presentations of continuous, disruptive, and discontinuous innovations, as illustrated in new Figure 3-4.
- The forces that limit full development of a product's market potential have been expanded from five to seven and now include *unrecognized need* and *hard to use* as barriers to reaching full market potential.
- The section entitled "Market Share Performance Metrics" has been expanded and now includes a discussion on building a share performance tree. Figure 3-16 shows a share performance tree with the share performance metrics typically used in figuring the

market share index and determining the amount of share leakage at the various levels of the tree. Figure 3-17 addresses the relationship between the market share index and the actual market share.

Chapter 4: The Customer Experience and Value Creation

■ The section "Total Customer Experience" is revised and now presents, along with new Figure 4-1, a new example of a company that is dedicated to improving the customer experience.

■ An expanded section now entitled "Mass Collaboration and Crowdsourcing" includes examples of the ways companies make use of the collective input of customers and experts to improve both products and the customer experience and to create customer value.

■ The section entitled "Life-Cycle Cost and Customer Value" has a revised discussion of the total cost of ownership, with a new example of a company that uses its web site to let customers compare the ownership costs of company products against those of competitors, as shown in new Figure 4-14.

■ In the section entitled "Price-Performance and Value Creation," a new method of estimating the customer value for products has been added. New Figures 4-16 and 4-17 illustrate this process for 10 digital cameras.

■ The discussion of relative performance has a new example of a product that offers superior value. New Figure 4-18 uses *Consumer Reports'* ratings of 61 computer printers in a price and relative performance value map.

■ A new marketing performance tool and application exercise was added to the section "Marketing Performance Tools and Application Exercises" for the customer value methodology presented in Figure 4-17.

Chapter 5: Market Segmentation and Segmentation Strategies

■ An examination of the importance of Millennials, with reference to a YouTube video, has been added. New Figure 5-1 illustrates the significance that this age-based segment has for marketing professionals.

■ In the discussion of forces that shape consumer market needs, an example of needs-based market segmentation ("Toothpaste Market Segmentation") is added. Four market segments are discussed, and new Figure 5-6 presents a summary description of each segment.

■ A revised discussion of adjacent-segment strategy places Toyota's strategy in its historical context. Revised Figure 5-17 maps Toyota products with respect to their first years of production and their relative levels of perceived quality and price.

Chapter 6: Competitive Position and Sources of Advantage

■ Added to the section entitled "Competitive Advantage" are three examples of companies with either a cost, differentiation, or marketing advantage. For these companies, new Figure 6-3 shows the results of key metrics for financial performance, asset management, and marketing performance.

■ In the discussion of market share advantage, a revision includes search engines as examples, and revised Figure 6-12 compares their relative market shares.

■ In the revised discussion of a sample competitor analysis, five competing airlines are used for the analysis. New Figure 6-19 benchmarks the marketing and financial performance of Southwest Airlines relative to four competitors.

- Figure 6-20 is new. It offers a broad view of the performance of five competing airlines by benchmarking against 200 Fortune 500 companies with respect to marketing ROS, marketing ROI, and operating income as a percentage of sales.

Part III: Marketing Mix Strategies

Chapter 7: Product Positioning, Branding, and Product Line Strategies

- In the chapter introduction and in the section entitled "Brand Expansion Strategies," Starbucks is presented as a new example of a company that plans to expand its branding to additional markets.
- In the discussion of product positioning, a new business-to-business positioning strategy for an industrial product is presented, along with new Figure 7-3. New Figure 7-5 depicts the repositioning strategy of a major consumer electronics company.
- New Figure 7-9, in the discussion of product performance and differentiation, presents the product differentiation and pricing of General Electric appliances.
- New Figure 7-11, in the discussion of service quality and differentiation, uses Les Schwab Tire Centers as an example of a company whose service quality is a source of differentiation.
- New Figure 7-12, in the discussion of branding and brand management strategies, lists nine brand-encoding strategies with examples.
- Figures 7-13 through 7-17 are new, comprehensive examples of company branding strategies.
- The chapter has a new section entitled "Protecting Your Brand Name and Intellectual Property." New Figure 7-19 illustrates the branding of a new product, and new Figure 7-20 presents images of examples discussed in the text.

Chapter 8: Value-Based Pricing and Pricing Strategies

- The chapter's new introduction has a chart that presents the results of a price survey of Mac and PC users, and the text contrasts Apple's new-product pricing strategy for the iPad with that of the iPod. New Figure 8-1 presents the iPod's product positioning, branding, and customer value.
- A new section entitled "Cost-Based Pricing: Overpricing and Lower Profits" has an expanded discussion of this topic, and new Figures 8-3 and 8-4 contrast cost-based pricing with market-based pricing and illustrate the consequences of cost-based under- and overpricing.
- In the section entitled "Life-Cycle Value Pricing," the revised discussion presents the net present value of a customer's total cost of purchase as a new value-pricing tool. New Figure 8-7 provides an example of this value-based pricing concept.
- The chapter has a new section entitled "Customerization Value Pricing" that uses the purchase of a laptop computer as an example in the discussion and in new Figures 8-13 and 8-14. The section covers a product's full-feature reference price and the advantages of a top-down, as opposed to a bottom-up, price presentation.
- The discussion of multi-segment pricing has been revised and includes two new examples of companies that use this form of pricing. New Figures 8-19 and 8-20 illustrate multi-segment pricing strategies used by General Electric and Comcast.

Chapter 9: Marketing Channels and Channel Mapping

■ A new introduction presents Cisco Systems' marketing channel collaboration tools: what they are, how Cisco uses them, and how they increase sales, lower costs, and reduce problem-solving time for companies, channel partners, and customers. The chart and table in the introduction and Figure 9-1 are new.

■ A new section entitled "Channel Value Proposition" discusses why companies need a value proposition not only for customers, but for channel intermediaries.

■ The discussion of business-to-consumer and business-to-business channels has been revised in a new section entitled "Consumer and Business Channels." New Figure 9-6 shows the B2C and B2B marketing channels used by technology companies. Channel financing to improve channel liquidity and grow channel partner sales is described, and new Figure 9-7 serves as an illustration of channel financing.

■ In the section entitled "Alternative Marketing Channels," the discussion of indirect channels presents the worldwide channel strategy used by Yum Brands. New Figure 9-14 lists the company's major brands, the number of countries served by each brand, and the number of U.S. and international outlets.

Chapter 10: Marketing Communications, Social Media, and Customer Response

■ A new introduction discusses Volkswagen's strategy for a television and YouTube commercial that the company produced for the 2011 Super Bowl. An image includes a screenshot of the commercial and summarizes the company's strategy.

■ A new section entitled "Marketing Communications and Customer Response" covers the three major types of marketing communications: brand-image, brand-information, and brand-action communications. New Figures 10-1 through 10-4 present examples.

■ The chapter has a new section entitled "Digital Marketing Communications," with supporting examples in new Figures 10-5 and 10-6.

■ A new section entitled "Social Media Marketing Communications" highlights the use of Facebook, YouTube, Twitter, LinkedIn, and blogs. New Figures 10-7 through 10-12 illustrate many of the ways that companies use social media marketing communications.

■ The section entitled "Pull Communications and Customer Response" presents new material on the relationship between advertising and sales. The discussion uses Hart Schaffner Marx as an example to illustrate the strength of the relationship, as well as to shed light on advertising elasticity and advertising carryover effects.

Part IV: Strategic Marketing

Chapter 11: Portfolio Analysis and Strategic Market Planning

■ A new introduction presents a company portfolio example that illustrates Yum Brands' five store brands (KFC, Taco Bell, Pizza Hut, A&W, and Long John Silver's) with respect to segment share (competitive position) and opportunity for growth (market attractiveness).

■ In the section entitled "Portfolio Analysis and Strategic Marketing," Figure 11-1 and the accompanying discussion are new. They present the changes in Toyota's U.S. product portfolio from 1964 to 2010.

■ In the section entitled "Marketing Mix Strategy and Performance Plan," revised Figure 11-20 presents Zi-Tech's performance plan for the company's four product markets.

Chapter 12: Strategic Offensive Strategies

■ A new introduction discusses Apple's offensive strategies for growing sales with innovative additions to its product portfolio from 2005 to 2010. The introduction includes a chart ("Product Growth Portfolio") and a performance table.

■ A new section entitled "Apple's Product Portfolio and Offensive Growth" continues the introductory discussion. New Figure 12-1 illustrates Apple's product life-cycle portfolio and presents data on product sales.

■ A new section entitled "When Growth Stalls" discusses how strategically offensive companies rebound from a sales stall after a long period of sales growth. New Figures 12-10 and 12-11 use the experiences of Fortune 500 companies to illustrate what happens after a sales stall. Starbucks is held up as an example of a company that adopted an offensive growth strategy after a stall. New Figure 12-12 shows Starbucks' growth and profitability from 2005 to 2009.

Chapter 13: Strategic Defensive Strategies

■ A new introduction presents General Motors' defensive strategic market plan that included the restructuring of its product portfolio in 2010. New images in the introduction show GM's brand portfolio (before and after brand reorganization), the company's performance from 2006 to 2010, the company's defensive plan in the context of a product life-cycle portfolio, and the relationship between the company's operating income and marketing profits.

Part V: Marketing Plans and Performance

Chapter 14: Building a Marketing Plan

■ The Stericycle Sample Marketing Plan (Figures 14-5, 14-9, and 14-13) is updated and includes a forecast of sales and marketing profits for 2013. As each new edition of this book is published, a new sample marketing plan has been created that allows for a comparison of planned performance against actual performance in the chapter's introduction.

■ A new situation analysis was conducted for Stericycle on the basis of the company's 2010 performance and information presented in its 2010 annual report. Figure 14-5 (six pages) is revised with new text, charts, graphs, and tables.

■ Figure 14-13 (six pages), which presents the sample plan's new marketing strategies, is revised with new text, charts, graphs, and tables.

■ A new performance plan was conducted for Stericycle on the basis of the revised situation analysis and the new marketing strategies. Figure 14-13 (five pages) is revised with new text, charts, graphs, and tables.

Chapter 15: Marketing Metrics, Performance, and Strategy Implementation

■ A new introduction discusses the improvement in marketing profitability by four companies following a series of marketing metrics training programs. The average increase in marketing profitability was over 30 percent.

■ In the section entitled "Marketing Metrics and Performance," new Figure 15-1 shows a web site that provides access to information, training, and other resources related to marketing metrics, including a *Marketing Metrics Handbook*.

■ The chapter has a new section entitled "Forward-Looking versus Backward-Looking Metrics." New Figure 15-6 presents the results of a key forward-looking marketing metric (customer satisfaction), and new Figure 15-7 presents the results of a key backward-looking marketing metric (customer retention).

Chapter 16: Market-Based Management and Financial Performance

■ The introduction has been revised to include Stericycle's 2010 financial and marketing profitability performance. A new chart illustrates Stericycle's performance relative to that of Fortune 500 companies with respect to marketing ROI and operating income as a percentage of sales.

■ In the section entitled "Financial Impact of Marketing Profitability," new Figure 16-1 illustrates the high correlation between Stericycle's net marketing contribution and operating income from 2000 to 2010.

■ All Stericycle marketing and financial performance metrics discussed in the chapter were updated on the basis of 2010 results presented in the Stericycle 2010 annual report.

■ In the section entitled "Shareholder Metrics," new Figure 16-12 provides an estimate of marketing profits, earnings per share, and Stericycle's stock price for 2011, 2012, and 2013.

INSTRUCTIONAL SUPPORT

Supplements are available for instructors to download at www.pearsonhighered.com/irc. The site includes detailed descriptions of the supplements. Registration is simple and gives the instructor immediate access to new titles and new editions. Pearson's dedicated technical support team is ready to help instructors with the media supplements that accompany this text. The instructor should visit http://247.pearsoned.com/ for answers to frequently asked questions and for toll-free user support phone numbers. Supplements include the following:

■ Instructor's Manual
■ Test Item File and TestGen software
■ PowerPoint Set
■ Online Marketing Performance Tools
■ MBM Blog
■ ˈMBM Sample Marketing Plan

CourseSmart Textbooks were developed for students looking to save on required or recommended textbooks. Students simply select their eText by title or author and purchase immediate access to the content for the duration of the course, using any major credit card. With a CourseSmart eText, students can search for specifi c keywords or page numbers, take notes online, print out reading assignments that incorporate lecture notes, and bookmark important passages for later review. For more information or to purchase a CourseSmart eTextbook, visit www.coursesmart.com.

ABOUT THE AUTHOR

Roger Best is an Emeritus Professor of Marketing at the University of Oregon. He earned a Bachelor of Science in Electrical Engineering from California State Polytechnic University and, following graduation, joined the General Electric Company where he worked in engineering, product management, and marketing. While at GE, he received a patent and completed his M.B.A. at California State University, Hayward. He went on to obtain a Ph.D. in Business from the University of Oregon while continuing to work with GE in corporate consulting and marketing education. He taught at the University of Arizona from 1975 to 1980 and the University of Oregon until 2000.

Over the past 35 years, he has published more than 50 articles and won numerous teaching awards. He is the coauthor of *Consumer Behavior* (10th ed.). In 1998, he received the American Marketing Association's Distinguished Teaching in Marketing Award. In 1988, the Academy of Marketing Science voted an article on marketing productivity by Del Hawkins, Roger Best, and Charles Lillis as the Outstanding Article of the Year. Dr. Best developed the Marketing Excellence Survey, an assessment tool used to benchmark the marketing knowledge of marketing managers, and MarkPlan, a software program for building performance-driven marketing plans. Both of these products are now owned and operated by the Corporate Executive Board Company.

Dr. Best has also worked extensively with a variety of companies in marketing consulting and executive education. These companies include 3M, General Electric, Dow Chemical, Dow Corning, DuPont, Eastman Kodak, Hewlett-Packard, Lucas Industries, Tektronix, Textron, ESCO, Pacific Western Pipe, James Hardie Industries, and many others. He has also taught many executive management education programs at INSEAD, Fontainebleau, France.

ACKNOWLEDGMENTS

A book such as this is an assimilation of knowledge from many sources. It is an integration of perspectives intended for a particular audience. An author's added value is in the focus, integration, and presentation, but the basic knowledge is derived from many sources. I would like to acknowledge specific individuals whose knowledge contributed to my understanding of marketing and shaped many of the ideas presented in this sixth edition of *Market-Based Management*. These individuals include Stewart Bither, George Day, Del Hawkins, Jean-Claude Larreche, and Charles Lillis.

Second, I would like to acknowledge the valuable feedback I received from the following reviewers for the sixth edition. Their thoughtful reviews and suggestions for improvement are appreciated and greatly enhanced this edition.

Mary Albrecht, Maryville University

Richard (Mike) Dailey, University of Texas at Arlington

Brent Goff, University of Houston–Downtown

Chickery Kasouf, Worcester Polytechnic Institute

Norm Mcelvany, Johnson State College

Chip Miller, Drake University

Julianne Pfister, Fashion Institute of Los Angeles

Lucille Pointer, University of Houston–Downtown

Jason (Qiyu) Zhang, Loyola University

The sixth edition would not have been possible without the painstaking support and thoughtful assistance of Robert Lofft. His participation and contributions were critical to every aspect of this edition and are greatly appreciated. I would also like to acknowledge Peter Vomocil, a valued colleague who provided insightful guidance throughout this revision and helped extensively with the social media and digital marketing additions to the sixth edition. Finally, my wife, Robin, deserves a great deal of credit for enduring my ups and downs in writing one more edition of *Market-Based Management*.

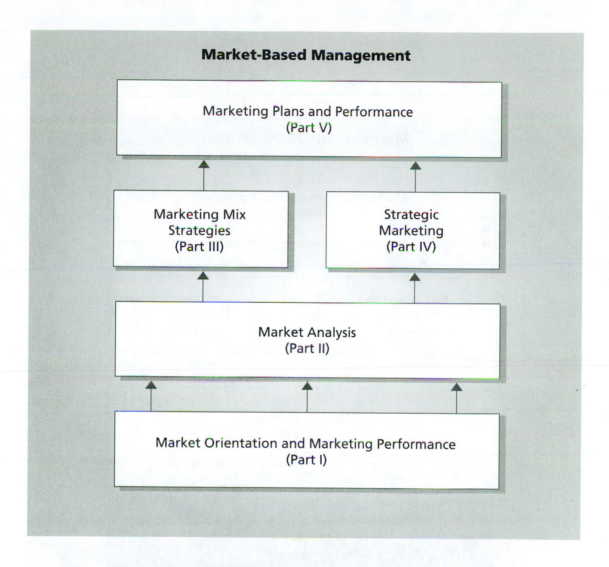

Market-Based Management

Marketing Plans and Performance
(Part V)

Marketing Mix
Strategies
(Part III)

Strategic
Marketing
(Part IV)

Market Analysis
(Part II)

Market Orientation and Marketing Performance
(Part I)

This model represents both the logic of market-based management and the organization of this book. Market Orientation and Marketing Performance (Part I) are the bedrock of market-based management and foster a Market Analysis (Part II) built around customer needs, market trends, and competition.

A commitment to a market orientation and ongoing market analysis allow the development of focused Marketing Mix Strategies (Part III) and Strategic Marketing (Part IV). Marketing Plans and Performance (Part V) are the culmination of this process.

Successful implementation of this process improves customer value, which in turn enhances customer satisfaction, customer loyalty, and profitability.

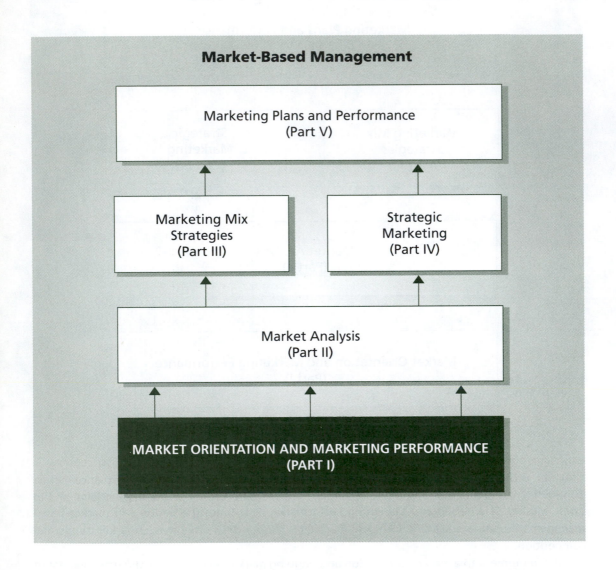

Market-Based Management

Marketing Plans and Performance
(Part V)

Marketing Mix
Strategies
(Part III)

Strategic
Marketing
(Part IV)

Market Analysis
(Part II)

MARKET ORIENTATION AND MARKETING PERFORMANCE
(PART I)

Market Orientation and Marketing Performance

■ Being market-driven means that everything done by everyone in the company is driven by the needs of the target market(s) you serve.[*]

A market-based business has a strong market orientation that all functions and employees of the organization reflect. Whereas the marketing personnel have the primary responsibility for creating marketing excellence, in a market-based business all members of the organization are market oriented. All members are sensitive to customers' needs, are aware of competitors' moves, and work well across the organization's structure toward a timely market-based customer solution. What's the payoff? Market-based businesses are more profitable.

Part I demonstrates the connectivity that exists among market orientation, customer satisfaction, profitability, and market-based management. Chapter 1 examines the fundamental components of a market orientation and explores how each is related to customer satisfaction and retention. From this perspective, we will calculate the profit impact of customer life,

as well as the high cost of customer dissatisfaction. We will see that a strong market orientation is intended primarily to improve a business's chances for long-run survival, but marketing efforts to improve customer satisfaction and retention also can increase short-run profits.

A strong market orientation cannot be created by mere proclamation. To attain a strong market orientation, a business needs to adopt a market-based management philosophy. The organization restructures itself around markets rather than products or factories, and it develops an employee culture responsive to customers and changing market conditions. Market-based management also requires a business to use marketing performance metrics to measure profits at the market level and to track a variety of other market-related performance indicators. These topics and their relation to marketing strategies and profitable growth are discussed in Chapter 2.

[*]M. Frichol, "Marketing in a 'Market-Driven' Company," *The Marketing Mélange,* http://marketing.infocat.com/2009/02/marketing-in-market-driven-company.html, retrieved February 12, 2009.

Customer Focus, Customer Performance, and Profit Impact

■ Customer satisfaction is a leading indicator of company financial performance.[1]
— *American Customer Satisfaction Index, University of Michigan*

CUSTOMER SATISFACTION AND PROFITABILITY

"Very satisfied" customers have the greatest impact on profitability. Although results vary by industry, "very satisfied" customers often account for a major portion of a business's profits, as illustrated in the bar chart.

Managing dissatisfied customers is equally important, as dissatisfied customers are often unprofitable and likely to share their dissatisfaction. Social networking sites and other Internet communication channels make it easier than ever for dissatisfied customers to share their experiences with large numbers of other individuals.

In today's globally competitive world, customers expect more, have more choices, and are less brand loyal. Sears, Eastman Kodak, and General Motors are examples of companies that at one time seemed invincible in terms of their market domination. Each of these companies had to restructure (reengineer) its organization to address changing customer needs and emerging competitive forces. In the long run, the survival of every business is at risk. Although companies such as Intel, Dell, Microsoft, and Wal-Mart were business heroes of the 1990s, and Google, Apple, and Netflix were heroes of the 2000s, there is no guarantee that these same companies will continue to dominate over the next decade. The only constant is change:

- Customers will continue to change in needs, demographics, lifestyle, and consumption behavior.
- Competitors will continue to change as new technologies emerge and barriers to foreign competition shift.
- The environment in which businesses operate will continue to change as economic, political, social, and technological forces shift.

The companies that survive and grow will be the ones that understand change and that lead or create change. Others that are slower to comprehend change will follow with reactive strategies, while still others will disappear, unaware that change was even occurring.

CUSTOMER FOCUS AND PROFITABILITY

Businesses that have embedded a strong customer focus into their business culture are forward looking and experience continuous improvement as a result of their passion to fully understand the customer experience. Customer-focused businesses are in synch with customers' needs, competitors' strategies, changing environmental conditions, and emerging technologies, and they seek ways to continuously improve the customer solutions they bring to target customers. This process enables them to move with—and often lead—change.

The major benefit of a strong customer focus is long-run survival. Western cultures have long been criticized for their extremely short-term perspective. A business with a short-term perspective usually lacks a strong customer focus and is less motivated to build long-term customer relationships as a primary management goal. Managers are often judged on last quarter's results and not on their efforts to ensure the long-run survival of the business. Likewise, shareholders are more interested in immediate earnings than in long-run survival.

Although the long-run benefits of a strong customer focus are crucial to business survival and to the nation's economic health, the purpose of this chapter is to demonstrate both the short-run and long-run benefits of a strong customer focus. Businesses with a strong customer focus not only outperform their competition over the long term by consistently delivering higher levels of customer satisfaction, they also realize higher profits over the short term. A customer-focused business creates greater customer value and manages customer loyalty as a way to create above-average profits and greater shareholder value. A strong customer focus and market orientation also create a market-measurement culture in which a business uses a wide variety of marketing performance metrics to measure external conditions related to the business's marketing performance and profitability.[2]

How to Underwhelm Customers and Shareholders

Perhaps the best way to understand the marketing logic that links customer focus to shareholder value is to examine the sequence of events that occurs when a business has little or no customer focus. A business with a weak customer focus underwhelms both customers and shareholders. It has only a superficial understanding of customer needs and the competition.

FIGURE 1-1 UNDERWHELMING CUSTOMERS AND SHAREHOLDERS

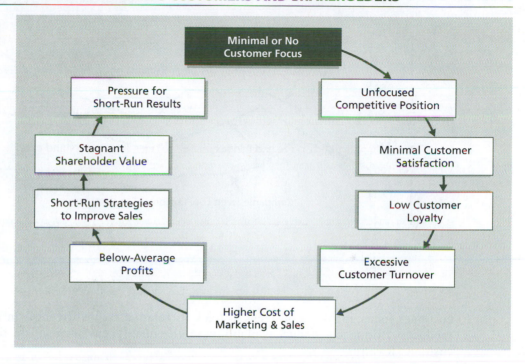

Moving clockwise from the top in Figure 1-1, we can see that little or no customer focus translates into an unfocused competitive position and minimal customer satisfaction. The result is a low level of customer loyalty because customers are easily attracted to competitors, which lowers customer retention. Marketing efforts designed to minimize customer switching are expensive, as are efforts to acquire new customers to replace lost customers.[3] Low levels of customer loyalty and higher marketing costs contribute to disappointing profits. In response, the company implements short-term sales tactics and accounting maneuvers to bolster short-run financial results. But investors and Wall Street analysts are able to see through these facades, and shareholder value generally stagnates. Perhaps even worse, managers come under greater pressure to produce short-run profits, diminishing their time and motivation to understand customer needs and unravel competitors' strategies. The result is a vicious circle of poor performance.

Customer Focus, Customer Satisfaction, and Profitability

In contrast with the situation presented in Figure 1-1, a business that has a strong customer focus stays in close contact with customers in an effort to deliver a high level of customer satisfaction and build customer loyalty. Marketing strategies in these businesses are centered on meeting customer needs and achieving customer satisfaction. The strength of a business's customer focus also depends on how well it understands key competitors and evolving competitive forces. This aspect of

FIGURE 1-2 STOCK PRICE INDEX AND CUSTOMER SATISFACTION

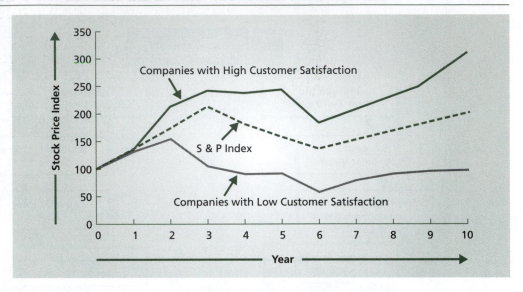

customer focus enables a business to track its relative competitiveness in pricing, product performance, product availability, service quality, customer satisfaction, and customer loyalty.

American Customer Satisfaction Index

The American Customer Satisfaction Index (ACSI) provides an excellent customer satisfaction database from which managers can gain important insights. It measures customer satisfaction for over 200 companies in 43 industries. The ACSI company database may be used to place companies into four classes according to their level of customer satisfaction and improvements in their customer satisfaction index. To show the great impact of customer satisfaction on profit, Figure 1-2 illustrates how the stock price index varies for companies with high and low levels of customer satisfaction.[4]

For each company, a stock price index was created in year 1 based on the company's end-of-year stock price. This way, all companies have the same starting stock price index of 100. The average stock price index for high-customer-satisfaction companies increased from 100 to roughly 300 in 10 years. For the portfolio of companies with low customer satisfaction, the average stock price index ended slightly below where it had started 10 years earlier. The S&P 500 stock price index for the same period of time increased from 100 to roughly 200.

A strong customer focus and a high level of customer satisfaction contribute to a high level of customer loyalty. Keeping good customers is the first priority of market-based managers. A business with a strong customer focus is well positioned to develop and implement strategies that deliver high levels of customer satisfaction and loyalty. In turn, customer satisfaction and loyalty drive customer profitability. We will see in this chapter that very satisfied, loyal customers are the ones who shape the profitability of a business.

FIGURE 1-3 CUSTOMER FOCUS, CUSTOMER PERFORMANCE, AND PROFITABILITY

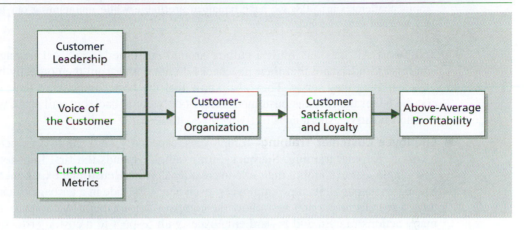

Building a Strong Customer Focus

A strong customer focus is built from the top down and includes all employees in the organization. As shown in Figure 1-3, customer leadership, attention to the voice of the customer, and the use of customer metrics are the driving forces that underlie a business with a strong customer focus. Each of these key forces is associated with behaviors and practices that individually contribute to a customer focus and customer satisfaction. Leadership, organizational training, a customer measurement mentality, and some level of investment are required to bring about full acceptance of the key forces of a customer focus across a business. The extent to which a business lives by these behaviors and practices determines its performance and the profit benefits that a strong customer focus can achieve.

Customer Leadership

Customer leadership is essential to a strong customer focus. Although customer leadership starts at the top, it is important for all managers and employees to be engaged in a customer focus and realize that they have a job because customers buy the company's products. It is very simple. If customers stop buying, jobs start disappearing. A company may take various approaches in making a strong customer focus part of its culture, but we believe that senior management leadership, employee customer training, and customer involvement are essential parts of customer leadership. A brief explanation of each with regard to "best practices" follows.

- **Senior Management Leadership**—It always starts at the top. Senior management sets the tone with respect to a company's customer focus. If senior managers are not fully committed to a strong customer focus, it is unlikely that the rest of the organization will adopt one. Lower-level managers and employees have an internal compass that senses what is important and what is not important. Senior management sets the tone and sends the signals. This view is evident in the following excerpt from a letter to shareholders that appeared in the *Southwest Airlines 2008 Annual Report*:

  To attract new and retain loyal customers, we launched a new and innovative boarding system, coupled with a Business Select product offering, and improved the customer airport experience. The customer response has been overwhelmingly favorable. So, despite enormous challenges in 2008, we have remained profitable while maintaining our legacy of Culture and Customer Service.[5]

Southwest Airlines has built a culture around customer focus. All managers and employees understand that their paychecks do not come from the company but from the customers they serve. They also know that the better they serve their customers, the better the chances customers will not only come back but will share with others their positive experiences of flying on Southwest.

■ **Employee Customer Training**—Employees, especially new employees, need some level of customer training. Starbucks, for example, spends the first four hours with new employees explaining their role in creating a positive customer experience. Waste Management has all its new employees, even new VPs, ride in a garbage truck for one day to see customers and learn how the company serves them. A company can take many actions to train and reward employees with respect to a customer focus. However, one thing is certain: If a business does nothing in the area of employee customer training, it is unlikely that employees will make extra efforts to create positive customer experiences. Those companies that engage employees in understanding customer needs and sources of customer satisfaction are able to build a much stronger customer focus.[6]

■ **Customer Involvement**—Customer feedback, good and bad, is shared across the organization. Employees learn how their job affects the customer, how customers use the company's products, and what frustrations and problems customers encounter. For example, FedEx tracks 10 areas of service failure and reports the company's performance to managers and employees each day. Other companies, like Worthington Steel, have customer field trips for employees so they can see how their products are used by customers. Many companies also use focus groups and videos of customer experiences to communicate to employees the frustrations that customers might encounter in using their products.

Voice of the Customer

Only 8 percent of customers describe their experience as superior, yet 80 percent of companies believe the experience they provide is indeed superior.[7]

This quote tells us a lot about the importance of the voice of the customer and the level of insight that businesses generally have regarding the customer experience. No report or management presentation can replace the words articulated by a customer. Without the voice of the customer, companies may believe they are creating a superior customer experience when in fact they are not. Customers have a different language and express both their satisfaction and frustrations in words that only they can voice. In order to build a customer-focused organization, businesses must capture the voice of the customer and share it across the organization to keep management and employees sensitized to what customers are thinking and saying about the company's products and services. The following list summarizes several ways that a business can capture and communicate the voice of the customer.

- **Customer Experience**—The best way to understand the customer experience is to see it. Intuit, makers of QuickBooks and other software products, have a "Follow the Customer Home" program to observe how customers install and use the company's products. From these observations and customer comments on how they would like to do things, Intuit is able to improve its products and enhance the customers' experiences in using the company's products. For high-tech and business-to-business customers, "A Day in the Life of a Customer" examines how products are acquired, used, maintained, and replaced in order to understand the total customer experience.

- **Customer Solutions**—Companies often become overly focused on building and selling products they believe their customers want, whereas customers are often seeking somewhat different solutions to their usage situation. A product may need additional features or services to provide the solution that customers are actually seeking. For example, General Electric was selling an innovative micron filter but discovered its customers needed a filter holder that made the new product easier to use. 3M observes and talks with lead users of their products, as these customers are trying to use the products in ways that go beyond their design capabilities. Understanding the adaptations that lead users have made or would like to have helps 3M develop its next-generation products. Apple has set up online customer chat rooms for customers to discuss features that they would like to see Apple develop in its products. Customers' suggestions in the chat rooms have led to innovations in the iPod, iPhone, and iPad.

- **Customer Complaints**—Most businesses view complaints as negative feedback and would prefer not to hear them. These businesses often make the resolution process overly difficult for customers.[8] That may be the natural response, but it's not the way a customer-focused business thinks. A business with a strong customer focus views negative customer feedback as an opportunity to understand the sources of customer dissatisfaction and to address them. Domino's Pizza listened hard to customers who said its product tasted like cardboard and improved its product. In 1 year Domino's increased revenue by 18.4 percent and profit by 3.2 percent.[9] The explosion of social media platforms has afforded numerous mechanisms that make it easy for companies to solicit candid feedback from customers in the spirit of ongoing product and process improvement.

Customer Metrics

Most company performance metrics are internal company metrics, such as return on sales, asset turnover, accounts receivable as a percent of sales, employee turnover, manufacturing defects, late deliveries, and many more. In contrast, customer metrics, such as customer satisfaction, customer retention, and customer loyalty, are external metrics that provide a completely different view of company performance. These customer metrics include several forward-looking metrics that can act as leading indicators of company sales and profitability metrics. For example, sales and profits could be going well, but if customer intentions to repurchase are declining, future sales and profits are likely to decline. Firms that aim to increase the value of their customer base should report forward-looking customer metrics to better align corporate goals with future customer performance.[10]

■ **Customer Satisfaction**—The level of customer satisfaction is a key customer performance metric for any customer-focused organization. The percentage of customers who are "very satisfied," as opposed to simply "satisfied," and the percentage who are dissatisfied have a significant impact on profits, as we will demonstrate later in this chapter. The following quote is a great illustration of the way that a customer-focused organization views customer satisfaction.

> Satisfied is not good enough. Completely satisfied—that's a big deal. A completely satisfied customer is at least three times more likely to return than one who's just satisfied.
> — *Andrew Taylor, CEO, Enterprise Rent-A-Car*[11]

Enterprise Rent-A-Car, a company with over 6,500 offices and 600,000 vehicles, is committed to having "completely satisfied" customers. Every month, Enterprise interviews a sampling of customers from each of its rental offices to determine the level of customer satisfaction. Company promotions go to those managers whose offices have above-average levels of customer satisfaction. If a customer who is being interviewed mentions an employee by name, the next morning that employee receives a copy of the customer's comments. If a customer mentions that the vehicle was dirty or expresses any other dissatisfaction, the comment goes to the manager of the office where the customer rented it. Enterprise trains its new personnel not only in its procedures for renting vehicles to the public but in the company's philosophy of customer focus. All employees learn what's important to customers and what's important in terms of being a good team member.

■ **Customer Retention**—The longer a business keeps a customer, the more profitable that customer becomes. For most businesses, the cost of acquiring a customer is 5 to 10 times more than retaining one. For a given customer base, higher customer retention means less money is spent replacing lost customers. Netflix, for example, increased its customer retention from 72 to 85 percent. Because it needed fewer new customers to replace lost customers, Netflix had more money for increasing its customer base.[12] Later in the chapter we will demonstrate how the profit impact of customer retention can be used to determine the lifetime value of a customer in monetary terms.

■ **Customer Loyalty**—Loyal customers typically have long histories with a company, buy more than the average customer, and would be more likely than the average customer to recommend a company's products to potential customers. Loyal customers usually account for a large percentage of overall customer profits. But companies must also make efforts to improve relationships with their less loyal customers and build relationships with their new customers.

Companies that use customer performance metrics are able to identify their unprofitable customers. These are the customers the company has attracted but cannot really satisfy based on their needs and the company's product benefits and price. These customers leave before the business can recover its investment in acquiring them. For any business, knowing which customers *not* to attract is just as important as knowing which customers to attract.

FIGURE 1-4 AMERICAN CUSTOMER SATISFACTION INDEX

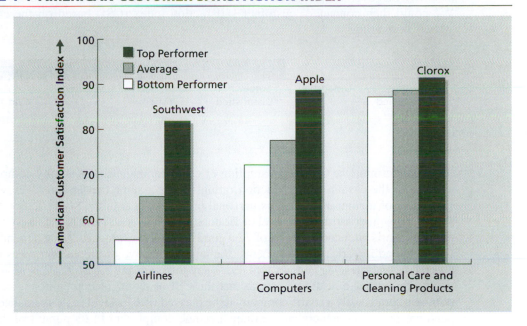

CUSTOMER SATISFACTION—A KEY MARKETING PERFORMANCE METRIC

Figure 1-4 shows the top and bottom performers with respect to customer satisfaction for three distinctly different industries, along with the industry average.[13] The airline industry has the largest variance in customer satisfaction, with an average much lower than the bottom performers for personal computers and personal care and cleaning products. The American Customer Satisfaction Index for Southwest Airlines is considerably higher than for the average airline and average personal computer company. For personal computers, the top performer is Apple, and its customer satisfaction index is well above average. The personal care and cleaning products sector has a high average, with a relatively small difference between the top and bottom performers. The bottom performer in this business sector produces a customer satisfaction index that is close to the top performer for personal computers and above the top performer for the airline industry.

Measuring Customer Satisfaction

One of the many ways to measure customer satisfaction is based on customers' ratings of their overall satisfaction. The six-category scale shown here ranges from "very dissatisfied" to "very satisfied." The levels of customer satisfaction are rated from zero for "very dissatisfied" customers to 100 for "very satisfied" customers. The scale could be used to rate the satisfaction of a sample of customers for a given product or service. It could also be used by a governmental agency or service, such as the U.S. Postal Service or Medicare. We could then compute a customer satisfaction index (CSI) based on the customer satisfaction ratings.

Very Dissatisfied	Dissatisfied	Somewhat Dissatisfied	Somewhat Satisfied	Satisfied	Very Satisfied
0	20	40	60	80	100

To determine the CSI for a sampling of customers, a business simply computes the average of the customers' satisfaction ratings. Let's assume that an interview with 100 customers of a company that sells personal printers results in a CSI of 72. By itself, an average customer satisfaction level of 72 does not tell us much and is not likely to attract management's attention. Is a CSI of 72 a good level of performance? That depends on the CSI obtained in earlier measurements, the target objective of the current measurement, and the CSIs of leading competitors. Let's say the company's CSI of 72 is an improvement over earlier measurements and that the CSI of its major competitor is 62. Those numbers could easily lead the company to be pleased with its level of performance among personal printer customers and perhaps become complacent in its pursuit of customer satisfaction. In addition, because efforts to increase customer satisfaction cost money, some may argue that the incremental benefit is not sufficient to justify the cost. That argument, however, would not have any merit for the company or any other business where customer satisfaction is a top corporate performance metric and a top priority. To really understand customer satisfaction and how to leverage its profit potential, we need to expand our view of it.

A Wide-Angle View of Customer Satisfaction

A company may view a customer satisfaction index of 72 (where 100 is the maximum) as acceptable or even very good. However, simply managing to achieve an average or even a very high CSI can mask the opportunities that a broad view of customer satisfaction offers to increase profits.[14] If we expand our view of customer satisfaction by including the percentage for each category on our customer satisfaction scale, a more meaningful set of insights emerges. As illustrated in Figure 1-5, the CSI of 72 was derived from 80 percent of customers who reported varying degrees of satisfaction and 20 percent of customers who reported varying degrees of dissatisfaction. The 20 percent who were "somewhat satisfied" are certainly vulnerable to competitor moves, but it is the 20 percent who reported various levels of dissatisfaction who are serious candidates for exit as customers. Management's immediate concern should be the "somewhat dissatisfied," "dissatisfied," and "very dissatisfied" customers.

Customer satisfaction is a valuable marketing performance metric because it can forecast future revenues and profits. This metric deserves our high regard because customer satisfaction is a forward-looking indicator of business success that measures how well customers will respond to the company in the future. Other measures of market performance, such as sales and market share, are backward-looking measures of success or failure. They tell how well the firm has performed in the past, but not how well it will do in the future.

FIGURE 1-5 CUSTOMER SATISFACTION—A WIDE-ANGLE VIEW

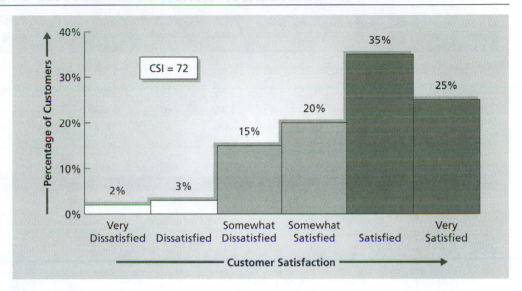

Even a business that has recently produced excellent financial results may be disappointing customers. In markets where customers cannot switch to alternatives, dissatisfied customers may stay in the short run but will exit eventually. When they exit, sales and profits are likely to decline.

For many businesses, quarterly measures of customer satisfaction are an effective way to project future performance. If customer satisfaction is declining, this early warning sign gives management time to take preemptive action before real damage is done. Of course, if a business does not track customer satisfaction, it remains unaware of any coming decline in its customer base and foregoes the opportunity to correct performance problems before sales and profits also decline.

De-averaging Customer Satisfaction and Customer Profitability

De-averaging a CSI provides a wide-angle view of customer satisfaction and allows managers to see more completely the opportunities for improvement. De-averaging, however, is even more important in understanding customer profitability.[15] In the example in Figure 1-6, the average customer revenue is $655. More important is the fact that "very satisfied" customers spend an average of $1,200 per year—almost twice the average.

Even more impressive is the role that "very satisfied" customers play in profitability.[16] Whereas the average annual customer profitability is $250, "very satisfied" customers produce a profit of $620. "Very satisfied" customers not only buy more, they often buy higher-margin products and services, which results in a higher percent margin on total sales.

"Somewhat satisfied" customers are profitable but are below the average customer profitability, which is largely determined by the profit impact of "very satisfied" customers. De-averaging customer satisfaction demonstrates the importance of "very satisfied" customers to the overall profits of a business. When we chart customer profitability against customer satisfaction in Figure 1-6, we see that the "very satisfied" customers are the ones who drive profitability.

FIGURE 1-6 CUSTOMER SATISFACTION AND PROFIT IMPACT

Customer Satisfaction	Customer Percent	CSI Score	Customer Revenue	Percent Margin	Gross Profit	Retention Cost	Customer Profit
Very Satisfied	25%	100	$1,200	60%	$720	$100	$620
Satisfied	35%	80	$800	50%	$400	$100	$300
Somewhat Satisfied	20%	60	$300	40%	$120	$100	$20
Somewhat Dissatisfied	15%	40	$80	40%	$32	$100	–$68
Dissatisfied	3%	20	$60	40%	$24	$100	–$76
Very Dissatisfied	2%	0	$50	40%	$20	$100	–$80
	100%	72	$655	49%	$350	$100	$250

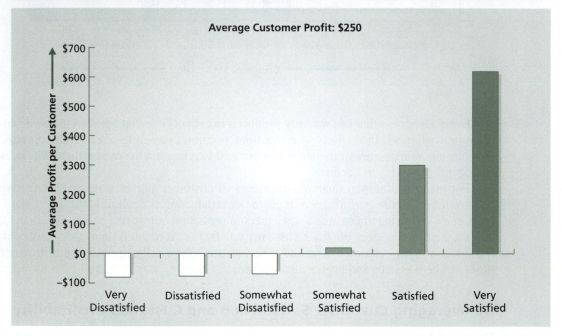

This type of analysis reveals how an effort to reduce customer dissatisfaction and improve the percentage of satisfied customers could raise the overall level of customer satisfaction. Just an 8-point increase in the CSI from 72 to 80 would increase the average profit per customer from $250 to $328, a 31 percent increase. Using this analysis, a manager can evaluate many different customer satisfaction scenarios with respect to overall customer satisfaction and average profit per customer.

Managing Customer Dissatisfaction

Dissatisfied customers buy smaller amounts of product and often buy low-margin or promotional products. In the example in Figure 1-6, after the cost of marketing is subtracted from the customer gross profit, it is apparent that these customers lose the company money.

FIGURE 1-7 CUSTOMER SATISFACTION, COMPLAINT BEHAVIOR, AND CUSTOMER RETENTION

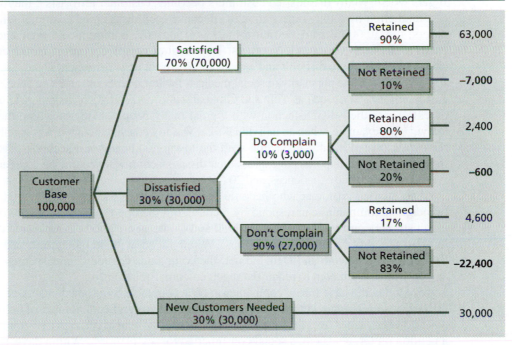

Yet, despite the less significant role that dissatisfied customers play in profitability, a market-based management business gives its dissatisfied customers as much attention as its "very satisfied" customers. When a dissatisfied customer leaves, a business suffers several economic consequences that lower profits. But mainly because it costs much more to attract a new customer than to retain a current customer, a market-based management business knows it cannot neglect its dissatisfied customers.

Dissatisfied customers usually do not complain, but they do walk and they do talk. Well-documented studies have found that a surprisingly small percentage of dissatisfied customers complain to a business.[17] In Figure 1-7, of the 27,000 dissatisfied customers who do not complain, 22,400 of them—or 83 percent—will exit. Exiting customers directly erode market position, and because they each tell an average of 8 to 10 other people about their dissatisfaction, they make it more difficult to attract new customers.

Figure 1-7 illustrates the importance of focusing on the dissatisfied customers who do not complain. The business in this example has 100,000 customers, 70 percent satisfied and 30 percent dissatisfied. Each year, the business loses 30,000 customers who must be replaced to maintain the customer base of 100,000. Of the 70,000 satisfied customers, the business loses only 7,000. The other 23,000 lost customers are dissatisfied customers, most of whom do not complain. In this example, 10 percent of the 30,000 dissatisfied customers complain and, of these, 80 percent (2,400) are retained. By contrast, 90 percent of the dissatisfied customers (27,000) do not complain and, of these, only 17 percent are retained (4,600) and 83 percent are lost (22,400). A quick calculation tells us that the dissatisfied customers who do not complain represent fully 75 percent of the customers lost by the business each year.

Dissatisfied Customer Revenge and the Use of Social Media

It gets worse. Many dissatisfied customers become "customer terrorists": they vent their dissatisfaction by telling others about it. Because each dissatisfied customer tells 8 to 10 others, the 30,000 dissatisfied customers will verbally communicate their bad experiences to about a quarter million others. This level of negative word-of-mouth communication makes it more difficult and expensive to attract new customers.[18]

Even worse, the popularity of social media—Twitter, Facebook, and YouTube, as well as customer rating sites such as Yelp and Groubal—allows dissatisfied customers to easily and quickly share their dissatisfaction with a great many people, many of whom they do not know.[19] For example, when an individual's car was towed even though it was legally parked, the owner posted his dissatisfaction with the towing company on Facebook. His post led more than 10,000 supporters to express their dissatisfaction with the towing company. Many related their own bad experiences, and 20 formal complaints were filed over a 3-year period.[20]

Dissatisfied customer who become "consumer terrorists" pose a potential threat to brands, but companies can respond by recognizing the opportunity to convert these ranting customers into raving customers. Dell and Comcast are good examples of companies that turned threats into opportunities. When faced with harsh online criticism on ComcastMustDie.com and DellHell.net, the companies created ComcastCares (Twitter) and DellIdeaStorm.com to repair damaged customer relationships.

Social media have forced companies to be accountable for product or service issues. In 2010, Fry's Electronics canceled without explanation a significant number of online orders that had been placed over the Thanksgiving weekend. About 1,100 angry customers signed a petition on Groubal.com, a social consumer advocacy platform. Within days, Fry's publicly agreed to honor all the transactions, apologized to customers, and resolved the issue.[21]

To prevent a poor reputation from developing by word of mouth, a customer-focused business encourages dissatisfied customers to complain. For example, Domino's Pizza simply asks its dissatisfied customers to complain.[22] The company's effort to encourage complaints produces feedback from 20 percent of its dissatisfied customers. Domino's is able to resolve 80 percent of the problems within 24 hours. When complaints can be resolved quickly, 95 percent of the complaining customers are retained. When complaints cannot be resolved within 24 hours, the retention rate falls to 46 percent.

Although it may seem odd at first, the job of a market-based management team includes not only tracking customer satisfaction but also encouraging dissatisfied customers to complain. Only after learning the details of a customer complaint can a business take corrective action.

Profit Impact of Customer Dissatisfaction

MBNA America, now merged with Bank of America, was a Delaware-based credit card company that became frustrated with its level of customer dissatisfaction and customer defection. The company brought all 300 of its employees together in an effort to understand the problem and develop methods of delivering greater levels of customer satisfaction in order to retain more customers. At the time, MBNA America had a 90 percent customer retention rate. After dedicating itself to improved customer satisfaction and retention for several years, the company raised its customer retention to 95 percent. That may seem like a small difference, but the impact on profits was a 16-fold increase, and the company's industry ranking went from 38th to 4th.[23] The marketing efforts to satisfy and retain customers paid off far more than we might have expected from only a 5 percent increase in customer retention. As we saw in Figure 1-7, most dissatisfied customers do not complain. They just walk away and tell others, leaving the business with the task of replacing them in order to retain its market share.

PROFIT IMPACT OF CUSTOMER RETENTION

The two tables in Figure 1-8 build on the data from the customer retention tree in Figure 1-7 to demonstrate the sales and profit impact of an increase in customer retention. For two different levels of customer retention, the tables show the average annual revenue, margin, and marketing and sales expenses per customer for retained customers, lost

FIGURE 1-8 CUSTOMER RETENTION AND PROFITABILITY

70% Customer Retention Sales and Profit Performance	Retained Customers	Lost Customers	New Customers	Overall Performance
Sales (millions)	70,000	30,000	30,000	100,000
Revenue per Customer	$1,000	$300	$500	$940.0
Sales (millions)	$70.0	$9.0	$15.0	$94.0
Percent Margin	45%	35%	30%	42%
Gross Profit (millions)	$31.5	$3.2	$4.5	$39.2
Marketing & Sales Expenses per Customer	$100.00	$50.00	$500.00	$180.77
Marketing & Sales Expenses (millions)	$7.0	$1.5	$15.0	$23.5
Net Marketing Contribution (millions)	$24.5	$1.7	–$10.5	$15.7
Other Expenses (millions)				$10.0
Profit Before Tax				$5.7
Pre-Tax Return on Sales				6.0%

80% Customer Retention Sales and Profit Performance	Retained Customers	Lost Customers	New Customers	Overall Performance
Number of Customers	80,000	20,000	20,000	100,000
Revenue per Customer	$1,000	$300	$500	$960.0
Sales (millions)	$80.0	$6.0	$10.0	$96.0
Percent Margin	45%	35%	30%	43%
Gross Profit (millions)	$36.0	$2.1	$3.0	$41.1
Marketing & Sales Expenses per Customer	$110.00	$55.00	$500.00	$165.83
Marketing & Sales Expenses (millions)	$8.8	$1.1	$10.0	$19.9
Net Marketing Contribution (millions)	$27.2	$1.0	–$7.0	$21.2
Other Expenses (millions)				$10.0
Profit Before Tax				$11.2
Pre-Tax Return on Sales				11.7%

customers, and new customers. The retained customers are the profit driver of this business. With the company's current customer retention rate of 70 percent, the retained customers account for 74.4 percent of the sales revenue and 80 percent of the gross profit. They produce a net marketing contribution of $24.5 million (gross profit minus marketing and sales expenses), while lost customers produce a net marketing contribution of $1.7 million. Because the cost of acquiring new customers is high, and because new customers generally buy less, their net marketing contribution is a negative $10.5 million. After other fixed expenses of $10 million are taken into account, a 70 percent level of customer retention produces a profit before tax of $5.7 million and a pre-tax return on sales of 6 percent.

In this example, the business increased its marketing and sales expenses per customer by 10 percent for retained and lost customers, improving its overall customer retention rate to 80 percent. We can readily see that the profit before tax and the pre-tax return on sales are almost double those for the 70 percent customer retention rate. The math is simple. The marketing cost of retaining customers is much lower than the cost of replacing them. Because the business has fewer lost customers and needs fewer new customers to replace them, it can improve profits derived from retained customers and reduce the losses associated with acquiring new customers.

Obviously, efforts to retain customers are not free. In this example, the marketing and sales expenses for retained and lost customers increased from $8.5 million to $9.9 million. But the marketing and sales expenses devoted to acquiring new customers to replace lost customers dropped from $15 million to $10 million. In the end, the overall marketing and sales budget decreased from $23.5 million to $19.9 million.

The immense potential for increased profits and cash flow is evident. Every additional customer who is retained increases a business's net profit. The costs associated with serving dissatisfied customers and the costs of acquiring new customers to replace them are reduced. Placing a high priority on satisfying and retaining customers can provide tremendous financial leverage.

Customer Satisfaction and Customer Retention

The relationship between customer satisfaction and customer retention is intuitively easy to discern. Different competitive conditions, however, modify this relationship.[24] For example, in less competitive markets, customers are more easily retained even with low levels of customer satisfaction because substitutes are few or switching costs are high. In markets where relatively few choices are available—such as water service, electricity service, and hospital care—customers stay even when they are dissatisfied. Businesses that have no or limited competition have high levels of customer retention even if they have low levels of customer satisfaction. In highly competitive markets, however, even high levels of customer satisfaction may not prevent customer defection. Grocery store, restaurant, and bank customers can switch quickly when they are not completely satisfied. Although the time between purchases is longer, customers who periodically buy personal computers, automobiles, appliances, and electronic products can also easily move to another brand. In these and similar markets, customer retention is much more difficult, and a very high level of customer satisfaction is needed to ensure a high percentage of retained customers.

FIGURE 1-9 ESTIMATING CUSTOMER RETENTION

How likely are you to buy this product or brand again on your next purchase?

Definitely Will Not Repurchase	Will Not Repurchase	Probably Will Not Repurchase	Probably Will Repurchase	Plan to Repurchase	Definitely Will Repurchase

Intention to Repurchase	Percent	Probability
Definitely Will Repurchase	25%	1.00
Plan to Repurchase	35%	0.80
Probably Will Repurchase	20%	0.60
Probably Will Not Repurchase	15%	0.40
Will Not Repurchase	3%	0.20
Definitely Will Not Repurchase	2%	0.00
Total:	**100%**	**0.72**
Customer Retention		**72%**

Estimating Customer Retention

Banks, wholesale suppliers, and other businesses that engage in recorded customer transactions can figure their customer retention rates fairly easily. Many businesses, however, are one step removed from end-user customers and cannot determine their customer retention rates on the basis of customer transaction records. To estimate their retention rates, these businesses can use a customer survey as outlined in Figure 1-9.

Customer Retention and Customer Life Expectancy

Customer satisfaction and retention are important linkages to a market-based strategy and to profitability. The ultimate objective of any marketing strategy should be to attract, satisfy, and retain target customers. If a business can accomplish this objective with a competitive advantage in attractive markets, it will produce above-average profits.

The customer as a critical component in the profitability equation is completely overlooked in financial analyses and annual reports. Customers are a marketing asset that businesses have yet to quantify in their accounting systems, even though the business that can attract, satisfy, and keep customers over their lifetimes of purchases is in a powerful position to deliver superior levels of profitability. Businesses that lack a market orientation see customers as individual purchase transactions. A market-based management business sees them as lifetime partners. The *New York Times*, a good example of the latter business model, tracks its customer retention and the retention rates of competing newspapers by length of subscription.[25] Among mature subscribers—those subscribing longer than 24 months—the *New York Times* has a retention rate of 94 percent. Its closest competitor has an 80 percent retention rate.

The higher the customer retention rate, the greater the profit impact. In the short run, we showed this to be true on the basis of increased profits from retained customers, reduced losses from defecting customers, and the subsequent lower cost of attracting new

FIGURE 1-10 NETFLIX—CUSTOMER RETENTION AND CUSTOMER LIFE

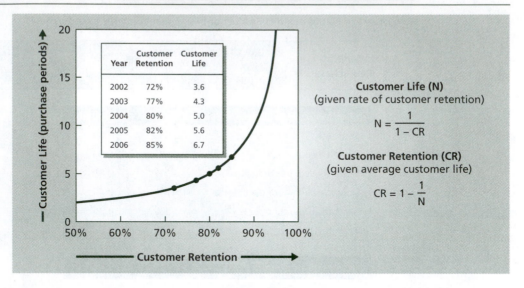

Year	Customer Retention	Customer Life
2002	72%	3.6
2003	77%	4.3
2004	80%	5.0
2005	82%	5.6
2006	85%	6.7

Customer Life (N)
(given rate of customer retention)

$$N = \frac{1}{1 - CR}$$

Customer Retention (CR)
(given average customer life)

$$CR = 1 - \frac{1}{N}$$

customers to maintain the customer base. But higher levels of customer retention also have a long-term positive impact on profits because a higher rate of retention lengthens the average life of customers, increasing their lifetime value.

A business that has a 50 percent customer retention rate has a fifty-fifty chance of retaining any one customer from one year to the next. This fact translates into an average customer life of 2 years, as shown here:

$$\text{Average Customer Life} = 1 / (1 - \text{Customer Retention}) = 1 / (1 - 0.5)$$
$$= 1 / 0.5 = \textbf{2 years}$$

As customer retention increases, the customer's life expectancy increases. More important, customer life expectancy increases exponentially with customer retention. As shown in Figure 1-10, Netflix improved its customer retention each year from 2002 to 2006.[26] Over this 5-year period, the ever-higher retention rates increased the average customer life from 3.6 to 6.7 years.

As an example, the average rate of customer retention among health care providers is 80 percent.[27] This level of retention produces an average customer life of 5 years. If a health care provider could increase its customer retention rate to 90 percent, the increase would produce an average customer life of 10 years. We can see that as a business moves to higher levels of customer retention, the life expectancy of a customer grows dramatically.

CUSTOMER LIFETIME VALUE

A loyal Lexus customer who buys a $45,000 Lexus and replaces it every 5 years for 30 years (seven purchases) could be worth more than $300,000 during that 30-year period. If Lexus loses that customer after the first purchase, it loses more than $250,000 in future sales. To replace that lost customer, Lexus would need to attract a new customer, which

FIGURE 1-11 LIFETIME VALUE OF A CUSTOMER

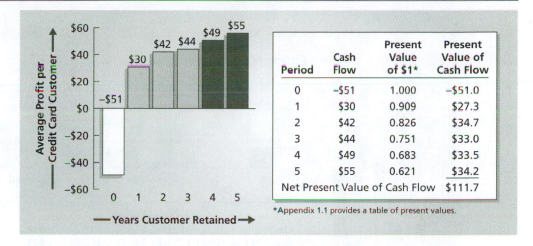

Period	Cash Flow	Present Value of $1*	Present Value of Cash Flow
0	–$51	1.000	–$51.0
1	$30	0.909	$27.3
2	$42	0.826	$34.7
3	$44	0.751	$33.0
4	$49	0.683	$33.5
5	$55	0.621	$34.2
Net Present Value of Cash Flow			$111.7

*Appendix 1.1 provides a table of present values.

is an expensive process, as we saw in Figure 1-8. The cost of marketing and sales efforts to ensure customer satisfaction is small, then, compared with the current and future benefits of customer purchases, as well as the cost of replacing customers who become dissatisfied and leave. In general, it costs five times more to replace than to keep a customer.

Figure 1-11 illustrates the average profit per credit card customer generated over a 5-year period. Acquiring and setting up accounts for new credit card customers nets an annual loss of $51 per customer. Newly acquired credit card customers are also slow to use their cards; new customers produce an average profit of $30 the first year, $42 the second year, and $44 the third year. By year 5, the average profit obtained from a credit card customer is $55. The value of a credit card customer, then, grows fairly significantly over time. Of course, if a credit card company loses a customer after year 4 because of customer dissatisfaction, the company incurs the cost of replacing the customer. The cost in the first year following customer exit is a considerable $106, which includes the $55 in lost profit from the exiting customer and the $51 loss associated with attracting a replacement customer. In this example, the average customer life is 5 years. Working backward, we can estimate the customer retention to be 80 percent:

$$\textbf{Customer Retention} = 1 - \frac{1}{N} = 1 - \frac{1}{5} = \textbf{0.80 (or 80\%)}$$

To estimate the lifetime value of a customer at this rate of retention, we need to compute the net present value of the customer cash flow shown in Figure 1-11. The $51 cost of acquiring this customer is immediately gone. Because it takes a year to achieve the initial $30 in profit, the customer's present value is less than an immediate $30 profit. In this example, the business uses a discount rate of 10 percent. Therefore, the present value of $1 received after 1 year is $0.909 (the rate at which $1 is discounted for 1 year at 10 percent). Accordingly, $30 to be received 1 year later has a present value of $27.30 ($30 × 0.909). The discounting is performed for each year's customer profits, and the values are totaled to provide the net present value of this cash flow. When each year's customer cash flow is properly discounted, the sum of the discounted amounts equals

FIGURE 1-12 VALUE OF ONLINE CUSTOMERS

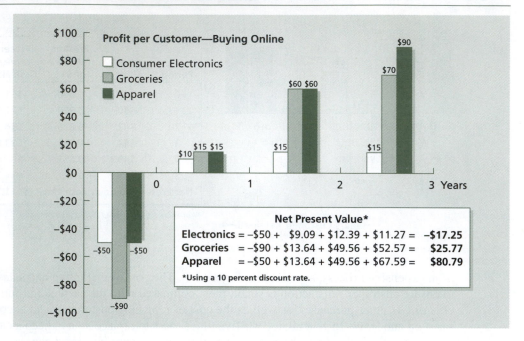

$111.70, the amount that this customer is worth in today's dollars. This example assumes a 5-year life expectancy; if the customer life expectancy were only 3 years, the customer lifetime value (net present value) would be considerably smaller. The higher the rate of customer retention, the longer the average customer life expectancy and the greater the customer lifetime value.

To better understand this concept, let's look at the customer lifetime value (net present value) over a 3-year period for online shoppers for consumer electronics, groceries, and apparel, as illustrated in Figure 1-12.[28] The cost of acquiring an online grocery customer is almost twice the cost of acquiring an online consumer-electronics or apparel customer. After 3 years, the average online grocery customer has a positive net present value of $25.77, whereas the online consumer-electronics customer has a negative net present value of $17.25. The average online apparel customer is the most profitable, with a net present value of $80.79 after 3 years.

CUSTOMER LOYALTY

Most businesses have a mix of customers with varying levels of loyalty and customer profitability. Loyal customers have a longer customer history, are more committed to the company brand, buy more, and are more likely to recommend the brand to others. Repeat customers also have a long history but are less committed to the brand, buy less, and are less likely to recommend the brand to others.

Unfortunately, most businesses also have dissatisfied "captive customers," but often a business does not know who these customers are. On the basis of their long customer history and their purchase amounts, they look like repeat customers, but they are less than satisfied, have a low level of product preference, and would like to switch to another company's product if they could. They would not recommend the brand, and many would advise not buying it.

Because customer satisfaction and retention have a positive impact on profitability, a business will always have customers it wants to keep. But it can also have customers it should abandon.[29] Likewise, when a business is trying to attract new customers and manage them to a level of customer loyalty, there are potential customers the business should not pursue. Attracting the right customers is part of customer relationship marketing.

We can facilitate the effective management of customer relationships with regard to customer retention by classifying customers on the basis of customer loyalty and profitability.[30] Not all customers are the same. Some are loyal and profitable, some are profitable but not loyal, some are loyal but not profitable, and others are neither loyal nor profitable. But we first need a measure of customer loyalty.

Measuring Customer Loyalty

Customer loyalty varies on the basis of the five customer loyalty components included in Figure 1-13. Each of these customer loyalty components is assessed using three levels of customer behavior. The average of these five loyalty components provides a customer loyalty index that varies from zero to 100. The higher the customer loyalty index, the more loyal a customer is. A customer loyalty index of 80 would be considered a high level of loyalty despite a few average scores.

$$\text{Customer Loyalty Index} = \frac{\text{Customer History} + \text{Purchase Amount} + \text{Desire to Repurchase} + \text{Product Preference} + \text{Would Recommend}}{5}$$

$$= 100\,(\text{Long}) + 50\,(\text{Average}) + 100\,(\text{High}) + 100\,(\text{Strong}) + 50\,(\text{Maybe})$$
$$= 400/5$$
$$= \mathbf{80}$$

"Customer history" is measured as simply *long*, *average*, or *short* relative to the average customer history for a company. A loyal customer has a long history, whereas a new customer has a short history. In the example calculation of customer loyalty, the customer has a long customer history.

"Purchase amount" varies from *below average* to *above average*. A loyal customer usually has an above-average purchase amount, whereas a less-than-loyal customer probably has a below-average purchase amount. The customer in the customer loyalty calculation has an average purchase amount.

FIGURE 1-13 CUSTOMER LOYALTY—LOYALTY COMPONENTS AND MEASUREMENTS

Customer History	Loyalty Index	Purchase Amount	Loyalty Index	Desire to Repurchase	Loyalty Index	Product Preference	Loyalty Index	Would Recommend	Loyalty Index
Long	100	Above Avg.	100	High	100	Strong	100	Yes	100
Average	50	Average	50	Average	50	Average	50	Maybe	50
Short	0	Below Avg.	0	Low	0	Weak	0	No	0

"Desire to repurchase" varies from *low* to *high*, with *average* reflecting a moderate commitment to buying again from the business. A loyal customer has a high score, a repeat customer an average score, and a dissatisfied customer a low score. In the calculation, the customer is very likely to buy again from the business.

"Product preference" varies from *weak* to *strong*. A loyal customer has a strong level of product preference relative to competing products, whereas a nonloyal repeat customer has a weak level of preference for the company's product over a competitor's and would buy either. A dissatisfied customer has a low product preference score and would switch to another product if possible. In the example calculation of the customer loyalty index, the customer has a strong preference for the company's product.

"Customer recommendation," or referral to potential customers, is also a critical factor in determining the degree of customer loyalty. Loyal customers with a long history and a strong product preference usually recommend the company's product to others. Repeat customers are generally less likely to recommend the product, and new customers are even less likely to recommend it to others because their experience with the product is very limited. In our example, the customer rated the likelihood of recommendation as *maybe*. Although this lowers the customer's loyalty index, an overall loyalty index of 80 still warrants classifying the customer as loyal.

Customer Loyalty Classifications

Measuring the loyalty of individual customers usually generates a wide range of customer loyalty scores, varying from zero to 100. Naturally, the higher the loyalty score, the more loyal the customer, and the lower the score, the less loyal the customer. Because customer profitability is correlated with customer loyalty, a higher score normally means higher customer profitability, and a lower score means lower customer profitability.

For the sample company in Figure 1-14, the mix of loyalty scores and the percentage of customers in each "customer classification" produces an overall loyalty score of 50. Sixty percent of the customers are loyal, repeat, or captive customers. Forty percent are either new or unprofitable customers. The company would not know any of this without measuring customer loyalty. But because the company's marketing managers do measure customer loyalty and have the information in Figure 1-14, they can develop marketing programs for each classification of customer loyalty. These

FIGURE 1-14 SAMPLE COMPANY—CUSTOMER LOYALTY SCORES

Customer Classification	Loyalty Scores	Percent Customers	Customer History	Purchase Amount	Desire to Buy Again	Product Preference	Would Recommend	Loyalty Index
Loyal	70 to 100	20%	90	80	95	80	80	**85**
Repeat	50 to 69	30%	80	65	90	40	45	**64**
Captive	Under 50	10%	75	55	20	10	0	**32**
New	0 to 60	20%	10	20	50	50	50	**36**
Unprofitable	0 to 40	20%	25	15	15	20	0	**15**
Customer Loyalty Index								**50**

tailored marketing programs improve customer profitability, which in turn improves company profitability. One goal of customer relationship marketing is to manage these five customer loyalty classifications to obtain a higher level of overall loyalty and customer profitability.[31]

Loyal Customers

A loyal customer could have an individual loyalty score as high as 100, but it is likely that a score of less than 100 in at least one of the five loyalty aspects will result in an overall loyalty score lower than 100. For example, a loyal customer could have scores of 100 on the first four aspects of loyalty, but for personal reasons would not be likely to recommend the product to others. To be classified as a loyal customer, a customer should have a loyalty score between 70 and 100. Twenty percent of the customers of the sample company in Figure 1-14 are classified as loyal. Using the average score for each loyalty component for this set of loyal customers yields an overall average loyalty index of 85. Because of their above-average loyalty and customer profitability, these customers account for a large portion of the business's profits. The following range of scores is what we would expect for a loyal customer.

Loyal Customers—Range of Behaviors

Customer History	Purchase Amount	Desire to Repurchase	Product Preference	Would Recommend	Loyalty Index	Lifetime Value
Avg. to Long	Avg. to High	High	Strong	Maybe to Yes	High	Above Average
50 to 100	50 to 100	100	100	50 to 100	70 to 100	

Loyal customers need to be managed differently.[32] They should be rewarded for their loyalty with special offers and services that are not offered to other customers. Marriott, for example, offers its loyal customers a variety of extra services and room upgrades in order to reward and maintain their loyalty. The loyalty program should include precautions against demoting loyal customers. It is better to keep them in the loyalty program even if their purchase amounts drop into a lower range.[33] Their loyalty goes beyond their purchase amounts. Many loyal customers produce a referral value that is over three times their customer lifetime value.[34]

Repeat Customers

Many repeat customers are simply "big spenders." They buy a lot from many companies and do not have a strong preference for one over the other. Big-spender repeat customers buy at above-average levels and frequently purchase products for others. They are "satisfied" or "very satisfied" customers with an excellent retention rate, but they are less likely than loyal customers to recommend the product of a specific business.

Repeat customers are loyal customers in waiting. They have high profit potential, and their product preference is average to high. They may or may not recommend a company's product to others. As Figure 1-15 shows, repeat customers have an average to above-average customer lifetime value, but one that is lower than that of loyal customers. Repeat customers often make up 15 to 20 percent of a business's

FIGURE 1-15 CUSTOMER LOYALTY AND CUSTOMER LIFETIME VALUE

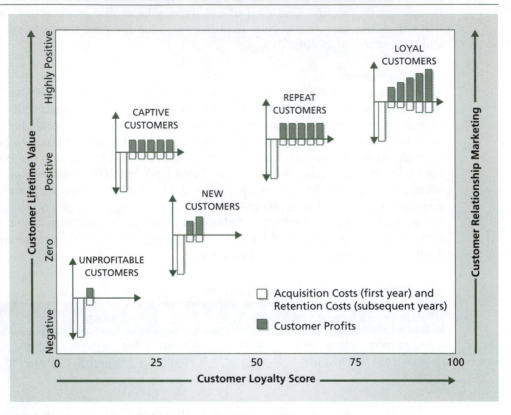

customer portfolio. A repeat customer has a loyalty index between 50 and 69 and a positive customer lifetime value, as shown in Figure 1-15. The following range of scores is what we would expect for a repeat customer.

Repeat Customers—Range of Behaviors

Customer History	Purchase Amount	Desire to Repurchase	Product Preference	Would Recommend	Loyalty Index	Lifetime Value
Avg. to Long	Low to Avg.	Avg. to High	Avg. to Strong	Maybe to Yes	Moderate	Average to Above Avg.
50 to 100	0 to 50	50 to 100	50 to 100	50 to 100	40 to 90	

Companies often mismanage repeat customers and overlook opportunities to upgrade them to loyal customers. Because competitors can easily lure them away, these customers are at risk of becoming lost customers. Companies should make an effort to build loyalty among high-potential repeat customers in order to retain them and the profits they produce. One objective of customer relationship marketing is to strengthen customers' loyalty by offering them benefits that are designed to increase their satisfaction and retention. It is important to expand loyalty programs to repeat customers even when they have average and below-average purchase amounts.[35]

Many businesses have found that repeat customers increase their purchase amounts, which raises their customer lifetime value, when they are included in loyalty program benefits.

Captive Customers

Captive customers are dissatisfied customers who have an average to long customer history. They have a low desire to repurchase but are unable to move easily to another company's product. They are likely to have a weak product preference and would not recommend the product to others. A PC customer who is frustrated with Microsoft Office really has no place to go and, as a result, continues to repurchase despite being dissatisfied. Many airlines with low levels of customer satisfaction, especially those serving small markets, still see the same faces, as their captive customers do not have the choice of flying on a customer-oriented airline. A public utility or group health insurance company that is unresponsive to its customers has many captive customers. In most cases the customers are locked into their next purchase or simply cannot switch. Captive customers exhibit the following range of behaviors:

Captive Customers—Range of Behaviors

Customer History	Purchase Amount	Desire to Repurchase	Product Preference	Would Recommend	Loyalty Index	Lifetime Value
Avg. to Long	Avg. to High	Low	Weak	No	Low	Average to Above Avg.
50 to 100	50 to 100	0	0	0	20 to 40	

In Figure 1-14, captive customers have an average to above-average customer history and a positive cash flow. Their customer lifetime value is average to above average, as shown in Figure 1-15, but the future of their cash flow is at risk because they desperately want to switch. Businesses with captive customers often have no idea that their captive customers exist; frequently, such business also lack awareness of the frustrations with which these customers live. To make matters worse, captive customers are likely to share their frustrations with others, making the company's efforts to acquire new customers harder.

Because many companies are unaware of the customer experience, they blissfully assume that all is well. The revenue continues to flow, and then comes the day when the dissatisfied customers up and leave. But those companies whose marketing efforts include the early detection of captive customers can manage them with respect to their customer dissatisfaction, thereby greatly reducing the possibility that they will switch to a competitor when they are able to do so.

New Customers

New customers can be first-time customers or returning customers. They have a low to average customer history and a below-average to average customer lifetime value. Their loyalty is low, as they have not had time to form a customer history or develop a strong product preference. Hence, they are less likely to recommend the product to others at this stage of their customer life. With respect to customer relationship marketing, they require "critical care." These customers have high expectations that need to be carefully managed in an effort to lift them to a higher level of customer loyalty. They could represent 15 to 20 percent of a business's customer portfolio.

New Customers—Range of Behaviors

Customer History	Purchase Amount	Desire to Repurchase	Product Preference	Would Recommend	Loyalty Index	Lifetime Value
Short to Avg.	Low to Avg.	Low to High	Weak to Avg.	No to Maybe	Low	Below Avg. to Average
0 to 50	0 to 50	0 to 100	0 to 50	0 to 50	0 to 60	

First-time customers should fit the business's profile for target customers. They should possess many of the same traits of loyal and repeat customers. How they are managed as new customers will determine how their purchasing patterns and customer loyalty develop. It is essential for the company to provide them with a positive customer experience in order to build customer satisfaction, retention, and loyalty.

Returning customers are also considered to be new, even though they have a previous customer history. Most often they are repeat customers who switched to a competitor, usually because they were mismanaged, and have for various reasons returned. Returning customers are often referred to as "win-back customers."[36] They already know the business's products and services and are likely to resume their former purchasing patterns. As Figure 1-16 shows, in 5 years the "second lifetime value" of a win-back customer has a net present value almost three times higher than the average lifetime value of an entirely new customer. For a company, the return of a former customer is a lost opportunity that has reappeared—a second chance to develop a loyal customer.

FIGURE 1-16 LIFETIME VALUE OF WIN-BACK CUSTOMERS

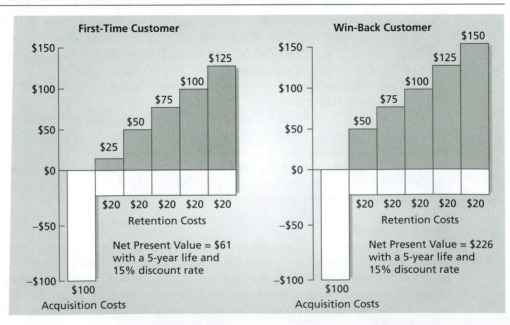

Unprofitable Customers

Unprofitable customers are the result of mismanaged customer selection.[37] They are unprofitable and unlikely ever to be loyal. Unprofitable customers are a drain on a business's profits because the cost of acquiring them can never be recovered, as shown in Figure 1-15. They can be 30 to 35 percent of a business's customer portfolio. A business with a strong and well-managed customer focus can significantly reduce its percentage of unprofitable customers and improve customer retention and loyalty with proper customer selection as a part of its customer relationship management program. As shown in the table that follows, unprofitable customers have low to average ratings for customer history, desire to repurchase, and product preference, and they have a low purchase amount. They have little or no inclination to recommend the company or its product to others. Their loyalty index is 0 to 40, and their lifetime value is negative to below average.

Unprofitable Customers—Range of Behaviors

Customer History	Purchase Amount	Desire to Repurchase	Product Preference	Would Recommend	Loyalty Index	Lifetime Value
Low to Avg. 0 to 50	Low 0	Low to Avg. 0 to 50	Weak to Avg. 0 to 50	No to Maybe 0 to 50	Low 0 to 40	Negative to Below Avg.

Some unprofitable customers are known as "misfits." They may be wonderful people and even great customers—for some other business. The offerings of the current business do not fit their needs. Although they were initially attracted to this business and its value proposition, they will never be satisfied.[38] They are unlikely to be retained no matter how hard the business tries. The best approach, and often the hardest, is to help them leave.

"Spinners" are another group of unprofitable customers. These customers buy one time and then exit. Typically, they buy because a product is being offered at an attractive price or with a promotional incentive. Telecom companies, for instance, are known for their incentives, and for their spinners. AT&T found that 1.7 million of its customers switched carriers an average of three times a year.[39] Improved customer selection management, with better targeting of promotions, would keep the number of a business's spinners to a minimum. We know that a business can do better if it avoids attracting unprofitable customers. By being aware of the general characteristics of its former unprofitable customers, a business can market more selectively to its target customers. Consider the following quote:

> I will know when our businesses have done a good job of market segmentation when they can tell me to whom we should not sell.[40]
>
> — *Dr. Charles Lillis, Former CEO of MediaOne*

Understanding the differences between target and nontarget customers is an important aspect of customer relationship marketing.[41] A profile that identifies people who are not target customers is just as valuable as a profile that identifies people who are target customers. A customer-acquisition process that profiles unprofitable customers and helps the company avoid them will lower the total cost of attracting new customers and improve the business's customer retention rate. In contrast, unrestrained customer acquisition will attract many customers who will be neither loyal nor profitable, resulting in a negative rather than positive impact on profits due to the cost of customer acquisition with little offsetting income.

Every business loses customers at one time or another. Some were profitable customers whom the business would like to win back. Most of them were mismanaged customers who switched to a competitor due to dissatisfaction. But some were abandoned because they were unprofitable.

Managing Customer Loyalty

Managing customer interactions is a vital aspect of managing customer loyalty and profitability. Successful customer relationship marketing involves managing all customer relationships based on the customer's level of loyalty and profit potential. An effective program starts by identifying the target customers a business can acquire and retain, and it includes strategies for managing new customers and abandoning

FIGURE 1-17 CUSTOMER LOYALTY AND CUSTOMER PROFITABILITY

Customer Classification	Loyalty Scores	Percent Customers	Customer Revenue	Percent Margin	Mktg. & Sales Exp. per Customer	Average Customer Profit
Loyal	70 to 100	20%	$1,000	50%	$100	$400
Repeat	50 to 90	30%	$750	40%	$75	$225
Captive	20 to 40	10%	$600	40%	$75	$165
New	0 to 60	20%	$400	30%	$100	$20
Unprofitable	0 to 40	20%	$100	30%	$50	–$20
Total/Average		**100%**	**$585**	**38%**	**$80**	**$164**

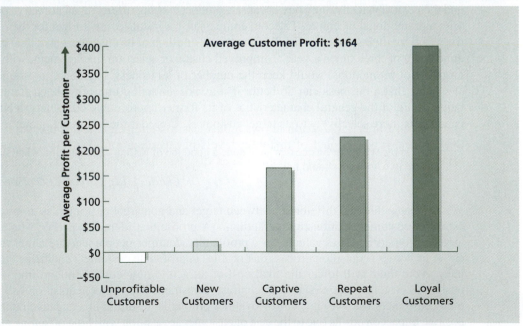

unprofitable ones. Each customer relationship has an impact on overall retention levels and profitability.

Customers who make referrals can have a higher customer lifetime value if we take into account the value of the new customers they bring to the company. Customers who refer others are special and should be rewarded for their efforts. For example, Scott Trade, an online brokerage, offers three complimentary trades valued at $7 per trade to both referring and referred customers. Sprint Nextel offers a $20 service credit for any customer referral and an additional $10 service credit for referrals who become actual customers.

Figure 1-17 illustrates how to evaluate the profit impact of different levels of customer loyalty. The percentage of customers in each customer classification can vary, affecting profit. We can expect that managing the marketing and sales expenses per customer for different loyalty classifications will pay off in greater profitability. Each category of customers requires a different strategy for managing loyalty, with the goal of growing both the overall loyalty index and profitability of the business.

■ Summary

A business's effectiveness in developing market-based strategies that deliver high levels of customer satisfaction depends on the strength of its customer focus. A few years ago, many managers considered that statement to be a nice academic philosophy that nonetheless did not have any practical application for a company trying to improve its profits. Today, however, the evidence shows that businesses with a strong customer focus deliver higher levels of customer satisfaction and above-average profits. Developing a customer focus requires customer leadership, which is evident in senior management leadership, employee customer training, and customer involvement. Letting the voice of the customer be heard is also a necessary part of customer focus; it can be achieved by striving to understand the customer experience, encouraging customer complaints, and seeking to develop customer solutions, not just products. Customer metrics, such as customer satisfaction, customer retention, and customer loyalty, are key performance metrics that measure the success of a customer-focused organization.

The customer satisfaction metric has been shown to be related to profitability. A high overall customer satisfaction score is nice, but unbundling the score into different levels of customer satisfaction allows a business to better understand its overall average and the profit impact of different levels of customer satisfaction. This analysis allows a business to see the percentages of customers who are "dissatisfied" and "somewhat satisfied." Efforts to better understand customer dissatisfaction can be greatly enhanced when a business encourages dissatisfied customers to complain. Allowing them to share their complaints provides both an opportunity to understand causes of customer dissatisfaction and a way to retain customers who otherwise would be lost. Various social media platforms have provided new forums for customers to complain and an opportunity for companies to respond with efforts to repair damaged customer relationships.

Customer satisfaction affects customer retention. And higher levels of customer retention deliver higher customer profits—not only annual profits but future profits as well, due to a longer customer life. It is much more expensive to acquire a new customer than to retain a current customer. Improving customer retention from 67 to 75 percent increases the customer life from 3 to 4 years. This adds one more year of sales and profits and spares the company the high acquisition cost of finding a new customer to replace each lost customer. In addition, customers generally buy more from a business the longer they stay with the business.

The ultimate goal of a customer-focused business is a high level of customer loyalty. A loyal customer has a long purchase history, an above-average purchase amount, a high desire to repurchase, and a strong product preference. A loyal customer would recommend the business's products to others. Loyal customers are highly profitable and have an above-average customer lifetime value. Repeat customers could have an above-average lifetime value and long customer history but are less committed to the business's product and less likely to recommend it to others. Nevertheless, they are very important to the business's profitability and need to be carefully managed with respect to customer retention. The goal is to move them to a higher level of customer loyalty.

Many businesses have captive customers but do not know it. These customers may have a long customer history and average or better lifetime value. But they are not happy and would switch to a different company if they could. As one might guess, they also share their frustrations with others and are more likely to advise others not to buy from the company.

New customers may be first-time customers or returning customers. A customer-focused business knows the customer history and purchase behavior of the returning customers and should manage them accordingly (i.e., differently from the first-time customers). Both types of new customers offer a business the opportunity to move them up in customer loyalty over time and improve profits with a higher customer profit and customer lifetime value.

Finally, some customers are unprofitable. What they need and are willing to pay does not match the business's offerings. These customers were expensive to acquire and are unlikely to ever be profitable. Another group of unprofitable customers are those chasing deals. They will never be loyal; they switch from one product offering to another, usually based on a lower price or a price promotion. The goal of a customer-focused business is to understand all levels of customer loyalty and develop the right customer marketing relationship program for each type of customer in order to better manage the overall profitability of the business.

■ Market-Based Strategic Thinking

1 How would a business like Enterprise Rent-A-Car manage its customer focus using the customer-focus behaviors and practices presented in Chapter 1?

2 Why would a strong customer focus and high levels of customer satisfaction allow Southwest Airlines to be more profitable than other airlines?

3 Why would a very satisfied Apple Mac customer be more profitable than a somewhat satisfied Apple Mac customer?

4 Why would companies with high levels of customer satisfaction produce larger gains in their stock prices than the average S&P 500 company?

5 Lexus is known for high levels of customer satisfaction. How does this affect customer retention over time?

6 If Lexus has an average customer retention of 80 percent, how many purchases does the average customer make over their life as a Lexus customer?

7 If a new coffee company had above-average profits its first couple of years but intentions to repurchase (see Figure 1-9) were declining, with customer retention expected to fall from 67 to 50 percent, what would be the likely impact on future profits?

8 Why would extending the life of an online fashion retail customer from 4 to 5 years affect profits?

9 What makes an Apple customer loyal, and why are loyal customers more profitable than other customers?

10 How could a frequent-flyer airline customer become a captive customer? How do captive airline customers contribute to current and future company profits?

11 How would you manage a repeat McDonald's customer who had a below-average (low) purchase amount?

12 What could cause a business to attract unprofitable customers?

13 How could a repeat customer with a low lifetime value be more valuable than a repeat customer with a high lifetime value?

14 How should a first-time machine tool customer be managed differently from a returning customer?

15 For an industrial supply company, how could a returning new customer have a higher customer lifetime value than a first-time customer?

Marketing Performance Tools and Application Exercises

The four interactive marketing performance tools and application exercises outlined here will add to your understanding of the ways customer performance affects profitability. To access them, go to **rogerjbest.com**. You can determine the answers to the questions listed for each marketing performance tool by entering data included in the questions. You can also enter other data to see the results, and you can save your work. Each marketing performance tool is based on the Chapter 1 figure referenced in parentheses.

1.1 Customer Satisfaction and Profitability (Figure 1-6)
  A. How would average customer sales and average customer profit change for a business with 10 percent "very satisfied" customers, 35 percent "satisfied" customers, and 55 percent "somewhat satisfied" customers?

  B. How would the average customer sales and average customer profit change if this business was able to shift customer satisfaction to 35 percent "very satisfied," 35 percent "satisfied," and 30 percent "somewhat satisfied"?

1.2 Customer Retention (Figure 1-7)
  A. How would customer retention change if the percentage of all dissatisfied customers decreased to 15 percent and the percentage of all satisfied customers increased to 85 percent?

  B. Using the original data, how would customer retention change if the percentage of customers who complained increased from 10 to 50 percent?

1.3 Customer Lifetime Value (Figure 1-11)
  A. How would the lifetime value of the average customer change if the customer life was shortened from 5 to 4 years?

B. How would the lifetime value change if the customer life was extended from 5 to 6 years and in year 6 the net cash flow was $60?

1.4 Customer Loyalty and Profitability
(Figure 1-17)
A. How would the average customer profitability change with 25 percent loyal and 25 percent repeat customers?

B. How would the average customer profit change with the following customer loyalty: 30 percent loyal, 35 percent repeat, 5 percent captive, 20 percent new, and 10 percent unprofitable?

Notes

1. E. Anderson, C. Fornell, and S. Mazvancheryl, "Customer Satisfaction and Stock Valuation," *Journal of Marketing* (October 2004): 172–85.
2. S. Singh, *Market Orientation, Corporate Culture and Business Performance* (Ashgate, 2004); and G. Gebhardt, G.S. Carpenter, and J.F. Sherry, Jr., "Creating a Market Orientation: A Longitudinal, Multifirm, Grounded Analysis of Cultural Transformation," *Journal of Marketing* (October 2006): 37–55.
3. F.F. Reichheld and W.E. Sasser, Jr., "Zero Defections: Quality Comes to Services," *Harvard Business Review* (September–October 1990): 106–11; and F.F. Reichheld, "Loyalty-Based Management," *Harvard Business Review* (March–April 1993): 64–73.
4. L. Aksoy, B. Cooil, C. Groening, T.L. Keiningham, and A. Yalcin, "The Long-Term Stock Market Valuation of Customer Satisfaction," *Journal of Marketing* (July 2008): 105–22.
5. *2008 Southwest Airlines Annual Report* (February 9, 2009) 2.
6. C. Homburg, J. Wieseke, and T. Bornemann, "Implementing the Marketing Concept at the Employee-Customer Interface: The Role of Customer Knowledge," *Journal of Marketing* (July 2009): 64–81.
7. C. Meyer and A. Schwager, "Understanding Customer Experience," *Harvard Business Review* (February 2007): 118.
8. E. Yellin, *Your Call Is (Not That) Important to Us* (Free Press, 2009).
9. N. Bomey, "Redesigned Recipe Leads to Sales Increases for Domino's Pizza," AnnArbor.com LLC (May 5, 2010): www.annarbor.com, retrieved June 2010.
10. T. Wiesel, B. Skiera, and J. Villanuveva, "Customer Equity: An Integral Part of Financial Reporting," *Journal of Marketing* (March 2008): 1–14.
11. "Enterprise Asks What Customers Are Thinking and Acts," *USA Today* (May 22, 2006).
12. T. Wiesel, B. Skiera, and J. Villanueva, "Customer Equity: An Integral Part of Financial Reporting," *Journal of Marketing* (March 2008): 1–14.
13. American Customer Satisfaction Index, www.theacsi.org; data used in Figure 1-4 retrieved June 2011.
14. P. Byrne, "Only 10% of Companies Satisfy Customers," *Transportation and Distribution* (December 1993); and T. Eck, "Are Customers Happy? Don't Assume," *Positive Impact* (July 1992): 3.
15. L. Seldon and G. Colvin, *Angel Customers and Demon Customers* (Portfolio, 2003): 45–59.
16. P. Doyle, *Value-Based Marketing* (Wiley, 2000): 8–85.
17. TARP, "Consumer Complaint Handling in America: An Update Study," White House Office of Consumer Affairs, Washington, DC, 1986; TARP, "Consumer Complaint Handling in America, Final Report," U.S. Office of Consumer Affairs, Washington, DC, 1979; and K. Rhoades, "The Importance of Customer Complaints," *Protect Yourself* (January 1988): 15–18.
18. A.M. McGahan and P. Ghemawat, "Competition to Retain Customers," *Marketing Science* 13 (Spring 1994): 165–76; and M.H. McCormack, "One Disappointed Customer Is One Too Many," *Positive Impact* 4 (September 1993): 7–8.
19. D. Ariely, "The Customers' Revenge," *Harvard Business Review* (December 2007): 31–36.
20. R. Rubin, "Should Your Company Sue Over Social Media Comments?" *Inc.* (April 21, 2010).
21. M. Bard, "Does Social Media Affect Consumer Complaints?" *SmartBlog* (January 5, 2011), retrieved January 2011.
22. T. Lucia, "Domino's Theory—Only Service Succeeds," *Positive Impact* (February 1992): 6–7.
23. F.F. Reichheld and W.E. Sasser, Jr., "Zero Defections: Quality Comes to Services," *Harvard Business Review* (September–October 1990): 106–11; and F.F. Reichheld, "Loyalty-Based Management," *Harvard Business Review* (March–April 1993): 64–73.
24. T. Jones and W.E. Sasser, Jr., "Why Satisfied Customers Defect," *Harvard Business Review* (November–December 1995): 88–89.
25. F.F. Reichheld and P. Schefter, "E-Loyalty: Your Secret Weapon on the Web," *Harvard Business Review* (July–August 2000): 105–13.
26. T. Wiesel, B. Skiera, and J. Villanuveva, "Customer Equity: An Integral Part of Financial Reporting," *Journal of Marketing* (March 2008): 1–14.

27. R. Clarke, "Addressing Voluntary Disenrollment," *CDR Healthcare Resources* (1997): 10–12.

28. M. Johnson and A. Gustafsson, *Improving Customer Satisfaction, Loyalty, and Profit* (New York: Jossey-Bass, 2000).

29. P. Nunes and B. Johnson, "Are Some Customers More Equal than Others?" *Harvard Business Review* (November 2001): 37–50.

30. S. Smith and J. Wheeler, *Managing the Customer Experience* (Prentice Hall, 2002).

31. M. Nykamp, *The Customer Differential* (AMACOM, 2001); and S. Gupta and D. Lehmann, "Customers as Assets," *Journal of International Marketing* (2003).

32. W. Reinartz and V. Kumar, "The Mismanagement of Customer Loyalty," *Harvard Business Review* (July 2002): 86–94.

33. T. Wagner, T. Hennig-Thurau, and T. Rudolph, "Does Customer Demotion Jeopardize Loyalty?" *Journal of Marketing* (May 2009): 69–85.

34. V. Kumar, J.A. Petersen, and R.P. Leone, "How Valuable Is Word of Mouth?" *Harvard Business Review* (October 2007): 139–46.

35. Y. Liu, "The Long-Term Impact of Loyalty Programs on Customer Purchase Behavior and Loyalty," *Journal of Marketing* (October 2007): 19–35.

36. J. Griffin and M. Lowenstein, *Customer Winback* (Jossey-Bass, 2001).

37. V. Mittal, M. Sarkees, and F. Murshed, "The Right Way to Manage Unprofitable Customers," *Harvard Business Review* (April 2008): 95–102.

38. R. Dhar and R. Glazer, "Hedging Customers," *Harvard Business Review* (May 2003): 86–92.

39. S. Schriver, "Customer Loyalty—Going, Going, …" *American Demographics* (September 1997): 20–23.

40. Quotation from conference addresses by Charles M. Lillis. Used with permission.

41. E. Sullivan, "Just Say No," *Marketing News* (April 15, 2008): 17.

Present Value Table

Period (N)	DR = 8%	DR = 9%	DR = 10%	DR = 11%	DR = 12%	DR = 13%	DR = 14%	DR = 15%
0	1.000	1.000	1.000	1.000	1.000	1.000	1.000	1.000
1	0.926	0.917	0.909	0.901	0.893	0.885	0.887	0.870
2	0.857	0.842	0.826	0.812	0.797	0.783	0.769	0.756
3	0.794	0.772	0.751	0.731	0.712	0.693	0.675	0.658
4	0.735	0.708	0.683	0.659	0.636	0.613	0.592	0.572
5	0.681	0.650	0.621	0.593	0.567	0.543	0.519	0.497
6	0.630	0.596	0.564	0.535	0.507	0.480	0.456	0.432
7	0.583	0.547	0.513	0.482	0.452	0.425	0.400	0.376
8	0.540	0.502	0.467	0.434	0.404	0.376	0.351	0.327
9	0.500	0.460	0.424	0.391	0.361	0.333	0.308	0.284
10	0.463	0.422	0.386	0.352	0.322	0.295	0.270	0.247
11	0.429	0.388	0.350	0.317	0.287	0.261	0.237	0.215
12	0.397	0.356	0.319	0.286	0.257	0.231	0.208	0.187
13	0.368	0.326	0.290	0.258	0.229	0.204	0.182	0.163
14	0.340	0.299	0.263	0.232	0.205	0.181	0.160	0.141
15	0.315	0.275	0.239	0.209	0.183	0.160	0.140	0.123
16	0.292	0.252	0.218	0.188	0.163	0.141	0.123	0.107
17	0.270	0.231	0.198	0.170	0.146	0.125	0.108	0.093
18	0.250	0.212	0.180	0.153	0.130	0.111	0.095	0.081
19	0.232	0.194	0.164	0.138	0.116	0.098	0.083	0.070
20	0.215	0.178	0.149	0.124	0.104	0.087	0.073	0.061

$$\textbf{Present Value Formula: } PV = \frac{1}{(1 + DR)^N}$$

PV = Present Value of $1.00
DR = Discount Rate (cost of borrowing or desired rate of return)
N = Number of periods before the $1.00 will be received

Example I: N = 5 periods and the Discount Rate (DR) = 10%

$$PV = \frac{1}{(1 + 0.1)^5} = \frac{1}{1.611} = 0.621 \ (\$1.00 \text{ received in 5 years is worth } \$0.621 \text{ today})$$

Example II: N = 2.33 periods and the Discount Rate (DR) = 10%

$$PV = \frac{1}{(1 + 0.1)^{2.33}} = \frac{1}{1.249} = 0.801 \ (\$1.00 \text{ received in 2.33 years is worth } \$0.801 \text{ today})$$

Marketing Metrics and Marketing Profitability

■ The reason for marketing's low level of credibility is largely its lack of disciplined financial-return measures to assess the value of its contribution to the enterprise.[1]

Marketing *metrics* measure marketing performance. Marketing *analytics* are the tools and data used to create marketing metrics. The system used to measure customer satisfaction in Chapter 1 is a marketing analytic. The overall customer satisfaction index is a marketing metric, as is the percentage of "very satisfied" customers.

Marketing metrics and marketing profitability are related to business unit and company profitability, as shown in the flowchart. It is essential for marketing and product managers to demonstrate their contributions to a company's profit. Measures of marketing profitability enable them to do so. These metrics have added importance in that they directly relate to business and company profit.

MEASURING PERFORMANCE

BioTronics is a $390 million business that manufactures high-tech specialty electronics equipment for the biotechnology industry. Three years ago, a new management team was put in place after the company delivered several years of disappointing performance. The new management team reorganized the business and designed programs to lower unit costs, control overhead expenses, and facilitate better management of assets. In addition, the new management team implemented an extensive sales training program that improved the productivity of the sales force from $5 million to $7.5 million per salesperson.

FIGURE 2-1 BIOTRONICS' PERFORMANCE AND FINANCIAL METRICS

BioTronics' Performance (millions)	Base Year	Year 1	Year 2	Year 3
Sales Revenues	$254	$293	$337	$390
Cost of Goods Sold	$127	$139	$157	$175
Gross Profit	$127	$154	$180	$215
Marketing & Sales Expenses	$61	$67	$74	$82
General & Administrative Expenses	$20	$23	$27	$31
Other Expenses	$30	$35	$40	$47
Pre-Tax Profit	**$16**	**$29**	**$39**	**$55**
Financial Metrics				
Pre-Tax Return on Sales	6.3%	9.9%	11.6%	14.1%
Sales-to-Assets Ratio	0.90	0.95	1.00	1.05
Pre-Tax Return on Assets	5.7%	9.4%	11.6%	14.8%

The results were sensational! In 3 years, the new management team increased sales by $136 million and, more important, more than tripled net profit before taxes. As shown in Figure 2-1, BioTronics' return on sales grew from 6.3 to 14.1 percent, and its return on assets increased from 5.7 to 14.8 percent. On the basis of the information in the table,

■ How would you rate BioTronics' performance over the 3-year period?
■ Which aspects of BioTronics' performance were most impressive?
■ Should BioTronics continue to follow the same strategy it used during this period?

Most of us would agree that BioTronics' performance over the 3-year period was outstanding. Who would not want to run a business with that level of profitable growth? Yet, despite the impressive increases in sales and profits, we could be making a mistake by judging BioTronics' performance solely on *financial* measures of performance. Sales revenues, net profit, return on sales, assets as a percentage of sales, and return on assets are certainly reliable measures of internal financial performance, but they do not provide an *external* or *market-based* view of performance. From the financial measures alone, we cannot tell how BioTronics performed relative to the external benchmarks of market growth, competitive pricing, relative product and service quality, and ability to satisfy and retain customers. The strategy that BioTronics used during the 3-year period may or may not have been the best way to achieve profitable growth, and continuing to follow that strategy may or may not achieve the best possible results in the future.

In actuality, as remarkable as the company's growth seems, BioTronics should have had $41 million in additional profits over the 3 years, profits that, in effect, the corporation and its shareholders lost. This information becomes apparent when marketing performance metrics are added to the company scorecard. Had BioTronics used these marketing performance metrics to help guide its strategic thinking, rather than relying on financial metrics alone, the company would have realized it was losing share in a rapidly growing market.

FIGURE 2-2 BIOTRONICS' MARKETING METRICS

Marketing Metrics	Base Year	Year 1	Year 2	Year 3
Market Metrics				
Market Growth (% dollars)	20.5%	22.5%	21.4%	21.3%
BioTronics' Sales Growth	15.3%	15.4%	15.0%	15.7%
Market Share	10.0%	9.4%	8.9%	8.5%
Competitiveness Metrics				
Product Performance	19	17	15	11
Service Quality	0	–3	–7	–9
Customer Value	28	25	16	8
Customer Metrics				
Customer Satisfaction Index	78	73	68	64
Customer Retention	77%	75%	69%	65%
Customer Lifetime Value	$103.0	$96.0	$67.0	$45.0

Applying Marketing Metrics

To complement its internal financial performance metrics, a business needs a parallel set of external marketing metrics to track its market-based performance.[2] Although these external measures of performance may lack some of the elegance associated with financial accounting, they provide a more strategic view of a business's performance.

Figure 2-2 includes a set of marketing performance metrics that paint a much different picture of BioTronics' performance than the one portrayed by the financial measures in Figure 2-1. These marketing metrics provide three significant insights.[3] First, although the corporation's sales showed impressive growth, the rate of growth did not match the overall rate for the rapidly expanding biotechnology market, as shown in Figure 2-3. During this period, then, BioTronics was losing market share. In all, the company's market share fell from 10 to 8.5 percent. The decline went undetected because BioTronics did not track external market metrics, such as market demand, market growth, and market share.[4]

Second, product and service performance each diminished *relative to competition*. These declines do not necessarily mean that BioTronics' product and service quality diminished. Competitors may have simply moved ahead in delivering superior product and service performance. The competition's more rapid progress caused BioTronics to lose ground in these two areas *relative* to its competitors, leading to a reduction in customer value.

Third, customer satisfaction declined, probably due in part to the diminished product and service quality, resulting in a decrease in the customer retention rate and average customer lifetime value.

Instead of the highly favorable impression that the financial metrics presented, we now have a much different assessment of BioTronics' 3-year performance. The corporation's performance was marked by increased profits, true, but also by customer defection, a decline in market share, and a greatly diminished customer value. From the financial metrics, BioTronics' management and shareholders know they performed

FIGURE 2-3 MARKET METRICS PROVIDE AN EXTERNAL VIEW OF PERFORMANCE

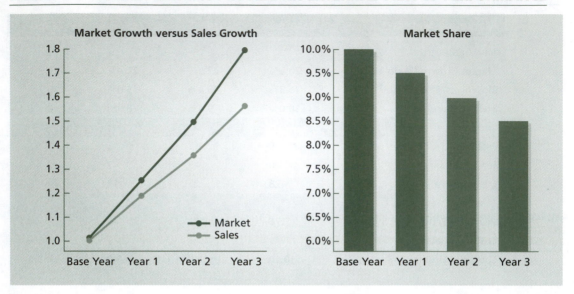

well, but, without the marketing metrics, they don't know how much they really lost and will continue to lose.

A Marketing-Metrics-Based Strategy

What would have been the impact of a BioTronics strategy to hold market share? To hold its base-year 10 percent share in the growing biotechnology market, the corporation should have invested more heavily in marketing, sales, and product development to keep pace with market demand and competitors. Had BioTronics adequately invested in marketing, sales, and R&D to maintain its 10 percent market share, it would have had a good chance of achieving the results in Figure 2-4.

A market-based strategy to hold share would have resulted in an increase in pre-tax return on sales (17%) and delivered approximately the same return on assets as the internally driven strategy, and it would have produced an additional $41 million in net profit (before taxes). This is $41 million that the corporation essentially gave up in bottom-line pre-tax profit. Furthermore, BioTronics' "lost" pre-tax profits will be greater over the next 3-year period even if halts the erosion of its market share, and even if market growth completely subsides. If BioTronics' market share continues to erode and the biotech market continues to grow, the "lost profits" over the next 3 years could easily amount to $100 million.

The BioTronics story underscores the importance of marketing performance metrics. They are the foundation of market-based management. The financial systems of most businesses are set up to track revenues, costs, factory overhead, accounts receivable, operating expenses, and profits, but they usually overlook the fact that a business's customers are its most important asset and the only significant source of positive cash flow. Not attracting new customers during a period of market growth simply means a business will have to work harder and spend more to regain its previous market share. It will need a sizeable expenditure to attract a large number of new customers.

FIGURE 2-4 MARKETING-METRICS-BASED STRATEGY TO HOLD SHARE

BioTronics' Performance (millions)	Base Year	Year 1	Year 2	Year 3
Market Demand	$2,540	$3,111	$3,777	$4,580
Market Share	10.0%	10.0%	10.0%	10.0%
Sales Revenues	$254	$311	$378	$458
Cost of Goods Sold	$127	$148	$176	$206
Gross Profit	$127	$163	$202	$252
Marketing & Sales Expenses	$61	$71	$83	$96
General & Administrative Expenses	$20	$23	$27	$31
Other Expenses	$30	$35	$40	$47
Pre-Tax Profit	**$16**	**$34**	**$52**	**$78**
Financial Metrics				
Pre-Tax Return on Sales	6.3%	11.0%	13.8%	17.0%
Sales-to-Assets Ratio	0.90	0.95	1.00	1.05
Pre-Tax Return on Assets	5.7%	10.4%	13.7%	17.9%
Lost Profits*	**$0**	**−$5**	**−$13**	**−$23**

*Pre-Tax Profit in Figure 2-1 minus Pre-Tax Profit in Figure 2-4

MARKETING METRICS

Metrics are really a big part of everyday life in every profession. Figure 2-5 lists three health care metrics routinely used during a visit to the doctor. These three metrics provide personal measurements from which your doctor can quickly determine if there are any variations from the benchmarks for body temperature, blood pressure, and pulse

FIGURE 2-5 WHY MARKETING METRICS ARE IMPORTANT

Analytics	Metrics	Important Things Metrics Tell Us
■ **Health Care**		
Thermometer	98.6	Normal Body Temperature
Blood Pressure	120/80	Normal Diastolic/Systolic Blood Pressure
Pulse Rate	65	Normal Pulse Rate for Patient's Age and Health
■ **Automobile**		
Gas Gauge	25%	Only a Quarter of a Tank Left
Speedometer	63 MPH	8 Miles per Hour over the Posted Limit of 55
Pressure Gauge	40 PSI	Tire Pressure at the Recommended Level
■ **Marketing**		
Customer Retention	67%	The Company is Losing 33% of its Customers Annually
Marketing ROI	150%	$1.50 in Marketing Profits per $1 in Marketing and Sales Expenses
Share Development Index	40	Only 40% of the Share Potential Has Been Developed

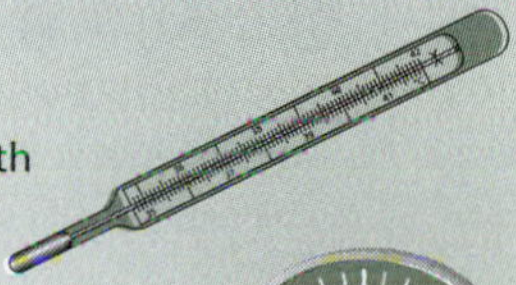

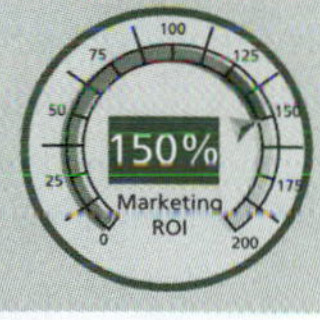

rate. Even more familiar are the metrics we use in operating our cars. The fuel gauge tells us roughly how much gas we have left, the speedometer tells us our speed, and an air pressure gauge lets us know if our tires are above, below, or right at the recommended pressure.

The marketing metrics listed in Figure 2-5 are just as important for a business's managers as the health care metrics are for a doctor and patient and as the metrics used in operating a car are for its driver. The marketing metrics gauge the business's performance and indicate how management can expect the business to perform in the future. For example, a market share of 10 percent lets managers know the share of the market that the company is attaining, whereas a relative market index of 1.0 means that a business is tied for the highest market share among competitors. A customer retention rate of 67 percent translates to an average customer life of 3 years. However, for that level of customer life, the customer lifetime value is negative, meaning the company is still losing money on its 3-year repeat customers as a group. A marketing return on investment (marketing ROI) of 150 percent means that for every dollar invested in marketing and sales expenses, the company is realizing $1.50 in marketing profits. Finally, a share development index of 40 means that the business or product has only obtained 40 percent of its share potential.

Each of these marketing metrics gives us important measurements of marketing's performance. Yet, in a CEO survey conducted by The Conference Board, 51 percent of CEOs responded that marketing lacks meaningful performance metrics.[5]

Financial Metrics versus Marketing Metrics

Most businesses have excellent financial performance metrics that report important ratios for profits, costs, and assets, as shown on the left side of Figure 2-6. These metrics help a business understand its performance and profitability. These *internal* metrics, however, do not provide the needed insight into how the business or a product is performing in the market. The marketing performance metrics[6] shown on the right side of Figure 2-6 are *external* metrics, many of which are leading indicators of future financial performance. For example, if customers' intentions to repurchase are declining, a business will know that declines in sales and profitability are also very likely unless it acts to prevent customer defections.

Marketing performance metrics are at the heart of market-based management because they tell us how a product or business is performing in the market.[7]

> Metrics should be necessary (i.e., the company cannot do without them), precise, consistent, and sufficient (i.e., comprehensive) for review purposes.[8]

They are important for two reasons. First, they provide measures of marketing performance, such as customer satisfaction, retention, and loyalty. Secondly, marketing performance metrics are correlated with profitability. Although they do not directly affect present profitability, they are a barometer of current and future financial performance. If customer retention is declining, for example, a business will need to attract more new customers to hold market share. Because it is more expensive to acquire new customers than to serve retained customers, profits may be expected to decline even if market share doesn't. Marketing performance metrics fall into four major catgories, as presented in Figure 2-6:

FIGURE 2-6 FINANCIAL METRICS VERSUS MARKETING METRICS

FINANCIAL METRICS	Performance	MARKETING METRICS	Performance
Profit Metrics		**Market Metrics**	
• Gross Profit	55.0%	• Market Growth Rate	22.5%
• Return on Sales	17.0%	• Market Share	8.5%
• Return on Assets	17.8%	• Market Development Index	40
Expenses Metrics		**Customer Metrics**	
• Marketing & Sales Expenses	21.0%	• Customer Satisfaction	64
• General & Administrative Expenses	8.0%	• Customer Retention	65%
• Other Expenses	12.0%	• Customer Lifetime Value	$45
Asset Management Metrics		**Competitiveness Metrics**	
• Sales-to-Assets Ratio	1.05	• Product Performance	11.0
• Accounts Receivable	15.0%	• Service Quality	−9.0
• Capacity Utilization	67.0%	• Customer Value	8.0
Shareholder Metrics		**Marketing Profitability Metrics**	
• Return on Equity	15.0%	• Net Marketing Contribution	$156
• Return on Capital	13.0%	• Marketing ROI	162%
• Earnings per Share	$2.00	• Marketing ROS	34.0%

1. **Market Metrics**—Market metrics measure a market with respect to current performance and profit impact. For example, the relative market share of a product or business is a market performance metric that assesses the market share of that product or business relative to its three top competitors. As shown in Figure 2-7, the higher a business's relative market share, the higher its profits. This market performance metric is discussed in Chapters 6 and 15. Other market performance metrics are presented in Chapters 3, 6, and 15.

2. **Customer Metrics**—Customer metrics gauge a business or product in terms of its performance with customers. In Chapter 1, we learned about several customer performance metrics, and others are discussed in Chapters 3, 9, and 15. We already know how they indirectly affect profitability. As shown in Figure 2-7, for example, a business that increases its customer retention rate can expect to improve its profits.

3. **Competitiveness Metrics**—These performance metrics index a business or product against benchmark competitors with respect to product performance, service quality, brand image, cost of purchase, and customer value. For example, in Figure 2-7 relative service quality has a positive correlation with profitability. This and other competitiveness performance metrics are presented in Chapters 4, 6, and 15.

4. **Marketing Profitability Metrics**—Marketing ROI is a key marketing profitability metric that measures the profit impact of an investment in marketing and sales expenses. Because it is a percentage metric, the marketing ROI of any of a company's divisions, regions, or product lines can be compared with the marketing ROIs of other divisions, regions, or product lines and with the company's overall marketing

FIGURE 2-7 FOUR SELECTED MARKETING METRICS AND PROFIT IMPACT

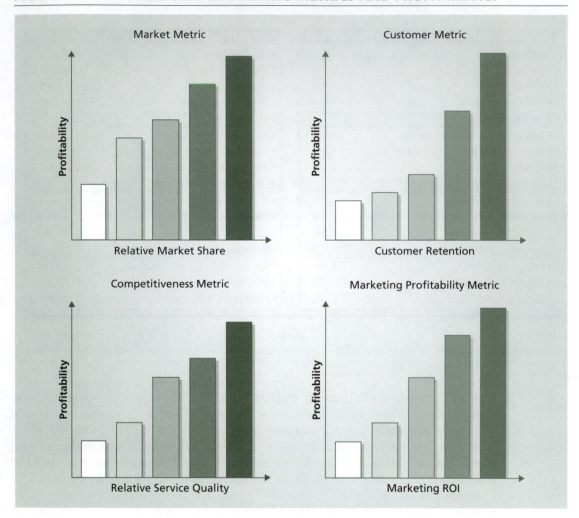

ROI. A company can also compare its marketing ROI with that of its competitors and benchmark publicly traded companies. Later in this chapter, we will learn about marketing ROI. We will also discuss two other marketing profitability metrics: net marketing contribution and marketing return on sales (marketing ROS).

Internal versus External Metrics

To track total performance, a business needs both *internal* and *external* performance metrics. As presented in Figure 2-8, internal company metrics typically track product defects, late deliveries, late payments, and inventory turnover. They also track unit costs, expenses, asset utilization, employee and capital productivity, and overall financial profitability.

FIGURE 2-8 INTERNAL VERSUS EXTERNAL METRICS AND FORWARD-LOOKING VERSUS BACKWARD-LOOKING METRICS

PERFORMANCE PERSPECTIVE	TIME HORIZON	
	Forward-Looking Metrics	Backward-Looking Metrics
INTERNAL Company Metrics	Company metrics applied during an operating period, such as: ■ Product Defects ■ Late Deliveries ■ Late Payments ■ Inventory Turnover	Company metrics reported at the end of an operating period, such as: ■ Sales Revenues ■ Percent Gross Profit ■ Net Profit Before Tax ■ Return on Assets
EXTERNAL Marketing Metrics	Marketing metrics applied during an operating period, such as: ■ Customer Awareness ■ Customer Satisfaction ■ Perceived Performance ■ Intent to Repurchase	Marketing metrics reported at the end of an operating period, such as: ■ Relative Market Share ■ Market Share ■ Customer Retention ■ Revenue per Customer

External marketing metrics provide a view of a company from a market-based perspective. They track the levels of awareness that customers have of a company's product, the customers' overall satisfaction, their perceptions of product performance, and their intentions to repurchase. These metrics also track the company's performance in its market, including market share, customer satisfaction, customer retention rate, and revenue per customer.

Although CPA firms have done an excellent job developing and applying internal measures of a business's performance, the next frontier for CPA firms, as well as market analysis firms, will be the development and application of standardized external measures of a business's market-based performance. With both sets of measures available to them, managers, financial analysts, and shareholders will be in a better position to evaluate a business's marketing effectiveness and overall financial performance.

Forward-Looking versus Backward-Looking Metrics

Some internal company metrics and some external marketing metrics are *forward-looking* metrics, whereas others in both groups are *backward-looking*, as indicated in Figure 2-8. The forward-looking metrics, such as late deliveries and customer satisfaction, indicate future performance and normally are applied at regular intervals *during* a company's reporting period. The backward-looking metrics, such as pre-tax net profit and market share, measure past performance and are applied *at the end* of the reporting period. These measures tell a company where it stands with respect to current performance but do not provide any insights on future performance.[9]

External Marketing Metrics

The primary purpose of marketing metrics is to maintain an ongoing measure of marketing performance and profitability.[10] The results of those metrics that serve as predictors of financial performance are then used to develop a strategy to improve performance. These forward-looking marketing metrics are especially important because they are indicators of future financial performance.[11] The backward-looking marketing metrics correspond more closely to past financial performance, for a fiscal period that has just ended.

Product awareness, intentions to purchase, product trial, and customer satisfaction, along with customer perceptions of relative product quality, service quality, and customer value, all serve as forward-looking marketing metrics. Significant changes in any of them, positive or negative, generally precede actual changes in customer purchasing behavior. As a result, these forward-looking measures of customer thinking and attitude are key indicators of future purchasing behavior and, hence, of future revenue and profits.

A business's customers, for example, may be satisfied but still perceive the value they derive from the business's product, relative to competing alternatives, to be steadily diminishing. The business may not have done anything to dissatisfy customers; instead, competitors may have simply improved in delivering customer value by adding benefits without implementing major price increases. The business's customers then perceive that the value derived from the business's product has diminished, and this change in perception makes customers more inclined to buy the competitors' products. With an early warning signal, a market-based business can take corrective action before customers switch. Without forward-looking marketing metrics, problems may go undetected until declines in financial performance make it clear, too late, that something went wrong.

Some of the backward-looking marketing metrics are relative market share, market share, customer retention, and revenue per customer. These marketing metrics are generally applied at the end of a financial performance period, and each provides a different set of performance diagnostics and insights.[12]

Let's assume sales revenues are increasing ahead of forecast and profits are higher than expected. Most businesses would be pleased with this performance. But if the backward-looking marketing metrics show that the business is losing share in a growing market and a poor customer retention rate is masked by new customer growth, management would have cause for concern. Without external marketing metrics, management has only the limited insights of an internal perspective on end-result performance.

NET MARKETING CONTRIBUTION—A MARKETING PROFITABILITY METRIC

Devising a marketing profitability metric is a significant step forward in providing a way for marketing and product managers to communicate their contribution to business unit and company profits. To be credible, it is important for a marketing profitability metric to operate within the boundaries of reported financial information. It also must clearly demonstrate the contribution that a marketing strategy and the investment in it make to the profit of a business. A marketing profitability metric also needs to be strategic. It must be an integral part of any marketing strategy to allow the marketing profitability of an overall strategy or a particular marketing tactic to be determined and reported with the same credibility as the results of a financial profitability metric.

FIGURE 2-9 ADDING MARKETING PROFITS TO THE INCOME STATEMENT

Income Statement—Traditional Area of Performance (millions)		Income Statement—With Marketing Profits Area of Performance (millions)	
Sales Revenues	$125.0	Sales Revenues	$125.0
Cost of Goods Sold	$76.5	Cost of Goods Sold	$76.5
Gross Profit	$48.5	Gross Profit	$48.5
Sales, General, & Admin. Expenses	$23.5	**Marketing & Sales Expenses**	**$18.5**
Other Operating Expenses	$15.0	**Net Marketing Contribution**	**$30.0**
Operating Income*	$10.0	General, Admin., & Other Operating Expenses	$20.0
Performance Metric		Operating Income	$10.0
Operating Income (% sales)	8.0%	**Performance Metric**	
*Also IBIT (Income Before Interest & Taxes)		**Operating Income (% sales)**	**8.0%**

Let's start with a very basic and traditional view of a business's accounting for profits and work toward a measure of its marketing profits.[13] The left table in Figure 2-9 presents the operating income for Santa Fe Sportswear, a company that manufactures and markets a narrow line of specialty clothing through high-end retail boutiques. Operating income is simply sales minus three major areas of business expense—the cost of the goods sold; sales, general, and administrative (SGA) expenses; and other operating expenses. These three major categories of business expense are defined in Figure 2-10.

FIGURE 2-10 DEFINING BUSINESS EXPENSES

Cost of Goods Sold (COGS)	
Variable Cost	An expense that changes on a per-unit basis when production volume increases or decreases, such as the cost of materials, labor, and packaging.
Manufacturing Overhead	Fixed expenses for a business's facilities, equipment, management, and other manufacturing needs, which do not vary for a given production capacity.
Sales, General, and Administrative (SGA) Expenses	
Marketing & Sales Expenses	Marketing and advertising expenses, plus costs related to all sales and customer support services.
General & Administrative Expenses	Costs associated with managing a business, such as senior managers' salaries, professional fees, management of the business's property, and office supplies.
Other Operating Expenses	
Research & Development Expenses	Costs associated with improving products and developing new ones.
Taxes and Interest	Income, property, and other taxes, and interest on borrowing.

$$\underset{\text{Income}}{\text{Operating}} = \text{Sales Revenues} - \text{Cost of Goods} - \text{SGA Expenses} - \text{Other Operating Expenses}$$
$$= \$125 \text{ million} - \$76.5 \text{ million} - \$23.5 \text{ million} - \$15 \text{ million}$$
$$= \mathbf{\$10 \ million}$$

By simply separating marketing and sales expenses from SGA expenses, we can obtain a measure of marketing's contribution to profit, as shown in the right table of Figure 2-9.[14]

Marketing and sales expenses (MSE) are the costs of marketing administration, sales, customer service, and advertising. Marketing and sales expenses do not include general and administrative expenses, research and development expenses, or other expenses. This metric allows us to understand more clearly how much a company is investing in marketing and sales each year to achieve a certain level of sales and percent gross profit.

$$\underset{\text{Income}}{\text{Operating}} = \text{Sales Revenues} - \text{Cost of Goods} - \boxed{\text{SGA Exp.}} - \text{Other Operating Exp.}$$
$$\downarrow$$
$$= \text{Sales Revenues} - \text{Cost of Goods} - \boxed{\text{MSE} - \text{G\&A Exp.}} - \text{Other Operating Exp.}$$
$$= \$125 \text{ million} - \$76.5 \text{ million} - \$18.5 \text{ million} - \$5 \text{ million} - \$15 \text{ million}$$
$$= \mathbf{\$10 \ million}$$

Because marketing and sales strategies impact prices and margins, we gain an even greater insight into the impact of marketing and sales by using the *percent gross profit* in the operating income equation. As shown in the following equation, percent gross profit is simply the percentage of sales that is gross profit.

$$\textbf{Percent Gross Profit} = (\text{Sales} - \text{Cost of Goods Sold})/\text{Sales} \times 100\%$$
$$= (\$125 \text{ million} - \$76.5 \text{ million})/\$125 \text{ million} \times 100\%$$
$$= \mathbf{38.8\%}$$

The next calculation uses information about sales, percent gross profit, and marketing and sales expenses and isolates the non-marketing and non-sales expenses (general and administrative expenses and other operating expenses) in the operating income equation.

$$\underset{\text{Income}}{\text{Operating}} = \boxed{\text{Sales} \times \text{Percent Gross Profit}} - \text{MSE} - \text{G\&A Exp.} - \text{Other Operating Exp.}$$
$$= \boxed{\$125 \text{ million} \times 38.8\% - \$18.5 \text{ million}} - \$5 \text{ million} - \$15 \text{ million}$$
$$= \mathbf{\$10 \ million}$$

With this information we can create a marketing profitability metric that we call *net marketing contribution (NMC)*. Using the performance of Santa Fe Sportswear from Figure 2-9, we apply the following equation to obtain the NMC. This metric is simply the gross profit (sales times the percent margin) produced by a marketing strategy, minus the marketing and sales expenses needed to produce that level of sales and gross profit. NMC is an important marketing performance metric because it provides a way for marketing and product managers to communicate the profit impact of a strategy to management. It also sets a benchmark from which to gauge improving or deteriorating marketing profitability.

FIGURE 2-11 SANTA FE SPORTSWEAR—NET MARKETING CONTRIBUTION AND PROFIT

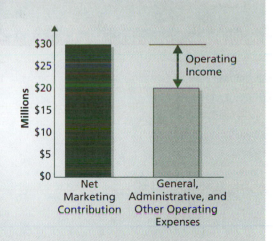

Performance (millions)	2009
Sales Revenues	$125.0
Percent Gross Profit	38.8%
Gross Profit	$48.5
Marketing & Sales Expenses (% sales)	14.8%
Marketing & Sales Expenses	$18.5
Net Marketing Contribution	$30.0
General & Administrative Expenses	$5.0
Other Operating Expenses	$15.0
Operating Income	$10.0
Performance Metric	
Operating Income (% sales)	8.0%

$$\text{Net Marketing Contribution} = \text{Sales Revenues} \times \text{Percent Gross Profit} - \text{Marketing \& Sales Expenses}$$
$$= \$125 \text{ million} \times 38.8\% - \$18.5 \text{ million}$$
$$= \mathbf{\$30 \text{ million}}$$

Santa Fe Sportswear's NMC of $30 million is derived from sales of $125 million and a gross profit of 38.8 percent margin. The gross profit ($48.5 million) is the amount that the strategies produced before the $18.5 million in marketing and sales expenses was subtracted After that subtraction, we have the net marketing contribution to profit of $30 million.

The NMC of $30 million is the only source of positive profit, as shown in Figure 2-11. All other expenses are deducted from this amount. For Santa Fe Sportswear, the $30 million produced in marketing profits paid for $5 million in general and administrative (G&A) expenses and $15 million in other operating expenses to produce $10 million in operating income—income before interest and taxes (IBIT).

$$\text{Operating Income} = \text{Net Marketing Contribution} - \text{G\&A Exp.} - \text{Other Operating Expenses}$$
$$= \$30 \text{ million} - \$5 \text{ million} - \$15 \text{ million}$$
$$= \mathbf{\$10 \text{ million}}$$

MARKETING AND SALES EXPENSES

Whether we are working within a company or evaluating a company's net marketing contribution from the outside, we all face the same unfortunate accounting problem: determining what to include in marketing and sales expenses in order to fairly assess

FIGURE 2-12 MARKETING AND SALES EXPENSES SEPARATED FROM SALES, GENERAL, AND ADMINISTRATIVE EXPENSES

Company	Sales, General, & Admin. Exp. (% sales)	Marketing & Sales Expenses (% sales)	General & Admin. Exp. (% sales)	Marketing & Sales Expenses (% SGA)
Adobe Systems	39.9%	31.1%	8.8%	78%
Campbell's Soup	22.1%	14.5%	7.6%	66%
Cisco Systems	27.3%	21.2%	6.1%	78%
Microsoft	29.5%	22.5%	7.0%	76%
Oracle	25.9%	21.1%	4.8%	81%
SAP	25.5%	20.7%	4.8%	81%
Yahoo	28.8%	20.4%	8.4%	71%
Average	**29.7%**	**22.3%**	**7.4%**	**74%**

the company's net marketing contribution. As a rule of thumb, marketing and sales expenses should include all costs associated with bringing products to market, as well as all expenses related to supporting these products. These expenses include costs of advertising, marketing, sales, product management, technical support, customer service, and any other expense that is directly related to products and markets served. As shown in Figure 2-11, general and administrative expenses and other operating expenses are not included.

Estimating Marketing and Sales Expenses

For most corporations, marketing and sales expenses (MSE) are included in the amount that the corporations report for sales, general, and administrative expenses. The seven companies shown in Figure 2-12 however, report MSE separately from their other expenses. The information provided on these seven companies gives us some insight into the portion of SGA expenses that we can use as an estimate of MSE in evaluating companies that do not report MSE separately. As shown, the MSE as a percentage of SGA expenses for the seven companies varies from 66 to 81 percent, with an average of 74 percent. When marketing and sales expenses are not reported, we therefore recommend using 75 percent of SGA expenses as a reasonable estimate. Obviously, if the marketing and sales expenses are known, that figure should be used to compute the company's NMC.

MARKETING PROFITABILITY RATIO METRICS

As with financial performance metrics, we need to convert the overall measure of marketing profitability to standardized ratios so that we may compare the results at different levels of sales. Two marketing profitability ratio metrics that serve this function are marketing return on sales (marketing ROS) and marketing return on investment (marketing ROI). Marketing ROS is simply marketing profitability (the NMC) as a percentage of sales. For

Santa Fe Sportswear, the marketing ROS is 24 percent, as calculated in the equation that follows. Because it is a ratio metric, the marketing ROS of the company can be compared easily with the marketing ROS of a specific product line or division within the company or to the marketing ROS of a competitor or a particular segment of the market.

$$\textbf{Marketing ROS} = \text{Net Marketing Contribution/Sales} \times 100\%$$
$$= \$30 \text{ million}/\$125 \text{ million} \times 100\%$$
$$= \textbf{24\%}$$

Marketing ROI is the marketing profitability (NMC) as a percentage of the marketing and sales expenses. Dividing the NMC by the investment in marketing and sales produces the marketing return on investment.[15] For Santa Fe Sportswear, the marketing return on investment is 162 percent.

$$\textbf{Marketing ROI} = \text{Net Marketing Contribution/Marketing \& Sales Expenses} \times 100\%$$
$$= \$30 \text{ million}/\$18.5 \text{ million} \times 100\%$$
$$= \textbf{162\%}$$

This means that for each dollar Santa Fe Sportswear invested in marketing and sales, the company's marketing strategies produced $1.62 in marketing profits. As with marketing ROS, we can compare the company's overall marketing ROI with that of one of its product lines, a division within the company, a competitor, or a particular segment of the market.[16]

Figure 2-13 illustrates how these two marketing profitability metrics, along with the net marketing contribution, provide marketing managers with a way to demonstrate

FIGURE 2-13 MARKETING PROFITABILITY AND RATIO METRICS

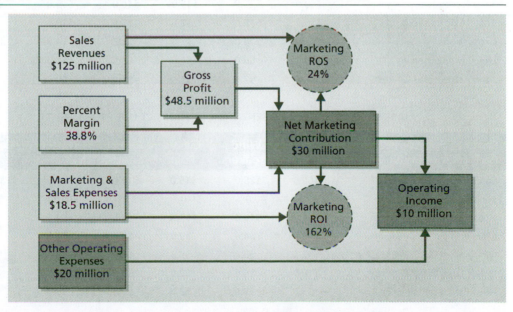

marketing's contribution to profits within the financial framework. The two marketing profitability ratio metrics offer important insights into what the company's investment in marketing and sales produced and how efficient that investment was. Used in addition to standard financial performance metrics, such as return on sales or return on assets, they allow a company to track how gains in marketing profitability affect operating income and how improvements in the marketing profitability ratio metrics contribute to improvements in the financial performance metrics. Let's next examine how the net marketing contribution and marketing ROS and marketing ROI might be used in a business discussion of product line profits.

MARKETING PROFITABILITY AND PRODUCT LINE MANAGEMENT

Santa Fe Sportswear has five product lines that contribute to the corporation's total sales of $125 million. Overall, the corporation is profitable, but two product lines are not performing well. To address this problem, the senior management team has scheduled a meeting to review product line profitability. In preparation for the meeting, the finance manager has developed a product line profitability summary, presented as the first part of Figure 2-14, and plans to make the following argument:

FIGURE 2-14 PRESENTING PRODUCT LINE PROFITABILITY

FINANCE MANAGER'S PRESENTATION OF PRODUCT LINE PROFITABILITY						
Santa Fe Sportswear Performance (millions)	Khaki Pants	Wind Breakers	Classic Polo	Casual Shorts	Knitted Sweaters	Company Total
Sales Revenues	$60.0	$25.0	$15.0	$10.0	$15.0	$125.0
Cost of Goods Sold	$36.0	$15.0	$7.5	$7.5	$10.5	$76.5
Gross Profit	$24.0	$10.0	$7.5	$2.5	$4.5	$48.5
Operating Expenses	$18.5	$8.0	$4.0	$3.5	$4.5	$38.5
Net Profit (before taxes)	$5.5	$2.0	$3.5	–$1.0	$0.0	$10.0

MARKETING MANAGER'S PRESENTATION OF PRODUCT LINE PROFITABILITY						
Santa Fe Sportswear Performance (millions)	Khaki Pants	Wind Breakers	Classic Polo	Casual Shorts	Knitted Sweaters	Company Total
Sales Revenues	$60.0	$25.0	$15.0	$10.0	$15.0	$125.0
Percent Margin	40.0%	40.0%	50.0%	25.0%	30.0%	38.8%
Gross Profit	$24.0	$10.0	$7.5	$2.5	$4.5	$48.5
Marketing & Sales Expenses	$8.5	$4.0	$2.0	$1.5	$2.5	$18.5
Net Marketing Contribution	$15.5	$6.0	$5.5	$1.0	$2.0	$30.0
Other Operating Expenses	$10.0	$4.0	$2.0	$2.0	$2.0	$20.0
Net Profit (before taxes)	$5.5	$2.0	$3.5	–$1.0	$0.0	$10.0

We are wasting resources on the casual shorts and knitted sweaters product lines. One makes no money and the other loses money. I recommend we drop both product lines and focus our efforts on the profitable product lines.

Would this be a good decision? How can the marketing manager present a different interpretation of the profit performance of the casual shorts and knitted sweaters product lines?

Using net marketing contribution as a measure of profitability, the marketing manager could present the same information as the finance manager, but with marketing and sales expenses separated from other expenses. The marketing manager could present the marketing profitability for each product line, shown in the second part of Figure 2-14.

Let's look more closely at the marketing profitability for just the casual shorts line. If this product line were dropped, what impact would the decision have on profit? Although the line's overall profit before taxes is a negative $1 million, this line is producing a positive marketing profit of $1 million. The marketing profits do not cover the $2 million in operating expenses that are unrelated to marketing and sales, but the casual shorts line does make a contribution to profit of $1 million. To fully understand marketing profitability and how marketing strategies affect it, we need to examine more closely the marketing elements that influence marketing profitability. To do this, we need to systematically break down the elements of profitability and the marketing strategy to examine how they interact.[17]

$$\begin{aligned}
\frac{\text{Operating}}{\text{Income}} &= \text{Sum of All Products' NMCs} - \text{G\&A Exp.} - \text{Other Oper. Exp.} \\
&= (\text{NMC 1} + \text{NMC 2} + \text{NMC 3} + \text{NMC 4} + \text{NMC 5}) - \text{G\&A Exp.} - \text{Other Oper. Exp.} \\
&= (\$15.5 \text{ mil.} + \$6 \text{ mil.} + \$5.5 \text{ mil.} + \$1 \text{ mil.} + \$2 \text{ mil.}) - \$5 \text{ mil.} - \$15 \text{ mil.} \\
&= \textbf{\$10 million}
\end{aligned}$$

Perhaps the best way to understand how the marketing profits from the casual shorts product line contribute to corporate profit is to compute overall net profit without the casual shorts line. As shown in the equation that follows, if the product line is dropped, overall marketing profits fall by $1 million, but the operating expenses remain at $20 million. As a result, net profit before taxes falls from $10 million to $9 million. Even worse, if both the casual shorts and the knitted sweaters product lines were eliminated, net profit before taxes would fall to $7 million.

$$\begin{aligned}
\frac{\text{Operating}}{\text{Income}} &= (\text{NMC 1} + \text{NMC 2} + \text{NMC 3} + \text{NMC 4} + \text{NMC 5}) - \text{G\&A Exp.} - \text{Other Oper. Exp.} \\
&= (\$15.5 \text{ mil.} + \$6 \text{ mil.} + \$5.5 \text{ mil.} + \$0 \text{ mil.} + \$2 \text{ mil.}) - \$5 \text{ mil.} - \$15 \text{ mil.} \\
&= \textbf{\$9 million}
\end{aligned}$$

Managing Marketing Profitability—A Product Focus

Viewing net marketing contribution from a financial perspective is important because it shows senior management and finance managers the contribution that marketing makes to corporate profits in a way that they can understand. But to fully manage marketing profitability, we need to expand the definition of NMC to include other factors that a marketing manager must consider in building a profitable marketing strategy. In addition to the financial perspective, we need to look at NMC from a *strategic* perspective.

The first step is to break down sales into more meaningful marketing variables, each of which has strategic importance in shaping the profit impact of a marketing strategy.[18] As the following equation shows, net marketing contribution can be separated into its component variables.

$$\begin{array}{c} \text{Net Marketing} \\ \text{Contribution} \end{array} = \underbrace{\begin{array}{c} \text{Market} \\ \text{Demand} \end{array} \times \begin{array}{c} \text{Market} \\ \text{Share} \end{array} \times \begin{array}{c} \text{Average} \\ \text{Selling Price} \end{array} \times \begin{array}{c} \text{Channel} \\ \text{Discounts} \end{array}} \times \begin{array}{c} \text{Percent} \\ \text{Margin} \end{array} - \begin{array}{c} \text{Marketing \&} \\ \text{Sales Expenses} \end{array}$$

$$= \begin{array}{c} \text{Net} \\ \text{Sales} \end{array} \times \begin{array}{c} \text{Percent} \\ \text{Margin} \end{array} - \begin{array}{c} \text{Marketing \&} \\ \text{Sales Expenses} \end{array}$$

Market Demand (units)—The size of the served market (number of units purchased annually).

Market Share (%)—The business's market share of the served market.

Average Selling Price ($ per unit)—The price paid by end customers who will use the product.

Channel Discount (1 – CD%)—The amount the company must pay to compensate channel intermediaries for channel services, such as sales, distribution, and customer service. One minus the percent channel discount is the percentage of the market sales that the company will obtain after paying channel intermediaries for services provided.

Percent Margin—Gross profit as a percentage. It may also be calculated as:

$$\text{Percent Margin} = (\text{Price} - \text{Unit Cost})/\text{Price} \times 100\%$$

Marketing and Sales Expenses ($)—The investment in marketing and sales that is needed to produce a certain market share and a net marketing contribution.

A company may want to employ a strategy to grow market demand for its product while maintaining the company's current market share. Depending on how much more the company would need to invest in marketing and sales to increase demand, this strategy could lead to improved marketing profitability. Ideally, the company would seek to increase demand while also growing its own share of the market, a strategy even more likely to be worth the additional investment needed in marketing and sales. Or the company might try holding market share while increasing price. To avoid losing a significant number of price-sensitive customers, the strategy would need to include a change in advertising. The new message would focus on the customer value that the company's product offers, based on superior product quality and brand reputation.

Let's take a strategic view of net marketing contribution with regard to Santa Fe Sportswear's khaki pants product line. As shown in Figures 2-15 and 2-16, the net sales of $60 million is the result of the market demand (12 million units), the market share (12.5%), the average selling price ($80), and the channel discount (50%). With an aver-

FIGURE 2-15 MANAGING PRODUCT LINE MARKETING PROFITABILITY

Santa Fe Sportswear Performance (millions)	Khaki Pants	Wind Breakers	Classic Polo	Casual Shorts	Knitted Sweaters	Company Total
Market Demand	12.0	10.0	16.7	20.0	6.7	65.4
Market Share	12.5%	5.0%	3.0%	2.0%	3.0%	4.7%
Unit Volume Sold	1.5	0.5	0.5	0.4	0.2	3.1
Average Selling Price (actual)	$80.00	$100.00	$60.00	$50.00	$150.00	$80.66
Channel Discount	50.0%	50.0%	50.0%	50.0%	50.0%	50.0%
Net Selling Price (actual)	$40.00	$50.00	$30.00	$25.00	$75.00	$40.33
Sales Revenues	$60.0	$25.0	$15.0	$10.0	$15.0	$125.1
Percent Margin	40.0%	40.0%	50.0%	25.0%	30.0%	38.8%
Gross Profit	$24.0	$10.0	$7.5	$2.5	$4.5	$48.5
Marketing & Sales Expenses	$8.5	$4.0	$2.0	$1.5	$2.5	$18.5
Net Marketing Contribution	$15.5	$6.0	$5.5	$1.0	$2.0	$30.0
G&A & Other Operating Expenses	$10.0	$4.0	$2.0	$2.0	$2.0	$20.0
Net Profit (before taxes)	$5.5	$2.0	$3.5	–$1.0	$0.0	$10.0
Marketing ROS	25.8%	24.0%	36.7%	10.0%	13.3%	24.0%
Marketing ROI	182%	150%	276%	67%	81%	162%

FIGURE 2-16 MARKETING PROFITABILITY—KHAKI PANTS PRODUCT LINE

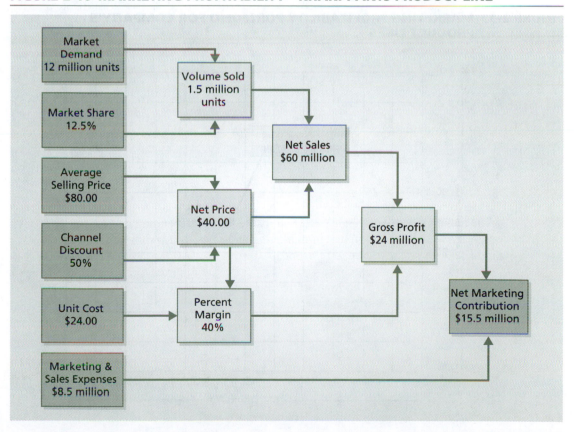

age margin of 40 percent, the product line produces a gross profit of $24 million. By deducting from this gross profit the cost of marketing and sales ($8.5 million), we arrive at a net marketing contribution of $15.5 million.

Our calculation of the net marketing contribution for Santa Fe Sportswear's khaki pants product line would look like this:

$$
\begin{aligned}
\text{NMC} \atop \text{Khaki Pants} &= \frac{\text{Market}}{\text{Demand}} \times \frac{\text{Market}}{\text{Share}} \times \frac{\text{Average}}{\text{Selling Price}} \times \frac{\text{Channel}}{\text{Discounts}} \times \frac{\text{Percent}}{\text{Margin}} - \frac{\text{Marketing \&}}{\text{Sales Expenses}} \\
&= \underbrace{12 \text{ million} \times 12.5\% \times \$80 \times (1 - 50\%)}_{\text{Net Sales} \atop \$60 \text{ Million}} \times 40\% - \$8.5 \text{ million} \\
&= \$60 \text{ million} \times 0.4 - \$8.5 \text{ million} \\
&= \mathbf{\$15.5 \text{ million}}
\end{aligned}
$$

The marketing ROS for khaki pants is 25.8 percent, and the marketing ROI is 182 percent, both above the product line averages for marketing ROS (24%) and marketing ROI (162%). As the numbers in Figure 2-15 show and the diagram in Figure 2-17

FIGURE 2-17 MARKETING PROFITABILITY PORTFOLIO FOR COMPANY'S PRODUCT LINES

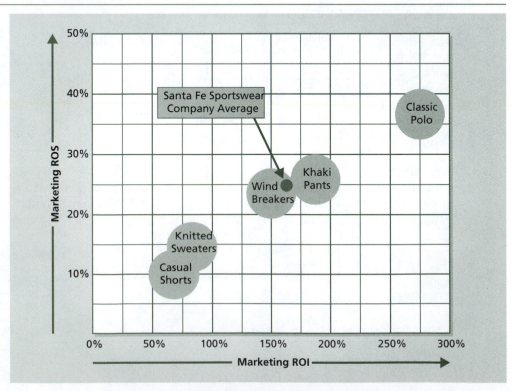

illustrates, the khaki pants product line is the second-best line with respect to these two marketing profitability metrics. The best is the classic polo line, which produces a marketing ROS of 36.7 percent and a marketing ROI of 275 percent. The casual shorts line produces the lowest marketing profitability ratios.

MANAGING MARKETING PROFITABILITY—A CUSTOMER FOCUS

The accounting systems of most businesses are built around production. Revenues and costs are associated with a product or service. Costs that are not directly related to production are allocated to the product or service using agreed-on accounting rules that have nothing to do with satisfying customers or making money. To develop marketing strategies that satisfy customers and grow profits, we need an alternate accounting system that will better serve the marketing function in managing marketing profitability. This system will be a more meaningful method for tracking a business's revenues, variable costs, fixed expenses, and profits.

Although it is convenient to report performance by product, we should also track performance by markets and customers. It is the customer who, when buying a product or service, produces cash flow for a business. Regardless of the appeal of a business's products or services, the number of potential customers in any given market is finite. The objective of a marketing strategy should be to attract, satisfy, and retain target customers in a way that grows the profits of the business.

By using customers and the market segments to which they belong as the accounting units, we can acquire a better understanding of market-based profitability and how to grow it. But let's first see what a market-based profitability statement would look like.

In Figure 2-18, we have rebuilt the performance of Santa Fe Sportswear around the three markets that the company serves. We notice at once that the product-based and market-based accounting approaches produce the same total revenue, gross profit, net marketing contribution, and net profit. Each approach, however, presents its own insights for market-based managers. Both approaches are important and meaningful. The product-focused accounting statement represented by Figure 2-15 helps us understand product unit volume, product price, and product unit margin. The customer-focused accounting statement represented by Figure 2-18 helps us understand customer demand, customer share, customer volume, revenue per customer, and variable cost per customer. The customer-focused approach shows us that all three market segments produced a positive net profit, but in the product-focused statement two product lines—casual shorts and knitted sweaters— did not produce a positive net profit. But because each of the three marketing segments in Figure 2-18 has a positive NMC, eliminating any product would result in a lower net profit for its market segment and lower overall profits for Santa Fe Sportswear.

PROFIT IMPACT OF MARKETING STRATEGIES

Recognizing the product or customer as a unit of analysis, we can evaluate different aspects of net marketing contribution in order to gain more insight into the development of marketing strategies that are designed to grow profitability.[19] As shown in Figure 2-19, each element of the NMC equation offers the potential to create a marketing strategy that

FIGURE 2-18 MARKETING PROFITABILITY OF CUSTOMER SEGMENTS

Santa Fe Sportswear Performance	Traditional Buyer	Fashion Seeker	Trend Setter	Company Total
Market Demand (customers)	7,000,000	5,890,000	8,000,000	20,890,000
Market Share	9.0%	3.5%	6.0%	6.3%
Customer Volume	630,000	206,150	480,000	1,316,150
Average Revenue per Customer	$180.00	$360.00	$130.00	$189.96
Channel Discount	50.0%	50.0%	50.0%	50.0%
Net Selling Price	$90.00	$180.00	$65.00	$94.98
Sales Revenues (millions)	$56.7	$37.1	$31.2	$125.0
Percent Margin	40.0%	35.9%	40.0%	38.8%
Gross Profit (millions)	$22.7	$13.3	$12.5	$48.5
Marketing & Sales Expenses (millions)	$7.0	$6.5	$5.0	$18.5
Net Marketing Contribution (millions)	$15.7	$6.8	$7.5	$30.0
G&A and Other Operating Expenses (millions)	$8.0	$6.5	$5.5	$20.0
Net Profit (before taxes)	$7.7	$0.3	$2.0	$10.0
Marketing ROS	27.7%	18.4%	24.0%	24.0%
Marketing ROI	224%	105%	150%	162%

will improve profit. The NMC of any proposed strategy must exceed the current NMC in order to increase a business's net profit, a fact that limits the number of fundamental marketing strategies a business can use.

Consider Santa Fe Sportswear's performance among traditional buyers, as presented in Figure 2-18. Traditional buyers produced an NMC of $15.7 million, derived from net sales of $56.7 million, a 40 percent margin, and $7 million in marketing and sales expenses. Sales revenues were the result of a market demand of 7 million customers, a 9 percent market share, an average revenue per customer of $180, and a 50 percent channel discount.

FIGURE 2-19 MARKETING STRATEGIES AND MARKETING PROFITABILITY

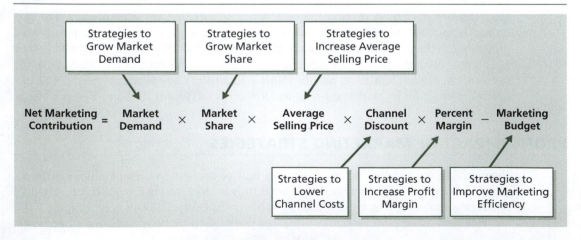

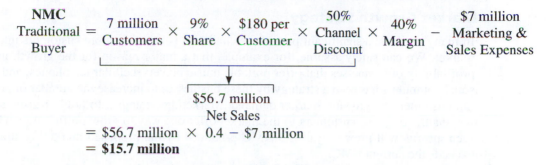

$$\begin{array}{c} \text{NMC} \\ \text{Traditional} \\ \text{Buyer} \end{array} = \begin{array}{c} 7 \text{ million} \\ \text{Customers} \end{array} \times \begin{array}{c} 9\% \\ \text{Share} \end{array} \times \begin{array}{c} \$180 \text{ per} \\ \text{Customer} \end{array} \times \begin{array}{c} 50\% \\ \text{Channel} \\ \text{Discount} \end{array} \times \begin{array}{c} 40\% \\ \text{Margin} \end{array} - \begin{array}{c} \$7 \text{ million} \\ \text{Marketing \&} \\ \text{Sales Expenses} \end{array}$$

$$\begin{array}{c} \$56.7 \text{ million} \\ \text{Net Sales} \end{array}$$

$$= \$56.7 \text{ million} \times 0.4 - \$7 \text{ million}$$
$$= \mathbf{\$15.7 \text{ million}}$$

Figure 2-20 illustrates how the different elements of the net marketing contribution equation fit together strategically for the traditional-buyer segment. A marketing strategy to grow the marketing profitability of traditional buyers could address market demand, market share, revenue per customer, channel discounts, the variable costs that affect margin, marketing and sales expenses, or any combination of these factors. We are now ready to discuss the market-based strategies suggested in Figure 2-19 and assess how selected strategies in each area might affect the profits of Santa Fe Sportswear.

FIGURE 2-20 MARKETING PROFITABILITY OF TRADITIONAL-BUYER SEGMENT

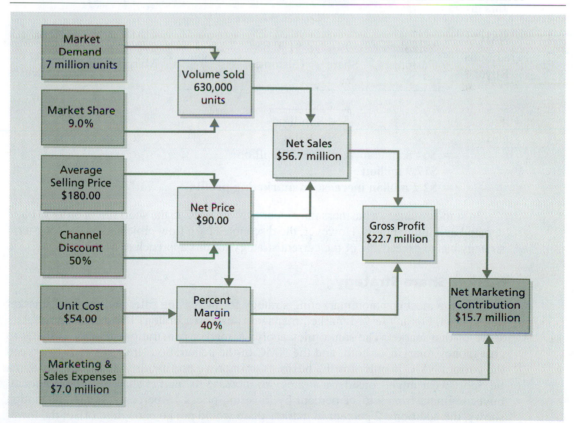

Market Growth Strategy

In many markets, a significant part of the challenge is bringing more customers into the market. We can safely assume, for example, that a major reason for the growth in the profitability of businesses that offer portable music players, cellular telephones, and personal computers has been a strategy by these businesses to increase the number of potential customers by growing market demand. Marketing strategies to hold or grow share while attracting new customers to the market offer one way to grow profits. As we have seen, profits will grow only if the NMC produced by the proposed marketing strategy exceeds the current NMC.

For example, the Santa Fe Sportswear's traditional-buyer marketing manager believes market demand could be grown from 7 to 8 million customers with a $1 million increase in marketing and sales expenses. If this growth in demand could be achieved, and Santa Fe Sportswear could maintain a 9 percent share among traditional buyers, the number of traditional buyers would grow from 630,000 to 720,000, an increase of 90,000 customers. But would this strategy improve the marketing profitability for the traditional-buyer segment and increase the business's overall profitability?

The following calculation shows that this would indeed be a worthwhile marketing strategy. NMC would increase by $2.2 million, from $15.7 million to $17.9 million. The gain of 90,000 new customers, with their additional contribution, would more than justify the additional $1 million in marketing and sales expenses required to achieve this growth.

$$= \$64.8 \text{ million} \times 0.4 - \$8 \text{ million}$$
$$= \textbf{\$17.9 million}$$
$$= \textbf{\$2.2 million \underline{increase} in marketing profits}$$

In some instances, a business may incur a lower NMC in the short run in order to build demand and future profits. However, the discounted cash flow projected by the long-term strategy has to exceed that of the current strategy for this approach to be viable.

Market Share Strategy

Perhaps the most common marketing strategy for increasing sales and profits is market penetration. For any served market, managers develop a strategy to grow the business's share of that market. The same rules apply: A market penetration strategy is likely to cost money, margin, or both, and the NMC of the penetration strategy needs to exceed the current NMC in order for the business to improve profitability. For example, Santa Fe Sportswear might consider a strategy to increase its market share of the traditional-buyer segment from 9 to 11 percent by lowering prices 10 percent. As the calculation shows, the additional 2 percent in market share would not be enough to offset the lower margin that would result from the 10 percent price reduction (the margin would fall from 40 to 33.3 percent). The outcome would be a $1.9 million decrease in NMC, from $15.7 million to $13.8 million.

$$\begin{matrix}\text{NMC} \\ \text{Traditional} \\ \text{Buyer}\end{matrix} = \begin{matrix}\text{7 million} \\ \text{Customers}\end{matrix} \times \begin{matrix}\text{11\%} \\ \text{Share}\end{matrix} \times \begin{matrix}\text{\$162 per} \\ \text{Customer}\end{matrix} \times \begin{matrix}\text{50\%} \\ \text{Channel} \\ \text{Discount}\end{matrix} \times \begin{matrix}\text{33.3\%} \\ \text{Margin}\end{matrix} - \begin{matrix}\text{\$7 million} \\ \text{Marketing \&} \\ \text{Sales Expenses}\end{matrix}$$

$$\underbrace{\qquad\qquad\qquad}_{\begin{matrix}\text{\$62.4 million} \\ \text{Net Sales}\end{matrix}}$$

$$= \text{\$62.4 million} \times 0.333 - \text{\$7 million}$$
$$= \textbf{\$13.8 million}$$
$$= \textbf{\$1.9 million decrease in marketing profits}$$

Customer Revenue Strategy

In a mature market with a strong share position, a business may find that it is unprofitable to grow market demand or market share. The business's customers, however, remain its best strategic asset, and an examination of customer needs might identify new products and services to better serve those needs and grow revenues. To evaluate the overall profit impact of such a marketing strategy, a business would project the required increase in the average cost per unit and the higher price that could be attained.

A business would also need to consider the likelihood of greater marketing and sales expenses. Additional advertising dollars would be necessary to make existing customers aware of new products, new services, or improvements in existing products or services. Managers must examine all aspects of a strategy to increase price per unit to ensure that the strategy leads to an increase in net marketing contribution.

To illustrate the profit impact of a strategy to build revenue per customer, suppose that most customers in the traditional-buyer segment are not fully aware of the high quality of the product line. With more effective advertising, the average revenue per customer could be increased from $180 to $200. Although this increases the margin from 40 to 46 percent, an additional $3 million in marketing and sales expenses would be needed to communicate the advantages of the company's product quality and unique product design. This marketing strategy would produce an NMC of $19 million for the traditional-buyer segment, an increase of $3.3 million over the current NMC of $15.7 million.

$$\begin{matrix}\text{NMC} \\ \text{Traditional} \\ \text{Buyer}\end{matrix} = \begin{matrix}\text{7 million} \\ \text{Customers}\end{matrix} \times \begin{matrix}\text{9\%} \\ \text{Share}\end{matrix} \times \begin{matrix}\text{\$200 per} \\ \text{Customer}\end{matrix} \times \begin{matrix}\text{50\%} \\ \text{Channel} \\ \text{Discount}\end{matrix} \times \begin{matrix}\text{46\%} \\ \text{Margin}\end{matrix} - \begin{matrix}\text{\$10 million} \\ \text{Marketing \&} \\ \text{Sales Expenses}\end{matrix}$$

$$\underbrace{\qquad\qquad\qquad}_{\begin{matrix}\text{\$63 million} \\ \text{Net Sales}\end{matrix}}$$

$$= \text{\$63 million} \times 0.46 - \text{\$10 million}$$
$$= \textbf{\$19 million}$$
$$= \textbf{\$3.3 million increase in marketing profits}$$

Cost Reduction Strategy

Another way to grow net profit is to lower the variable cost per unit. Perhaps a new distribution strategy for a given market segment could reduce transportation costs and sales commissions. This strategy would lower the variable cost per unit and increase margin per unit, but the business would need to be certain that the new distribution strategy would not adversely affect the level of customer satisfaction. If customer satisfaction declines, so will customer retention—and in the long run, net profit will erode even though the business achieves a lower variable cost and higher margin per unit. A successful marketing strategy must hold or increase customer satisfaction while growing net profit through increases in NMC.

For example, the marketing manager for the traditional-buyer segment of Santa Fe Sportswear is evaluating a new order-entry and billing system that would lower the variable cost of serving customers by an average of $9 per customer, thereby increasing margin from 40 to 50 percent. The marketing manager believes that the new system would significantly improve the accuracy and detail of customer bills, and it would make the ordering process easier and more pleasant for customers. This new system, however, would cost an additional $1 million annually in fixed marketing and sales expenses, raising a question as to whether it would truly improve profitability. By calculating the projected NMC, we find that the new order-entry and billing system would increase the net marketing contribution by $4.7 million. Putting the system in place makes good sense financially and probably in terms of customer satisfaction as well.

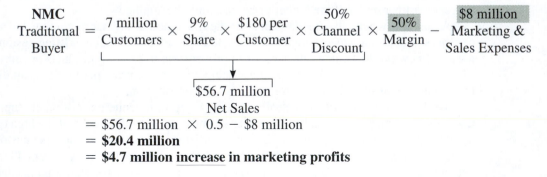

$$= \$56.7 \text{ million} \times 0.5 - \$8 \text{ million}$$
$$= \textbf{\$20.4 million}$$
$$= \textbf{\$4.7 million \underline{increase} in marketing profits}$$

Advertising Strategy

A business could also improve the profitability of its marketing efforts by using advertising to grow market share. Consider a proposed strategy that calls for an additional $2 million in marketing and sales expenses solely for advertising to increase market share from 9 to 10 percent. In this case, we will use the marketing profitability equation to solve for the market share that is needed to produce the current level of marketing profit (an NMC of $15.7 million).

As shown in the equation that follows, the strategy would require a 9.8 percent market share to pay for the increase in marketing and sales expenses just to maintain the same level of marketing profit. Even achieving the goal of a 10 percent market share would provide very little incremental profit. This strategy would lower marketing profit if the market share achieved was less than 9.8 percent. The risk of not obtaining the full 10 percent share outweighs the small profit that would result.

$$\begin{array}{c}\textbf{\$15.7 million}\\ \text{NMC}\\ \text{Traditional}\\ \text{Buyer}\end{array} = \begin{array}{c}\text{7 million}\\ \text{Customers}\end{array} \times \begin{array}{c}\textbf{Market}\\ \textbf{Share}\\ \textbf{(MS\%)}\end{array} \times \begin{array}{c}\$180\\ \text{per}\\ \text{Customer}\end{array} \times \begin{array}{c}50\%\\ \text{Channel}\\ \text{Discount}\end{array} \times \begin{array}{c}40\%\\ \text{Margin}\end{array} - \begin{array}{c}\textbf{\$9 million}\\ \text{Marketing \&}\\ \text{Sales Expenses}\end{array}$$

$15.7 \text{ million} = \text{MS\%} \times \$252 \text{ million} - \$9 \text{ million}$

$\quad\ \text{MS\%} = (\$15.7 \text{ million} + \$9 \text{ million})/\$252 \text{ million}$

$\quad\quad\quad\ = \textbf{9.8\% Market Share}$

With this market share, the business makes the <u>same</u> marketing profit of $15.7 million.

Channel Strategy

Still another way to improve the profitability of a marketing strategy is to bypass the channel and thereby eliminate most of the channel cost. In Figure 2-21, the current strategy for the traditional buyer produces market sales of $113.4 million. Half of these sales dollars are offset by the current indirect channel strategy, leaving $56.75 million in net sales. This results in a gross profit of $22.7 (40% margin). Subtracting the marketing and sales expenses of $7 million produces a net marketing contribution of $15.7 million.

An alternate channel strategy could make use of the Internet as the point of purchase. Using this direct channel strategy, the company might offer the product for an average

FIGURE 2-21 MARKETING PROFITABILITY—CHANNEL STRATEGY

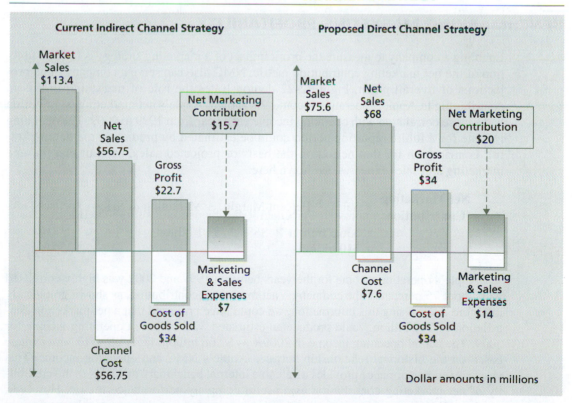

selling price of $120 rather than $180, shipping the product directly to customers. The channel cost in this case would drop to 10 percent of sales. Although prices would be reduced by 33 percent, eliminating most of the indirect channel discount of 50 percent allows the business to improve net sales from $56.75 million to $68 million. The gross profit would increase due to both higher net sales and a higher percent margin (from 40% to 50%). Marketing and sales expenses, however, would need to double to advertise the price reductions and the online purchasing venue more aggressively. If successfully implemented, this channel strategy would be more profitable than the current indirect channel strategy, as shown in the equation that follows. Perhaps an even better strategy would be to separate the traditional-buyer segment into two groups on the basis of preferred point of purchase and price and then use two channels to serve this market segment.

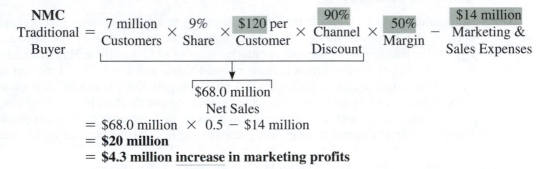

$$\begin{array}{l} \text{NMC} \\ \text{Traditional} \\ \text{Buyer} \end{array} = \dfrac{7\text{ million}}{\text{Customers}} \times \dfrac{9\%}{\text{Share}} \times \dfrac{\$120\text{ per}}{\text{Customer}} \times \begin{array}{l} 90\% \\ \text{Channel} \\ \text{Discount} \end{array} \times \dfrac{50\%}{\text{Margin}} - \begin{array}{l} \$14\text{ million} \\ \text{Marketing \&} \\ \text{Sales Expenses} \end{array}$$

$$\underbrace{\$68.0\text{ million}}_{\text{Net Sales}}$$

$$= \$68.0\text{ million} \times 0.5 - \$14\text{ million}$$
$$= \textbf{\$20 million}$$
$$= \textbf{\$4.3 million \underline{increase} in marketing profits}$$

BENCHMARKING MARKETING PROFITABILITY

Enabling a company to measure the profit impact of a marketing strategy is but one function of the net marketing contribution metric. NMC also can serve a company in its projections of overall profit. Figure 2-22 demonstrates the role of marketing profits in contributing to Apple's operating income. As shown, Apple's net marketing contribution had a close correlation with operating income each year from 1999 to 2009. The operating income for a future reporting period could be estimated by predicting the net marketing contribution for that period on the basis of projected sales, percent margin, and marketing and sales expenses, as shown here:

$$\begin{array}{l} \textbf{Net Marketing} \\ \textbf{Contribution} \end{array} = \text{Sales} \times \text{Percent Margin} - \text{Marketing \& Sales Expenses}$$
$$= \$36.5\text{ billion} \times 36\% - \$3.1\text{ billion}$$
$$= \textbf{\$10 billion}$$

Apple's operating income for the years between 1999 and 2009 was highly correlated with about 75 percent of the company's net marketing contribution, as shown graphically in Figure 2-22. Using this information, we could have projected that a net marketing contribution of $10 billion would produce an estimated $7.5 billion in operating income for 2009. The actual operating income in 2009 was $7.66 billion, fairly close to our estimate based on the historical relationship between Apple's NMC and operating income. This year-to-year performance provides a valuable internal benchmark that adds to the credibility of net marketing contribution as a useful company performance metric. However, Apple's NMC and the level of operating income it produces do not provide any insight

FIGURE 2-22 BENCHMARKING MARKETING PROFITABILITY TO OPERATING INCOME OVER TIME

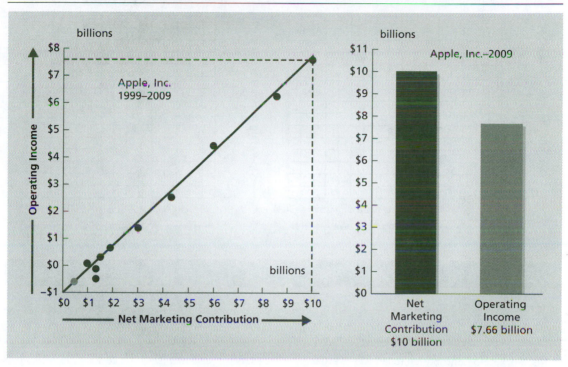

into *relative* performance. Is this level of marketing profitability above or below average for the technology industry? To address this question, we need to benchmark Apple's marketing ROS and marketing ROI against its competitors and other technology companies.

Benchmarking Marketing ROS

Using the two marketing profitability ratios—marketing ROS and marketing ROI—a company can compare itself with competitors to obtain a better understanding of its marketing efficiency in producing marketing profits. The first marketing profitability ratio we will benchmark is marketing ROS. This marketing profitability metric, as we saw earlier, is the net marketing contribution as a percentage of sales.

$$\textbf{Apple's Marketing ROS}\text{ (2009)} = \text{Net Marketing Contribution/Sales} \times 100\%$$
$$= \$10 \text{ billion}/\$36.5 \text{ billion} \times 100\%$$
$$= \textbf{27.4\%}$$

Apple's marketing ROS of 27.4 percent is derived from a net marketing contribution of $10 billion and a marketing and sales budget of $3.1 billion. Apple's operating income as a percentage of sales was 21 percent for the same annual accounting period, as shown here:

$$\textbf{Apple's Operating Income}\text{ (\% sales)} = \$7.66 \text{ billion}/\$36.5 \text{ billion} \times 100\%$$
$$= \textbf{21.0\%}$$

FIGURE 2-23 BENCHMARKING APPLE'S MARKETING PROFITABILITY METRICS

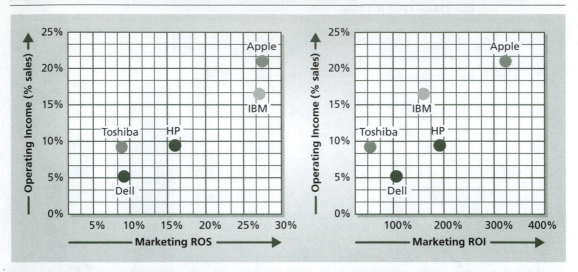

Performance–2009	Apple	Dell	HP	IBM	Toshiba
Sales (billions)	$36.5	$61.1	$118.4	$103.6	$69.9
Percent Margin	36.0%	17.9%	24.3%	44.1%	25.2%
Marketing & Sales Expenses (% sales)	8.5%	8.7%	8.3%	17.0%	16.3%
Net Marketing Contribution (billions)	$10.0	$5.6	$18.9	$28.1	$5.9
Operating Income (billions)	$7.7	$3.2	$10.8	$17.1	$6.2
Performance Metrics					
Operating Income (% sales)	21.0%	5.2%	9.1%	16.5%	8.9%
Marketing ROS	27.4%	9.2%	16.0%	27.1%	8.4%
Marketing ROI	323%	106%	192%	160%	52%

Note: Marketing and sales expenses in all cases have been estimated at 75% of SGA expenses, since these companies do not separately report their marketing and sales expenses.

But, how do these levels of marketing ROS and operating income as a percentage of sales compare with Apple's benchmark competitors?

In Figure 2-23, we can see how Apple's marketing ROS and operating income as a percentage of sales compare with Dell, Toshiba, HP, and IBM. Apple's marketing ROS of 27.4 percent and its operating income as a percentage of sales—21 percent—were both higher than those of the closest competitor and considerably higher than those of the other three competitors. In general, Figure 2-23 demonstrates that companies with higher levels of marketing ROS tend to have higher operating incomes as a percentage of sales.

Benchmarking Marketing ROI

Figure 2-23 also lists the marketing ROI for Apple and its four benchmark competitors. As we learned earlier, marketing ROI is simply the marketing profitability (net marketing contribution) as a percentage of the marketing and sales expenses. Dividing the net marketing contribution by the investment in marketing and sales produces the marketing return on investment. For Apple, the marketing ROI is 323 percent, as calculated here:

$$
\begin{aligned}
\textbf{Apple's Marketing ROI } (2009) &= \text{NMC}/\text{Marketing \& Sales Expenses} \times 100\% \\
&= \$10 \text{ billion}/\$3.1 \text{ billion} \times 100\% \\
&= \textbf{323\%}
\end{aligned}
$$

Apple's marketing ROI is derived from a net marketing contribution of $10 billion and a marketing and sales budget of $3.1 billion. Of the five companies represented in Figure 2-23, Apple has the highest marketing ROI and highest operating income as a percentage of sales. Toshiba and Dell have the two lowest marketing ROIs and two lowest operating incomes as a percentage of sales. Although many factors influence both marketing ROI and operating income as a percentage of sales, there is a correlation between these two metrics, as suggested by the relationship displayed in Figure 2-23.

BENCHMARKING COMPANY MARKETING PROFITABILITY METRICS

Figure 2-24 provides a much broader view of relative performance from which to draw a relationship between these marketing profitability ratio metrics and operating income as a percentage of sales. This graphic includes 169 well-known companies with publicly available financial statements. The companies are listed in the appendix to this chapter.

The average marketing ROS for this sample of Fortune 500 companies is 23.5 percent, and the median is 19 percent. The average operating income as a percentage of sales is 10.4 percent, and the median is 11.1 percent. As shown, Apple has a higher average for both performance metrics, with a marketing ROS of 27.4 percent and an operating income as a percentage of sales of 21 percent. Companies with very high levels of marketing ROS typically have very high operating incomes as a percentage of sales.

With regard to marketing ROI, the average for this sample of Fortune 500 companies was 163 percent and the median 135 percent. This suggests that the average for these companies is higher than for the typical company because some of them have very high levels of marketing ROI. Apple, with a 323 percent marketing ROI, is among the leaders in marketing ROI. As with marketing ROS, the higher a company's marketing ROI, the more likely the company will realize a higher operating income as a percentage of sales. In general, there is a reasonable relationship between marketing ROI and operating income as a percentage of sales.

Now that we have explored the relationships shown in Figure 2-24, we can see the value of marketing ROS and marketing ROI as useful marketing profitability metrics. The degree to which each correlates with the financial performance metrics, such as operating income as a percentage of sales, helps support the importance of these marketing profitability metrics. The same results are obtained when correlating the marketing profitability metrics to pre-tax return on assets.

**FIGURE 2-24 MARKETING PROFITABILITY CORRELATED
TO OPERATING INCOME**

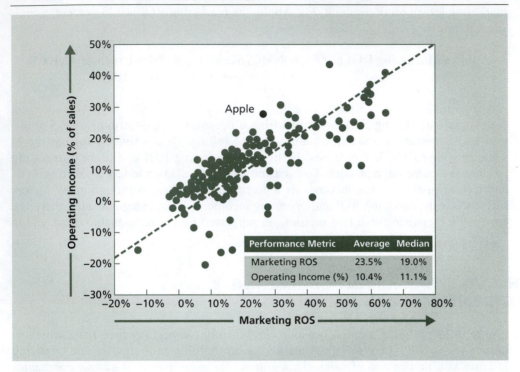

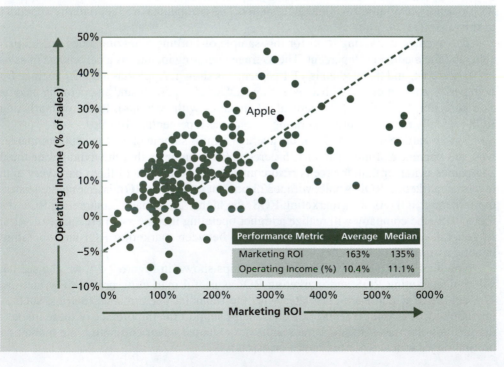

MANAGING MARKETING PROFITABILITY

Marketing and product managers play a strategic role in shaping the overall profits of a company. This role extends beyond sales, distribution, and advertising. Marketing and product managers also must be able to demonstrate the contributions that marketing makes to a business's financial performance. A market-based business thinks and behaves in terms of marketing performance because its managers know that success rests on marketing performance. Internal financial metrics are valuable in that they track what has happened in the past, but by themselves they provide a limited view of the reasons for a particular level of profit performance. The key to understanding the underlying forces contributing to financial performance, and the key to superior financial performance, are the marketing metrics we have been discussing, as well as others that we will examine in later chapters.

No matter how high the levels of marketing performance that marketing managers deliver, senior management and finance managers want tangible proof of how marketing and sales expenses contribute to overall profits. To meet this need, net marketing contribution offers a financially derived performance metric. Marketing profitability metrics have a direct linkage to company profits. It is pretty simple: The more money a marketing strategy produces, the more money there is for other expenses and profits.

■ Summary

A business that does not use marketing metrics to measure marketing profitability fails to demonstrate marketing's contribution to the business's profits. Marketing and product managers need to report their marketing performance and profitability in order to earn the respect of senior management and other organizational functions such as finance and manufacturing where performance metrics are a way of life.

BioTronics provides an excellent example of a high-growth business with impressive gains in sales and profits over a 3-year period. However, this performance was gauged largely on internal, financial metrics. The addition of marketing metrics provided an external view of performance that revealed declining market share, customer performance, and competitive position. Had these marketing metrics been in place and had the company maintained its 10 percent market share, we estimated that it would have earned an additional $41 million in profits before tax.

Marketing metrics are external performance metrics that provide a market-based view of company performance. In many instances, marketing metrics such as intentions to repurchase, customer satisfaction, and perceived performance are forward-looking metrics that are leading indicators of future sales and profits. Most financial metrics are backward-looking and report what has happened at the end of a financial reporting period. Forward-looking marketing metrics tell us what is happening now and predict what will happen with respect to external performance.

Net marketing contribution (NMC) was introduced as an important measure of marketing profitability. The NMC equation is simply:

$$NMC = Sales \times Percent\ Gross\ Margin - Marketing\ \&\ Sales\ Expenses$$

The net marketing contribution may be calculated for a company, region, business unit, market, market segment, product line, or product. It allows us to use the same measure of marketing profitability at all levels of the organization. The one problem we do have is that many businesses do not report marketing and sales expenses separately. These businesses include their marketing and sales expenses as part of sales, general, and administrative (SGA) expenses. However, for companies that do not report their marketing and sales expenses separately from SGA expenses, we can estimate that 75 percent of SGA expenses are marketing and sales expenses, which is about the average portion of SGA expenses spent on marketing and sales by companies that report their marketing and sales expenses separately. This estimate was used in the Apple examples and benchmarking graphics presented in Figures 2-23 and 2-24.

We also provided a strategic measure of net marketing contribution that further broke down NMC into market demand in dollars, market share, channel discounts, percent margin, and marketing and sales expenses. In addition, we presented a product-level measure of NMC that added average selling price and unit cost to the NMC equation. The addition of market and product measures of NMC allows us to better understand how a certain level of marketing profits is attained at the market or product level.

Marketing return on sales (marketing ROS) and marketing return on investment (marketing ROI) are easily computed using the net marketing contribution as a measure of marketing profitability:

Marketing ROS = Net Marketing Contribution/Sales × 100%
Marketing ROI = Net Marketing Contribution/Marketing & Sales Exp. × 100%

These two marketing profitability metrics, because they are ratio metrics, allow us to compare the marketing profitability across an organization that has large differences in sales magnitude for different products. These metrics can be used to determine the *relative* marketing profitability of a product, market segment, region, division or business unit, or the overall company. For example, we can compare Apple's marketing ROI of 323 percent and marketing ROS of 27.4 percent with any region, business unit, market segment, product line, or specific Apple product. We can also benchmark the company's marketing ROS and marketing ROI against other publicly owned corporations, as shown in Figure 2-24.

No matter how high the levels of marketing performance that marketing managers deliver, senior management and finance managers want tangible proof of marketing's contributions to overall profits. Net marketing contribution offers a financially derived performance metric to meet this need. Marketing profitability metrics have a direct linkage to company profits.

■ Market-Based Strategic Thinking

1 How could marketing metrics help General Motors turn around its decline in sales and profits?
2 If a company dominates a market the way Microsoft, Google, and Intel dominate their markets, why should that company bother to track marketing metrics?
3 How would marketing metrics help a company like McDonald's better manage its profitability?

4 How would Toyota use forward-looking marketing metrics to better understand future sales and profits in the U.S. market?

5 How could a Wall Street analyst benefit from access to a company's marketing metrics for a company like BioTronics?

6 Why are most financial metrics backward-looking metrics?

7 Why would chief financial officers and senior management be comfortable with net marketing contribution as a financial measure of marketing profitability?

8 Compute Apple's net marketing contribution for the company's last fiscal year and add it to Figure 2-22. Then explain how this level of net marketing contribution could be used in Apple's marketing plans to project Apple's operating income for the current year.

9 How would Vizio use net marketing contribution at the market level to increase its knowledge of the U.S. flat-panel television market?

10 How would Procter & Gamble use a product-level measure of net marketing contribution for the Tide brand in the U.S. market?

11 How could Apple's chief marketing officer use Figure 2-23 to explain to Apple's CFO the value of marketing ROS and marketing ROI as corporate performance metrics?

12 Shown here are HP's six major business segments and their percentages of sales for 2009. How would a marketing profitability portfolio (similar to Figure 2-17) help the HP chief marketing officer communicate to senior management the relative performance of each business segment when compared to the HP average?

HP Business Segments:	Personal Systems	Imaging & Printing	Enterprise Storage	HP Services	Software	HP Financial Services
Sales (%)	34%	20%	14%	28%	3%	1%

13 In 2009, Netflix had a marketing ROI of 178 percent. What does this mean in terms of the company's investment in marketing and sales?

14 For any airline of interest, compute its 2010 marketing ROS, marketing ROI, and operating income (as a percentage of sales) using the airline's 2010 income statement in its annual report. Assume marketing and sales expenses are 75 percent of SGA expenses. Then plot the results in Figure 2-24 and interpret the airline's performance.

15 Why would companies that sell energy and raw materials, such as ExxonMobil and Alcoa, have very large marketing ROIs?

Marketing Performance Tools and Application Exercises

The four interactive marketing performance tools and application exercises outlined here will strengthen your understanding of the profit impact of managing marketing profitability. To access the tools, go to **rogerjbest. com.** You may enter the data presented in each exercise to obtain the answers to the questions. You may also enter other data to see the results, and you may save your work. The figure numbers in parentheses are related examples in Chapter 2, but the lettered instructions pertain to the online exercises.

2.1 Company-Level Net Marketing Contribution (Figure 2-15)

A. Evaluate the profit impact of eliminating the casual shorts and knitted sweaters product lines.

B. What would be the profit impact of increasing market share from 2 to 3 percent for the casual shorts product line if marketing and sales expenses were doubled (from $1.5 million to $3 million)?

2.2 Market-Level NMC, Marketing ROS, and Marketing ROI (Figure 2-18)

A. Evaluate the profit impact of exiting the fashion-buyer segment.

B. In the fashion-buyer segment, how much market share would the business have to obtain to keep the same level of marketing profits if the business doubled marketing and sales expenses in that segment?

2.3 Company Net Marketing Contribution and Marketing ROI (Figure 2-13)

A. For a company of interest, obtain the required input from a company annual report. Evaluate the company's marketing profitability and how it contributes to net profit before taxes.

B. How would marketing profits and net profit change if sales increase by 25 percent?

C. Evaluate the profit impact of a strategy in which the percent margin is increased by 5 points and marketing and sales expenses are increased by 2 percentage points.

2.4 Benchmarking Marketing ROI versus Operating Income as a Percentage of Sales (Figure 2-23)

A. For a company of interest, go online and obtain the operating income and the data needed to estimate the company's marketing ROI. You will probably need to use 75 percent of SGA expenses as your estimate of marketing and sales expenses, because companies rarely report marketing and sales expenses separately in their financial statements.

B. Next, collect the same data for a major competitor. How does the first company compare with this competitor in terms of the marketing profitability metrics (marketing ROS and marketing ROI) and operating income as a percentage of sales? How would these results compare with the average performance shown in Figure 2-24?

Notes

1. P. Hyde, E. Landry, and A. Tipping, "Making the Perfect Marketer," *Strategy+Business* (Winter 2004).
2. B. Gale, "Tracking Competitive Position Drives Shareholder Value," *Global Management* (1992): 367–71.
3. P. Levy, "Measure for Measure," *Marketing News* (October 30, 2009): 6.
4. M. Krauss, "Which Metrics Matter Most?" *Marketing News* (February 2009): 20.
5. Hyde, Landry, and Tipping, "Making the Perfect Marketer."
6. T. Ambler, F. Kokkinaki, and S. Puntoni, "Assessing Marketing Performance: Reasons for Metrics Selection," *Journal of Marketing Management* (2004): 475–98; D. Brady and D. Kiley, "Making Marketing Measure Up," *Business Week* (December 13, 2004).
7. P. Farris, N. Bendle, P. Pfeifer, and D. Reibstein, *Marketing Metrics* (Wharton School Publishing, 2007).
8. T. Ambler, *Marketing and the Bottom Line: New Metrics of Corporate Wealth* (Prentice Hall, 2000).
9. C. Meyer, "How the Right Measures Help Teams Excel," *Harvard Business Review* (May–June 1994): 95–103.
10. R. Kaplan and D. Norton, "The Balanced Scorecard—Measures That Drive Performance," *Harvard Business Review* (January–February 1992): 71–79; R. Eccles, "The Performance Measurement Manifesto," *Harvard Business Review* (January–February 1991): 131–37.
11. D. O'Sullivan and A.V. Abela, "Marketing Performance Measurement Ability and Firm Performance," *Journal of Marketing* (April 2007): 79–93.

12. G. Cressman, "Choosing the Right Metric," *Drive Marketing Excellence* (November 1994), New York: Institute for International Research.

13. Y. Chen, J. Hess, R. Wilcox, and Z.J. Zhang, "Accounting Profits versus Marketing Profits: A Relevant Metric for Category Management," *Marketing Science* 18, No. 3 (1999): 208–29.

14. J. Shank and V. Govindarajan. "The Perils of Cost Allocation Based on Production Volumes," *Accounting Horizons* 4 (1988): 71–79; J. Shank and V. Govindarajan, "Making Strategy Explicit in Cost Analysis: A Case Study," *Sloan Marketing Review* (Spring 1988): 15–30.

15. D. Hawkins, R. Best, and C. Lillis, "The Nature of Measurement of Marketing Productivity in Consumer Durables*," Journal of the Academy of Marketing Science* 15, No. 4 (1987).

16. L.H. Moeller, S.K. Mathur, and R. Rothenberg, "The Better Half: The Artful Science of ROI Marketing," *Strategy+Business* (Spring 2003).

17. J. Shank and V. Govindarajan. *Strategic Cost Analysis* (New York: Irwin, 1989): 99–112.

18. M. Morris and G. Morris. *Market-Oriented Pricing* (New York: NTC Business Books, 1990): 99–100; D. Schultz, "Spreadsheet Approach to Measuring ROI for MCI," *Marketing News* 28 (February 1994): 12.

19. W. Christopher. "Marketing Achievement Reporting: A Profitability Approach," *Industrial Marketing Management* (New York: Elsevier North Holland, Inc., 1977): 149–62; P. Dunne and H. Wolk. "Marketing Cost Analysis: A Modularized Contribution," *Journal of Marketing* (July 1977): 83–94; S. Shapiro and V.H. Kirpalard, *Marketing Effectiveness: Insights from Accounting and Finance* (Needham Heights, MA: Allyn and Bacon, 1984): 377–424; J.-C. Larreche and H. Gatignon. MARKSTRAT (New York: Scientific Press, 1990): 22–23.

Companies Represented in Figure 2-24

3M
Abbott Laboratories
Adobe Systems
Agilent
Amazon
American Airlines
Apple
AutoZone
Avery Dennison
Avon Products
Barnes & Noble
BASF
Baxter International
Bayer
Becton Dickinson
Bed Bath & Beyond
Best Buy
Black & Decker
Blockbuster
BorgWarner
Brinks
Bristol-Myers Squib
Brunswick
Burlington Northern
   Santa Fe
Caterpillar
Circuit City Stores
Clorox
Coca-Cola
Colgate-Palmolive
ConAgra Foods
Continental Airlines
Cummins
Danaher
Darden Restaurants
Dean Foods
Dell
Delta Airlines

Dillard's
Dow Chemical
Dr Pepper Snapple
   Group
Dresser Rand
DuPont
Eastman Chemical
Eastman Kodak
Eaton
eBay
Eli Lilly
EMC
Emerson Electric
Estée Lauder
Family Dollar Stores
FedEx
Foot Locker
Ford Motor
Frito-Lay/PepsiCo
General Electric
General Mills
General Motors
Goodrich
Goodyear Tire &
   Rubber
Grace
Grainger
Great Atlantic &
   Pacific Tea
Greif
H.J. Heinz
Harley-Davidson
Hershey
Home Depot
Honeywell
   International
Hormel Foods
Hewlett-Packard

Huntsman
IBM
Illinois Tool Works
Ingersoll & Rand
Ingram Micro
International Paper
ITT
JC Penney
John Deere
Johnson & Johnson
Johnson Controls
Kellogg
Kennametal
Kimberly-Clark
Kohl's
Kraft
Kroger
Legg Mason
Limited Brands
Lowe's
Macy's
Mattel
McDonald's
McGraw-Hill
Medtronic
Merck
Microsoft
Molson Coors
   Brewing
Monsanto
Motorola
Nash-Finch
Navistar International
NCR
Netflix
Newell Rubbermaid
Nike
Nordstrom

Office Depot
Oshkosh
Owens Corning
Pantry
Papa John's
   International
Parker Hannifinn
PepsiCo
PepsiAmericas
PetSmart
Pfizer
Philip Morris
   International
Philips
Pilgrim's Pride
Pitney Bowes
Polo Ralph Lauren
PPG INDS
Praxair
Procter & Gamble
RR Donnelley
Rite Aid
Rockwell
   Automation
Rockwell Collins
Ross Stores
Safeway
SAP
Sara Lee
Sealed Air
Sears Holding
Seco Tools
Seimens
Sherwin-Williams
Smuckers
Southwest Airlines
Starbucks
Supelco

Target	Toshiba	United Parcel SVC	Whirlpool
Tenneco	Toyota	United Stationers	Whole Foods Market
Textron	Travel Centers of	United Technologies	Winn-Dixie Stores
The Gap	America	US Airways	Yahoo
Thermo Fisher	UAL	Wal-Mart Stores	Yum Brands
Scientific	Unilever	Wendy's	
Timken	Unisys	Westinghouse	

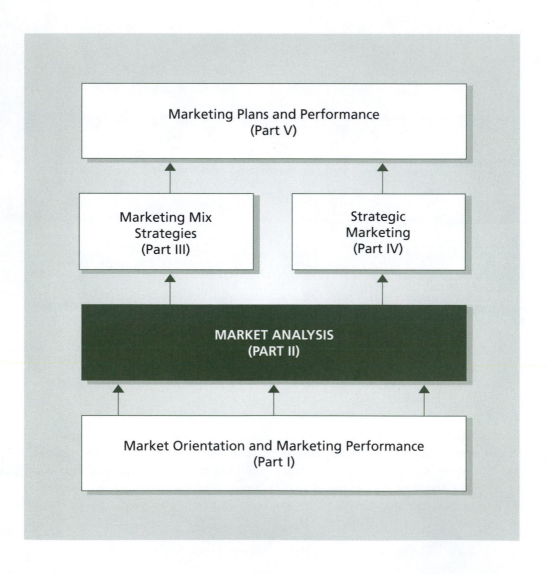

PART II

Market Analysis

■ Revenue growth looks great at 25 percent, but alarms should go off if that growth occurs in a market growing at 40 percent.[*]

Without conducting market analysis, a firm that has 25 percent sales growth might be very happy. However, if the market is growing 40 percent annually, the firm would be losing market share at a tremendous rate. Measurements of market share and market growth are just two of many marketing metrics that help businesses manage and plan their growth in sales and profits.

Market analysis is an essential aspect of the development of market-based management strategies that deliver superior levels of customer satisfaction and profitability. The continuous pursuit of customer needs, ongoing monitoring of competitors' moves and capabilities, and tracking market-based performance are the core competencies of a market-focused business.

Part II consists of four chapters that consider the fundamental inputs of market analysis: market demand, customer analysis, market segmentation, and competitor analysis. The first of these chapters, Chapter 3, examines market definition, market potential, market demand, and market share. Markets, however, do not buy products. *Customers* buy products. Chapter 4 focuses on customer analysis and the discovery of benefits that provide superior customer value.

Because customers in any market differ in many ways, rarely can one marketing strategy adequately serve all their needs. Chapter 5 addresses needs-based market segmentation and the development of segment strategies. Finally, Chapter 6 focuses on competitor analysis, competitive position, and sources of competitive advantage.

[*]Karen G. Strouse, "Planning, Measuring, Managing Market Share," January 2001, http://www.channelpartnersonline.com/articles/2001/01/planning-measuring-managing-market-share.aspx, retrieved August 2011.

CHAPTER 3

Market Potential, Market Demand, and Market Share

> ■ A narrow market definition limits your business opportunities. You have to see more to sell more.
> —*Jack Welch, CEO, 1981–2000*
> *General Electric Company*

arket potential, market demand, and market share are three very important marketing metrics. Without them, a business is unable to gauge its performance and adjust its marketing strategies and budgets to changing market conditions.

For example, the personal computer market has an estimated market potential of 450 million personal computers per year. Past that point, the market will grow slowly as the population grows. In 2010, the market demand for PCs was approximately 325 million.

As shown in the bar chart, market demand for the personal computer market is approaching saturation. In 2010, with a market share of about 12.8 percent, Dell was the second-largest share holder behind Hewlett-Packard in the global PC market. All three market metrics will play a key role in Dell's marketing strategy to manage profitable growth over the next 5 to 10 years as market demand slows.

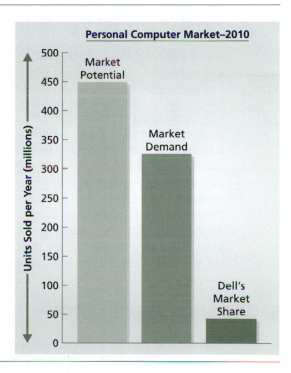

MARKET DEFINITION—WHAT BUSINESS ARE WE IN?

Perhaps the greatest threat to a business's survival, and a major cause of missed market opportunities, is a narrow focus on existing product-markets. Businesses that do not look at the broader picture of customers, market demand, and forces that shape unserved market demand expose themselves to this risk.[1] Theodore Levitt's perspective on marketing myopia applies today as much as it did when he first wrote on the subject some 50 years ago:

> A myopic vision of the potential markets a business might serve translates into a narrow product-focused market definition.[2]

Marketing professionals with a broad market vision see the world differently. Their view of market demand goes beyond existing products and customers and enables them to recognize untapped or emerging market opportunities that others overlook. With their unrestricted market vision, their businesses can move quickly to control their own destinies.[3]

A broad market vision enables a business to better serve the needs of its customers. But a broad market vision goes even further, enabling a business to see *unserved needs* that no one is addressing. Fred Smith, founder of FedEx, saw unserved customer needs that led him to conceive of a business which would provide overnight deliveries around the world, an idea that many bankers and industry experts said would never work. The broad market vision of Phil Knight, co-founder of Nike, led to a transformation of the athletic footwear and sports apparel markets. And Steve Jobs, co-founder of Apple, foresaw millions of people using computers in their daily lives, revolutionizing the way they work, communicate, and learn.

A broad market definition includes all potential substitute products. The likelihood that consumers will substitute one product in a certain market for another product in a different market is affected by how similar the markets are.[4] The more similar they are, the greater the possibility that consumers will substitute products.

Developing a broad vision of a market is the first step in understanding market demand.[5] A market vision limited to a particular product focus will only maintain the status quo. A business with a narrow market focus does not see beyond the *articulated needs* of served customers.[6] A market definition encompassing only the articulated needs of current customers will result in unfulfilled market potential as the business's served market moves left to right and becomes a greater part of the *unserved* market ignored by the narrow market definition. The inclination of many managers is to define their markets on the basis of the customers they currently serve, which limits the managers' perceptions and strategies. As a result, their businesses do not grow beyond the narrow view of the articulated needs of served customers, leaving a vast untapped market opportunity.

BROAD MARKET DEFINITION

Figure 3-1 shows the kinds of products that make up the nonalcoholic beverage market as it is today. Forty years ago, several of these products did not exist, while others had not yet reached their tipping point, the point where market demand moves from slow growth to exponential growth. Interestingly, the newer products quickly gained a significant share of the nonalcoholic beverage market as the result of strategies implemented by relatively small, innovative, new businesses.

The large beverage companies, almost without exception, were late in entering the product-markets of bottled water, sports drinks, fruit drinks, iced coffee, and energy

FIGURE 3-1 BEVERAGE PRODUCT-MARKET STRUCTURE AND MARKET GROWTH

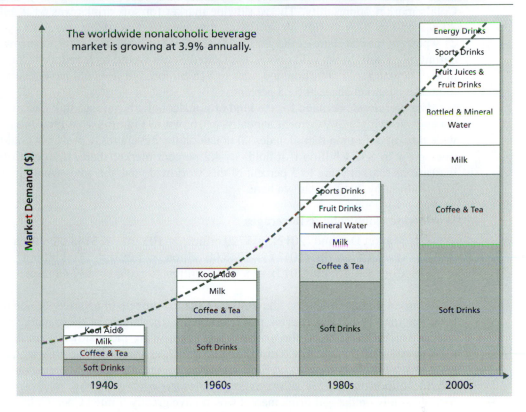

drinks. Their late entry serves as an excellent example of how short-term vision, with its limited view of a market, can overlook a chance to grow profits. It is especially likely for such opportunities to be missed when a company is doing well. Focused on their existing products, and feeling confident because the worldwide market for those products was rapidly expanding, the large beverage companies did not see the potential that alternative beverages held until they noticed the market success of the new products.

A broad market definition is essential for any business in order for its managers to understand and measure market demand, market potential, and market share. For a global company like Coca-Cola, a broad market definition includes the worldwide sales of all nonalcoholic beverages, which was $720 billion in 2009. As shown in the following table, Coca-Cola had a 4.2 percent market share and sales of $30 billion for 2009.

Coca-Cola (2009) Product Focus	Geographic Focus	Market Demand	Market Share	Coca-Cola Sales
Soft Drinks	United States	$30 billion	53.3%	$16 billion
Soft Drinks	Worldwide	$128 billion	21.9%	$28 billion
Nonalcoholic Beverages	Worldwide	$720 billion	4.2%	$30 billion

A market definition that includes only sales of soft drinks would greatly limit Coca-Cola's market opportunity. The worldwide market for soft drinks was $128 billion in 2009, and the 2009 worldwide soft drink revenues for Coca-Cola were $28 billion—a 21.9 percent market share of the worldwide soft drink market. For 2009, a narrow market definition of soft drinks sold only in the United States would have reduced Coca-Cola's market demand to $30 billion and sales to $16 billion, but it would have resulted in an impressive market share of 53.3 percent.

The worldwide demand for the kind of nonalcoholic beverages that Coca-Cola produces is growing at 3.9 percent annually, as shown in Figure 3-1. With a broad worldwide market definition that includes all nonalcoholic beverages, Coca-Cola could see its sales grow to $31.4 billion if it holds its 4.2 percent market share. If Coca-Cola could increase its market share to 5 percent of this worldwide market, sales would increase to $37.4 billion by 2012, as shown here.

Worldwide Nonalcoholic Beverages

$$\text{Market Demand (2012)} = \$720 \text{ billion} \times 103.9\% = \$748.08 \text{ billion}$$
$$\text{Coca-Cola Sales (2012)} = \$748.08 \text{ billion} \times 4.2\% = \$31.4 \text{ billion}$$
$$\text{Coca-Cola Sales (2012)} = \$748.08 \text{ billion} \times 5.0\% = \$37.4 \text{ billion}$$

A broad market definition allows Coca-Cola to compete in a variety of nonalcoholic beverage markets. The soft drink market, which is the largest of these markets and the one in which Coca-Cola is the market leader, is growing more slowly than the generic market, at 2 percent annually. Growth markets such as sports drinks, growing at 23 percent; energy drinks, growing at 31 percent; and other nonalcoholic beverage markets provide opportunities for above-average sales growth. A narrow market definition focused solely on the soft drink market would have greatly limited Coca-Cola's potential for future sales growth and increased profits.

NARROW MARKET DEFINITION

A narrow market definition, one adopted by design, is not always a limitation. Red Bull, a fast-growing Austrian company, has a 50 percent share of the European energy drink market, which was $2 billion in 2009. The worldwide energy drink market had sales of $12 billion in 2009, and Red Bull's share of it was 41.7 percent, as shown in the table that follows. The company recognizes that it is only part of the much larger nonalcoholic beverage market, but its market definition at this time is focused on energy drinks, with a strategy to hold its leadership position despite rapid new competitor entry into this segment of the nonalcoholic beverage market.

Red Bull (2009) Product Focus	Geographic Focus	Market Demand	Market Share	Red Bull Sales
Energy Drinks	Europe	$2 billion	50.0%	$1 billion
Energy Drinks	Worldwide	$12 billion	41.7%	$5 billion
Nonalcoholic Beverages	Worldwide	$720 billion	0.7%	$5 billion

The energy drink market is projected to grow at double-digit rates, and Red Bull will have to invest significantly in marketing resources to hold its leadership position. Remaining the share leader may be difficult because of the new competition. Coca-Cola, PepsiCo, and Anheuser-Busch are among the companies that have entered the market with brands like Full Throttle, SoBe, Adrenaline Rush, and 180. Holding its worldwide market share of 41.7 percent in the energy drink market could prove challenging for Red Bull. Gatorade successfully maintained an 80 percent share of the U.S. sports drink market for many years but recently saw its share fall to 71 percent in the face of the new competition.[7]

MARKET POTENTIAL

After a served market definition has been established, a business is in a better position to understand several important aspects of market potential.[8] The first and most crucial aspect is the potential market demand: How many customers make up the maximum potential for the served market definition?[9] This assessment of market demand includes a determination of the maximum unit and dollar potential if all potential consuming units entered the market.

At any point in time, a business has an *existing* pool of current and prospective customers who make up current market demand and a *potential* pool of prospective customers who provide the opportunity to grow market demand. But because for every product and service a fixed number of customers buy at a certain rate of purchase, any product or service will have a certain level of market demand at any point in time.

For example, the personal computer market emerged in the early 1980s but did not reach its tipping point[10] until the early 1990s, as illustrated in Figure 3-2. From then on,

FIGURE 3-2 PERSONAL COMPUTER MARKET DEMAND

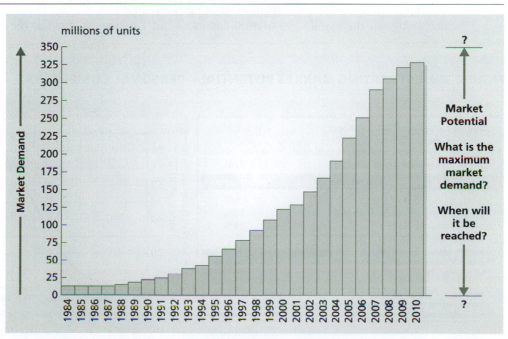

growth accelerated rapidly as products improved and prices came down. However, for any technology the market demand has an upper limit, a ceiling that cannot be exceeded without a change in technology or a new way of using the product. This is the market potential—the maximum number of units that can be consumed by the world population, or other defined market, at any point in time.

Knowing the maximum number of units that can be consumed by the defined market is of great strategic importance to a business: After a market reaches its full potential and saturates, new customers will be hard to find. For the personal computer market, the current full market potential is estimated at 450 million units per year, as shown in Figure 3-3. The worldwide market demand in 2010 was approximately 325 million personal computers. But what is the market potential for this product and when will it be reached? We need to keep in mind, too, that the market potential could change as the result of substantial price declines, radically new computer technology, or other unpredictable developments.

Published information on the market potential for any given market is difficult or impossible to find. But by using facts, logic, and assumptions, we can arrive at a reasonable estimate of a market's potential.[11] We should use no more than 10 years as the time horizon, because a market's potential can change significantly over time, for better or worse, in response to such influences as technological advances, changes in customer behavior, and regional or global economic conditions.

Figure 3-3 presents a systematic approach for estimating market potential. The first step is to define the geographical boundaries and the consuming units. The consuming units could be defined in terms of individuals, families, households, businesses, or other purchasing entities. For the personal computer, the market is worldwide, and individual users are its consuming units. The world's population is 7 billion people, but we can logically estimate that 2.5 billion of them are not old enough, lack the ancillary requirements, or are otherwise incapable of using a computer, so the maximum number of consuming units is 4.5 billion. This number is further reduced by the fact that a significant percentage of the world's population cannot afford a computer, even at the estimated

FIGURE 3-3 ESTIMATING MARKET POTENTIAL—PERSONAL COMPUTERS

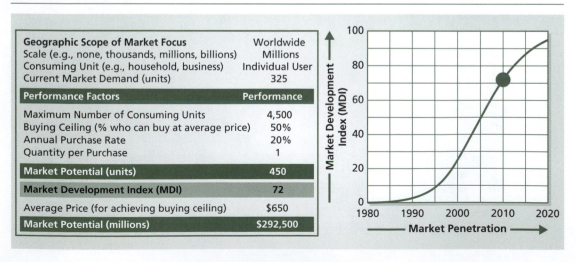

Geographic Scope of Market Focus	Worldwide
Scale (e.g., none, thousands, millions, billions)	Millions
Consuming Unit (e.g., household, business)	Individual User
Current Market Demand (units)	325
Performance Factors	**Performance**
Maximum Number of Consuming Units	4,500
Buying Ceiling (% who can buy at average price)	50%
Annual Purchase Rate	20%
Quantity per Purchase	1
Market Potential (units)	**450**
Market Development Index (MDI)	**72**
Average Price (for achieving buying ceiling)	$650
Market Potential (millions)	**$292,500**

average price of $650 for 2020. This price estimate is based on a long-running market trend of price declines of about 7 percent annually. Using economic data on the populations of the world's nations, we can estimate a buying ceiling of 50 percent, meaning that only about half of the maximum number of consuming units can afford to buy a personal computer. For the personal computer industry, then, 2.25 billion is the estimated worldwide number of personal computer users when the market saturates.

Market Potential = 4.5 billion potential × 50% buying ceiling = **2.25 billion users**

If we assume that each user has just one personal computer, and that users replace their computers on average every 5 years, the number of units sold per year at full market potential would be 450 million. At the estimated price of $650 per unit, the annual sales at full market potential would be $292.5 billion, barring any unpredictable major developments. These calculations are embodied in the following formula for figuring a market's annual sales when it reaches its potential:

$$\frac{\textbf{Market}}{\textbf{Potential}} = \frac{\text{Maximum}}{\text{Consuming Units}} \times \frac{\text{Buying}}{\text{Ceiling}} \times \frac{\text{Purchase}}{\text{Rate}} \times \frac{\text{Purchase}}{\text{Quantity}} \times \frac{\text{Average}}{\text{Price}}$$

$$\frac{\textbf{Market}}{\textbf{Potential}} = \frac{4.5 \text{ billion}}{\text{users}} \times \frac{50\%}{\text{buying ceiling}} \times \frac{20\% \text{ rebuy}}{\text{annually}} \times \frac{1 \text{ PC per}}{\text{user}} \times \frac{\$650}{\text{Price}}$$

$$= \textbf{\$292.5 billion annually}$$

For the U.S. soft drink market, retail sales at full market potential may be estimated in the same way. Of the 300 million people in the United States, we exclude very young children and other individuals whom we could not consider as potential consumers, leaving 80 percent of the population as the maximum number of consuming units. The average soft drink consumer buys 365 soft drinks a year. At an average price of $1 per drink, annual retail sales would be $87.6 billion if all potential consumers entered the market.

$$\frac{\textbf{Market}}{\textbf{Potential (\$)}} = \frac{300 \text{ million}}{\text{people}} \times \frac{80\%}{\text{ceiling}} \times \frac{365 \text{ units}}{\text{annually}} \times \frac{\$1 \text{ per}}{\text{unit}} = \frac{\textbf{\$87.6 billion}}{\textbf{annually}}$$

For flat-panel TVs, let's assume the number of households in the United States will grow to 120 million in 10 years. If we further assume that 80 percent of the households would buy a flat-panel TV at an average selling price of $500, and each household would buy one TV every 5 years, the market potential would be an estimated $9.6 billion annually. If the average price fell to $400, and the consuming units grew to 90 percent of the households, the market potential would drop to $8.6 billion.

$$\frac{\textbf{Market}}{\textbf{Potential (\$)}} = \frac{120 \text{ million}}{\text{households}} \times \frac{80\%}{\text{ceiling}} \times \frac{20\% \text{ rebuy}}{\text{annually}} \times \frac{1 \text{ unit per}}{\text{household}} \times \frac{\$500 \text{ per}}{\text{unit}} = \frac{\textbf{\$9.6 billion}}{\textbf{annually}}$$

To estimate the U.S. market potential for motorized golf carts, we would similarly rely on facts, logic, and assumptions. First, we would research various sources to find the information we need. Let's suppose we learn that the United States has 17,000 golf courses, that 5 percent of the courses do not have golf carts, that the other 95 percent have an average of 100 carts, that golf courses typically replace their fleets every 3 years, and that the cost of a new cart is $2,500. In this mature market, we can assume that the selling price will stay about same over the next 10 years.

$$\begin{array}{c}\text{Market} \\ \text{Potential (\$)}\end{array} = \begin{array}{c}17{,}000\text{ golf} \\ \text{courses}\end{array} \times \begin{array}{c}95\% \\ \text{ceiling}\end{array} \times \begin{array}{c}33.3\%\text{ buy} \\ \text{annually}\end{array} \times \begin{array}{c}100\text{ carts} \\ \text{per course}\end{array} \times \begin{array}{c}\$2{,}500 \\ \text{per cart}\end{array} = \begin{array}{c}\textbf{\$1.3 billion} \\ \textbf{annually}\end{array}$$

Because the golf cart market matured some time ago, the present market demand is close to the market potential. However, if a significant number of new courses are developed, market potential would increase. As golf's popularity continues to grow, many new courses are a strong likelihood. In addition, because an ever-increasing number of courses are requiring their golfers to use golf carts in order to increase the daily number of rounds that can be played, the average fleet size will probably increase.

HOW INNOVATION CHANGES MARKET POTENTIAL

Every product-market is on an innovation curve that allows products to be developed to their full extent. A new technology application essentially goes unnoticed until it reaches a tipping point[12] and then develops more rapidly through *continuous innovation*, as shown in Figure 3-4. Eventually a technology reaches a point of saturation with respect

FIGURE 3-4 INNOVATION AND MARKET POTENTIAL

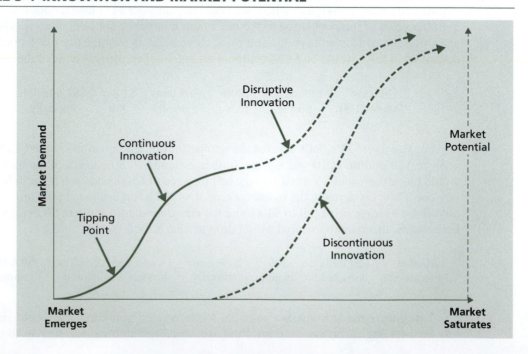

to its development, which limits market demand. In order for the market to develop further, there must be a *disruptive innovation* or a *discontinuous innovation*.[13] Each type of innovation is briefly summarized here:

- **Continuous Innovation:** The development of technology and improved products for a given product market. The mainframe computer, vacuum-tube television, and fountain pen were all improved over many years of continuous innovation.
- **Disruptive Innovation:** Change along the technology innovation curve that allows for the development of products that are less expensive, smaller, and often easier to use. The microcomputer, solid-state television, and ballpoint pen greatly expanded the market demand and market potential for computers, televisions, and pens.
- **Discontinuous Innovation:** A major shift from an old technology to a new technology that usually offers new customer benefits. New technology, for example, has led to the development of digital photography, which has largely replaced film photography. Similarly, flat-panel televisions have eroded the market for picture-tube sets.

Each type of innovation has the potential to expand the number of customers who can use the product, as well as the number of product applications. The flat-panel TV is now found in many homes, and it is also in airports, waiting rooms, restaurants, and bars. Flat-panel technology has led to a much greater use of televisions for entertainment and staying informed, and it has greatly changed the product's market demand and market potential.

MARKET DEVELOPMENT INDEX

Figure 3-5 illustrates the market development of several well-known product-markets. Each had a well-defined tipping point, followed by periods of rapid growth and eventually a leveling-off period as market demand approached its market potential. As shown earlier

FIGURE 3-5 MARKET DEVELOPMENT AND MARKET POTENTIAL

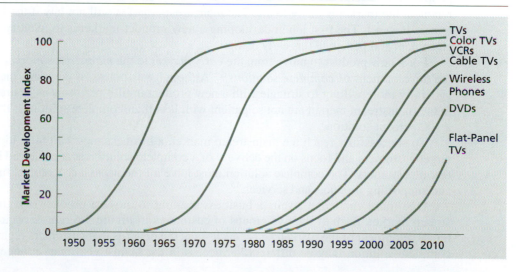

in Figure 3-3, the personal computer market is approaching its full market development. To help us understand the evolution of a market and to measure a market's potential for future growth, we can use a measurement called the *market development index (MDI)*. This index is simply a ratio of current market demand to market potential:

$$\underset{\text{Personal Computers}}{\textbf{Market Development Index}} = \frac{\text{Current Market Demand}}{\text{Market Potential}} \times 100$$

$$= \frac{325 \text{ million}}{450 \text{ million}} \times 100 = \textbf{72}$$

An MDI of less than 33, for example, would suggest considerable growth potential for a product's market. When the MDI is between 33 and 67, further development of the market is based on addressing product improvements, expanding distribution, and reducing prices. As the MDI goes beyond 67, the potential for growth remains, but the task will be more difficult because the business now faces strong forces that impede full market development.

MANAGING MARKET GROWTH

In order to eventually succeed in a new market, a business's first need is customers. For many products, finding those customers isn't easy. The risks associated with being an early buyer of a new product or service make most potential customers extremely reluctant. New products are usually priced high at first, customers may not know how to make them work, and early versions often quickly give way to much-improved versions. Some new products also encounter societal or cultural resistance because they represent too much of a change. They are just *too* different for most people. Emerging markets, then, are relatively small. They consist of *innovators* and *early adopters*, as shown in Figure 3-6. Customers who make up the early market possess more knowledge, are less price sensitive, are more benefit driven, and are less dependent on what others do or think than most people. These *lead customers* are critical. If they cannot be attracted, satisfied, and retained, the market is likely to die. The mainstream market will not buy if the lead customers haven't. The first job in developing a new product-market is to identify the lead customers and penetrate this early market.

For a new product to move from the *early market* to the *mainstream market* requires the development of *complete solutions*.[14] Although customers in the early market are generally more willing to struggle with a new product until it performs as desired, those in the mainstream market are not so patient with less-than-complete solutions; they want a 100 percent solution.

To successfully reach the mainstream market, a business must carefully identify its target customers and focus on the delivery of a complete solution as it is viewed by those target customers. The complete solution must have all the necessary features, functions, and supporting products and services.[15]

One more challenge awaits a business seeking to move a product into the mainstream market. Each of the five groups of customers in Figure 3-6 represents a stage in the development of the market, and at each stage the benefits that customers regard as the complete solution may be different.[16] Success in the mainstream market depends to a

FIGURE 3-6 FACTORS INFLUENCING FULL MARKET DEVELOPMENT

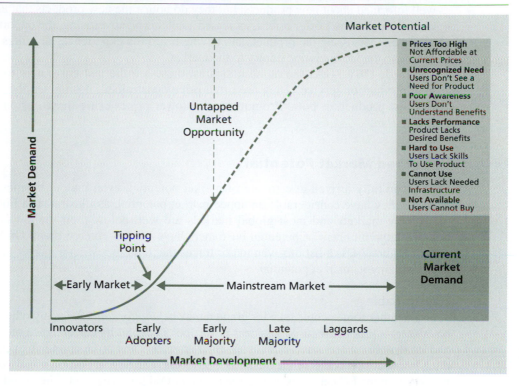

great extent on the experience of lead users—the innovators and early adopters—and their influence on potential mainstream customers. But success also requires adjustments to attract the potential mainstream customers. The more quickly a business addresses the complete solution needed for mainstream customers, the more quickly the market will grow. A look at the five customer groups will help us gain a better understanding of the kinds of adjustments that might be necessary.

1. **Innovators (2.5%)**—As the first to buy a new product or service, these customers see genuine value in it and are willing to pay a premium price, despite any deficiencies in ease of use, support services, and the set of features.
2. **Early Adopters (13.5%)**—Because they are well informed, these customers are aware of the innovators' experience and satisfaction with a new product or service. They are attracted to the product's benefits and are willing to pay a premium price even though the product or service lacks the refinements that will come later.
3. **Early Majority (34%)**—A product has penetrated the mass market when the early majority of customers have adopted it. The price is affordable, the product is useable, and the feature set is attractive. Until these product attributes are met, the market's development will be delayed. The early majority customers are quality conscious, fairly well informed, and somewhat price sensitive.
4. **Late Majority (34%)**—The customers in the late majority are skeptics. They wait to see whether the product or service will really deliver meaningful benefits. These

customers are more price sensitive than early majority customers and often are not as well informed about new products, but they do notice the new products that are being used around them. Lower prices, increased availability, advertising, the opportunity to observe others using the product, and having heard the experiences of others all contribute to the late majority's entry to the market.

5. **Laggards (16%)**—As the name indicates, these are the last customers to adopt a new product or service. They are often price constrained, do not see the need for the new product, or both. Promotions and lower prices bring these customers into the market.

Untapped Market Potential

With a carefully arrived-at estimate of market potential, even mature businesses may discover they have considerable untapped market potential, as illustrated in Figure 3-6. Many new markets and most global markets are well below their market potentials because large numbers of potential customers have not yet entered them. On the right side of Figure 3-6 is a list of seven major forces that tend to restrict a market or product from realizing its market potential.

Unaffordable

A product that some people take for granted may be *unaffordable* for many others. As we have seen, a product-focused business never looks beyond its current customer market, and its senior managers never challenge their engineers and production managers to produce lower-cost versions of the business's products. The largest portion of new-customer purchases in the PC market is now in the under $1,000 price segment. The introduction of a $100 computer, though it may be limited in capabilities, will greatly expand the market potential of PCs to include the many people worldwide who cannot afford the more expensive models.

Unrecognized Need

Full market development may be limited by the percentage of prospective customers who *do not perceive a need* for the product. In many cases, potential consumers shy away from a new product because they do not see the need for it. For example, a car owner might not recognize the need for a Triple A card until the car owner is stranded with a flat tire or dead battery, and as they grow older people may not see the need for nutritional supplements to help prevent certain diseases. Many undeveloped markets or underdeveloped market segments have a large percentage of customers who may be aware of a product but do not recognize a need for it.

Lack of Awareness

Consumer awareness means not just *product awareness*, but also a *complete comprehension of benefits*. Even potential customers who are aware of a product will not recognize its potential value to them if they do not fully understand its benefits. In the case of the personal computer, most potential customers in the worldwide market are aware of the product but may not realize all the benefits that personal computers offer. Because the product is complex and experiential, customers appreciate its most compelling benefits only after they have used it for a period of time.

Lacks Desired Performance

A product cannot reach its market potential if its *performance benefits are not appealing* to consumers. If the performance benefits of a product are not compelling enough, market demand will be limited. The benefit proposition is simply deficient—too weak to stimulate purchase regardless of the strength of other forces influencing a decision to buy. Because consumers have varied lifestyles and preferences, a product may be unable to accommodate all the needs and desired benefits in its market. In these cases, a practical limit is placed on market potential. But a practical limit can also restrict a market from reaching its maximum potential. Computer companies, for example, could easily have excluded older people from the potential PC market in the belief that older people would see no benefit in owning a computer. But now that e-mail, online banking, and online shopping are commonplace, and with a vast number of other online services and resources available, older people have become an important source of new customers for PC companies. Had the companies set a practical limit on their potential markets by excluding the older population, they would unnecessarily have limited the market potential for their products.

Consumers Lack Skills to Use

Many products require users to have a certain skill level. Market expansion may be restricted when a significant percentage of potential consumers *lack the skills* that are needed to use a product. Using personal computers, for example, may be second nature to many, but for people who have not been exposed to them, there is often a barrier to purchase based on the difficulty of using the product. But this barrier can also be an opportunity. Companies that are willing to develop learning solutions for those who lack usage skills can own that segment of new customers. Apple, Microsoft, and other information technology companies fund educational programs that benefit students and their communities and also contribute to the development of the personal computer market and the companies' share of that market. Similarly, in the early days of the microwave oven, some microwave manufacturers offered classes to show people how to cook with the new ovens. In this way, the manufacturers took a barrier to market development and made it a boost for market development, as well as a boost for the manufacturers' market share.

Insufficient Infrastructure

For many products, an *absent or insufficient infrastructure* restricts market growth. Before they can sell the high-speed trains that they manufacture, Alstom, Siemens, and Talgo must first sell their potential customers on building or upgrading the railway infrastructure. Likewise, the manufacturer of any electrical product, whether it is a light bulb or a computer, would find few customers in the remote but populous regions of the world that are not served by an electrical grid.

Unavailability

The last of the seven forces that restrict market demand is *unavailability*. For mature markets, product unavailability generally is not a significant factor in limiting market demand. But even in mature markets, market demand is hampered if products are in short supply, difficulties arise in distribution, or support services are inadequate. When the personal computer market was in its early stages, many individuals and businesses who saw the benefits of PCs were reluctant to buy because they did not have access to technical support services.

Market Potential and Market Growth

Recognizing that every market has some upper limit—its market potential—marketing managers naturally want to know how fast their markets will grow to their market potential. For marketing managers, any catalyst that might spur market growth provides the potential for sales growth.

Among the market growth curves shown in Figure 3-5 are growth curves for black-and-white televisions, color televisions, and VCRs. The upper limit in each case represents the market potential for each product-market. The rate at which customers enter a market is a market-specific phenomenon that is based on product attractiveness, customer characteristics, and marketing efforts.[17] However, the early pattern established by the rate of customer entry into a market offers enough information to project the market growth rate accurately in most cases.[18]

Three fundamental forces affect the rate of market growth and hence the shape of the market growth curve:

1. **Market Potential:** The maximum number of customers the market could attract, given a specific definition for the served market.
2. **Market Penetration:** The number of customers who have entered a market at a certain point in time.
3. **Rate of Entry:** The percentage of potential customers who enter the market during a given period.

These three elements define the parameters of a market's customer attraction and growth. They can vary greatly from one product-market to another. Some markets, we know, grow much faster and reach their potential much sooner than others. But why? What makes some product-markets grow quickly and others grow slowly? The next section addresses this question and provides marketing strategies for accelerating market growth.

Accelerating Market Growth

Developing and delivering a complete solution requires more than improving the product and making it affordable to the mainstream market. The rate at which the mainstream market adopts a new product also depends on customer characteristics, product positioning, and market influences. Given adequate product awareness, a number of forces can act to accelerate customer attraction and the rate of market growth.[19] As shown in Figure 3-7, there are five customer adoption forces and five product adoption forces affecting new product-market penetration.

Customer Adoption Forces

Customer adoption forces affect the rate at which customers enter a market. First, customers must *feel a need* for the product, although the strength of that felt need can vary. When the felt need for a product is low, customer attraction will be slow. For years, many potential customers simply did not feel a strong need to have a microwave oven, so the rate at which customers entered this product-market was slow.

In addition, many people saw a safety *risk* with the product, and this perception also slowed market growth. Customer perceptions of risk, the second of the five customer

FIGURE 3-7 CUSTOMER FORCES AND PRODUCT FORCES THAT SHAPE MARKET GROWTH

Customer Forces	Relative Importance	Customer Rating	Description of Customer Tipping Point
Need	30%	8	Strong, recognized need for this product.
Risk	10%	9	Little or no economic, social, or performance risk.
Buying	20%	3	May be purchased without the approval of others.
Observation	20%	6	Easily observed in use.
Trial	20%	3	Easy to try before purchase.
Total	100%	5.7	Overall score on scale from 0 to 10.

Product Forces	Relative Importance	Customer Rating	Description of Customer Tipping Point
Advantage	30%	9	Meaningful advantage over other products.
Affordable	20%	3	Price affordable for target customers.
Ease of Use	15%	6	Easy to install, use, and service.
Performance	20%	6	Meets customers' performance expectations.
Available	15%	8	Available where customers prefer to buy.
Total	100%	6.6	Overall score on scale from 0 to 10.

adoption forces, are not limited to safety risks. Customers might also envision risks associated with the loss of money or loss of status.

The third customer adoption force is the *buying decision*. If the decision to buy a product or service can be made without having to get the agreement or input of several people, market growth will develop more rapidly. An individual decision maker can act quickly if he or she does not first need the approval of others. Conversely, when decisions to purchase a product are likely to be group decisions, such as those by a married couple, an organization's governing board, or the managers or owners of a business, the rate of customer entry into a market is slowed.

The fourth influence on the growth of a product's market demand is the extent to which potential customers can *observe* the use of the product by current customers. The demand for products that are easily observed, such as televisions and fashionable sunglasses, grows faster than for products that are less observable, such as household cleaners and insurance programs.

Trialability is the fifth factor affecting market growth. Products that can be tried at the point of purchase or offered on a trial basis will penetrate their markets more quickly than products that customers cannot try before buying. The easier it is to try or sample a product before buying, the faster the rate of market penetration.

To help project a new product's rate of market penetration, we can measure the strength of the customer forces. As shown in the top portion of Figure 3-7, we first estimate the relative importance of each customer force and then assign each force a customer rating on a scale from 0 to 10, where 10 indicates the strongest possible appeal for a potential customer. We then multiply the relative importance rating for each force by its customer rating, adding the results to give us the overall average score. Naturally, the higher the overall score, the more rapid the market penetration. In our example, the customer adoption forces achieve an overall score of 5.7, which means that they are moderately favorable. This score for customer forces will contribute to a slightly above-average rate of market penetration, but five product adoption forces also play an equally important role in the rate of market development.

Product Adoption Forces

The strength of a product's positioning on the basis of its relative benefits has a major effect on the rate of market growth. The stronger the benefits *advantage* and the more *affordable* the price, the greater the customer value created by the product and the faster the rate of customer market entry.

Unfortunately, many businesses never go beyond creating a strong benefits package and setting an affordable price. These businesses fail to examine their products' *ease of use, desired performance,* and *preferred availability* as perceived by potential customers.

If a product is incompatible with the normal routines of potential customers, or if the potential customers think it would be difficult to use, they will be reluctant to purchase it. When microwave ovens were first introduced, they were expensive, but they had very attractive benefits. Some potential customers, as mentioned earlier, shied away from the product because they didn't feel the need for it or because they perceived risks associated with its use. Other potential customers were deterred by the price of early models. But undoubtedly a significant percentage of potential mainstream customers delayed buying a microwave because they didn't know how to use one. For many high-tech products, the relative advantages are enormous, but the perceived difficulty in using the products can discourage purchases.

Similarly, consumer doubts about the *performance* of a product will hurt market penetration. A perception that microwaved food is not as appetizing as conventionally cooked food is probably still keeping some consumers from entering the market.

The fifth and last product force is *availability*. Not only must the product itself be available to consumers at their preferred points of purchase, but any necessary support or maintenance services must also be readily accessible. A lack of after-sales customer service can kill product adoption. Because new products often present new challenges for customers, inadequate after-sales customer support can doom a new product by bad word-of-mouth reports. As with the overall score for customer forces, the higher the overall score for product forces, the more rapid the market penetration. In the bottom portion of Figure 3-7, the overall average score for product forces is 6.6. This favorable score means that the current strength of the product forces, while not exceptional, is nevertheless favorable for market penetration.

Figure 3-8 shows how overall scores for customer forces and product forces affect market growth. Products or services with weak overall scores for both customer forces and product forces, such as flood insurance and HIV drugs, experience very slow market growth. A relatively high overall score for customer forces but a relatively low score for product forces, such as for biofuels, leads to a somewhat faster market growth, but it is still slow. Similarly, moderately strong product forces but very weak customer forces, such as for eco-washers, produce faster growth but it is still relatively slow. The best results naturally occur when both the customer forces and the product forces are strong overall, as with flat-panel TVs, hybrid cars, the iPhone and iPad, and Facebook. Then market growth is

FIGURE 3-8 CUSTOMER AND PRODUCT FORCES DRIVING MARKET GROWTH RATE

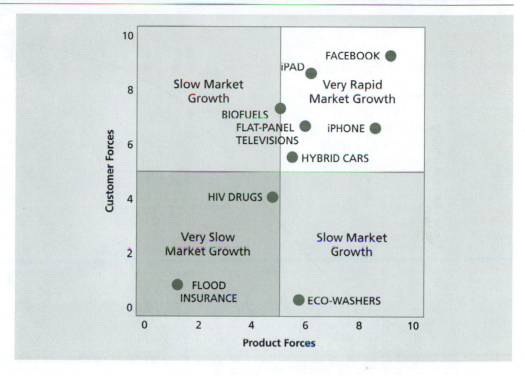

very rapid. Developing solutions for weak consumer and product forces allows a business to influence the rate of market growth. For example, a business could improve low scores for trial and ease of use for a new product category in order to accelerate market growth.

PRODUCT-MARKET VERSUS PRODUCT LIFE CYCLE

Every market has a generic product-market life cycle. The generic life cycle encompasses many product life cycles, as illustrated for the different Intel microprocessors in Figure 3-9. The generic market demand plotted on this graph is for the product life cycle of a product-market category—in this case, Intel microprocessors. By no means is a generic product-market life cycle the same as the product life cycle for a specific product. As the personal computer market has grown, along with the demand for greater speed and capacity, Intel has gone through entire product life cycles for several products, as the graph illustrates. In most cases, the newer products hastened the decline of the existing products.

In Figure 3-10, we clearly see the introductory and growth stages of a product life cycle. As the market demand approaches the market potential, growth slows. Eventually the market becomes a mature market with little or no growth. The product has now entered a critical phase in its life cycle. Whereas the volume during the product's introductory and growth stages was derived from both market demand and market share, in a mature market gains in volume can be achieved only with gains in market share. When a market fully matures, declining volumes are inevitable.

FIGURE 3-9 GENERIC PRODUCT-MARKET LIFE CYCLE VERSUS PRODUCT LIFE CYCLE

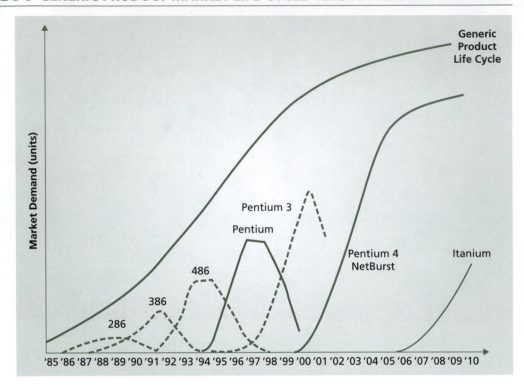

Product Life Cycle, Market Demand, and Profits

Because a business's volume depends on market demand and market share, any business would want to increase both demand and share by implementing an effective marketing and sales program. In the early stages of the product life cycle, as Figure 3-10 shows, the net marketing contribution (NMC) is negative. The negative NMC is the result of marketing and sales expenses exceeding gross profit during the introduction stage of the product life cycle.

As the product moves into the growth stage, it reaches a break-even NMC, with gross profit equaling marketing and sales expenses. Beyond that point, the annual NMCs grow and eventually peak in the late growth stage of the product life cycle. As the market matures, the combination of flat market demand, lower margins, and higher marketing and sales expenses results in lower NMCs. In the declining stage of the life cycle, marketing profits continue to fall with decreases in market demand, despite any efforts to milk the product for profits by reducing marketing and sales expenses.

Market Demand and Prices

One of the reasons that demand grows as a product moves from introduction through early adoption and into the growth and late growth stages is an ongoing decline in the average selling price of the product. Figure 3-11 shows the average prices for personal computers and printers sold in stores.[20] Prices decline steadily in the early stages of the

FIGURE 3-10 PRODUCT LIFE CYCLE, MARKET DEMAND, AND PROFITS

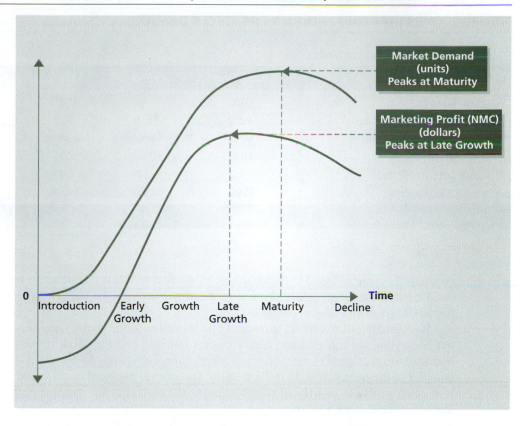

FIGURE 3-11 AVERAGE SELLING PRICE—PERSONAL COMPUTERS AND PRINTERS

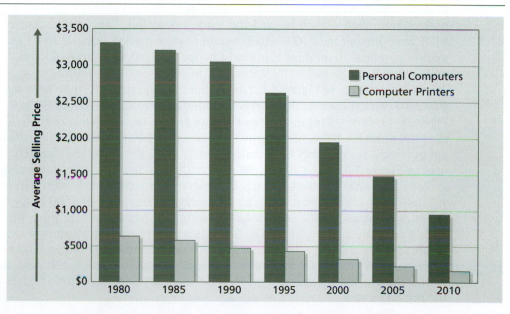

FIGURE 3-12 ESTIMATING PRODUCT LIFE-CYCLE DEMAND AND SALES

Market Potential: 20 Million Units				
	Base Year	Year 1	Year 2	Year 3
Market Growth	10%	10%	10%	10%
Market Demand (millions)	12.0	13.2	14.5	16.0
Market Development Index	60%	66%	73%	80%
Market Share	10%	10%	10%	10%
Volume Sold (millions)	1.2	1.32	1.45	1.6
Average Selling Price	$500	$475	$450	$425
Sales Revenues (millions)	**$600**	**$627**	**$653**	**$680**

product life cycle and tend to flatten out as products reach their mature stage of the product life cycle. Declining prices allow more customers to enter the market, increasing both market demand and sales revenues.

Recognizing that volumes grow and prices decline in the growth stages of the product life cycle, we can estimate future market demand and the MDI by projecting the assumed market growth rate over a 3-year planning period. In Figure 3-12, market demand in the base year is 12 million units. The market potential is estimated at 20 million units, giving us an MDI of 60. This means the market is just over the halfway point in its life cycle. If we assume that the market will grow 10 percent annually for the next 3 years, we can project market demand to reach 16 million in 3 years. At this point, the market will be at 80 percent of full development.

One of the important benefits of estimating market potential is the ceiling it places on market demand. Too often, a business that has enjoyed years of growth will project continued growth beyond the market potential. This could occur only if the MDI were greater than 100, which would require market demand to be greater than market potential, something that could happen only if the market potential has been underestimated.

In the example in Figure 3-12, the actual growth rate is likely to be lower than the stated 10 percent because the market is projected to reach an MDI of 80 in 3 years. As Figure 3-13 shows, sales revenue and market growth rates typically begin to level off as the MDI nears 80. If the market growth is indeed still 10 percent annually, then the market potential has probably been underestimated and should be re-estimated. The business in Figure 3-12 has a 10 percent market share in the base year, and management's strategy is to hold this market share. If the strategy succeeds, unit sales will grow from 1.2 million to 1.6 million units. With an average selling price of $500 in the base year, the sales revenues were $600 million. Assuming the average selling price will decrease by $25 annually, by year 3 it will be $425. In a market growing 10 percent annually, the combination of holding a 10 percent market share and reducing prices allows sales revenues to grow from $600 million in the base year to $680 in year 3. Any changes in market growth, market share, or price would naturally alter the estimated sales revenues for any given year.

FIGURE 3-13 ESTIMATING GROWTH FOR MARKET DEMAND AND SALES

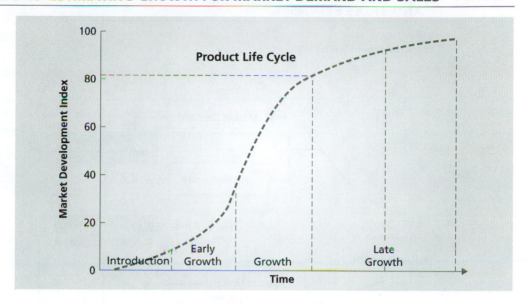

Product Life-Cycle Margins and Marketing Expenses

In addition to growth in volume sold and declines in the average selling price over the product life cycle, important changes occur in the average cost per unit sold and the marketing expenses needed to support market growth. As shown in Figure 3-14, prices tend to decrease faster than unit costs decrease. Thus, margins per unit tend to decline over the product life cycle.

Figure 3-14 also shows that marketing and sales expenses increase over the introductory and early growth phases of the product life cycle. These marketing and sales expenses are essential in creating product awareness and communicating product benefits to potential customers. Marketing and sales expenses as a percentage of sales tend to level off as a product approaches the maturity stage of its product life cycle, and they decrease during the decline stage.

Product Life-Cycle Sales and Gross Profits

Figure 3-15 illustrates how profits can vary over the product life cycle. In the case of personal computers, we can see continued growth beyond the life cycle's late growth stage in both sales revenues and market demand in units. However, slower growth in volume and declining prices will contribute to lower margins and lower industry gross profits. As shown, industry gross profits are expected to peak in 2010 and be somewhat lower by 2015. This modest decline occurs as the personal computer market moves from a stage of late growth to the maturity stage of its product-market life cycle.

Changes in technology, regional or global economic conditions, customer use of personal computers, and price could each redefine the market potential, as discussed earlier. In the 1950s, IBM estimated the market potential for computers at 50 per year, a striking

FIGURE 3-14 LIFE-CYCLE DEMAND, MARGINS, AND MARKETING AND SALES EXPENSES

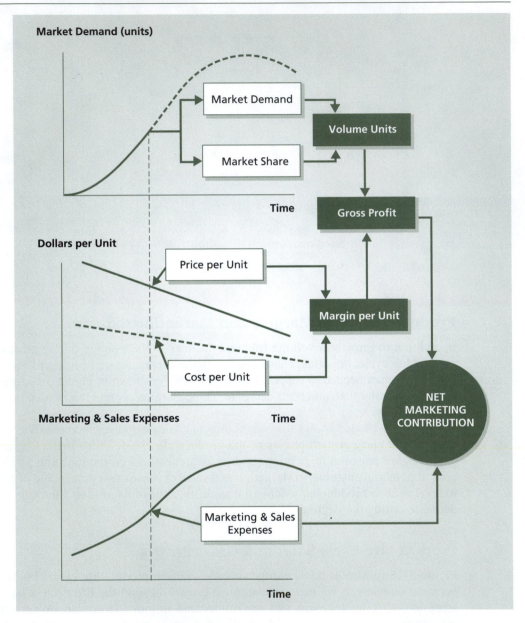

example of how changes in technology, product form, price, and customer usage can reshape market demand and market potential.

A good first step in developing a reliable estimate of sales is to develop a reliable estimate of market demand. The market demand sets an upper limit on sales. If a business had a 100 percent market share, then its sales would equal the total market demand.

FIGURE 3-15 PERSONAL COMPUTER LIFE-CYCLE SALES AND GROSS PROFIT

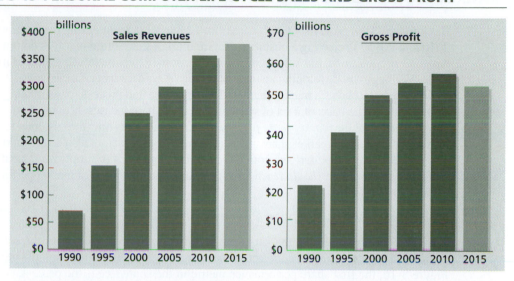

Industry Market Performance	1990	1995	2000	2005	2010	2015
Market Potential (millions)	450	450	450	450	450	450
Market Demand (millions)	24	58	132	207	325	400
Market Development Index	5	13	29	46	72	89
Average Selling Price	$2,950	$2,650	$1,900	$1,450	$1,100	$950
Industry Sales (billions)	$71	$154	$251	$300	$358	$380
Average Margin (%)	30%	25%	20%	18%	16%	14%
Industry Gross Profit (billions)	$21	$38	$50	$54	$57	$53

Following this logic, the current annual market demand times a business's current market share represents the volume of units that a business sells in a given year.

Volume Sold (units) = Market Demand (units) × Market Share

For example, Dell sold about 41.6 million PCs in 2010, based on Dell's 12.8 percent share of a market demand of 325 million PCs.[21] Over the next 5 years, the market is projected to grow to 400 million units.[22] If Dell can grow its market share to 15 percent, the combination of market growth and Dell's share growth would result in the sale of 60 million units in 2015.

Dell PC Unit Sales (2010) = 325 million units × 12.8% = **41.6 million units**
Dell PC Unit Sales (2015) = 400 million units × 15% = **60 million units**

Dell's future sales will depend on the same two factors: market demand and market share. By accurately projecting demand and share, Dell can more effectively plan for production volumes and achieve the lowest possible unit cost.

MARKET SHARE PERFORMANCE METRICS

But how will Dell grow its market share from 12.8 to 15 percent during the 5 years between 2010 and 2015? Projecting a business's future market share often involves complex mathematical propositions, but we can arrive at a reasonable estimate using simple marketing logic. We begin by developing an understanding of *how market share is achieved*.

Figure 3-16 shows a market share performance tree and process for estimating a *market share index* on the basis of a set of sequential market share metrics. Moving from bottom to top, each stage of the *market share performance tree* indicates how the customer response to a strategy influences market share.[23] Because many other factors also affect market share, the market share index derived from the customer responses is simply an indicator of the level that market share *should* reach, given certain expected levels of market performance.

Building a Market Share Performance Tree

The first step in building a market share performance tree is to identify the sequence of events that have to take place for a customer purchase to occur. In the example presented in Figure 3-16, the first share performance metric in the share tree is the percentage of target customers who are aware of the company's product. The metric is often referred to simply as *product awareness*. Currently, only 45 percent of target customers are aware of the company's product. This means that the company immediately loses 55 percent of its share

**FIGURE 3-16 MARKET SHARE PERFORMANCE TREE AND MARKET SHARE
                        PERFORMANCE METRICS**

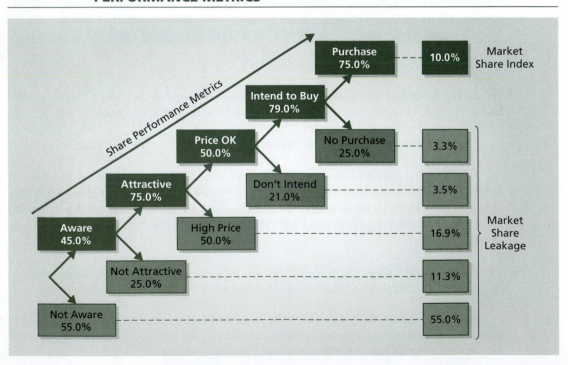

potential, which is the percentage of customers who cannot go to the next stage of assessing the product's attractiveness because they are not aware of the product.

Of the 45 percent of potential customers who are aware of the company's product, 75 percent find the features attractive and 25 percent do not find the features *attractive*. As a result, 25 percent of the 45 percent of people who were aware of the product are lost as customers, resulting in a market share leakage of 11.3 percent. The people who are attracted to the product (45% × 75% = 33.8%) next evaluate *price*. At this stage, 50 percent of the potential customers who were aware of the product and interested in it remain potential customers and 50 percent are lost, resulting in a share leakage of 16.9 percent.

As Figure 3-16 shows, most of the company's share leakage occurs at the lower end of the share tree. At the upper end, of those potential customers who find the price acceptable, 79 percent *intend to buy* the company's product. The share leakage due to this share performance metric is only 3.5 percent. Of those who intend to buy, 75 percent actually *purchase* the product. The share leakage at this stage of the share tree is only 3.3 percent. When all the positive metrics in the market share performance tree are multiplied together, the result is a market share index of 10 percent, as shown here.

$$\begin{aligned}
\text{Market Share Index} &= \text{Aware} \times \text{Attractive} \times \text{Price OK} \times \text{Intend to Buy} \times \text{Purchase} \\
&= 45\% \times 75\% \times 50\% \times 79\% \times 75\% \\
&= \mathbf{10.0\%}
\end{aligned}$$

Market Share Index

The market share tree and index that a business creates by modeling the market share performance tree in Figure 3-16 will rarely correspond exactly with the business's actual market share. Although a business's actual market share may be higher or lower, the market share index serves as a diagnostic approximation based on market share performance metrics that contribute to a certain level of market share. The index also provides three other important benefits:

- It helps identify the major causes of lost market share opportunity;
- It provides a mechanism for assessing market share change when improvement efforts are directed to an area of poor performance; and
- It enables a business to estimate a reasonable potential for its market share, given the levels of performance that the company believes it can attain for each share performance metric.

The market share index of 10 percent in our example is unlikely to equal the actual market share for a product, but it should be a good approximation. Figure 3-17 plots the market share indexes of several products against their actual market shares to show that the market share index is usually close to the actual market share, although the two can sometimes vary greatly. If the market share index is much higher than the actual market share, it is likely that share metric performance was overestimated or a key share performance metric has been overlooked. If the actual market share is much higher than the market share index, the business may have underestimated performance or included an unimportant aspect of performance that had a low level of performance. Finally, a business could gain some insights by adjusting the share performance estimates to achieve a market share index that closely equals its actual market share.

FIGURE 3-17 MARKET SHARE INDEX VERSUS ACTUAL MARKET SHARE

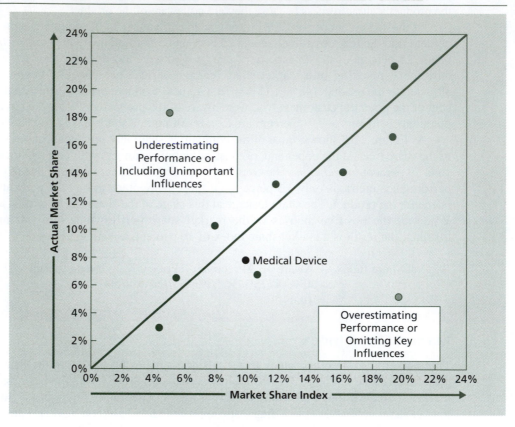

The importance of the market share index is that it gives us a basis for evaluating how the market share index would change with improved levels of market share performance. In our example, improving awareness from 45 to 60 percent would improve the market share index from 10 percent to 13.3 percent, as shown here.

$$\text{Market Share Index} = \text{Aware} \times \text{Attractive} \times \text{Price OK} \times \text{Intend to Buy} \times \text{Purchase}$$
$$= 60\% \times 75\% \times 50\% \times 79\% \times 75\%$$
$$= \mathbf{13.3\%}$$

This is a 33.3 percent improvement. If the actual market share were 8 percent, we might expect the actual market share to improve by 33.3 percent to 10.6 percent. Using the market share performance tree shown in Figure 3-16, we could evaluate a variety of market share strategies.

Market Share Potential Index

Figure 3-18 shows the market share performance gaps between *actual* customer response and *desired* customer response on the market share performance tree. For each level of the tree, the share performance gap indicates the extent of lost market share due to the lower

FIGURE 3-18 MARKET SHARE POTENTIAL INDEX AND PERFORMANCE GAPS

Share Performance Metric	Current Performance	Potential Performance	Performance Gap
Product Awareness	45%	80%	−35%
Feature Attractiveness	75%	80%	−5%
Price Acceptable	50%	60%	−10%
Intentions to Buy	79%	80%	−1%
Purchase Product	75%	80%	−5%
Market Share Index	10.0%	24.6%	−14.6%

customer response rates along the share performance path, as opposed to the desired response rates. On the basis of the share performance gaps in Figure 3-18, a business could estimate the share and revenue loss due to the lower than expected performance levels of its strategies.

Establishing a *desired level of response* at each level of the performance tree provides a basis for estimating market share potential. Using Figure 3-18, we can compute a *market share potential index* on the basis of the desired customer responses, as shown here.

$$\textbf{Share Potential Index} = \text{Aware} \times \text{Attractive} \times \text{Price OK} \times \text{Intend to Buy} \times \text{Purchase}$$
$$= 80\% \times 80\% \times 60\% \times 80\% \times 80\%$$
$$= \textbf{24.6}\%$$

A business that establishes a desired level of customer response performance at each stage of the market share performance tree and can then implement marketing strategies to reach those performance levels should achieve a market share index considerably greater than its current index. Using this process, a business can assess its actual market share relative to its market share potential, and it can determine the level of growth and profitability that it could achieve with the market share gains.

Share Development Index

Having determined its share potential index, the business is now in the position to assess its opportunity for market share development. In our example, the business's current market share is 8 percent, but it should be about 10 percent on the basis of the business's market share index. Obviously, secondary factors are keeping the actual market share at only 8 percent. We further estimated that the business's market share potential index would be 24.6 percent if the business could achieve the desired level of positive customer response at each phase of the market share performance tree in Figure 3-16. A ratio of the market share index to the market share potential index provides a share development index (SDI).

$$\textbf{Share Development Index} = \frac{\text{Market Share Index}}{\text{Share Potential Index}} = \frac{10\%}{24.6\%} \times 100 = \textbf{41}$$

The SDI of 41 means that the business is achieving only 41 percent of its potential market share performance. If the business can deliver a marketing strategy that will be effective in achieving the desired customer response rate at each phase of the market share performance tree, the market share index will equal the market share potential index, resulting in an SDI of 100.

GROWTH OPPORTUNITY PORTFOLIO

By combining the Market Development Index (MDI) with the Share Development Index (SDI), we can create a valuable planning matrix that will reveal opportunities for growth. Figure 3-19 shows a sample growth opportunity portfolio for five products. The vertical axis is the scale for the MDI, the degree to which the overall market for a product has been developed. The horizontal axis is the scale for the SDI, the level of market share development that the product has achieved. Combining the two indexes to create this matrix provides a way for a business to evaluate the growth opportunities for its products. The matrix will indicate for a particular product whether a business should concentrate on market development or share development or both, depending on the product's position in the growth opportunity portfolio.

We know that the product in our example has an SDI of 41, but we don't know the MDI for the product's market. We do know the current demand in this market is 1 million units. By researching facts and using logic and assumptions, we learn that the market potential—the level of demand if all potential customers enter the market—is about 2 million units. The ratio of current demand to maximum demand multiplied by 100 percent gives us the MDI, which is 50. The combined SDI and MDI places this business's product (product A) partially in the quadrant marked "Share Growth Opportunity" and

FIGURE 3-19 MARKET DEVELOPMENT INDEX VERSUS SHARE DEVELOPMENT INDEX

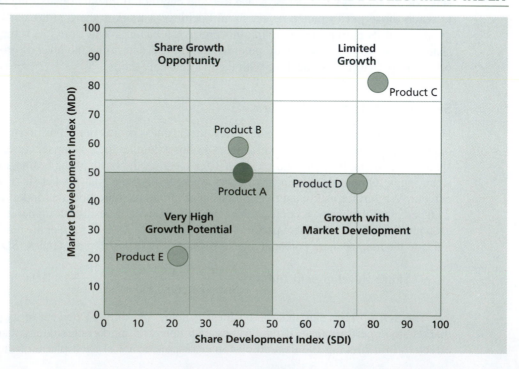

FIGURE 3-20 USING MARKET AND SHARE METRICS TO BUILD A SALES FORECAST

Sales Forecast				
Market Potential (units)	2,000,000			
Market Share Index	10.0%			
Share Potential Index	24.6%			
	Base Year	**Year 1**	**Year 2**	**Year 3**
Market Growth	5.0%	5.0%	5.0%	5.0%
Market Demand	1,000,000	1,050,000	1,102,500	1,157,625
Market Development Index	**50**	**53**	**55**	**58**
Market Share Plan	8.0%	8.5%	9.5%	10.5%
Market Share Index	10.0%	11.0%	12.0%	13.0%
Share Development Index	**41**	**45**	**49**	**53**
Volume Sold (units)	80,000	89,250	104,738	121,551
Average Net Price	$1,000	$975	$950	$925
Sales Revenues	**$80,000,000**	**$87,018,750**	**$99,501,100**	**$112,434,675**

partially in the quadrant marked "Very High Growth Opportunity." Further growth for this business could best be achieved if the business adopted a share development strategy combined with a market growth strategy.

Adding the market development index and share development index to a sales forecast provides a way to understand the potential for future sales growth. In Figure 3-20, the current-year market development index is 50 and, based on an assumed 5 percent annual rate of market growth over the next 3 years, the market development index will increase to 58 for the market potential estimated. This indicates that there is plenty of market growth beyond year 3 of the sales forecast.

The share development index for the current year is 41, with a projected increase to 53 in year 3 based on the planned change in the market share index and estimated share potential index. This also suggests plenty of growth with respect to market share beyond year 3. For this forecast, volume in expected to increase from 80,000 to 121,551 units, and prices are expected to decline from $1,000 to $925 by year 3. The net result is a forecasted increase in sales from $80 million to $112.4 million in 3 years.

■ Summary

A critical first step in formulating a marketing strategy is to determine the size of the market. A business with a narrow product focus considers only the products it sells in its current market. By adopting a broad, strategic view of its market, a business will see more possibilities for developing its market, and it will become aware of substitute products and of adjacent markets that might serve as new opportunities for growth.

A broad view of a business's defined market enables the business to determine the maximum potential of its market. The market development index (MDI) indicates the extent to which a market has reached its maximum demand. In some instances, the market may be well below its maximum demand potential. In an underdeveloped market, it is important to determine the sources of lost market demand: What are the factors that keep customers from entering the market? The strength of five customer adoption forces and five product adoption forces determine the rate of market growth.

In many instances, changes in technology can alter market potential. Some products are improved with continuous innovation; others are improved through disruptive innovations that often lower cost and improve ease of use to allow more new customers to enter the market. Discontinuous innovations, such as the flat-panel TV, iPod, and Internet search engines, create whole new market potentials for existing or new products. Market demand over time is an important aspect of market planning and strategy development. In many of today's markets, market demand is composed of both new customers and existing customers who are making replacement purchases.

Market demand can be projected over time using the rate at which new customers enter the market, the time it takes for all potential customers to enter the market, and the rate of product replacement. The rate at which a market approaches its full potential is a function of target customer characteristics, product positioning, and marketing effort. Each of these factors may be influenced by the marketing strategies developed by a business and its competitors.

Market demand typically grows slowly at first, with the product attracting only innovators and early adopters, together known as lead users. During this introductory stage of the product life cycle, before the product enters the mainstream market, marketing expenses exceed gross profit, resulting in a negative net marketing contribution. If the business uses successful strategies, the product emerges from this stage and growth in sales volume rapidly accelerates. During this stage of the product life cycle, prices and margins decline and marketing expenses increase. But the much greater volumes result in net marketing contributions that increase throughout the growth phase of the product life cycle. As growth slows, net marketing contributions peak and then begin a slow decline as the product life cycle enters its maturity stage. The market saturates, leaving little or no room for further market development.

The demand for a business's products is also based on the share of market it can extract from a given level of market demand. Market share is simply the proportion of sales a business can obtain from the total market demand at any given time, but a business needs to evaluate its share performance to avoid overlooking deficiencies in the market share performance tree. Factors that shape market share can be used to create the share tree and calculate a market share index based on the performance of these share performance metrics. The market share index helps a business understand where it is losing market share.

A share potential index can be created on the basis of estimates of superior performance for each share tree metric. Dividing the current market share index by the share potential index creates a share development index (SDI). This index varies from zero to 100. The lower the SDI, the greater the opportunity for market share growth.

Combining the MDI with the SDI to create a growth opportunity portfolio can reveal strategies for increasing sales revenues. For a given market, depending on the market's potential for development, a business can determine its best opportunities for sales growth, depending on its potential to grow share.

■ Market-Based Strategic Thinking

1 How does a product-focused market definition differ from a strategic market definition for a company like Coca-Cola?

2 How would a strategic market definition help a company like Nike?

3 Why is Facebook's market vision an important element of the market demand that Facebook creates?

4 Why is it important for Pampers to understand the market potential for disposable diapers?

5 How would you estimate the worldwide market potential for toothbrushes?

6 What is your estimate of the MDI for toothbrushes?

7 What forces restrict today's market demand for disposable diapers from reaching the maximum market demand?

8 What factors helped accelerate market growth and market demand for Apple's iPad? How could Apple influence these factors to further accelerate market growth?

9 How does an MDI help Dell forecast its sales of personal computers?

10 How do customer adoption forces accelerate or impede market penetration of electric cars like GM's Volt?

11 How do product adoption forces accelerate or impede market penetration of electric cars like the Volt?

12 How could Apple accelerate the rate of market penetration for iPads?

13 Why do iPod's sales volumes, prices, and margins vary over the product life cycle?

14 Referring to Figure 3-12, why would the NMC be negative in the introductory stage for GM's Volt car?

15 Why would the NMC for a personal computer peak during the late growth stage of the product life cycle?

16 What share performance metrics underlie the market share performance of Apple's Mac computer?

17 How would Toyota use an index of its current and potential market share to gauge the market share growth of the Prius?

18 What are the advantages of computing a market share index for a new printer?

19 Why would Netflix's actual market share differ from its market share index for a given target market?

20 How could a matrix combining the MDI and SDI be used to develop international marketing strategy for Gatorade?

Marketing Performance Tools and Application Exercises

The four interactive marketing performance tools and application exercises outlined here will strengthen your understanding of market potential, the MDI, the market share index, the SDI, the product life cycle as it relates to profit, and sales forecasting. To access the tools, go to **rogerjbest.com.** You can determine the answers to many of the questions by entering the data in the questions. You may also enter other data to see the results, and you can save your work. The figure numbers in parentheses are related examples in Chapter 3, but the lettered instructions pertain to the online exercises.

3.1 Market Potential and Market Development Index (Figure 3-3)

A. How would the market potential and market development indexes change if each person had an average of 1.25 personal computers (that is, every fourth person had two personal computers)?

B. Estimate the worldwide market potential for soft drinks, using reasonable assumptions.

3.2 Market Share Management (Figure 3-16)

A. How much would the market share index and SDI change if product attractiveness could be improved from 45 percent to 60 percent with more effective advertising?

B. How much would the market share index and SDI change if a product's purchase metric could be improved from 75 to 80 percent?

3.3 Product Life-Cycle Sales and Gross Profit (Figure 3-15)

A. How would product life-cycle profit change if the market grew at a slower rate between 2010 and 2015 such that in 2015 market demand would be 375 million units?

B. What would be the impact on product life-cycle profits if the average selling price dropped to $850 by 2015 and percent margins dropped to 13 percent?

3.4 Sales Forecasting (Figure 3-20)

A. How would sales and the MDI change if sales growth were adjusted downward to 3 percent annually?

B. What would be the sales impact if the business could hold prices at $1,000 per unit over the 3-year planning period but lost 0.5 share points each year?

Notes

1. N. Tichy and S. Sherman, *Control Your Destiny or Someone Else Will* (New York: Harper Business, 1993); and R. Ott, "The Prerequisite of Demand Creation," *Creating Demand* (Burr Ridge, IL: Business One Irwin, 1992): 3–10.

2. T. Levitt, "Marketing Myopia," *Harvard Business Review* (July–August 1960): 45–56.

3. J. Porras and J. Collins, "Successful Habits of Visionary Companies," *Built to Last* (New York: HarperCollins, 1994); and B. Nanus, *Visionary Leadership* (San Francisco: Jossey-Bass, 1992).

4. R.E. Bucklin and V. Srinivasan, "Determining Interbrand Substitutability Through Survey Measurement of Consumer Preference Structures," *Journal of Marketing Research* (February 1991): 58–71; "Car Makers Use Image Map as Tool to Position Products," *Wall Street Journal* (March 22, 1984): 33; and "Mapping the Dessert Category," *Marketing News* (May 14, 1982): 3.

5. P. Kotler and F. Trias de Bes, *Lateral Marketing* (New York: Wiley, 2003).

6. G. Hamel and C.K. Prahalad, *Competing for the Future* (Cambridge, MA: Harvard Business School Press, 1994): 103.

7. E.B. York, "Gatorade Changing Its Game Plan," *Los Angeles Times* (January 1, 2011): http://articles.latimes.com/2011/jan/01/business/la-fi-gatorade-20110101, retrieved January 2011.

8. D. Abell and J. Hanunond, *Strategic Market Planning* (Upper Saddle River, NJ: Prentice-Hall, 1979): 185–86.

9. P. Kotler, *Marketing Management*, 7th ed. (Upper Saddle River, NJ: Prentice Hall, 1991): 240–60.

10. M. Gladwell, *The Tipping Point* (New York: Little, Brown and Company, 2000).

11. J. Pfeffer and R. Sutton, "Why Managing by Facts Works," *Strategy+Business* (Spring 2006).

12. Gladwell, *op. cit.*

13. S.D. Anthony, M.W. Johnson, J.V. Sinfield, and E.J. Altman, *Innovator's Guide to Growth—Putting Disruptive Innovation to Work* (Cambridge, MA: Harvard Business School Press, 2008).

14. G. Moore, *Inside the Tornado* (New York: HarperCollins, 1985): 11–26.

15. W. Davidson, *Marketing High Technology* (New York: Free Press, 1986).

16. J. Naisbitt, *Global Paradox: The Bigger the World Economy, the More Powerful Its Smallest Players* (New York: Morrow, 1994).

17. R. Calantorte, A. di Benedetto, and S. Bhoovaragha-van, "Examining the Relationship Between the Degree of Innovation and New Product Success," *Journal of Business Research* 30 (June 1994): 143–48; and F. Sultan, J. Farley, and D. Lehmann, "A Meta-Analysis of Applications of Diffusion Models," *Journal of Marketing Research* (February 1990): 70–7.

18. F. Bass, T. Krishonan, and D. Jain, "Why the Bass Model Fits Without Decision Variables," *Marketing Science* 13 (Summer 1994): 203–23.

19. D. Hawkins, R. Best, and K. Coney, *Consumer Behavior—Implications for Marketing Strategy*, 8th ed. (New York: Irwin, 2001): 250–51.

20. "Market Share Alert: Preliminary PC Market Results, Worldwide, 2Q10," Gartner, Inc. (July 12, 2010): http://www.gartner.com/technology/home.jsp (Document ID: G00205579), retrieved January 2011.

21. "Market Share Alert," *ibid.*

22. "Worldwide PC Market," eTForecasts (not dated): etforecasts.com, retrieved January 2011.

23. D. Schaffer, "Competing Based on the Customer's Hierarchy of Needs," *National Productivity Review* (Summer 1995).

The Customer Experience and Value Creation

■ Only 8 percent of customers describe their experience as superior, yet 80 percent of companies believe the experience they provide is indeed superior.[1]

Lenox Tools uses a YouTube video to compare the customer experience of using one of its saw blades and a competitor's blade. The short video is a side-by-side comparison of the two products, which shows that the Lenox blade lasts over three times longer. This longer product life translates into considerable savings for any business or individual who uses saws regularly.

The customer savings comes in two forms: less money spent on blades, and less work time spent changing them. Both sources of savings affect the total cost of ownership of a Lenox blade and determine the customer value that the company offers when compared to competing products.

THE TOTAL CUSTOMER EXPERIENCE

Southwest Airlines is dedicated to improving the customer experience. Southwest's focus on its customers is reflected in a value proposition that communicates the savings the airline offers by not charging extra fees for checked baggage, in-flight services, and other items. The graphic shown in Figure 4-1 is based on a Southwest advertisement showing how a customer for a particular flight could save over 50 percent by flying Southwest rather than a competing airline.

FIGURE 4-1 SOUTHWEST AIRLINES—CUSTOMER EXPERIENCE AND CUSTOMER VALUE

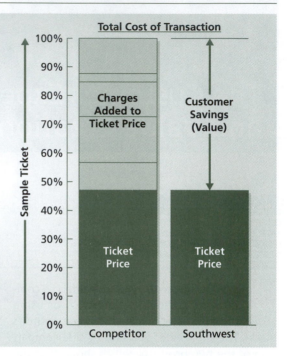

■ To attract new and retain loyal customers, we launched a new and innovative boarding system, coupled with a business select product offering an improved Customer Airport Experience. We strengthened our brand further by refusing to "nickel and dime"our Customers as our competitors have done. Our "No Hidden Fees" campaign underscores both our commitments to low fares and to customer service.

> — *Gary C. Kelly*
> *Chairman and CEO*
> *Southwest Airlines*
> *2009 Annual Report*

Southwest Airlines' print ads typically show how much a passenger can save. The main goal of the ads is to communicate the customer value the airline offers relative to competing airlines. The graph here, based on a Southwest ad for a particular trip, shows that the airline offers a 53 percent customer savings.

Understanding the total customer experience gives a business the opportunity to discover sources of customer frustration and disappointment in the experience that the business's product or service provides. This chapter explores the customer experience and the ways that a business can offer customers greater value than its competitors.

The total customer experience consists of much more than the interactions a customer has with a company. The customer experience, as shown in Figure 4-2, includes the purchase experience with respect to information, evaluation, order placement, and payment.[2] During the purchase experience, most customer touch points are proactive: a company, in its interactions with potential customers, reaches out to them and tries to

FIGURE 4-2 THE TOTAL CUSTOMER EXPERIENCE

Purchase Experiences	Usage Experiences	Replacement Experiences
Information Gathering Prioritizing Needs Evaluating Alternatives Order Placement & Payment	Delivery & Installation Product Usage Product Maintenance Product Repair	Product Upgrades Returns and Warranty Product Replacement Product Disposal

Total Customer Experience →

meet their needs. The usage experience is at a greater distance and more difficult to observe, but it is during this stage that the true value of a product becomes apparent. Yet few businesses have a good knowledge of their customers' user experience. The last stage of the customer experience is the replacement stage. As customers consider replacing or upgrading their products, a business has the opportunity for additional touch points. For some businesses, this stage includes product disposal. It's another opportunity for customer interaction, especially if disposal is difficult and becomes a barrier to repurchasing.

A customer's level of satisfaction depends on all three stages of the customer experience in Figure 4-2. These separate stages offer a framework that a business can use to identify areas of satisfaction and dissatisfaction. When a business knows its weaknesses at any stage, it can discover ways to improve its product and service benefits. An effective way to improve recognition of customer desires and needs is to become the customer.[3] Customers' statements of their preferences are important, but when they are asked, customers often do not mention the frustrations they encountered in the purchase and use of a product.

For this reason, Honda's effort to improve customer value includes observation of customers' actual experiences. To understand the difficulties that people have in loading their car trunks, for instance, Honda sent a crew to supermarket parking lots to take videos of people loading their groceries. The videos showed that most people arranged their bags to keep them from falling over. Some first leaned the bags against the rear-end wall of the compartment well, but these people then found they couldn't close their trunk doors. The videos gave Honda engineers a way to put themselves "in the customers' shoes." By seeing and feeling users' experiences, the engineers could then envision better trunk designs.

Filming customer product use is one form of the *empathic design*. It is an observational approach to understanding customer needs and discovering the problems that customers commonly encounter in acquiring, using, and disposing of a product. Intuit, the maker of the personal finance software Quicken, has a Follow-Me-Home program. Product developers obtain permission from first-time buyers to observe their initial experience with the software in their own homes. In this way, Intuit's product developers see the other software applications on the customer's system and learn whether those applications are compatible with Quicken. From their in-home observations, Intuit product developers learned that many small business owners used Quicken to keep their accounting books. That discovery led to a new product line called QuickBooks.

Empathic design gives a business the opportunity to learn more about the customer's usage experiences, depicted in the center box of Figure 4-2. But empathic design alone does not provide full insight into the total customer experience.

The Customer Experience—Actual versus Ideal

Although actual observation is a good way to understand the customer experience, it isn't possible to observe customers in many consumer, business, and industrial markets. As an alternative, a business could create two "hypothetical videos" of the customer experience.[4] Video 1 would be a scripted sequence of scenes that describe a typical customer's experiences with respect to the acquisition, installation, use, maintenance, and disposal of the product. When preparing the script for a hypothetical video, the business pays particularly close attention to the parts of each scene that, on the basis of interviews with customers, hold the greatest satisfaction, as well as to those parts that present problems and frustrations. Hypothetical Video 1 is not product specific; it is a narrative of the process a customer goes through in acquiring and using the current solution for that customer and usage situation.

In hypothetical Video 2, the script describes from the customers' perspective their ideal product with regard to its features. The company uses information from customer interviews to present the ideal product without constraints, even though the product description may include features that are not possible. The end result is a good picture of how customers would like the product to work in their usage situation.

To fully understand this approach and improving customer value, let's examine how Weyerhaeuser Corporation, a leading wood products company, applied it to the use of particleboard by furniture makers. The initial prompt for creating hypothetical Video 1 occurred when a Weyerhaeuser marketing team visited a large furniture maker to learn more about the product benefits that the furniture maker wanted in particleboard. The furniture maker was clear that it mainly wanted consistent high quality and a low price. Weyerhaeuser presented a compelling case for the high quality of its product, but the customer, who also wanted that low price, was not swayed. The Weyerhaeuser representatives could not offer a value because they could not compete on price against a competitor that had a considerable cost advantage.

This is where most businesses would have stopped in their analysis of customer needs. Weyerhaeuser, however, put together a multifunctional team to revisit the furniture maker to gain a better understanding of the processes the manufacturer employed in purchasing, inventorying, modifying, and using particleboard in making furniture. This time, Weyerhaeuser sought to understand how the furniture maker used particleboard, not just what purchase criteria the furniture maker used.

By focusing on the actual *use* of a product, rather than just on the product, Weyerhaeuser discovered two major shortcomings in the particleboard that was then available to furniture makers. One was the grit that the particleboard contained. A high level of grit, Weyerhaeuser's hypothetical video would show, requires more production downtime for sharpening saw blades, as well as more expense due to shorter blade life. Heavy grit also often resulted in an unsatisfactory surface, requiring that pieces be sanded to achieve the desired smoothness.

The second shortcoming of the particleboard was that it was too thin for many applications. The furniture maker often had to laminate pieces of particleboard to obtain the thickness needed for some furniture. Figure 4-3 summarizes the customer's current use, frustrations, and associated costs as uncovered during the customer visit to create the hypothetical Video 1.

With these insights into customer use, Weyerhaeuser responded with hypothetical Video 2, a sequence of scenes in which the furniture maker has the benefit of a less gritty, thicker particleboard. In the video's script, the lower level of grit lessens blade wear and greatly reduces

FIGURE 4-3 HYPOTHETICAL VIDEO I: CURRENT CUSTOMER EXPERIENCE

Customer Use Process	Customer Frustration	Cost to Customer
Cut the particleboard	Saw blades wear out quickly from excess grit	Production downtime and saw blade sharpening and replacement
Build furniture	Need to use thicker pieces	Lamination process to glue pieces
Produce finished product	Desired finish not achieved	Requires sanding for desired finish

FIGURE 4-4 HYPOTHETICAL VIDEO II: DESIRED CUSTOMER EXPERIENCE

Customer Process	Ideal Solution	Benefit to Customer
Cut the particleboard to size	Saw blades last longer due to less grit	Less production downtime and lower saw blade expense
Build furniture	Buy thicker pieces	Eliminate lamination process
Produce finished product	Smoother finish	Less sanding required for finish

the sanding, and the increased thickness eliminates the laminating. Although it is more costly to purchase, this new product offers a substantial overall savings for the customer. Figure 4-4 indicates how the product benefits would translate into meaningful customer value, and Figure 4-5 represents one way that Weyerhaeuser communicated this customer value.

The Customer Experience of Lead Users

Not all customers use products the same way. Some are new users who lack experience with the product, and others are occasional users with somewhat limited experience. Observing or querying these customers for sources of dissatisfaction usually results in minimal insight. Many products, however, have *lead users*—highly knowledgeable and skilled users who often extend the boundaries of a product's application to achieve a more desired customer solution.

FIGURE 4-5 COMMUNICATING PRODUCT FEATURES AND CUSTOMER BENEFITS

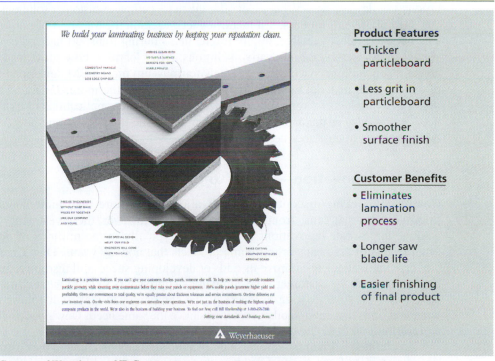

Product Features

- Thicker particleboard
- Less grit in particleboard
- Smoother surface finish

Customer Benefits

- Eliminates lamination process
- Longer saw blade life
- Easier finishing of final product

Courtesy of Weyerhaeuser NR Company.

FIGURE 4-6 LEVERAGING LEAD USER CUSTOMER EXPERIENCE

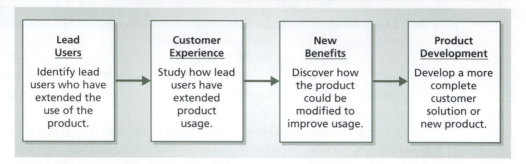

Studying the experience of lead users provides insights for improving a product by adding new features or modifying it in other ways. A good understanding of lead users' needs and desired solutions can result in major improvements in product benefits and customer value. Lead users of cellular phones, for example, devised ways to extend the capabilities of the phones beyond their intended application by using them to access the Internet—a technology that has spawned many new products and companies.

Figure 4-6 shows the four steps in developing new customer solutions with the help of a product's lead users.[5] Identifying these users is the first step. Discovering how they use the product to solve their own problems, step two, opens the door to insights on how a product may be adapted for a more complete customer solution. At step three, a business considers developing value-added features, functions, and services. Step four involves reengineering products or developing new ones that offer the more complete customer solutions.

In applying this process, 3M identified lead users in the transport of museum pieces. The need to protect valuable, highly fragile items during transport had led museum personnel to devise several innovative solutions. After learning how these lead users had adapted conventional packaging materials for museum pieces, 3M developed a new line of off-the-shelf material for packaging fragile items.[6] Furthermore, 3M found that developing new products by researching and refining lead user applications of existing products can produce as much as eight times more revenue than generating new products by other analyses of customer needs.[7]

Reverse Innovation—Invent to Order

Companies seeking discontinuous innovations need more than incremental product improvements that come from lead user analysis. However, the investment required to achieve large-scale innovations is expensive, typically in the millions of dollars, and often results in dead ends or intriguing products that nobody wants. Dow Chemical uses "reverse innovation" to improve its odds of developing successful disruptive innovations by starting with the customer. The company's approach is to learn *what customers want but cannot get from existing products.* If the company can make what these customers want and finds that enough other customers have the same need, Dow goes to the lab with a prescription it calls "invent to order."[8]

As outlined in Figure 4-7, reverse innovation starts by listening to the customer experience and identifying product benefits that are not provided by any existing products.

FIGURE 4-7 REVERSE INNOVATION—INVENT TO ORDER

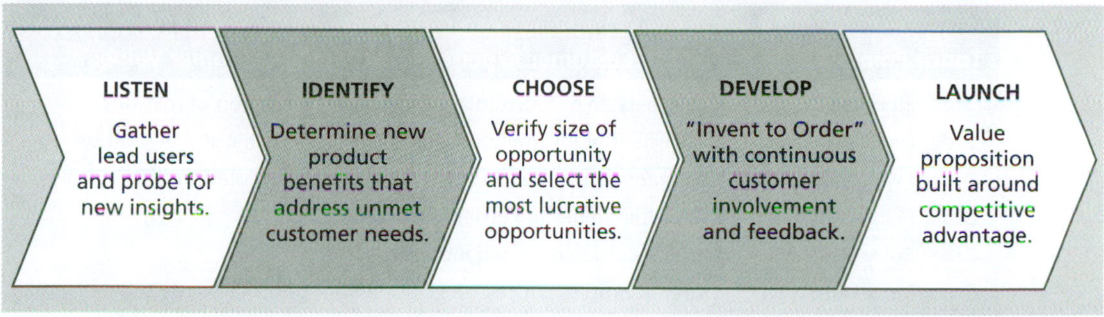

LISTEN
Gather lead users and probe for new insights.

IDENTIFY
Determine new product benefits that address unmet customer needs.

CHOOSE
Verify size of opportunity and select the most lucrative opportunities.

DEVELOP
"Invent to Order" with continuous customer involvement and feedback.

LAUNCH
Value proposition built around competitive advantage.

Each proposed product benefit needs to be carefully analyzed with respect to market and profit potential. Then an "invent to order" is specified. Throughout the development process, the company keeps customers involved. As a product evolves from concept to physical form, it typically undergoes many design changes in response to customer feedback. The first Lexus car went through 1,000 design changes, mostly based on customer input, before its design was finalized. Finally, launch and commercialization of the product must communicate and deliver a value proposition that is built around these unique customer benefits, features that are not found in competing products.

Dow pioneered reverse innovation in the 1990s when its plastics business was performing poorly. By 2004, Dow had an intense customer focus and Dow plastics had achieved four times its previous volume sold and three times its normal sales. More recently, the company used reverse innovation to address an unmet need in the apparel industry, successfully launching a product with more stretch, less shrinkage, better wrinkle resistance, and more texture than competing products.

Managing Customer Touch Points

During a customer's process of buying and using a product, a business has several opportunities to affect the customer's experience. The business can either respond proactively by anticipating possible problems and reaching out to and helping the customer at the various touch points, or it can respond reactively, letting the customer make the first contact. A business could, for instance, take a close look at its customer ordering process from the customer's viewpoint, with the objective of uncovering any potential problems or sources of frustration in the purchasing process. This day-in-the-life-of-a-customer approach might be described as "stapling yourself to an order"[9] in an effort to discover the touch points where a business can improve the customer experience.

The customer experience outlined in Figure 4-8 involves tracking the customer order process from the early stages of order planning to the resolution of complaints whenever after-purchase problems arise. Each step of the ordering cycle has the potential to cause customers problems or frustrations. The earlier problems or frustrations occur, the less likely a customer is to buy from that business. Problems or frustrations that emerge later in the process hurt the chances of repurchase, lowering the customer retention rate.

A business could begin its assessment of its ordering process by asking, "What are the worst things that could happen to a customer at each stage of the customer order cycle?"

FIGURE 4-8 CUSTOMER TOUCH POINTS

Customer Touch Points	Customer Problems and Interaction Opportunities to Improve the Customer Experience and Build Customer Value
Order Planning	Customers do not recognize the business's solution as relevant
Order Development	Insufficient or incomplete information for meaningful evaluation
Order Evaluation	Customers encounter difficulties/frustrations in placing orders
Order Placement	Difficulties in placing order
Order Entry	Order recorded or priced incorrectly
Order Processing	Order in process but customer not aware of order status and delivery
Order Delivery	Product delivered late or damaged; wrong product delivered
Customer Invoice	Bill has errors, no one to contact, and calls lead to "voicemail hell"
After-Sale Services	Problems after purchase with no one to call; calls not returned
Product Usage	Inadequate instructions; no hotline offered
Product Problems	Product does not work and must be returned at customer's expense
Returns and Claims	Customer has to fight to get warranty claim resolved

On the basis of the level of customer frustration that these actions or omissions would create, and the frequency with which they could occur, a market-based business would identify and implement preventive measures and look for other ways to add customer value by improving the purchasing process. A market-based business with a strong customer focus can use its order cycle to create important sources of customer value that the business's product-focused competitors will never see.

The efforts of Weyerhaeuser, Intuit, Honda, Dow, and 3M to create additional customer benefits went beyond product-focused thinking. Each of these companies engaged in an analysis of the customer experience and the problems customers encountered. With a better knowledge of customer usage, these businesses were able to engineer customer solutions for needs that were poorly met by the then-available products.[10] Whereas product-focused businesses are providers of products, market-based businesses are providers of solutions.[11] To be a provider of customer solutions requires a broad view of customers' underlying problems, a view that transcends products or services to include a comprehensive understanding of the total customer experience.

MASS COLLABORATION AND CROWDSOURCING

In the past, companies relied on the suggestion box to obtain ideas for improving products and processes. Today the suggestion box has been replaced by the Internet, a much more efficient and far-reaching means for businesses to tap into the knowledge and experience of consumers, professionals, suppliers, and employees. For many companies, the Internet has become a venue for collective idea generation and collaboration—resulting in a broad base of ideas and an intimate connection with the marketplace. The result has been two major developments in the area of product and process improvement known as mass collaboration[12] and crowdsourcing.[13] As Figure 4-9 shows, mass collaboration is

FIGURE 4-9 MASS COLLABORATION AND CROWDSOURCING

the use of collective intelligence in a collaborative environment, whereas crowdsourcing uses collective intelligence to solve specific problems or solicit ideas—often as part of a competition or for a reward.

Mass Collaboration

Mass collaboration can take many different forms and involve different kinds of collaborators, but the main purpose is to collaborate with a large group of people who have expertise and diverse perspectives that extend beyond the walls of the organization. The main difference between crowdsourcing and mass collaboration is the level of multidirectional interaction. Through mass collaboration, a business not only solicits the contributions of people all over the globe but collaborates with them on initiatives that add significant value.

A business could seek the collaborative input of a unique group of individuals, such as scientists in a specific field, or it could look to a broad spectrum of individuals, such as all current and prospective users of a particular product. The four groups that businesses most frequently involve in mass collaboration are prosumers, professionals or specialists, suppliers, and employees, as discussed in the next four sections.

Prosumers—Customers as Co-Inventors

Prosumers are consumer product-inventors. The customers in this unique subset of consumers take product usage beyond its intended capability. They often modify a product in a way that improves performance or serves an altogether new purpose. Businesses that engage prosumers in product development through mass collaboration frequently discover innovative ways to increase the customer value of their products.

For example, among automobile enthusiasts, BMW enjoys a reputation for reliability and high-quality design. BMW has thousands of R&D professionals, many dedicated to specific aspects of automotive design. But when it came time to rethink the company's telemetric features, such as GPS navigation, BMW released a digital design kit on its web site and asked for proposals from customers. Thousands responded with features they envisioned, and BMW's engineers used many of the proposals in developing value-added benefits. Figure 4-9 shows how the mass collaboration process leads to possible solutions.

Apple also used mass collaboration for improving the iPod, and LEGO involved its target customers—children—in the design of LEGO Robots. As might be expected,

LEGO's collaborative web site also attracted many engineers who offered some good ideas, too. However, it is important to recognize that prosumers are advanced users who do not always represent the needs of an overall target market.

Partnerships—Engaging Professionals

What small business wouldn't want to partner with BMW? But how likely is it that such a partnership would actually come about, especially if the small business is in a remote part of the world, far removed from any of BMW's operations? The odds of such a partnership are exceedingly small. Or at least they used to be. BMW now hosts a virtual design agency on its web site that gives small and medium-size businesses an opportunity to submit ideas that could lead to ongoing relationships with BMW.

Consider a Canadian gold mine that had seemingly depleted the gold from one of its properties over a 50-year period. Like any large mining company, this company employed its own geologists, and for years they had explored the possibility of extracting the "unavailable" gold from the property. Then, using a Wiki site, the company presented its problem to geologists around the world. This worldwide audience of professionals reviewed the property's geology, the company's activities to date, and the recommendations and comments of one another. From this group of geologists came new ideas that resulted in an extraction that equaled the entire output of the mine during the previous 50 years.

Eli Lilly and IBM are other examples of companies that use mass collaboration. Eli Lilly's Wiki site allows scientists around the world to participate in developing cures and preventive treatment for diseases. IBM estimates that its collaboration with open-source communities saves the company almost $1 billion annually over the cost of maintaining an in-house operation that would produce the same results.

Businesses must dedicate resources to filtering and aggregating partner contributions. The reward is that mass collaborations with outside professionals and specialists lead to product enhancements in less time and at a lower cost than the conventional closed approach.

Suppliers—Leveraging Supplier Participation

In the world of mass collaboration, suppliers must also have the opportunity to share their ideas on product and process improvement. Using the traditional approach, a company would develop the design specifications for a product and the suppliers would use those specifications in preparing their bids—a process that greatly limited the use of suppliers' creativity. With mass collaboration, suppliers become part of the design process.

Boeing's sleek, fuel-efficient 787, for example, is the result of a collaborative effort among some 100 suppliers in six countries. Boeing structured this truly collaborative design effort as a horizontal network of partners who worked together to produce a product with an exceptionally high level of performance. By targeting suppliers as its collaborators, Boeing gained access to the best ideas and capabilities in the worldwide aircraft industry.

Channel intermediaries are another group that businesses frequently involve. An intermediary that sees customers daily develops a good knowledge of their likes and dislikes, as well as a keen awareness of their needs. For businesses with indirect sales channels, the collaboration of intermediaries can rapidly lead to products with greater customer value.

Employees—An Under-Leveraged Opportunity

A business's frontline employees are perhaps in the best position to see possibilities for improvements to products and processes. These employees, however, can rarely break through the firewall surrounding the high-level employees who evaluate ideas and take steps to adopt new product benefits and processes. By encouraging employee participation through mass collaboration, a business overcomes the invisible barrier between the front line and the front office.

At a large company, the employees are also often consumers of the company's products. Many Procter & Gamble employees, for instance, undoubtedly use the company's products in their daily lives. Why wouldn't management want to hear from them about how the products might be improved?

Perhaps a maintenance supervisor has found a way to extend the life of an expensive piece of equipment on the product floor. If the supervisor has an effective way to share that information with other maintenance managers, the business would realize a tremendous cost savings. Mass collaboration of this type provides yet another source of value creation for businesses and customers.

Crowdsourcing

The Internet has provided a platform for companies to leverage the collective intelligence of their customer bases and experts. Participants are motivated by a reward system and often take pride in being a part of the community. Crowdsourcing initiatives—unlike open-source projects—typically have a specific purpose or problem to solve. In this respect, the process is far more focused and typically yields results more quickly.

The Netflix Prize is one of the best-known and successful examples of crowdsourcing to date. Netflix offered a $1 million reward for every 10 percent improvement in the company's movie recommendation algorithm.[14] Having reached a limit with its internal capabilities, Netflix sought to harness the power of collective intelligence to significantly and quickly improve its product offering. The 3-year contest garnered interest and participation from around the world. By the conclusion of the Netflix Prize, there were 51,051 contestants on 41,305 teams from 186 countries. In total, Netflix received 44,014 valid submissions.[15] At the conclusion of the contest, two teams that finished within 20 minutes of each other had developed a number of elements that Netflix soon integrated into its recommendation algorithm. Netflix CEO Reed Hastings told the *New York Times* of the process, "You look at the cumulative hours and you're getting Ph.D.'s for a dollar an hour. . . . We strongly believe this has been a big winner for Netflix."[16]

A number of companies have taken the idea of leveraging collective intelligence one step further and have built their business models around crowdsourcing. Quirky.com, Threadless.com, and Local Motors are all examples of companies that harness the power of the crowd to solicit market-generated product ideas and improvements.

Quirky.com is a unique product design firm that leverages collective intelligence to bring user-generated product ideas to market. Users are invited to submit ideas, vote for their favorites, and engage in the improvement process. Community members earn "influencer" points based on their contributions to the refinement of the product. These people are then rewarded with a royalty stream based on the significance of their improvements. According to Quirky.com, "The world influences our business in real-time, and we share our revenue directly with the people who helped us make successful decisions."[17] Users are motivated by the potential monetary rewards, but they are also driven by the sense of contribution and community involvement. Beyond user motivation, the products are developed by a community of eager buyers who are ultimately consumer evangelists. The company has also significantly reduced its manufacturing risks by implementing a pre-order trigger point that must be met before the design is sent to the factory.[18]

Threadless.com employs a similar community-based model but limits its product offering to user-generated T-shirt designs. Users submit designs to a weekly contest and vote for their favorites. On the basis of the community feedback, the winning designs are selected and produced. The winning designers receive a monetary reward, a royalty stream, and bragging rights. In this way, the company harnesses the collective intelligence of a community of over 500,000 people to design and select T-shirts.[19]

"The auto industry was extremely out of whack with what customers were looking for . . . I wanted to see car companies adapt more quickly," said Jay Rogers, co-founder of Local Motors.[20] The company was founded around an old idea—car kits. But this old idea was transformed by innovation when the company offered a community of enthusiasts and potential customers a chance to be involved in the design and engineering process. Local Motors also sponsors contests to further refine components of its Rally Fighter. In addition, the company provides a web destination for users to connect with one another and share their stories and photos of their modifications.

Procter & Gamble is one of the many companies using mass collaboration and crowdsourcing to develop improved products. An example aired on National Public Radio illustrates the process. P&G's own scientists are working on research and development, but in order to quickly find a molecule that would remove red wine and similar stains from fabric, the company decided to crowdsource the problem, offering a cash award to the first scientist anywhere in the world who could produce an effective and safe molecule. The reasoning behind the decision makes sense: Would the discovery of the new molecule more likely come from the relatively few scientists working for P&G or from the hundreds of thousands of scientists worldwide? By crowdsourcing ideas, P&G gained access to expertise and creativity far beyond its own domain and was likely to find a solution quickly and with a smaller investment.

LIFE-CYCLE COST AND CUSTOMER VALUE

Customers are willing to pay more for products and services that have an economic value, or, more plainly, for products and services that save them money. To determine a product's economic value, we first need to determine its *life-cycle cost*, which is the sum of the purchase price and the costs of acquiring, using, owning, maintaining, and disposing of the product.

$$\text{Life-Cycle Cost} = \frac{\text{Price}}{\text{Paid}} + \frac{\text{Acquisition}}{\text{Costs}} + \frac{\text{Usage}}{\text{Costs}} + \frac{\text{Ownership}}{\text{Costs}} + \frac{\text{Maintenance}}{\text{Costs}} + \frac{\text{Disposal}}{\text{Costs}}$$

To arrive at a product's economic value, a company then compares its product's life-cycle cost with that of the main competing product. The difference in the two products' life-cycle costs is the economic value of the company's product. Because customer value is essentially a product's total benefits minus the cost of acquiring those benefits, a product with economic value, despite its higher price, typically has more customer value than a competitor's similar product. Delivering *economic value* requires that the customer achieve a *net economic gain* over the product's life cycle.

$$\text{Economic Value} = \text{Competing Product's Life-Cycle Cost} - \text{Our Product's Life-Cycle Cost}$$

FIGURE 4-10 LIFE-CYCLE COST AND ECONOMIC VALUE

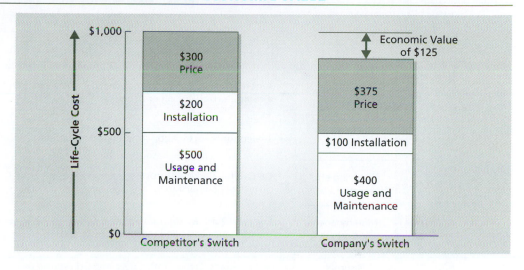

We saw how Weyerhaeuser developed a product with economic value for furniture makers. Weyerhaeuser's conventional product, even though it was of high quality, could not compete on cost among furniture makers, but the new product—in essence a specialty product—can now do so. Even though Weyerhaeuser's new product costs more than competitors' products, its economic value is greater. The money that furniture makers save by using the Weyerhaeuser product, instead of a competitor's less expensive product, more than offsets the higher purchase price. Weyerhaeuser gained a competitive edge by first looking for an unmet customer solution, then providing the solution.

In Figure 4-10, the total life-cycle cost of a competing telecommunications switch is $1,000. This cost is derived from a $300 price per unit, a $200 installation cost, and a $500 usage and maintenance cost. The company's switch, despite its higher price, offers an economic value of $125 because the other costs contributing to its life-cycle cost are lower.[21]

Economic Value = $1,000 Life-Cycle Cost (Competitor) − $875 Life-Cycle Cost (Company)
= **$125**

In this case, both the customer and the company win. The customer saves $125 per switch, and the company receives a price that is $75 higher than that of a competing product. Both the customer and the company will be more profitable as a result.[22]

Figure 4-11 outlines the six major cost categories that contribute to the life-cycle cost. The purchase price for a product or service stands out as the most obvious cost, and it is the one that businesses most commonly use in communicating economic value to customers. Customers have no difficulty understanding that a product of the same quality as a competitor's product but with a lower price offers more economic value. But other sources of value can, from a customer's perspective, be even more important. Customers may immediately recognize that they can save more money by choosing a product with a benefit that eliminates a time-consuming step than by choosing a lower priced

FIGURE 4-11 SOURCES OF ECONOMIC BENEFIT AND VALUE CREATION

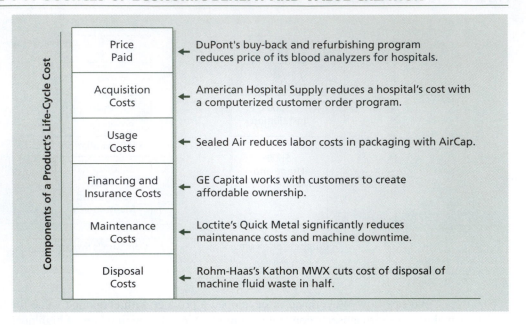

product. By spending a day in the life of a customer, marketers can discover the value-creation opportunities that may be present in any of the six major cost categories of the life-cycle cost.

Price Paid

Quite often, the price or payment terms destroy customer value. A product may offer an excellent customer solution, but its price may be too high relative to the benefits provided. For example, DuPont found that large hospitals could justify the higher price of its more expensive blood analyzers in light of the overall benefits they offered. Small hospitals, however, had lower volumes of blood chemistry work—not enough to justify purchasing the more sophisticated and more costly blood analyzers. DuPont ran into another problem when it rolled out a still more advanced blood analyzer. The company met resistance from the large hospitals, which said they could not justify the expense because their present blood analyzers were adequate and still fairly new. This situation led to a strategy in which DuPont offered to buy back the large hospitals' current blood analyzers when the hospitals purchased new analyzers. DuPont then refurbished the analyzers it bought back and resold them to small hospitals. In this way, the company created a combination of benefits that was affordable for both large and small hospitals.

Acquisition Costs

American Hospital Supply found that half of every dollar spent by hospitals on pharmaceuticals, chemicals, and equipment went to the purchasing process and inventory of these products. Acquisition costs, as shown in Figure 4-11, are a part of the total life-cycle cost. By placing computers in hospitals to streamline order entry, logistics, and inventory procedures, the company created economic value for its products by making them less expensive for hospitals to order, track, and inventory. As a result, American Hospital Supply won a large share of the market for its products.

Usage Costs

A product that will eliminate or significantly reduce the usage costs that customers presently incur offers a substantial economic value. For many businesses, this is the source of their products' economic value. By reducing the manufacturing costs for furniture makers and thereby giving its product economic value, Weyerhaeuser was able to deliver superior customer value with its new particleboard, even at a higher price. The same is true for the telecommunications switch in Figure 4-10. The competitor's switch had a total life-cycle cost of $1,000. The purchase price was only $300, but installation and start-up costs amounted to an additional $200, and usage and other after-sale costs came to $500. The new switch offered customers a solution that would cut start-up costs in half and reduce the usage cost by $100. This solution would create an economic value of $200 at the same $300 price as the competitor's switch. However, the product had to be priced in a way that offered customer value while improving profit. In response, the company set a price of $375, compared with the $300 price for the existing customer solution. The price was $75 higher, but it created a customer solution that reduced the life-cycle cost by $125 per switch.

Figures 4-12 and 4-13 present another example of creating economic value by reducing usage costs. The lower freight and labor costs made possible by a particular packaging material more than offsets its higher price. Sealed Air's AirCap packaging material costs

FIGURE 4-12 ECONOMIC VALUE ANALYSIS

Life-Cycle Cost Components	Specific Cost	Company AirCap	Competitor Cardboard	Cost Difference
Price Paid	Direct Purchase	$1.05	$0.80	$0.25
Discounts/Rebates (negative number)				
Delivery	Shipping Cost	$2.40	$2.60	−$0.20
Installation				
Shipping Materials	Shipping Carton	$0.55	$0.55	$0.00
Inventory (Holding Cost)				
Financing Cost (Loan Interest)				
Owning Cost (Insurance)				
Usage Cost (Cost of Use)	Labor per Shipment	$0.13	$0.83	−$0.70
Maintenance Cost				
Replacement Cost				
Disposal Cost				
Resale Value (negative number)				
Life-Cycle Cost		$4.13	$4.78	−$0.65
Life-Cycle Period for Product: 1 Shipment				

FIGURE 4-13 COMMUNICATING ECONOMIC VALUE

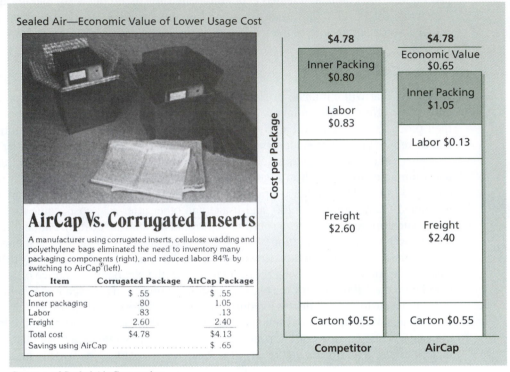

Sealed Air—Economic Value of Lower Usage Cost

AirCap Vs. Corrugated Inserts

A manufacturer using corrugated inserts, cellulose wadding and polyethylene bags eliminated the need to inventory many packaging components (right), and reduced labor 84% by switching to AirCap®(left).

Item	Corrugated Package	AirCap Package
Carton	$ .55	$ .55
Inner packaging	.80	1.05
Labor	.83	.13
Freight	2.60	2.40
Total cost	$4.78	$4.13
Savings using AirCap	. . . .	$ .65

Courtesy of Sealed Air Corporation.

the manufacturer 25 cents more per carton to buy than a competing product, but AirCap produces an economic value of 65 cents with each carton the manufacturer ships to a customer. This means that, compared with the lower priced competitor's product, the AirCap material saves the manufacturer 65 cents per shipment.

One more example of a company that reduces usage costs for its customers is Kyocera. To communicate the savings, Kyocera created its TCO Tracker web site where potential customers can compare the total cost of buying and using a Kyocera printer with that of any competing printer.[23] As explained in Figure 4-14, site users input their printing needs, and the site shows the TCO (total cost of ownership) for the best-suited Kyocera printer and any competing printer for a 3-year product life. As Figure 4-14 shows, the Kyocera printer in the example offers a customer savings of $808 over the competing model. Potential customers immediately see that they would save not only on the purchase price but also on the cost of color and black inks over the 3 years.

Financing and Insurance Costs

Products with high ownership costs are typically expensive items that buyers finance and insure. The interest and premiums paid over time account for the high ownership costs. Many years ago, General Electric (GE) developed GE Capital to create affordable ownership with financing. GE Capital became highly successful and today is a large business that serves both GE and non-GE customers. A business that can make owning its product

FIGURE 4-14 TOTAL COST OF OWNERSHIP AND ECONOMIC VALUE

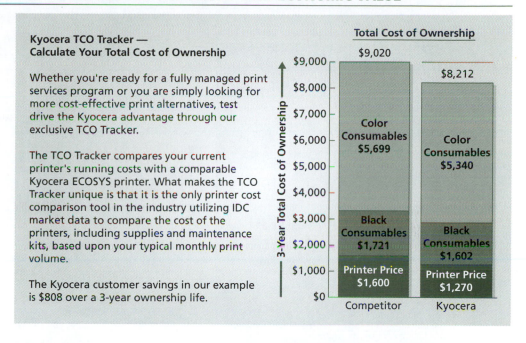

less expensive than owning a competitor's similar product gives its product economic value. The initial purchase price of the product might be more, but the total life-cycle cost to the customer is less because ownership costs are lower.

Maintenance Costs

Maintenance and repair is another area where economic value can be added to a product. Products with good performance records or those with all-inclusive warranties may cost more to buy but will have a lower total cost of ownership. To guarantee lower maintenance costs, many products come with a manufacturer's warranty and maintenance contract. Electronic document processing equipment, for example, can be expensive to repair. In response to this risk, Xerox created a customer satisfaction program that guarantees product performance for an extended period.

In addition, any product that can reduce a customer's maintenance and repair costs has economic value for the customer. Loctite's Quick Metal, one of the examples in Figure 4-11, can be applied to worn or cracked machine parts to avoid an extended shutdown. Quick Metal's value proposition, *"Keep the machinery running until the new part arrives,"* tells customers how Quick Metal can create a major savings (economic value) for them.

Disposal Costs

Another source of potential economic value lies in the disposal costs of a product. By reducing or eliminating a customer's disposal cost, a business creates economic value in the product. FP International (FPI), a manufacturer of styrene packaging materials, picks

FIGURE 4-15 LOWER DISPOSAL COSTS AS A SOURCE OF ECONOMIC VALUE

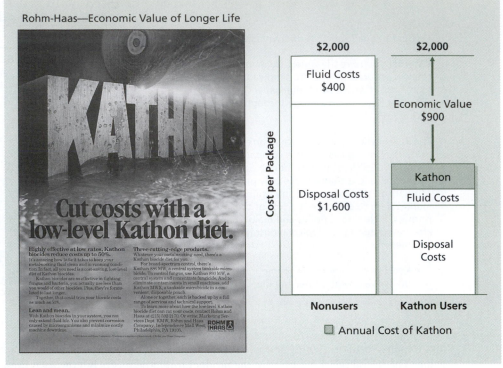

Courtesy of Rohm and Haas Company.

up waste styrene packaging from its customers and then sells the recycled packaging back to its customers at a premium price. Because FPI lowers the total cost of the product by solving its customers' problem of disposing of the waste packaging, the company can charge a higher price and still offer an attractive customer value.

Figure 4-15 describes another example. Kathon is a product that creates economic value for machine shop owners by extending the life of metalworking machine fluids. The longer life of the fluids reduces the annual cost of machine fluid disposal.

PRICE-PERFORMANCE AND VALUE CREATION

Although economic value provides a powerful basis for creating a cost-based customer value, some aspects of product performance are more difficult to quantify in assessing product performance. Performance can also include product features and functions that do not save money but enhance usage and, in that way, create customer value. A car can have cost-based value for its owner if it has good fuel economy, low maintenance requirements, and high resale value. A car can also offer customer value with comfort and safety features. Although these latter forms of customer value are difficult to quantify with respect to the total cost of owning a car, they can be evaluated with respect to performance. *Consumer Reports,* which rates the performance of many products and their features, can help buyers evaluate the price-performance of competing products.

FIGURE 4-16 PERFORMANCE VERSUS PRICE AND CUSTOMER VALUE

Competing Digital Cameras	No.	Performance Rating	Product Price	Fair Price	Customer Value
Canon A590	1	80	$180	$224	$44
Canon SD790	2	90	$300	$246	–$54
Canon SD870	3	80	$280	$224	–$56
Casio EX-29	4	70	$150	$202	$52
Casio EX-280	5	50	$180	$157	–$23
Fuji J10	6	70	$130	$202	$72
Kodak M1033	7	80	$200	$224	$24
Kodak V1073	8	60	$230	$179	–$51
Nikon P60	9	70	$230	$202	–$28
Pentax M50	10	70	$180	$202	$22
Average		**72**	**$206**	**$206**	**$0**

Figure 4-16 shows 10 digital cameras that cover a span of *Consumer Reports* performance ratings from 50 to 90, with an average rating of 72.[24] Prices for these 10 models range from $130 to $300, with an average price of $206. The first question is, what is the relationship between price and performance? Figure 4-17 plots the 10 cameras on the basis of their respective performance ratings and prices. The higher performing cameras

FIGURE 4-17 CUSTOMER VALUE AND VALUE MAP

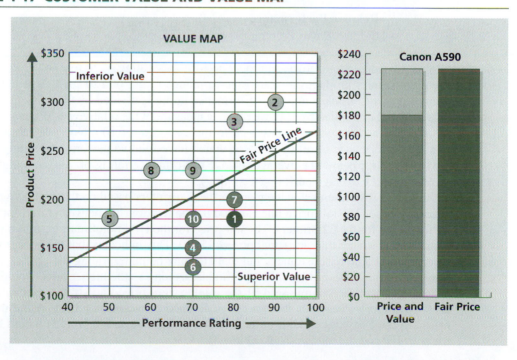

generally have higher prices, but this relationship is far from perfect. Cameras 1, 3, and 7 have the same performance rating of 80, but their prices range from $180 to $280. So, which one of the 10 cameras would be the best value?

To answer this question we need to dig deeper into the price-performance relationship. The fair price line in Figure 4-17 is an estimate of the price-performance relationship based on the data provided. For the Canon A590 (number 1), the fair price based on these price-performance data is $224. The selling price is $180. Relative to the other nine cameras in the value map, the Canon A590 has a customer value of $44, the difference between the fair price and the camera's actual price. Using a different set of comparison cameras would likely result in a different fair price line and a different customer value for the Canon A590. Of the cameras shown, the Fuji J10 (number 6) at $130 offers the best value ($72). If a customer wanted higher performance but still a relatively low price, the Canon A590 would be a great alternative with respect to customer value.

Relative Performance

In many instances, relative performance is a preferred metric over a performance rating. This metric is easily created by dividing the performance rating of a product by the average performance rating of all products in the market. The performance ratings for 62 printers according to *Consumer Reports* produces an average rating of 61 and an average price of $148.[25] This measurement of a product's relative performance helps us more readily assess performance around a benchmark average of 100, as in the following formula.

$$\text{Relative Performance} = \frac{\text{Product Performance Rating}}{\text{Average Performance Rating}} \times 100$$

$$\begin{array}{c}\textbf{Relative Performance}\\ \text{HP PhotoSmart Premium}\end{array} = \frac{73}{61} \times 100 = \textbf{120}$$

As the calculation shows, a product performance rating of 73 for the HP PhotoSmart Premium printer produces a relative performance rating of 120 for this printer. When each printer's *Consumer Reports* performance rating is divided by the average of all ratings (61) and multiplied by 100, we obtain a measure of the relative performance for each product against an average relative performance rating of 100. Now we can assess the relative performance of all 62 printers, which have relative performance ratings from a low of 70 (30% below the average relative performance rating of 100) to a high of 120 (20% above the average performance rating).

Figure 4-18 presents a value map for the 62 printers based on their relative performance and price. The fair price line is based on the relationship between price and relative performance for the 62 printers. The fair price for the HP PhotoSmart Premium printer is considerably higher than its actual price of $140. This indicates that the printer provides a very good value for customers, but that HP may be underpricing the printer. A higher price could make the product more profitable, as long as the higher price would not significantly affect the volume sold. If the printer were priced at $149, it would still be a great customer value, with about a $50 difference between the fair price and the actual price. At the $149 price, the profitability of this above-average product would be better for both HP and the retailers that sell it.

FIGURE 4-18 PRICE AND RELATIVE PERFORMANCE VALUE MAP

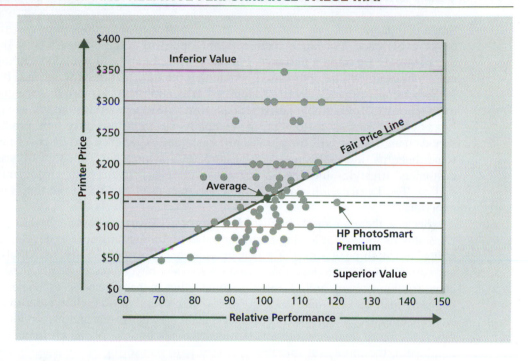

Perceived Customer Value

In many instances, customers consider more than product performance when they assess the overall value of a product. The service provided and brand reputation can also be important considerations for many buyers. The decision to buy a particular car is very often made on the basis of the car's product performance, service quality, and brand reputation. As a result, our measure of relative performance may be expanded to include these other aspects of value.

Other factors might also be important customer considerations, such as the cost of ownership and resale value. Our relative price metric can be expanded to a relative-cost-of-purchase metric, which includes nonprice ownership costs that are important in assessing a product's customer value. As a result, our value equation can be redefined as shown here.

$$\textbf{Perceived Customer Value} = \text{Relative Performance} - \text{Relative Cost of Purchase}$$
$$= 125 - 90$$
$$= \textbf{35}$$

The relative performance of 125 is based on a weighted average of product performance, service quality, and brand reputation. A relative performance of 125 means that the product is 25 percent better than the average relative performance rating (100). The relative cost of purchase is based on the product's price plus operating costs relative to all products. A relative cost of purchase of 90 means that this product's cost of purchase is 10 percent lower than the average relative cost of purchase (100) for all products in the market. The difference of 35 is a value index that is the perceived measure of customer value.

PERCEIVED PERFORMANCE AND VALUE CREATION

Some companies believe that adding more features to a product improves the customer experience. For some customers, the opposite may be true.[26] They find that extra features are often a nuisance. For this reason, Lexus will not add a feature to its automobiles unless the company is certain that the new feature will enhance the driving experience. Figure 4-19 illustrates the Lexus approach to improving the customer experience by looking beyond its product to its customers. With the knowledge that Lexus gains from its customers, the company can then introduce new product and service benefits that will truly add to the customer experience. To discover new customer benefits, the Lexus marketing team knows it must have good awareness of its customers' lifestyles and demographics, as well as the features that customers like or dislike. The Lexus team wants to know as much as it can about the total customer experience.

Because there are rarely published ratings of performance beyond product performance, this method of assessing customer value requires a business to develop its own ratings based on perceptions of product performance, service quality, brand reputation, and various costs of purchase that customers consider beyond price. Ideally, these ratings come from customers and potential customers, but managers and salespeople within a company may also estimate the ratings. It is often useful to do both in order to see how well the employees in the company understand customer needs and perceptions. Obviously, the more deviation there is between the perceptions of the customers and the employees, the more valuable this approach is to measuring and managing customer value. In this section, we will examine the ways that we can use customer perceptions of a broad range of performance and cost to infer customer value in a business's products or services.

FIGURE 4-19 LEXUS CUSTOMER EXPERIENCE AND CUSTOMER VALUE

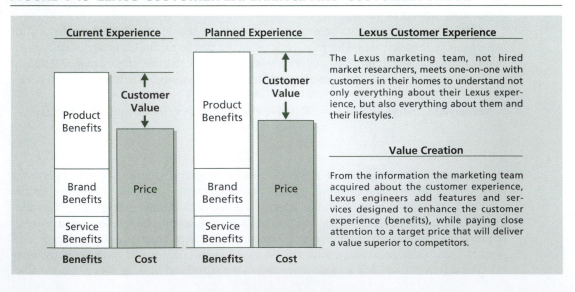

FIGURE 4-20 PRODUCT PERFORMANCE INDEX

Product Performance Attributes	Relative Importance	Business Rating	Competitor A	B	C	Relative Advantage
Machine Uptime	40	8	7	5	6	27
Print Speed	30	9	8	5	5	20
Image Quality	20	7	7	7	6	0
Ease of Use	10	4	6	7	6	−10
	100					37

Relative Product Performance Index: 100 + 37 = 137

Perceived Product Performance

Value creation is logically affected by perceptions of product performance. These perceived product performance attributes cannot be plotted as obvious, tangible, and objectively rated economic and performance benefits; yet it is customer perceptions that drive purchase behavior. We therefore need a method for measuring customer perceptions of product benefits, and we need a way to determine the relative value derived from customer perceptions in comparison with a competitive benchmark.[27]

Figure 4-20 shows four aspects of product performance that customers seek in commercial copiers. Each benefit is weighted with respect to its relative importance. For example, "machine uptime" is twice as important as "image quality" and four times as important as "ease of use." To determine the degree to which a relative advantage is created by delivering these product benefits, a business evaluates the performance of its product relative to competing products. In this case, three competitors are used to benchmark each area of perceived product performance, thereby enabling the business to determine the product's overall relative advantage.

The product performance ratings shown for the business and the three competitors are based on a scale that ranges from zero points (disastrous) to 10 points (outstanding). If a business's product performance outperforms a competitor by more than one point, it receives all of the relative importance points allocated to that area of product performance. As an example, for "machine uptime" a business might be rated only one point above competitor A but more than one point above the other two competitors. With only one point of difference, the business has no perceived advantage over competitor A, so it receives zero relative importance points with respect to that competitor. But because the business is perceived as better than competitors B and C by more than one point in both cases, it receives from each of the two competitors the 40 relative importance points allocated for "machine uptime." When the three perceived performance impacts are averaged, we obtain an overall relative advantage score of 27 for machine uptime. For "print speed," the business also outperformed two of the competitors by more than one point. The business therefore received two-thirds of the relative importance points allocated for "print speed." For "image quality," the business had no perceived relative advantage, and with respect to "ease of use" the business was rated more than one point below each of the three competitors. The 10 relative importance points allocated for "ease of use" were therefore awarded to each of the three competitors—a total of −30 points from the business's

FIGURE 4-21 SERVICE QUALITY INDEX

Service Quality Performance Attributes	Relative Importance	Business Rating	Competitor A	B	C	Relative Advantage
Repair Time	60	5	7	6	5	−20
Response Time to Problems	30	5	5	6	2	10
Quality of Service	10	7	7	6	8	0
	100					−10

Relative Service Quality Index: 100 − 10 = 90

perspective—which made the business's relative advantage score for this product benefit −10 (−30 divided by 3).

$$\text{Relative Advantage Machine Uptime} = \frac{0 + 40 + 40}{3} = 27$$

When the relative advantage scores for all four product benefits are totaled, the result is the business's overall relative advantage, which in this case is 37. The score of 37 means that, on the basis of perceived ratings of product benefits relative to the competition, the business produces 37 percent greater benefits. When this overall relative advantage is added to a base index of 100, the result is a relative product performance index of 137.

Perceived Service Quality

For many markets or segments, product differentiation is minimal because competitors are able to emulate the best features of each other's products. Whenever product features are basically identical from competitor to competitor, service quality becomes a crucial source of differentiation and competitive advantage.[28] To measure a business's perceived service quality we can use the same approach we used for perceived product performance.

Figure 4-21 provides a measure of perceived service quality for the same business that was evaluated in Figure 4-20. With respect to repair time, the business is about equal to two of its benchmark competitors and slightly below one of them. But this position detracts from the business's overall perceived service quality because 60 percent of all relative importance points are allocated to repair time. For response time to problems, the business roughly matches competitors A and B, and it outperforms competitor C. The net result is a slight advantage. Because the average competitor performance with respect to response time is already somewhat weaker than the business's performance, the business has an excellent opportunity to move ahead in this aspect of service quality. The business's current relative advantage score for response time to problems is figured as follows:

$$\text{Response Time to Problems} = \frac{0 + 0 + 30}{3} = 10$$

With respect to quality of service, the business failed to capture any relative advantage. Overall, the business produced a service quality index of 90, which means that the

FIGURE 4-22 COMPANY OR BRAND REPUTATION INDEX

Company or Brand Reputation Attributes	Relative Importance	Business Rating	Competitor A	B	C	Relative Advantage
Customer Commitment	60	8	7	6	4	40
Reputation for Quality	40	9	8	9	8	0
	100					40

Relative Company of Brand Reputation Index: 100 + 40 = 140

business is 10 percent less attractive than its competitors in delivering service quality to customers.

Perceived Company or Brand Reputation

A third source of perceived performance is the reputation of the company or brand name with the public. Whether the company is Nordstrom or Hewlett-Packard, and whether the brand is Lexus or Perrier, the name itself can be a benefit for many customers. The Nordstrom name is practically a byword for customer service, an added benefit that goes beyond actual customer service, and many HP customers value that company's reputation for innovation, a benefit that is neither product nor service specific. The names Lexus and Perrier convey an element of status that many customers find appealing.

To measure a business's perceived company reputation from its company or brand reputation, we follow the same method that was used for measuring perceived product performance and service quality. The company's brand reputation in Figure 4-22 was driven by two factors: customer commitment and the reputation for quality. In this case, the business leads two of its three benchmark competitors in customer commitment but has no relative advantage in reputation for quality. The net result of these customer perceptions is an overall index of 140 for relative company reputation.

Overall Performance Index

To arrive at an overall measure of perceived relative performance, we need a way to combine the three sources of customer-perceived performance. Combining perceived product performance, perceived service quality, and perceived company or brand reputation requires weighing the relative importance of each group. In Figure 4-23, the most weight

FIGURE 4-23 OVERALL PERFORMANCE INDEX

Core Area of Performance	Relative Importance	Relative Advantage	Overall Performance
Product Performance	0.60	137	82
Service Quality	0.30	90	27
Company or Brand Reputation	0.10	140	14
	1.00		123

Overall Performance Index = 123

FIGURE 4-24 COST OF PURCHASE INDEX

Customer Cost of Purchase Component	Relative Importance	Business Rating	Competitors' Ratings			Relative Advantage
			A	B	C	
Purchase Price	40	7	8	5	5	27
Service and Repair	30	5	6	7	6	−10
Toner	20	5	8	7	5	−14
Paper	10	6	6	5	5	0
	100					3

Relative Cost of Purchase Index = 100 + 3 = 103

is given to product performance (0.60), less weight to service quality (0.30), and the least weight to company reputation (0.10). When these relative importance ratings are weighted by the respective relative areas of performance indexes, we obtain an overall index of perceived performance. In this case, the overall perceived performance score of 123 means that the business is 23 percent ahead of its competition in delivering the three areas of perceived customer performance.

But has the business created a superior customer value? We still don't know. The level of perceived customer value cannot be determined until we determine the perceived cost of acquiring these levels of performance.

Cost of Purchase Index

In order to determine the overall level of value that is created for customers, we must first determine the perceived relative cost of purchase, a process similar to computing perceived relative benefits. We begin by identifying the components of the purchase cost that a typical customer would consider in a decision to buy, and then we assign each component relative importance points on a percentage basis.

Figure 4-24 lists four sources of cost that copier customers would likely consider. The purchase price logically has the most relative importance, and 40 points are allocated to it. Three other costs—for service and repairs, toner, and paper—are also component costs of the perceived total cost of purchase. As we figure the cost of purchase index, we must keep in mind that the *higher* the rating for each cost component, the *higher* the cost with respect to that component. The rating scale, then, is the opposite of the scale that is used for determining the indexes for product, service, and company or brand benefits. Accordingly, the *higher* the business's relative advantage score for each cost component, the *weaker* its competitive position.

In this example, the business's purchase price is rated at 7, about equal to competitor A's rating of 8. Because the difference in the two ratings is not more than one point, the business does not lose the 40 relative importance points. But because the business is rated more than one point higher than both competitors B and C, the business is assigned 40 points from each of them. The business's high relative advantage score of 27 for purchase price, figured as follows, indicates that the business charges a premium price for its product and, as a result, has a weak competitive position with regard to the cost of purchase component. For the cost of toner, which has a relative importance of 20, the company is rated more than one point lower than both competitors A and B and equal to competitor C. The relative advantage score for this cost component, −14, means that the toner for the business's copier is less expensive for customers than the average cost of toner for the competitors' copiers. More than half of the 27 relative advantage points charged to the business because of its high purchase price are offset by the lower toner costs.

$$\frac{\text{Relative Advantage}}{\text{Purchase Price}} = \frac{0 + 40 + 40}{3} = 27$$

$$\frac{\text{Relative Advantage}}{\text{Cost of Toner}} = \frac{-20 + -20 + 0}{3} = -14$$

We also can compute the business's relative advantage with respect to service and repair costs and paper costs. The overall relative advantage score—the sum of the relative advantage scores for each cost component—is 3, which results in a relative cost of purchase index of 103. The index of 103 means that the total cost of purchase for the business's copier is 3 percent less attractive to customers than is the average total cost of purchase for competing copiers.

Perceived Customer Value Index

After it has determined customers' perceptions of overall benefits and total cost of purchase, a business can evaluate the level of value that it creates for its customers.[29] Figure 4-25 shows the customer value created by the copier company. Each area of

FIGURE 4-25 PERCEIVED CUSTOMER VALUE AND VALUE MAP

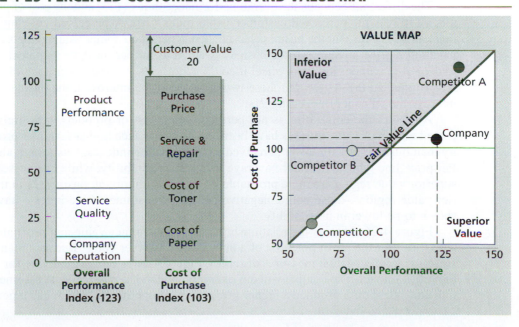

FIGURE 4-26 PERCEIVED VALUE AND PROFIT IMPACT

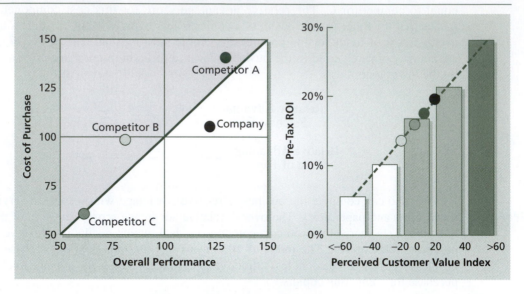

perceived product performance is plotted in the first bar using the relative advantage scores in Figure 4-23. The sum of the scores is the overall performance index. For the cost of purchase index, which is computed differently than the overall performance index, the bar shows the overall relative cost of purchase; the index equals the sum of the scores for each cost area plus 100, as presented in Figure 4-24. The individual cost areas are not plotted because, as we saw, their relative advantage scores inversely reflect competitive advantage—the higher the score, the lower the advantage.

The difference between the overall performance index (123) and the cost of purchase index (103) is the perceived customer value index (20). A perceived customer value index of 20 means that the business has created superior customer value while still commanding a price premium. If the business wanted to further improve its perceived customer value without lowering price, it could address its weaknesses in ease of use and repair time. To the degree that these two areas could be improved, the business would improve the value it offers customers.

Although the correlation is not perfect, businesses or products with higher perceived customer value indexes have been shown to produce higher levels of profitability than businesses with lower perceived customer value indexes. Businesses along the fair price line typically produce average levels of profitability, while businesses in the superior value region are more profitable. Perhaps as important, businesses in the inferior value region—those with a negative perceived customer value index—have been shown to be lower in profitability.

Figure 4-26 presents the relationship between customer value and profitability as a way to infer the profit potential of a business's customer value. Because many other factors can affect actual measures of return, Figure 4-26 is only a guideline for assessing profit impact. The company in our example, which has a perceived customer value index of 20, should produce a higher profit than competitor B, which has a perceived customer value index of −21.

EMOTIONAL BENEFITS AND VALUE CREATION

So far, we have looked at customer benefits that we might describe as *rational* benefits. The rational appeal of an automobile, for instance, includes price, fuel economy, maintenance costs, safety features, and resale value. Less tangible rational benefits include the quality of repair service, the friendliness of service personnel, and the manufacturer's reputation. Certain products also offer *emotional* benefits tied to the customer's personal psychological needs. The same can be true in many business-to-business purchases in which emotional benefits might be tied to security, reputation, or friendship. To be thorough in our examination of customer benefits and value creation, we need to consider sources of emotional customer benefits and the ways that they contribute to customer value.

Emotional Benefits and Psychological Value

We know that every individual has both physical and psychological needs. Physical needs such as food, shelter, sleep, and safety naturally are priorities. After those necessities have been met, we can devote more attention to our psychological needs, such as close relationships, affiliation, recognition, respect, enjoyment, and self-fulfillment. Because many products have, in a sense, "personalities" that serve our psychological needs, we can say they have emotional benefits. The psychological needs of customers frequently draw them to the products with the types of brand personalities that would satisfy those needs.[30]

Customers' Psychological Needs → Brand Personality → **Emotional Benefits**

For example, an individual with a need to be seen as rugged and self-sufficient might be attracted to a Chevy pick-up advertised as durable, powerful, and "like a rock." Individuals with a need to receive recognition and respect would likely be more attracted to a Mercedes. Products that project a "brand personality" can create customer value by delivering emotional benefits.

Brand Personality and Value Creation

Figure 4-27 lists five dominant brand personalities identified by a comprehensive study of human personality and brand personality.[31] In a market or segment where two or more brands meet a consumer's rational needs—those related to price, product, and service

FIGURE 4-27 BRAND PERSONALITY AND PERSONALITY TRAITS

Brand Personality	Brand Example	Personality Traits
Sincerity	Betty Crocker	Down-to-Earth, Honest, Wholesome, Cheerful
Excitement	Nike	Daring, Spirited, Imaginative, Up-to-Date
Competence	Hewlett-Packard	Reliable, Intelligent, Successful
Sophistication	Lexus	Upper Class, Charming, Sophisticated
Ruggedness	Timberline	Rugged, Outdoorsy, Tough

benefits—the consumer will be drawn to the brand with the personality that most fully corresponds to the consumer's emotional needs.

Let's suppose that several years ago Nike used UCLA's famous coach John Wooden instead of Chicago Bulls star Michael Jordan to endorse Nike Air basketball shoes, later named Air Jordan. The personality of the Nike brand of basketball shoes at that time would have been quite different, and the emotional benefits created by the product would have been considerably less for the product's target customers.

Products do have personalities. The development of those personalities, of course, is largely a function of advertising that often associates products with well-known, real-life personalities. Consumers in turn derive a measure of satisfaction or enjoyment, or have other psychological needs met, by using products that project a particular image or set of personal attributes. To the degree that a business delivers such emotional benefits in its product, it contributes to the overall value that customers derive from purchasing and using that product.

IDENTIFYING VALUE DRIVERS

We have seen that a business can create customer value in several ways, but determining exactly which aspects of customer value are the key value drivers can be challenging for any business. Asking customers directly is one approach, but businesses have found that customers cite a wide range of benefits. From a customer's perspective, anything or everything can be important. We can more accurately determine the benefits that customers value by asking them to choose among products that have different benefits and different prices. By examining how customers make trade-offs when choosing among various combinations of price and benefits, we can create a set of preference curves using *conjoint analysis*.[32]

The company Silent Floor tested customer reaction to nine hypothetical flooring systems that included four dimensions of potential value, as presented in Figure 4-28.[33] Each of the nine flooring options offered different combinations of different levels of labor savings, warranty life, price, and callback frequency. Home builders were asked to assume the role of flooring buyers and to rank the nine Silent Floor systems according to their preferences. Figure 4-28 includes the results of the builders' rankings, and Figure 4-29 presents preference curves derived from a conjoint analysis of the rankings.

Customer Preferences

In the Silent Floor example, the preference curves represent the value that home builders placed on varying levels for the four attributes of the flooring. The higher the number on the value axis (.00 to 1.00) for each of the three levels of an attribute, the more important that level of the attribute was for the builder.[34]

We can see, for example, that the builders considered a 40 percent labor savings (1.00) to be considerably more important than a 20 percent labor savings (0.33). The larger the range from low score to high score on an attribute's preference curve, the more important that attribute was to the builders when they ranked the nine options. The low-to-high ranges for warranty life and callback frequency are both 0.58, which means that these two attributes were equally important to the builders. But these two ranges are not as large as the ranges for the more important attributes of price (a maximum range of 1.00) and labor savings (a range of .83).

FIGURE 4-28 ALTERNATIVE FLOORING SYSTEMS

Flooring System A
Labor Savings..............None
Product Warranty.......5 years
Delivered Price...........Competitive
Customer Callbacks....Some
Customer Ranking: 5

Flooring System B
Labor Savings..............None
Product Warranty.......10 years
Delivered Price...........+20%
Customer Callbacks....Often
Customer Ranking: 6

Flooring System C
Labor Savings..............None
Product Warranty.......None
Delivered Price...........+40%
Customer Callbacks....None
Customer Ranking: 8

Flooring System D
Labor Savings..............20%
Product Warranty.......10 years
Delivered Price...........Competitive
Customer Callbacks....None
Customer Ranking: 1

Flooring System E
Labor Savings..............20%
Product Warranty.......None
Delivered Price...........+20%
Customer Callbacks....Some
Customer Ranking: 7

Flooring System F
Labor Savings..............20%
Product Warranty.......5 years
Delivered Price...........+40%
Customer Callbacks....Often
Customer Ranking: 9

Flooring System G
Labor Savings..............40%
Product Warranty.......None
Delivered Price...........Competitive
Customer Callbacks....Often
Customer Ranking: 3

Flooring System H
Labor Savings..............40%
Product Warranty.......5 years
Delivered Price...........+20%
Customer Callbacks....None
Customer Ranking: 2

Flooring System I
Labor Savings..............40%
Product Warranty.......10 years
Delivered Price...........+40%
Customer Callbacks....Some
Customer Ranking: 4

Builders' Preference Ranking: D, H, G, I, A, B, E, C, F
Conjoint analysis used in this ranking to create the preferences curves.
(See Appendix 4.1 for details)

The percentage next to the attribute's name above each of the four preference curves in Figure 4-29 represents the relative importance that attribute had for the builders. We can calculate the relative importance percentage by dividing an attribute's low-to-high range by the sum of all four ranges. Price, the most important factor for the builders, accounted for 34 percent of the overall influence on the builders' rankings. Labor savings was the second most important attribute, with 28 percent of the overall influence. Warranty life and callback frequency each accounted for 19 percent of the influence.

Customer Value

To determine the value driver of any flooring system, we need to create a *customer value index* (CVI) for a specific flooring system, which we will call the "conventional flooring system." This system offers a competitive price but no labor savings and no warranty, and it entails frequent callbacks. The CVI for the conventional flooring system is derived from the performance features and price of the system and the extent to which the home builders valued the performance features and price as scored on the performance curves in Figure 4-29. For the conventional flooring system, price is clearly the value driver (1.00) because it makes up 60 percent of the total CVI of 1.67.

FIGURE 4-29 PREFERENCE CURVES FOR FLOORING SYSTEM ATTRIBUTES

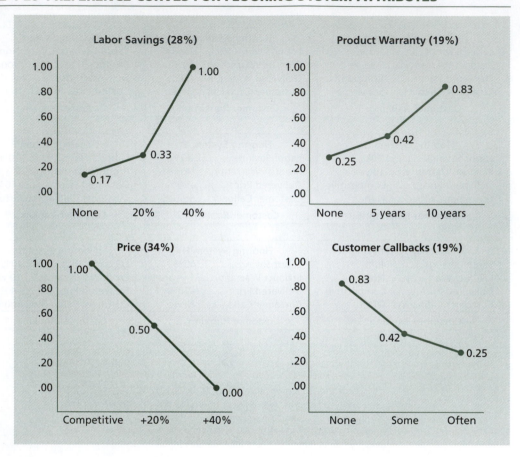

$$\text{Customer Value Index} = \text{Labor Savings} + \text{Warranty} + \text{Price} + \text{Callbacks}$$

CVI of Conventional Flooring System $= \text{None } (.17) + \text{None } (.25) + \text{Competitive } (1.0) + \text{Often } (.25)$

$$= \mathbf{1.67}$$

Another flooring system, one that offers a 40 percent labor savings and no customer callbacks, could be positioned in two ways. Strategy A in Figure 4-30 has the full labor savings and customer callback benefits, along with a 10-year warranty and a price that is 40 percent higher than the current conventional flooring system. This combination produces a CVI of 2.66, 59 percent higher than the CVI produced by a conventional flooring system. Home builders, then, would find Strategy A more attractive than the conventional system. The value driver for this strategy is the labor savings (1.00 of 2.66) because it is the largest contributor to the overall customer value index.

Strategy B provides the same labor savings and customer callback performance as Strategy A, but it is priced only 20 percent higher than the conventional flooring system and offers just a 5-year warranty. The CVI for this combination of performance features

FIGURE 4-30 CUSTOMER PREFERENCE AND CUSTOMER VALUE

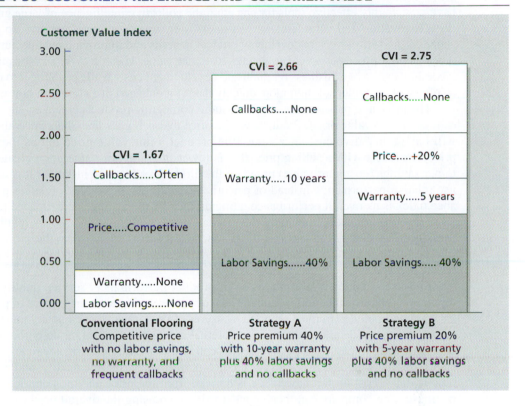

and price is 2.75, 65 percent higher in value than the conventional flooring system. The value driver for Strategy B is also labor savings. Strategies A and B are both superior to the conventional flooring system in terms of customer value, but Strategy A is likely to be more profitable because it has a substantial price premium.

■ Summary

A strong customer focus and an ongoing commitment to understanding customers' needs and the problems that customers encounter are at the core of any market-based strategy. Too often, businesses oversimplify the analysis of customer needs by narrowly focusing on specific product features and price. Although such assessment is valuable, it is more important for a business to look beyond current product features and price to understand the complete customer experience. Knowing the total customer experience—encompassing the customer's acquisition, use, and disposal of a product—enables a business to add meaningful customer value to its product. Using empathic design, experiencing "a day in the life of a customer," conducting lead user analysis, and managing customer touch points are all practical ways for managers to see customers' needs and respond with new product and service benefits that will add to customer value and raise the business's CSI.

With the advent of mass collaboration and crowdsourcing, market-based businesses have new, highly effective tools for engaging the collective intelligence of large groups to drive innovation and value creation. Businesses engage prosumers, partnership groups, suppliers, and employees in developing product benefits and improving manufacturing and other internal processes to create greater customer value. Using a Wiki site for mass collaboration can save a business research and development costs while enabling it to develop an effective customer solution more quickly than if it engaged in a closed, in-house effort.

The price and performance for 10 or more competing products create enough data to estimate a fair-value price. Products with a price that is higher than their fair-value price will have a negative customer value (the product's fair-value price minus the selling price). Products with a selling price that is lower than the fair-value price create a customer savings (customer value) based on the difference. In some instances it is useful to use relative performance instead of performance ratings. A product's relative performance index is its overall performance rating divided by the average performance rating of all competing products, including the product itself, multiplied by 100. A relative performance index of 120 means that the product is 20 percent better than the average relative performance (100), whereas an index of 90 means that the product is 10 percent below average.

End-user customers are interested in product performance, service quality, brand reputation (emotional benefits), and the cost of purchase. Because these areas of performance are not included in most reported measures of performance, a company must collect its own customer data, create data from internal manager estimates, or do both. From the data, an overall measure of performance—called the overall performance index—is created using the weighted averages for product performance, service quality, and company reputation. A cost of purchase index is derived from the price and the nonprice costs of purchase. The company can then create a value map using the overall product performance index and the cost of purchase index.

We examined three kinds of benefits—economic benefits, perceived benefits, and emotional benefits—and the way that customers derive value from these benefits. Economic benefits result in measurable differences in savings for the customer and a stronger competitive financial position for the business. A lower price is an obvious source of economic value, but other sources of economic benefit can be created. Savings from lower acquisition costs, usage, ownership, maintenance, and disposal costs offer ways to lower the total cost of purchase, thereby creating more customer value.

But not all benefits can be quantified into an economic value expressed in dollar savings. Customer benefits derived from a product's appearance, exceptional service, or reputation are more difficult to quantify in dollars. Likewise, customer perceptions of performance have a strong influence on product preference and purchase behavior. By measuring customer perceptions of product performance, service quality, and brand reputation relative to competition, we are able to develop an overall performance index for a business's product. By also measuring customer perceptions of price and nonprice costs of purchase of a product relative to its competition, we can develop an overall cost of purchase index. The difference between total perceived benefits and cost provides a measure of perceived customer value. The larger the customer value, the greater is the potential to attract, satisfy, and retain customers.

A third area of customer benefit and customer value creation is emotional benefits. Products that serve an underlying psychological need, match the personality type, or express the personal values of customers have emotional benefits that enhance customer value. Understanding these aspects of a target market is essential in positioning a product and enhancing its perceived value. Products, like people, have personalities, and the better a business can position its product with respect to the target customer's emotional needs, the greater will be the product's customer value.

Finally, trade-off analysis (conjoint analysis) helps quantify the value created by different combinations of price and product positioning. The customer trade-off process enables us to uncover the degree to which different aspects of a product are driving customer preferences. This analysis in turn enables a business to index the value it creates relative to key competitors and to evaluate the impact that alternative positioning strategies would have on customer preference and relative value. Overall, customer analysis and value creation are important inputs in developing marketing strategies that are designed to yield high levels of customer satisfaction.

■ Market-Based Strategic Thinking

1 What is the advantage of understanding the customer's total experience for a brand such as Kyocera?

2 Why is it more valuable for Lexus managers themselves, rather than a market research firm, to interview customers in order to understand a customer's total experience?

3 How could Apple use empathic design to discover customer problems and new opportunities for value creation for the iPhone?

4 What would be the purpose of a printer manufacturer spending a day in the life of a customer at a company that has over 100 printers in its office building?

5 Why is understanding the total customer experience of a lead user of an iPad potentially more valuable than spending the same amount of time with an average iPad customer?

6 Why would understanding the customer experience of a lead user of an iPad result in better product improvements than those that Apple engineers might design on their own?

7 How could a bank improve the customer experience by managing customer touch points?

8 How could a business that manufactures and sells hardwood flooring through building supply stores make the best use of mass collaboration to improve product performance and service quality?

9 Why should the two hypothetical videos of a day in the life of a customer using a digital camera go beyond the product and focus on the customer's use of the digital camera?

10 How would you assess the economic value of two SUVs?

11 How could a business selling firewood create a more attractive economic value?

12 How would you explain to HP management the fair price line in Figure 4-18 and HP's perceived customer value for the HP PhotoSmart premium printer? How would you discuss with HP the fact that its printer may be underpriced?

13 Why is it important for McDonald's to measure all aspects of perceived performance and perceived cost of purchase?

14 In what ways can HP improve the perceived value of its personal computers?

15 How should customer preference and purchase behavior change as perceived value increases or decreases for vacation packages to Hawaii?

16 Why are emotional benefits important to a brand like Nike or Rolex?

17 How do psychological motives help shape emotional benefits and customer perceptions of value?

18 How does the personality of a spokesperson used in advertising help shape the emotional benefits of a product?

19 Using Figure 4-27 as a guide, discuss the brand personalities of Kodak, Mountain Dew, and Prudential Insurance, and describe how these brand personalities were created.

20 What is automobile trade-off analysis? How would it help Ford understand customer preferences, price sensitivity, and value drivers?

21 How could a restaurant determine whether its customers would prefer a proposed premium service that would cost customers 10 percent more for their meals?

Marketing Performance Tools and Application Exercises

The four interactive marketing performance tools and application exercises outlined here will add to your understanding of economic value, price-performance value mapping, customer value, and price-performance trade-offs as they relate to customer value. To access the tools, go to **rogerjbest.com.** For many of the questions, you can enter the data presented to obtain the answers. You may also enter other data to see the results, and you can save your work. The figure numbers in parentheses are related examples in Chapter 4, but the lettered instructions pertain to the online exercises.

4.1 Economic Value Analysis (Figures 4-12 and 4-13)

A. If Sealed Air sold its AirCap product for the same price as the competing product, how would the economic value change? Why shouldn't Sealed Air do this, as a price equal to the competitor's price creates more economic value for the customer?

B. What price would Sealed Air charge for its AirCap product to produce a zero economic value? This would make more money for Sealed Air, but why would this be an unwise move?

4.2 Price-Performance Value Mapping (Figures 4-16 and 4-17)

A. How would the customer value change if the price of the Canon A590 increased from $180 to $199?

B. How much could the price of the Fuji J10 be increased if Fuji wanted the camera to have a $10 value advantage over the next best customer value in the market?

4.3 Customer Value Analysis (Figures 4-20 to 4-26)

A. How would the company's customer value change if it raised its repair time rating from 5 to 7? How would this affect the competitors' customer values?

B. What would be the value impact of improving the ease-of-use product benefit from 4 to 6? Would this improve perceived customer value more than addressing the repair time benefit problem in the previous question?

4.4   Price-Performance Trade-Offs and Customer Value (Figures 4-28 to 4-30)

A. Create a trade-off analysis that considers three levels of hamburger quality (poor, average, and good), service quality (poor, average, and good), and price (25% lower than average, average, and 25% higher than average).

Rank your preferences for the nine options from 1 (most preferred) to 9 (least preferred). Which aspect of price or performance is most important and which is least important?

B. Which aspect of an average product would you change to improve the overall value?

Notes

1. C. Meyer and A. Schwager, "Understanding Customer Experience," *Harvard Business Review* (February 2007): 118.

2. J. Womack and D. Jones, "Lean Consumption," *Harvard Business Review* (March 2005).

3. D. Leonard and J. Rayport, "Spark Innovation through Empathic Design," *Harvard Business Review* (November–December 1997).

4. M. Lanning, *Delivering Profitable Value* (Reading, MA: Perseus Books, 1998): 228–53.

5. E. von Hippel, "Lead Users: An Important Source of Novel Product Concepts," *Management Science* 32, No. 7 (July 1986): 791–805.

6. C. Henderson, "Finding, Examining Lead Users Push 3M to Leading Edge of Innovation," *Practice Case Study Series*, American Productivity & Quality Center, 2000.

7. G. Lillien, P. Morrison, M. Sonnack, and E. von Hippel. "Performance Assessment of the Lead User Idea Generation Process for New Product Development," working paper, ISBM No. 4-2001, The Pennsylvania State University.

8. R. Kneten and D. Rudes, "Inventing to Order," *Business Week* (July 5, 2004): 84–5.

9. B. Shapiro, V.K. Rangan, and J. Sviokla, "Staple Yourself to an Order," *Harvard Business Review* (July–August 1992): 113–22.

10. R. Yeager, "Customers Don't Buy Technologies; They Buy Solutions: Here's How Five Advanced Technology Marketers Saw the Light and Avoided Becoming High-Tech Commodities," *Business Marketing* (November 1985): 61–76.

11. M. Hammer, *The Agenda* (New York: Crown Business, 2001).

12. B.D. Tapscott and A.D. Williams, *Wikinomics: How Mass Collaboration Changes Everything* (New York: The Penguin Group, 2006).

13. J. Howe, "The Rise of Crowdsourcing," Condé Nast Digital (June 2006): http://www.wired.com/wired/archive/14.06/crowds.html, retrieved February 20, 2011.

14. S. Lohr, "The Crowd Is Wise (When It's Focused)," *New York Times* (July 19, 2009): http://www.nytimes.com/2009/07/19/technology/internet/19unboxed.html, retrieved February 20, 2011.

15. "Netflix Prize," Netflix, Inc. (not dated): http://netflixprize.com/leaderboard, retrieved February 24, 2011.

16. S. Lohr, "A $1 Million Research Bargain for Netflix, and Maybe a Model for Others," *New York Times* (September 22, 2009): http://www.nytimes.com/2009/09/22/technology/internet/22netflix.html, retrieved February 24, 2011.

17. "We Make Invention Accessible," Quirky, Inc. (not dated): http://www.quirky.com/about, retrieved March 11, 2011.

18. S. Bynghall, "How Quirky.com Uses Crowdsourcing to Make Inventors' Dreams Reality," The Insight Exchange (October 25, 2010): http://futureofcrowdsourcingsummit.com/blog/how-quirky-com-uses-crowdsourcing-to-make-inventors-dreams-reality/, retrieved February 24, 2011.

19. T.W. Malone, R. Laubacher, and C. Dellarocas, "The Collective Intelligence Genome," Massachusetts Institute of Technology (April 1, 2010): http://sloanreview.mit.edu/the-magazine/2010-spring/51303/the-collective-intelligence-genome/, retrieved February 23, 2011.

20. S. Weinberger, "Pentagon Goes Wiki With Crowdsourced Tech Project," AOL, Inc. (July 30, 2010): http://www.aolnews.com/2010/07/30/pentagon-goes-wiki-with-crowdsourced-tech-project/, retrieved February 24, 2011.

21. J. Forbis and N. Mehta, "Value-Based Strategies for Industrial Products," *Business Horizons* (May 1981): 32–42.

22. G. Smith and T. Nagle, "A Question of Value," *Marketing Management* (July–August 2005), 39–43.

23. Kyocera TCO Tracker, http://usa.kyoceramita.com/americas/jsp/Kyocera/tcotracker.jsp (December 2010).

24. "Digital Cameras," *Consumer Reports* (April 2010).

25. "Printers," *Consumer Reports* (April 2010).

26. B. Schwartz, "More Isn't Always Better," *Harvard Business Review* (June 2006).

27. G. Smith and T. Nagle, "Measuring the Unmeasurables," *Marketing Management* (May–June 2005) 39: 12–13.

28. M. Holbrook, "The Nature of Customer Value: An Axiology of Services in the Consumption Experience," *Service Quality: New Directions in Theory and Practice*, R. Rust and R. Oliver, ed. (London: Sage Publications, 1991): 21–71.

29. B. Gale, *Managing Customer Value* (New York: Free Press, 1994).

30. D. Hawkins, R. Best, and K. Coney, "The Changing American Society: Values and Demographics," in *Consumer Behavior: Implications for Marketing Strategy*, 6th ed. (New York: Irwin, 1995): 66–88.

31. J. Aaker, "Dimensions of Brand Personality," *Journal of Marketing Research* (August 1997): 347–56.

32. D. Tull and D. Hawkins, *Marketing Research: Measurement and Method*, 6th ed. (New York: Macmillan, 1993): 406–18; and M. Agarwal and P. Green, "Adaptive Conjoint Analysis versus Self-Explicated Models," *International Journal of Research* (June 1991): 141–46.

33. J. Morton and H. Devine, "How to Diagnose What Buyers Really Want," *Business Marketing* (October 1985): 70–83.

34. J. Axelrod and N. Frendberg, "Conjoint Analysis," *Marketing Research* (June 1990): 28–35; P. Green and V. Srinivasan, "Conjoint Analysis in Marketing Research," *Journal of Marketing* (October 1990): 3–19; D. Wittink and P. Cattin, "Commercial Use of Conjoint Analysis," *Journal of Marketing* (July 1989): 19–96; and A. Page and H. Rosenbaum, "Redesigning Product Lines with Conjoint Analysis," *Journal of Product Management* (1987): 120–37.

Trade-Off Analysis Computations

Step 1. Determine individual scores for each attribute (factor/level) by summing the scores for that attribute.

Labor Savings	Price		
	Same	+20%	+40%
None	Some 5 years (A) 5	Often 10 years (B) 6	None None (C) 8 = 19
20%	None 10 years (D) 1	Some None (E) 7	Often 5 years (F) 9 = 17
40%	Often None (G) 3	None 5 years (H) 2	Some 10 years (I) 4 = 9
	= 9	= 15	= 21

Product Warranty

None	= 8 + 7 + 3	= 18
5 years	= 5 + 9 + 2	= 16
10 years	= 6 + 1 + 4	= 11

Customer Callbacks

None	= 8 + 1 + 2	= 11
Some	= 5 + 7 + 4	= 16
Often	= 6 + 9 + 3	= 18

Step 2. Rank attributes and summed attribute scores from lowest to highest (X's below).

	X	Y
+40% Labor Savings	9	1.00
Same Price	9	1.00
10 Years Product Warranty	11	0.83
No Callbacks	11	0.83
Price +20%	15	0.50
5 Years Product Warranty	16	0.42
Some Callbacks	16	0.42
+20% Labor Savings	17	0.33
No Product Warranty	18	0.25
Often Callbacks	18	0.25
No Labor Savings	19	0.17
Price + 40%	21	0.00

Step 3. Determine the maximum score, minimum score, and difference between the maximum and minimum scores.

Step 4. Rescale the raw scores (X's) using the following Normalization Formula:

$$Y = \frac{X_{max} - X}{X_{max} - X_{min}}$$

$$Y = \frac{21 - X}{21 - 9}$$

$$Y = \frac{21 - X}{12}$$

Now, all scores will vary between zero and one, depending on their overall attractiveness to this customer segment.

Market Segmentation and Segmentation Strategies

■ The 90 percent failure rate of 30,000 new products is due to poor market segmentation.[1]

© thinkstock

MILLENNIALS

Millennials are a lifestyle segment comprising 840 million of the worldwide population. They are uniquely defined by their age, 18 to 24 years, and their strong interest in innovation, identity, and separating themselves from mainstream stereotypes. They exert enormous influence over the global demand for music, clothing, food, beverages, hairstyles, movies, food, and electronic media. Millennials are the "connected generation" and are heavy users of Facebook, Twitter, YouTube, blogs, and other social media that keep them in contact with one another. This segment is not only large, it also influences younger and older age-based segments.

Their high connectivity and influence on other age groups make it especially important for marketers to pay close attention to how Millennials are likely to respond to new products and services. In today's digital world, Millennial consumers can easily share their experiences and opinions with a great many others, including their unvarnished opinions about companies and products should their experiences be unsatisfactory. For a better understanding of this age-based segment and the influence it has on today's product-markets, we recommend the YouTube video, *We All Want To Be Young*.

We All Want To Be Young (http://vimeo.com/16638983), Lena Maciel, Lucas Liedke, and Rony Rodrigues, Zeppelin Films.

FIGURE 5-1 THE INFLUENCE OF THE 18–24 AGE SEGMENT

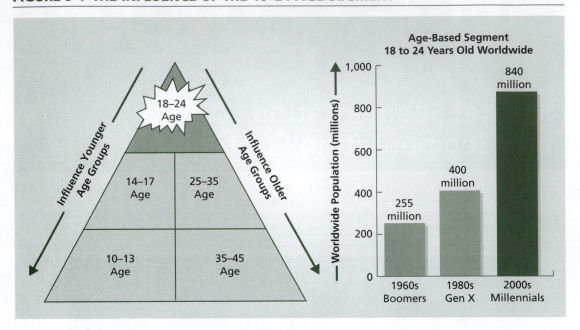

Each of the three lifestyle generations represented in the bar chart on the right side of Figure 5-1 was composed of people aged 18 to 24 years. In the 1960s and 1970s, they were the Baby Boomers, young adults who were born in the postwar era. In the 1980s and 1990s, the age group of the time was called Generation X or simply Gen X, and today, in the 2000s, the age group is referred to as Gen Y or the Millennials. The self-defined lifestyle and unique product needs of each each generational age-based group have influenced both younger and older consumers. As shown on the left side of Figure 5-1, the Millennials today influence the teens who are younger and have an influence on people who are older than they are. The Millennials' sphere of influence over people aged 14 to 35 years is 2.3 billion people, 36.6 percent of the world population in 2010.

For many products, age is a factor that drives certain customer needs. Younger people, for example, do not have much need for health products, insurance, and family vacation packages. As people age and their family situations change, their needs for products and services change. But the preferences of young consumers for clothing, hairstyles, beverages, music, electronic media, and communication devices do influence those who are younger and older than they are. Millennials are uniquely different than the earlier generations of that same age-based segment, and their numbers—about 840 million worldwide—are far greater.

Some brands that have recognized the power of Millennials in the United States include Apple, Scion, Converse, Facebook, Red Bull, Jamba Juice, Zipcar, and, surprisingly, Herbal Essences, Target, and Grape Nuts.[2] Procter & Gamble, the maker of Herbal Essences shampoos, has done a great job of updating what was an aging mass-market brand to appeal to Millennial women. Target has tailored its messages to Millennials, focusing on affordable prices, stylish products, and socially responsible values. The tag line of a television spot featuring two college roommates dancing and decorating their dorm room with Target products was "Happy together, design together, save together." Grape Nuts' advertising and its web site reflect one of the Millennials' favorite themes: "Give it to me straight but don't bore me."

NEEDS-BASED MARKET SEGMENTATION

Millennials are a lifestyle segment that is defined by its age. In this case, their particular stage of life creates certain needs for creativity, identity, and fun. The needs of Millennials are unique and driven by age-related outlooks and behaviors. There are other age-related segments for insurance, housing, entertainment, health care, and food products. When segmenting a market, however, it is best to start with customer needs and then determine which demographics influence those needs.[3]

The market segmentation process should begin with the benefits that customers are seeking in order to solve a particular customer problem. Because different customers seek different solutions for the same problem, our first challenge is to identify and understand the various customer needs that drive product consideration and preferences. After we have grouped customers into *needs-based segments,* we can then ask, "What are the demographics, usage behaviors, and psychographics that distinguish one group of customers from another?" Knowing the factors that differentiate one segment from another helps us identify the segments. Figure 5-2 shows how we might divide the market for home siding into two segments that have different needs: a price-sensitive segment and a quality-conscious segment. Needs-based segmentation provides the basic guidelines for product positioning strategies and marketing communications. With the market properly segmented, we can now develop specific segment value propositions that will attract new customers and retain existing ones.

FIGURE 5-2 NEEDS-BASED MARKET SEGMENTATION

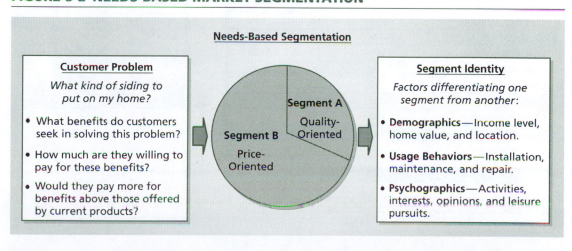

CUSTOMER NEEDS, PRICE, AND PRODUCT BENEFITS

Let's consider another example, the purchase of a laptop computer whereby the customer can choose from many product-price configurations. Figure 5-3 shows a laptop computer with a base price of $800. This price can be adjusted should the customer want more or fewer features or different levels of performance. But to understand customer needs, including price, we need to let customers select the features and performance levels they prefer in view of the price they want to pay. As we see in Figure 5-3, a price-sensitive customer who needs less performance could buy this laptop for as little as $550. If the number of customers who buy below the $800 base price is significant, then the company might want to target a separate market segment consisting of price-sensitive customers.

At the other extreme, customers who want all of the extended features would pay $1,550 for their laptops. The needs of these customers are different, and they are willing to pay more to obtain the high performance that a fully configured laptop offers. Again, if the number of customers paying well over $800 is significant, a market segment for potential customers who want extra features and high performance would be in order. Although there are 6,561 combinations of product features and prices for this particular product, clusters of product-price configurations create meaningful needs-based market segments.

FIGURE 5-3 CUSTOMER PREFERENCES FOR FEATURES VERSUS PRICE

Product Features	Level 1	Level 2	Level 3
Processor Speed (MHz)	X	1.5X	2X
Cost Adjustment	$0	$150	$300
Memory (GB)	X	2X	4X
Cost Adjustment	–$100	$0	$100
Hard Drive (GB)	X	2X	3X
Cost Adjustment	–$50	$0	$50
Media Drive	CD-ROM	DVD	DVD+RW
Cost Adjustment	–$50	$0	$100
Operating System	Basic	Plus	Pro
Cost Adjustment	$0	$50	$100
Carrying Case	None	Nylon	Leather
Cost Adjustment	–$50	$0	$50
Warranty	90 Days	1 Year	3 Years
Cost Adjustment	$0	$25	$50

Customer Feature Preference	Lowest Price	Highest Price
Base Price	$800	$800
Processor Speed	$0	$300
Memory	–$100	$100
Hard Drive	–$50	$50
Media Drive	–$50	$100
Operating System	$0	$100
Carrying Case	–$50	$50
Warranty	$0	$50
Total Price	**$550**	**$1,550**

Price	Total
Base Price	$800
Cost Adjustment	$0
Price to be Paid	$800

Given this set of features and prices, there are 6,561 possible product–price configurations.

The right one for any given customer will depend on the customer's needs and price preference.

The purpose of needs-based segmentation is to offer product benefits that satisfy the needs, including price, of different sets of target customers. Or, with a multiproduct segment strategy, various products are designed for the needs of different segments, each of which has target customers who differ meaningfully in the product benefits they desire and the price they can afford.

Customer Needs

Many companies forget that solving customer problems requires knowing who their target customers are and what they need.[4] Understanding customer needs is the first step in successful market segmentation. A business with a strong market orientation seeks to understand the needs of its target customers and then develops strategies to attract, satisfy, and retain them. Because potential customers will rarely have all the same needs, a business with a strong market orientation divides its served market into customer segments.

Both consumers and businesses have market needs, but the factors influencing their needs differ in important ways. Understanding why customers have different needs is helpful in determining how to divide a market into useful needs-based market segments.

Forces That Shape Consumer Market Needs

Consumers differ in a great many ways. Obviously people have different preferences in automobiles, toothpaste, and entertainment. Not so obvious are the factors that influence those preferences. Although many factors contribute to these differences,[5] three primary forces shape the needs of consumers, as summarized in Figure 5-4.

Demographic Influences

Needs and preferences often shift as a person moves *demographically* from one life situation to another. Changes in income, occupation, and educational level all contribute to a changing set of customer needs for a variety of products. Consider how customer needs and preferences for an automobile change as a person moves from college student to

FIGURE 5-4 FORCES THAT SHAPE CONSUMER NEEDS

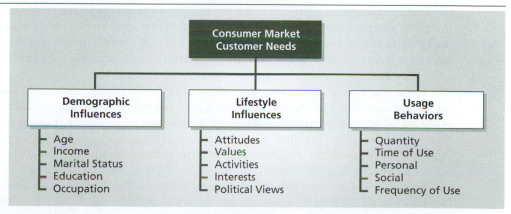

management trainee. A few years later, the same person may marry and start a family, and changes in marital status and household will once again shift automobile needs and preferences. Because of the many demographic differences among individuals and households, we should expect a wide array of differences in what consumers need, can afford, and buy. To the extent that demographics reflect the needs and preferences of customers, they can be used to identify market segments.

Lifestyle Influences

Demographics are not alone in shaping customer needs and market demand. Lifestyle forces created by differences in values, attitudes, and interests also contribute to differences in customer needs. Two consumers who are demographically the same may differ significantly in their attitudes and value orientations. A consumer with strong environmental values is likely to prefer a different car than a demographically identical person whose values are focused on fun, enjoyment, and personal gratification. Differences in lifestyle, including different values, attitudes, and interests, are forces that create different needs and product preferences among customers. To the extent that lifestyle attributes reflect the needs and buying preferences of customers, they can be used to identify market segments.

Usage Behaviors

A third major force in shaping customer needs is *usage behavior*. How the product is used, when it is used, and how much it is used are all forces that shape customer needs for a great many products. A family with two children under age 10 will have a different set of usage behaviors for an automobile than a family with two children over age 16. In addition, if parents are buying a first car for their child as a graduation gift, their needs are likely to be different from those of buyers who are purchasing a car for the family or for business use. To the extent that usage behaviors reflect the needs and buying preferences of customers, they can be used to identify market segments. Figure 5-4 presents a list of characteristics commonly used in consumer markets to identify segments.

Example: Toothpaste Market Segmentation

Toothpaste is one of the most dynamic segments of the oral care market. The frequency of product launches in existing segments of the market and the ongoing genesis of new product introductions contribute to the market's continuous evolution. The sales growth in oral hygiene products worldwide has largely resulted from an increasing awareness of the benefits of oral hygiene and its related products. Advances in product design and science have led to a variety of high-priced, value-added multifunctional products in several oral care categories.

For major toothpastes, preventing tooth decay is no longer enough. Major brands now also promote fresher breath, healthier gums, and whiter teeth. These added benefits, made possible by the industry's scientific advancements in recent years, have altered toothpaste products so that they now offer benefits to customers in addition to just fighting cavities.[6] Whitening toothpastes and other products with multiple functions are driving growth in the dentifrices segment.

Shown in Figure 5-5 are four needs-based segments for the toothpaste market. Each has a core need for decay prevention, but there's a secondary differentiating benefit for

FIGURE 5-5 TOOTHPASTE CUSTOMER NEEDS AND MARKET SEGMENTS

Segment Name	Worrier	Sociable	Sensory	Independent
Core Need	Prevent Decay	Prevent Decay	Prevent Decay	Prevent Decay
Differentiating Benefit	Oral Hygiene	Whitening	Taste/Flavor	Value
Segment Size	50%	30%	15%	5%
Key Demographic	Families/Adults	Teens/Young Smokers	Children	Single Male
Lifestyle Factor	Conservative	Active/ Sociable	Self-Involvement	Autonomy
Price Paid	Medium	High	Medium	Low
Product Size	Large Canisters	Large Tubes	Medium Tubes	Small Tubes
Sample Product	Crest	Ultrabrite	Aquafresh	Private Label

each segment that defines it. "Worriers" want complete oral hygiene, whereas "sociables" want whitening, and "sensory" customers seek a brand that tastes good. "Independents" prefer a brand with the best combination of benefits at a low price.

Each segment is also different with respect to demographics, lifestyle factors, and usage behavior. As shown, each also has different preferred brands. Of course, it is possible for a toothpaste producer to serve more than one segment with a differentiated brand for each segment's customer needs.

Forces That Shape Business Market Needs

Quite often, discussions of market segmentation are limited to consumer markets, and as a result managers in business-to-business, industrial, high-tech, and commercial markets are left to extrapolate how segmentation might apply to their markets. Much like consumer markets, business-to-business markets are influenced by demographics, lifestyle (company culture), and usage behaviors. Figure 5-6 shows these three fundamental forces, along with the factors that contribute to these forces.

FIGURE 5-6 FORCES THAT SHAPE BUSINESS-TO-BUSINESS CUSTOMER NEEDS

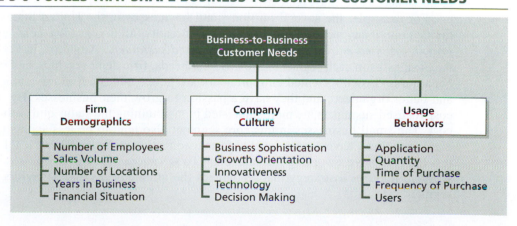

Firm Demographics

In consumer markets, a key force that shapes a market is demographics. In business-to-business markets, we use the term *firm demographics*. Differences in the size of a commercial or industrial customer with respect to both employees and sales are likely to contribute to differences in customer needs. Industries can also be identified by the Standard Industrial Classification (SIC) code. These industry differences often correspond to different product applications and different needs for products. The newness of a business, the number of locations that it has, and its financial stability are also important firm demographics that may play a role in shaping customer needs in nonconsumer, business-to-business markets.

Company Culture

Just as consumer markets have lifestyles, commercial markets have *cultures* (styles) that can have a profound impact on customer needs. Two commercial customers that are similar in firm demographics may have very different needs due to major differences in their corporate style or culture. A company such as Apple with a strong technological base and growth orientation has a different set of needs than a commodity business with limited aspirations for growth. Other differences in attitudes with respect to innovation, risk, and centralized versus decentralized decision making can also shape customer needs in business-to-business markets.

Usage Behaviors

Finally, as in consumer markets, usage behavior often has a significant role in shaping the needs of commercial customers. How much a business buys, how often it purchases, who uses the product, and how it is used all influence the specific needs of a business-to-business customer and affect its choice of one vendor or product over another. Commercial customers are interested not merely in the products they are buying but also in the technical support, service, and integrity of the supplier companies.

As with consumer segments, business segments are created on the basis of product and price needs that are unique to each segment. However, to make the segments actionable we need to identify each segment according to its own combination of firm demographics, business culture (style), and usage behaviors. In an effort to identify needs-based segments in business markets, we can modify Figure 5-2 by using the forces that shape business needs to create Figure 5-7.

For example, the several million small businesses in the United States can be divided into many narrow segments, but they broadly fall into just two core segments: *growth-oriented entrepreneurs* and *cost-focused sustainers*. As shown in Figure 5-7, the businesses in each segment have different needs, firm demographics, and purchase behaviors. Growth-oriented entrepreneurs are better educated, more sophisticated, and better organized, and they have a passion to grow their businesses. By contrast, cost-focused sustainers are more interested in maintaining the status quo at the lowest cost. The small businesses in this core segment also tend to be less sophisticated in their operations, have a lower level of formal education at the leadership level, and are less likely to have a working financial plan. To sell successfully to businesses in either segment requires a strategy that recognizes the unique needs and behaviors of each segment.

FIGURE 5-7 MARKET SEGMENTATION OF THE SMALL BUSINESS MARKET

Growth-Oriented Entrepreneurs

Core Business Need
 Ways to invest and grow

Firm Demographics
 Medium size
 More sophisticated
 Higher in education
 Ongoing financial plan

Purchase Behavior
 Products that enhance productivity
 High revenue per customer
 Willing to buy value-added solutions

Value Proposition
 Solutions that help you grow
 your business

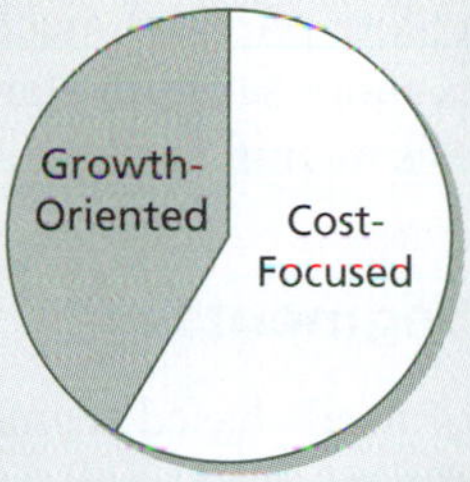

Cost-Focused Sustainers

Core Business Need
 Ways to continue and save

Firm Demographics
 Small in sales/employees
 Less sophisticated
 Lower in education
 Limited or no financial plan

Purchase Behavior
 Products that lower cost
 Low revenue per customer
 Confused by value-added solutions

Value Proposition
 Solutions that save your
 business money

(Pie chart: Growth-Oriented / Cost-Focused)

NEEDS-BASED MARKET SEGMENTATION—PROCESS

Understanding customer needs is a basic tenet of market-based management. Although demographics, lifestyle, and usage behaviors help shape customer needs, they are not always the best ways to identify groups of similar customers. Too many variables and too many meaningless combinations exist. Instead, the market segmentation process should start with customer needs: A business groups its customers according to their similar needs and then determines which of the many demographics, lifestyle forces, and usage behaviors make each group distinct from the other groups.

In this way, a business allows customer needs to drive the market-segmentation process, and then the business identifies the unique combination of external forces that shape each segment. This approach reduces the possibility of an artificial segmentation of the market by a combination of demographics and usage behaviors that are not key forces in shaping customer needs. But before we proceed with our discussion of needs-based segmentation, let's first examine the demographic trap.

The Demographic Trap

Marketers new to market segmentation will often fall into the demographic trap. Given the strong role that demographics, lifestyle, and usage play in shaping customer needs, it seems logical to segment a market on the basis of these differences. For example, in the consumer financial services market, we could segment the market on the basis of differences in income, education, and age, as well as differences in the amount invested, frequency of transactions, and type of investments purchased. If we created three meaningful categories for each of these six variables, we would have 729 possible market segments!

$$\text{Number of Segments} = (3 \text{ categories per variable})^6 = \textbf{729}$$

That number of segments is far too many to consider if we are to develop a meaningful marketing strategy for each customer group, and a good portion of the 729 segments would not have much relevance to customer needs. It may be convenient to group customers into demographic, lifestyle, or usage categories, but the demographics selected may or may not be relevant in shaping customer needs. Although markets are heterogeneous, and people differ in demographics, personal attitudes, and life circumstances, demographic segmentation seldom provides much guidance for product development or message strategies.[7] It makes more sense to start the market-segmentation process by grouping customers on the basis of similar needs.

Needs-Based Market Segments

To illustrate the importance of needs-based segmentation, consider again how we might segment the market for investment services. Relevant demographics that might be considered to cause differences in needs could include income, assets, age, occupation, marital status, and education. Relevant use behaviors might include experience with investments, size of investment portfolio, portfolio diversification, and amount of average transaction. We could legitimately argue that each of these demographic factors is an important force in shaping customer needs, but attempting to segment this market on the basis of all of these differences would be a hopeless task. Instead, the first step in the market segmentation process outlined in Figure 5-8 is to determine customers' investment needs and the benefits they hope to derive from their investment decisions. A study of female investors' needs, for example, produced three *needs-based segments*.[8]

■ **Segment A:** Female investors who seek minimally taxed investments that outperform inflation.

FIGURE 5-8 NEEDS-BASED SEGMENTATION PROCESS

Steps in Segmentation Process	Description
1. Needs-Based Segmentation	Group customers into segments based on similar needs and benefits sought by customer in solving a particular consumption problem.
2. Segment Identification	For each needs-based segment, determine which demographics, lifestyles, and usage behaviors make the segment distinct and identifiable (actionable).
3. Segment Attractiveness	Using predetermined segment attractiveness criteria, determine the overall attractiveness of each segment.
4. Segment Profitability	Determine segment profitability (net marketing contribution).
5. Segment Positioning	For each segment, create a "value proposition" and product-price positioning strategy based on that segment's unique customer needs and characteristics.
6. Segment Strategy "Acid Test"	Create "segment storyboards" to test the attractiveness of each segment's positioning strategy.
7. Marketing Mix Strategy	Expand segment positioning strategy to include all aspects of the marketing mix: product, price, promotion, place, and service.

- **Segment B:** Female investors who want investments that provide appreciation with limited risk.
- **Segment C:** Female investors who desire a good income from their investments but also want limited risk.

It would not take much for a financial adviser to figure out which type of investments would best suit each segment of investors. But on the basis of needs alone, we do not know who these customers are. The main benefit of needs-based market segmentation is that the segments are based on specific customer needs. The main disadvantage is that we cannot identify in advance the individual customers who would fall into each segment. We need to determine the observable demographics and behaviors that differentiate one segment from another in order to make the needs-based segmentation actionable.

Segment Identification

After dividing a market into needs-based segments, the next step in the segmentation process is segment identification. For a segmentation strategy to be actionable, it must identify and characterize segments by demographics or other measurable variables for the purposes of targeting and positioning.[9] For each needs-based segment, we must determine the demographics, lifestyles, and usage behaviors that make one segment meaningfully different from another. The key descriptive factors that distinguish segment A from the other female investor segments are career orientation, occupation, college education, and above-average income, as shown in Figure 5-9. Women in this segment are also more likely to be self-confident and individualistic and to have interests outside the home. On the basis of these characteristics, this segment is labeled the *career woman* segment. With accurate delineation of segment needs and identification, we can begin to visualize a self-confident career woman who has discretionary income to invest but wants her investments to grow at a rate greater than inflation without the burden of additional taxes.

Although segment B is in the same general age category as segment A, customers in segment B have lower incomes, are more likely to have young children, and are less likely to be married. They have less experience with investments and are more likely to be apprehensive of investment decisions. This is the *single-parent* segment, named in view of both the unique family situation and the lifestyle orientation that together help identify and characterize it.

Segment C is called the *mature woman* segment because of the older age, conservative outlook, and wealth level that that characterize it. These female investors look for investments that can deliver a good return, in the form of current income, with limited risk. We see, then, that all three segments have unique needs and unique identities that enable us to accomplish the first two steps in the needs-based segmentation process outlined in Figure 5-8.

Segment Attractiveness

What makes one segment attractive and another unattractive? Although every business in a particular market might answer this question somewhat differently, when we step back and look more broadly at the factors that make a segment attractive, we find that the level

FIGURE 5-9 SEGMENT IDENTIFICATION—FEMALE INVESTOR MARKET SEGMENTS

Segment Name	Career Woman	Single Parent	Mature Woman
Core Need	Growth Without Taxes	Appreciation with Minimal Risk	Income with Minimal Risk
Demographics			
Age	35–45	35–55	Over 55
Income > $50,000	86%	3%	63%
Working	100%	43%	17%
Professional	83%	9%	13%
Married	56%	13%	35%
Youngest Child < 5	24%	83%	5%
College Educated	78%	23%	17%
Lifestyle			
Investment Attitude	Confident	Concerned	Conservative
Interests	Sports/Reading	Family	Leisure
Entertainment	Concerts	Movies	Television
Key Value	Individualistic	Cooperative	Traditional
Usage Behaviors			
Experience	Some/Extensive	None/Limited	Limited/Moderate
Risk Preference	Moderate/High	Low	Low/Moderate
Net Worth	Growing	Fixed	Fixed

of attractiveness is based primarily on three important considerations. Common to most assessments of segment attractiveness are assessments of *market demand*, *competitive intensity*, and *market access*.

Market Demand

As Figure 5-10 shows, to assess market demand we consider the present size of the segment, its rate of growth, and its market potential. Large, growing segments with the potential for long-term future growth are naturally more attractive than small, static segments that show no indication of future growth. Market size, growth rate, and growth potential all influence a business's prospect for improved performance. A first step in assessing segment attractiveness is to determine the extent to which these key market forces contribute to the attractiveness of the segment.

Competitive Intensity

The number of competitors, the number of substitutes, and the level of competitive rivalry affect the attractiveness of a segment. Even if a segment is attractive because of favorable market-demand forces, intense rivalry among the segment's competitors could more than offset the favorable demand and make the segment unattractive. Numerous competitors and relatively low barriers to entry also diminish the attractiveness of a segment because these conditions make it more difficult to achieve market share and margin

FIGURE 5-10 FORCES THAT SHAPE SEGMENT ATTRACTIVENESS

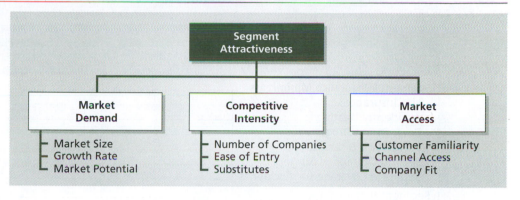

objectives. In addition, in a segment with many substitute products and limited product differentiation, margins will be further compressed and profits reduced. An attractive segment is one with relatively few competitors, minimal price competition, few substitutes, and high barriers to competitor entry.

Market Access

To be attractive, a segment has to be accessible. The first requirement is having access to channels that reach target segment customers. Without customer awareness of a company's product and access to marketing channels, the opportunity that the products have for success is greatly reduced. Accessing a market also requires that the core capabilities of a business fit well with the needs of its target segment. The better the match between customer needs and a business's sources of advantage, the easier it is to access markets. Without sufficient marketing resources, market access is seriously impeded. Segment attractiveness is greatly enhanced when a business has cost-effective access to customers and when the business's sources of competitive advantage are in good alignment with the needs of target customers.

The importance of market segmentation and segment attractiveness is highlighted in Figure 5-11. The health insurance company in this example attempted to sell to all willing commercial buyers without first segmenting the market. However, a later market segmentation based on the insurance customer needs revealed that the business's greatest market penetration was in the least profitable segment, segment I. Given the relative attractiveness of the other two segments, both of which had more revenue per customer, the health insurance carrier revised its marketing efforts to target segments II and III.

A key benefit of market segmentation is identifying segments that should not be pursued. This is a point that former MediaOne CEO Dr. Charles Lillis often emphasizes when he is asked to speak on market segmentation:

> A willingness on the part of sellers to construct their offerings in a way that clearly targets the most desirable customers almost always gets diluted because they just can't convince themselves that they shouldn't be at least "sort of" attractive to all buyers. Most often this lack of discipline harms profits because the costs of attempting to serve all segments is very high.[10]

FIGURE 5-11 SEGMENTATION OF THE BUSINESS HEALTH INSURANCE MARKET

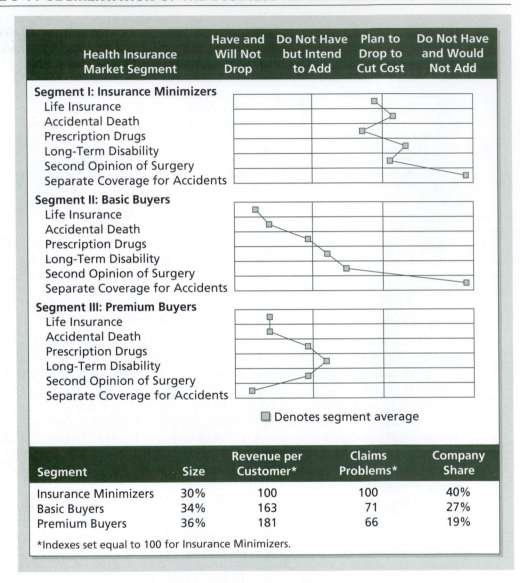

Segment	Size	Revenue per Customer*	Claims Problems*	Company Share
Insurance Minimizers	30%	100	100	40%
Basic Buyers	34%	163	71	27%
Premium Buyers	36%	181	66	19%

*Indexes set equal to 100 for Insurance Minimizers.

Segment Profitability

Although the market attractiveness of a segment may be acceptable, a business may elect not to pursue that segment if it does not offer the desired level of profit potential. In order to assess segment profitability, a business estimates the net marketing contribution that is expected at a certain level of segment market penetration.

For example, the market for silicon sealants can be divided into three segments based on customer needs and product usage, as illustrated in Figure 5-12. Although the silicon-based product is the same in each market segment, the segment strategies are customized

FIGURE 5-12 SEGMENT MARKETING PROFITABILITY

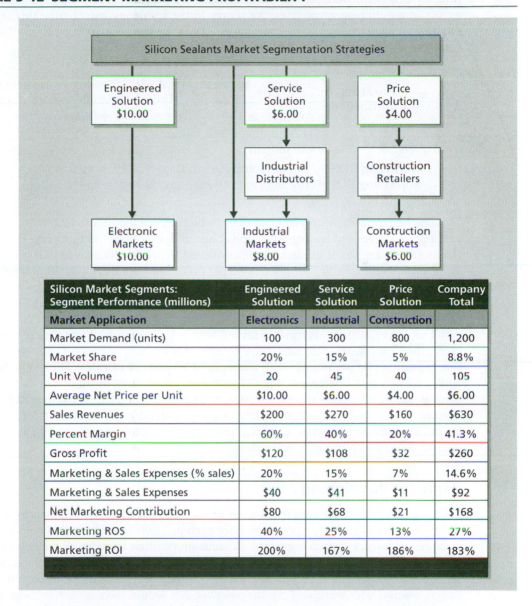

Silicon Market Segments: Segment Performance (millions)	Engineered Solution	Service Solution	Price Solution	Company Total
Market Application	**Electronics**	**Industrial**	**Construction**	
Market Demand (units)	100	300	800	1,200
Market Share	20%	15%	5%	8.8%
Unit Volume	20	45	40	105
Average Net Price per Unit	$10.00	$6.00	$4.00	$6.00
Sales Revenues	$200	$270	$160	$630
Percent Margin	60%	40%	20%	41.3%
Gross Profit	$120	$108	$32	$260
Marketing & Sales Expenses (% sales)	20%	15%	7%	14.6%
Marketing & Sales Expenses	$40	$41	$11	$92
Net Marketing Contribution	$80	$68	$21	$168
Marketing ROS	40%	25%	13%	27%
Marketing ROI	200%	167%	186%	183%

around different customer needs for (1) product amount, (2) product package, (3) product applicator, (4) engineering support, (5) technical service, (6) availability, and (7) price.

The *engineered solution segment*, the smallest of the three segments, buys 100 million pounds per year. The manufacturer has captured a 20 percent market share with a segment strategy that is designed for engineering applications. This segment is served with easy-to-use smaller containers of the product, a special product applicator, and technical service in the form of a one-on-one relationship between the company and the customer. With this level of product customization and service, the company has set a premium price of $10 per pound. At this price, margins are 60 percent and marketing and sales expenses are 20 percent of sales. As shown in the following calculation, this segment strategy yields a net marketing contribution of $80 million, a marketing ROS of 40 percent, and a marketing ROI of 200 percent.

$$
\begin{aligned}
\text{Net Marketing Contribution} &= \frac{\text{Segment}}{\text{Demand}} \times \frac{\text{Segment}}{\text{Share}} \times \frac{\text{Price per}}{\text{Unit}} \times \frac{\text{Percent}}{\text{Margin}} - \frac{\text{Marketing \&}}{\text{Sales Expenses}} \\
&= 100 \text{ million} \times .20 \times \$10 \times .6 - \$40 \text{ million} \\
&= \$120 \text{ million} - \$40 \text{ million} \\
&= \mathbf{\$80\ million}
\end{aligned}
$$

$$\text{Marketing ROS} = (\$80 \text{ million} / \$200 \text{ million}) \times 100\% = \mathbf{40\%}$$
$$\text{Marketing ROI} = (\$80 \text{ million} / \$40 \text{ million}) \times 100\% = \mathbf{200\%}$$

The *service solution segment* strategy, which serves the industrial market is differentiated on the basis of package size, applicator, and direct sales and support. To enhance this strategy, companies use industrial distributors to provide local availability and delivery. For this segment, the net price is $6 per pound and the margin is 40 percent of the selling price. Marketing and sales expenses in the service solution segment are 15 percent of sales. As shown in Figure 5-12, this yields a marketing ROS of 25 percent and a marketing ROI of 167 percent.

The *price solution segment* is served with a large-size package that is sold indirectly through construction retailers with no end-user sales or support. The net price in this segment is $4 per pound, with a margin of 20 percent of sales. The marketing and sales expenses are 7 percent of sales. This yields a marketing profit of $21 million. The price solution segment's marketing ROS is 13 percent, and the marketing ROI is 186 percent. Although the segment strategies vary considerably across these three segments according to customer needs, each segment strategy is profitable and contributes to the overall marketing profit of $168 million.

Segment Positioning

Each target segment presents its own set of marketing challenges. A business needs to develop a customized *value proposition* for each positioning strategy that delivers value to target customers in each segment.[11] A value proposition includes all the key elements of the situation and the benefits the target customer is seeking in this purchase. For the female investor market described in Figure 5-9, segment A included middle-aged professional women who were seeking investments that would have above-average growth with minimal tax consequences. The value proposition for this segment might be *How to beat inflation and taxes.* Ideally, the value proposition for a segment should capture the key benefits sought by the target customer. As a result, the value propositions for segment B and segment C would differ from segment A because of the different needs, benefits, and purchase behaviors of these segments.

To develop a segment positioning strategy for each of the three segments, let's return to Figure 5-9 as a guide. Because the three segments differ in primary needs, demographics, lifestyle, and purchase behaviors, it is important to use all this information when developing a customized positioning strategy for each segment.

FIGURE 5-13 SEGMENT STORYBOARDS FOR ACID TEST OF SEGMENT STRATEGIES

Investment Program A	Investment Program B	Investment Program C
How to Beat Inflation and Higher Taxes	*Special Help for Women with Unique Money Problems*	*Safe Investment Solutions that Pay Good Income*
Key Benefits	**Key Benefits**	**Key Benefits**
• Capital Appreciation • Minimal Taxation	• Growth/Appreciation • Safety	• Safety • Income
Products	**Products**	**Products**
• Growth Stocks • Municipal Bonds • Growth Funds	• Growth Mutual Funds • Blue-Chip Stocks • High-Grade Bonds	• Utility Stocks • High-Grade Bonds • High-Dividend Stocks

Potential customers are instructed to examine each "segment storyboard" and select the one that best fits their investment needs. The degree to which target segment customers select the storyboard designed for them enables a business to judge the extent to which the segment positioning strategy will work.

Figure 5-13 presents a storyboard for each of the three segments. Storyboards are a tool that marketing managers use to assess the merits of a proposed marketing communication and the strategy behind the communication. Each of the three storyboards in this example outlines a value proposition and positioning strategy that is designed to meet its segment's unique needs. Product differences based on segment needs are relatively easy to determine. This is the first sign of an effective segmentation effort. If a business can readily link customer needs to specific product features and benefits, then it is on the right track to a successful segment strategy. If this linkage is difficult or arbitrary, target customers will be less likely to recognize the uniqueness of a segment strategy. Because pricing is less important in the investment market than in, for example, the retail market, it is not a key part of the segment positioning strategy for any of the three segments. Had a segment emerged as price sensitive, then pricing would have been critical to both the value proposition and the segment positioning strategy.

Promotion is essential in delivering the value proposition and in communicating to potential customers. Both the ad copy and the media selected for advertising communications will affect customer response. For segment A, the ad copy would portray a career woman in a business setting; media where the ad would be placed could include *Business Week* and *The Wall Street Journal*. Segment B requires a different approach because the family plays a larger role, and because the target audience has limited experience in financial planning. Meanwhile, the promotion strategy for segment C has to be carefully customized to the needs, lifestyle, and usage behavior of mature female investors. To reach customers in any of these segments, a business must be sensitive to the needs and lifestyle of the target customer. For the career woman segment, lunchtime seminars at or near the workplace could be used to deliver the value proposition and product portfolio that would best serve this segment's needs and desired benefits. Morning or evening seminars at local schools could be a way to reach the single-parent segment. Seminars designed for the mature woman segment might be held in a meeting room at a hotel. Interestingly, seminars targeted at the mature segment are sometimes offered aboard cruise ships, enabling participants to write off a portion of their trip expenses.

Segment Strategy Acid Test

To test our understanding of segment needs and our ability to translate that understanding into a value proposition, the next step in the segmentation process is the "acid test" of our strategy.[12] To conduct the acid test, we will use the storyboards in Figure 5-13. Each storyboard delineates a different value proposition and segment positioning strategy.

Our first step is to recruit a group of female investors and use a set of questions to assign each of them to one of our three segments. We then ask them to critique each segment's storyboard and select the one that most appeals to them. Our marketing strategy holds promise for success if most of the potential customers in each target segment select the storyboard that was created to appeal to them. The higher the percentage of correct classifications, the more likely the segment strategy will succeed. Of course, if a majority of target customers indicates that none of the segment storyboards fits their needs, then we have failed on all accounts to translate segment needs into a meaningful value proposition and segment positioning strategy.

A telecommunications business used this acid test and learned that five out of six segments found the storyboards created for them attractive, although the participants had suggestions on how to improve them. One segment failed to find any of the segment storyboards attractive. The business needed to probe deeper into the overall needs of the customers in the segment that failed to find an attractive storyboard. After doing additional customer research and repeating the acid test, the business was able to develop storyboards that were attractive for all segments of target customers, and it then moved forward in the segmentation process.

Another example of using the segment strategy acid test involved a bank that wanted to be certain of its segment strategies. One segment of the bank's customers rejected the storyboard designed for them because it did not include the cost of a new service. A revised value proposition included both the benefits and the cost of the service. In all cases, an important part of the acid test is to ask customers for ways in which the value proposition can be improved to better fit their needs, usage behaviors, and lifestyles.

Segment Marketing Mix Strategy

Customer research, the storyboard process, and a careful assessment of a proposed strategy won't guarantee success. Despite the best preparations, failure is a certainty when a segment strategy is poorly executed. To be successful, the strategy needs to be expanded to include all elements of the marketing mix. The segment positioning strategy may include both product and price, but a complete marketing mix strategy needs to include promotion (communications) and place (sales and distribution) strategies as well.[13] If target-segment customers are not adequately aware of the segment value proposition or cannot acquire the product at preferred points of purchase, the segment strategy will fail. For example, in Figure 5-14 we can see how DuPont developed different advertisements to execute a strategy to sell Kevlar to two different segments. Note the attention to distinct

FIGURE 5-14 DUPONT—SEGMENT VALUE PROPOSITIONS AND POSITIONING STRATEGIES

Commercial Fishing

Aircraft Design

Value Proposition: *This boat hull of Kevlar saves fuel, gets there faster, and can carry more fish.*

Value Proposition: *Our L-1011 is 807 pounds lighter because of Kevlar 49.*

Advertising and photo courtesy of DuPont.

segment value propositions and the product positioning differences that are unique to each target segment.[14] A generic ad highlighting product features would not have had the impact of each segment-specific ad.

SEGMENTATION STRATEGIES

Taking into consideration segment attractiveness, profit potential, and available resources, businesses may choose among several segment strategies. As Figure 5-15 shows, segment strategies can range from a *mass-market* strategy, which has no segment focus, to *subsegment* strategies, which have numerous niche segments within segments.

Mass-Market Strategy

When differences in customer needs are small or demographics are not distinctive, a business may elect to use a mass-market strategy. This strategy presents a generic value proposition that is built around the core customer need and the business's generic positioning strategy. Wal-Mart, for example, pursues a mass-market strategy built around a low-cost value proposition that has worked effectively for over 30 years. Coca-Cola,

FIGURE 5-15 MARKET SEGMENTATION STRATEGIES

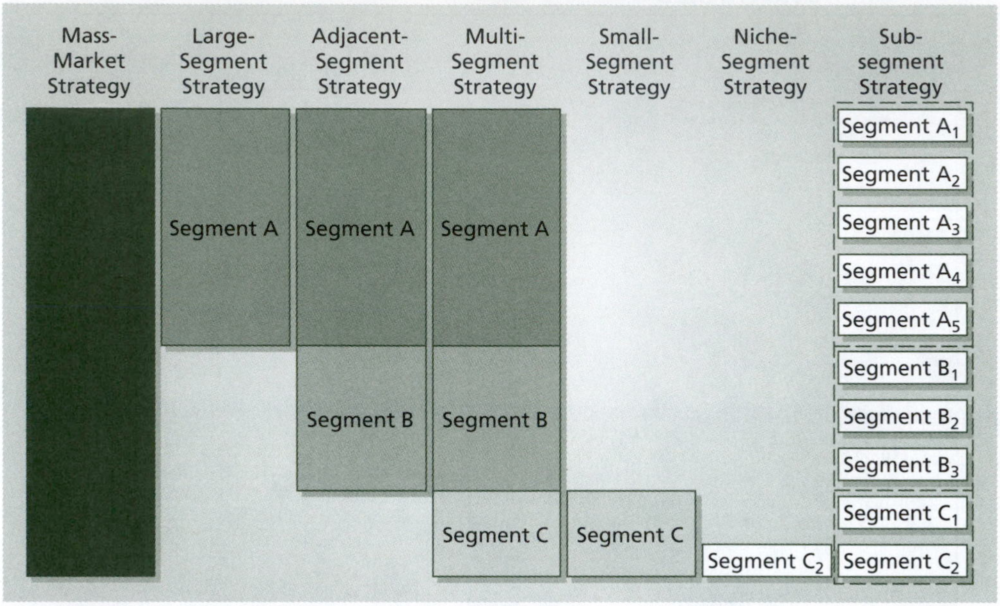

Mass-Market Strategy	Large-Segment Strategy	Adjacent-Segment Strategy	Multi-Segment Strategy	Small-Segment Strategy	Niche-Segment Strategy	Sub-segment Strategy
						Segment A_1
						Segment A_2
	Segment A	Segment A	Segment A			Segment A_3
						Segment A_4
						Segment A_5
						Segment B_1
		Segment B	Segment B			Segment B_2
						Segment B_3
						Segment C_1
			Segment C	Segment C	Segment C_2	Segment C_2

Caterpillar, Sony, Marlboro, ConocoPhillips, Toyota, Volvo, and Kodak are some of the many well-recognized global brands that use a global marketing strategy, although they sometimes modify their products and market communications to meet specific customer needs in different international markets.

Let's take a look at a company that shifted from a mass-market strategy to a segmentation strategy. James Hardie Industries is the market leader in the manufacturing and sales of fiber cement siding for homes and commercial buildings. For many years the company viewed its product as a commodity and sold it with a mass-market strategy at a price that was competitive with other siding products, as presented in Figure 5-16.

As the company grew, its managers became aware that customers were frustrated with the difficulty of achieving superior results when priming and painting the siding, as well as with the lack of finished trim for high-quality homes. James Hardie's customer research revealed that 30 percent of its customers would pay two to three times more per square foot for finished products. This led the company to offer preprimed and prepainted siding and a finished trim kit. The new products were aimed at customers who placed a high value not just on durability but also on the attractiveness of their homes and commercial buildings.

James Hardie divided its market into two segments: a quality segment for 30 percent of the market and a price segment for 70 percent of the market. The company's segmentation strategy for the quality segment, which had a higher average price per square foot, enabled percent margins, sales, and profits to grow at a faster rate.

Large-Segment Strategy

When a market is segmented and marketing resources are limited, a business could elect to pursue a large-segment strategy. As illustrated in Figure 5-15, a mass-market strategy

FIGURE 5-16 JAMES HARDIE—MASS-MARKET VERSUS SEGMENTATION STRATEGIES

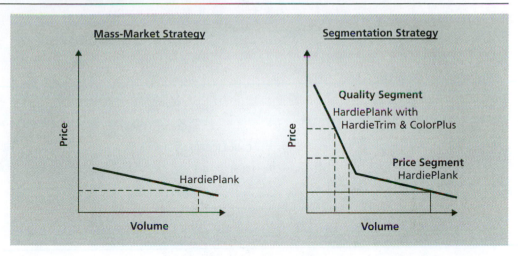

could divide a market into three core segments. A large-segment strategy would focus on segment A, because it is the largest, representing 50 percent of the market. Unlike a mass-market strategy, a large-segment strategy addresses one set of core customer needs. It engages the benefits of market segmentation and also provides a relatively large market demand. Chevy's truck strategy is a large-segment strategy. Because market demand is somewhat limited and a large segment exists, this strategy provides a cost-effective way to reach a large number of target customers.

Adjacent-Segment Strategy

Businesses quite often find that they have pursued a single-segment focus but have reached the point of full market penetration. When this is the case, an adjacent-segment strategy offers an attractive opportunity for market growth. Whenever resources are limited, the company markets to a closely related attractive segment first. Using profits derived from this segment, it then addresses the next most attractive adjacent segment.

In Figure 5-15, segment B is most similar to segment A. When a business has reached full penetration in segment A with a large-segment strategy, it may pursue new growth by entering segment B, an adjacent segment with respect to product and price needs. An example of this segmentation strategy was Toyota's adjacent-segment strategy in the U.S. car market between 1960 and 2000. Toyota entered the U.S. market in the late 1950s with the Corona, which was priced at the low end of the market (today the Yaris serves this segment). As Toyota penetrated the low-price segment, it moved to an adjacent segment in terms of price and quality by adding the Corolla in 1966, as shown in Figure 5-17. In the 1970s and 1980s, Toyota developed higher priced models for the quality-conscious segments. Next came entry into the luxury-car segment with the Lexus brand, an adjacent segment for the full-size Avalon, and then with the Prius the hybrid segment, in which Toyota has been a pioneer. Over a 40-year period, Toyota effectively used an

FIGURE 5-17 TOYOTA—ADJACENT-SEGMENT STRATEGY FOR PASSENGER CARS

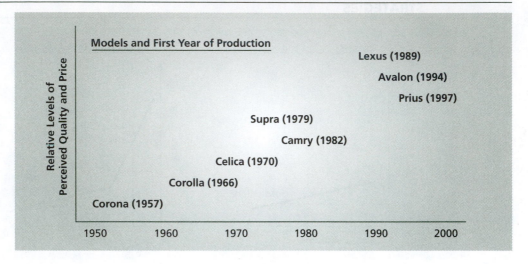

adjacent-segment strategy. Today—with more than 70 models of cars, sport utility vehicles, vans, and trucks—the company enjoys a strong position in nearly all segments of the automotive market.

Multi-Segment Strategies

Market segmentation opens the door to multiple market-based strategies and greater marketing efficiency. For decades, gas stations operated on the fundamental belief that gasoline purchases were made primarily on the basis of price, and it was this belief that guided their marketing strategy. However, a study of the needs of gas station customers uncovered five distinct segments, only one of which could be described as price shoppers.[15] The top three segments illustrated in Figure 5-18 were more concerned with quality, service, and the availability of other products, such as coffee, soft drinks, sandwiches, and snack foods. In addition, each of the top three segments in the figure (*road warriors, generation F3*, and *true blues*) produced more revenue per customer than *homebodies* (convenience buyers) and *price shoppers*. These three target segments, which make up 59 percent of gas station customers, produce more revenue per customer because they buy more gas, premium products, and food and beverages. In addition, the average margin per customer in each of these segments is higher than in the other two groups because the products they buy often have higher margins. By focusing on these three segments, a gasoline retailer could implement a series of marketing strategies to better serve the needs of these target segments and, if successful, could grow revenues and profits.

   An electrical equipment manufacturer developed an even more challenging multi-segment marketing strategy. Some 7,000 entities make up the electrical power generation and distribution market in the United States. A segmentation study of this market produced 12 distinct needs-based segments that differed in customer needs, firm demographics, and usage behavior,[16] as shown in Figure 5-19. At one extreme was a segment that included big, publicly owned utilities that had large engineering and maintenance staffs,

FIGURE 5-18 SEGMENTATION OF GASOLINE STATION CUSTOMER MARKET

Segment	Size (%)	Core Customer Needs	Usage Behavior	Key Demographics
Road Warriors	16	Premium Products and Quality Service	Drive 25,000 to 50,000 miles a year, buy premium gas, drinks, and sandwiches.	Higher income, middle-aged men.
Generation F3	27	Fast Fuel, Fast Service, and Fast Food	Constantly on the go; drive a lot, snack heavily, and want fuel and food fast.	Upwardly mobile men and women, half under 25.
True Blues	16	Branded Products and Reliable Service	Brand and station loyal; buy premium gas, pay cash.	Men and women with moderate to high income.
Homebodies	21	Convenience	Use whatever gasoline is conveniently located.	Usually housewives who shuttle children during day.
Price Shoppers	20	Low Price	Neither brand nor station loyal.	Usually on tight budget.

and at the other extreme were small co-ops that produced electricity for rural areas. One segment included businesses that produced electricity for their own consumption and sold excess power to the local utilities. The Los Angeles Performing Arts Center is a customer in this segment. The electric equipment manufacturer found that all identified segments were attractive to their target markets and already had sales to customers in each of them. The only difference was that, before the segmentation study, the business used a mass-market strategy and treated all customers roughly the same. After the study, it designed 12 separate marketing programs to meet the unique needs of each segment. The 12 different product-positioning and marketing approaches built a strong value proposition for each segment.

One regional vice president elected not to participate in the implementation of the multi-segment marketing strategy, so that region was designated the control group. The year that the multi-segment strategy was implemented, the overall market experienced a decline of 15 percent in sales. Despite the market's overall decline, regions A and B had significant sales increases, and region C, the control group, had a nominal increase, as shown in Figure 5-19. The business as a whole achieved a sales growth of more than 10 percent in a year that saw the market decline by 15 percent in sales volume. It is also important to note that this increase was achieved with essentially no change in marketing budget—simply a clearer market focus and a better allocation of marketing resources.

Small-Segment Strategy

Although a market may offer opportunities in several segments, a business with limited resources and certain capabilities may elect to compete in only the smallest segment. The

FIGURE 5-19 MULTI-SEGMENT STRATEGY FOR POWER GENERATION MARKET

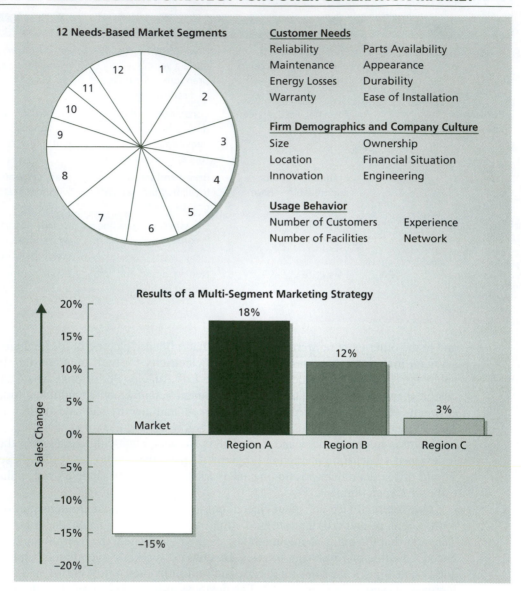

smallest segment, represented by segment C in Figure 5-15, is often ignored by large competitors, who may use mass-market or large-segment strategies. Even businesses with a multi-segment strategy may not be able to compete effectively with a business that has a singular-focus small-segment strategy. For many years, Mercedes used a small-segment strategy focused on the luxury car market. Having built a certain prestige in this market, Mercedes was reluctant to move into lower price-quality adjacent segments. However, because of the growing attractiveness of adjacent segments, Mercedes now pursues a dual-segment strategy.

Niche-Segment Strategies

Dividing a market into *homogeneous segments*—groups of customers with similar needs—is never a perfect process. Even when customers in a given segment share common needs, they still have differences in demographics or usage behaviors that cannot be addressed fully by a strategy designed for that segment. This situation provides an opportunity for another business to carve out a niche within the segment, using a highly refined marketing effort directed at this overlooked small group of target customers.

Consider the case of Sub-Zero refrigerators.[17] This business, which has less than a 2 percent share of the U.S. refrigerator market, competes with industry giants that have large economies of scale and marketing resources. But Sub-Zero holds 70 percent of the "super-premium" segment, a niche segment within the refrigerator market. It specializes in very expensive built-in refrigerators that start at $3,500. Target customers claim, "To own a Sub-Zero refrigerator is to have something special." It is hard to outperform niche competitors such as Sub-Zero because all their marketing resources are focused on the specific needs of a certain type of customer. Sub-Zero stays completely focused on a *niche market* that consists only of high-end customers who are seeking a super-premium refrigerator. For Sub-Zero, a needs-based market strategy is customized to the specific needs, lifestyle, and usage behavior of its niche customer.

Subsegment Strategies

Whether a market is divided into two segments or a dozen, as in Figure 5-19, it is always possible to identify additional customer differences. We might ask, then, "How many segments are enough?" A better question is: "Are there meaningful differences in customer needs within segments that are not being met with the current segmentation?"

If the answer to the second question is yes, then further needs-based segmentation is warranted. If the answer is no and core needs are met, then no further needs-based segmentation is required. Yet it is still possible that subsegments within a core segment could be addressed with more precise marketing strategies to better serve customer needs in those subsegments.

Figure 5-15 shows a market divided into three needs-based core segments: A, B, and C. Within each core segment are subsegments that could be served with more customized marketing programs according to differences in product use or demographics. In this illustration, the segmentation strategy for segment A could be further customized to the use situation experienced for each of the five subsegments (A_1, A_2, A_3, A_4, and A_5). Each one represents an opportunity to refine the core segment marketing strategy, tailoring it to the individual needs of the target customers in those subsegments.

For example, in Figure 5-20 we have expanded the two needs-based core segments of the fiber-cement home siding market presented in Figure 5-16 to include subsegments within each core segment. In the quality segment, the custom-home buyers and spec-home builders generally have greater need for high-quality appearance. Because architects and custom-home builders are important members of this subsegment, a subsegment strategy could be developed to better serve their application needs. James Hardie developed

FIGURE 5-20 CORE AND SUBSEGMENTS IN THE FIBER-CEMENT SIDING MARKET

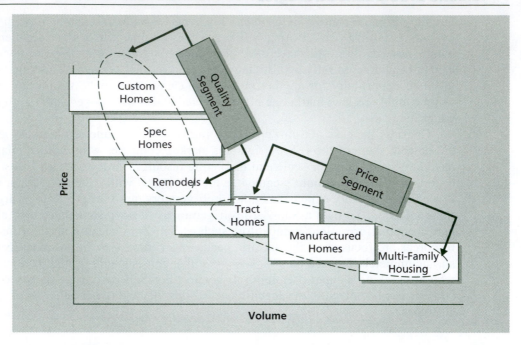

the ColorPlus and HardiTrim products to better serve the needs of these subsegment customers. Also within the same quality segment are remodeling projects by builders and home owners who both want a quality appearance but have slightly different needs. Subsegment strategies could be developed to better serve the unique needs of the remodeling subsegment.

The price segment is also divided into three subsegments. Although they are all driven primarily by price and installation costs, these subsegment customers differ from one another because they encounter different problems in using fiber-cement siding in tract homes, manufactured homes, and multi-family housing units. Appropriate subsegment strategies could be developed to meet the needs of each of these smaller customer groups. Any subsegment that does not warrant a specific marketing strategy is served with the core strategy for the price segment.

The addition of subsegment customization allows a business to add value to its product and build customer loyalty. But there is a trade-off between the cost of extending extra benefits to subsegments of a core segment and the incremental financial benefit to the company. In some instances, the improvement in customer profitability and loyalty may be so slight that it does not justify the creation of a separate subsegment strategy. When this is the case, the subsegment customers may be served using the core-segment strategy created for that segment's needs and usage behaviors. As the profit potential for any given subsegment increases, it becomes more advantageous for a business to reach these subsegment customers with personalized marketing communications.

CUSTOMER RELATIONSHIP MARKETING

Many businesses work hard to acquire new customers, but this is where the effort to promote good customer relations often stops. By contrast, customer relationship marketing is more focused on what happens after a customer is acquired. The goal of customer relationship marketing is to develop a long-term customer relationship that benefits both the customer and the company. Consider how Wells Fargo looks at individual customer relationships:

> Much of the time, the opening of a new customer account is simply an opportunity to lose money. Most single-account households are unprofitable. We have to build a relationship to make a profit. If we can build a relationship, then we can keep customers through relationship building—not pushing products. They will reward us by buying more, buying profitably, and keeping more of their money with us.[18]

As the potential for greater company value and customer value increases, the company gains an opportunity to extend its market segmentation to individual customers. As shown in Figure 5-21, customer relationship marketing includes three different strategies for three different groups of customers as determined by company value and customer value.

FIGURE 5-21 CUSTOMER RELATIONSHIP MARKETING STRATEGIES

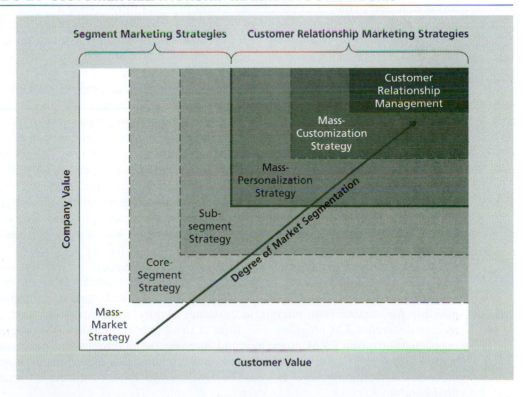

Customer relationship marketing is often called customer relationship management, but these two terms have distinct meanings:

- *Customer relationship marketing (CRM)* is a range of one-on-one relationship marketing programs based on the level of company and customer value, as illustrated in Figure 5-21.
- *Customer relationship management* is a high-level CRM program for developing ongoing individualized relationships with certain customers when both company and customer value are high enough to warrant this level of marketing effort.

Customer Value versus Company Value

Before going any further, we will define company value and how it differs from customer value. Customers achieve greater customer value when the overall perceived benefits they derive from products, services, and brand exceed by a meaningful margin the cost of obtaining these benefits (see "Customer Value Index" in Chapter 4). CRM attempts to create additional customer value through personalized communications, extra services, customized products, and special price offerings. Of course, these added customer benefits come at some cost to the customer. When customers perceive that the overall benefits exceed the overall costs by a meaningful margin, there is an attractive level of customer value in the relationship that a business has built with its customers.

Companies view value in more economic terms. As we saw in Chapter 1, higher levels of repeat purchase extended over longer periods of time create a higher customer lifetime value. As customer loyalty grows and customer retention increases, the lifetime value of the customer relationship also increases. Highly satisfied loyal customers have been shown to be more profitable. They typically buy more and often buy premium-priced products and services. The combination of higher customer profitability and higher customer loyalty creates a higher customer lifetime value based on the discounted cash flow over the life of the customer (see "Customer Lifetime Value" in Chapter 1).

Figure 5-21 indicates that as customer value and company value grow to the benefit of both, a business may engage in higher levels of customer relationship marketing. Within any given segment or subsegment, not all customers will have the potential for high levels of company value and customer value. For example, perhaps only 10 percent of all the builders and architects in the custom-home subsegment of the fiber-cement siding quality-market segment will offer the right combination of company value and customer value to warrant a customer relationship management program. The other 90 percent of the custom-home subsegment could be served with a mass-personalization strategy, as shown in Figure 5-21.

CRM requires a higher level of marketing effort and expense, so the company must be certain it is warranted before undertaking it. When both customer value and company value are favorable, a business can justify a one-on-one CRM marketing program. It is possible for customers to migrate in customer loyalty and profitability and thereby receive different CRM programs over time. A mass-personalization CRM program or a mass-customization CRM program could increase the purchases and profitability of some customers to a point at which a customer relationship management program of individualized customer services would be developed for those customers to further build their loyalty.

Database Marketing

At the core of customer relationship marketing is *database marketing*.[19] Each customer is treated as unique in CRM, and the goal is to build a more personal relationship between the business and the customer. The only two differences in the three basic kinds of CRM programs are the level of company effort and the level of customer benefit. To determine how much effort a customer deserves, a business must have enough data to know each customer's individual needs, buying behavior, and individual product preferences.

Advances in database marketing technologies have lured many businesses down a side road where technology is seen as the solution instead of as a tool for implementing the solution. Without a solid commitment to serving individual customer needs, these businesses can fall into a *technology trap*. Many millions of dollars have been wasted in developing technological approaches for marketing to customers without first strategizing a CRM program.

The amount of customer data that is required depends on which CRM strategy will be used. Some customers may be targeted with a *mass-personalization* program that relies on personalized communications. Others may be served with a *mass-customization* strategy based on their buying behavior and individual needs for product and service customization. Still others who have high levels of customer value and company value may be good candidates for an individualized customer relationship management program.

Certain customers across segments may be excellent candidates for one of the three CRM programs. For example, with regard to Figure 5-20, it is possible that certain contractors in the tract-home building subsegment would be best served with a mass-personalization strategy, whereas others warrant a customer relationship management program. The overall goal of CRM is to serve customer needs as much as possible, subject to the cost of serving these needs (extra marketing and sales expenses), in light of the results (customer loyalty and long-term customer profitability). The rest of this chapter discusses the three CRM programs that make up the field of database marketing.

Mass Personalization

The first level of customer relationship marketing is a *mass-personalization strategy* that recognizes individual customers by name, needs, and buying behavior. In order to implement this strategy, a business's database marketing system must be able to track individual customers and their buying history, segment needs, and segment value proposition. This information is then used to develop personalized marketing communications for target customers.

American Express is a good example of a company that has had success with a mass-personalization strategy. The company has a core market segment labeled *zero spenders*.[20] Zero spenders are customers who hold an American Express Card and pay the annual fee but rarely or never use their cards. These customers are marginally profitable and are the most likely to defect. But not all customers in this segment are the same. Some are not using the card because they can't afford much discretionary spending, while others are using cash or a competitor's card. American Express developed a mass-personalization promotional program for this core segment in the hope of distinguishing the high-potential subsegment customers. High-potential customers who were attracted to these promotions self-select to participate in them, which enables American Express to identify this subsegment for future promotions in an effort to build card usage and customer loyalty.

Another example is the United Airlines Frequent Flyer Mileage Plus program. This mass-personalization program allows customers to extend their involvement with United Airlines by joining the Frequent Flyer Program, which in turn allows United to establish personalized communications and mileage awards based on the level of each customer's travel. Customers who travel more are given more customer benefits. Frequent flyers can migrate to United Premium, Executive Premium, and 100K customer status. At each level, customer personalization increases with respect to mileage bonuses, ticket class upgrades, and personalized services, including access to exclusive toll-free numbers for faster customer reservations and problem solving.

United Airlines is striving to build customer retention and customer profitability with this mass-personalization program that adds value for its frequent flyers. The goal is to personalize customer interaction with the company, extending different levels of benefits to target customers based on the potential for growing customer loyalty and customer profitability. As United expands these marketing efforts to include extra services or modified product offerings that build one-on-one marketing relationships, the company is moving closer to a mass-customization program.

Mass Customization

Market segmentation and subsegmentation recognize that customers value a product's benefits differently; in fact, some customers within a segment are willing to pay more for extra benefits.[21] It is difficult, however, to offer customers in the same segment different product-price configurations. Mass customization allows a company to do this because the marketing mix is customized to the level of individual customer product preferences, extended services, and prices. Mass customization allows each customer to build a custom product to meet that customer's specific needs, personal constraints, and price considerations.

Perhaps the most successful example of mass customization is Dell, Inc. On Dell's web site, customers can choose from a variety of options to create their own computer configurations, which are then built to order and shipped within a short time.

Figure 5-22 illustrates how mass customization can be applied to the purchase of a notebook computer. Customers start with a base model and customize it with options that fit their needs and budget. A great many different configurations are possible for a notebook computer, and this process lets potential customers weigh the costs and benefits of each option before selecting the ones that are best suited for their personal situations.

The use of mass customization essentially allows customers to become their own individual market segments. This is good for the customer as well as the business, because even the same customer, as we have seen, may have different needs over time. A number of companies are launching programs of mass customization, giving some validity to the word "customer." Products ranging from a Lexus to a Barbie doll can now be individualized to suit a buyer's unique tastes. The whole point of mass customization is to let customers "build their products" according to their individual needs and price sensitivity. Mass customization combines the advantages of a niche-segment

FIGURE 5-22 MASS CUSTOMIZATION FOR THE ONLINE PURCHASE OF A LAPTOP COMPUTER

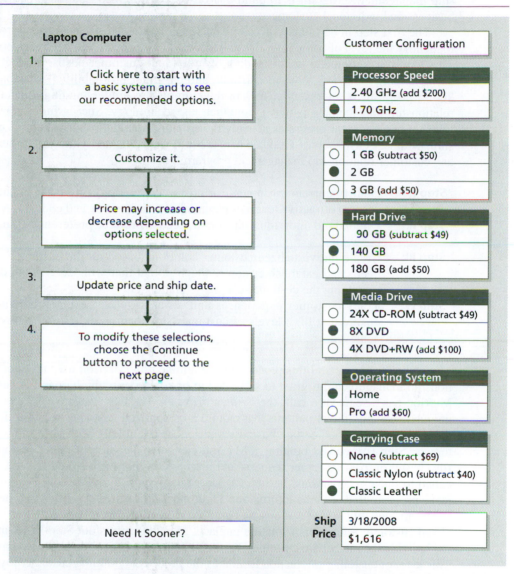

strategy with the breadth of opportunity that is available with multi-segment marketing strategies.

Customer Relationship Management

When the potential exists for high levels of both customer value and company value, the company can justify using a customer relationship management program. Although needs-based market segmentation strives to build programs around target customers' needs in an effort to satisfy and retain customers, the ultimate goal of a customer relationship management program is to build one-on-one customized relationships between a business and individual customers.[22]

The first step in building a successful customer relationship management program is to identify the level of company value and the level of customer value for each customer. This requires a complete understanding of individual customer needs, product preferences, buying behaviors, customer loyalty, and customer profitability. A database marketing program is an essential tool in developing this understanding, but customer relationship management is much more than just technology. Successful customer relationship management programs actually develop and maintain individualized relationships with key customers.[23] Outlined here are four steps that are critical to the success of any customer relationship management program.

Step I: Qualify current customers for customer relationship management on the basis of attractive levels of potential customer value and company value.

Step II: Understand individual customer needs, product preferences, and usage behaviors.

Step III: Create individualized customer solutions based on the customer's unique needs and establish customer touch points that will serve in building and sustaining the customer-company relationship.

Step IV: Track customer experiences and all aspects of customer satisfaction to ensure that high levels of customer satisfaction and customer loyalty are achieved.

To better understand this process, let's examine how Marriott uses a customer relationship management program to serve its top performers and high-potential customers. Marriott has a segment it calls the *business traveler*. The business traveler customer has unique needs and travel patterns that require a customized customer solution. In Step I, the company identified certain business travelers as potentially profitable and loyal customers. Step II involved building a Marriott customer database of target customer profiles based on past customer requests and preferences that were stored when customers called to make reservations. In Step III, Marriott developed its Personal Planning Service, a program that uses the information about individual customer needs to schedule tee times, arrange dinner reservations, and propose recreation itineraries. With this individualized customer relationship solution in place, Marriott carries out Step IV by maintaining individual contact with customers to measure all aspects of their customer experience. This level of customer interaction facilitates the process of building customer loyalty and tracking customer performance.

For Marriott, high customer-satisfaction scores have translated into higher levels of repeat business and customer loyalty. Marriott has learned that customers who participate in its Personal Planning Service produce significantly higher customer-satisfaction scores and spend an average of $100 per day *more* on services beyond the room rate. The program has not only improved customer loyalty among business travelers who spend more on supplementary services, it has also resulted in an occupancy rate that is 10 percent higher than the industry average.

An important concept in customer relationship management is *customer touch points*. Every interaction with a customer or a potential customer is a *touch point*. Customer touch points include in-store interactions, web sites, voice mail systems, direct-mail advertising, mass e-mail messages, order desks, return counters, and service calls. Indirect customer touch points are less obvious but sometimes even more important in turning potential customers into actual customers. These are often informational contacts, such as news articles and word-of-mouth advertising. They are powerful forces in shaping the beliefs and attitudes of potential customers toward the business and its products and services.

At every point of contact—before, during, and after a sale—a business's communication affects its relationships with customers and potential customers. The way a business manages each customer relationship from the first touch point determines the long-run profit potential of that customer.

■ Summary

Millennials represent a worldwide lifestyle segment that is defined by age (18–24 years) and driven by fundamental needs for creatively, identity, and having fun. With 840 million Millennials worldwide, this age group is a significant consumer segment. The segment's importance is amplified by the influence Millennials have on younger and older consumers, which extends the Millennials' sphere of influence to 2.3 billion people. To reach Millennials and other consumer segments, companies conduct market segmentation.

Skillfully executed market-segmentation efforts lie at the heart of market-based management. Market segmentation is the core of a market-based strategy because it is built around unique customer needs, different lifestyles, and different usage behaviors. To the extent that a business understands differences in its customers' needs, lifestyles, and product usage, it can translate them into actionable segment strategies. The segmentation process we examined in the most detail emphasized the identification of needs-based segments. Although it may be easy to create segments based on differences in demographics or behavior, doing so can lead to a marketing strategy that does not deliver a needs-based customer solution. Demographics shape customer needs, and demographics often (but do not always) serve as a measurable way to identify needs-based market segments. The first step is to identify segments based on needs. Then a business should identify needs-based segments by demography and create actionable strategies for each segment.

These first two steps are critical. The next steps in the segmentation process require that we index overall segment attractiveness and estimate segment profit potential to select target segments. A value proposition and marketing mix strategy must be developed for each target segment selected. The segment "acid test" is one way to ensure that we have accurately translated target customer needs and identity characteristics into our positioning strategy (value proposition and marketing mix). The test enables a business to determine whether a segment's target customers are adequately attracted to the segment value proposition and the segment strategy designed for them. Customer feedback can contribute to the development of a revised strategy.

In some instances, resources may be limited and the company may only be able to pursue a single segment or niche (subsegment) within a segment. In other instances, a business may have the resources and capabilities to implement a multi-segment strategy. But the more segments a business has, the more difficulty it encounters in maintaining a distinct marketing strategy for each. By using database marketing, a business can take either a single-segment strategy or a multi-segment strategy one step further with a customer relationship marketing (CRM) program. CRM programs include mass-personalization strategies, mass-customization strategies, and customer relationship management strategies. The first type of strategy allows a business to personalize its marketing communications to target customers, using a refined value proposition. The second essentially lets customers design the product for their individual needs. An effective mass-customization program enables a multi-segment business to obtain the advantages of a niche marketer; it can serve not only its larger segments, but also subsegments and even additional subsegments, or niches, within those subsegments.

A logical extension of mass customization is customer relationship management. The ultimate goal of customer relationship management is to develop an ongoing individual relationship between a business and its most profitable individual customers. Because not all customers can be served by a business's customer relationship management program, we first determine the levels of customer value and company value for each customer. After customers for the program have been identified, the business develops customized solutions for their product or service needs and uses touch points to maintain ongoing relationships with the customers in an effort to increase their loyalty and profitability.

■ Market-Based Strategic Thinking

1   Why are Millennials important to a company like Apple or Campbell's Soup?
2   How have the lifestyles of Millennials influenced the use of social media and iPhones among older consumers?
3   Why would Coca-Cola advertise in magazines read by Millennials?
4   Why should customer needs be the driving force in segmenting the toothpaste market?
5   What kind of problems could occur if a manufacturer of large machine tools segments its market on the basis of firm demographics?
6   For an automobile purchase, how are customer needs shaped, and what role do these forces play in the segmentation process?
7   What happens when an insurance company is able to segment a market on the basis of needs for automobile insurance but unable to identify the segments by demography or behavior?
8   How do firm demographics help shape business-to-business customer needs for commercial printers?
9   What forces shape market attractiveness for the iPad, and how should they be measured in order to develop an overall index of market attractiveness?
10   What criteria should be used in determining the segments that an insurance company should pursue for its automobile insurance policies?
11   How did market segmentation help James Hardie in its marketing strategy?
12   What would be a segment value proposition for the quality segment served by James Hardie (see Figure 5-16)? Why is it a crucial part of the segmentation process?
13   How would you develop a value proposition for a retail gasoline segment presented in Figure 5-18?
14   How does the marketing mix strategy differ for each of the three segments of the female investor services market presented in Figure 5-9?

15 How would you conduct a segment strategy "acid test" using the three storyboards presented in Figure 5-13? What are the advantages of applying the test?

16 How did DuPont create an effective multi-segment strategy for Kevlar?

17 What would be an adjacent-segment strategy in the toothpaste market (see Figure 5-5)?

18 Why would a business pursue an adjacent-segment strategy when several other segments are also attractive and offer good profit potential?

19 Why would a new business pursue a single-segment strategy?

20 Why is it often difficult for competitors to outperform a niche strategy as used by Pajamagram (pajamagram.com) or Vermont Teddy Bear (vermontteddybear.com)?

21 Why does Dell use mass customization? How could a large company using a mass-customization strategy match the effectiveness of a niche competitor?

22 How could customer relationship marketing be used by a travel agency, and why would it likely improve the travel agency's customer satisfaction and retention?

23 Why is market segmentation a critical first step in building a customer relationship marketing program for Lexus?

24 What are customer touch points for a regional bank, and what role do they play in customer relationship marketing?

Marketing Performance Tools and Application Exercises

The five interactive marketing performance tools and application exercises outlined here will strengthen your understanding of segmentation strategies and customer relationship marketing. To access the tools, go to **roger-jbest.com.** For many of the questions, you can determine the answers by entering data included in the questions. You may also enter other data to see the results, and you can save your work. Each application exercise is based on the Chapter 5 figure in parentheses.

5.1   Needs-Based Segmentation (Figure 5-3)

A. Using the laptop product-price configuration provided, create a needs-based segment for laptop users who have home businesses and work on their laptops 4 to 6 hours a day, including while on out-of-town business trips.

B. Next, using the laptop product-price configuration provided, create a needs-based segment for a high school student with a limited budget who wants to buy a laptop for school assignments, e-mail, and entertainment.

5.2   Segment Identification (Figure 5-4)

A. For the home business segment, edit the consumer profile characteristics and indicate which consumer demographics, lifestyle, and usage behaviors make this type of potential customer identifiable.

B. For the high school student segment, edit the consumer profile characteristics and indicate which consumer demographics, lifestyle, and usage behaviors make this type of potential customer identifiable.

C. What are the most important characteristics that differentiate one segment from the other? How would knowing those characteristics help a business develop its marketing communications strategy?

5.3   Segment Profitability

A. For the price segment, what would be the profit impact of a 10 percent decrease in price if market share could be increased from 2 to 3 percent?

B. For the quality segment, what would be the profit impact of a strategy to increase the marketing budget from 10 to 15 percent of sales in an effort to increase market share from 2 to 3 percent?

5.4   The "Acid Test" for Segment Strategies (Figure 5-5)

A. For the "worrier" segment, create a storyboard similar to the ones in Figure 5-13. If possible, add a picture from a magazine that represents the customer identity of this segment.

B. Do the same for the "sociable" segment.

C. Create a third storyboard with no segment identity, average product features, and a mid-range price.

5.5   Customer Relationship Marketing

A. Using the data provided, estimate how customer profitability and lifetime value change for the mass-personalization program if the customer retention dropped from 67 to 60 percent.

B. At what percent margin would the mass-customization program no longer produce a positive customer profit?

Notes

1. C.M. Christensen, S. Cook, and T. Hall, "Marketing Malpractice: The Cause and the Cure," *Harvard Business Review* (December 2005): 74–83.

2. C. Phillips, "What Appeals to Millennials? Ten Brands That Hit the Mark," Brand Amplitude LLC (September 3, 2008): http://brandamplitude.com/millennial_marketing/millennial_marketing.htm, retrieved January 2011.

3. D. Yankelovich and D. Meer, "Rediscovering Market Segmentation," *Harvard Business Review* (February 2006): 131.

4. R. Gulati, "Silo Busting: How to Execute on the Promise of Customer Focus," *Harvard Business Review* (May 2007): 98–108.

5. D. Hawkins, R. Best, and K. Coney, *Consumer Behavior: Implications for Marketing Strategy*, 6th ed. (New York: Irwin, 1995): 4–25.

6. M. McDonald, "Needs-based Market Segmentation—The Unchanging Bedrock of Successful Strategy," Oxford College of Marketing (February 12, 2010): http://blog.oxfordcollegeofmarketing.com, retrieved January 2011.

7. M. Greenberg and S.M. Schwartz, "Successful Needs/Benefits Segmentation: A User's Guide," *Journal of Consumer Marketing* (Summer 1989): 29–36.

8. "Merrill Lynch Campaign Targeted at Women Stresses Investment Options," *Marketing News* (November 30, 1979): 11.

9. S. Gupta and P. Chintagunta, "On Using Demographic Variables to Determine Segment Membership in Logit Mixture Models," *Journal of Marketing Research* (February 1994): 128.

10. Quotation from conference addresses by Charles M. Lillis. Used here with permission.

11. M. Lanning, *Delivering Profitable Value* (Reading, MA: Perseus Books, 1998): 39–88.

12. W. Band, "Customer-Accelerated Change," *Marketing Management* (Winter 1995): 19–33.

13. P. Dickson and J. Ginter, "Market Segmentation, Product Differentiation, and Marketing Strategy," *Journal of Marketing* (April 1987): 1–10.

14. G. Coles and J. Culley, "Not All Prospects Are Created Equal," *Business Marketing* (May 1986): 52–9.

15. A. Sullivan, "Mobil Bets Drivers Pick Cappuccino Over Parties," *Wall Street Journal* (January 30, 1995): B1.

16. D. Gensch, "Targeting the Switchable Industrial Customer," *Marketing Science* (Winter 1984): 41–54.

17. J. Levine, "Cool!" *Forbes* (April 1996): 98.

18. M. Nykamp, *The Customer Differential* (New York: AMACOM, 2001): 11.

19. S. Rapp and T. Collins, *MaxiMarketing* (New York: McGraw-Hill, 1987); J. Berry, "Database Marketing—A Potent New Tool for Selling," *Business Week* (September 5, 1995): 56; and R. Buzzell and R. Sisoda, "Information Technology and Marketing," *Companion Encyclopedia of Marketing*, Michael Baker, ed. (Los Angeles: Rutledge, 1995).

20. L. O'Brien and C. Jones, "Do Rewards Really Create Loyalty," *Harvard Business Review* (May–June, 1995): 75–82.

21. J. Gilmore and J. Pine II, "The Four Faces of Mass Customization," *Harvard Business Review* (January–February 1997): 91–103.

22. D. Peppers and M. Rogers, *The One-On-One Future: Building Relationships One Customer at a Time* (New York: Doubleday, 1997).

23. D. Peppers and M. Rogers, *One to One B2B: Customer Development Strategies for the Business to Business World* (New York: Doubleday, 2001).

CHAPTER 6

Competitive Position
and Sources of Advantage

■ Value, instead of cost, must be used in
analyzing competitive position.[1]

Shown in the price-performance value map is the competitive position of 10 competing midsize SUVs. The positioning of the SUVs is based on *Consumer Reports'* ratings of 2010 models, along with each model's average selling price.[2]

Value maps provide insights into competitive position and customer value. Brand 3 clearly offers the best customer value. It has slightly above-average performance and the price is $5,600 below the fair price line (the price a buyer would expect to pay for that level of performance). Brand 4 offers a good value for buyers who are looking for performance significantly above average. The brands above the fair price line have a negative value. Appendix 6.1 identifies each brand, along with its overall performance, average selling price, fair price, and customer value.

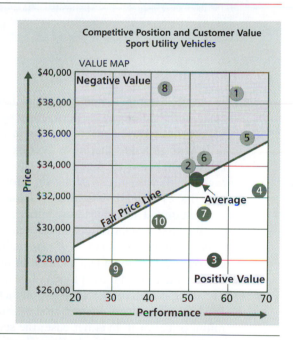

Competitive Position and Customer Value
Sport Utility Vehicles

COMPETITIVE ADVANTAGE

A competitive advantage results in some level of superior customer value, as summarized by Michel Porter in his highly recognized book, *Competitive Strategy*.

Competitive advantage grows fundamentally from the value a firm is able to create. Value is what buyers are willing to pay, and superior value stems from offering lower prices than competitors for equivalent benefits or providing unique benefits that more than offset higher prices.[3]

FIGURE 6-1 COMPETITIVE ADVANTAGE, CUSTOMER VALUE, AND PROFITABILITY

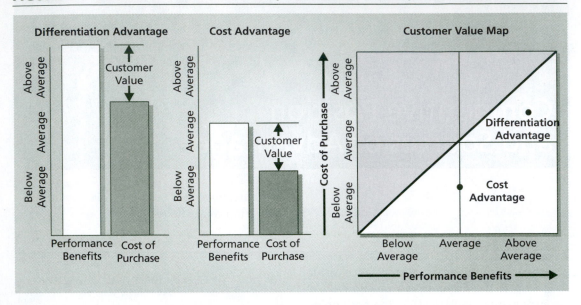

A competitive advantage results in some level of superior customer value based on a customer's preference for performance benefits, the cost of the purchase, and the ease of the purchase. Businesses with a *cost advantage* are able to create superior customer value even with products that have average performance benefits if the businesses offer the products at below-average cost. Businesses that have a meaningful *differentiation advantage* are likewise able to create superior customer value with above-average performance benefits, even at above-average prices.

Figure 6-1 illustrates how either low cost of purchase or high performance benefits can create customer value and how customer value can be mapped. Businesses that have either of these two sources of competitive advantage find it easier to attract and retain customers. It is important to keep in mind, however, that the two sources of customer value attract two different kinds of customers.

Price-sensitive customers are attracted by a lower purchase price, and performance-conscious customers are attracted by superior performance and are willing to pay a premium price for it. In either case, the superior customer value results in superior profits. As Figure 6-2 illustrates, businesses with above-average customer value produce higher levels of pre-tax return on investment. Businesses with an average customer value, where the cost of purchase equals performance benefits, produce average pre-tax profits. The businesses in this second group need to spend more to acquire customers, and they have more difficulty retaining customers because their value propositions are merely average. The net result is average profits.

Businesses with a negative customer value, where the cost of purchase exceeds performance benefits, produce a negative value and have difficulties attracting customers and even greater difficulties keeping them. These businesses have been shown to produce lower profits and tend to lose market share.

FIGURE 6-2 COMPETITIVE ADVANTAGE, CUSTOMER VALUE, AND PROFITABILITY

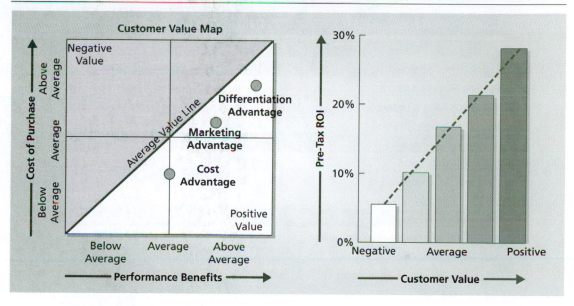

Either a cost advantage or a differentiation advantage improves a business's competitiveness. A third source of competitive advantage takes the form of a *marketing advantage*. Businesses that can create a superior customer value with high levels of market share and brand awareness, along with broad product lines and highly effective distribution systems, have a marketing advantage. Businesses that have a marketing advantage as the result of high levels of brand awareness and brand preference have a positive customer value, as shown in Figure 6-2.

In many instances, a business with a marketing advantage will have a market share that is considerably higher than its closest competitor. Its strong market presence creates high brand awareness and brand recognition, enabling it to attract new customers more easily. Although such a business does not offer lower cost or greater benefits, it does create customer value with a high brand reputation, a broad product line offering a variety of choices, and excellent product distribution that lowers customers' transaction costs. As Figure 6-2 shows, businesses with a marketing advantage typically have prices at or slightly above average prices. The combination of high share (high volume) and slightly higher prices (higher margins) contributes to above-average profits.

To achieve above-average profits, a business has to develop some source of competitive advantage that provides target customers with positive customer value. Figure 6-3 presents three aspects of performance for three well-known companies, each of which is pursuing a different source of competitive advantage.

■ **Dell—Cost Advantage:** Dell's low-cost direct-marketing strategy is well known and has allowed the company to emerge from being unknown to being among the share leaders in the personal computer market. Compared with the other two companies

FIGURE 6-3 COMPANY SOURCES OF ADVANTAGE AND COMPANY PERFORMANCE

Company Performance (2010)	Dell	Apple	Nike
Source of Advantage:	Low Cost	Differentiation	Marketing
Financial Performance			
Percent Gross Margin	19.1%	42.9%	55.9%
Return on Sales (pre-tax)	4.2%	29.8%	20.3%
Return on Assets (pre-tax)	6.5%	24.5%	12.5%
Asset Management			
Sales-to-Assets Ratio	1.57	0.82	1.32
Accounts Receivable (days)	40	58	24
Inventory (days)	7	6	28
Marketing Performance			
Marketing & Sales Expenses (% sales)	9.2%	6.7%	23.8%
Marketing Return on Sales	9.9%	36.3%	32.1%
Marketing Return on Investment	107%	545%	135%

shown in Figure 6-3, Dell's percent gross margin in 2010 was much lower, but its sales-to-assets ratio was the highest. Efficient asset management is a key part of a low-cost producer strategy. Dell produces $1.57 in sales for every dollar in assets.

■ **Apple—Differentiation Advantage:** Apple's product innovation and brand loyalty put it in a special class of companies that have realized success with a differentiation strategy. As Figure 6-3 shows, Apple has achieved superior financial performance and outstanding marketing performance, producing a marketing ROI of 545 percent. The company's return on sales and return on assets are far higher than its competitors, primarily because its products are premium priced as they offer highly specialized performance benefits as part of their product differentiation advantage.

■ **Nike—Marketing Advantage:** Nike is a powerful marketing company. It builds brands with innovative advertising and dominates channels with an aggressive sales force. Nike's products are produced abroad, lowering Nike's investment in assets, and they command premium prices, so the company realizes very attractive margins. With its emphasis on marketing, however, the cost of marketing and sales are considerably higher as a percentage of sales, as Figure 6-3 shows. In 2010 the company produced $1.32 in sales for every dollar in assets.

Sustainable Advantage

Dell, Apple, and Nike are examples of companies that were just beginning to emerge in the 1970s and 1980s. Although the three companies have seen stellar sales growth and performance during the past 20 years, there is no guarantee that they will have the same success over the next 20 years. Sustaining a source of competitive advantage is a challenge not to be taken lightly. Many great companies have come and gone as their sources of competitive advantage were nullified by competitors. In many instances, those competitors did not even exist prior to the mid-1970s.

The successes of Dell, Apple, and Nike are impressive. But even for these businesses, maintaining a competitive advantage is difficult because the competitive environment is always changing. To stay ahead, these companies must continuously update their customer and competitor knowledge and monitor their level of competitive advantage. Consider General Motors, NBC, or Sears: the strong competitive position held by each of these market leaders for so many years has changed dramatically. For General Motors, it was foreign competition that eroded its competitive position—first with lower prices and then with higher levels of product quality. For NBC, as well as for CBS and ABC, it was first ESPN, CNN, and Fox, and then a multitude of cable networks and the Internet. For Sears and other long-established large retailers of consumer goods, it was Wal-Mart, Target, Best Buy, and Costco.

In each case, the market leader once held an almost impenetrable competitive position. And in each case, when new competitive forces emerged, the competitive position of the market leader seriously eroded. It is important to recognize that in each example, the market leader had not lowered quality, raised prices, or curtailed marketing efforts. On the contrary, each made intense efforts to improve products, reduce prices, and expand marketing efforts to retain customers. But in each case, the competitive forces brought to bear on its market first challenged, and then eroded, the market leader's competitive position.

The challenge of sustainable competitive advantage led former Intel CEO Andrew Grove to write a book titled *Only the Paranoid Survive*.[4] The core message of Dr. Grove's book is that a company in pursuit of a stronger competitive advantage never rests. Attaining a competitive advantage is a continuous process of innovation and a never-ending effort to understand customer needs, both the needs being met and the needs remaining unfulfilled. To date, Dell, Apple, and Nike have done a great job as they continue to expand their product lines while leveraging their core sources of competitive advantage. However, the daunting challenge is that they can never stop. If they do, they will be on the road to losing their sources of competitive advantage.

SOURCES OF COMPETITIVE ADVANTAGE

As a business begins to more fully grasp its position relative to key competitors, it gains more insight into potential sources of competitive advantage. For a source of relative advantage to be a competitive advantage requires that (1) the area of relative advantage be meaningful to target customers, and (2) the relative advantage be sustainable (not easily copied by competitors). Wal-Mart, for example, has developed a cost advantage that has enabled it to attract and satisfy target customers by offering lower prices. Hewlett-Packard has built a differentiation advantage with product innovation and quality, and Nordstrom has built a differentiation advantage with service quality. All three companies attract and satisfy customers with differentially superior products or services. Nike and Procter & Gamble, on the other hand, have developed their marketing advantages by building their brand reputations and using creative retailing that attracts and satisfies target customers. In each case, the business developed a source of competitive advantage that is meaningful to target customers. This source of competitive advantage becomes an area of daily focus for managers in order to sustain their business's level of competitive advantage.

FIGURE 6-4 SOURCES OF COMPETITIVE ADVANTAGE

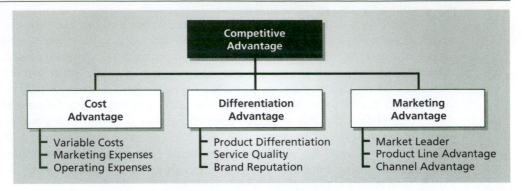

With Dell, Apple, and Nike, we saw three primary sources of competitive advantage. The three sources are shown in Figure 6-4 and may be summarized in this way:

- **Cost Advantage:** A significantly lower cost position from which to create lower prices while still achieving desirable profit margins.
- **Differentiation Advantage:** A meaningful differentiation that creates desired performance benefits at a level superior to those of competitors.
- **Marketing Advantage:** A market position and marketing effort that dominates the competition in brand recognition, product line, and channels of distribution.

COST ADVANTAGE

A business can achieve three different types of cost advantage, as listed in Figure 6-4. It can achieve a lower variable cost per unit sold, a lower level of marketing and sales expenses, or a lower level of operating and overhead expense. Each type of cost advantage can be achieved in several ways. As demonstrated in Figure 6-5, a cost advantage relative to competition contributes to higher levels of profitability.

Variable Cost Advantage

Businesses with a lower unit cost are able to achieve the same (or better) margins at lower prices than competing businesses. Unit or variable costs include manufacturing costs and costs associated with distribution, such as discounts, sales commissions, transportation, and other transaction costs.

But how does a business achieve a variable cost advantage? Volume is a key factor. Businesses with a substantial market share advantage (volume) can generally achieve a lower unit cost.[5] As volume increases, the cost per unit generally decreases. For example, as demonstrated in Figure 6-6, the cost of providing cellular phone service to each customer decreases by 20 percent every time the volume of customers in a geographic market doubles. For example, when a cellular business doubles its customer base from 400,000 to 800,000, the unit cost decreases by 20 percent. The cellular service company that attains the largest customer penetration (volume) achieves the lowest unit cost.

FIGURE 6-5 COST ADVANTAGE AND PROFITABILITY

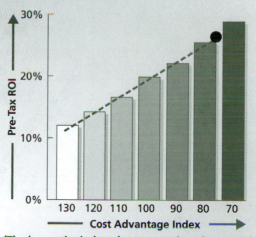

Profit Impact

Businesses with a cost advantage relative to competitors have been shown to be more profitable.

In contrast, businesses with above-average cost relative to competitors are, in general, less profitable.

$$\text{Cost Advantage Index} = \frac{\text{Business (\% Cost of Goods Sold)}}{\text{Average (\% Cost of Goods Sold) for Top Three Competitors}} \times 100$$

$$\text{Cost Advantage Index} = \frac{50\%}{(60\% + 65\% + 70\%)/3} \times 100 = \frac{50\%}{65\%} \times 100$$

$$= 77$$

Note: When competitors differ significantly in size (sales), a weighted average based on sales should be used for the top three competitors.

A larger unit volume allows for production and purchasing economies that lower the per-unit manufacturing cost of a product, thereby creating a *scale effect*. By making large volume purchases, Wal-Mart has been able to negotiate a lower cost of goods. The same scale effect occurs for a manufacturer who doubles production capacity. As Honda has increased its production capacity, the company has seen a reduction in unit cost due to a scale effect for a certain component product, as illustrated in Figure 6-7.

Likewise, when a business adds products to its product line that have similar manufacturing processes and that are made of the same purchased materials as its other products, the business can lower the average unit cost of all products. This is a *scope effect*. For Honda, the cost of ignition switches is lower than for some other manufacturers because the same ignition switch components are used in cars, motorcycles, lawn mowers, all-terrain vehicles, snowblowers, snowmobiles, jet skis, and generators. Honda's extension of its product line has provided a cost advantage across products due to the increased volume, and hence the reduced cost, of the common component parts.

Finally, as a business builds more of the same product, there is a greater opportunity for *learning effects*. These nonscale, nonscope effects contribute to lower costs through process improvements that are the result of learning. Each unit produced provides additional learning

FIGURE 6-6 UNIT COST AND EXPERIENCE CURVE—CELLULAR SERVICE

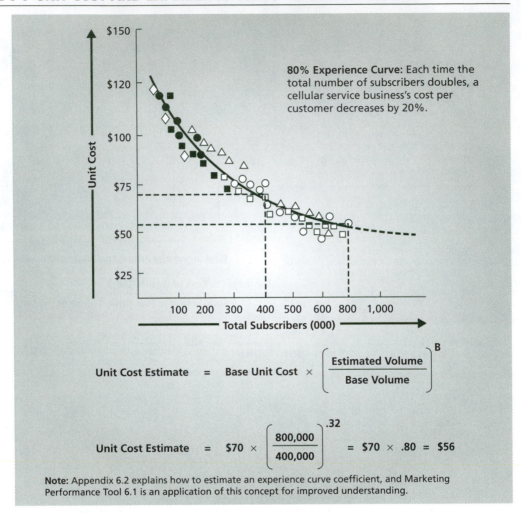

Note: Appendix 6.2 explains how to estimate an experience curve coefficient, and Marketing Performance Tool 6.1 is an application of this concept for improved understanding.

and the opportunity to build the next unit more efficiently. Naturally, the business with the most production experience has had the best opportunity to learn from experience. This learning normally leads to improvements in processes that lower the cost per unit.

Marketing Cost Advantage

Quite often, businesses fail to look beyond variable costs for sources of a cost advantage. Many of these businesses could benefit from marketing cost efficiencies derived from product line extensions, which is another way to gain a cost advantage. For example, it takes a certain number of salespeople to adequately cover a target market. As the sales force is given more products to sell to the same customers, a *marketing cost scope effect* is created. As illustrated on the left side of Figure 6-8, Procter & Gamble's sales force expense per pound of detergent sold should decrease as it adds more brands of detergent

FIGURE 6-7 IGNITION SWITCH COST ADVANTAGE DUE TO SCALE AND SCOPE EFFECTS

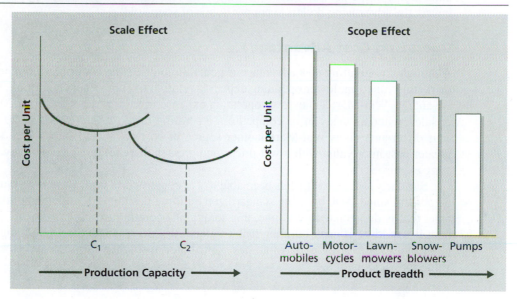

to its product line. A competitor with far fewer brands would need to have the same sales call frequency to adequately serve retailers and, therefore, would experience a higher cost per pound sold because it has fewer brands to sell.

Another area of marketing cost advantage is derived from the advertising cost efficiency of a brand extension strategy, as the right side of Figure 6-8 illustrates for the extensive product line offered by Campbell's Soup. Each time an individual soup is

FIGURE 6-8 PRODUCT SCOPE AND MARKETING COST ADVANTAGE

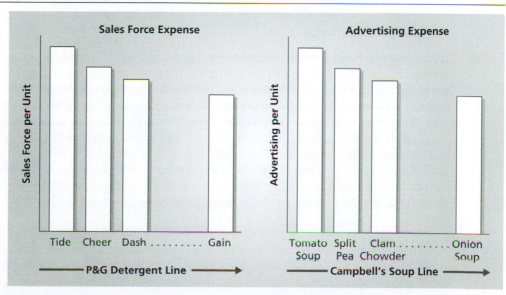

advertised, the ad reinforces top-of-the-mind awareness of Campbell's Soup brand and other soups in the product line. In this way, the scope effect created by additional soups lowers the advertising dollars spent per ounce of soup sold.

Operating Cost Advantage

Although an operating cost advantage is generally outside the control or influence of the marketing function, lower operating expenses relative to competitors contribute to a cost advantage. Wal-Mart achieves an operating expense to sales ratio of less than 20 percent of sales, whereas many of its competitors' operating expenses are well over 20 percent. This difference gives Wal-Mart another source of cost advantage from which to create greater customer value with lower prices and greater shareholder value with lower operating expenses.

Similarly, McDonald's has been able to cut construction costs of new restaurants by 50 percent since 1990 by using standardized building designs. Because the building is an asset that is depreciated over time, this source of operating expense is drastically lower than it would be if each building had a unique design. A standardized building design, along with rapid store expansion, has contributed to higher earnings and shareholder value for McDonald's.

DIFFERENTIATION ADVANTAGE

Every business must manage its costs, but not every business can have a cost advantage. To achieve above-average profits, a business needs some source of competitive advantage. A differentiation advantage with respect to product, service, or brand reputation is a potential source of competitive advantage, as we have seen. But like every source of competitive advantage, a differentiation advantage has to be meaningful to target customers as well as sustainable (not easily duplicated by competitors).

Product Advantage

A business can build a differentiation advantage around any of a product's many aspects. A product's durability, reliability, performance, features, appearance, and conformance to a specific application each have potential to be a differentiation advantage.[6] ESCO Corporation, for example, is a manufacturer of earth-moving equipment parts that are used in very demanding mining and construction applications. The company has developed a differentiation advantage in the wear life of its products due to proprietary steel chemistry and product design. Its products last longer and are less likely to break than are the products of its competitors. Both of these product benefits save the customer money even when the products are sold at a higher price. Overall, businesses with a relative advantage in product quality produce higher levels of profitability, as illustrated in Figure 6-9.

Service Advantage

A business can achieve a differentiation service advantage in the same way it can achieve a differentiation product advantage.[7] The same baseline conditions are required. First, the

FIGURE 6-9 PRODUCT DIFFERENTIATION ADVANTAGE AND PROFITABILITY

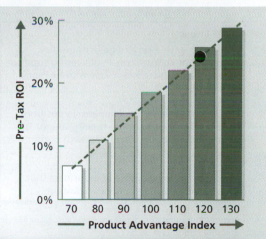

Profit Impact

Businesses with a product advantage that outperforms competitors in delivering superior product benefits have been shown to be more profitable.

In contrast, as in this example, an inferior competitive position with respect to product benefits sought by target customers has been correlated with poorer financial performance.

Intel, Microsoft, and Apple have each built a product advantage in the markets they serve.

Product Benefits (Voice of the Customer)	Relative Importance	Our Business	Competitors			Product Advantage
			A	B	C	
Reliable Performance	50	7.7	7.5	7.4	6.7	17
Ease of Use	30	5.6	5.1	7.7	4.9	−10
Product Life	20	7.6	6.8	5.2	6.1	13
	100					20

Product Advantage Index = 100 + 20 = 120

service advantage has to be meaningful and important to target customers, and second, it has to be sustainable. FedEx tracks its performance on 10 service quality indicators (each weighted by the "customer pain" that a failure creates). This service quality index is carefully monitored each day to help FedEx maintain a service quality advantage. As its service quality index improves, customer satisfaction improves and the overall cost per package decreases. By tracking its service performance each day, FedEx is able to create greater overall customer satisfaction with fewer errors, lower costs, and greater profits for shareholders. As Figure 6-10 shows, businesses with a service advantage produce higher levels of profitability.

Reputation Advantage

Another source of differentiation competitive advantage is brand reputation. Although competing watchmakers may match the quality of a Rolex watch, they cannot easily match Rolex's brand reputation advantage. Brands such as Chanel, Nikon, and Perrier also have built reputations that provide a source of competitive advantage in their ability to attract target customers. For these companies, the stature of their brand names adds a dimension of appeal that is an important customer benefit for many less price-sensitive, more image-conscious consumers.

A brand reputation advantage can be measured in the same way as a product or service advantage. Businesses with an advantage in brand reputation can both attract

FIGURE 6-10 SERVICE DIFFERENTIATION ADVANTAGE AND PROFITABILITY

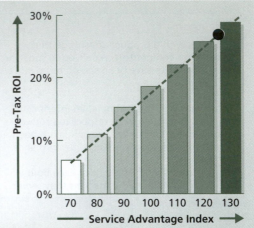

Profit Impact

Businesses with a service advantage that outperforms competitors in delivering superior service quality have been shown to be more profitable.

In contrast, an inferior competitive position with respect to the service quality sought by customers has been correlated with poorer financial performance.

Nordstrom is an example of a business that has strived to build a service advantage.

Service Quality (Voice of the Customer)	Relative Importance	Our Business	Competitors			Service Advantage
			A	B	C	
Parts Availability	60	7.2	6.3	4.3	6.7	20
Competent Service	20	6.5	6.8	6.6	5.5	0
Response to Problems	20	7.2	6.3	5.2	6.6	7
	100					27

Service Advantage Index = 100 + 27 = 127

customers and obtain a price premium. As Figure 6-11 shows, the reputation of a consumer product or service can have an impact on price premiums. The strong brand reputation of the Apple iPod, for example, translates into a price premium. Even in business-to-business markets, an advantage in brand or company reputation helps to support price and margins.

MARKETING ADVANTAGE

A business that dominates markets with a relative advantage in sales coverage, distribution, or marketing communications can control (and often block) market access. A marketing advantage can be a business's best source of competitive advantage. Whether through sales, distribution, or marketing communications, Nike, Procter & Gamble, Campbell's Soup, and many other companies have developed solid competitive advantages as a result of their marketing expertise.

Market Share Advantage

Market leaders often do not pose a strong differentiation or cost advantage. Their competitive advantage is derived from market dominance. As Figure 6-12 shows, the more dominant the share leader is with regard to market share compared with its top three competitors, the greater are the share leader's profits. In this example, Google is the share leader among

FIGURE 6-11 BRAND ADVANTAGE AND PROFITABILITY

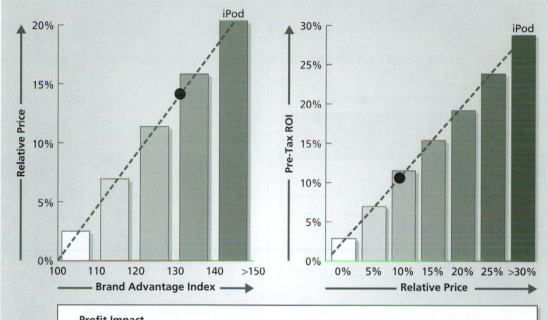

Profit Impact

Businesses with a brand advantage command a price premium, which often means higher margins. This, in turn, contributes to higher levels of profitability.

Brand Benefits (Voice of the Customer)	Relative Importance	Our Business	Competitors A	B	C	Brand Advantage
Most Respected Brand	50	7.7	7.5	5.4	6.7	17
Known for Quality	50	7.5	6.7	6.6	3.5	17
	100					34

Brand Advantage Index = 100 + 34 = 134

search engines and has a relative market share of 199. Yahoo, number two in market share, has a relative market share of 19, and number three AOL has a relative market share of 2. For this industry, relative market share partially explains large differences in company profitability. Market leaders have well-known, trusted brands; many variations in their product lines; and highly effective distribution systems.

Like Google, Nike is also a market share leader with a considerable marketing advantage. The main thing that makes Nike a tough competitor is the level of market awareness it has developed with creative ad copy, pervasive promotion of the Nike swoosh, careful selection of product spokespersons, and heavy advertising. This level of marketing advantage makes it difficult for competitors to succeed, even those who might have a better product or lower prices with comparable quality.

This type of competitive advantage, like all others, is relevant only when the communications created are meaningful and important to target customers. It takes more than simply spending advertising dollars to obtain and sustain a marketing communications

FIGURE 6-12 MARKET SHARE ADVANTAGE AND PROFITABILITY

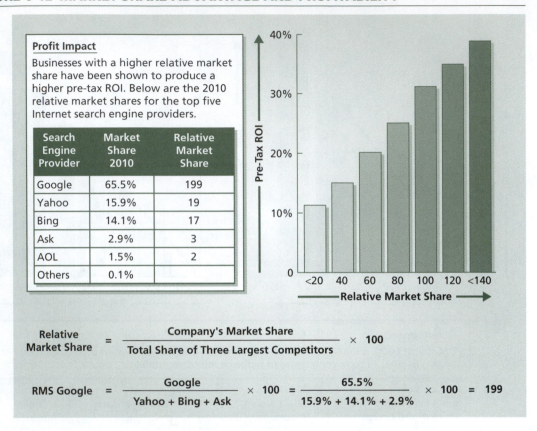

Profit Impact

Businesses with a higher relative market share have been shown to produce a higher pre-tax ROI. Below are the 2010 relative market shares for the top five Internet search engine providers.

Search Engine Provider	Market Share 2010	Relative Market Share
Google	65.5%	199
Yahoo	15.9%	19
Bing	14.1%	17
Ask	2.9%	3
AOL	1.5%	2
Others	0.1%	

$$\text{Relative Market Share} = \frac{\text{Company's Market Share}}{\text{Total Share of Three Largest Competitors}} \times 100$$

$$\text{RMS Google} = \frac{\text{Google}}{\text{Yahoo} + \text{Bing} + \text{Ask}} \times 100 = \frac{65.5\%}{15.9\% + 14.1\% + 2.9\%} \times 100 = 199$$

advantage. The challenge goes right to the core of market-based management: who are our customers, what do they want, and how do we communicate our product in a way that best serves their needs?

Product Line Advantage

The more products a business has to sell, the more ways it has to attract and satisfy customers. A broad line of products creates more selling opportunities for the sales force and channel partners. A business with a narrow line of products has to be more focused in order to be cost effective in its marketing efforts. Because a broad product line gives a business more prospective customers and the potential to sell more to each customer, this type of marketing efficiency translates into more sales and higher levels of profitability. Figure 6-13 shows that businesses with broad product lines are more profitable during the emerging and growing stages of a product life cycle than are businesses with narrow product lines. It is particularly important, then, to expand a business's product line during these stages of the product life cycle.

Quite often, a company wants to expand from one market segment into an adjacent segment in order to grow sales and profits. Product line expansion requires considerable

FIGURE 6-13 PRODUCT LINE ADVANTAGE AND PROFITABILITY

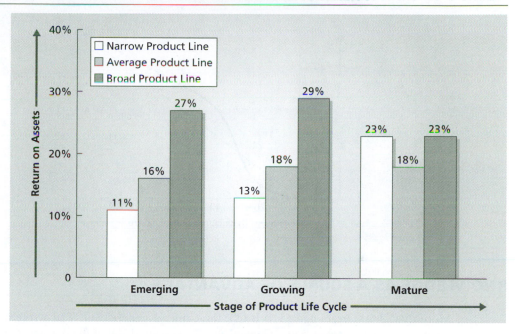

product differentiation and careful positioning because the same company then needs to ask a different price for a different combination of product, service, and brand benefits. Toyota sequentially expanded its product line from a low product-price segment in the 1960s to its current full line of vehicles, each with a different product-price position and a unique brand-name identity.

In the beer market, Anheuser-Busch's product line strategy utilizes separate brand names for each of the several positioning strategies it has pursued. Each brand has a distinct product-price position that is attractive to different types of customers or different use situations. In recent years, Anheuser-Busch has expanded its product line to the microbrew segment with the introduction of Michelob Bavarian Style Wheat, added Kirin and other foreign brands to create an import brand position, and developed Budweiser Select for the low-calorie, low-carbohydrate segment.

Channel Advantage

Businesses that need distribution in order to gain market access have a limited number of distributors, whether they are retailers in consumer markets or dealers in business-to-business markets. There are only a few top-notch distributors. Therefore, a business that has exclusive access to these distributors can control channels in a given market and, to some degree, can control market access. A channel advantage is a source of competitive advantage that is independent of a cost or differentiation advantage.

Figure 6-14 shows the relationship between distributor share and market share. As a business is able to dominate the channels to market, it is able to achieve a larger relative market share, and a larger relative share in turn corresponds with greater profitability.[8]

FIGURE 6-14 CHANNEL ADVANTAGE AND PROFITABILITY

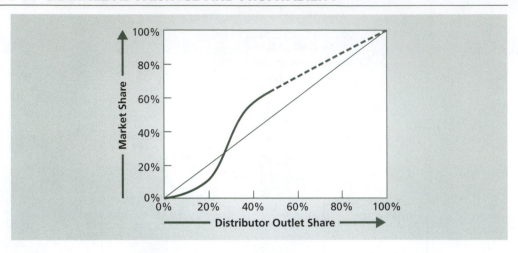

KNOWLEDGE AS A SOURCE OF ADVANTAGE

More than 2,500 years ago (510 B.C.), the Chinese general Sun Tzu wrote a military manual called *The Art of War*.[9] General Sun Tzu concluded that the out-and-out destruction of an enemy resulted in greater *losses* than *gains*. He believed that deception, restraint, and minimalism were the best ways to defeat an enemy. Though it seems paradoxical, the major premise of *The Art of War* is that the best policy is to neutralize and subjugate a competitor into following one's own group, not to fight the competitor. Today, *The Art of War* is among the world's most widely read books, and its principles of competition are studied by many major corporations.[10]

In his manual, General Sun Tzu presents competitive strategy as the process of developing a *knowledge advantage* and then attacking obliquely, almost unnoticeably, in a way that eventually causes your competitor to follow you. He believed that a less confrontational approach could achieve better results without significant losses than direct warfare. Focused on a knowledge advantage, he built competitive strategies based on superior knowledge of both the terrain (customers) and the enemy (competitors).

In any competitive environment, knowledge is the principal source of competitive advantage. In business, attracting customers is the mission a business seeks to accomplish, and the competitors are the forces it is fighting to achieve its mission. Without adequate knowledge of both customers and competitors, a business is severely handicapped in developing strategies to gain customers and grow market share. A company needs a knowledge advantage in order to develop a successful oblique strategy. Partial knowledge may seem like an advantage, but it often results in *reactive strategies*, as presented in Figure 6-15. A business with excellent customer knowledge but limited competitor knowledge will likely overreact to customer demands. Similarly, having excellent competitor knowledge without adequate customer knowledge will likely result in an overreaction to competitors' moves.

As Figure 6-15 shows, businesses that lack both customer knowledge and competitor knowledge are working with an *inside-the-box strategy* as they make competitive moves

FIGURE 6-15 COMPETITIVE STRATEGY BASED ON KNOWLEDGE ADVANTAGE

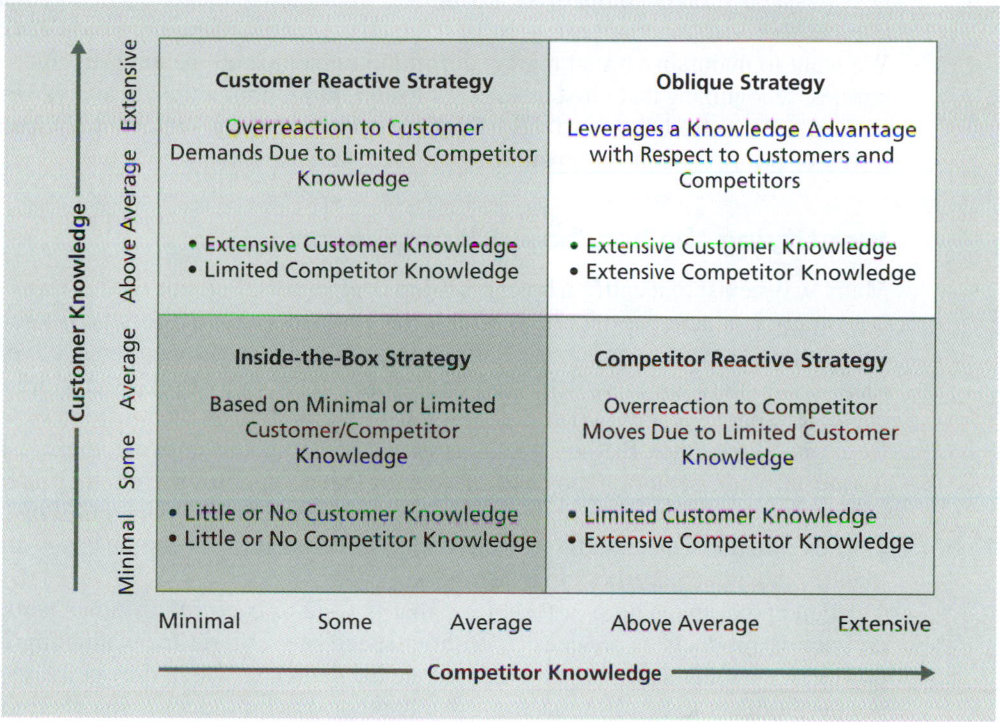

Customer Reactive Strategy Overreaction to Customer Demands Due to Limited Competitor Knowledge • Extensive Customer Knowledge • Limited Competitor Knowledge	**Oblique Strategy** Leverages a Knowledge Advantage with Respect to Customers and Competitors • Extensive Customer Knowledge • Extensive Competitor Knowledge
Inside-the-Box Strategy Based on Minimal or Limited Customer/Competitor Knowledge • Little or No Customer Knowledge • Little or No Competitor Knowledge	**Competitor Reactive Strategy** Overreaction to Competitor Moves Due to Limited Customer Knowledge • Limited Customer Knowledge • Extensive Competitor Knowledge

Customer Knowledge (vertical axis): Minimal — Some — Average — Above Average — Extensive

Competitor Knowledge (horizontal axis): Minimal — Some — Average — Above Average — Extensive

from an internal perspective with no real market knowledge. These businesses can only make blind attempts at success, usually in the end losing more ground than they gain. Other businesses with partial knowledge of customers or competitors are likely to employ reactive strategies, which is the normal response to customer or competitor pressures when a business sees only one aspect of the marketplace. The best strategy is an oblique strategy, which requires superior knowledge of both customers and competitors.

With a knowledge advantage, a business can devise a market-based strategy to achieve desired gains without sustaining excessive losses. Following General Sun Tzu's approach, the business can implement market-based strategies that leverage a knowledge advantage with respect to both customers and competitors, a nonconfrontational approach that minimizes losses. We have labeled this an oblique strategy because it seeks to gain a competitive advantage without direct confrontation. A competitive strategy with limited or partial customer and competitor knowledge could more easily slide into a frontal attack strategy—a direct attack on a competitor's position.

COMPETITOR INTELLIGENCE

Selecting competitive environments that favor profit potential is a key aspect of the industry analysis that a business conducts when it considers entry into new markets. But no matter how attractive a new market may be in light of the competition, developing a strong competitive position is still critical.[11] To understand the degree to which a business has a position of competitive advantage, we need to engage in a detailed analysis of competitors. An important question is, "Which competitors should a business analyze?" We want to maintain a broad market definition to include all meaningful competing substitutes, recognizing that most businesses would find it impractical to analyze every competitor.[12] We therefore need a mechanism to help us identify a relevant competitor set as a way of prioritizing the competitors to analyze and benchmark.

Identifying the Benchmark Competitors

Many ways exist to identify a business's top competitors. Perhaps the best way is to have customers evaluate the degree to which they consider competitors as interchangeable substitutes. The more similar two competitors are from a customer perspective, the more likely customers are to switch from one to the other. Conversely, the more dissimilar customers perceive any two competitors, the less likely it is that customers will switch from one to the other. Businesses can survey a sampling of their customers, asking them to rate each competitor on the basis of how far that competitor is from their ideal product or supplier. From these customer perceptions, we can create a *perceptual map* that will give us a better understanding of the competitive position of the business and help us identify the key competitors to benchmark.

Perceptual mapping is a technique that is used to capture customer perceptions of competing products or services.[13] Without specifying criteria for evaluating competing products, customers are simply asked to rate the degree to which they perceive two competing products to be different from one another. Each product is matched one-on-one with every competing product, so customers evaluate the differences between only two competing products at a time, as with the luxury cars in Figure 6-16. In this figure, Volvo, Mercedes, BMW, Lincoln, Honda, and Buick are competing substitutes. Customers perceived Volvo and BMW to be very similar, whereas they perceived Lincoln and Honda to be very dissimilar.

By also asking customers to rate each car on the extent to which it approaches their ideal car, we can gain a better understanding of competitive position and key competitors. In the example in Figure 6-16, the customer ratings relative to the ideal car produced two different segments. Two different sets of customer needs and product preferences were operating in this sample market. The ideal car for segment A is almost equidistant from Honda, Buick, BMW, and Volvo. These four competitors would be the most likely choices for customers in segment A. If we were on the marketing team for Buick, we would then view Honda, Volvo, and BMW as our key competitors in serving segment A, even though Mercedes and Lincoln are equally close to Buick. However, if we were more interested in serving segment B, Lincoln and Mercedes would be the competitors to benchmark.

A business can use a variety of multidimensional scaling programs to create a perceptual map,[14] such as the one at the bottom of Figure 6-16. In this example, interbrand differentiation is graphed in two dimensions.[15] In most applications, over 90 percent of competitor differentiation can be captured in two dimensions. By looking at a perceptual map of its competition, a business can easily discern two things: (1) who its competitors will be in a particular market segment, and (2) its competitive position relative to these competitors in attracting and satisfying customers in this segment. However, to improve

FIGURE 6-16 CUSTOMER PERCEPTIONS OF INTERBRAND DIFFERENTIATION

Competing Alternatives	Degree of Perceived Differentiation										
	Very Similar								Very Different		
	0	1	2	3	4	5	6	7	8	9	10
Mercedes—Volvo	0	1	2	3	4	5	(6)	7	8	9	10
Mercedes—Lincoln	0	1	(2)	3	4	5	6	7	8	9	10
Mercedes—Honda	0	1	2	3	4	5	6	7	8	(9)	10
Mercedes—Buick	0	1	2	3	4	5	(6)	7	8	9	10
Mercedes—BMW	0	1	2	(3)	4	5	6	7	8	9	10
Mercedes—Ideal A	0	1	2	3	4	5	(6)	7	8	9	10
Mercedes—Ideal B	0	1	(2)	3	4	5	6	7	8	9	10
Volvo—Lincoln	0	1	2	3	4	5	6	(7)	8	9	10
Volvo—BMW	0	1	2	(3)	4	5	6	7	8	9	10
Volvo—Buick	0	1	2	3	(4)	5	6	7	8	9	10
Volvo—Honda	0	1	2	3	4	(5)	6	7	8	9	10
Volvo—Ideal A	0	1	(2)	3	4	5	6	7	8	9	10
Volvo—Ideal B	0	1	2	3	4	(5)	6	7	8	9	10
Lincoln—Honda	0	1	2	3	4	5	6	7	8	9	(10)
Lincoln—BMW	0	1	2	3	(4)	5	6	7	8	9	10
Lincoln—Buick	0	1	2	3	4	5	(6)	7	8	9	10
Lincoln—Ideal A	0	1	2	3	4	5	6	7	(8)	9	10
Lincoln—Ideal B	0	1	(2)	3	4	5	6	7	8	9	10
BMW—Honda	0	1	2	3	4	5	6	7	(8)	9	10
BMW—Buick	0	1	2	3	4	(5)	6	7	8	9	10
BMW—Ideal A	0	1	2	3	4	(5)	6	7	8	9	10
BMW—Ideal B	0	1	2	(3)	4	5	6	7	8	9	10
Buick—Honda	0	1	2	3	4	(5)	6	7	8	9	10
Buick—Ideal A	0	1	(2)	3	4	5	6	7	8	9	10
Buick—Ideal B	0	1	2	3	(4)	5	6	7	8	9	10
Honda—Ideal A	0	1	2	3	(4)	5	6	7	8	9	10
Honda—Ideal B	0	1	2	3	4	5	6	7	8	(9)	10

Perceptual Map

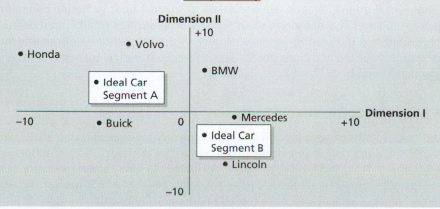

or maintain a position relative to competitors and the customers' ideal car, a business must also know on what basis target customers are differentiating competing products.

Competitor Analysis

After a business has identified which competitors it should benchmark, the business then needs to conduct a more detailed analysis of them. A detailed competitor analysis is a difficult undertaking, something that most businesses are inclined to do only periodically. However, because of its strong market orientation, a market-based business gathers competitor intelligence all the time and, as a result, has continuously evolving competitor profiles from which to evaluate its own competitiveness and competitive advantages.[16]

Obtaining Competitor Intelligence

A great deal of competitive intelligence is public information and readily available from dealers, the trade press, the business press, industry consultants, trade shows, financial reports, industry reports, the general press, government documents, and customers.[17] But unless a business has created a market-based culture in which everyone in the organization is an information gatherer, sources of competitive intelligence that are more valuable but also more difficult to find will slip by unnoticed.

Figure 6-17 presents a list of competitor behaviors that signal when a competitor is in trouble or lacks marketing leadership. This type of competitor intelligence is readily available from published articles, financial reports, and information that salespeople could observe in customer visits or while talking with distributors. In each case, the competitive behavior opens the door to marketing strategies that could be implemented at a time when it would be difficult for the competitor to respond. If a competitor is investing less in research and development, for example, it would be an excellent time for a business to accelerate new-product introductions. If a competitor is changing ads and ad agencies often, it is a good time for a business to further promote its own value proposition to customers.

In today's expanding information age, ever more information on markets and competitors is becoming available. As an illustration of just how much competitor intelligence can be gathered, consider the success of a reference librarian at Multnomah County Library in Portland, Oregon. He was asked to spend 1 hour gathering competitor intelligence to answer five questions about Merix Corporation, a small circuit board manufacturer. Outlined in Figure 6-18 is a summary of the competitive information and sources used to answer the questions posed. The reference librarian answered all five questions adequately in 1 hour.[18]

A Sample Competitor Analysis

Let's use Southwest Airlines (SWA) as our company focus and benchmark its performance in 2010 against four major competitors: American Airlines (AA), Continental Airlines (CO), Delta Airlines (DL), and United Airlines (UA), as shown in Figure 6-19. Southwest is number two in market share with 14 percent of the U.S. market, 1.3 share points behind market leader Delta but almost 2 share points above the average for all four competitors.[19] Southwest is ahead of all its competitors in customer satisfaction by 8 to 19

FIGURE 6-17 KNOWING WHEN A COMPETITOR IS IN TROUBLE

Behaviors exhibited by a competitor *under pressure to improve profits/cash flow:*

- Laying off employees and closing plants or sales offices
- Making across-the-board price increases without market justification
- Reducing advertising and not attending trade shows
- Cutting investment in research and development
- Increasing the average days in accounts payable
- Taking on more debt/increasing debt-to-equity ratio
- Tightening the terms of sale and payment conditions
- Not recruiting new people as employees retire; shrinking workforce
- Paying salespeople to collect unpaid bills

Behaviors exhibited by a competitor that *lacks marketing leadership/market focus:*

- Frequently changing advertising message; changing ad agencies often
- Having lower-than-average sales per salesperson
- Having higher-than-average marketing and sales expenses as a percent of sales
- Having frequent new-product failures
- Communicating a hollow or vague value proposition
- Using cost-based pricing, unaware of its product's customer value
- Frequently cutting prices to increase volume
- Frequently changing senior management/marketing management

points on the American Customer Satisfaction Index,[20] and it is 15 points above the competitors' average customer satisfaction index.

Using publicly available financial information, Southwest can extend its benchmark competitor analysis to better understand marketing profits and financial performance. As shown in Figure 6-19, Southwest's gross margins are close to the competitor average, whereas its spending on marketing and sales as a percentage of sales (25%) is 3.6 points lower than the competitor average. The lower marketing and sales expenses allow Southwest to achieve an above-average marketing ROS (16.8%) and marketing ROI (67%). The company's marketing performance in 2010 had a positive impact on its financial performance: a 2.5 percent return on sales, and a 1.7 percent return on assets. With regard to Southwest's sales to assets ratio, however, the airline earned only 69 cents in sales for every dollar in assets, whereas the average for the four competitors was 90 cents in sales for every dollar in assets.

Figure 6-20 provides an even broader view of benchmark performance. The figure provides airline industry averages for the five airlines referenced in Figure 6-19. The averages are compared with the performance of 200 well-known Fortune 500 companies. As shown, the averages for the five airlines are well below the averages and median performances for operating income, marketing return on sales, and marketing return on investment for the 200 Fortune 500 companies. This level of analysis suggests that all of the competing airlines are performing at the lower level of company performance.

FIGURE 6-18 COMPETITOR INFORMATION SEARCH

Outlined here are the questions posed and the sources of information from which competitive intelligence was gathered in 1 hour by a research expert.

1. How big is the circuit board market served by Merix, and what is its current market share?

The *Market Share Reporter* gives market size and share of hundreds of sectors in the economy, but Merix did not appear. *Predicast* provides market sizes and reference to *SMT Trends* (a trade journal) that reports the market share statistics of the top 10 circuit board producers, but not Merix. However, the *Corp Tech Dictionary of Technology Companies* turned out to be the mother lode. It gives Merix's SIC (standard industrial classification) and lists other companies in that sector. From this information, an estimate of market size and share was computed.

2. Merix has been dependent on a few large customers. Is it adding to its customer base?

A search of a local newspaper uncovered an article "Merix Wants More Customers." It quotes the company as saying 70 percent of revenues come from its top five customers. Merix's most recent annual report also states that 69.3 percent of revenues come from four customers. In addition, the SEC Edgar Web site reports not much progress has been made in adding new customers to Merix's customer base.

3. Develop a biographical profile of Merix's CEO and her approach to business.

Standard & Poor's *Register of Directors and Executives* provides a short bio on the CEO, Debi Coleman, and her e-mail address. The *Biography and Genealogy Master Index, Dun & Bradstreet Reference Book of Corporate Management, Who's Who,* and *Who's Who of American Women* provide no details. However, *Who's Who in Finance and Industry* provides a detailed résumé.

4. Will Merix have a booth at any upcoming trade shows? If so, where and when?

Trade Shows Worldwide and the current editions of *Trade Show and Exhibits Schedule and Trade Show Week Data Book* provide the answers needed.

5. Merix hired a new chief operating officer. What biographical information is available?

Predicast reported that a chief operating officer was hired, and *Business Wire* press releases provided a bio on the new COO.

Other sources considered but not used included *Business News Bank* (a CD-ROM database), *Business Index* (another CD-ROM database), *Value Line,* and *Red Chip Review.* Had time permitted, the *Manufacturers Register* (every state has one) and trade magazines would have been used.

FIGURE 6-19 COMPETITOR ANALYSIS—SOUTHWEST AIRLINES VERSUS COMPETING AIRLINES

Area of Performance	SWA	Competitor Avg.	AA	CO	DL	UA
Market Share	14.0%	12.1%	13.8%	9.0%	15.3%	10.3%
Customer Satisfaction Index	79	64	63	71	61	60
Gross Margin (% sales)	41.8%	41.1%	34.2%	54.0%	40.6%	35.6%
Marketing & Sales Exp. (% sales)	25.0%	28.6%	24.1%	37.6%	22.0%	30.8%
Marketing ROS	16.8%	12.5%	10.1%	16.4%	18.6%	4.8%
Marketing ROI	67%	46.5%	42%	44%	84%	16%
Financial Performance						
Return on Sales (pre-tax)	2.5%	0.9%	2.1%	−1.2%	7.3%	−4.5%
Return on Assets (pre-tax)	1.7%	0.2%	2.0%	−1.2%	4.7%	−4.6%
Sales-to-Assets Ratio	0.69	0.90	0.94	0.99	0.65	1.04

FIGURE 6-20 BENCHMARKED AIRLINE PERFORMANCE—MARKETING PROFITABILITY VERSUS OPERATING INCOME

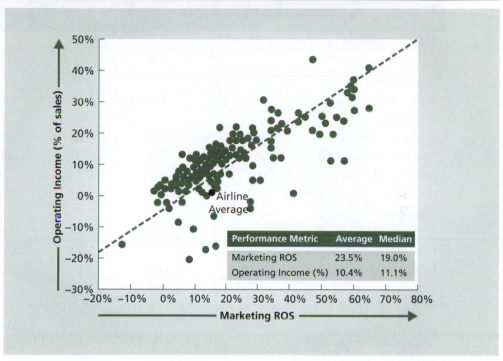

Performance Metric	Average	Median
Marketing ROS	23.5%	19.0%
Operating Income (%)	10.4%	11.1%

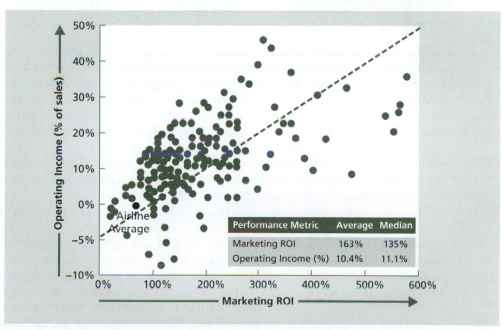

Performance Metric	Average	Median
Marketing ROI	163%	135%
Operating Income (%)	10.4%	11.1%

FIGURE 6-21 COMPETITOR ANALYSIS FOR AN INDUSTRIAL BUSINESS

Dimension of Competitiveness	Business Performance	Competitor Performance	Performance Gap*
Market-Based Performance			
Market Share (%)	6	17	11 behind
Relative Price	115	100	15 higher
Relative Product Quality	115	105	10 better
Relative Service Quality	93	113	20 worse
Number of Distributors	87	261	174 fewer
Sales Force (number)	36	60	24 fewer
Advertising & Promotion (% of sales)	2.0	2.0	0 equal
Sales, General, and Administrative (% of sales)	16.0	17.0	1.0 lower
Operating Performance			
Cost of Goods Sold (% of sales)	48.0	50.8	2.8 lower
Direct Materials (% of sales)	26.0	17.6	8.4 higher
Overhead (% of sales)	12.0	10.0	2.0 higher
Return on Assets (%)	17.1	19.5	2.4 lower
Return on Sales (%)	7.4	11.1	3.7 lower
Asset Turnover	2.3	1.6	0.7 higher
Accounts Receivable (days)	46	38	8 higher
Sales per Employee	$1.5 mil	$2.1 mil	0.6 lower

*Performance Gap = Business Performance − Competitor Performance

The level of detail included in a competitor analysis can vary considerably. In the example shown in Figure 6-21, the competitor analysis is broken down into two categories: market-based performance and operating performance. Each area is further broken down into more specific performance metrics that are applied for the business and a benchmark competitor. In this example, the business has about one-third of the market share of the benchmark competitor. This competitive gap corresponds closely with a similar competitive gap in the number of distributors. The business also has a significant gap in sales force coverage. To close its share gap, the business undoubtedly needs to address adverse competitive gaps in distribution and sales coverage.

Overall, the business is behind its benchmark competitor in most aspects of market-based performance. The competitive gaps shown help create performance targets and management incentives to close those gaps. This, of course, is a key input into the development of a successful market-based strategy. From an internal perspective, this business is also poorly positioned in almost all areas of operating performance. Higher overhead costs and accounts receivable, as well as a lower return on sales per employee, contribute to lower profitability and productivity. Each of these gaps may be difficult to close, and competitors are not likely to cooperate by sharing information on the methods they use for achieving better performance. To successfully close these important competitive gaps, the business may need to go outside its industry to find better competitive practices.

FIGURE 6-22 COMPETITIVE BENCHMARKING—XEROX BILLING ERRORS

Competitive Benchmarking	Xerox: Billing Errors
1. Identify a key area of competitive weakness.	1. Xerox found billing errors were more frequent than those of competitors.
2. Identify a benchmark company.	2. Xerox looked at Citicorp, AT&T, and American Express.
3. Track the benchmark company's process advantage.	3. With the cooperation of American Express, Xerox developed new systems to reduce billing errors.

Competitive Benchmarking

By going outside its industry to benchmark a business that is known to be superior in a particular process, a company almost always gains insight into its own operations. General Mills' experience is a good example. The company uses the same production lines to make a variety of related food products. For instance, it uses the same production line for scalloped potatoes as for au gratin potatoes. Making the necessary equipment changes between production runs once took as long as 12 hours. General Mills made extensive efforts to reduce downtime during production changeovers, but those efforts brought only small, incremental improvements. The company then decided to benchmark a NASCAR pit team's process for changing equipment when a race car comes off the track for servicing. A better example of preparedness, precision, and quickness would have been hard to find. What General Mills learned enabled it to implement a new process that reduced changeover time to as little as 20 minutes.

Competitive benchmarking is a process that was developed initially at Xerox to improve its competitive position relative to key competitors. The idea is for a business to identify a key area of competitive weakness, such as billing errors, as shown in Figure 6-22, and then benchmark a business or other entity outside its industry that is recognized as a world-class performer in this area.[21] In this way, a business may gain insights into the underlying processes that produce this best practice and may develop a system that has the potential to be better than that of its key competitors.

The first step in competitive benchmarking is to identify a key area of competitive weakness that affects customer satisfaction or profitability or both. For Xerox, a large number of billing errors was a serious competitive weakness. It was a source of considerable customer frustration, and it hurt overall perceptions of performance and lowered customer satisfaction. The second step was to identify several companies that were among the best in the world in this area of performance. Xerox identified Citicorp, American Express, and AT&T. After talking with these companies, Xerox chose to focus on American Express and gained its cooperation in order to study its billing system, which at the time had a significantly lower error rate and many more transactions than Xerox.

Xerox observed the systems and processes used by American Express that led to a more error-free billing system. Then it used this knowledge to develop several programs that made Xerox more competitive in this key area of competitive weakness. It set performance benchmarks in an effort to decrease billing errors. It took time, but Xerox reached its goal and turned a competitive weakness into a competitive strength. Xerox achieved similar success in competitive benchmarking of order cycle time (the time it takes to deliver the product after the customer places the order), using L. L. Bean as the benchmark company.

INDUSTRY ANALYSIS

To prepare an industry analysis, a business first determines the attractiveness of the competitive environment. In an unattractive market, a business can encounter low profitability even when its competitive position is relatively strong.[22] Choosing the right markets (industries) in which to compete is a crucial step in market analysis and strategy development.

Figure 6-23 lists the industry forces that shape the attractiveness of a competitive environment. Each of these industry forces can be evaluated along a continuum from unfavorable to favorable. As the sum of these forces favors a more attractive competitive environment, the potential for profit is greater. A new business with a favorable set of industry forces has a far better chance of succeeding than a business in a market with low barriers to entry, high barriers to exit, high levels of customer and supplier power, many substitutes, or intense rivalry among competitors.

Barriers to Entry

Market entry may be blocked in many ways. International markets are often blocked by political barriers. These barriers reduce competition and enhance profit potential for

FIGURE 6-23 INDUSTRY ANALYSIS—INDUSTRY FORCES AND PROFIT POTENTIAL

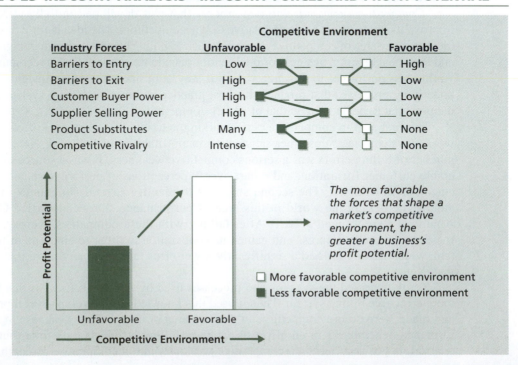

protected competitors. Technology or low-cost manufacturing can also create barriers to entry. Businesses with a superior technological or cost advantage have built competitor barriers to entry of their own. Another barrier to entry might be the substantial resources it would take for a new business to succeed in a given market. A market that necessitates high start-up and operating costs for a business considering entry to that market helps preserve the market for the businesses that are already in it. An example is the pharmaceutical industry: heavy investments in R&D, costs related to patents and federal approval, high advertising expenses, and the large sales forces needed for marketing to physicians deter the entry of new competitors, making the competitive environment more attractive for those already in the market.

Barriers to Exit

The competitive environment is also enhanced when weak competitors can easily exit a market. Legal barriers, specialized assets, or the strategic importance of a business often prevent businesses from exiting markets when they should. A pharmaceutical company that is losing money on a particular prescription drug may want to exit the market for that drug, but legal, political, or social forces could create an environment in which market exit would be difficult.

Likewise, a business that has invested in specialized assets (capital, people, or both) may find it difficult to exit a market because these assets are not easily sold or transferred to another business application. Businesses that have specialized in nuclear fuel reprocessing, for instance, find market exit difficult because of their specialized assets. Finally, a business that depends on products which are strategically important to its image or ability to market other products may not exit a market even though its profits on the strategically important products are lower than desired.

Customer Buying Power

When relatively few customers buy in large quantities and can easily switch suppliers, the customers' strong buying power diminishes market attractiveness. Large, concentrated groups of customers possess a buying power that enables them to negotiate lower prices or better terms and conditions of sale. Likewise, when customers can easily switch from one supplier to another, they force increased competition, which can lower prices and increase the cost of serving customers. In addition, when the purchased product or service is of limited importance to the customer, supplier dependence is much lower.

For the pharmaceutical industry, customer buying power is relatively low. Patents protect many well-known prescription drugs well into the future, and customers who benefit from these drugs usually have few, if any, alternatives. As a result, the pharmaceutical industry has relatively low customer buying power, which enhances the competitive environment and profit potential.[23]

Supplier Selling Power

The flip side of customer buying power is supplier selling power. If a business is a large purchaser of a commodity product (less important to the buyer) and is in an industry where switching costs are low, supplier power is generally low. For a business, this is a favorable market condition, one that strengthens industry attractiveness and profit potential. Because businesses in the pharmaceutical industry purchase supplies in large volumes and have fairly low switching costs, supplier seller power is relatively weak, contributing to the overall attractiveness of the industry.

Product Substitutes

The more substitute products that are available to customers, the easier it is for them to switch. Ease of switching intensifies competition and lowers profit potential and industry attractiveness.

In the soft drink industry, product substitutes are numerous, making premium pricing impossible. With the market definition broadened to include mineral water, fruit drinks, juice drinks, energy drinks, and coffee drinks, this level of choice places enormous pressure on competitors serving these markets. A business with a broad market definition, as presented in Chapter 3, recognizes the impact of substitutes in evaluating industry attractiveness. Stiff competition is the rule in industries with many substitutes, such as the automotive and beverage industries, but competitors have little to fear from one another in industries where substitutes are few, such as the petroleum and pharmaceutical industries.

Competitive Rivalry

The more competitors an industry has, the lower will be the differentiation among those competitors, and low differentiation increases competitive rivalry. Excess capacity within an industry can also cause competitors to intensify their moves against one another. The greater the excess capacity, the more intense the moves will likely be. Intense competitive rivalry invariably leads to lower prices and margins, as well as to higher marketing and sales expenses for attracting and retaining customers. The net effect is an unattractive industry, one in which the profit potential is relatively low.

FIGURE 6-24 PERFORMANCE IMPACT OF PRICE RIVALRY AND THE PRISONER'S DILEMMA

Business's Price Strategy	Competitor's Price Strategy	
	Hold Price	**Lower Price 5%**
Hold Price	Market Share = 10% Volume = 1 million units Price = $100 per unit Margin = $40 per unit Total Contribution = $40 million	Market Share = 8% Volume = 800,000 units Price = $100 per unit Margin = $40 per unit Total Contribution = $32 million
Lower Price 5%	Market Share = 12% Volume = 1.2 million units Price = $95 per unit Margin = $35 per unit Total Contribution = $42 million	Market Share = 10% Volume = 1 million units Price = $95 per unit Margin = $35 per unit Total Contribution = $35 million

The personal computer industry has a much higher level of competitive rivalry today than during the 1980s and early 1990s. Since that time, the industry has attracted many competitors that have considerable capacity. In addition, product differentiation has become minimal. Add to these factors the slowdown in the growth of the personal computer market, and we have the perfect conditions for fierce competitive rivalry. By contrast, the pharmaceutical industry has relatively few competitors, product differentiation is high and very often protected by patents, and the market for pharmaceuticals keeps growing. As a result, competitive rivalry in this industry is relatively low.

The Prisoner's Dilemma

Intense competitive rivalry can evolve into what is known as *the prisoner's dilemma*.[24] In such situations, downward price moves by one competitor force "follower moves" by other competitors in order to minimize lost profits. Actually, all the competitors would be better off if none of them cut prices to begin with.

Consider the example presented in Figure 6-24. In the current situation, both the business and its competitor are holding their prices steady, which yields a total contribution (margin per unit multiplied by unit volume) of $40 million for the business. If the competitor cuts its price by 5 percent and the business keeps its price the same, the business will lose two share points and $8 million in total contribution due to lost demand. Of course, if the business were to lead with a price cut against its competitor and the competitor does not follow, the business could gain two share points and $2 million in total contribution. The worst outcome of the prisoner's dilemma, from an industry-wide perspective, occurs when the competitor cuts price and the business matches the cut. Although the loss to the business's contribution is $3 million less than if it had held price, the competitor's profits also fall, resulting in severely diminished profits for the industry as a whole. Yet, if the business does not match its competitor's cut, its own profits will fall more.

■ Summary

Competitive position drives profitability. Businesses or products that lack a competitive advantage are less profitable and those with a discernable competitive advantage are more profitable. A competitive advantage can be achieved in three ways: superior differentiation, low cost, or superior marketing. Apple is a company with a differentiation advantage based on the uniqueness of its products, brand loyalty, and product innovation. Dell has achieved success with a low-cost competitive advantage through careful management of product costs, marketing and sales expenses, and assets. Nike has built success with superior marketing through brand building, advertising, and channel management.

In all cases, however, the real challenge is sustaining a competitive advantage. Companies that do not seek continuous improvement around their core source of competitive advantage eventually will be replaced by competitors, often innovative companies that are new to their markets.

Competitor analyses are an important aspect of formulating a marketing strategy and strengthening a business's market orientation. A high level of marketing knowledge with respect to competitors is a source of competitive advantage just as a good knowledge of customers is. A business that has a knowledge advantage can pursue an oblique, indirect strategy that forces competitors to follow. An oblique strategy is more profitable than a direct frontal attack, which requires greater resources and may or may not result in a market share gain.

There are three primary dimensions to competitor analysis: assessing the sources of a business's competitive advantage, engaging in competitor intelligence, and assessing industry attractiveness. A market-based management business includes this last assessment in its market analysis. Industry forces such as competitor entry and exit, number of substitutes, buyer and supplier power, and competitive rivalry all affect profit potential. When the collective sum of these forces is favorable, the profit potential is greater. Conducting a competitor analysis helps a business understand its competitive position in a given market. A complete competitor profile, including information obtained by intelligence gathering, enables a business to see its key strengths and main weaknesses.

Businesses frequently overlook fundamental weaknesses that affect their competitive positions. A competitor gap analysis is intended to expose any major weaknesses. Often, a competitor gap analysis will reveal an operational or process weakness that needs to be examined in depth for ways to strengthen it. The business then goes outside its market to observe the highly effective practices of a noncompeting business. This process, called *competitive* benchmarking (as opposed to *competitor* benchmarking) gives a business insights into the steps it must take to correct the weakness and gain a competitive advantage.

■ Market-Based Strategic Thinking

1 How would a market leader such as Google use a cost advantage to build customer value and above-average profits in an emerging market?

2 What is the iPad's primary source of competitive advantage? How does this source of competitive advantage help build a superior customer value for iPad and above-average profits for Apple?

3 How would Coca-Cola use its marketing advantage to build customer value and profitability in the consumer market?

4 How would a marketing knowledge advantage be a source of competitive advantage in the cell phone market for a company like Nokia?

5 What areas of competitive advantage does Wal-Mart use to drive its competitive position? How should Target and Sears develop their competitive positions?

6 Why are businesses with a competitive advantage in market share, unit cost, or product performance more profitable than businesses with no advantage in any of those areas?

7 For each area of differentiation advantage, identify a business that has a competitive advantage in that area. Explain how each business's source of differentiation advantage helps the business attract and satisfy target customers.

8 Identify businesses that have developed different types of marketing advantage, and explain for each how this advantage affects profitability.

9 How could a business with a niche market strategy develop a marketing advantage as a source of competitive advantage?

10 How has the Internet affected competitor intelligence gathering?

11 What is the benefit of a competitor gap analysis for General Motors? How could it use the results in its strategy development?

12 What is the main difference between *competitor* benchmarking and *competitive* benchmarking? When should a business engage in competitive benchmarking, and what are its benefits?

13 Cost and differentiation are well-known sources of competitive advantage, but why is a marketing advantage also a potential source of competitive advantage?

14 What are the various ways that a business like Kia can achieve a cost advantage?

15 Why do share leaders like Wal-Mart, Google, and Intel often have a cost advantage?

16 How might the industry forces for a regional phone company be different from the industry forces for a regional bank?

17 How will the industry change as competitors enter the regional phone market? How will profit potential be affected?

18 What impact would Procter & Gamble's everyday-low-price strategy have on competitive rivalry and the prisoner's dilemma?

Marketing Performance Tools and Application Exercises

The four interactive marketing performance tools and application exercises outlined here will add to your understanding of competitor analysis and sources of competitive advantage. To access the tools, go to **rogerjbest.com.** You may determine the answers to many of the questions by entering data offered. You may also enter your own data to see the results, and you can save your work. Each marketing performance tool is based on the Chapter 6 figure referenced in parenthesis.

6.1 Cost Advantage (Figure 6-6 and Appendix 6.2)

A. Estimate the experience curve coefficient for a cost curve with an initial unit cost of $100, an initial cumulative volume of 50,000 units, a current unit cost of $70, and a cumulative volume of 300,000 units.

B. What is the estimated unit cost when the business hits a cumulative volume of 1 million units?

C. What cost advantage will the business have at a cumulative volume of 1 million units if we assume that the business's closest competitor is on the same experience curve with a cumulative volume of 500,000 units?

6.2 Differentiation Advantage (Figure 6-9)

A. Create three product attributes for an MP3 player and indicate the relative importance of each, with the sum of the relative values equaling 100.

B. Use Apple's iPod as the company product and specify three competing MP3 players. Then rate each product attribute of Apple's iPod and each attribute of the three competing products on a scale that ranges from 0 (disastrous) to 10 (outstanding), where 5 is average.

C. What is Apple's product advantage index, and what does it imply with respect to customer value and profitability?

6.3 Marketing Advantage (Figures 6-12, 6-13, and 6-14)

A. How would the market share advantage change for the company that increased its market share from 20 to 23 percent while competitors each lost one share point? How would this affect profitability?

B. This same company is in a growing market and is willing to invest in expanding its product line from an average position to a broad product line position. How would this affect its marketing advantage and profitability?

C. How would the company's market share and profits change if it increased its distributor outlet share from 25 to 30 percent?

6.4   **Industry Analysis** (Figure 6-23)

A. Rate the industry attractiveness for the iPad and personal computer.

B. How does the overall industry attractiveness differ for each?

C. Which industry is likely to be more profitable?

Notes

1. M. Porter, *Competitive Strategy* (New York: Free Press, 1985): 38.
2. "Best and Worst New and Used Cars," *Consumer Reports* (2011): 43.
3. Porter, *op. cit.*: 3
4. A. Grove, *Only the Paranoid Survive: How to Exploit the Crisis Points That Challenge Every Company* (rev. ed.) (New York: Doubleday, 1999).
5. W. Boulding and R. Staelin, "A Look on the Cost Side: Market Share and the Competitive Environment," *Marketing Science* (Spring 1993): 144–66.
6. D. Garvin, "Competing on the Eight Dimensions of Quality," *Harvard Business Review* (November–December 1987): 101–9.
7. B. Gale, *Managing Customer Value* (New York: Free Press, 1994): 309.
8. R. Buzzell and B. Gale, *The PIMS Principles: Linking Strategy to Performance* (New York: Free Press, 1987).
9. Sun Tzu, *The Art of War, A Reader's Companion* (New York: Spark Publishing, 2003).
10. G. Gagliardi, *The Art of War Plus the Art of Marketing*, 2nd ed. (Seattle: Clearbridge Publishing, 2002).
11. G. Day and P. Nedungadi, "Managerial Representations of Competitive Advantage," *Journal of Marketing* (April 1994): 31–44; R. Rumelt, "How Much Does Industry Matter?" *Strategic Management Journal* (March 1991): 67–86; and R. Boscheck, "Competitive Advantage: Superior Offer or Unfair Dominance," *California Management Review* (Fall 1994): 132–51.
12. J. Porac and H. Thomas, "Taxonomic Mental Models of Competitor Definition," *Academy of Management Review* 15 (1990): 224–40.
13. H. Devine, Jr., and J. Morton, "How Does the Market Really See Your Product?" *Business Marketing* (July 1984): 70–9.
14. D. Tull and D. Hawkins, *Marketing Research: Measurement and Method*, 6th ed. (New York: Macmillan, 1993): 431.
15. G. Urban and S. Star, *Advanced Marketing Strategy* (Upper Saddle River, NJ: Prentice Hall, 1991): 144.
16. S. Slater and J. Narver, "Does Competitive Environment Moderate the Market Orientation–Performance Relationship?" *Journal of Marketing* (January 1994): 46–55; and J. Narver and S. Slater, "The Effect of Market Orientation on Business Competitor Analysis and Profitability," *Journal of Marketing* (October 1990): 20–35.
17. L. Fuld, *The New Competitive Intelligence—The Complete Resource for Finding, Analyzing, and Using Information about Your Competitors* (New York: John Wiley & Sons, 1995).
18. "Intelligence," *Oregon Business* (May 1988): 28–32.
19. "Airline Domestic Market Share–December 2010," Bureau of Transportation Statistics, Research and Innovative Technology Administration, U.S. Department of Transportation (not dated): http://www.transtats.bts.gov/, retrieved January 2011.
20. "Scores by Industry—Airlines," American Customer Satisfaction Index (not dated): http://www.theacsi.org/index.php?option=com_content&view=article&id=147&catid=&Itemid=212&i=Airlines, retrieved January 2011.
21. R. Camp, *Benchmarking—The Search for Industry Best Practices That Lead to Superior Performance* (Milwaukee: Quality Press, 1989); K. Leibfried and C. McNair, *Benchmarking: A Tool for Continuous Improvement* (New York: Free Press, 1992); J. Main, "How to Steal the Best Ideas Around," *Fortune* (October 9, 1992): 102–6; G. Watson, *Strategic Benchmarking* (New York: Wiley, 1993); and G. Watson, *Benchmarking for Competitive Advantage* (Portland, OR: Productivity Press, 1993).
22. M. Porter, *Competitive Strategy* (New York: Free Press, 1980).
23. A. McGahan, "Industry Structure and Competitive Advantage," *Harvard Business Review* (November–December 1994): 115–24.
24. S. Oster, "Understanding Rivalry: Game Theory," in *Modern Competitive Analysis*, 2nd ed. (Kinderhook, NY: Oxford, 1994): 237–51.

Competitive Position and Customer Value for 10 Competing Mid-Size SUVs

Make and Model	Value Map Number	Overall Performance[1]	Average Price	Fair Price[2]	Customer Value[3]
Toyota Highlander	1	62	$38,578	$34,281	−$4,297.00
Hyundai Veracruz SE	2	50	$33,870	$32,726	−$1,144.15
Nissan Xterra S	3	57	$28,000	$33,633	$5,633.02
Kia Sorento EX (V6)	4	68	$32,390	$35,059	$2,668.58
Honda Pilot EX-L	5	65	$35,830	$34,670	−$1,160.21
Subaru Tribeca Ltd	6	53	$34,270	$33,115	−$1,155.36
GMC Terrain SLT-1 (V6)	7	54	$30,985	$33,244	$2,259.23
Jeep Grand Cherokee (V6)	8	44	$39,010	$31,948	−$7,061.73
Dodge Journey SXT (V6)	9	31	$27,320	$30,264	$2,943.53
Jeep Wrangler Sahara	10	42	$30,375	$31,689	$1,314.08
Average		**53**	**$33,063**	**$33,063**	**$0.00**

1. Based on *Consumer Reports* ratings; does not include value of service quality or brand reputation.
2. Based on least-squares regression of average price (dependent variable) and overall performance.
3. Fair price minus average price.

Estimating an Experience Curve Coefficient and the Percent Experience Curve

Variables	Symbol	Example
Unit Cost at Time 1	UC1	$100
Unit Cost at Time 2	UC2	$80
Cumulative Volume at Time 1	CV1	40,000
Cumulative Volume at Time 2	CV2	120,000

Estimating Experience Curve Coefficient (B)

$$B = \frac{\ln(UC2 / UC1)}{\ln(CV2 / CV1)} = \frac{\ln(80 / 100)}{\ln(120{,}000 / 40{,}000)} = \frac{-0.223}{1.10}$$

$$B = \boxed{-0.203}$$

Percent Experience Curve $= (2)^B \times 100\% = (2)^{-.203} \times 100\% = \boxed{87\%}$

Forecasting Unit Cost

$$\text{Unit Cost (at 600,000)} = \$100 \times (600{,}000 / 40{,}000)^{-.203} = 0.577103$$
$$= \$100 \times .5771$$
$$= \boxed{\$57.71}$$

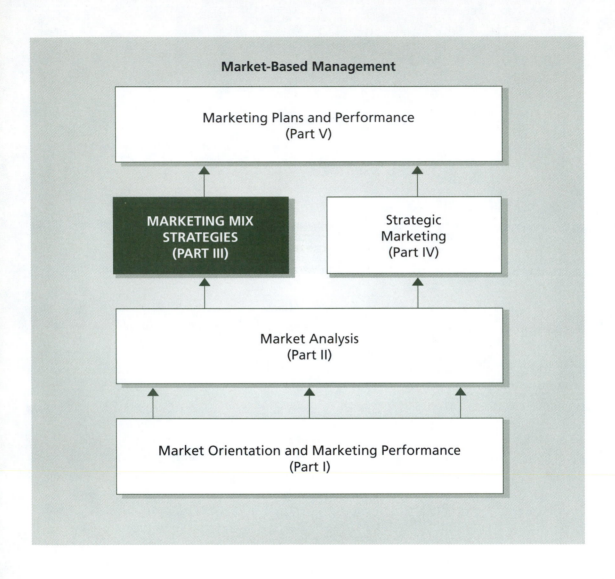

Market-Based Management

Marketing Plans and Performance
(Part V)

MARKETING MIX
STRATEGIES
(PART III)

Strategic
Marketing
(Part IV)

Market Analysis
(Part II)

Market Orientation and Marketing Performance
(Part I)

PART III

Marketing Mix Strategies

■ The marketing mix is the combination of a business's products, prices, promotions, and places (distribution channels). Short- and long-term marketing mix strategies can greatly affect a business's profits and its ability to survive over the long term.[*]

Businesses that lack a market orientation are likely to price their products simply by modeling the competition or marking up costs to achieve a desired profit margin. These businesses are more likely to hurt their customer value, market share, and profits. A market-based business, however, sets its prices on the basis of customer needs and the strength of its product position relative to competitors to create a desired level of customer value.

Part III focuses on short-term tactical marketing strategies designed around the marketing mix for a particular target market. The market analysis concepts presented in Part II are a prerequisite for developing tactical marketing strategies. These strategies are based on market demand and the needs of a target segment, and they must be formulated within the context of a competitive environment.

Chapter 7 examines product positioning and differentiation, branding and brand management, and product line strategies. Chapter 8 presents alternative market-based pricing strategies.

In the previous chapter, we saw how the combination of product performance and price creates a certain level of customer attraction for a business's product position. A business's share potential, however, cannot be fully realized unless the business also makes a strong marketing effort through advertising, promotion, sales, and distribution. Chapter 9 considers the various marketing systems (channels and sales) that businesses use to reach target customers, and Chapter 10 focuses on the role of marketing communications in delivering a successful marketing mix strategy.

[*]B. Kyle, "7 Ways to Improve Profit Through Both Long- and Short-Term Strategies," Web Marketing Place, LLC (not dated): http://www.websitemarketingplan.com/small_business/marketingmix.htm/, retrieved March 2011.

Product Positioning, Branding, and Product Line Strategies

■ A strong umbrella brand creates a base from which line extensions can achieve a faster market penetration at a lower cost.[1]

1971

1987

1992

2011

Starbucks has evolved from a regional brand from its beginnings in 1971 to a well-known international brand today. The Starbucks logo has also changed along the way. Although the company has been a coffee brand for 40 years, its current positioning strategy, launched in January 2011, is aimed at broadening Starbucks' product line beyond coffee. The new umbrella logo, without the words "Starbucks" and "coffee" enables the company to brand its additional products as it enters markets that are unrelated to coffee.

The marks "Starbucks" and "Starbucks Coffee" still appear sometimes in conjunction with the company's logo, but in many cases the new logo now stands alone, giving Starbucks flexibility in branding its new noncoffee products.

BRAND EXPANSION STRATEGIES

For Starbucks, the new logo paves the way for the company to move into new markets and expand its product line, opening up new opportunities for sales and profitable growth. But brand expansion also can take the form of a natural progression within a company's own market. Intel is a good example. Starting with memory chips in the 1970s and the 286, 386, and 486 microprocessors in the 1980s, Intel grew into a global company during the early

FIGURE 7-1 INTEL—PRODUCT POSITIONING, BRANDING, AND CUSTOMER VALUE

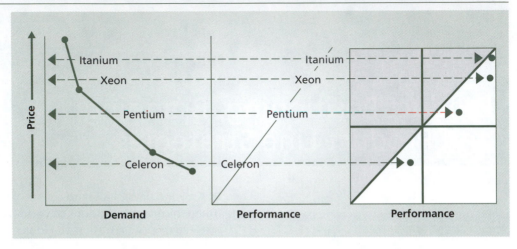

1990s with its Pentium processors. In the mid 1990s, as illustrated in Figure 7-1, new opportunities emerged for the company to sell more powerful processors at higher prices, which led Intel to design and introduce the Xeon processor. The Xeon was positioned at a higher price-performance point than the Pentium, offering more customer value at a higher price.

Fighter Brands

In the late 1990s, the lower priced personal computer (PC) market emerged prompted by the rise of Intel's competitor, Advanced Micro Devices (AMD). Intel could have responded by lowering the price on Pentium processors. Instead, to compete with AMD in the lower price segment, Intel held the Pentium's price and launched the Celeron processor at a lower price-performance point. In the early 2000s, the Celeron was a fighter brand.[2] It was designed to fight low-price competitors in order to serve the lower-price segment of the market, as well to protect the market share position of the Pentium, which would lose sales without the Celeron fighter brand. This product line and brand management strategy has enabled Intel to remain competitive and to grow with market demand while maintaining a market share of more than 80 percent.

Black & Decker took a different approach, positioning its new cordless drill products on the basis of differences in price and performance. The cordless drill market is partitioned into five needs-based segments, as shown in Figure 7-2.[3] At the low end are light-duty cordless drills, which are relatively low in power, torque, and endurance. At the other extreme are heavy-duty power cordless drills, which are high in power, torque, and endurance. Sears has elected to position products in each of the five price-performance segments. Black & Decker, on the other hand, has positioned itself in four of the five cordless drill segments at much lower prices. Black & Decker also used the same branding and product positioning strategy for DeWalt, a brand that Black & Decker owns. The set of DeWalt brands was positioned higher than Sears in four of the five segments. Although Sears' product-positioning strategy covers all five price-performance segments, its relative position is not the same in all five segments. At the low-price end of the market (light duty), Sears is priced higher than Black & Decker for roughly the same level of performance. At

FIGURE 7-2 PRODUCT LINE POSITIONING—CORDLESS DRILLS

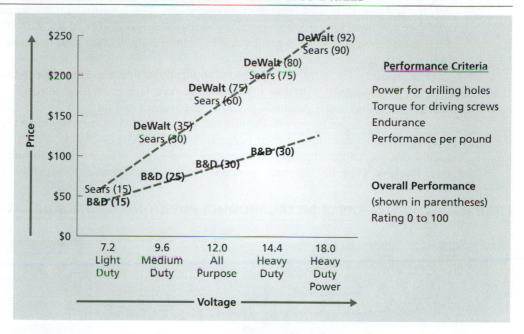

the high-price end of the market (heavy-duty power), Sears is priced just below DeWalt. In the mid-price segments (medium duty, all purpose, and heavy duty), Sears' performance rating and price are slightly lower than DeWalt's. Black & Decker's performance rating and price are significantly lower in the all-purpose and heavy-duty segments. In effect, the entire Black & Decker line consists of fighter brands that are designed to serve price-oriented customers while protecting the price and share position of the DeWalt product line.

Product Positioning

Product positioning starts with target customers, not company engineers or product managers. The needs of target customers—the benefits they seek in usage and the prices they are willing to pay—should drive product positioning. Working from this perspective, a business positions its product around customer needs for product performance service, and price. Product positioning also includes developing a brand name that communicates a desired brand image and marketing communications that correspond to target customer message and media preferences. It sounds easy, but successful product positioning strategies can be elusive in complex organizations that have many different perspectives and company traditions. To better understand this challenge, let's examine an industrial product that offers tremendous potential with respect to customer benefits and value.

Loctite is a well-established producer of industrial adhesives, owned by Henkel, a worldwide leader in adhesive brands and technologies. Many years ago, Loctite introduced a product called RC-601, an innovative substance that when applied to cracked or worn metal parts could perform as well as the metal itself. The application was not intended to be a permanent solution to a problem but merely a temporary fix for a broken machine part until it could be repaired or replaced, saving machine downtime and keeping production going. Loctite targeted RC-601 at production engineers who controlled the supplies and materials used in production operations. The advertising message consisted largely of technical data that supported the strength and reliability of RC-601. The price of a 6-ounce tube was $9.95, a good value in light of a study that found one tube saved a company 800 hours of machine downtime.[4]

The product worked well in its intended applications, but in less than a year disappointing sales led Loctite to withdraw it from the market. However, the company's product managers believed in the product's potential and wanted to find out why the market had rejected it. They began by personally interviewing selected customers to gain a full understanding of their needs and of their perceptions of RC-601. Loctite's product managers quickly discovered that they should target not production engineers but machine maintenance workers. Typically, the maintenance workers at the companies to which Loctite mar-

FIGURE 7-3 LOCTITE—QUICK METAL PRODUCT POSITIONING COMMUNICATION

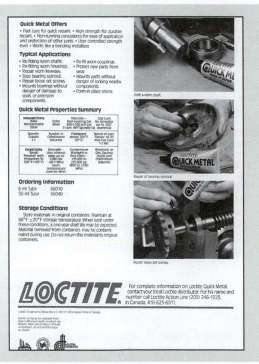

Product Positioning	Initial Positioning	Repositioning Strategy
Target Customer	Production Engineers	Machine Maintenance Workers
Brand Name	RC-601	Quick Metal
Ad Message	Technical Data	Pictures of How to Use
Price (6-ounce tube)	$9.95	$19.95
Packaging	None	In Silver Box
Value Proposition	Strong as Steel	Keep the Machines Running

FIGURE 7-4 PRODUCT-PRICE POSITION, MARKETING EFFORT, AND MARKET SHARE

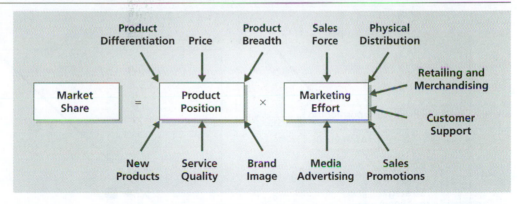

keted had the authority to make small purchases of materials and supplies. Loctite's managers also learned the maintenance workers disliked technical data, preferring instead pictures of when and how to use products. Researching the needs of the maintenance workers led Loctite to develop the repositioning strategy shown here. The product was rebranded as Quick Metal to better communicate its main product performance benefits (strength and speed). The advertising message shown in Figure 7-3 included pictures of five typical user applications and a list of many more possible applications. Loctite used distinctive packaging for Quick Metal that communicated the new brand name and logo. The packaging also made it easier for maintenance workers to store the product and then find it when needed. The repositioned product went on to set a record for first-year sales for new products.

Product Positioning and Market Share

The goal of a positioning strategy is to create a product-price position that is attractive to target customers and to provide a good source of cash flow for the business. Achieving greater market share is a primary indicator of the success of a marketing strategy, and the extent that market share grows depends on the strength of a business's product positioning and marketing effort. As shown in Figure 7-4, market share is represented as the business's product position multiplied by its marketing effort. A weak product position with a strong marketing effort will fail to deliver the desired level of market share. An attractive product position with a weak marketing effort will also fail to achieve the desired share.

To be successful, a business needs both an attractive product position and a strong marketing effort. Figure 7-4 shows the factors that contribute to a business's product position and marketing effort. Product differentiation, price, product breadth, new products, service quality, and brand image all strengthen a business's overall product position. As these influences on product positioning outperform those of competitors, the strength of a business's product position increases, and the product becomes more attractive to target customers.

To illustrate how product positioning affects marketing and profit performance, consider Samsung's successful repositioning of its consumer electronics products. Samsung had traditionally positioned its products at lower prices. Product quality and performance were generally lower than the quality and performance of competing products, and the products were sold through high-volume retailers like Wal-Mart. In 1997, sales were $22.6 billion but pre-tax profit was a negative $800 million, a negative 3.5 percent of sales.

FIGURE 7-5 SAMSUNG'S PRODUCT REPOSITIONING AND PERFORMANCE

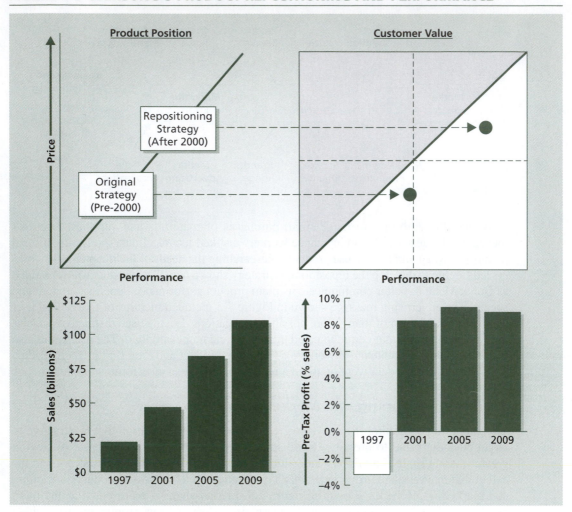

Samsung senior management then put in place a strategy to reposition the business as a higher quality, higher priced brand. All aspects of the product positioning and market-ing effort shown in Figure 7-4 had to be changed to accomplish the repositioning objec-tive. The effort entailed a massive investment in product development, with major expenses in research and development, but it paid off by 2001. As Figure 7-5 shows, sales more than doubled to $46.4 billion and pre-tax profit was $3.8 billion, 8.2 percent of sales. By 2005, the repositioning strategy produced sales of $85.4 billion and a pre-tax profit of $8 billion, 9.4 percent of sales. In 2009, sales continued to grow, but pre-tax profits as a percentage of sales stalled at 9 percent.

Product Positioning Strategies

Creating an attractive product position and achieving a desired level of market share and profitability require a company to make several ongoing product management efforts.

FIGURE 7-6 PRODUCT POSITIONING STRATEGIES

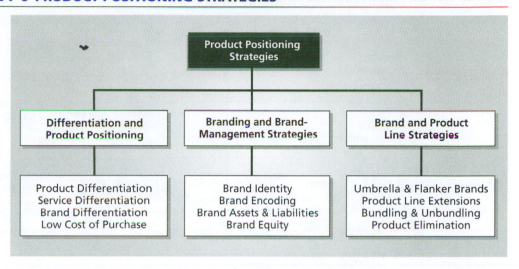

The first is the development of a positioning strategy based on target customers' needs. To do this, the company must answer two questions: "Who is our target customer?" and "How do we offer superior value for target customers?" For a particular target price, a business needs to develop a position based on either a low price or some source of differentiation and product positioning that is meaningful to target customers. As we saw in the previous chapter and as we see again in Figure 7-6, a differential advantage can be based on some combination of cost, product, service, and brand.

A second important area of product management involves branding and brand management strategies. How broad should the product line be? How should brands communicate a consistent image and desired target-market identity? How may a brand's assets and liabilities be managed to create higher levels of brand equity?

A third area of product management includes brand and product line strategies. To what degree should other brands be added as extensions of a strong umbrella brand? And when should a business bundle or unbundle products in order to attract and satisfy target customers? From a core product positioning strategy, these types of product line strategies need to be developed in order to fully leverage a business's capabilities and profit potential.

PRODUCT POSITIONING AND DIFFERENTIATION

On the basis of target customer needs, a business must develop a product position that is differentially superior to competitors' product positions. In a price-sensitive market, product positioning generally requires a lower price because this is the only source of differentiation that target customers value. For markets in which differentiation is possible and valued by target customers, a variety of strategies are possible. Product, service, and brand-image differences that are meaningful to target customers and differentially superior to those of competitors offer the potential to create a more attractive product position. Regardless of the product-positioning strategy pursued, the goal is to create customer value that is superior to that of competitors, as illustrated in Figure 7-7.

FIGURE 7-7 DIFFERENTIATION AND CUSTOMER VALUE

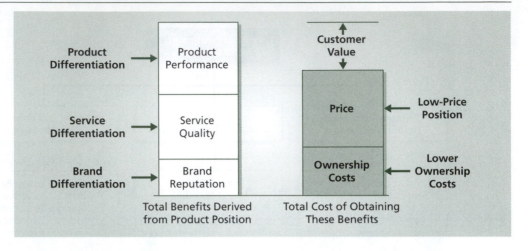

Product Performance and Differentiation

Many customers are willing to pay a higher price for products that deliver important performance benefits. Enhancements in product performance can attract customers who are seeking products that perform better than average. There are eight dimensions of product performance that can serve as a basis for product differentiation.[5] These dimensions may be arranged into four hierarchical categories of product performance, as shown in Figure 7-8. If a business fails to deliver acceptable or expected levels of reliability and conformance, an advantage in other dimensions of product performance will not matter. At the other extreme, quality aesthetics as a source of differentiation are of value only when all other aspects of quality are met with respect to customer quality expectations.

FIGURE 7-8 PRODUCT PERFORMANCE AND DIFFERENTIATION

■ **Product Performance Requirements**

Reliability   The length of time before failure or malfunction of the product.

Conformance   Incidence of defects that should not have occurred.

■ **Product Performance Differentiators**

Improvements   Operational characteristics that distinguish product performance.

Durability   Product life and ability to endure demanding use conditions.

■ **Product Performance Enhancements**

Features   Number and types of options that can be added.

Serviceability   Ease, speed, and costs of maintenance and repair.

■ **Product Performance Emotional Enhancements**

Apperance   The fit, finish, and overall appearance of the product.

Reputation   The image created by the brand name or comapany.

Product Quality Requirements

Customers expect products to be reliable and conform to specifications. Reliability and conformance to specifications are necessary if customers are even to consider purchasing the product. Poor reliability and conformance are quality killers. Whether customers are buying a computer, an automobile, or a jet plane, they expect reliability and conformance. For example, to enable its product to conform to customer expectations (i.e., specifications) worldwide, Nescafé creates different blends of coffee to match customers' taste preferences in different international markets.

Customers also expect products to operate reliably. Companies such as General Electric (GE), Motorola, and Honeywell have engaged in Six Sigma programs. The name *Six Sigma* is derived from a statistical term referring to the probability of product failure. At two sigma, a business with one million products would experience 40,000 failures. At six sigma, the product is close to failure-free. GE has spent $1 billion to ensure that all its divisions follow Six Sigma principles. Higher conformance to specifications and fewer failures have enhanced GE's customer retention rate and improved the company's profitability.

Product Performance Differentiators

Continuous improvement is one the workhorses of product performance. The automotive industry strives for continuous improvements in performance, as seen in the advances in steering, braking, and fuel economy. BMW adds an extra coat of paint to the vehicles that it sells in Japan in order to meet the quality expectations of the Japanese luxury-car buyer. Manufacturers who cannot keep pace with performance improvements will lose market share over time. Those who can lead with improved product performance will see their positions improve due to product differentiation and a competitive advantage. Intel, for example, seeks to stay ahead of competitors by continuously improving its products. For over three decades, Intel has been validating an axiom known as *Moore's Law*. Named after Intel co-founder Gordon E. Moore, the axiom states that the number of transistors that can be inexpensively placed on an integrated circuit doubles about every 2 years. Its pursuit of continuous performance improvement has enabled Intel to dominate its market with an 80 percent market share.

Durability is the other workhorse of product performance. Customers have expectations with respect to how long the product should last or how well it should stand up under normal usage. A business that fails to meet customer expectations with respect to product durability will have difficulty attracting new customers and retaining existing customers. Durability is a common source of advantage for industrial products used in demanding situations. ESCO Corporation, the specialty steel manufacturer that makes wear parts for front-end loaders and buckets for mining and earth-moving applications, offers customers greater product durability than its competitors through proprietary steel chemistry and product designs. Durability—the low breakage rate and long life of the products—is a quality driver that has strong appeal for ESCO's customers.

Product Performance Enhancements

A product that meets customer expectations with respect to conformance, reliability, performance, and durability can be differentiated with enhanced product and service features. Additional options that improve the ease of use, safety, or enjoyment of a product may be important sources of product differentiation. Air bags, entertainment systems, cruise control, and onboard navigation systems are examples of features that have been

FIGURE 7-9 GE APPLIANCE PRICE-PERFORMANCE—MAJOR PRODUCT LINES

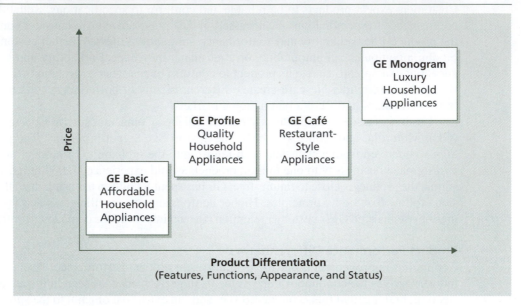

added to automobiles to enhance their quality. Optional features become more important as a source of differentiation when a business serves primarily affluent segments of the market. These customers often want more than the basic elements of product performance.

Serviceability is another differentiation enhancer. Products that are easier to maintain and repair save time and money. The Saturn was engineered to make repairs easier and less time consuming, resulting in lower repair costs. The Saturn design also has resulted in lower insurance premiums for owners due to lower than normal repair costs in the event of an accident. Both factors lower the total cost of ownership of a Saturn.

Product Performance Emotional Enhancements

The appearance of a product and its reputation can also serve as sources of product differentiation. In Japan, the appearance of a product and its packaging can have an enormous impact on its success. A British stereo manufacturer, for example, introduced a high-quality system into the Japanese market but failed to earn profits because the box in which the system was packaged did not match the quality of the product inside.

The image that a brand projects also can be important in many markets. The products made by Porsche, Rolex, and Chanel are judged not only on their functional characteristics, but also on their aesthetic characteristics and the image they project. A watch that is comparable on all seven other aspects of quality listed in Figure 7-8, but not made by Rolex, would fail to attract the customers who value the Rolex name and the image that a Rolex watch projects.

General Electric appliances all meet reliability requirements while offering customers a wide range of product-price performance, as shown in Figure 7-9. The basic GE product line is positioned with competitive prices and good quality, whereas the GE Profile product line offers more differentiating features and functions at a slightly higher price. The GE Café line is priced the same but offers GE Profile products in a restaurant-style

FIGURE 7-10 SERVICE QUALITY AND DIFFERENTIATION

■ **Service Quality Requirements**

Service Reliability	Ability to deliver the promised service dependably and accurately.
Service Assurance	Employee competence with respect to knowledge and courtesy.

■ **Service Quality Differentiators**

Performance	Able to outperform competitors and customers' service expectations.
Responsiveness	A service obsession to get it right when things go wrong.

■ **Service Quality Enhancements**

Extended Services	Extra customer services that enhance the ease of purchase.
Customer Empathy	Individual attention to customer needs.

■ **Service Quality Emotional Enhancements**

Appearance	The décor of facilities and the appearance of employees.
Reputation	The superior reputation built by a service-oriented business.

design. The GE Monogram product line offers a more limited line of luxury appliances products at a higher price. These products have a greater emphasis on status (emotional benefits). This product line strategy allows GE to create products and price points for a variety of customer needs. Extending the GE product line to this degree requires a careful assessment of revenues and expenses to ensure that a product line this broad is more profitable than one much more limited.[6] Companies sometimes grow their product lines without a careful consideration of profits, leading to a decline in profitability. In such cases, reducing the product line can restore the former level of profits.

Service Quality and Differentiation

Service can also be an important source of differentiation when it comes to positioning strategies. Nordstrom, FedEx, and Caterpillar are examples of businesses that have attained a superior position with a service differentiation. Because competitors can carry the same brand name products and can match the atmosphere found in Nordstrom stores, Nordstrom's superior service is a critical element in the company's positioning strategy. Service quality has dimensions similar to product performance as shown in Figure 7-10.

Les Schwab Tire Centers is a regional company with 430 locations in eight western states. The company's tires are of the best quality, but the performance attribute that differentiates Les Schwab from competitors is its exceptional service. Every Les Schwab store provides the same high level of reliable and fast service, and every store offers the service quality differentiators and emotional enhancements listed in Figure 7-11. Every customer interaction is an opportunity to positively affect the Les Schwab customer experience. These and other service enhancements contribute to Les Schwab's high level of customer satisfaction and high customer retention rate, the key drivers of a successful business.

Service Quality Requirements

One of the basic requirements of service quality is *service reliability*. Unreliable service is a quality killer.[7] Customers expect reliability first and foremost as a measure of service

FIGURE 7-11 LES SCHWAB—SERVICE QUALITY IS A COMPANY COMMITMENT

LES SCHWAB Tires – Service Quality

• **Service Reliability**
Les Schwab offers the same high level of
service at all of its 430 locations.

• **Service Quality Differentiator**
Fast, high-quality service and competitive prices
have differentiated Les Schwab from other tire
stores.

• **Service Quality Enhancements**
The company offers free flat-tire repair, and
customers who buy snow chains at Les
Schwab can return them if not used.

• **Emotional Enhancements**
All Les Schwab employees are neatly attired
with white shirts and run to customers' vehicles
as they are parking.

quality. For FedEx, the promise of *"when it absolutely, positively has to get there"* communicates the company's service position, a position based on reliability. A second service-quality killer is poor *service assurance*. Service assurance includes the competence and courtesy of service personnel. Caterpillar has sought to strengthen its competitive position and customer benefits with a differential advantage in responsive service. Offering a 24-hour parts and repair service available anywhere in the world and around-the-clock service has helped Caterpillar differentiate itself from its competitors.

Service Quality Differentiators
Nordstrom has always sought to achieve an unparalleled service quality advantage. This position of superior service—offering customers higher levels of service *performance* and *responsiveness*—differentiates the company from its competitors. Nordstrom is legendary in delivering service at levels that go beyond customer expectations, always satisfying customer wants in a timely fashion. The company's focus on satisfying customers may mean replacing a sweater that a customer shrank in the dryer despite a clearly labeled warning to line-dry only. By going beyond customers' expectations of service, Nordstrom delivers greater customer value to target customers.

Service Quality Enhancements
Extended services and individualized customer attention (*customer empathy*) are other aspects of service quality through which a business can seek to build a differentiation advantage. For example, Marriott's customer relationship marketing program focuses on individual customer needs and preferences, such as prearranging tee times for guests who golf. Marriott's highly customized attention to the service needs of its customers creates a differentiation advantage based on service quality. Likewise, Nordstrom offers its customers

the services of a "personal shopper" who meets with them to learn about their tastes and preferences in design, color, and other characteristics. Nordstrom's personal shoppers then make individualized recommendations.

Service Quality Emotional Enhancements

The *appearance* and *reputation* of the service quality can also affect perceptions of service quality and differentiation. At Les Schwab Tires, the nearest employee hurries to greet every customer who drives up; in the service area, all personnel move quickly in performing their tasks. The quickness of the service personnel conveys to customers an exceptional quality of service and leverages a small difference in employee behavior into a large differentiation advantage in its service quality and positioning.

Brand Differentiation

In many consumer and business-to-business purchases, customers are influenced by the status of a brand name or by the assurance of a well-known company. Brands like Lexus and Mercedes have strong associations with prestige or status. The importance of brand reputation to many target customers enhances the companies' positioning and differentiation advantage.[8]

Brand differentiation provides another way to position a business's products relative to competitors and to create incremental customer benefits and value, as illustrated in Figure 7-7. For example, Marriott estimated that adding its name to Fairfield Inn increased Fairfield Inn's occupancy by 15 percent. Kellogg's found that in matched product tests, customer choice of corn flakes cereal increased from 47 percent when the brand was not known to 59 percent when the Kellogg's name was identified. And when Hitachi and a competitor joined forces as strategic partners to jointly manufacture televisions in England, Hitachi sold its televisions at a $75 price premium and achieved a higher market share.[9] Each of these examples illustrates the importance of brand benefits to target customers and the brand equity that these brand reputations create for the business.[10]

A strong brand enhances positive evaluations of a product's quality, maintains a high level of product awareness, and provides a consistent image or brand personality. A strong brand, such as Coca-Cola, extends these attributes to brand extensions that include Coke Classic, Diet Coke, Caffeine-Free Coke, and Cherry Coke. Brand extensions are an effective source of differentiation, one that extends the positioning benefits of a core brand to related brands. However, there are limits to brand extensions.[11] At some point, it may be necessary to create new brand names and build another area of brand equity, as Coca-Cola did when it entered the sports drink market with Powerade and the energy drink market with brands that have no association with the company name.

Low Cost of Purchase

So far, we have focused on differentiation and the customer benefits it provides. A business can also create a source of advantage with low costs, making it possible for the business to offer a lower purchase price. Businesses with a low-cost advantage in markets in which price is an important determinant of customer value can use low prices as a basis for product positioning. In these market situations, however, a business cannot ignore product performance, service quality, or brand reputation issues. It must still meet customer expectations in these areas, even though the strength of its product position is based on an attractive price.

Low-Price Position

Wal-Mart is an example of a retailer that uses low prices to create an attractive position relative to competitors. With a low-price positioning strategy, Wal-Mart achieves a lower cost of buying, inventorying, and retailing the products it sells. This positioning strategy requires Wal-Mart to continuously find ways to contain or lower costs in order for its prices to remain a source of competitive advantage, while still meeting target customer needs for product, service, and brand. With this positioning strategy, Wal-Mart creates customer value and obtains a competitive advantage.

Whereas Wal-Mart uses large assortments of brand-name products and massive retail outlets, Trader Joe's is an upscale specialty food and wine chain with smaller stores but prices that are still below average. With over 350 existing stores and 20 new stores every year, Trader Joe's carries 2,500 items, 80 percent of which are private-label products. The average grocery store carries 25,000 branded products and only about 16 percent private-label goods. Wines for $3.99 are common at Trader Joe's, and the stores' promotion wine, Charles Shaw—nicknamed "Two Buck Chuck" when Trader Joe's introduced it in 2002 at a price of $1.99—still sells for just $2.99 at most Trader Joe's locations. Trader Joe's is a discount gourmet food store chain. The main source of Trader Joe's advantage—low price—is not easily copied, as it is a combination of a low-cost structure and thousands of personally developed relationships with private-label producers all over the world.

Lower Ownership Costs

The total cost of purchase also includes a customer's ownership costs, as shown in Figure 7-7. Ownership costs are expenses other than the purchase price that are associated with the acquisition and use of a product. A business can build a low-cost advantage and customer value by lowering these nonprice costs of purchase. For example, in Chapter 4 we saw that American Hospital Supply discovered that 50 cents of every dollar a hospital spent on equipment was for acquiring and inventorying the equipment. In response, American Hospital Supply developed a computerized ordering and inventory management system that would lower a client hospital's cost of acquiring and inventorying equipment by 50 percent. By lowering these ownership costs, American Hospital Supply created a greater customer value and developed a source of advantage that enabled the company to become the market share leader in the hospital equipment market.

BRANDING AND BRAND MANAGEMENT STRATEGIES

To fully capture the total value of a product's positioning, it is important to brand a product in a way that communicates its intended positioning. A brand name gives an identity to a product or service, providing customers with a way to quickly comprehend the brand's primary benefits, whether rational or emotional.

Brand Identity

The successful management of brands is built around sound marketing practices. A business with a strong market orientation that has segmented its target markets and tracks customer behavior by segment is in the best position to build a successful brand.[12] An internally focused business simply does not have the market intelligence it needs to build

FIGURE 7-12 BRAND-ENCODING STRATEGIES

Encoding Strategy	Examples
Company Logo	The "swoosh" (Nike), an apple with a bite (Apple, Inc.), a lizard (La Coste)
Company Color	John Deere (green), Caterpillar (yellow), IBM (blue), Coca-Cola (red)
Company Letters	3M, BMW, FedEx, GE, HP, IBM, PPG, J&J, P&G
Company Name	Ford, Boeing, Kellogg, Canon
Product Name	GE Jet Engines, Heinz Tomato Ketchup, Victoria Salsa
Umbrella Brand	Mac, Oreo, Grand Cherokee, Canon PowerShot, Cessna
Subbrand Name	Laredo (Jeep Grand Cherokee), Cessna Citation Mustang, CanoScan LiDE
Brand Benefit	Lean Cuisine, Campbell's Low-Sodium Soup, Oral-B Cavity Defense Toothbrush
Numbers/Letters	Cessna Citation CJ1+, Canon PowerShot SX30 IS, Canon PIXMA MG8120

a brand identity that would be meaningful to target customers. The first step in developing a brand identity is to define the desired product positioning and value proposition for a specific target market. Without these specifications, the branding identification process would quickly deteriorate into an internal process that was built around product features rather than customer benefits.

Brand Encoding

A great deal of strategic thinking goes into the branding process and the creation of specific brand names.[13] Because brand names take a variety of forms and serve a variety of functions, a brand-encoding system will help us understand how to position a product with a brand name for a specific market and desired image. The encoding system is presented as a hierarchy of possible naming components, as shown in Figure 7-12, starting with the company name, followed by a brand name, and enhanced or modified by subbrand names, numbers, letters, product names, and benefits. A brand may be as broad as a company name like Dell, as narrow as a specific version of a product like Microsoft Windows 7, or as abstract as Altoids.

Company brand names such as Nike and General Electric carry an image and serve as umbrella brands under which important benefits may be communicated to diverse product-markets. The Nike name evokes competitiveness and winning across product-markets that include track, golf, soccer, football, and basketball. General Electric's reputation for reliability and good value reaches across light bulbs, appliances, medical equipment, power-generation systems, electric motors, transportation equipment, electrical distribution equipment, jet engines, and financial services. Companies such as Sony, Intel, and Ford have created specific brand names to supplement their company names and to enhance the identities and positions of their products. Ford, for example, brands its cars with names such as Explorer, Taurus, and Mustang. Intel adds a product name to its company name and brand name to further distinguish its product positioning for Pentium, Celeron, and Xeon processors. Other companies use only a brand name, as Procter & Gamble does with Tide, Cheer, Bold, Bounce, Gain, and Ivory Snow. Some combination of elements from the brand-encoding system allowed each of these companies to achieve

FIGURE 7-13 GENERAL ELECTRIC COMPANY—PRODUCT BRANDING STRATEGY

General Electric Product Areas	GE's Branding of Appliance Products				
Appliances ⟶	**Appliances**	**GE**	**GE Profile**	**GE Café**	**GE Monogram**
Aviation	Air Conditioners	X			
Business Finance	Compactors	X			
Consumer Finance	Cooktops	X	X		X
Electrical	Dehumidifiers	X			
Electrical Distribution	Dishwashers	X	X	X	X
Energy	Disposals	X			
Healthcare	Freezers	X			
Lighting	Microwaves	X	X	X	X
Media & Entertainment	Ranges	X	X	X	X
Oil & Gas	Refrigerators	X	X	X	X
Rail	Toasters	X			
Software & Services	Wall Ovens	X	X		X
Water	Warming Drawers	X	X		X
	Washers & Dryers	X	X		X
	Water Filters	X			
	Water Heaters	X			
	Water Softeners	X			
	Wine Refrigerators	X			

the desired product positioning for each brand and build a portfolio of brands that has both meaning and synergy.[14] A brand name may or may not use all of the elements in the coding system. Choosing the specific elements to include is a matter of determining which combination is most likely to exert full power to position a product, as discussed under each of the following brand-encoding strategies.

Company and Product Name

General Electric (GE) serves a diverse set of product-markets that include aviation, consumer goods, energy, healthcare, electrical equipment, lighting, media, transportation, and financial services. The GE name and logo are key factors in communicating the company's long tradition of providing quality products and services at prices that deliver high customer value. However, General Electric has elected not to include the brands NBC Universal (co-owned with Comcast) and CNBC under the GE flagship brand. For strategic reasons, GE has preferred to minimize the association between the GE name and the NBC Universal and CNBC names.

As shown in Figure 7-13, the GE company name is the umbrella brand for the company's products and services. In the table, major GE product-markets are listed under the GE umbrella name. GE appliance products are branded by product names, such as GE Cooktops or GE Washers and Dryers. The GE Profile line is made up of uniquely branded

FIGURE 7-14 TOYOTA COMPANY NAME AND BRANDING STRATEGY

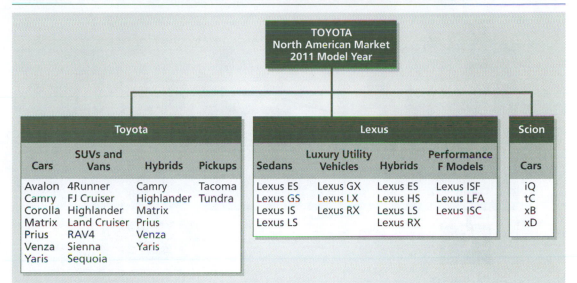

GE appliances, such as the GE Spacemaker Microwave. The GE Café line consists of restaurant-grade appliances. The GE Monogram class of appliances is a higher perform-ance, luxury brand.

To illustrate the power of a well-known company brand name, customer surveys in the 1980s found that GE was rated among the best in gas cooktops, even though at the time the company did not make gas cooktops. GE went on to leverage its brand power by adding gas cooktops to its product line.

Company and Brand Name

Major automotive companies such as Ford, Honda, and Toyota have used their company name as a prominent part of their branding strategy. Figure 7-14 lists the many brand names that Toyota uses for its vehicles. The Toyota company name served as its only umbrella brand until 1990 when the company introduced the Lexus. Toyota later started Scion, another division brand, and sold the first vehicles in 2003 in California.

In deciding to market Lexus and Scion without the Toyota brand, the company sought to broaden its overall appeal by distancing the new vehicles from the general pub-lic conceptions about the Toyota brand at the time. In 1990 Toyota had limited brand equity in the luxury car market, so it launched its new luxury cars under the Lexus brand without the Toyota name. By 2000, Toyota vehicle buyers in North America were mostly in their middle years or older, so Toyota began work on the Scion to appeal to young buy-ers. The Scion models, which range in size from a microcar to a coupe, are marketed with many accessories and a simplified purchasing process. For Lexus, the branding strategy has proven a great success, with Toyota growing its Lexus product line from one model to the array of Lexus brands shown in Figure 7-14. The Scion division is also growing, and the cars are now sold across the U.S. and Canada. A third umbrella brand may be in the offing at Toyota; there have been reports that the company is considering dropping the Toyota name in branding the Prius.

FIGURE 7-15 CESSNA'S BRAND AND SUBBRAND POSITIONING STRATEGY

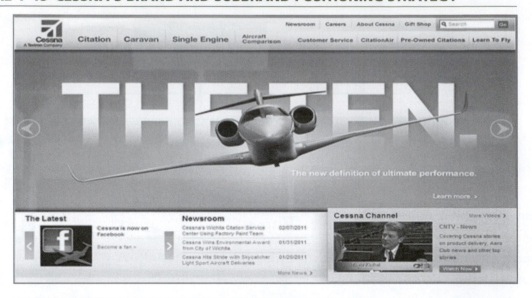

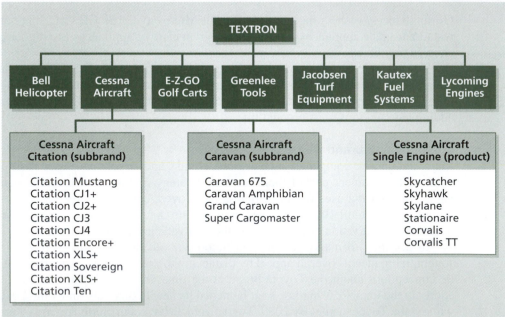

Umbrella Brand and Subbrands

Textron is a $10 billion-plus company that is unknown to most people. But the brands that Textron owns, like Bell Helicopter, Cessna, and E-Z-GO Golf Carts, are well-known umbrella brands. As shown in the bottom portion of Figure 7-15, Textron has seven major umbrella brands under which it markets many subbrands. Its flagship brand is Cessna, the major source of Textron sales and profits. The Cessna brand has two major subbrands: Citation and Caravan. Both subbrands have several brand names, such as Cessna Citation

FIGURE 7-16 YUM BRANDS—ENCODING WITH BRAND NAME ONLY

Yum Brands – 2011	KFC	Pizza Hut	Taco Bell	A&W	Long John Silver's	Total Stores
Before 4th Quarter 2011	16,264	13,281	5,627	637	1,024	36,833
After 4th Quarter 2011	16,264	13,281	5,627	0	0	35,172

Mustang or Cessna Caravan Amphibian. A third subbrand category, called Single Engine, consists of small planes that are individually branded with names such as Cessna Skycatcher, Skyhawk, and Skylane. This strategy has allowed Textron to acquire new companies with strong brand names under which the companies can grow by adding new subbrands.

Shown in top portion of Figure 7-15 is Cessna's home page, which provides details and photos of the company's product line and is integrated with Cessna's social media activities. Cessna's Facebook page (see Figure 10-8 in Chapter 10) gives customers a forum for sharing their experiences, love of flying, and enthusiasm for Cessna planes.

Brand Name and Product/Benefit

Braun has successfully branded the Oral-B toothbrush. Taking advantage of the well-known name and its image for quality, Braun extended the Oral-B brand name by including primary benefits that differentiate the brands. Oral-B Ultra Plaque Remover is clearly targeted at customers who are seeking the benefit of plaque removal; customers can quickly differentiate this from the intended benefit of the regular Oral-B toothbrush. Some of the many other brand names that include key product benefits are Lean Cuisine, DieHard, Easy-Off, Loctite, Red Bull, Healthy Choice, and Slim-Fast.

Brand Name Only

Yum Brands is not a well-known company among consumers. But its brands as shown Figure 7-16 are very well known worldwide. Yum Brands has more than 35,000 stores in over 100 countries, with about 20,000 of the stores in the United States. Each store brand has a variety of products that make up several product lines. Yum Brands added the Wing Street brand of buffalo wings to 1,000 Pizza Hut locations in 2007 and planned to have 4,000 locations of the combined brand by 2010. In 2011, Yum Brands announced the sale of A&W (637 stores) and Long John Silver's (1,024 stores). Yum Brands' divestment strategy will enable the company to devote more resources to the three remaining brands, each of which has far more stores than either of the other two brands.

Procter & Gamble and Unilever also use a brand-only product positioning strategy. As shown in Figure 7-17, P&G has a total 114 brands: 83 U.S. and 31 international brands. The figure shows the three major brand categories. The 24 detergents include nine individual brand names. This branding strategy allows P&G to better target specific customer needs and dominate the store shelf space with individual brands.

Brand Name Development

Whether naming a new company, a new brand, or a new subbrand, it can be a challenge to come up with a name that has meaning with respect to positioning a product, as well as

FIGURE 7-17 PROCTER & GAMBLE PRODUCT BRANDING

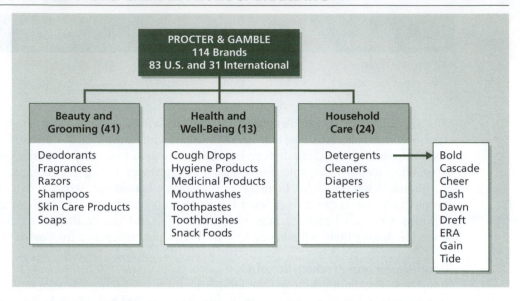

being short and easy to remember. Summarized here and in Figure 7-18 are five ways for creating a new company, brand, or subbrand name.[15]

1. **Founder and Owner Names:** Not surprisingly, many company names (core brands) are the names of company founders or owners, such as Dell, Inc. (Michael Dell), Ford Motor Company (Henry Ford), Calvin Klein, Estée Lauder, and Hilton Hotels (Conrad Hilton). Other names are derivations of founders' names, like Wal-Mart (derived from Sam Walton). These brands had to build their brand equity without any association with a core customer benefit.

2. **Functional Names:** These names are derived from the basic benefit provided by the product. Duracell (long lasting), Federal Express (fast delivery), Lean Cuisine (low calorie), Sub-Zero (stays cold), and Microsoft (microcomputer software) each strived to build an association between the brand name and core function of the brand. Federal Express eventually shifted to a name morpheme (FedEx).

FIGURE 7-18 BRAND NAME DEVELOPMENT

Founder Brand Names	Functional Brand Names	Invented Brand Names	Experiential Brand Names	Evocative Brand Names
Wal-Mart Sam Walton	**Duracell** Long Lasting	**Kleenex** Sanitary, Clean	**Big Bertha** Power, Long Drives	**Apple** Friendly, Easy to Use
Dell Michael Dell	**E-Z-GO Golf Carts** Easy to Operate	**Noxzema** Skin Cleanser	**Kodak EasyShare** Share Photos Easily	**Victoria's Secret** Sexual, Seductive
Levi's Levi Strauss	**Microsoft** PC Software	**Fresca** Citrus, Freshness	**Land Rover** Exploration	**Virgin Airlines** Excitement

FIGURE 7-19 BRANDING A NEW EAR PROTECTION PRODUCT

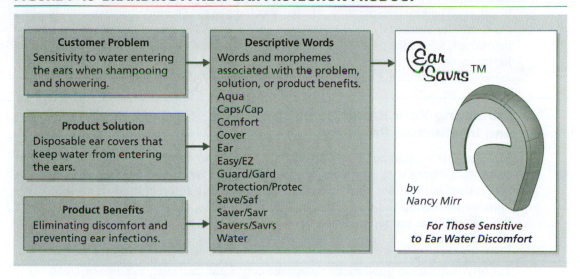

Customer Problem	**Descriptive Words**	
Sensitivity to water entering the ears when shampooing and showering.	Words and morphemes associated with the problem, solution, or product benefits.	

Descriptive Words list:
Aqua
Caps/Cap
Comfort
Cover
Ear
Easy/EZ
Guard/Gard
Protection/Protec
Save/Saf
Saver/Savr
Savers/Savrs
Water

Product Solution
Disposable ear covers that keep water from entering the ears.

Product Benefits
Eliminating discomfort and preventing ear infections.

Ear Savrs™

by Nancy Mirr

For Those Sensitive to Ear Water Discomfort

3. **Invented Names:** There are two kinds of invented names: those which are built from root words and morphemes, and those which are poetic constructions based on the rhythm or experience of saying them. Agilent and Alliant are invented company names from roots that mean "agile" and "ally." Poetically created brand names include Oreo, Kleenex, Snapple, and Google. Google is actually derived from the mathematical term *googol*. Ketchup is an invented word created in China in the 1690s as Kê-chiap. The word evolved to Kechap in Malaysia and Singapore (early 1800s) and eventually became Ketchup in the United States.

4. **Experiential Names:** These are company or brand names associated with an experience, such as the experience of discovery, success, movement, or good health. The Internet browsers Explorer, Magellan, Navigator, and Safari are names created to communicate the experience of surfing the web. Big Bertha, Red Bull, Path Finder, and Silk Soy Milk are also brand names that convey meanings based on people's experience.

5. **Evocative Names:** Companies also create names that evoke a positive attribute or a feeling. Examples include Apple, Yahoo, and Virgin Airlines.

Creating a New Brand Name

Recognizing the various approaches to brand-name development, a business or management team ultimately needs to develop a specific name for a specific business situation. Figure 7-19 illustrates the process of creating a brand name for a new product. The product's inventor experienced personal discomfort with water getting into her ears during visits to her hair salon. Research found that other people also were prone to discomfort when water entered their ears, including infants and children. The product solution was to create a disposable rubber ear cover. The product benefits included eliminating discomfort and reducing the potential for ear infections.

Branding the new product was important. Selecting the right name, one that conveyed its use and benefits, would help position the product in its market. The product's creators came up with several words and morphemes and evaluated many different combinations. The brand name they selected was Ear Savrs. The logo used an outline of an ear to further communicate the product's application. The target market was primarily hair salons, where the product could be offered to those customers who were sensitive to having water enter their ears during a shampoo, or even to all customers. A secondary market was a children's version that would come in a variety of fun colors.

Protecting Your Brand Name and Intellectual Property

Many people want to be their own boss, start their own company, and become the next Mark Zuckerberg with a product like Facebook. The Internet provides a new platform for product innovation, whether people are creating an Internet product such as Facebook or marketing their products online. In all cases, entrepreneurs need to protect their intellectual property. Listed here are five ways to protect a brand name or new product idea.

1. **Copyright:** It's a good idea to place the copyright date (i.e., the date of creation) at the bottom of each page. Then register your work with the U.S. Copyright Office by sending a "deposit," which in many cases is a copy of your work, along with information about the work, the author's name, and date of creation. Submit a copy of each page with the copyright notice on each page. For the *Marketing Metrics Handbook* shown in Figure 7-20, this process required approximately 300 pages of screen prints. The computer code used to create this interactive product was also copyrighted.
2. **Trademark:** Add the TM initials next to your brand name and logo and submit them to the U.S. Patent and Trademark Office. If the trademark is approved, change the TM emblem to the registration emblem (®) to indicate a registered trademark. The logos and brand names were registered for four of the products shown in Figure 7-20.
3. **U.S. Patent:** In order to patent your idea and the unique features of the product, submit careful documentation, including drawings and descriptions, to the Patent and Trademark Office. The process of patent approval can take several years. In the interim you can use the "U.S. Patent Pending" notice. We performed a patentability search and filed a U.S. patent application for the *Marketing Metrics Handbook*, which allows us to mark it "U.S. Patent Pending."
4. **Licensing:** Licensing is a good option for products that are difficult to produce or that would be better manufactured and marketed by a company which has the necessary capabilities. Licensing allows owners of intellectual property to obtain payment for their creations in a lump sum, plus royalties.
5. **Assignment:** Assignment of the rights to a product formalizes the transfer of rights held by one party—the *assignor*—to another party—the *assignee*. The financial terms may consist of a single payment, a series of payments over time, royalties, or a combination of these options.

Of the several products developed by the author in Figure 7-20, the first two were the can topper (1968) and the pop-top filter holder (1972). The author documented the idea

FIGURE 7-20 PROTECTING INTELLECTUAL PROPERTY

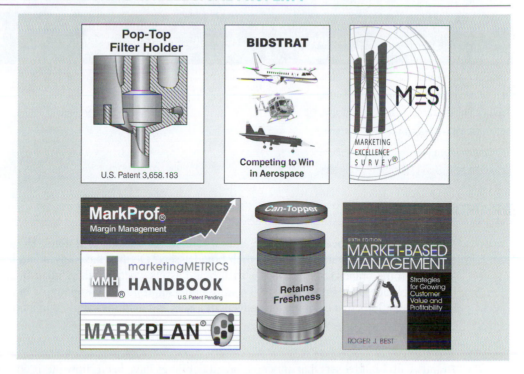

for the can topper by mailing a description of the product and its benefits, along with an illustration, to himself. At the time plastic lids and containers had not been developed, and the can topper product would have been used to seal cans whose contents—such as tomato paste, refried beans, and canned fruit—had been only partially used. The can topper name was never trademarked and no patent application was submitted. However, on a piece of paper, the author included his illustration of the product, the description of how it worked, and a statement of its product benefits. He then folded the sheet of paper in thirds, sealed it with cellophane tape, and mailed it. The envelope was postmarked September 17, 1968. Although the envelope and its contents are not a legal document, they do establish the date that the inventor originated the idea. The envelope remains sealed after more than 40 years.

The pop-top filter holder was conceived in 1970 and patented in 1972. The patent was assigned to General Electric Company where the author worked as an engineer. Googling the product's name will show the many applications that it has today.

BIDSTRAT (1990) was licensed to Stratx International. The author copyrighted and obtained trademarks for MES (1990), MarkProf (2000), MarkPlan (2005), and the *Marketing Metrics Handbook* (2009). The Marketing Excellence Survey and MarkPlan were assigned to the Corporate Executive Board in 2007 for a single payment. *Market-Based Management* was first published in 1996, and all rights were assigned to the publisher in exchange for royalties. Each of these new products required a brand name to help position the product on the basis of its application and benefits. Each product also was given some level of legal protection to ensure its intellectual property ownership.

FIGURE 7-21 BRAND ASSETS SCORECARD

Brand Assets	Relative Importance	Very Low 0	Below Average 25	About Average 50	Above Average 75	Very High 100	Brand Asset Score
Brand Awareness	20%					X	20.0
Emotional Connectedness	10%			X			5.0
Brand Loyalty	20%				X		15.0
Product Line Extensions	30%			X			15.0
Price Premium	20%			X			10.0
Overall Brand Assets	**100%**						**65.0**

BRAND EQUITY

Brand names like Coca-Cola, Apple and GE are worth billions of dollars. How did they achieve this level of value? What are their brand assets? Do they have any brand liabilities? Why are some brands able to leverage their brand assets whereas others incur brand liabilities that reduce their brand equity? To fully understand how a company or brand builds brand equity, let's first examine the concept of assets and liabilities applied to a brand name.

Brand Assets

Brands with brand assets that outweigh brand liabilities have been shown to produce higher levels of sales growth and customer commitment.[16] Like a business's financial assets, the brand name itself has different kinds of assets.[17] A brand like Coca-Cola creates brand assets based on its market leadership and high level of awareness. Brand assets that affect brand value are also derived from an exceptional reputation for quality, brand relevance, and high levels of customer loyalty. Although a variety of other influences could create brand assets,[18] the five brand assets in Figure 7-21 may be found to some degree in all top brand names.

1. **Brand Awareness:** Companies with high brand awareness can more easily introduce new products and enter new markets. Nike began with athletic shoes but now has a wide range of apparel products and accessories.
2. **Emotional Connection:** A superior reputation for quality is a brand asset for brands such as Lexus. A brand name that relates to consumers on an emotional level can be a highly valuable brand asset. Over the past 20 years, Lexus has gained brand relevance among luxury-car buyers, and Cadillac has lost brand relevance as the lifestyle and demographics of this market have changed.
3. **Brand Loyalty:** For brands like Apple, high customer loyalty creates a profitable brand asset that lowers marketing and sales expenses and increases customer profitability.
4. **Product Line Extensions:** The Honda name, once primarily identified with motorcycles, now appears on products ranging from SUVs to outboard motors. Many product line extensions carrying the brand name convey a company's confidence in its products and in turn inspire customer confidence.
5. **Price Premium:** Being able to command a price premium is a valuable asset for a brand. Companies such as Apple, Brooks Brothers, and Rolex hold strong positions in their markets, even with their higher prices.

One way to measure these brand assets is with a brand assets scorecard shown in Figure 7-21. Using the scorecard, we can rate each brand asset by comparing it with the average among competitors in the same market. Individual brand asset scores can range from 0 to 20. When we combine the scores for the five kinds of assets, the overall brand asset score ranges from 0 to 100. An average brand attains an overall brand asset score of 50. Brands with large brand equity, such as Coca-Cola, Apple, and GE, produce brand asset scores much greater than 50.

To understand how the scorecard works, consider how we might assess each of the brand assets presented in Figure 7-21 for Cadillac and Lexus. In the luxury-car market in 1990, Lexus was a relatively new brand, and Cadillac was the market leader with a 30 percent market share. Most luxury-car buyers in 1990 would have rated Cadillac higher than Lexus, so the overall brand asset score for Cadillac would have been much higher that year than the score for Lexus. But if we had scored the two brand names every 3 or 4 years since 1990, we would have seen Lexus climb in brand assets and Cadillac slide, with its market share eroding to below 20 percent.[19]

Brand Liabilities

Brands can also incur brand liabilities due to product failure, lawsuits, or questionable business practices. A good example is Arthur Andersen, once among the world's top accounting firms. Before the Enron collapse, an assessment of Arthur Andersen's brand liabilities would have been highly favorable. But publicity about the firm's questionable practices at Enron led to substantial customer dissatisfaction. Arthur Andersen's brand liabilities escalated. Simultaneously, a loss of market share, an eroding reputation for quality, and declining brand loyalty caused its brand assets to plummet. The firm's legal problems stemming from Enron eventually led to its demise. More recently, we can understand how Toyota's brand liabilities increased with massive product-failure recalls and an extensive investigation of Toyota quality assurance. Product failure is one of five kinds of brand liabilities that could potentially harm a company's brand equity.

1. **Customer Dissatisfaction:** High levels of customer complaint and customer dissatisfaction detract from brand equity. Customer dissatisfaction with large banks has created an increasing brand liability for Bank of America and others.
2. **Product or Service Failures:** Product failures, like the ones reported with respect to Toyota product failures, are a serious brand liability, one that can greatly diminish even a powerful brand.
3. **Questionable Practices:** Business practices that lead to allegations, lawsuits, or prosecution also hurt brand liability. During the early 2000s, a flurry of prosecutions involving top executives of major corporations diminished the brand equity of those companies.
4. **Poor Record on Social Issues:** Businesses with a poor record of social responsibility may face eroded brand equity. Oil companies that become associated with poor environmental practices, and consumer goods companies whose "sweatshop" conditions at overseas manufacturing facilities are publicized, see declines in the equity of their brands.
5. **Negative Associations:** A brand that becomes identified in the public's mind with a disreputable individual, an unpopular venture, or an unpleasant event loses brand

FIGURE 7-22 BRAND LIABILITIES SCORECARD

Brand Liabilities	Rel. Imp.	Very Low 0	Below Average 25	About Average 50	Above Average 75	Very High 100	Brand Liabilities Score
Customer Dissatisfaction	20%		X				5.0
Product or Service Failures	20%		X				5.0
Questionable Practices	20%			X			10.0
Poor Record on Social Issues	20%	X					0.0
Negative Associations	20%		X				5.0
Overall Brand Liabilities	**100%**						**25.0**

equity. For this reason, most companies are quick to shed their affiliation with a celebrity advertising spokesperson if the person suddenly becomes embroiled in negative publicity.

Brand liabilities can be assessed using the brand liabilities scorecard in Figure 7-22. For strong brands, brand assets will exceed brand liabilities. Using the brand liabilities scorecard, we could assess Arthur Andersen's brand liabilities before and after the Enron debacle. We would find that our estimate of the brand liabilities increased after the Enron scandal. For Arthur Andersen, then, the Enron scandal decreased its brand assets and increased its brand liabilities, both of which contributed to a significant drop in brand equity.

Brand Equity

In a business, the owner's equity is the value of the owner's holdings in the company. It is determined by the difference between the company's assets and its liabilities. The larger the ratio of assets to liabilities, the greater the owner's equity. As Figure 7-23 shows, brand equity can be viewed in the same way. To calculate brand equity, simply subtract the total brand liabilities score from the total brand assets score. Tracking changes in brand equity over time is an important part of the brand management process, because brand equity is not static.

For businesses such as Enron, Arthur Andersen, and WorldCom, we can easily envision how brand equity quickly eroded as brand assets declined and brand liabilities grew. Likewise, it is easy for us to understand how the brand equity of companies such as Apple, Lexus, and Target has grown over the last 15 years without burdensome brand liabilities that would have limited that growth. In either situation, the brand equity model is a useful way to understand and manage a brand's equity.

Building brand equity requires a significant effort, and some companies use alternative means of achieving the benefits of a strong brand. For example, brand equity may be borrowed by extending the brand name to a line of products in the same product category or even to other categories. In some cases, especially when there is a perceptual connection between the products, such extensions are successful. In other cases, the extensions are unsuccessful and can erode the original brand equity.

FIGURE 7-23 BRAND BALANCE SHEET AND BRAND EQUITY

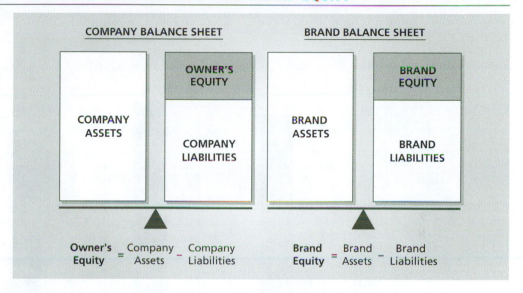

BRAND AND PRODUCT LINE STRATEGIES

We have seen that the more products a business has to sell, the more ways it has to attract and satisfy customers. A broad line of products creates more selling opportunities for the sales force and channel partners. A business with a narrow line of products has to be more focused in order to be cost effective in its marketing efforts.

Because a broad product line gives a business more prospective customers and the potential to sell more to each customer, this type of marketing efficiency translates into more sales and higher levels of profitability. For example, in Figure 7-24 we can see that businesses with broad product lines are more profitable during the emerging and growing stages of the products' life cycles than are businesses with a narrow product line. It is particularly important, then, to expand a business's product line during these stages of a product life cycle. This is exactly what Microsoft did in the 1980s and 1990s in growing the computer software market.

Product Line Development

When a business expands from one market segment into an adjacent segment in order to grow sales and profits, product line expansion requires considerable product differentiation and careful positioning. The business now asks a different price for a different combination of product performance, service quality, and brand reputation. In Chapter 6, we saw that Toyota sequentially expanded its product line from a low product-price segment in the 1960s to today's full line of vehicles, each with a different product-price position and a unique brand-name identity, as illustrated in Figure 7-25.

We also saw in Chapter 6 that Anheuser-Busch's product line strategy uses separate brand names for each of the many positioning strategies it pursues, as also presented in Figure 7-25. The brands have distinct product-price positions that are attractive to different

FIGURE 7-24 BREADTH OF PRODUCT LINE AND RETURN ON INVESTED ASSETS

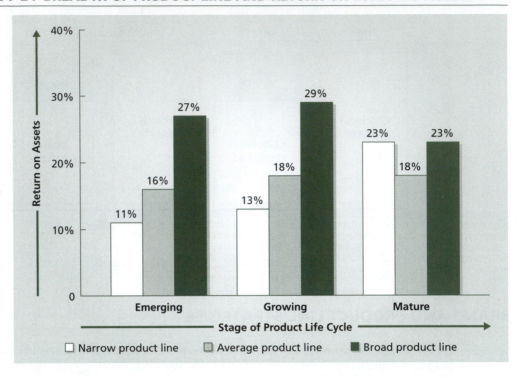

FIGURE 7-25 PRODUCT LINE, BRANDING, AND DIFFERENTIATION STRATEGY

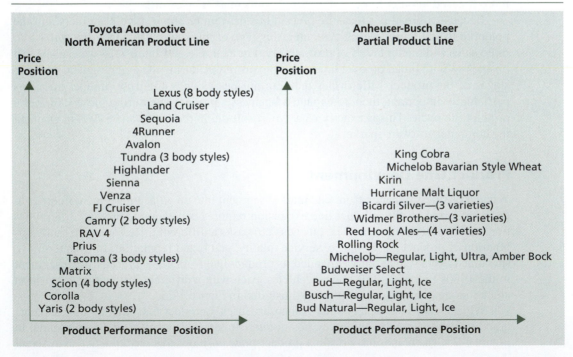

types of customers. In recent years, Anheuser-Busch has expanded its product line to the microbrew segment with Michelob Bavarian Style Wheat, added Kirin to create an import brand position, and introduced Budweiser Select to create a product position with a low-calorie, low-carbohydrate beer. In the 2000s, Anheuser-Busch added the regional brewery Rolling Rock to its product line portfolio. Although this last addition may not seem significant, with Anheuser-Busch's marketing expertise and resources, a strong regional brand has every promise of growing into a strong national brand.

Umbrella Brands and Product Line Extensions

An *umbrella brand* is the core product of a business. For American Express, the core product is credit cards; for Whirlpool, it's washers and dryers; and for Johnson & Johnson, it's baby shampoo. From a consumer's point of view, the core product is the most visible embodiment of the brand name. Accumulated exposure of consumers to the core product and their experiences with it solidify a certain image and quality expectation for this product.

Umbrella branding involves the transfer of quality perceptions derived from a core product or brand to product line extensions that use the same brand name. The intent of umbrella branding is to enhance the effectiveness of marketing programs and to increase demand for product line extensions by transferring brand awareness and perceptions of quality from the umbrella brand.[20] For example, the umbrella brands of potato chips, corn chips, and cheese snack sold by Frito-Lay capture 59 percent of the U.S. snack-chip market. The sales growth of the Frito-Lay brands has been due largely to the introduction of new products under the core brands of Frito's Corn Chips, Lay's Potato Chips, Cheetos Cheese Snacks, Tostitos Tortilla Chips, and Doritos Tortilla Chips, as illustrated in Figure 7-26. These umbrella brands create a base from which to introduce line extensions that enhance market penetration at a lower cost.[21] Line extensions have also been shown to have much shorter take-off periods due to within-brand and cross-brand communications, which further improves profits and cash flow for the new products and the product line as a whole.[22]

Summarized here are four ways that an addition to business's product line benefits from a strong umbrella brand and adds to the business's overall profitability:

1. **Brand Awareness:** The high level of market awareness attained by the core brand acts as an umbrella under which the new product can be introduced at a much lower cost of advertising.

FIGURE 7-26 FRITO-LAY UMBRELLA AND FLANKER EXTENSIONS

Frito's Corn Chips	Lay's Potato Chips	Ruffles Potato Chips	Cheetos Cheese Snacks	Tostitos Tortilla Chips	Doritos Tortilla Chips	Rold Gold Pretzels	Cracker Jack
Frito's	Lay's		Cheetos		Doritos		
Twist	Bistro		Mystery		Extremes		
	Gourmet		Colorz		Tortilla		
	Chips		Snacks		Chips		
	Stax						

2. **Known Quality:** The product line extension shares in the core brand's reputation for high quality, which helps to jump-start sales.
3. **Market Reach:** Retailers are more inclined to give precious shelf space to well-known brands. As a result, a product line extension under a well-known umbrella brand gains easier access to retail outlets.
4. **Product Experience:** A product line extension under an umbrella brand provides customers with more variety, enabling them to buy variations of the core brand without having to switch to competing brands.

The purpose of line extensions under an umbrella brand is to leverage the awareness and image of the umbrella brand. But a company must take care that the new products will not erode the reputation of the umbrella brand and adversely affect profits. Line extensions may not grow market demand and can even cannibalize the core brand or other extensions, at the same time as they raise the total cost of marketing. Careful product line accounting is needed to ensure that product line extensions are profitable and that they improve the profitability of the entire product line.[23]

Product Line Extensions

Vertical Brand Extensions

A successful brand can often be "franchised," meaning it can be extended to other versions of the product. Franchising is most easily accomplished with *vertical brand extensions* of the core brand. Lean Cuisine manufactures low-calorie frozen food entrees, dinners, and snack products. Under the umbrella brand of Lean Cuisine are the seven horizontal brands shown in Figure 7-27. The original brand, Casual Cuisine, was launched in 1981 with 10 products and grew to 52 products by 1993.[24] Other horizontal brands were added to better group brands into food categories, and vertical brand extensions

FIGURE 7-27 LEAN CUISINE—HORIZONTAL AND VERTICAL BRAND EXTENSIONS

Horizontal and Vertical Brand Extensions						
Horizontal Brand Extensions →						
1	2	3	4	5	6	7
Casual Cuisine	Market Creations	Spa Cuisine	Café Cuisine	Comfort Cuisine	Simple Favorites	Dinnertime Cuisine
Pizzas (11)	Chicken (9)	Chicken (12)	Beef (3)	Chicken (4)	Chicken (6)	Chicken (7)
Sandwiches (10)	Tortelloni (3)	Ravioli (1)	Chicken (15)	Turkey (3)	Bread Pizza (3)	Steak (2)
Snacks (3)	Shrimp (2)	Beef (1)	Fish (3)	Pot Roast (1)	Quesadilla (2)	Turkey (1)
		Shrimp (1)	Shrimp (2)	Lasagna (1)	Broccoli (2)	Shrimp (1)
		Salmon (1)	Steak (1)	Steak (1)	Pot Stickers (1)	Meatballs (1)
			Rigatone (1)	Meatloaf (1)	Pomodoro (1)	
					Beef (1)	
					Potato (1)	
					Fettuccine (1)	

(Vertical Brand Extensions, rows 1–9, shown along the left axis)

FIGURE 7-28 HONDA'S PRODUCT LINE AND PRODUCT LINE EXTENSIONS

Product Line	Product Line Offerings
Automobiles	Accord, Civic Sedan, Civic Coupe, Civic Hybrid, Insight, Odyssey, Pilot, S-2000
Motorcycles	Standard, Touring, Sport Touring, Sport, Cruiser, Moto-Cross, Off-Road
Scooters	Silver Wing, Reflex, Elite 80, Metropolitan, Metropolitan II
Jet Skis	Aqua Trax F-12, Aqua Trax F-12X
All-Terrain Vehicles	Utility, Sport
Lawn and Garden	Lawn Mowers, Trimmers, Tillers
Snowblowers	Wheel-Drive, Track-Drive, Lightweight
Pumps	Construction, De-Watering, Multipurpose, Submersible
Generators	Handheld, Economy, Industrial, Super Quiet, Deluxe
Engines	GX Series, GC Series, Mini 4-Stroke

were added to each horizontal brand. The Casual Cuisine product line now has 24 vertical brand extensions, and Lean Cuisine's full product line consists of more than 100 branded products.

Horizontal Brand Extensions

Horizontal brand extensions within a product class are additions of complementary products. For Lean Cuisine, this meant adding seven horizontal brand extensions, as shown in Figure 7-27. The Simple Favorites horizontal brand extension led to nine vertical product line extensions. Each of these combinations leveraged the Lean Cuisine brand, which enabled growth in sales and profits.

New Product-Market Brand Extensions

Vertical and horizontal brand extensions provide excellent opportunities for growth within a given product-market. However, eventually a business will hit a point of diminishing returns and will need to examine the potential of its proven brand name in other product-market applications. Honda initially built a reputation in the motorcycle and automobile markets for reliable, high-quality products. The company's brand reputation allowed easy entry to other product-markets, often at a price premium. The Honda brand name is so strong that it has easily been transferred to such product-markets as lawn mowers, snowblowers, pumps, generators, and jet skis, as illustrated in Figure 7-28. Each product-market has a "related relevance" to the Honda core brand, and the benefits of the core brand—its reputation for quality and its other brand assets—has carried over to these new products.

Cobranding

A business can also leverage a strong brand by entering another product-market with cobranding, rather than creating a brand extension. One example is Yoplait yogurt's cobranding with Trix, a children's cereal, to create Yoplait Trix yogurt for children.[25] High awareness and brand preference for Trix among children quickly led to a high volume of sales for Yoplait Trix yogurt, even though the new product was not advertised.

Another example is General Mills' cobranding of Reese's Peanut Butter Cups with a new cereal called Reese's Puffs. The cereal carries all the imagery of the Reese's Cups.

Cobranding takes advantage of the potential synergy of two brands that share a common market space. Healthy Choice has long had many brand extensions in the frozen dinner market. When it entered the cereal market, cobranding with Kellogg's cereals saved considerable advertising money and gave the product easier access to cereal shelf space in retail stores. The composite product—"Healthy Choice from Kellogg's"— uses the Healthy Choice logo, colors, and packaging. Cobranding provided Healthy Choice with easy access to the already crowded cereal market, and it gave Kellogg's a credible product line extension that included a dimension of weight loss and health, a product concept that had previously failed when it was launched without the Healthy Choice name.

Yoplait Trix and Healthy Choice from Kellogg's are examples of cobranding by combining two brands to name a single product. Cobranding can also include ingredient cobranding strategies. "Intel Inside" is a classic example of ingredient cobranding. The Intel microprocessor chip is an ingredient, a key component, of a personal computer. Intel's reputation for quality adds perceived quality to personal computers that carry the Intel logo. This cobranding strategy helped Dell grow its sales of personal computers and helped Intel grow its sales of microprocessors. Using the "Intel Inside" logo on all personal computers built with Intel microprocessors is a low-cost way to keep the Intel name in front of personal computer users.

Bundling and Unbundling Strategies

Products are often enhanced with additional features and services to provide customers with more complete solutions. Most personal computers are purchased with a variety of pre-installed software programs, such as word-processing and spreadsheet applications, an Internet browser, and other common programs. But some customers who already have their own specialty software seek to purchase a personal computer without the standard programs (i.e., unbundled) in order to lower the total cost of purchase. A computer company could use the bundling strategy to enhance the product's benefits or the unbundling strategy to lower the computer's cost, or the company could appeal to both customer types by making use of both strategies.

Product Bundling

Bundling products creates a complete customer solution that has the potential to provide a superior customer value and attract customers. Products such as living room sets, entertainment packages, and software applications that come with a new computer are product bundles that can create a superior value (economic and perceived) for target customers. There are two approaches to product bundling: pure bundling and mixed bundling.

A *pure product bundling strategy* involves the sale of two or more products at an overall price that is lower than the total price that a customer would pay to purchase the products separately. Even when the products are offered individually at a discounted price that makes the total cost equal to the bundled purchase price, customers rate the bundled offering higher in perceived value.

A *mixed bundling strategy* offers the customer the opportunity to purchase each of the items separately at a sale price or bundled with an additional level of savings. There is evidence that when both options are available, customer perceptions of value exceed those produced with a pure bundling strategy.[26] In addition, mixed bundling strategies have been shown to be more profitable than pure bundling strategies.[27]

Product Unbundling

Unbundling a set of products that is normally sold as an integrated bundle or system may also attract and satisfy customers. Many consumers of complex industrial and commercial products may want to purchase individual products or components and integrate them into a certain configuration that best serves their needs.[28] In some instances, value-added resellers (VARs) fill this role. For specialized applications in architecture, agriculture, or chemical processing, VARs will purchase unbundled products and integrate them in a customized bundle that best suits the target customers' application. HP may have an attractive product bundle, but it cannot meet the specific needs of all customers. By unbundling and selling individual products or component products to VARs and systems integrators, HP has been able to create value for its customers and sales growth opportunities for the business.

In the early evolution of a market, customer needs are generally less fragmented than in the later stages, and bundled product solutions are often very attractive. However, as markets grow and new customers enter them, new segments of the market emerge, and more customized product solutions are needed to satisfy different customers.[29] As a market matures, unbundling often becomes more important in attracting and satisfying customers.[30]

■ Summary

For any specific target segment, a business needs to develop a tactical marketing strategy for positioning its product with respect to product features and price, and then marketing the product with respect to promotion and place. This chapter focused on product positioning, product line strategies, branding, and brand extensions. A successful marketing strategy requires an integrated mix of product, price, promotion, place, and service.

Product positioning and differentiation are key parts of a successful marketing strategy. How should a business position its products relative to customer needs and competitors? And what source of differentiation is needed to make this product position differentially superior to competitors' products?

A low-price differentiation is important to any business that serves a price-sensitive market. A company can also achieve a price advantage by lowering the customer's ownership costs. For markets in which differentiation is possible, a business could build its differentiation around a product or packaging advantage, a service advantage, or an advantage in brand reputation. To be successful, the differentiation underlying the positioning strategy must be meaningful to target customers and sustainable (not easily duplicated by competitors).

A positioning strategy is enhanced by the brand name that is used to identify a product. Businesses with many products in many diverse markets need to take special care in encoding brand names to ensure both meaning and consistency across the product line. Commonly used brand-encoding systems include (1) company and brand name; (2) brand and subbrand name; (3) company and product name; (4) company, brand, and product name; (5) company and brand name, followed by numbers or letters or a combination; (6) brand name and performance benefit and (7) brand name only. Each of these brand-encoding systems has advantages and disadvantages with respect to distinctiveness, consistency, and communicating the product's positioning.

The creation of a new brand name follows one of five major strategies. Founder names, such as Dell, Ford Motor Company, and Wal-Mart Stores, are one option. Functional brand names, such as Duracell and DieHard, communicate the brands' functional benefits. Invented brand names, like Kleenex and Google, are new words intended to convey a certain image or create an association with a concept. Experiential brand names, such as Kodak EasyShare or Land Rover, communicate the experience the brand hopes to provide. Evocative brand names, such as Victoria's Secret or Virgin Airlines, evoke a feeling or emotion.

A new brand name should reflect the problem application, the customer solution the product offers, or the benefit it provides. Drawing up a list of words and morphemes (part words) that are associated with the use or benefits of the product is helpful in coming up with a good name. The words and morphemes may be arranged in many combinations to generate a list of candidate brand names. Testing these brand names, of course, should be part of the process to ensure that the brand name eventually selected will communicate the intended message and help position the product. Protecting your brand name and intellectual property is critical. Obtaining copyrights, trademarks, registered trademarks, patents, and licensing are all important considerations in establishing ownership of intellectual property.

To grow, a business needs to leverage its product knowledge, production capabilities, marketing systems, and brand equity. Product line strategies provide an excellent opportunity to grow and leverage current assets and expenses. Related product line extensions, both horizontal and vertical, are important ways to achieve profitable growth. A business can leverage a high brand assets score for its core product by creating new, related products as product line extensions, or by expanding the brand into new, unrelated markets. Customer perceptions of the umbrella brand will carry over to the new products. But when it extends a product line, a business must be mindful of possible sales cannibalization as a result of substitution by customers along the product line and of the diminishing returns produced by too many related products. A business must also be careful not to damage the image of the core brand with products that may prove to be a detriment to the business's customer satisfaction index. Product bundling and unbundling are also product strategies that can enhance customer attractiveness in certain markets.

Adding brands as line extensions offers the potential for scale effects when no investment in additional production, personnel, and marketing and sales expenses is necessary. Leveraging excess production capacity and fixed marketing and sales expenses helps ensure the profitability of new products and improves overall performance.

■ Market-Based Strategic Thinking

1 What was the logic behind Apple's product-price strategy for the launch of the iPad?

2 Why didn't Apple use the same launch strategy for the iPod?

3 What is the product line logic for both the iPad and the iPod?

4 How did Intel's branding strategy help the company grow, and how does the strategy help the company maintain a dominant market share?

5 What role does a "fighter brand" play in Intel's product line strategy?

6 Does Apple have fighter brands for the iPod and the iPad?

7 How would you evaluate the product line positioning of Black & Decker relative to Sears in terms of customer choice and customer value?

8 Why did Samsung's repositioning strategy yield higher sales and profits?

9 How does General Electric use product performance quality differentiation in its product line of household appliances?

10 How does a business such as McDonald's develop a positioning strategy around some aspect of service differentiation? How would this strategy compare with the service differentiation achieved by Les Schwab Tire Centers?

11 Why do brand names like Kodak, Disney, or Coca-Cola create customer value and provide a basis for product line positioning and differentiation?

12 Why does the occupancy of a Fairfield Inn increase by 15 percent when the Marriott name is added to the building?

13 Why does an extension of a product line to include a small number of related products contribute to higher levels of profitability?

14 What does Starbucks hope to achieve by dropping its name and the word "coffee" from the company's logo?

15 What is the logic of Textron in branding the Cessna product line? Why doesn't Textron use its company name as a major part of the branding and product line strategy?

16 Why would a business use an experiential brand name versus an evocative brand name?

17 What are morphemes and how were they used in developing brand names such as InfoSeek, Duraflame, and Compaq Computer?

18 What is the marketing logic that underlies Anheuser-Busch's product line and the company's marketing strategy for the beer market?

19 What are the advantages of a strong core brand when a company wishes to develop a marketing strategy for new products, either as product line extensions in the same market or as products for an altogether different market? Under what conditions could this strategy fail?

20 Why are vertical brand extensions less expensive than horizontal brand extensions?

21 How does a well-known brand help in the marketing and profitability of new products?

22 Why did Healthy Choice cobrand with Kellogg's to introduce a new breakfast cereal? How did Kellogg's also benefit?

23 How might product line substitution effects have contributed to the sales of Intel Pentium microprocessors when the Xeon and Celeron brands were introduced?

24 Frito-Lay introduced Stax to compete with Pringles in 2003. Assuming the company had excess production capacity, how would the profits of other Frito-Lay chip products be affected by the success of Stax?

25 Under what conditions would eliminating a brand with a negative pre-tax profit from a product line result in lower overall pre-tax profit?

Marketing Performance Tools and Application Exercises

The three interactive marketing performance tools and the application exercises outlined here will strengthen your understanding of product positioning, brand name development, and brand equity. To access the tools, go to **rogerjbest.com**.

7.1 Product Positioning (Figure 7-3)

A. Use the Strategy 1 column to create a product positioning strategy for a new fast food restaurant, Teriyaki Rice Bowl. The product will be healthier, meat or meatless, and cost the same as a large hamburger and small fries.

B. Use the Strategy 2 column to create a product positioning strategy for Teriyaki Rice Bowl but for a different target customer. Use the comments section to discuss which strategy is more likely to succeed with respect to sales.

7.2 Brand Name Development (Figure 7-19)

A. Modify the marketing performance tool for Ear Savrs and create three new brand names for consideration.

B. For a new fast food restaurant, Teriyaki Rice Bowl, use this marketing performance tool to create a brand name. The product will be healthier, meat or meatless, and cost the same as a large hamburger and small fries. Use the comments section to explain the logic of your brand name strategy.

7.3 Brand Equity (Figures 7-21 to 7-23)

A. Estimate the brand assets and brand liabilities for a brand that you believe to be strong.

B. Estimate the brand assets and brand liabilities for a brand that you believe to be weak.

C. Compute the brand equity for each and discuss how a difference in brand equity could impact sales and profits.

Notes

1. M. Hatch and M. Schultz, "Are the Strategic Stars Aligned for Your Corporate Brand?" *Harvard Business Review* (February 2001): 128–34.
2. M. Ritson, "Should You Launch a Fighter Brand?" *Harvard Business Review* (October 2009): 87–94.
3. "Drills for All Reasons," *Consumer Reports* (November 1997): 24–8.
4. D. Garvin, "Competing on Eight Dimensions of Quality," *Harvard Business Review* (November–December 1987): 101–5.
5. B. Abrams, "Consumer-Product Techniques Help Loctite Sell to Industry," *Wall Street Journal* (April 2, 1991).
6. D. Evans and K. Webster, "Design the Right Product Offerings," *MIT Sloan Management Review* (Fall 2007): 45–50.
7. V. Zeithaml, A. Parasuramon, and L. Berry, *Delivering Quality Service* (New York: Free Press, 1990): Chapter 1.
8. B. Gale, "Creating Power Brands," *Managing Customer Value* (New York: Free Press, 1994): 153–74.
9. P. Farquhar, "Managing Brand Equity," *Marketing Research* (September 1989): 24–33.
10. D. Aaker, *Managing Brand Equity: Capitalizing on the Value of a Brand Name* (New York: Free Press, 1991).
11. D. Sheinin and B. Schmitt, "Extending Brands with New Product Concepts: The Role of Category Attribute Congruity, Brand Affect, and Brand Breadth," *Journal of Business Research* 31 (1994): 1–10.
12. D. Aaker, *Building Strong Brands* (New York: Free Press, 1996): 356–7.
13. D. D'Alessandro, *Brand Warfare* (New York: McGraw-Hill, 2001).
14. S. Hill, C. Lederer, and K. Keller, *The Infinite Asset: Managing Brands to Build New Value* (Boston: Harvard Business School Press, 2001).
15. "Name Development," Igor International (not dated): http://igorinternational.com/, retrieved 2004.
16. J.D. Berg, J.M. Mathews, and C.M. O'Hare, "Measuring Brand Health to Improve Top-Line Growth," *MIT Sloan Management Review* (Fall 2007): 61–8.

17. S.M. Davis, *Brand Asset Management* (San Francisco: Jossey-Bass Inc., 2000).

18. K. Keller, "The Brand Report Card," *Harvard Business Review* (January–February 2000): 147–57.

19. C. Lederer and S. Hill, "See Your Brands Through Your Customers' Eyes," *Harvard Business Review* (June 2001): 125–33.

20. T. Erdem, "An Empirical Analysis of Umbrella Branding," *Journal of Marketing Research* (August 1998): 339–51; D. Aaker, *Building Strong Brands* (New York: Free Press, 1995); P. Dacin and D. Smith, "The Effect of Brand Portfolio Characteristics on Consumer Evaluations of Brand Extensions," *Journal of Marketing Research* (May 1994): 229–42; and A. Rangaswamy, R. Burke, and T. Oliver, "Brand Equity and Extendibility of Brand Names," *International Journal of Research in Marketing* (March 1993): 61–75.

21. M. Hatch and M. Schultz, "Are the Strategic Stars Aligned for Your Corporate Brand?" *Harvard Business Review* (February 2001): 128–34.

22. B. Libai, E. Muller, and R. Peres, "The Role of Within-Brand and Cross-Brand Communications in Competitive Growth," *Journal of Marketing* (May 2009): 19–34.

23. B. Hardle, "The Logic of Product-Line Extensions," *Harvard Business Review* (November–December 1994): 53–62.

24. "Lean Cuisine History," Wikipedia (not dated): http://en.wikipedia.org/wiki/Lean_Cuisine, retrieved January 2011.

25. D. Aaker, *Building Strong Brands* (New York: Free Press, 1996): 298–300.

26. M. Yadav and K. Monroe, "How Buyers Perceive Savings in a Bundle Price: An Examination of a Bundle's Transaction Value," *Journal of Marketing Research* (August 1993): 350–8.

27. W. Adams and J. Yellen, "Commodity Bundling and the Burden of Monopoly," *Quarterly Journal of Economics* (August 1976): 475–98; and R. Schmalensee, "Gaussian Demand and Commodity Bundling," *Journal of Business* 57 (1984): 211–30.

28. L. Wilson, A. Weiss, and G. John, "Unbundling of Industrial Systems," *Journal of Marketing Research* (May 1990): 123–38.

29. R. Best and R. Angelmar, "Strategies for Leveraging Technology Advantage," *Handbook on Business Strategy* (Boston: Warren, Gorham, and Lamont, 1989): 2-1–10.

30. B. Jackson, *Winning and Keeping Industrial Customers* (Lanham, MD: Lexington Books, 1985); and M. Porter, *Competitive Advantage* (New York: Free Press, 1985).

Value-Based Pricing and Pricing Strategies

■ If you win a customer on price, you will lose that customer on price; if you win a customer on value, you will keep that customer on value.[1]

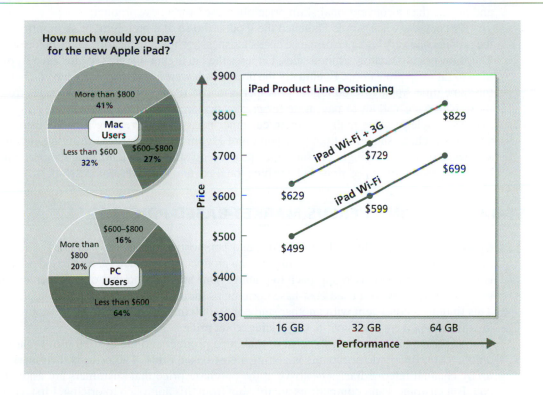

How much would you pay for the new Apple iPad?

rior to the launch of the iPad, the technology blog Retrevo conducted a price survey to determine how much buyers would pay for an Apple tablet.[2] As shown in the pie chart above, 41 percent of Macintosh owners but only 20 percent of PC owners reported that they would pay over $800. At the other extreme, only 32 percent of Mac owners but 64 percent of PC owners would not pay more than $600.

Apple launched the iPad with a wide range of customer choices. The entry price of $499 provided a base level of performance (16 gigabytes) with Wi-Fi but lacking a 3G benefit. This option would appeal to 32 percent of the Mac owners and 64 percent of the PC owners surveyed. But those who were willing to pay more to get more could trade up to 3G ($629), 32 GB ($599), or both ($729), as shown in the figure. Customers also had two other options priced at $699 and $829.

In 2010, Apple sold 7.46 million iPads at an estimated average net price of $665 (the price Apple obtains after retailer discounts) which resulted in $4.96 billion in first-year sales.

APPLE'S PRICING STRATEGIES

Apple's launch strategy for the iPad was a great margin management price strategy because the margin was likely to be more for the higher priced iPads. Offering only one or two high-price options at launch would have allowed Apple to create a traditional skim pricing strategy with great margins but lower volumes, as many target customers would not buy at a high price. But Apple's decision to offer different performance levels at several price points undoubtedly produced considerably more volume, sales revenues, and profits than a conventional skim price often used for a new product.

By contrast, when Apple launched the iPod, it did so at a premium, or skim, price, as the product had very high performance characteristics, as shown in the top half of Figure 8-1. The skim-pricing strategy limited sales, but it resulted in higher margins. It also gave Apple time to ramp up production. Eventually the price was lowered to attract more buyers, but at the same time Apple offered higher price-performance iPod models to capture sales from those who were willing to pay more for greater performance. This product line strategy allowed Apple to serve many different customer needs while creating a good customer value for each, as shown in the lower portion of Figure 8-1. Because of differing circumstances, Apple used a single product-price positioning strategy in launching the iPod and multiple product-price positions in launching the iPad, and both were successful.

COST-BASED PRICING VERSUS MARKET-BASED PRICING

Cost-based pricing is logical from a financial perspective and is easy to do, but it has nothing to do with what customers will pay for a product. Unfortunately, cost-based pricing is the most commonly used approach to pricing.[3] One study found that over 60 percent of the businesses surveyed used cost-based pricing as their primary basis for setting price.[4] This finding is consistent with another study of 50,000 managers from over 100 countries in which 64 percent used cost-based pricing to set price.[5]

As shown in Figure 8-2, the cost of making a product and the desired profit margin are the two primary determinants in setting a cost-based price. The price is then marked up by channel intermediaries to arrive at the purchase price that customers are asked to pay. But customers and competitors are missing from this approach to pricing. First, cost-based pricing ignores customer performance needs and what they will pay for a desired level of product performance. Second, this approach to pricing overlooks both competitors' offerings relative to customer needs and price sensitivity.

Value-based pricing, in contrast, starts with customer needs, competitors' product-price positioning, and company product-price positioning.[6] Taking into consideration

FIGURE 8-1 APPLE—IPOD'S PRODUCT-PRICE POSITIONING, BRANDING, AND CUSTOMER VALUE

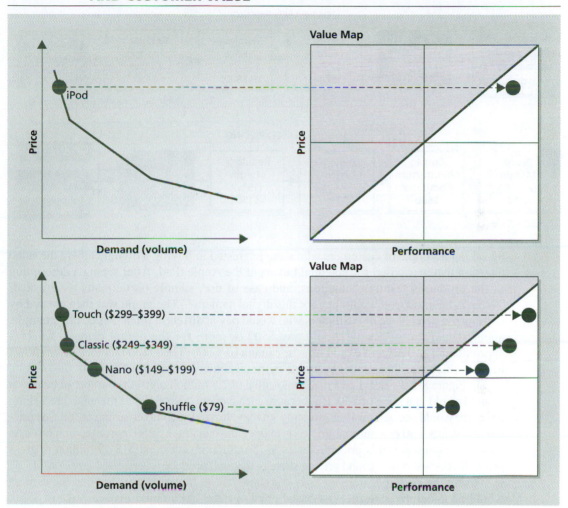

customer needs, customers' price sensitivity, and competing products, a company develops its price around a product's relative strengths to create greater value than competing products offer. Although pricing needs vary, there are certain basic factors that tend to play into most value-pricing strategies.

The value drivers that seem to come to the surface are product performance, quality of customer service, brand reputation, and price.[7]

Cost-Based Pricing: Underpricing and Lower Profits

Let's look at an example of how cost-based pricing can lead to underpricing and lower profits. Figure 8-3 depicts a typical price-customer purchase curve. The curve was derived

FIGURE 8-2 COST-BASED PRICING VERSUS MARKET-BASED PRICING

by asking a sample of customers who were interested in buying a digital camera the same question that was posed for potential buyers of the Apple iPad. After seeing a description of the product's features, functions, and ease of use, sample participants were asked: "What is the most you would pay for this digital camera?" The graph was then created by plotting the percentage of customers who would pay at different price points. For example, about 10 percent of people would pay $500 or more for the digital camera, whereas approximately 50 percent would buy the camera for $300. The graph included prices down to $50, which was the amount everyone in the customer sample would pay for the camera.

In Figure 8-3 we assumed a market potential of 2.5 million units, the number of units that would be sold at a price of $50. But because each camera costs $125 to manufacture, selling it for $50 would not be a profitable pricing strategy. Instead, a company using cost-based pricing that wants a 50 percent margin needs to price the camera at $250, twice the unit cost. As shown in Figure 8-3, this price produces $375 million in sales and $187.5 million in gross profit. It appears to be a sound pricing strategy that will produce a very good gross profit.

Using the customer-derived price-purchase curve, however, we find that the camera would be underpriced at the cost-based price of $250. At a market-based price of $350, the company would sell 500,000 fewer cameras and have $25 million less in sales, but the gross profit would be $225 million. This is no small difference, as the gross profit would be $37.5 million more. Serving fewer customers who value the product at the higher price of $350 is much more profitable, with a gross profit margin of 64.3 percent, than selling the digital camera at the cost-based price of $250 with a 50 percent margin.

Cost-Based Pricing: Overpricing and Lower Profits

Cost-based pricing can also lead to lower profits due to overpricing. Figure 8-4 shows the same digital camera price-purchase curve and the same market potential of 2.5 million units. However, in this example the unit cost is $250. Using cost-based pricing logic and desiring a margin of 50 percent would lead the company to price its digital camera at $500. Although this pricing strategy provides a good margin, only 10 percent of the potential market would buy the digital camera at that price. At a price of $500,

FIGURE 8-3 DIGITAL CAMERA—COST-BASED UNDERPRICING

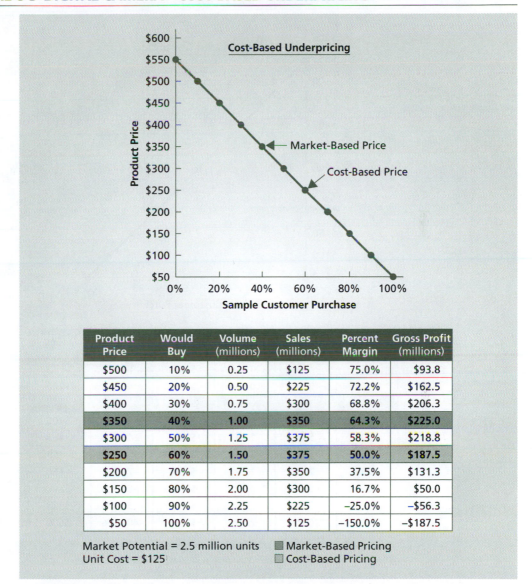

Product Price	Would Buy	Volume (millions)	Sales (millions)	Percent Margin	Gross Profit (millions)
$500	10%	0.25	$125	75.0%	$93.8
$450	20%	0.50	$225	72.2%	$162.5
$400	30%	0.75	$300	68.8%	$206.3
$350	40%	1.00	$350	64.3%	$225.0
$300	50%	1.25	$375	58.3%	$218.8
$250	60%	1.50	$375	50.0%	$187.5
$200	70%	1.75	$350	37.5%	$131.3
$150	80%	2.00	$300	16.7%	$50.0
$100	90%	2.25	$225	–25.0%	–$56.3
$50	100%	2.50	$125	–150.0%	–$187.5

Market Potential = 2.5 million units   ■ Market-Based Pricing
Unit Cost = $125   □ Cost-Based Pricing

the company would achieve $125 million in sales and a gross profit of $62.5 million. But using our market knowledge of how customers value this camera at the different price levels shown in Figure 8-4, we can see that a price which is $100 lower ($400) with a margin of 37.5 percent yields significantly higher levels of sales and gross profit. Sales of $300 million would earn the company $175 million more, and the gross profit of $113 million is almost double that earned from using the $500 cost-based price.

In companies where the finance function sets price, the customer-derived price-purchase curve is essential to winning the argument that a market-based price would be much more profitable than a company policy of pricing to achieve a 50 percent margin.

FIGURE 8-4 DIGITAL CAMERA—COST-BASED OVERPRICING

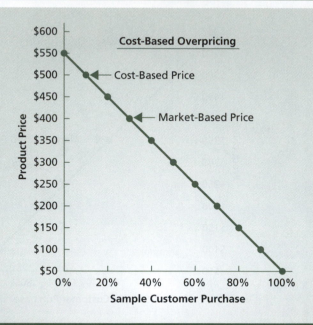

Product Price	Would Buy	Volume (millions)	Sales (millions)	Percent Margin	Gross Profit (millions)
$500	**10%**	**0.25**	**$125**	**50.0%**	**$63**
$450	20%	0.50	$225	44.4%	$100
$400	**30%**	**0.75**	**$300**	**37.5%**	**$113**
$350	40%	1.00	$350	28.6%	$100
$300	50%	1.25	$375	16.7%	$63
$250	60%	1.50	$375	0.0%	$0
$200	70%	1.75	$350	−25.0%	−$88
$150	80%	2.00	$300	−66.7%	−$200
$100	90%	2.25	$225	−150.0%	−$338
$50	100%	2.50	$125	−400.0%	−$500

Market Potential = 2.5 million units   ☐ Cost-Based Pricing
Unit Cost = $250   ▨ Market-Based Pricing

VALUE PRICING

Market-based pricing requires extensive customer and competitor intelligence.[8] Without having high levels of both, it is simply not possible to implement this kind of pricing. Market-based pricing starts with a good understanding of customer needs and the benefits that a product offers relative to competitors' products.[9] On the basis of product performance benefits, the price is set relative to competition to create a superior value. In this way, the price is determined in the market, not at the factory or in the finance department. This section discusses five kinds of value pricing:

1. **Value-in-Use Pricing**—Price is set to provide customers with an attractive savings after considering the life-cycle costs of acquiring, owning, using, maintaining, and disposing of a product.
2. **Life-Cycle Value Pricing**—Price is set with respect to the total cost of ownership over the life cycle of a product on the basis of the net present value of the difference between the company's and a competitor's life-cycle ownership costs.
3. **Perceived-Value Pricing**—Price is set on the basis of the value that customers realize when they compare the price and benefits of the company's product with those of a key competitor's product.
4. **Performance-Based Pricing**—Price is set on the basis of customer preferences for different levels of price and performance and taking into consideration how the company and competitors are positioned with respect to delivering both price and performance.
5. **Customerization Value Pricing**—Price is set by unbundling a product's features or performance levels, placing a price on each, and then allowing customers to select the features and performance that they want at a price that they are willing to pay. The price of the top-performing product that has all features serves as the reference price. Customers who buy the product with only the features and performance level they desire have an inferred savings (value) relative to reference price.

Understanding Total Cost of Ownership

Price is the most visible cost of any purchase, whether it is a new car, computer, insurance policy, vacation trip, or simple household cleanser. All customers are price sensitive to some degree. Some customers, however, are willing to pay more for extra benefits. These benefits often include reduced costs in other areas of product ownership. The other costs of owning a product are much less obvious than the purchase price. As shown in Figure 8-5, price is only the tip of the iceberg; the other costs of ownership are beneath the surface. Value-in-use pricing considers the annual cost of ownership for a competitor's product and the annual cost of ownership for the business's product in determining the business's customer value.[10]

This does not necessarily mean lowering prices. By considering the total cost of ownership that is incurred by target customers, a business can use value-in-use pricing to offer them an attractive savings (economic value) while maintaining a premium price. For example, in Figure 8-6, the price of a business's product is higher than the price of the competitor's product, but the total cost of ownership for the business's product is lower than the competitor's product. Because of lower acquisition, use, and other costs, the value in use of the business's product is higher than that of the competing product, and the customer saves money.

When a company uses value-in-use pricing, the price is based on the attractive savings that customers realize over the life of the product, not just on the costs of manufacturing and marketing the product. Customers are interested in overall savings, or economic value, and the higher the savings, the more attractive the business's product. The more attractive the product, the higher the purchase price can be, regardless of manufacturing and marketing costs. Chapter 4 discussed the various ways that a business can

FIGURE 8-5 PRICE IS ONLY THE TIP OF THE ICEBERG IN VALUE-IN-USE PRICING

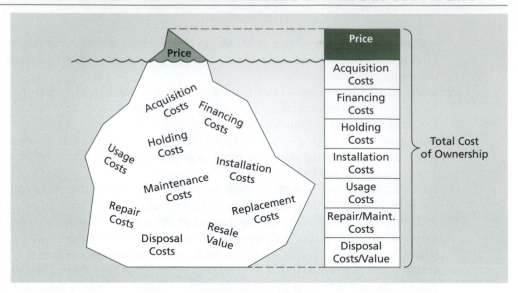

lower the cost of ownership and thereby achieve higher price levels while still creating a superior value for target customers.

Value-in-Use Pricing

A business tends to remain focused on price until it realizes how customers acquire, finance, use, maintain, and dispose of or resell its product. The business then understands that pricing is not the only option it has to create a competitive advantage. By looking more deeply into the costs of ownership, a business can discover new opportunities for customer savings and value creation. Let's begin with Figure 8-6, a total-cost-of-ownership analysis of a material that a company hoped to sell in the automotive manufacturing market. This market is highly price competitive, and customers simply do not pay price premiums. To do business in the market, the company was told it would need to set a price below the going price of $2 per pound. Had the company been a typical business, it would then have focused on ways to lower its price so its product would be attractive to the automotive industry. However, an analysis of the company's and competitors' ownership costs, as shown in Figure 8-6, reveals that a customer's total cost per pound for the competitor's product is $6. The $2 purchase price is only one third of the total cost of purchase; the other two thirds are costs associated with acquiring and using the product.

The company's total cost of ownership at a price equal to the competitor's price of $2 results in a $5.05 total cost of purchase. The lower total cost of purchase would save customers 95 cents per pound over the competitor's product. The value-pricing question is: "Can the company capture a price premium and still deliver a meaningful economic value to customers?"

Price premiums can be difficult to explain when customers look only at the purchase price, but the company set its price at $2.20, a 10 percent price premium, in the belief that customers in its market would readily see the substantial savings they would realize in a

FIGURE 8-6　VALUE-IN-USE PRICING

Ownership Costs	Competitor	Company	Savings
Price	$2.00	$2.20	$0.20
Shipping Cost	$0.07	$0.05	–$0.02
Handling	$0.10	$0.13	$0.03
Inventory	$0.05	$0.01	–$0.04
Financing	$0.00	$0.00	$0.00
Usage	$3.50	$2.80	–$0.70
Quality Control	$0.03	$0.01	–$0.02
Waste	$0.10	$0.02	–$0.08
Disposal	$0.15	$0.03	–$0.12
Total Costs	$6.00	$5.25	–$0.75

Value-Pricing Strategy

In this example, the company felt it could price its product 10% higher, at $2.20 per pound, and still save the customer 75 cents. The savings represents a 13% lower total cost of ownership despite the 10% higher purchase price.

Value-Pricing Strategies	VP1	VP2	VP3	VP4	VP5	VP6
Company Price	$2.00	$2.10	$2.20	$2.30	$2.40	$2.50
Competitor Price	$2.00	$2.00	$2.00	$2.00	$2.00	$2.00
Price Premium	$0.00	$0.10	$0.20	$0.30	$0.40	$0.50
Customer Value	$0.95	$0.85	$0.75	$0.65	$0.55	$0.45
Percent Value Advantage	16%	14%	13%	11%	9%	8%

product that cut overall costs by 75 cents per pound.[11] If a customer used 10,000 pounds of the product per month, the customer's monthly savings would be $7,500—or $90,000 annually. If the customer used 100,000 pounds per month, the yearly savings would be $900,000. With savings at that level, any supplier business would strategize that the higher price is justified due to the customer value it provides. Even at a price of $2.30, which would save 65 cents per pound, a customer with monthly volumes of 100,000 would still save $780,000 annually.

Life-Cycle Value Pricing

We can take the value-in-use pricing presented in Figure 8-6 one step further to demonstrate perceived value for products that have a usage life of several years. Figure 8-7 presents the net present value and cost of ownership for a medical apparatus sold by BioTronics at a price of $60,000, which is $10,000 more than the major competitor's price. Both products have an expected 5-year life. Purely on a price basis, the customer would be inclined to buy the competitor's product, saving $10,000. Doing so, however, would end up costing the customer more because of the greater cost of operating the equipment over 5 years.

FIGURE 8-7 LIFE-CYCLE VALUE PRICING

Competitor	Year 0	Year 1	Year 2	Year 3	Year 4	Year 5
Price	$50,000.00					
Operating Costs		$15,000	$15,000	$15,000	$15,000	$15,000

BioTronics	Year 0	Year 1	Year 2	Year 3	Year 4	Year 5
Price	$60,000.00					
Operating Costs		$8,000	$8,000	$8,000	$8,000	$8,000

	Year 0	Year 1	Year 2	Year 3	Year 4	Year 5
Cost Difference	−$10,000.00	$7,000	$7,000	$7,000	$7,000	$7,000
Discount Factor	1.000	0.833	0.694	0.579	0.482	0.402
Present Value	−$10,000.00	$5,831	$4,858	$4,053	$3,374	$2,814
Net Present Value	$10,930.00					
Discount Rate	20%					

Cost of Ownership	BioTronics	Competitor
Price	$60,000	$50,000
Annual Usage Costs		
Analysis Cost	$4,500	$8,000
Equipment Uptime	$1,000	$2,000
Quality Control	$1,250	$2,000
Re-Work	$500	$1,500
Documentation	$750	$1,500
Total Annual Usage Cost	**$8,000**	**$15,000**

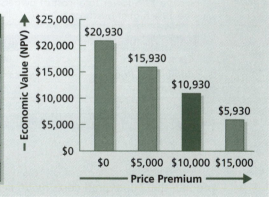

As shown in Figure 8-7, the competitor's product costs $15,000 a year on the basis of the five usage costs considered. The BioTronics product has an annual operating cost of $8,000. When we look at the net present value of the total cost of ownership for the Bio-Tronics product using a 20 percent discount rate for the $7,000 difference in annual usage costs for 5 years, we see that the net present value is $10,930. This is the economic value that the BioTronics product offers. Over 5 years, a customer would save $10,930 even though the purchase price of the BioTronics product is $10,000 more. The bar graph shows the economic value (net present value) that the company creates at three other levels of price premium. BioTronics has a clear opportunity to capture a higher margin with a price premium while still offering a very compelling value proposition.

Perceived-Value Pricing

Some customer benefits are more difficult to quantify in terms of economic value, yet they have an important perceived value.[12] These perceived customer benefits give us

FIGURE 8-8 COMPETITIVE ADVANTAGE IS THE KEY TO VALUE PRICING

Product Performance (Voice of the Customer)	Relative Importance	Our Business	Competitors A	B	C	Product Advantage
Reliable Performance	50	7.3	7.5	5.4	6.7	17
Ease of Use	30	5.6	5.1	7.7	4.9	–10
Product Life	20	6.6	5.2	5.2	6.1	13
	100					120

Service Quality (Voice of the Customer)	Relative Importance	Our Business	Competitors A	B	C	Service Advantage
Parts Availability	60	7.2	6.3	4.3	6.7	20
Competent Service	20	6.5	6.8	6.6	5.5	0
Response to Problems	20	7.2	6.3	5.2	6.6	7
	100					127

Brand Reputation (Voice of the Customer)	Relative Importance	Our Business	Competitors A	B	C	Brand Advantage
Most Respected Brand	50	7.7	7.5	5.4	6.7	17
Known for Quality	50	7.5	6.7	6.6	3.5	17
	100					134

another approach to value pricing, known as *perceived-value pricing*. In Chapter 4, we learned to calculate and interpret the indexes for product performance, service quality, and brand reputation. For the business in Figure 8-8, the perceived benefits derived from product performance (120), service quality (127), and brand reputation (134) each outperform the competition. In this case, each area of perceived benefits is a source of competitive advantage. When the amounts are weighted by the relative importance of each source of benefits, as in Figure 8-9, the overall customer benefits value index is 123, a 23 percent advantage over competitors with respect to all perceived benefits. The perceived-value-pricing question is "How much of a price premium can the business charge and still deliver a meaningful level of customer value?"

We can answer this question by first considering other costs of purchase that are important to the customer. Figure 8-9 lists service and maintenance costs and the depreciated value (how fast the equipment depreciates in value) as two other components, in addition to price, of the total cost of purchase (life-cycle cost). The business has some advantage in the area of service and maintenance costs but no advantage in depreciated value. If the business were to price its equipment at $5,000, it would have a cost advantage relative to its three competitors (60), resulting in a very high perceived value index of 64. Even an index of 25 would be good. The business, then, should not sell at a lower price but should set a price that results in a perceived value index close to 25.

As shown in the table at the bottom of Figure 8-9, increasing the $5,000 purchase price by increments of $250 up to $5,750 lowers the perceived value index to 43. At a purchase price of $6,000, the value index drops to 23, close to the target index of 25. The business chose the price of $6,250, as it also produced a perceived value index of 23. At this price,

FIGURE 8-9 PERCEIVED-VALUE PRICING (PERCEIVED BENEFITS MINUS COST)

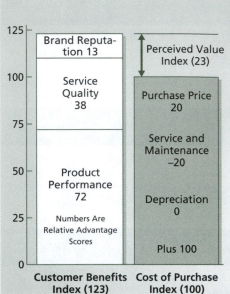

Customer Benefits (Voice of the Customer)	Relative Importance	Our Business's Performance	Overall Benefits
Product Performance	60	120	72
Service Quality	30	127	38
Brand Reputation	10	134	13
Customer Benefits Index	100		**123**

Cost of Purchase (Voice of the Customers)	Rel. Imp.	Our Bus.	Competitors A	B	C	Overall Cost
Price of Equipment	60	7.5	7.2	6.7	4.9	20
Service & Maint. Costs	30	5.1	7.2	7.1	5.3	−20
Depreciated Value	10	5.5	4.5	5.5	5.7	0
Cost of Purchase Index	100					**100**

Perceived-Value Pricing

Using this approach to value pricing, the business set its price at $6,250, and customers gave it a perceived-price rating of 7.5. Customers rated competitor A, with a $6,000 price, slightly lower at 7.2. Competitor B, with a $5,750 price, was rated 6.3, and competitor C was rated 4.9 with a $5,000 price.

The business's product has a premium price but the business's perceived value index is 23, which means the business offers 23% more value than its competitors as a group.

Value-Pricing Strategies	VP1	VP2	VP3	VP4	VP5	VP6
Company Price	$5,000	$5,250	$5,500	$5,750	$6,000	$6,250
Company Rating	5.0	5.5	6.0	6.5	7.0	7.5
Competitive Position	−20.0	0.0	0.0	0.0	20.0	20.0
Cost of Purchase Index	60	80	80	80	100	100
Perceived Value Index	64	43	43	43	23	23

customers rated the price of equipment at 7.5. Competitor A, who offered a price of $6,000, was rated at 7.2. Competitor A's product had a lower price but also had subpar customer benefits, as shown in Figure 8-8. Because its product has a higher price than that of all three competitors, the business must ensure that it communicates the value of its product's benefits so customers will know the higher price is more than offset by better value.

Performance-Based Pricing

If we were to ask a business's customers to name those things that most influence their purchase decisions, they would generally say *everything*. If we were to ask, "Is price important?" the answer would almost always be *yes*. So, what will customers pay for? And how do we determine whether our product has more value than our competitors' products at their prices?

Conjoint analysis, which was introduced in Chapter 4, is a method that marketing managers use to address these questions. The number of performance aspects that can be

FIGURE 8-10 PERFORMANCE-BASED PRICING—CUSTOMER PREFERENCES

Performance and Price Levels

Finish Trim	Paint		
	Unpainted	Primed	Color
None	$1 sq. ft.	$2 sq. ft.	$3 sq. ft.
Basic	$3 sq. ft.	$1 sq. ft.	$2 sq. ft.
Full	$2 sq. ft.	$3 sq. ft.	$1 sq. ft.

Creating Customer-Choice Alternatives

Choice A	Choice B	Choice C
· Finish Trim...None	· Finish Trim...None	· Finish Trim...None
· Paint............Unpainted	· Paint............Primed	· Paint............Painted
· Price............$1 sq. ft.	· Price............$2 sq. ft.	· Price............$3 sq. ft.

Choice D	Choice E	Choice F
· Finish Trim...Basic	· Finish Trim...Basic	· Finish Trim...Basic
· Paint............Unpainted	· Paint............Primed	· Paint............Painted
· Price............$3 sq. ft.	· Price............$1 sq. ft.	· Price............$2 sq. ft.

Choice G	Choice H	Choice I
· Finish Trim...Full	· Finish Trim...Full	· Finish Trim...Full
· Paint............Unpainted	· Paint............Primed	· Paint............Painted
· Price............$2 sq. ft.	· Price............$3 sq. ft.	· Price............$1 sq. ft.

evaluated in a price-performance trade-off analysis is limited. But we can use a simplified design, with two performance drivers across three levels of performance and three levels of price, to determine the value that customers place on different levels of performance and different levels of price.[13]

Figure 8-10 illustrates three levels of performance for two areas of product performance and three levels of price for fiber-cement construction siding. Customers can purchase the siding without the finish trim, with basic trim, or with full trim, and they can buy the siding unpainted, primed, or painted. The three price levels that the customers are asked to consider are $1, $2, and $3 per square foot. Although there are 27 possible combinations, the table in Figure 8-10 fairly represents these combinations with nine alternatives. Note that no performance level or price is repeated in any column or row. Using this set of hypothetical choices, the business asks a sampling of target customers to rank the nine alternatives from *most preferred* to *least preferred*. Using the conjoint measurement process explained in Appendix 4.1, we can derive the performance curves that are presented in Figure 8-11.

In this example, a sample of quality-conscious customers placed most value on trim (50%), second-most value on the siding's finish (43%), and least importance on price (7%).

FIGURE 8-11 PERFORMANCE-BASED PRICING: QUALITY-CONSCIOUS CUSTOMERS

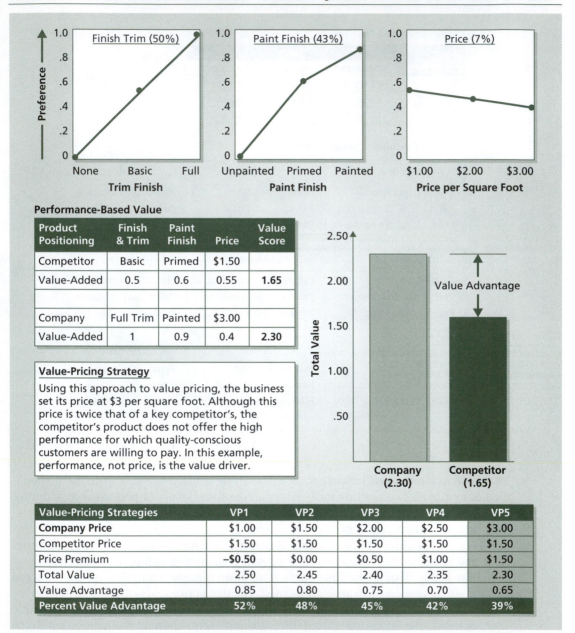

Performance-Based Value

Product Positioning	Finish & Trim	Paint Finish	Price	Value Score
Competitor	Basic	Primed	$1.50	
Value-Added	0.5	0.6	0.55	**1.65**
Company	Full Trim	Painted	$3.00	
Value-Added	1	0.9	0.4	**2.30**

Value-Pricing Strategy

Using this approach to value pricing, the business set its price at $3 per square foot. Although this price is twice that of a key competitor's, the competitor's product does not offer the high performance for which quality-conscious customers are willing to pay. In this example, performance, not price, is the value driver.

Value-Pricing Strategies	VP1	VP2	VP3	VP4	VP5
Company Price	$1.00	$1.50	$2.00	$2.50	$3.00
Competitor Price	$1.50	$1.50	$1.50	$1.50	$1.50
Price Premium	−$0.50	$0.00	$0.50	$1.00	$1.50
Total Value	2.50	2.45	2.40	2.35	2.30
Value Advantage	0.85	0.80	0.75	0.70	0.65
Percent Value Advantage	52%	48%	45%	42%	39%

Using these results, the company can compare its competitive position with that of a key competitor. Currently the business offers full trim (1.0), a painted finish for the siding (0.9), and a price at $3 per square foot (0.4). The business's value score is 2.30. Its key competitor offers a product with basic trim (0.5), primed siding (0.6), and a price of $1.50 per square foot (0.55), resulting in a value score of 1.65. The difference (0.65) is the value advantage that the business has over its competitor.

FIGURE 8-12 PERFORMANCE-BASED PRICING: PRICE-SENSITIVE CUSTOMERS

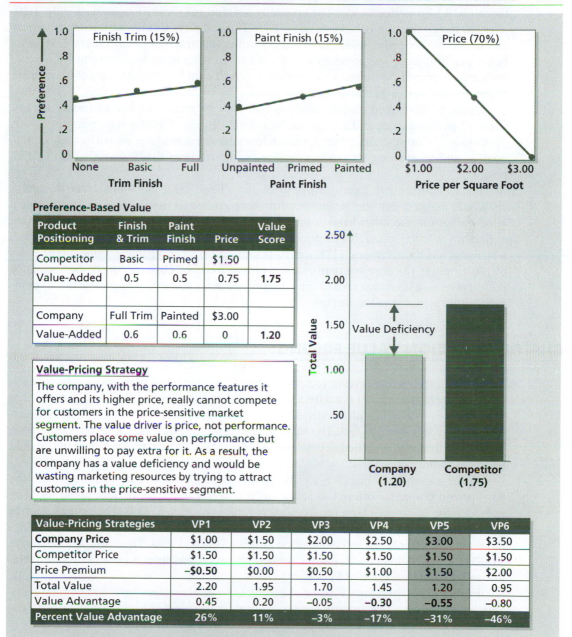

Preference-Based Value

Product Positioning	Finish & Trim	Paint Finish	Price	Value Score
Competitor	Basic	Primed	$1.50	
Value-Added	0.5	0.5	0.75	**1.75**
Company	Full Trim	Painted	$3.00	
Value-Added	0.6	0.6	0	**1.20**

Value-Pricing Strategy

The company, with the performance features it offers and its higher price, really cannot compete for customers in the price-sensitive market segment. The value driver is price, not performance. Customers place some value on performance but are unwilling to pay extra for it. As a result, the company has a value deficiency and would be wasting marketing resources by trying to attract customers in the price-sensitive segment.

Value-Pricing Strategies	VP1	VP2	VP3	VP4	VP5	VP6
Company Price	$1.00	$1.50	$2.00	$2.50	$3.00	$3.50
Competitor Price	$1.50	$1.50	$1.50	$1.50	$1.50	$1.50
Price Premium	−$0.50	$0.00	$0.50	$1.00	$1.50	$2.00
Total Value	2.20	1.95	1.70	1.45	1.20	0.95
Value Advantage	0.45	0.20	−0.05	−0.30	−0.55	−0.80
Percent Value Advantage	26%	11%	−3%	−17%	−31%	−46%

For customers in the quality-conscious segment of the siding market, the current product has more value than the competitor's product even though it costs 65 cents more, on the basis of the customers' performance preferences and the customers' low level of price sensitivity. But in Figure 8-12, a different set of customer price-performance preferences yields a different set of performance curves for the market's price-sensitive segment. In this case, the customer is highly price sensitive (70%) and places less importance (30%) on performance. The company's value for these customers is only 1.20, whereas the competitor offers a value of 1.75. The company's value deficiency is largely due to the higher price, which makes the product unattractive to customers despite its better performance. The company could elect to create a more basic product at a more competitive price to lessen its value deficiency, or it could simply decide not to compete in the market's price-sensitive segment.

Using sophisticated conjoint analysis software programs, we can add more dimensions of performance, and we can include more levels of performance in any given dimension.[14] Conjoint analysis programs allow a business to test price-performance preferences and to evaluate its product's value on the basis of the business's competitive position.

For a business with a competitive price and a large value advantage, such an analysis would suggest that the business could charge more for its product and still offer a good value. On the other hand, a business with a competitive price and a large value deficiency would realize that its price is high relative to the value it offers. In this case, a business has three options: (1) lower its price to create a comparable value on the basis of positioning; (2) improve performance on the basis of customer price-performance preferences to a level that creates meaningful customer value; or (3) choose not to compete in this segment of the market.

CUSTOMERIZATION VALUE PRICING

Customerization value pricing requires unbundling price and performance features to levels of performance and price for the major aspects of performance. In Figure 8-13, a new laptop is available with the standard processor speed, a speed that is 1.5 times faster, or a speed that is twice as fast. The standard speed is offered at the computer's base price of $500. If that's all a particular customer wants to pay, no performance upgrades would be added to the sale price.

In the example in Figure 8-13, the customer needed better performance than the base-priced computer offered and was willing to pay extra for certain upgrades. The upgrades the customer chose resulted in a purchase price of $1,000. The reference price is the price charged for the flagship model, the laptop with all the performance upgrades the company offers. The reference price in this case is $1,500. The customer who pays $1,000 for the computer with just the needed upgrades may infer a savings of $500, relative to the reference price of $1,500.

Figure 8-14 presents five of the 6,561 possible price-performance laptops. Customerization value pricing allows customers to select the performance configurations that fit their needs and price budgets. We would expect very few customers to buy the flagship product. So why show it? It *needs* to be shown, because the full-featured product sets the reference price. Without it, customers would not see their savings. Any price-performance configuration that is purchased at a lower price has an inferred savings based on the difference between the reference price and the price paid.

If we used the basic laptop at $500 as the reference price, then the customer would see any performance upgrades as an *added* expense. For our example in Figure 8-13,

FIGURE 8-13 CUSTOMERIZATION PRICE BASED ON PERFORMANCE

Product Features	Basic	Plus	Advanced
Processor Speed	X	1.5X	2X
Cost Adjustment	$0	$150	$300
Memory (GB)	X	2X	4X
Cost Adjustment	$0	$100	$200
Hard Drive (GB)	X	2X	3X
Cost Adjustment	$0	$50	$100
Media Drive	CD-ROM	DVD	DVD+RW
Cost Adjustment	$0	$100	$150
Operating System	Basic	Plus	Pro
Cost Adjustment	$0	$50	$100
Carrying Case	None	Nylon	Leather
Cost Adjustment	$0	$50	$100
Warranty	90 Days	1 Year	3 Years
Cost Adjustment	$0	$25	$50

Customer Preference	Reference Price	Purchase Price
Base Price	$500	$500
Processor Speed	$300	$150
Memory	$200	$100
Hard Drive	$100	$50
Media Drive	$150	$100
Operating System	$100	$50
Carrying Case	$100	$0
Warranty	$50	$50
Total Price	$1,500	$1,000
Customer Savings	$0	$500

Customer Savings = Reference Price − Price
= $1,500 − $1,000
= $500

Price $1,000

Savings
$500

the customers would infer that they had to pay $500 more over the basic laptop to get the performance they wanted. Numerous studies have researched the price impact of a top-down versus bottom-up price presentation.[15] When prices are presented to customers from the top down, they tend to buy at a higher price point than when the price presentation is from the bottom up. The psychological reason is simple: the customer perceives one presentation in terms of savings (top down) and the other in terms of extra cost (bottom up).

PRODUCT LIFE-CYCLE PRICING STRATEGIES

Pricing from a market point of view is the primary pricing orientation of a market-based business. Different phases of the product life cycle, however, call for different pricing strategies. The same is true as a company's positioning evolves or business conditions change.[16] Figure 8-15 shows eight pricing strategies and the phases of the product life cycle when businesses are likely to implement them. Each pricing strategy has its own positioning strategy and value proposition, and each pricing strategy affects profits in a different way. This section examines these pricing strategies—when and why to apply them, and how they impact profits.

FIGURE 8-14 FULL-FEATURE REFERENCE PRICE AND CUSTOMER VALUE

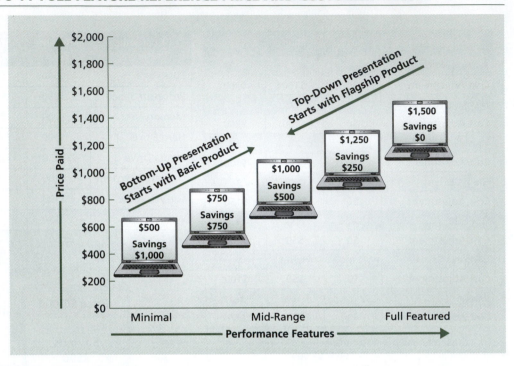

FIGURE 8-15 PRODUCT LIFE-CYCLE PRICING STRATEGIES

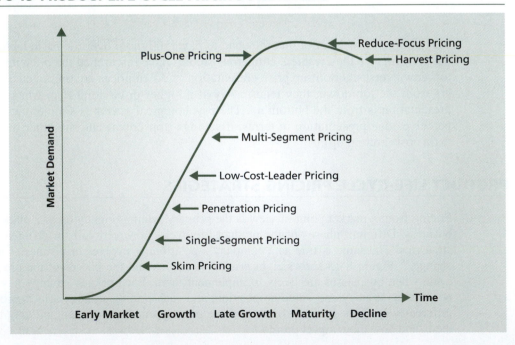

FIGURE 8-16 SKIM PRICING

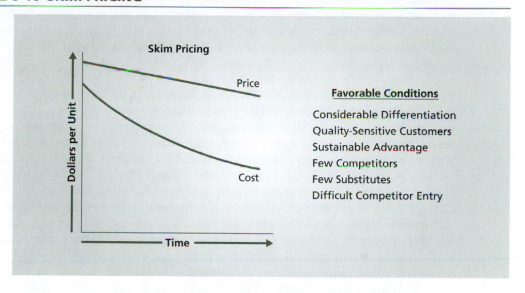

Skim Pricing

Skim pricing is the strategy that businesses often implement during the early stages of the product life cycle, as illustrated in Figure 8-15. This is the phase when conditions can be best for a skim-pricing strategy. As summarized in Figure 8-16, when a business has a considerable and sustainable differentiation advantage in a quality-sensitive market with few competitors, and entry to the market is difficult, skim pricing is a viable pricing strategy. When it is feasible, skim pricing allows a business to penetrate a market systematically as the business builds production capacity. As demand in the high-priced segment becomes saturated, the price may be gradually lowered to attract more customers, eventually reaching a level that is affordable to most potential customers.

Often a business has a proprietary-product advantage relative to competition because it holds a patent for its product or because the product's capability cannot be duplicated for other reasons. In such cases, a business usually pursues a skim-pricing strategy well into the market's growth stage. The skim-pricing strategy, which is really a temporary premium-pricing strategy, can be highly profitable as long as it delivers superior customer value. A business can use a skim-pricing strategy until its competitors are able to match the business's source of competitive advantage. Many prescription drugs, for example, are protected under patents, and the patent holders charge premium prices. During the patent period, the pharmaceutical company has a price umbrella. It is protected from price rivalry because any would-be competitors cannot match the business's relative advantage.

Single-Segment Pricing

As its product moves into the growth stage of its life cycle, a business will need to find a way to lower the cost to potential customers in order to attract their purchase volume. But this does not necessarily mean lowering prices. By considering the total cost of owner-ship that is incurred by target customers, a business can utilize *single-segment pricing*, which is a value-based pricing strategy, to produce an attractive savings (economic value) while maintaining a premium price. For example, in Figure 8-7, the price of BioTronics' product is higher than the price of its competitor's product, but the customer's total cost of purchase, or cost of ownership, is much lower than for the competitor's product. Because of lower usage costs over the life of the product, its value in use is higher than that of the competing product, and the customer saves money.

In other words, to use single-segment pricing, the company bases the price of a prod-uct on the attractive savings that customers realize over the life of the product, not just the costs of manufacturing and marketing the product. Customers are interested in overall savings, or economic value, and the higher the savings they realize, the higher the com-pany may set the purchase price, regardless of manufacturing and marketing costs. In Chapter 4, we examined various ways that a business can lower the cost of ownership and achieve higher price levels while still creating a superior value for target customers. We need to keep in mind, too, that single-segment pricing, because it is based on value-in-use pricing, is only possible when the company has a good understanding of customer needs and competitors' positions. Customer and competitor knowledge along with a company's positioning, is where all value-based pricing starts.

Penetration Pricing

Businesses that are focused on building volume may use a *penetration-pricing* strategy. As illustrated in Figure 8-15, this pricing strategy is most likely to be employed during the market's growth stage when volumes are rapidly increasing in response to lower prices. The primary objective of penetration pricing is to build volume to drive down cost, as illustrated in Figure 8-17.

Penetration pricing is a mass-market strategy. It is most effective in the growth stage of the product life cycle because this is when product differentiation is diminishing, poten-tial customers are price sensitive, many competitors or substitutes exist, and competitor

FIGURE 8-17 PENETRATION PRICING

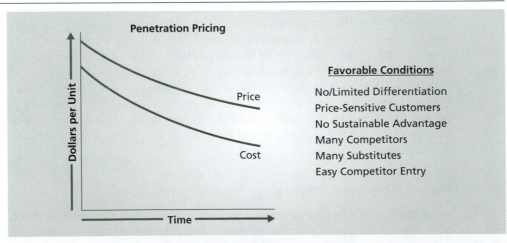

FIGURE 8-18 DRAM PRICE CURVE

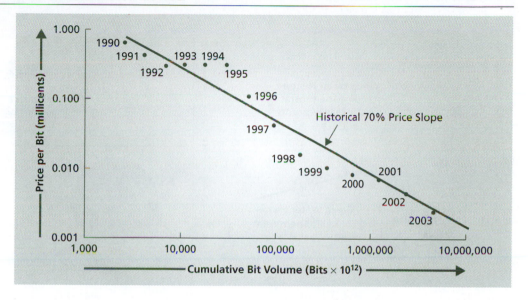

entry is easy. The volume leader often can gain a cost advantage and continue to lower prices, discouraging competitor entry and encouraging competitor exit. A volume leadership position, then, enables a business to use penetration pricing to build market share.

The price of dynamic random access memory (DRAM) chips is a good example of volume-sensitive pricing, as illustrated in Figure 8-18. In this product-market, prices decrease by 30 percent every time cumulative volume doubles.[17] The DRAM chip maker that is lowest on the cost curve, because it has the highest volume, can price its product lower than competitors do and still maintain a desirable margin. In any market where cost reduction is volume sensitive and product differentiation is minimal, a penetration pricing strategy can be a viable path to market leadership and profitable growth.

Low-Cost-Leader Pricing

The maker of BIC pens and lighters has always tried to keep its costs as low as possible and to offer a price that no competitor can beat. Likewise, from its beginnings Wal-Mart has sought to establish itself as the low-cost leader in retail by using a variety of management systems for reducing its cost for the goods it sells and for minimizing operating expenses. Both BIC and Wal-Mart have a volume advantage that contributes to their cost-reduction efforts, but a market's low-cost leader does not need to be the market's volume leader. Companies with smaller volumes can gain a cost advantage by having highly efficient operations, using superior technology, having highly motivated employees, and outsourcing parts of their operations. Even a low-share business can move into the low-cost-leader position.

Multi-Segment Pricing

A primary goal of market segmentation is a form of market-based pricing known as *multi-segment pricing*. Customers in different segments of a product's market generally have different needs and different price sensitivities. A price-sensitive segment is

FIGURE 8-19 MULTI-SEGMENT PRICING—GE WATER HEATERS

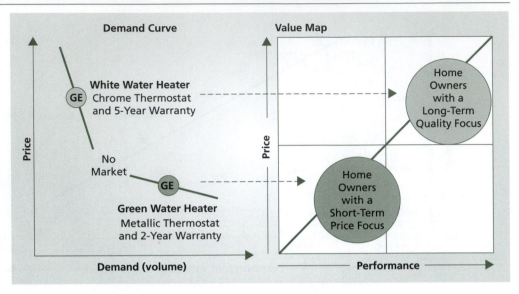

attracted to a product with a low price regardless of the product, service, or brand benefits offered by a higher priced model, whereas customers in a quality-conscious segment are willing to pay more for the additional benefits.

GE found that there was no middle market for household water heaters—just two segments at the high- and low-price points, as shown in Figure 8-19. The low-price segment consisted of buyers looking for a low-cost solution. GE served this segment with a green water heater that had a metallic thermostat and a 2-year warranty. The high-price segment was served with a white water heater that had a chrome thermostat and a 5-year warranty. In this quality-conscious segment, buyers seeking a reliable, long-term solution were willing to pay more for the higher quality product. GE performed well in both segments by providing GE-branded water heaters that met customer product needs at two price points.

To adequately serve the digital television cable market, Comcast has developed three segment-pricing strategies, as shown in Figure 8-20. Customers in the *basic service segment* pay $29.99 a month with a 2-year agreement and have access to 80-plus digital channels. Customers in the *basic-plus segment* pay $39.99 a month with a 2-year agreement and have access to 100-plus digital channels. Customers in the *premium service segment* pay $84.99 for the first 6 months and have access to 200-plus digital channels and many additional movie channels. These three Comcast pricing strategies address customer price needs with three different levels of digital television cable service. As Figure 8-15 shows, multi-segment pricing is most likely to be used during the growth stage of the product life cycle.

Plus-One Pricing

As markets mature, competitors are able to emulate the best features of a business's product and, as a result, it becomes ever more difficult for the business's product to stand out as unique. To succeed in a mature market, a business needs some source of differentiation in

FIGURE 8-20 MULTI-SEGMENT PRICING—COMCAST DIGITAL CABLE SERVICE

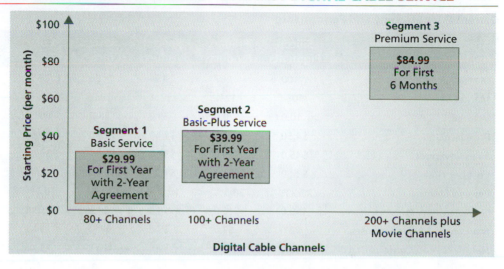

order to maintain its product position. To do this, it can establish a plus-one product position[18] in order to justify a value-based price with a slight premium relative to competing products.

Plus-one pricing can be used when a business's product position is the about the same as competitors' positions in every area of product and service quality, except that in one area of meaningful performance the business's product position is clearly superior. For example, Volvo first strives to meet customer expectations in all aspects of luxury-car performance. The company then uses safety as its plus-one product-differentiation strategy to set a value-based price relative to competing luxury cars. The safety features that Volvo has designed into its cars are the business's source of differentiation and are central to Volvo's product-price positioning and value proposition. On the other hand, Lexus uses performance as its plus-one pricing strategy, and Mercedes uses its reputation. As Figure 8-15 illustrates, a plus-one pricing strategy is the value-based pricing strategy that a business is most likely to use in the late stages of the product life cycle.

Reduce-Focus Pricing

As a market moves into its mature stage, prices and margins are often further eroded by intense competition. Because a business's product is still profitable in a mature market, it is not yet time for a harvest-pricing strategy. Instead, the business should apply a *reduce-focus pricing* strategy to manage price and improve profits.[19]

A reduce-focus pricing strategy calls for price increases with the intent of reducing volumes and market share in exchange for higher margins. After the first price increase, many price-sensitive customers leave, and subsequent price increases further diminish their numbers. The goal is to raise prices incrementally to the point where the best combination of volume and margin is achieved.

For example, in Figure 8-21, a chemical company's paint division was in a mature market with low margins.[20] In this case, the average for the margins across the product line was 20.5 percent. Just three of the products produced enough gross profit to cover their marketing and sales expenses. The reduce-focus pricing strategy resulted in the company's market share dropping from 11.7 to 8.6 percent. The share reduction corre-

FIGURE 8-21 REDUCE-FOCUS PRICING STRATEGY AND PROFIT IMPACT

Current Price Strategy and Performance

Area of Performance (millions)	Silicon Pigments	Primary Products	Special Products	Basic Colors	Color Enhancers	Overall Total
Market Demand	100	167	154	96	556	1,073
Market Share	10%	12%	13%	26%	9%	11.7%
Volume	10.0	20.0	20.0	25.0	50.0	125.0
Price per Unit	$4.50	$2.80	$1.60	$0.80	$0.60	$1.46
Sales Revenues	$45.0	$56.0	$32.0	$20.0	$30.0	$183.0
Cost per Unit	$3.50	$2.00	$1.30	$0.70	$0.54	$1.16
Percent Margin	22.2%	28.6%	18.8%	12.5%	10.0%	20.5%
Gross Profit	$10.0	$16.0	$6.0	$2.5	$3.0	$37.5
Marketing & Sales Expenses	$2.0	$7.0	$5.0	$3.0	$4.5	$21.5
Net Marketing Contribution	$8.0	$9.0	$1.0	–$0.5	–$1.5	$16.0

Reduce-Focus Pricing Strategy and Performance

Area of Performance (millions)	Silicon Pigments	Primary Products	Special Products	Basic Colors	Color Enhancers	Overall Total
Market Demand	100	167	154	96	556	1,073
Market Share	8.6%	10.3%	10.7%	17.1%	6.0%	8.6%
Volume	8.6	17.2	16.5	16.4	33.4	92.1
Price per Unit	$4.95	$3.20	$1.90	$0.98	$0.75	$1.85
Sales Revenues	$42.6	$55.0	$31.3	$16.1	$25.0	$170.0
Cost per Unit	$3.50	$2.00	$1.30	$0.70	$0.54	$1.25
Percent Margin	29.3%	37.5%	31.6%	28.6%	28.0%	32.1%
Gross Profit	$12.5	$20.6	$9.9	$4.6	$7.0	$54.6
Marketing & Sales Expenses	$2.0	$7.0	$4.5	$2.0	$3.0	$18.5
Net Marketing Contribution	$10.5	$13.6	$5.4	$2.6	$4.0	$36.1

sponded with a drop in overall volume from 125 million to 92.1 million units. However, the average price for the product line increased from $1.46 to $1.85 per unit. More importantly, the average margin rose from 20.5 to 32.1 percent. This combination of volume and margin produced a gross profit of $54.6 million, which was $17.1 million higher than before the company implemented the reduce-focus pricing strategy. The company also curtailed the marketing and sales expenses for three products, which further increased marketing profits. As shown in Figure 8-21, the company's overall net marketing contribution more than doubled, from $16 million to $36.1 million.

Harvest Pricing

During the late stages of a product's life cycle, margins are often low and volumes flat or declining. The net result is poor profits with little prospect for improvement. Many businesses in this situation are in the decline phase of the product life cycle, as illustrated in Figure 8-15.

FIGURE 8-22 HARVEST PRICING AND PROFITABILITY

Market Situation	Price	Volume	Sales	Unit Cost	Margin per Unit	Gross Profit
Late in life cycle	$10.00	10 million	$100 million	$10.00	$0	$0
15% price increase	$11.50	7 million	$80.50	$10.00	$1.50	$10.5 million
10% price increase	$12.65	6 million	$75.90	$10.00	$2.65	$15.9 million
10% price increase	$13.92	6 million	$83.52	$10.00	$3.92	$23.5 million

On the basis of cost and the need for higher margins, such a business will raise prices in order to reduce volume even more quickly than is typical of the late stage of a product's life cycle. Subsequent cost-based price increases will result in higher margins as volume continues to fall. The business normally continues the sequence of price increases and volume reductions until it reaches a price that customers simply will not pay and exits the market.

Harvest pricing, however, has an interesting twist. In many instances a business will raise price to improve margins, expecting to lose volume. This was true for an automobile components manufacturer that raised prices 15 percent and lost the anticipated 30 percent of its business volume. A subsequent price increase of 10 percent, however, resulted in only a modest decrease in volume, and a third 10 percent price increase a year later resulted in no decrease in volume. At this combination of price and volume, the business had uncovered a profitable niche market and was able to manage price and volume to produce an attractive gross profit, as illustrated in Figure 8-22.

PRICING AND PROFITABILITY

Sales growth is an obsession in most businesses. Marketing and sales managers, as well as general managers and CEOs, generally believe that more is better: "If those in marketing can deliver more volume, more market share, and more sales revenues, then we can grow profits." This may be true in many cases, but managers need to be especially careful when using price to achieve this objective. Let's examine a fairly common business situation.

A business's senior management has challenged the marketing and sales team to grow sales revenues at a rate greater than 10 percent. The business's product-markets are price sensitive, and the marketing and sales team judges that a 10 percent price decrease would result in a volume gain of 25 percent, with sales revenues increasing from $10 million to $11.25 million, as shown in Figure 8-23.

FIGURE 8-23 PRICE–VOLUME SALES STRATEGY

Performance Factor	Metric	Current	Strategy	Impact
Market Demand	units	50,000	10% Price Decrease	50,000
Market Share	%	20.0%		25.0%
Volume Sold	units	10,000	→	12,500
Average Selling Price	$/unit	$1,000		$900
Net Sales	$	$10,000,000		$11,250,000

FIGURE 8-24 PRICE–VOLUME STRATEGY AND PROFIT IMPACT

Performance Factor	Metric	Current	Strategy	Impact
Market Demand	units	50,000	10% Price Decrease	50,000
Market Share	%	20.0%		25.0%
Volume Sold	units	10,000	➡	12,500
Average Selling Price	$/unit	$1,000		$900
Net Sales	$	$10,000,000		$11,250,000
Unit Cost	$/unit	$700		$700
Percent Margin	%	30.0%		22.2%
Gross Profit	$	$3,000,000		$2,500,000

The problem with this sales-oriented approach is that the strategy would lose money! As the analysis in Figure 8-24 illustrates, this lower-price strategy would indeed grow sales revenues, but it would not grow gross profits. In fact, it would lead to a significant decline in profit. The 25 percent increase in volume would not offset a 33.3 percent reduction in margin. In this example, a pricing strategy to grow sales 12.5 percent would lower gross profit by almost 16.7 percent. Because all other fixed manufacturing, marketing, and operating expenses would not change, the pricing strategy would lower overall profit. Marketing strategies that deliver superior sales growth but fail to contribute to profit will eventually bankrupt a company.[21] The lesson is that the goal of a pricing strategy should be to increase profit—not to increase sales or volumes.

To continue with our example, the first question the marketing and sales team should ask before changing the price is "How much volume do we need to maintain the current level of profitability?" As illustrated in the calculation that follows and in Figure 8-25, to maintain a gross profit of $3 million, a strategy that lowers the product's price by 10 percent would require a 50 percent share gain (from 20% to 30%), assuming there was no change in market demand. A 50 percent share gain would in turn produce a 50 percent volume gain. The required increases in share and volume are double those projected by the marketing and sales team.

FIGURE 8-25 PRICE–VOLUME PROFITABILITY

Performance Factor	Metric	Current	Strategy	Impact
Market Demand	units	50,000	10% Price Decrease	50,000
Market Share	%	20.0%		30.0%
Volume Sold	units	10,000	➡	15,000
Average Selling Price	$/unit	$1,000		$900
Net Sales	$	$10,000,000		$13,500,000
Unit Cost	$/unit	$700		$700
Percent Margin	%	30.0%		22.2%
Gross Profit	$	$3,000,000		$3,000,000

$$\text{Gross Profit} = \text{Market Demand} \times \text{Market Share} \times (\text{Unit Price} - \text{Unit Cost})$$

$$\textbf{Market Share Needed} = \frac{\text{Gross Profit Desired}}{(\text{Market Demand})\,(\text{Unit Price} - \text{Unit Cost})}$$

$$= \frac{3{,}000{,}000}{(50{,}000)\,(900 - 700)} = \frac{3{,}000{,}000}{(50{,}000)\,(200)} = \frac{3{,}000{,}000}{10{,}000{,}000} = .3 = \textbf{30\%}$$

Although it is often difficult to estimate price elasticities, we can accurately determine the price elasticity that is needed to produce a profitable pricing strategy. In the example we have been using, the business would maintain its current gross profit with a 10 percent price reduction and a 50 percent volume gain. The calculation that follows shows that the business's product has a price elasticity of −5. This means that for every 1 percent price decrease, volume increases 5 percent. A 10 percent price decrease, then, would produce a 50 percent volume increase.

$$\textbf{Price Elasticity} = \frac{\text{Percentage Change in Volume}}{\text{Percentage Change in Price}}$$

$$= \frac{5{,}000 \,/\, 10{,}000}{-100/1000} = \frac{0.5}{-0.1} = \textbf{−5}$$

Price elasticity is almost always a negative number due to the inverse relationship between price and volume. As prices go up, volumes go down, and as prices go down volumes go up. The degree to which volume changes when price changes is the product's price elasticity, which is measured from zero (no price elasticity) to −10 (a very high level of price elasticity) and sometimes larger. A few products have a positive elasticity, such as prestige products that can see an increase in demand when their prices are increased. Price elasticities between zero and -1 are considered inelastic, as the percentage change in volume is less than the percentage change in price. Price elasticities between −1 and −10 are elastic because the percentage change in volume is greater than the percentage change in price. When the price elasticity equals −1, we have unitary elasticity where the percentage change in volume is equal to the percentage change in price.

The price elasticity of −5 is the elasticity that is needed for the business in our example to maintain current profits. To increase profits at a 10 percent price reduction, the price elasticity of the business's product would need to be larger than −5 (−6 for example). Price elasticities of this magnitude are rare, as would be a 10-point share gain with only a 10 percent price decrease. A very high price elasticity, such as −5, indicates that buyers are extremely sensitive to price moves—they will buy far less if the price goes up and much more if it goes down.

PRICE ELASTICITY AND PROFITABILITY

In most markets, market demand and market growth depend on price level. High prices deter customers from entering a market, as we saw in Chapter 3, and low prices attract customers. As prices for cell phone service, DVD players, and computers have fallen,

FIGURE 8-26 TELECOMMUNICATIONS SERVICE PRICE ELASTICITY

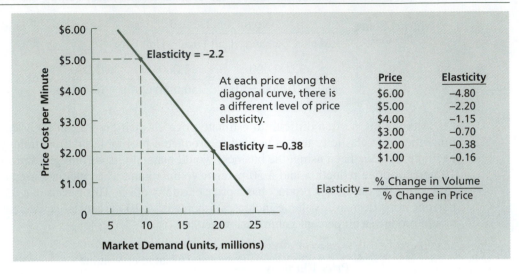

Price	Elasticity
$6.00	−4.80
$5.00	−2.20
$4.00	−1.15
$3.00	−0.70
$2.00	−0.38
$1.00	−0.16

$$\text{Elasticity} = \frac{\% \text{ Change in Volume}}{\% \text{ Change in Price}}$$

more customers have entered those markets. In one sense, price governs both the size of a market and how fast it will grow.

Figure 8-26 shows how market demand for voice messaging varies as a function of price. A telecommunications business that wants to limit initial demand for this service until it has the capacity to serve a large number of customers decides to price the service at $5 per minute. This price produces an estimated demand of 9,000 customers in a particular geographic market. At this price, the price elasticity is −2.2 which means that for each 1 percent change in price, demand will change by approximately 2.2 percent. A 10 percent price reduction from $5 to $4.50 should yield a 22 percent increase in customer demand (from 9,000 to 10,980).

A business might continue to lower price to grow demand, but once the price elasticity reaches −1, sales revenue has reached its maximum potential. At this point, a price change either up or down would lower sales revenue. This price point would be ideal for a nonprofit organization that conducts fundraising events, because the organization would be maximizing its revenues. A business, however, would price above or below this price point in an effort to maximize its profits.

Inelastic Price Management

As shown in Figure 8-27, when a price is inelastic, a price increase improves all aspects of performance. A price decrease, however, hurts sales, margins, and gross profit even though it increases unit volume. For example, Yellow Pages advertising is known to be price inelastic, with an elasticity of approximately −0.7. What would be the consequence of a Yellow Pages business lowering the price on its $100 ads by 10 percent? Assume the business normally sells one million of those ads and its variable cost is $50 per ad. The results are a unit margin of $50, sales revenues of $100 million, and a gross profit of $50 million.

FIGURE 8-27 PRICE ELASTICITY—VOLUME, SALES, AND PROFITABILITY

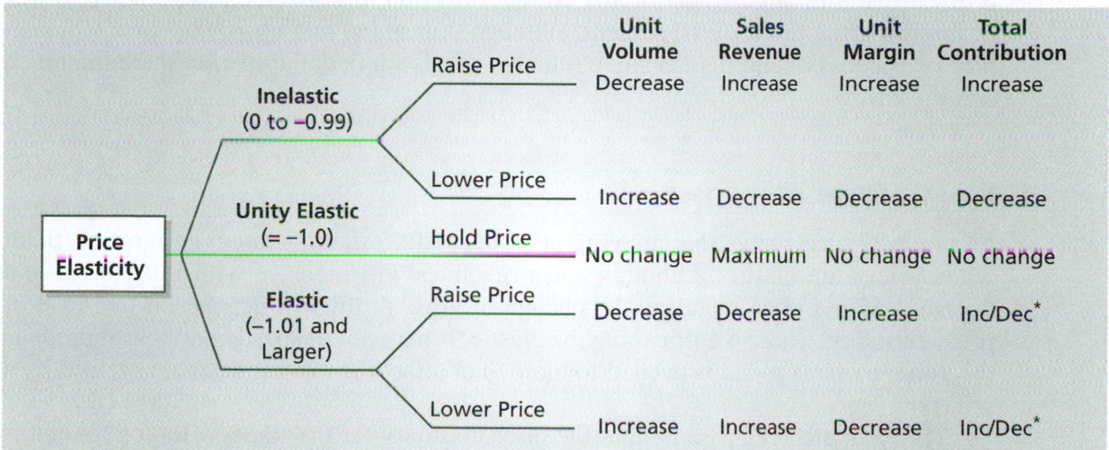

			Unit Volume	Sales Revenue	Unit Margin	Total Contribution
	Inelastic (0 to −0.99)	Raise Price	Decrease	Increase	Increase	Increase
		Lower Price	Increase	Decrease	Decrease	Decrease
Price Elasticity	Unity Elastic (= −1.0)	Hold Price	No change	Maximum	No change	No change
	Elastic (−1.01 and Larger)	Raise Price	Decrease	Decrease	Increase	Inc/Dec*
		Lower Price	Increase	Increase	Decrease	Inc/Dec*

*The gross profit could increase or decrease, depending on the level of elasticity, unit margin, and cost structure (variable and fixed costs).

Current Price Situation

Price per Ad = $100	Variable Cost per Ad = $50
Ad Volume = 1 million ads	Margin per Ad = $50
Sales Revenue = $100 million	Gross Profit = $50 million

A decision to lower prices by 10 percent when the price elasticity is equal to –0.7 would produce the following performance:

Lower-Price Strategy

Price per Ad = $90	Variable Cost per Ad = $50
Ad Volume = 1.07 million ads	Margin per Ad = $40
Sales Revenue = $96.3 million	Gross Profit = $42.8 million

The decision to lower price by 10 percent when prices are inelastic would lower margins by $10 per ad, lower sales by $3.7 million, and lower gross profit by $7.2 million, even though volume would increase. This would be a disastrous pricing decision. A business that does not know that its price is inelastic could easily follow a strategy of lowering prices in response to competitor moves or customer concerns about price.

The correct strategy in this case would be to raise price, because the price is inelastic. A strategy to raise price by 10 percent when the price elasticity is –0.7 would produce the following estimate of performance:

Raise-Price Strategy

Price per Ad = $110	Variable Cost per Ad = $50
Ad Volume = 0.93 million ads	Margin per Ad = $60
Sales Revenue = $102.3 million	Total Contribution = $55.8 million

This strategy would increase margins by $10 per ad, sales by $2.3 million, and gross profit by $5.8 million. Knowing the correct direction to move the price improved this business's gross profit by 10 percent, although it meant giving up 70,000 ads. Although there was a loss of unit market share (number of ads sold), dollar market share improved significantly.

Elastic Price Management

Figure 8-27 also shows that arriving at a successful pricing strategy is more difficult when prices are elastic. Although sales revenues will increase with a price cut and decrease with a price increase, the change in gross profit will depend on the level of price elasticity. Though a price may be elastic, it may not be elastic enough to produce the volume increase that is needed to more than offset the margin decrease created by a price cut.[22]

For example, let's assume that the price elasticity for the same Yellow Pages ad is −1.5. This is clearly an elastic price, and one that could lead many businesses to lower price to grow sales and volume. However, as the following estimate shows, a strategy to lower price by 10 percent would lower the gross profit by $4 million.

Lower-Price Strategy

Price per Ad = $90	Variable Cost per Ad = $50
Ad Volume = 1.15 million ads	Margin per Ad = $40
Sales Revenue = $103.5 million	Gross Profit = $46 million

A strategy to raise prices by 10 percent when the price elasticity is −1.5 would reduce the ad volume and sales revenue, but it would produce higher margins and a larger gross profit.

Raise-Price Strategy

Price per Ad = $110	Variable Cost per Ad = $50
Ad Volume = 0.85 million ads	Margin per Ad = $60
Sales Revenue = $93.5 million	Total Contribution = $51 million

The biggest challenge in using price elasticities is not performing the calculations; it is estimating a value for price elasticity. Every time a business changes its price, it has the opportunity to compute the actual price elasticity. It must do this computation, because market conditions change and those changes affect price elasticity.

PRICE AND BREAK-EVEN ANALYSIS

Break-even analysis is generally viewed as an accounting concept, but it is extremely useful in evaluating the profit potential and risk associated with any pricing strategy or marketing strategy.[23]

Price and Break-Even Volume

For a given pricing strategy and marketing effort, it is useful to determine the number of units that need to be sold in order to break even—that is, to produce an operating income equal to zero. Let's assume a business has a margin per unit of $2 and total fixed expenses (marketing, sales, general, administrative, and other pre-tax expenses) of $50 million. We see immediately that the business needs to sell 25 million units in order to break even: A margin of $2 per unit on 25 million units produces $50 million, the amount needed to equal the fixed expenses and give the business a zero operating income.

An actual business's fixed expenses and margin per unit are not likely to be round numbers that would make it easy to compute the break-even volume in our heads, so let's extrapolate a formula for calculating the break-even volume from the formula that we used for figuring the operating income.

$$\text{Operating Income} = \text{Volume} \times \text{Margin per Unit} - \text{Fixed Expenses}$$

$$\textbf{Volume} = \frac{\text{Operating Income} + \text{Fixed Expenses}}{\text{Margin per Unit}}$$

$$= \frac{\$0 + \$50 \text{ million}}{\$2 \text{ per unit}}$$

$$= \textbf{25 million units}$$

To calculate the break-even volume, we want to set the operating income equal to zero in the equation. A zero used as an addend (a number that is added to another number) does not affect the outcome of the calculation, so we can simplify the formula. The lower the break-even volume is relative to manufacturing capacity or expected sales volume, the greater the profit potential for a product or business.

$$\text{Break-Even Volume} = \frac{\text{Fixed Expenses}}{\text{Margin per Unit}}$$

Price and Break-Even Market Share

Because break-even volume is an unconstrained number, we must consider whether the break-even volume is reasonable. Market share, in contrast, is constrained between 0 and 100 percent, and so break-even market share provides a better framework for judging profit potential and risk. Computing the break-even market share requires only that we divide the break-even volume by the size of the target market.

$$\text{Break-Even Market Share} = \frac{\text{Break-Even Volume}}{\text{Market Demand}}$$

If the break-even volume is 25 million units and the market demand for the product is 200 million units per year, then the break-even market share would be 12.5 percent. The business has a 24 percent market share, which is 11.5 share points above the break-even

FIGURE 8-28 BREAK-EVEN VOLUME AND BREAK-EVEN MARKET SHARE

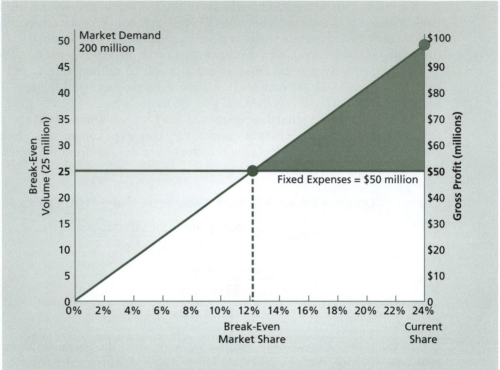

Note: The graph assumes a $2 margin per unit that remains constant as volume grows, although a significant rise in volume normally leads to a lower variable cost per unit, which improves margin. Ever-greater margins would result in more gross profit than shown.

point, as shown in Figure 8-28. If the business had only a 15 percent share of its target market, the risk of a loss would be greater because the business's share would be closer to the break-even share.

PRODUCT LINE PRICING

As a business adds more products to its product line, it enhances sales growth but also increases the risk of cannibalizing existing product sales. It is necessary, then, to know both a product's price elasticity and the degree to which it has cross-price elasticity with other products. Products that have a positive cross-price elasticity are substitutes; lowering the price of one product will decrease the demand for the other product. Products that have a negative cross-price elasticity are complementary products; lowering the price for one product will increase the demand for both products. Because the margins may be different for alternative products in a product line, a business needs to give careful consideration to any price change to ensure that the total profits for the entire product line will increase.

FIGURE 8-29 PRICE ELASTICITIES AND CROSS-PRICE ELASTICITIES OF COMPETING DETERGENTS

Brand	Share (%)	Wisk	Tide	Surf	Era	Solo	Cheer	Bold	All	Fab
Wisk	22.7	-1.37	0.31	0.37	0.23	0.11	0.12	0.09	0.08	0.07
Tide	21.5	0.33	-1.39	0.37	0.23	0.11	0.13	0.09	0.08	0.07
Surf	19.5	0.48	0.46	-1.91	0.33	0.16	0.16	0.12	0.11	0.09
Era	13.5	0.36	0.33	0.39	-1.57	0.11	0.12	0.10	0.08	0.07
Solo	5.9	0.36	0.34	0.41	0.25	-1.78	0.13	0.11	0.10	0.07
Cheer	4.9	0.46	0.47	0.47	0.31	0.15	-2.20	0.12	0.13	0.09
Bold	4.4	0.49	0.44	0.49	0.34	0.18	0.16	-2.32	0.11	0.10
All	3.6	0.48	0.46	0.50	0.32	0.17	0.20	0.12	-2.36	0.10
Fab	3.6	0.50	0.50	0.49	0.33	0.16	0.17	0.14	0.12	-2.41

Elasticities: A 1% price change in the brand column creates the percent change in market share for each row of brands.

Pricing Substitute Products

When it extends its product line, a business must recognize that some cannibalization will occur if customers can easily substitute one product in the line for another. Figure 8-29 shows the price elasticities and market shares for nine laundry detergents, along with their cross-price elasticities.[24] The results of this empirical study illustrate the price elasticity of each brand of detergent, as well as the cross-price elasticity of substitutes. As shown, the cross-price elasticities are much higher for the higher-share brands.

- **Tide Price Increase:** A 10 percent increase in Tide's price would lower Tide volume by 13.9 percent and increase the volume of Surf by 3.7 percent.
- **Surf Price Decrease:** A 10 percent decrease in Surf's price would increase Surf volume by 19.1 percent and lower Tide volume by 4.6 percent.

To fully understand the effects of product line substitutes, let's examine two types of coffee sold in the same coffee shop: the shop's regular coffee, priced at $1.50 a cup, and a specialty coffee, priced at $2.50 a cup. The regular coffee is price elastic (elasticity equal to –2), whereas the specialty coffee is inelastic (–0.8). Regular coffee drinkers generally would be inclined to switch to the specialty coffee if the specialty coffee price were lowered, as the cross-price elasticity is 0.4. However, specialty coffee drinkers generally would not be inclined to switch to regular coffee if the price for the specialty coffee were raised, as the cross-price elasticity is 0.2. Although many pricing strategies could be tested, a 10 percent increase in the price of the specialty coffee should increase the coffee shop's monthly gross profit.

Pricing Complementary Products

Of course, products that complement a certain product will also be affected whenever that product's price changes. Software, printers, and scanners are products that complement personal computers, and so the demand for these products varies with the price of personal computers. If the cross-price elasticity between PCs and spreadsheet software were 0.6, then for each 1 percent change in the price of PCs, there would be a 0.6 percent change in the demand for spreadsheet software. If computer industry prices decrease by 10 percent, the demand for spreadsheet software should go up by 6 percent. Conversely, if the price of personal computers were to increase by 10 percent, the demand for spreadsheet software would go down by 6 percent.

■ Summary

Customer value and business profitability depend on effective pricing strategies. High prices do wonders for margins but often result in low customer value, especially when a product's perceived benefits are less than its perceived price. In competitive markets where product differentiation is high, value-based pricing presents a pricing logic that is designed to deliver superior value for customers and high profitability for businesses.

Market-based pricing starts with customer needs, competitors' positions, and the business's product positioning and then works backward to margin. In contrast, cost-based pricing starts with the cost of the product and a desired margin and then works forward to a market price. Cost-based pricing often leads to under- and overpricing in markets where significant product differentiation is possible. But in markets where differentiation is minimal and customers are price sensitive, cost-based pricing can be a viable approach to pricing. In this chapter we presented five value-based pricing methodologies:

1. **Value-in-Use Pricing**—Price is set to provide customers with an attractive savings after considering the ownership costs of acquiring, owning, using, maintaining, and disposing of a product.
2. **Life-Cycle Value Pricing**—Price is set with respect to the total cost of ownership over the life cycle of a product on the basis of the net present value of the difference between the company's and a competitor's total costs of ownership.
3. **Perceived-Value Pricing**—Price is set on the basis of the value that customers realize when they compare the price and benefits of the company's product with those of a key competitor's product.
4. **Performance-Based Pricing**—Price is set on the basis of customer preferences for different levels of price and performance and taking into consideration how the company and competitors are positioned with respect to delivering both price and performance.
5. **Customerization Value Pricing**—Price is set by unbundling a product's features or performance levels, placing a price on each, and then allowing customers to select the ones they want. The price of the top-performing product serves as the reference price. Customers who buy the product with only the features they desire have an inferred savings relative to the reference price.

Different value-based and cost-based pricing strategies are especially suitable for particular phases of the product life cycle. During the early stages of the life cycle, skim pricing, single-segment pricing, and penetration pricing are usually the appropriate strategies. As markets enter their growth phase, many companies focus on multi-segment value-added pricing, whereas low-cost leaders create value with a low price. As its product moves into the mature phase of the life cycle and becomes more commoditized, a business may use a plus-one strategy to differentiate the product on the basis of a benefit that is meaningful to customers. Other businesses may pursue a reduce-focus pricing strategy in an effort to shed price-sensitive customers to the point where a price-volume combination yields lower sales but higher profits. In the decline stage of the product life cycle, a business may need to pursue a harvest-pricing strategy, raising prices systematically and reducing its marketing effort in anticipation of exiting the market. But after implementing a harvest-pricing strategy, some businesses discover a profitable niche market that prompts a return to premium pricing.

Changes in price affect both volume and margin. A price decrease that grows volume and sales but results in a decrease in total contribution adversely affects a business's profits. The goal of any pricing strategy should be to grow or at least maintain profits. A business always needs to determine beforehand how a price change will affect gross profit.

Because price affects margin, and because a certain level of fixed expenses is needed to achieve a certain level of market penetration, a business needs to assess the profit potential and risk of any pricing strategy it considers. A break-even volume analysis is helpful in assessing profit potential and risk, but not as helpful as a break-even market share analysis. Because a business's market share is always constrained between 0 and 100 percent, whereas volumes are unconstrained, the break-even market share is a better relative index by which profit potential and risk can be judged. Break-even market share enables a business to gauge the profit potential and risk of a pricing strategy by considering the target share in light of the difference between the business's current share and its break-even market share. For businesses that are operating below the break-even point, a market share break-even analysis will also show the feasibility of achieving a break-even volume within a market context.

Price-volume relationships are made more complex by varying degrees of price elasticity. Price elasticity is a measure of price sensitivity among buyers. When prices are inelastic, price increases reduce volume but increase sales revenue and profits. Price decreases in this situation increase volume but reduce sales revenue and lower profits. When prices are elastic, a price decrease will increase volume and sales revenue, but profits may go down if margins are low.

Product line pricing decisions need to consider cross-price elasticity. The price elasticity for a product may signal a particular pricing strategy, but when there is cross-price elasticity between products in the same line, a business needs to carefully analyze the profit impact of a price change. The demand for products that are substitutes will change in the direction of the price change of the substitute. The demand for complementary products will change inversely to a price change in the product they complement.

■ Market-Based Strategic Thinking

1   How could cost-based pricing lead to a price that is lower than the one customers would have paid? How does this affect the profit of a business?

2   How could cost-based pricing lead to a price higher than target customers are willing to pay? How does this affect the profit of a business?

3   How does value-based pricing differ from cost-based pricing? What should a business do if the value-based price is not high enough to deliver desired levels of profitability?

4 How would an earth-moving equipment manufacturer use value-in-use pricing to determine the customer value of its product?

5 How would the earth-moving equipment manufacturer use the net present value of a customer's total cost of ownership to set a value price?

6 How would Toyota use perceived-value pricing to set a price for the Prius? How would Toyota select a specific price that delivered a meaningful customer value?

7 At what price would the Prius not have any perceived customer value?

8 How could Toyota use performance-based pricing to determine a price that would create a good value for customers and a good price for Toyota?

9 How could Subaru use customerization pricing for the Subaru Outback and benefit from a top-down price presentation of price-performance options?

10 Why would Apple use a skim-pricing strategy for a new Apple product?

11 What kind of pricing strategy is single-segment pricing? Why is single-segment pricing used early in the growth stage of the product life cycle?

12 Why would a business use a penetration-pricing strategy instead of a single-segment strategy? How does the penetration-pricing strategy create customer value?

13 How does a low-cost-leader-pricing strategy differ from a penetration-pricing strategy?

14 Why would a business use multi-segment pricing early in the late-growth stage of the product life cycle?

15 What is plus-one pricing and why is a business more likely to use it in the mature stage of the product life cycle?

16 What is reduce-focus pricing? How can a business possibly be more profitable with fewer customers and lower volumes?

17 Why would a business use harvest pricing? Why do many businesses using harvest pricing never exit the market?

18 How would a business estimate the price elasticity needed for a price decrease that would maintain the current level of profits?

19 Why should a business always raise price when it is inelastic?

20 When price elasticity is –1.5 to –2, why would a price reduction result in larger volumes, higher market share, and greater sales but lower profits?

21 Why is break-even market share more useful than the break-even volume?

22 What happens to a substitute product when the price of another product in a business's product line is increased by 10 percent when the cross-price elasticity is 0.4? Why would a business intentionally shift sales volume from one product to another in its product line?

23 What happens to a complementary product when the price of the product that it complements is decreased by 10 percent and the cross-price elasticity is 0.4?

Marketing Performance Tools and Application Exercises

The four interactive marketing performance tools and the application exercises outlined here will add to your understanding of value-based pricing, pricing strategies, price elasticity, and break-even analysis. To access the tools, go to **rogerjbest.com**. For the questions, you can enter the data presented to obtain the answers. You may also enter other data to see the results, and you can save your work. The figure numbers in parentheses are related examples in Chapter 8, but the lettered instructions pertain to the online exercises.

8.1 **Value-in-Use Pricing** (Figure 8-6)

A. The ownership costs for a business's products that extend the life of machine fluids appear in the first example. Assess the economic value for several price points and select a price that creates a meaningful value for customers.

B. In this example, let's assume that the usage cost for the business's product is further reduced to $2.50 per pound. How would this affect customer value and the perception of the value price of $2.45?

8.2 **Perceived-Value Pricing** (Figures 8-8 and 8-9)

A. Assume the business can improve its ease of use from a 5.6 rating to a 7.5 rating. How would this change the overall benefits and customer value at the current price of $6,250?

B. With this higher ease-of-use rating, how would the customer value index change if the business raised its price to $6,500 and the business's rating on price of equipment increased from 7.5

to 8.0? Would you recommend this price increase?

8.3 **Performance-Based Value Pricing** (Figures 8-11 and 8-12)

A. Replace the existing data with two car performance factors each with three levels of performance (e.g. <20 MPG, 25 MPG, and >30 MPG) and a price factor with three price levels (e.g. $20,000, $25,000 and $30,000). Then rank the nine alternatives from 1 (most preferred) to 9 (least preferred) and interpret the performance and price curves.

B. Input the product positioning (position on each performance factor and price) for your company auto and competing auto. Interpret the value index for each automobile and how each might influence market share.

8.4 **Price-Volume Pricing** (Figures 8-23 to 8-25)

A. The price elasticity for personal computers is estimated to be –2. For the PC manufacturer shown, evaluate the sales and profit impact of a 10 percent price increase and a 10 percent price decrease.

B. For each pricing strategy, determine the break-even market share and discuss the profit risk associated with it.

Notes

1. Quotation from the Value Pricing and Profitable Growth Workshops led by R. Best, 1995–2005.
2. "Step Aside Apple Fans, Apple Needs to Sell Tablets to the PC Crowd," *Retrevo Blog* (February 23, 2009): http://www.retrevo.com/content/blog/apple-tablets-pc-users, retrieved December 2010.
3. P. Noble and T. Gruca, "Industrial Pricing: Theory and Managerial Practice," *Marketing Science*, 18, 3 (1999): 435–54.
4. G. Cressman, Jr., "Commentary on Industrial Pricing: Theory and Managerial Practice," *Marketing Science*, 18, 3 (1999): 455–57.
5. R. Best, "Marketing Excellence Survey," https://www.mes.executiveboard.com/Public/Default.aspx, retrieved September 2004.
6. A. Cleland and A. Bruno, *The Market Value Process* (San Francisco: Jossey-Bass, 1996): 106; and D. Kirkpatrick, "The Revolution at Compaq Computer," *Fortune* (December 14, 1992): 80–8.
7. E. Sullivan, "Value Pricing," *Marketing News* (January 15, 2008): 8.
8. M. Morris and G. Morris, *Market-Oriented Pricing* (Lincolnwood, IL: NTC Business Books, 1990): 93–100.

9. R. Dolan and H. Simon, *Power Pricing* (New York: Free Press, 1966): 82–3.

10. T. Nagle and J. Hogan, *The Strategy and Tactics of Pricing* (Upper Saddle River, NJ: Prentice Hall, 2006): 27–44.

11. G. Smith and T. Nagle, "A Question of Value," *Marketing Management* (July–August 2005): 39–43.

12. B. Gale, *Managing Customer Value* (New York: Free Press, 1994).

13. J. Morton and H. Devine, "How to Diagnose What Buyers Really Want," *Business Marketing* (October 1985): 70–83.

14. J. Axelrod and N. Frendberg, "Conjoint Analysis," *Marketing Research* (June 1990): 28–35; P. Green and V. Srinivasan, "Conjoint Analysis in Marketing Research," *Journal of Marketing* (October 1990): 3–19; D. Wittink and P. Cattin, "Commercial Use of Conjoint Analysis," *Journal of Marketing* (July 1989): 19–96; and A. Page and H. Rosenbaum, "Redesigning Product Lines with Conjoint Analysis," *Journal of Product Management* (1987): 120–37.

15. K.N. Rajendran and G. Tellis, "Contextual and Temporal Components of Reference Price," *Journal of Marketing* (January 1994): 22-34; C. Donoho, "Purchase Price and Order of Presentation" (Unpublished Dissertation, University of Oregon, 1991).

16. T. Nagle and J. Hogan, *The Strategy and Tactics of Pricing* (Upper Saddle River, NJ: Prentice Hall, 2006): 265–74.

17. *California Technology Stock Letter* (February 4, 1999): 4.

18. G. Moore, *Inside the Tornado* (New York: HarperCollins, 1985).

19. K.R. Harrigan, "Strategies for Declining Industries," *Journal of Business Strategy* (Fall 1980): 20–34.

20. G. Seiler, "Colorful Chemicals Cuts Its Losses," *Planning Review* (January–February 1987): 16–22.

21. G. Smith and T. Nagle, "Financial Analysis for Profit-Driven Pricing," *Sloan Management Review* (Spring 1994): 71–84.

22. R. Dolan and H. Simon, *Power Pricing* (New York: Free Press, 1996): 222–41.

23. T. Nagle and J. Hogan, *The Strategy and Tactics of Pricing* (Upper Saddle River, NJ: Prentice Hall, 2006): 175–204.

24. G. Tellis, "The Price Elasticity of Selective Demand: A Meta-Analysis of Econometric Models of Sales," *Journal of Marketing Research* (November 1988): 331–41.

Marketing Channels and Channel Mapping

■ Marketing channels are the conduits that create customer access to a company's products.

Partner-to-Partner (P2P) Channel Collaboration Program

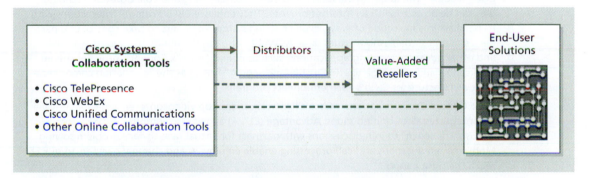

Cisco Systems Collaboration Tools

- Cisco TelePresence
- Cisco WebEx
- Cisco Unified Communications
- Other Online Collaboration Tools

Distributors → Value-Added Resellers → **End-User Solutions**

Cisco Systems		Channel Partners		Customers	
↑	100% Increase in Expert Productivity	↑	31% Increased Revenues from P2P Collaboration	↓	Reduced Issue Resolution Time (from days to minutes)
↓	55% Decrease in Travel Expenses	↓	$370,000 Travel Avoidance (observed by one partner)	↑	Improved Service Quality from Cisco and Partners
↑	Increased Sales (>50% in one example)	↑	20% Improvement in Partner Productivity	↑	Improved Customer Satisfaction

Cisco Systems relies on the channel system that is presented in the above channel map to provide end-user customer solutions. Cisco's partners in the channel system are large distributors with sales in the billions and value-added resellers that number in the thousands and have average annual sales of $15 million. Cisco and its channel partners work together, along with their end customers, to find better ways to share information. By using collaboration technologies such as Cisco TelePresence, Cisco WebEx, and Cisco Unified Communications, channel partners can better meet their customers' needs for specialized expertise and personalized service.

The net impact of Cisco's use of collaboration technologies in its marketing channel system is higher productivity, increased sales, lower travel costs, higher quality of service, improved customer relationships, and higher levels of customer satisfaction.

Figure 9-1 describes the channel collaboration tools that Cisco and its distributors use.

FIGURE 9-1 CHANNEL COLLABORATION TOOLS

Cisco's Collaboration Tools
Key Technologies Cisco and Its Partners Use

- **Cisco TelePresence**—This high-definition videoconferencing technology facilitates more frequent virtual face-to-face encounters among key people. It broadens the audience for special meetings and enables high-quality interaction. Cisco uses TelePresence to conduct quarterly business reviews with partners, to deliver its Virtual Experts program, and to host day-to-day meetings and discussions with partners.

- **Cisco WebEx**—This family of versatile, web-based conferencing and collaboration technologies can be accessed with an Internet browser. They enhance Cisco's remote interactions with its partners in a multitude of ways, even enabling system engineers to take control of a partner's system to troubleshoot issues directly. WebEx also has the ability to support webcasts and other advanced meeting applications, such as polling. WebEx Connect, provides shared workspaces and cross-organization instant messaging, serving as the foundation communications architecture for Cisco's Partner Connect program.

- **Cisco Unified Communications**—Cisco's lightweight desktop videoconferencing capability via the integrated Cisco Unified Video Advantage (CUVA) allows Cisco employees to be spontaneously "dialed in" to join discussions with partners for virtual face-to-face problem solving. Mobile communications and call processing enable employees and channel partners to quickly reach the right person.

- **Other Online Collaboration Tools**—Industry-standard tools for hosting discussion forums, wikis, videos on demand, blogs, and other social networking utilities round out the suite of collaboration technologies.

Cisco Systems uses a particular channel system to deliver products and services to value-added resellers who build customized solutions for end-user customer applications around the world. Channel partner collaboration is a way for Cisco to build relationships with channel partners and end-user customers, helping them to succeed and grow.

Source: "The Next Frontier in Collaboration: Transforming How Cisco and Channel Partners Work Together," from the *Business Transformation Series*, Cisco Systems Inc., San Jose (2009).

CHANNEL VALUE PROPOSITION

Companies (suppliers) need a value proposition for both end-user customers and channel partners.[1] Like end-user customers, channel intermediaries must have a good reason to buy and market a company's products. The basic question that every channel intermediary asks is "How will I be better off by carrying this company's line of products?" The answer can take into account many considerations, depending on the sophistication of the supplier and channel members and the intensity of the competition for a share of the channel. The following are among the most important considerations:

- **Sales Growth**—A company should emphasize the level of demand for its products or services and the investment that the company will continue to make in order to stimulate demand and grow channel partners' sales.
- **Profitability**—A company should show prospective intermediaries the margins, contributions, utilization of overhead, and net profitability that offering the company's products or services will deliver. The company could augment an intermediary's profitability by funding activities carried out by the channel member (such as placing items on display and emphasizing them in advertising) or offering rewards for performance (such as achieving volume thresholds and reaching a specific segment of the market).
- **Return on Capital**—A company should demonstrate how the productivity of the channel member's investments in inventory, working capital, and fixed assets will improve by engaging with the supplier. For example, a fast-selling product will accelerate inventory turnover, increasing the productivity of the intermediary's warehouse, shelf space, and web site.
- **Brand Leverage**—A company should show how an association with it will empower the channel member's own brand or allow it to "borrow" or leverage the supplier's brand. Small dealers and retailers, for example, could place the company's authorized-reseller emblems on their printed materials and in their premises to demonstrate credibility to customers.

Competent suppliers research their channel partners' needs to ensure that they tune their channel value propositions to those needs, thereby gaining traction in winning a share of the channel while keeping costs to a minimum.

No matter how great the benefits of a product may be, how attractive its price, and how alluring the communication of the value proposition, without marketing channels there can be no sales. Marketing channels make it possible for target customers to buy the product at their desired points of purchase. For some customers, the preferred point of purchase is a retail store; others may prefer to buy online, through a catalog, or from the business's sales representative.

Marketing channels connect businesses with their target customers. The purpose of this chapter is to understand how channel partners affect marketing channel performance and to examine the ways that marketing channels can be configured to reach customers with different needs. In this chapter, we also will explore the ways that marketing channels can serve as a source of competitive advantage. Finally, we will examine the impact of alternative channel systems on a business's overall financial performance.

CHANNEL MAPPING

The right marketing channel strategy for a company depends on a variety of company, product, and channel factors. Hewlett-Packard sells its products through all the channel paths shown in Figure 9-2. Costco provides its products to the consumer market

FIGURE 9-2 BASIC MARKETING CHANNELS

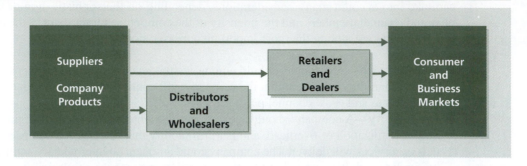

with a wholesale channel, while Dell is a manufacturer that relies primarily on direct marketing, bypassing the channel intermediaries shown. Wal-Mart, as a mass merchandise retailer, prefers direct relationships with companies that bypass distributors and wholesalers.

A diagram of the types of purchase points that a business uses is called a channel map. Figure 9-3 shows the channel map for a large electronic components manufacturer. The business uses a direct sales force to reach and serve the needs of its large accounts, those customers who make major purchases. In the diagram, the average purchase amount of large-account customers is $10,000. The company employs the sales force and pays all expenses related to direct sales to these customers. Independent sales agents call on the medium accounts. The average purchase amount of customers in this category is $3,000.

FIGURE 9-3 CHANNEL MAP FOR AN ELECTRONIC COMPONENTS COMPANY

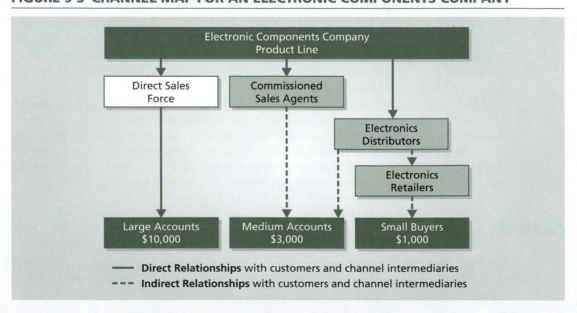

FIGURE 9-4 MAPPING CHANNEL PRICING AND POCKET PRICE

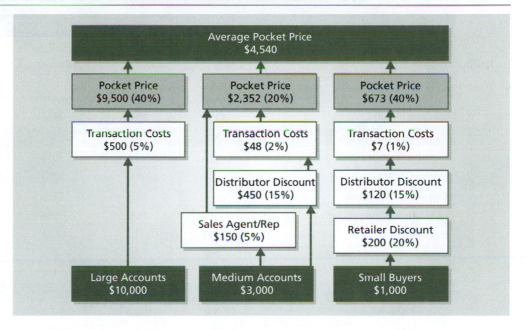

The sales agents for the medium accounts represent the company but not as employees. They receive commissions on their sales. After a sale is final, the products are shipped by a distributor, which is more efficient than shipping from the company. In the small-buyers market, the average purchase amount is $1,000. These customers typically buy a limited portion of the company's product line. To reach them, the company uses distributors that supply electronic components retailers.

As Figure 9-4 shows, each channel to the market produces a different level of sales revenue and has its own set of costs. The channel costs may include discounts to intermediaries, transaction costs, and commissions. The large-accounts direct channel has no costs in the form of discounts for intermediaries, but there is a 5 percent transaction cost for order processing, handling and shipping, invoicing, and bookkeeping. The average sale is $10,000 per purchase, so the average pocket price is $9,500. For the medium accounts, the sales reps receive a 5 percent commission, which equates to an average commission of $150 per purchase, and the distributors that ship the products receive a 15 percent discount, an average of $450 per shipment. After subtracting a 2 percent transaction cost, the average pocket price for this channel is $2,352.

For the small-buyer market, retailers receive a 20 percent discount (an average of $200 per purchase), and the distributors that ship to retailers take 15 percent of the wholesale price to retailers (an average $120 per shipment). After subtracting a 1 percent transaction cost, the channel pocket price on a $1,000 purchase is $673. In Figure 9-4, the percentage figure after the pocket price for each channel is the percentage of sales that the company obtains in that channel. The average pocket price for the company, across all channels, is the average of the three pocket prices weighted by the percentage of sales. In this case, the overall average pocket price is $4,540.

FIGURE 9-5 CHANNEL STRATEGIES AND CHANNEL TRANSACTION PROFITABILITY

Area of Performance	Direct	Mixed	Indirect	Total
Channel Strategy	Direct Sales	Agent & Dealer	Wholesaler & Dealer	
Target Customer	Large Accounts	Medium Accounts	Small Buyers	Served Market
Percent of Sales	40%	20%	40%	100%
Revenue per Purchase	$10,000	$3,000	$1,000	$5,000
Retailer Discount			20%	
Wholesale Price		$3,000	$800	
Distributor Discount		15%	15%	
Sales Agent Commission		5%	0%	
Net Price	$10,000	$2,400	$680	$4,752
Company Sales Commission	0%	0%	0%	
Transaction Cost	5%	2%	1%	
Pocket Price	$9,500	$2,352	$673	$4,540
Cost of Goods Sold	$6,000	$1,500	$500	$2,900
Percent Margin	36.8%	36.2%	25.7%	36.1%
Marketing & Sales Expense (%)	15.0%	8.0%	5.0%	9.6%
Marketing & Sales Expense ($)	$1,425	$188	$34	$436
Net Marketing Contribution	$2,075	$664	$140	$1,204
Marketing ROS	21.8%	28.2%	20.8%	26.5%
Marketing ROI	146%	353%	415%	276%

Knowing the pocket price of each channel allows a business to determine the profitability of each channel on the basis of the cost of goods sold and the marketing and sales expenses allocated to each channel for marketing communications, sales, service, and technical support. Figure 9-5 shows the costs and marketing profits of each channel. After deducting the cost of goods sold from the pocket price for each channel, we see that the margins were higher for the large-account and medium-accounts channels (margins of 36.8% and 36.2%) and lower in the small-buyer channel (a margin of 25.7%). The overall margin was 36.1 percent. One way to improve the overall profit margin would be to shift sales away from the small-buyer channel to the other channels. For example, a sales mix of 45 percent direct sales, 25 percent agent-distributor, and 30 percent distributor-retailer would increase the pocket price from $4,540 to $5,065 and increase margin from 36.1 to 42.7 percent.

But the profit margin is only one aspect of channel profitability. To fully understand channel profits, we need to know, for each channel, the marketing and sales expenses that are required to maintain or achieve a certain market share. The direct-sales strategy for the large accounts is the most expensive in dollars, costing 15 percent of channel sales ($1,425 of the pocket price of $9,500). This channel has the highest net marketing contribution ($2,075 per transaction) but the lowest marketing ROI (146%).

FIGURE 9-6 MARKETING CHANNELS FOR HIGH-TECHNOLOGY PRODUCTS

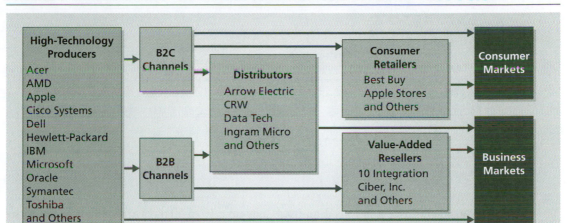

The agent-distributor channel is much less profitable than the direct sales channel in net marketing contribution, but it is more efficient, with a marketing ROS of 28.2 percent and marketing ROI of 353 percent. Shifting sales to the agent-distributor channel would increase the overall net marketing contribution, the overall marketing ROS, and the overall marketing ROI. As a way to improve pocket price, margins, and profits, this change in channel strategy would be worth consideration.

Consumer and Business Channels

Many high-technology manufacturers have a much more complex marketing channel system, as illustrated in Figure 9-6. The biggest contributor to the complexity is the need to serve both the consumer market (B2C) and the business market (B2B). For the consumer market, marketing channels include direct channels (the Internet and direct marketing) and indirect channels that either flow through distributors and wholesalers to retailers or flow directly to retailers. For the business market, direct channels include the Internet and direct marketing, and the indirect channels include distributors and value-add resellers (VARs).

Different companies use different combinations of these approaches. For example, Apple uses primarily Apple stores and Apple-authorized retail partners to reach the consumer market, but it uses VAR partners in the business market. Dell sells primarily direct in the consumer market but has direct and VAR sales in the business market. Hewlett-Packard utilizes all of the channel options shown in Figure 9-6 to reach different segments of both the consumer and business markets with its wide array of computers, printers, technical services, and storage devices.

Complex marketing channels involve a flow of products, information, services, and money. The money part of the channel can be quite complicated and contentious, as each partner in the system wants to receive payment for products and services in a reasonable amount of time. For example, in the hi-tech channel shown in Figure 9-7, the companies sell products to distributors and want to be paid in 30 to 60 days. The distributors carry the hi-tech company's inventory and sell to VARs, who need time to build and install

FIGURE 9-7 CHANNEL FINANCING IMPROVES CHANNEL LIQUIDITY

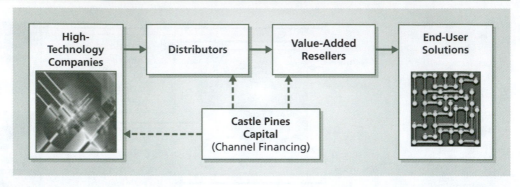

customized end-user solutions. End-users may take 30 to 60 days to pay their invoices, so the whole system is operating under intense cash flow pressure, resulting in late payments, short-term loans, and restricted sales due to a lack of money. With channel financing, a hi-tech company can improve channel liquidly and still be paid in a timely manner.

Figure 9-7 illustrates one way that a company with a strong brand can improve channel partner sales, profits, and return on capital. Using a firm like Castle Pines Capital to manage its accounts receivables with distributors, a hi-tech company can allow distributors 60 days to pay their bills while still receiving the payments in 30 days. The arrangement allows distributors to extend financing to their VARs, which lowers the VARs' cost of short-term borrowing and gives them more working capital to finance aggressive sales and marketing programs. The net result of the channel financing service has been a 20 percent increase in sales for many hi-tech companies and channel partners, lower accounts receivables for the hi-tech companies, and less contentious relationships with channel partners.

MARKETING CHANNEL PERFORMANCE

Marketing channel performance is based on the three areas shown in Figure 9-8: customer reach, operating efficiency, and service quality. To achieve the desired levels of sales and profits, a channel must do well in all three areas.[2] Consider the relationship between sales and the number of dealerships owned by a large car dealer, as represented

FIGURE 9-8 CHANNEL PERFORMANCE

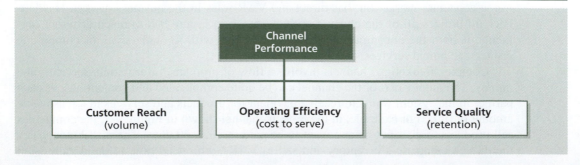

FIGURE 9-9 SALES AND CHANNEL CUSTOMER REACH

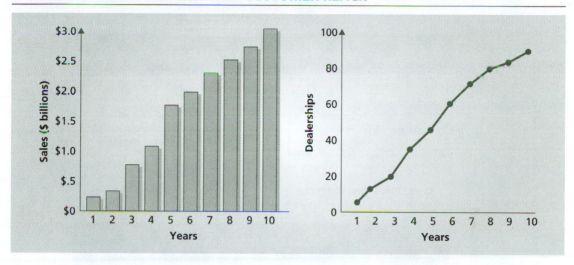

in Figure 9-9. The multiple dealerships strategy has allowed this particular car dealer to become the eighth largest dealer in the United States. For the automobile companies whose vehicles this channel intermediary carries, the strategy has produced significant sales. The goal of the channel intermediary is $11 billion in sales by 2014, which it hopes to achieve by adding more dealerships across the United States.[3]

Poor performance in any one of the three areas causes the channel to perform poorly overall. If a channel's operations are inefficient, the cost of serving customers will be too high for the channel to be profitable, regardless of how many customers it attracts or how good its service is. And if customer service is inferior, customer satisfaction will suffer and retention will decline, negating any initial benefits the business derived from the channel's good customer reach and high operating efficiency.

Customer Reach and Digital Marketing Channels

A primary objective of a marketing channel is to reach target customers. With direct marketing channels, a business engages with its customers by directly marketing and selling to them. Traveling sales representatives, direct mail, media advertising, trade shows, telemarketing, and digital marketing are some examples of direct channels. With indirect marketing channels, a business uses wholesalers, distributors, retailers, original equipment manufacturers (OEMs), VARs, and other intermediaries to reach customers. The nature of a business, its stage of development, and its target customer profile are the factors that most influence a channel strategy.

To illustrate the impact of digital marketing channels on customer reach and sales, let's examine how Dow Chemical modified its channel strategy for epoxies. The worldwide business-to-business (B2B) market demand for epoxy is $5 billion. The market consists of 2,000 customers, of which 20 percent account for 80 percent of the purchases. These 400 customers each provide average annual revenue of $10 million. As Figure 9-10 shows, Dow Chemical serves this group of customers with a direct marketing channel. This channel is profitable for the major customers, but it would not be a cost-effective

FIGURE 9-10 REACHING NEW CUSTOMERS WITH A DIGITAL MARKETING CHANNEL

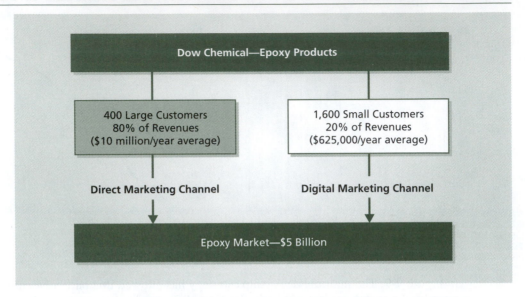

channel for reaching the other 1,600 epoxy customers around the world who buy much less. The cost of selling directly to a small customer, especially one in a distant location, would make the direct marketing effort unprofitable.

To reach a significant number of these 1,600 small customers in a cost-effective way, Dow invested $2 million in a digital marketing channel that it named e-epoxy. com. The web site attracted 1,400 new visitors and 700 repeat visitors during its first 7 weeks. Two-thirds of the orders came from customers who had never done business with Dow.[4] The end results were increased sales, a gain in market share, and many new customers that the company could now directly manage for retention and loyalty.

The marketing channel with the most potential for expanding customer reach is the digital marketing channel. The ability to reach a world of prospective customers at a low marketing cost has led nearly every business, large and small, to invest in digital marketing. The digital marketing channel that General Electric launched to supplement its traditional marketing channels saw immediate results. The channel generated $7 billion in first-year sales and twice as much the following year. A large portion of the digital marketing channel sales for those years was attributable to new customers.[5]

The digital marketing channel is playing an ever greater role in new consumer retail sales. As shown in Figure 9-11, in 2004 online U.S. consumer sales were $70 billion and 3.5 percent of all retail sales. By 2006, online retail sales grew to $106 billion and 5.2 percent of all retail sales. One market research firm projected that by 2014 U.S. online retail sales would reach $248.7 billion, about 8 percent of all retail sales.[6] Global online consumer sales are also rapidly increasing, and the growing popularity of smartphones worldwide—about 20 percent of online orders now originate with smartphone users—is expected to fuel that increase.

A company's web site does more than generate online sales. Findings vary somewhat from one market research firm to another, but it has become apparent that a great

FIGURE 9-11 ONLINE SALES AS A PERCENTAGE OF ALL RETAIL SALES

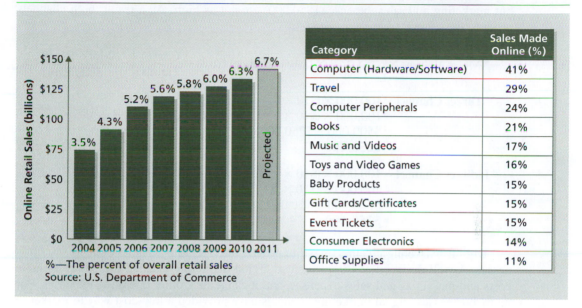

Category	Sales Made Online (%)
Computer (Hardware/Software)	41%
Travel	29%
Computer Peripherals	24%
Books	21%
Music and Videos	17%
Toys and Video Games	16%
Baby Products	15%
Gift Cards/Certificates	15%
Event Tickets	15%
Consumer Electronics	14%
Office Supplies	11%

%—The percent of overall retail sales
Source: U.S. Department of Commerce

many in-store purchases are influenced by information that customers see on company web sites. Today, customers routinely use the Internet to learn about product benefits, pricing, and where to buy. Rather than ordering online and waiting for delivery, customers often do research online and then buy their selected products from a nearby retailer.

In addition to showing the annual increases in online sales, Figure 9-11 lists the product categories that are most engaged in digital marketing.[7] Roughly two of every five purchases of computers and software programs are made online, and about one of every four computer peripherals is bought online. The level of online buying for computers and related products illustrates how important the digital marketing channel is to companies serving this market and how important it is for them to improve the customer experience in these purchases. Traditional retailers have responded to this competing channel by upgrading the interiors of their stores and improving customer services in an effort to make the in-store experience uniquely satisfying and enjoyable for customers.

Operating Efficiency

Just as different marketing channels vary in customer reach, they also vary in cost structure. A direct marketing channel produces higher margins, but the business must bear the cost of channel management and all marketing and sales expenses. An indirect marketing channel produces lower margins, but the costs of channel management and marketing are lower.

In the following example, the net marketing contribution of each channel is the same but the revenue and cost structures differ. Each channel produces sales of 100,000 units. The direct marketing channel has a higher margin per unit ($5) but incurs higher marketing expenses ($250,000). The indirect marketing channel has a lower margin per unit ($3), but marketing and sales expenses ($50,000) are not as high. As a result, both channels produce the same marketing profitability.

$$\text{NMC} = \text{Volume} \times \left[\frac{\text{End-User}}{\text{Price}} \times (1 - \% \text{ Channel Cost}) - \frac{\text{Cost of}}{\text{Goods}} \right] - \frac{\text{Marketing \&}}{\text{Sales Exp.}}$$

$$
\begin{aligned}
\textbf{Direct Channel} &= 100{,}000 \times [\$10 \times (1 - 0) - \$5] - \$250{,}000 \\
&= 100{,}000 \times (\$10 \times 1 - \$5) - \$250{,}000 \\
&= \$500{,}000 - \$250{,}000 \\
&= \mathbf{\$250{,}000}
\end{aligned}
$$

$$
\begin{aligned}
\textbf{Indirect Channel} &= 100{,}000 \times [\$10 \times (1 - .2) - \$5] - \$50{,}000 \\
&= 100{,}000 \times (\$10 \times .8 - \$5) - \$50{,}000 \\
&= \$300{,}000 - \$50{,}000 \\
&= \mathbf{\$250{,}000}
\end{aligned}
$$

Digital marketing channels have improved the operating efficiency of many businesses. A well-designed and implemented digital marketing channel can lower variable costs and marketing and sales expenses, and it can reduce other operating expenses. For many businesses, digital marketing channels have provided a low-cost way to market to smaller, hard-to-reach customers. GE's cost to serve customers, for example, decreased by $1 billion soon after the company implemented its digital marketing channels. Online buying also saved GE $1 billion on the company's purchase of goods and services in its second year of implementation. Hewlett-Packard also improved its operating efficiency when it introduced e-sourcing for conducting electronic requests for proposals, price quotes, and other information. The digital marketing channel has also reduced HP's costs and time in its procurement of products and services.

Service Quality

Every channel has different levels of service quality. When they use direct marketing channels, businesses control service quality because they, not channel intermediaries, interface with the customer at this and at all other customer touch points. This advantage allows them to make service enhancements, streamline their service procedures, and respond quickly to customer problems.

Indirect marketing channels remove a business from the end-user customer. As a result, the business is dependent on channel partners to deliver the desired levels of customer service. Channel intermediaries usually represent many different lines of products and have a good knowledge of them, but they may not fully understand the customer value that a specific product offers in meeting customer needs.

Digital marketing channels that improve the ordering process and track deliveries without multiple phone calls have lower costs and improve customer satisfaction. Many businesses have enhanced their digital marketing channels with a customer relationship marketing (CRM) system, as described in Chapter 5. A CRM system facilitates one-on-one customer relationships by enabling a company to dialogue with its customers to identify and resolve problems and obtain suggestions about how it can improve its service quality.

ALTERNATIVE MARKETING CHANNELS

A business first decides whether to use a direct, indirect, or mixed channel system.[8] All things being equal, most businesses prefer to sell and distribute directly to target customers. A direct channel system gives businesses full control when interfacing with customers, and it offers the greatest potential for value-added sales and services. On the other hand, a business that lacks the expertise and resources it needs to implement and fund a direct channel system might elect to reach target customers through an indirect channel system. Or a business may choose to use a mixed channel system—a combination of direct and indirect channels—in order to reach different target markets cost effectively or to deliver the service level expected by customers. These three channel systems are shown in Figure 9-12.

Direct Channels

As Figure 9-13 illustrates, a direct approach in business-to-consumer (B2C) markets can include a direct sales force, direct marketing, telemarketing, digital marketing, and manufacturer's representatives. In each case, the business retains ownership of the products and the responsibility for distribution, service, and collection of payment for products

FIGURE 9-12 ALTERNATIVE CHANNEL SYSTEMS

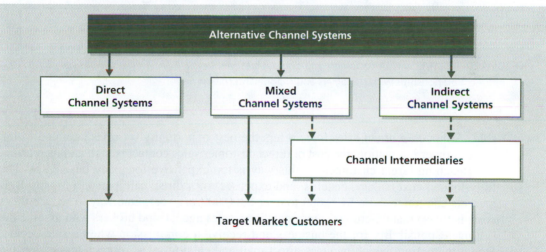

— **Direct Relationships** with customers and channel intermediaries
--- **Indirect Relationships** with customers and channel intermediaries

- **Direct Channel Systems** use one or more direct channels to reach customers, with the business interfacing with customers at all contact points and retaining ownership (title) of the product until delivery.
- **Indirect Channel Systems** use one or more indirect channels, with the channel intermediaries taking ownership of the product and interfacing with customers at all customer contact points.
- **Mixed Channel Systems** use a combination of direct and indirect channels. A business reaches, sells to, and services some customers directly but has channel intermediaries perform these functions for other customers, or a business and its intermediaries separately interface with the same customers at different contact points.

FIGURE 9-13 ALTERNATIVE B2C MARKETING CHANNELS

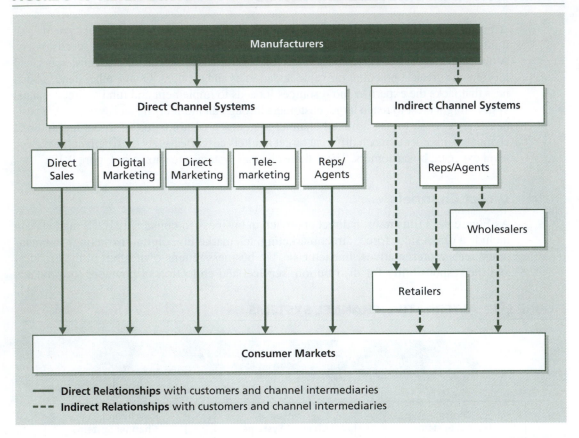

sold. Although a direct sales force offers the best opportunity for sales communication and customer interaction, the cost of direct customer sales contact is high and increasing.

Reaching target customers in this way is too expensive for many businesses. The fully loaded cost (salary, benefits, and expenses) of a direct salesperson in many B2B markets can range from $100,000 to over $300,000 per year. One way to reduce these costs is to use manufacturers' representatives, sales agents, and brokers who assume the selling responsibility for the business and receive a commission when a sale occurs. Direct marketing, which includes direct mail and catalog sales, offers a less expensive alternative, but the opportunity for sales communication is more limited. Telemarketing provides a better opportunity for a sales communication but is more labor intensive and usually more expensive than direct marketing. Digital marketing channels, when implemented well, are a highly efficient means of greatly enhancing customer reach, customer interactivity, information searches, purchasing, and after-sale customer service.[9]

Indirect Channels

Because using a direct channel system is often expensive, it limits the number of customers a business can profitably reach. Customers who make small purchases usually

FIGURE 9-14 YUM BRANDS' RETAIL STORE BRANDS

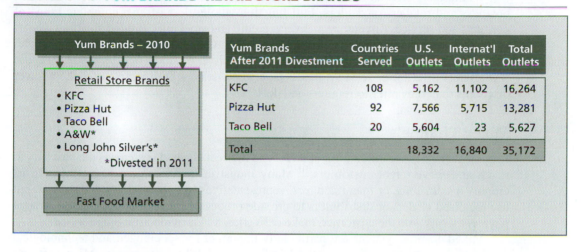

Yum Brands After 2011 Divestment	Countries Served	U.S. Outlets	Internat'l Outlets	Total Outlets
KFC	108	5,162	11,102	16,264
Pizza Hut	92	7,566	5,715	13,281
Taco Bell	20	5,604	23	5,627
Total		18,332	16,840	35,172

Yum Brands – 2010

Retail Store Brands
• KFC
• Pizza Hut
• Taco Bell
• A&W*
• Long John Silver's*
            *Divested in 2011

Fast Food Market

cannot be profitably served with a direct channel system. Yum Brands, Inc., is a pure indirect channel company with several well-known store brands. For the five major store brands shown on the left side of Figure 9-14, sales in 2009 were $10.8 billion across 36,833 outlets, an average of $293,215 per store. For these five brands in 2009, 46.6 percent of the retail locations were outside the United States and the top three brands accounted for 95 percent of them. Serving the marketing channels and managing the other marketing activities for the company's brands in many different countries creates significant challenges. In 2011, Yum Brands announced the sale of A&W and Long John Silver's. These two brands had a total of 1,661 stores, a relatively small portion of Yum Brands' total outlets. As shown in the table on the right side of Figure 9-14, after the 2011 divestment the company still had a total of 35,172 stores for its three core brands. The divestment will enable Yum Brands to sharpen its focus on growing its core brands internationally.

Each country in which Yum Brands has outlets is somewhat different in its distribution systems and food and store preferences due to cultural differences. Of KFC's 11,102 international locations, 2,872 are in China where KFC has been able to achieve a high margin (20.2% versus 13.9% in the Unites States). Given the market potential of China and its above-average margins, that country has become a key part of Yum Brands' growth strategy. Logically, the penetration of markets is a function of store location growth and increasing sales per location. Yum Brands plans to do both as it continues to develop its brands in the worldwide market. In 2011, the company introduced KFC in Nairobi, Kenya, the first fast food restaurant in East Africa.

An indirect channel system is inherently more complex because it involves at least one intermediary that takes over both ownership of the product and most, if not all, of the control in both sales and distribution. As shown in Figure 9-13, an indirect channel system may include retailers, manufacturers' representatives or agents, dealers, and wholesalers. Retailers take over the sales and point-of-purchase distribution in consumer markets, and distributors or dealers assume this responsibility in B2B markets. Compensation for their services is usually in the form of discounts, which typically range from 10 to 50 percent, but sometimes more, of the customer's purchase price.

Wholesalers offer an intermediate point of sales and physical distribution between a business and retailers or dealers. Full-function wholesalers offer a complete range of products and services (inventory, delivery, credit, and stocking); limited-function wholesalers offer a narrow range of products and services. One kind of limited-function wholesaler is cash-and-carry wholesalers, which do not deliver products or offer credit. Because wholesalers offer fewer services than retailers and dealers, businesses offer them lower discounts than they offer to retailers and dealers.

Mixed Channels

In some instances, a combination of direct and indirect channel systems is the best way to reach and serve target customers.[10] Many industrial and business-to-business firms employ a sales force or manufacturers' representatives to perform the sales contact, but use localized dealers or distributors to provide product availability information, arrange payment terms with the customer, make deliveries, and provide after-sale service.

Mixed channel systems are particularly important for specialized and technological products for which customers need localized availability or service. Microsoft and Hewlett-Packard, for example, have direct sales forces that call on large corporate accounts, often referred to as enterprise customers. Whereas the technical sales team works with the customer to create the desired customer solution, the local reseller of the companies' products handles the actual sale, delivery, and after-sale service.

B2C Channels

Businesses in different kinds of consumer markets need different channel systems—direct, indirect, or mixed—and different kinds of channels within those systems to reach customers, meet their needs, and produce acceptable levels of profitability. Figure 9-13 outlines the various B2C channel systems that businesses use. Traditionally, businesses in consumer markets have used indirect channels, mainly wholesalers and retailers, to reach target customers effectively and cost efficiently. However, advances in computer software beginning in the 1970s have opened new and attractive direct channels.

Direct marketing through consumer catalogs, mailings, telemarketing, and digital marketing has grown as the result of advances in computers and software programs, and future technological improvements will add to the effectiveness and use of these direct channels. Cost-effective printing and database technology enable companies like Esprit, Eddie Bauer, and L.L. Bean to use catalogs to market directly to the huge consumer apparel market. But some businesses in large consumer markets have long relied on another direct marketing channel. Mary Kay Cosmetics, Electrolux, and Amway are examples of businesses that, since early in their development, have reached their target consumers though direct sales distributors. Although the distributors are independent, in effect they are the sales forces for these businesses.

Online retail has opened up a new type of indirect B2C channel. Like brick-and-mortar retail, online retailers buy their products from manufacturers or wholesalers and resell them to consumers over the Internet. Easy price comparisons and "anytime shopping" make online stores very convenient for consumers. This indirect channel works particularly well for standard products that customers do not need to inspect before they buy, such as books or CDs.

FIGURE 9-15 CHANNEL MAP FOR A WELDING ROD MANUFACTURER

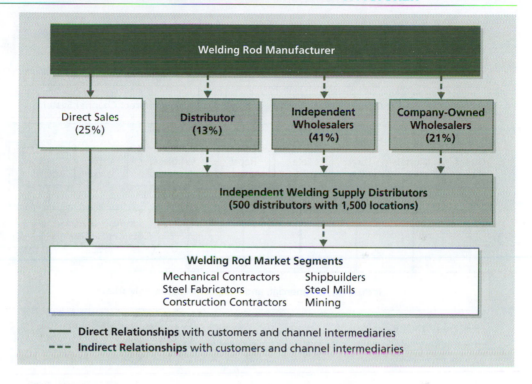

Direct Relationships with customers and channel intermediaries

Indirect Relationships with customers and channel intermediaries

B2B Channels

Most businesses, as noted earlier, would prefer to sell and distribute with a direct channel system. Direct channels provide a greater degree of control and specialized knowledge that can be customized for the end-user customer. But for manufacturers of industrial products, as illustrated in Figure 9-15, only 25 percent of sales are generated by direct channel systems.[11] This relatively low percentage is partly the result of the cost of a business-to-business direct sales call, which typically ranges from $100 to $300. In industrial markets, businesses derive about 50 percent of all sales from the combination of manufacturers' reps or sales agents and industrial distributors. Manufacturers of inexpensive industrial and commercial products generally sell through wholesalers. For example, a manufacturer may sell hospital supply products to a large hospital supply wholesaler that sells directly to hospitals and other medical institutions.

Unique to the business-to-business market, as included in Figure 9-16, are value-added resellers (VARs) and original equipment manufacturers (OEMs). VARs purchase a variety of components from several manufacturers and package them as a system. A VAR often provides the total system, as well as specialized services, to help the customer learn, use, maintain, and upgrade the system. For example, a VAR in the agricultural market may purchase computers, printers, modems, and telecommunications equipment from several manufacturers, along with specialized software, to produce an information and management system for use in farming, a system that would encompass planting, fertilizing, irrigation, and rotation requirements for a wide variety of crops. The agricultural

FIGURE 9-16 ALTERNATIVE B2B MARKETING CHANNELS

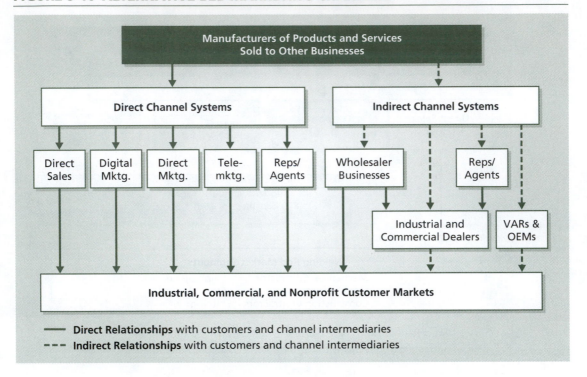

customers could buy all these products separately, but they prefer to purchase a complete (bundled) system that is customized to their specific needs.

An OEM is similar but actually creates a new product manufactured from components it buys. Ford, IBM, and Caterpillar are examples of OEMs that buy parts from other manufacturers and assemble them to make their products. Ford purchases many components, from body parts to tires, for manufacturing its vehicles. The tires come from Firestone and other tire makers, which also operate company-owned retail stores, but the automobile industry is an all-important indirect channel sales opportunity for the tire companies. IBM buys disk drives from Seagate and processors from Intel, but it also makes its own. Like Ford, Caterpillar has to purchase special tires, batteries, and many parts to manufacturer its earth-moving equipment.

Virtually all B2B businesses have some digital marketing capability. Many aspects of a digital marketing channel are informational; others facilitate order placement and solicit delivery preferences.

B2B and B2C Marketing Channels

Software manufacturers like Adobe and Microsoft serve both business and consumer customers. As illustrated in Figure 9-17, software manufacturers use a direct marketing channel to reach and serve large enterprises, such as Fortune 500 companies. To reach medium-sized and small businesses and individual consumers, software companies use online marketing as part of their direct channel systems, but more often they use indirect

FIGURE 9-17 MARKETING CHANNELS USED TO REACH B2B AND B2C CUSTOMERS

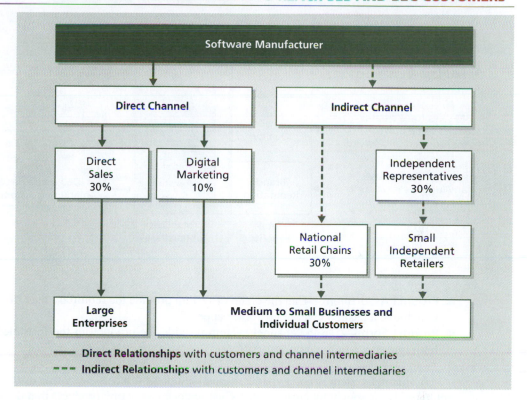

— **Direct Relationships** with customers and channel intermediaries
--- **Indirect Relationships** with customers and channel intermediaries

channels, including independent, commissioned representatives. Each of the channels has different levels of cost, control, sales contact, and ownership.

MARKETING CHANNELS THAT IMPROVE CUSTOMER VALUE

A business's channel system can consist of one or many channels, and a system with multiple channels can have all direct, all indirect, or any combination of direct and indirect channels. To be successful, however, a channel system must enhance customer value, as shown in Figure 9-18, by increasing customer benefits, lowering customer cost of purchase, or both.

Product Performance

If a business's product is perishable or easily damaged, it must use channels that can deliver the product to customers in a condition that meets or exceeds their expectations. Before selecting a channel system, a business needs to consider how that channel system either enhances or detracts from the following aspects of product performance:

- **Product Quality**—Can the channel system deliver the product with the quality level that is required and expected by customers?

FIGURE 9-18 HOW MARKETING CHANNELS CONTRIBUTE TO CUSTOMER VALUE

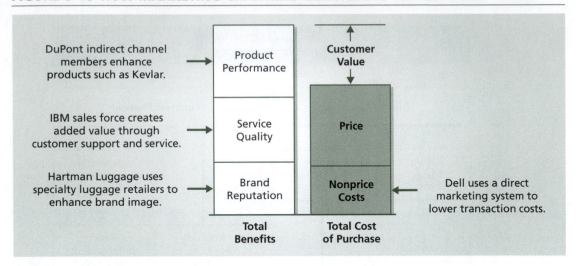

- **Product Assortment**—Can the channel system provide the required range of products to achieve a desired level of customer appeal?
- **Product Form**—Can the channel system provide the product, in the form needed, to both intermediaries and customers?

A channel system is not a viable alternative unless it meets every one of these product benefits, as sought by customers.[12] Customers will not buy products that do not meet their purchasing needs, as they can almost always find competing alternatives.

Service Quality

Every channel has advantages and limitations with respect to service. The need to provide delivery, installation, training, technical support, repair, terms of payment, credit, and easy return of faulty products are all service quality features that a business must consider in selecting a particular channel system. To determine whether a channel system is viable, a business has to evaluate the following points with respect to a customer's service needs and expectations.

- **After-Sale Services**—What after-sale services are critical to achieving total customer satisfaction with the product or service?
- **Availability and Delivery**—To what degree do customers benefit from quick access to goods or services and immediate delivery?
- **Transaction Services**—Can the channel system accommodate the customers' credit needs, terms of payment, warranty needs, desire for delivery at no charge, and easy return of faulty products?

All three of these points are important aspects of a channel system. A business with a better product may not achieve market success if it fails to provide the service benefits

FIGURE 9-19 HOW MARKETING CHANNELS ADD VALUE TO A FIBER-CEMENT SIDING PRODUCT

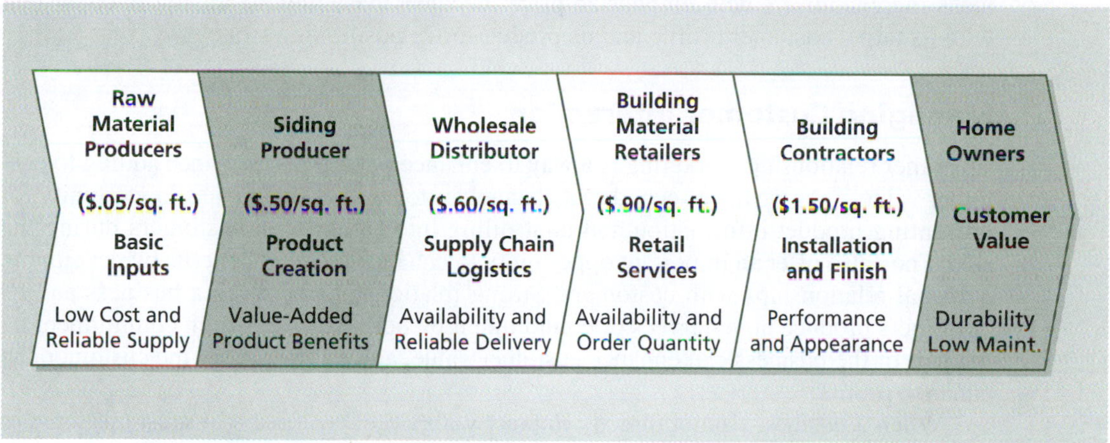

Raw Material Producers	Siding Producer	Wholesale Distributor	Building Material Retailers	Building Contractors	Home Owners
($.05/sq. ft.)	($.50/sq. ft.)	($.60/sq. ft.)	($.90/sq. ft.)	($1.50/sq. ft.)	Customer Value
Basic Inputs	Product Creation	Supply Chain Logistics	Retail Services	Installation and Finish	
Low Cost and Reliable Supply	Value-Added Product Benefits	Availability and Reliable Delivery	Availability and Order Quantity	Performance and Appearance	Durability Low Maint.

required by target customers. To be successful in meeting customer expectations, a business has to make the product available at the target customer's desired point of purchase. In addition, it must meet or exceed each of its customer's product and service requirements, whether the customer is an end user or a channel intermediary.

Let's consider again the fiber-cement construction siding discussed in previous chapters, this time in view of the way marketing channels can add value to the product. The product is made from a combination of paper and cement. As shown in Figure 9-19, these raw materials are needed at a low cost on a reliable basis in order to serve a growing market demand for fiber-cement siding. Manufacturers add roughly 45 cents per square foot by transforming these raw materials into a semifinished product. However, in this form, at the point of production, the product has no value to homeowners. A marketing channel is needed to reach the end-user customer. Producers sell to wholesalers who have a system of distribution in place that reaches the many construction retailers around the United States. Wholesalers add 10 cents per square foot to the price of the product in exchange for their logistic and distribution services. Construction retailers add 30 cents per square foot for providing localized inventories, desired purchase quantities, and customer service that includes offering information on the product and directing purchasers to contractors who can install the product. Contractors add trim and paint the product to achieve the desired performance and appearance. The net result is a cost to homeowners of roughly $1.50 per square foot of siding, a superior customer value in light of the product's benefits—resistance to fire, bug infestation, and rot, and a 50-year warranty—plus the value added by the channel intermediaries.

Company or Brand Reputation

Another important consideration is how a channel system will affect the image of a product or manufacturer. Hartman Luggage, for example, manufactures a high-quality line of luggage and has built an image among quality-conscious customers. Hartman is selective in choosing retailers who will support or enhance this brand image. Likewise, Perfume de

Paris manufactures and markets perfume at about one-third the price of Chanel and other high-priced perfumes. It is important for Perfume de Paris to sell its product through mass merchandisers who emphasize price, because mass merchandising is consistent with its target customer profile and its product-price positioning strategy.

Managing Customer Interaction

Customer relationship marketing is a way to enhance overall performance adding to customer value.[13] As we have seen, direct channel systems offer the greatest opportunity for presenting product information and controlling interaction with customers during the sale. They also offer an important opportunity to enhance the total benefits by developing personal relationships with customers. Strong relationships between a business and its customers produce high degrees of commitment by both parties. A high commitment on the part of the business can enhance customer value, and on the part of the customer can enhance profits.

When a business cannot directly interact with target customers, it must take care to select a channel system that is conducive to building effective customer relationships.[14] For a given product and customer profile, the inclusion of the right channels in the channel system requires a certain level of product knowledge, sales and negotiation skill, call frequency, and after-sale service. In the end, any channel system that does not provide effective sales interaction with target customers will be of little value.

Digital marketing channels are particularly well suited for customer interaction with a business. They can be extended with a CRM system that enables a business to develop a one-on-one relationship with each customer. A business with 10,000 customers that uses digital marketing should view its customers not as a segment of 10,000 customers but as 10,000 segments, each with one customer. Whether a company is a consumer business with millions of customers or an industrial business with hundreds of customers, the use of customer relationship and digital marketing enables it to interact with customers, make customized offerings, and build customer loyalty.

Dow Corning has been the market leader in silicon technology applications for many decades. Its products have a multitude of industrial uses, as well as many applications in the electronics, health care, and construction markets. As would be expected, though, many of Dow Corning's products are less competitive in the mature stage of the product life cycle. The company's traditional full-service consultative engineering approach does not work well for these products. In response to this problem, Dow Corning has augmented its overall marketing strategy with a new and radically different marketing channel.[15]

In order to develop this new marketing channel, Dow Corning researched the silicon-based product market and found that two segments could still be served profitably with the company's traditional marketing approach. As Figure 9-20 shows, the company chose to serve the innovation technology segment directly and use intermediaries for the service quality segment. A direct channel was appropriate for new applications, as was an indirect channel for high-growth applications. But Dow Corning needed a new marketing channel that could accommodate highly competitive prices through reduced sales and service expenses, so it developed a digital marketing channel for the price-sensitive segment. Because this strategy was a major departure from the company's core product positioning, Dow Corning decided to sell the 400 silicon-based products targeted for the digital marketing channel strategy under a new brand name, Xiameter.

FIGURE 9-20 MARKETING CHANNELS THAT ENHANCE VALUE PROPOSITIONS (VPs)

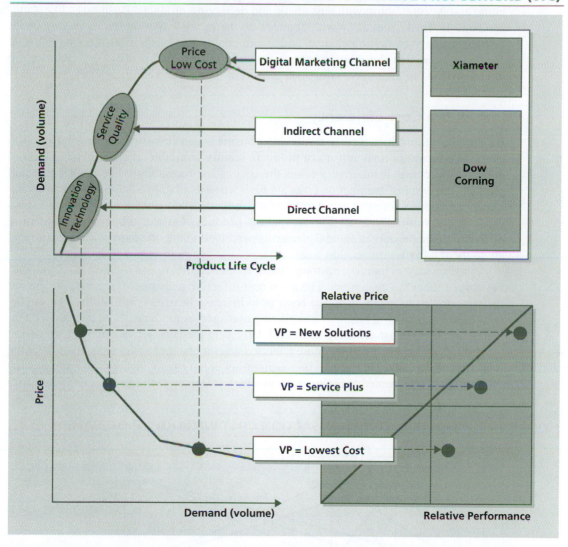

The Xiameter digital marketing channel lets customers compare Xiameter's prices with competitors' prices, a feature that any price-sensitive customer would find appealing. Customers order online, and each order has a guaranteed shipping date. Xiameter's success is directly linked to its cost-effective digital marketing channel applications for products that are in the mature stage of their life cycles, when prices generally fall.

For long-established businesses like Dow Corning, General Electric, and Charles Schwab, digital marketing complements their other marketing channels. It gives these companies one more way to attract new customers while serving present ones. The businesses find that digital marketing is cost-effective because it leverages existing brand equity, supply chain capabilities, and operating systems that are already in place. But many businesses that have formed since the advent of the Internet have chosen to rely almost exclusively on digital marketing, using it as their primary means for building brand equity, interfacing with customers, and delivering products. Businesses like Amazon.com, E*Trade, and eBay were founded on the premise that digital marketing could be their primary marketing channel and a core component of their business model. The customer value that these businesses create and the sales and profits they generate are directly related to their successful management of digital marketing.

Improving Cost Efficiency

By making its product readily available, a business can lower customers' transaction costs. If a business does not make products readily available at customers' preferred points of purchase, it inherently raises the cost of the transaction. For undifferentiated products, customers' transaction costs are high when availability is limited because customers must make an extra effort to find the products. Many customers will instead purchase a conveniently available competing product. On the other hand, the more differentiated a product is and the greater its perceived value, the more willing customers are to incur a higher transaction cost.

Another way to increase customer value (total benefits minus total costs) is to lower the cost of reaching customers. The more cost-effective a channel system is, the greater the opportunity to lower customer costs or to increase business profitability. An important responsibility for a business's marketing managers is to identify and develop a channel system that is cost-effective while still delivering the benefits sought by customers.

It is often assumed that the more intermediaries a channel system has, the higher the total cost of purchase. In general, this assumption is not true. Consider, for example, the channel system presented in Figure 9-21, in which 100 manufacturers in a certain industry

FIGURE 9-21 INDUSTRY-WIDE TRANSACTION COST WITHOUT WHOLESALERS

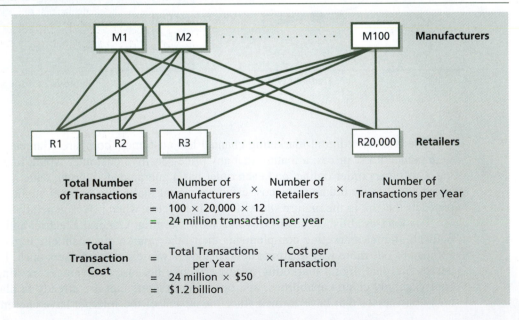

FIGURE 9-22 INDUSTRY-WIDE TRANSACTION COST WITH WHOLESALERS

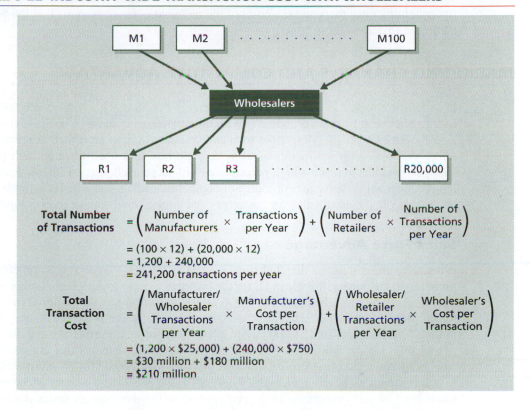

each contact 20,000 retailers once a month. With this channel system, each manufacturer incurs a $50 monthly transaction cost per retailer for order placement, handling, delivery, and billing. The net result is an industry that has an overall channel system transaction cost of approximately $1.2 billion, as shown.

When an extra layer—wholesalers—is added to the channel system, each of the 100 manufacturers can now sell to the wholesalers at a cost of $25,000 per month, as illustrated in Figure 9-22. For the manufacturers, the cost per transaction is much higher when they sell to the wholesalers than when they sell to retailers because much more merchandise is handled and delivered to the wholesalers each month. But there are far fewer transactions. In this channel system, the wholesalers then distribute to the 20,000 retailers each month. The wholesalers' cost is $750 per transaction, which is also much higher than the manufacturer-to-retailer cost in Figure 9-21 because wholesalers, who represent a large number of retailers, ship many more products at a time. But the number of wholesaler-to-retailer transactions in Figure 9-22 is only 10 percent of the manufacturer-to-retailer transactions in Figure 9-21. Adding wholesalers to the channel system reduces the total annual transaction costs for the industry by 82.5 percent, to only $210 million, or almost $1 billion less than the channel system without a wholesaler function.

Although a business generally builds customer value through a combination of product, service, and image benefits, or offers the product at a low price or with low transaction costs, any given channel system can add to or detract from the delivered customer value. Selecting a channel system, then, requires both careful consideration of the benefits sought by customers and the costs of the different channel systems that the business could use to deliver those benefits.

MARKETING CHANNELS AND COMPETITIVE ADVANTAGE

In order for any sale to occur, customer contact is essential. This contact can take many forms, whether it is direct or indirect. With direct channel systems, a business must have a sufficient number of salespeople to establish and maintain an effective level of customer contact. With indirect channel systems, a business must have enough retail or wholesale outlets to reach a high percentage of its target customers. Either a direct or an indirect channel system can be a source of competitive advantage when it is implemented in a manner that creates value for customers and a relative advantage over competitors.

Sales Force Advantage

When a business selects a direct channel system as the best way to reach and effectively serve target customers, it is essential for the business to have a sufficient number of salespeople. Assume that a business has 1,000 target customers and the required rate of customer contact for sales effectiveness and customer satisfaction is two customer visits per month. This translates into 24,000 customer contacts per year. Further assume that a salesperson in this particular industry can make three customer visits per day and can spend 4 days per week making customer calls. This translates into a need for 38 salespeople.

If competitors have an average of only 20 salespeople, they cannot accomplish the same level of sales coverage. These competitors will either contact fewer customers or contact the same number of customers less frequently. In either case, the business with 38 salespeople is able to reach more customers and better serve their needs, and both factors are sources of competitive advantage.

The quality of a business's sales force can also be a source of competitive advantage. A sales force with exceptional product knowledge and a strong market orientation is in a good position to serve target customer needs. Of course, the behavior and attitudes of the sales force are in part influenced by the market orientation of the business.[16] As a result, a business with a strong market orientation is in a better position to build customer relationships that enhance customer satisfaction and retention. The sales force is, in fact, creating a source of competitive advantage when this level of sales effort is valued by customers and cannot be matched by competitors.[17]

Sales Productivity

Businesses that have a high level of sales productivity can also develop a source of competitive advantage. A business with a more efficient sales force, in terms of sales per salesperson, will have a lower cost per sale than a less productive business that generates the same sales revenue. An efficient sales force translates into higher levels of profitability per sales dollar and a source of competitive advantage.

But how does a business develop high levels of sales productivity? Businesses with high-quality products, broad lines of related products, and efficient sales administrative

FIGURE 9-23 DISTRIBUTION OUTLET SHARE VERSUS MARKET SHARE

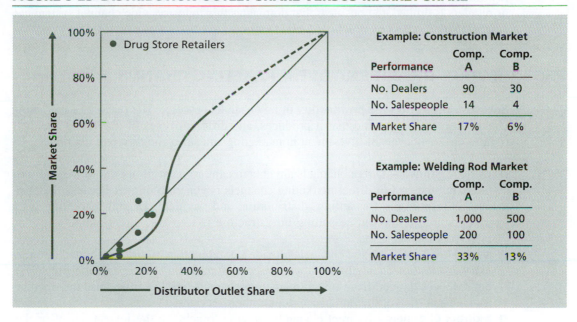

Example: Construction Market

Performance	Comp. A	Comp. B
No. Dealers	90	30
No. Salespeople	14	4
Market Share	17%	6%

Example: Welding Rod Market

Performance	Comp. A	Comp. B
No. Dealers	1,000	500
No. Salespeople	200	100
Market Share	33%	13%

systems produce high levels of sales per salesperson. High-quality products are easier to sell than low-quality products, and they often can be sold at price premiums. A broad product line provides more sales opportunities per sales call—and the use of computer networks and other telecommunications systems has been shown to improve sales administrative efficiency and to allow the sales force to have more contact with customers.

Distribution Advantage

For markets in which indirect channel systems are the dominant channel system that is used to reach target customers, share of distributor outlets can be directly linked to market share. In general, the higher a drug store chain's outlet share, the higher is its market share, as shown in Figure 9-23. Empirical studies have shown that the relationship between outlet share and market share is nonlinear and generally S-shaped, as in the figure. A small distributor share produces proportionately smaller market shares. However, as outlet share grows, market share grows at a faster rate until it exceeds outlet share. Then, as outlet share continues to increase, the rate of market share growth decreases.

There are only a few cases in which extremely high outlet and market shares have been observed. The lower part of the curve, below a 50 percent outlet share, is well documented.[18] However, because market share must equal 100 percent when outlet share equals 100 percent, the upper half of the curve in Figure 9-23 can be extrapolated with some confidence. When indirect retail or dealer channel systems are required to reach and serve target customers, businesses with dominant distribution shares have a source of competitive advantage. Why? Because in any given market, there is a finite number of distributors, and there are fewer good ones. Because the number of available distributors or retailers is limited, the business that dominates this industry-wide channel system can control market access by blocking market entry.

PROFIT IMPACT OF ALTERNATIVE MARKETING CHANNELS

Several factors affect the profitability of any channel strategy. The reach of a marketing channel affects the volume that it produces, and different types of marketing channels require different levels of investment in marketing and sales and different net prices.

- **Direct Channels**—Direct channels are able to capture most, if not all, of the end-user price, but the cost of direct marketing channels is generally higher because the business is responsible for selling, distribution, and payment. Digital marketing is an exception: after the online selling infrastructure is in place, direct online sales can yield very high margins.
- **Mixed Channels**—Mixed channels provide a combination of direct sales and intermediary distribution channels and lower the cost of marketing (as a percentage of sales), but revenues derived from mixed marketing channels are lower because intermediaries take a portion of the purchase price for their services.
- **Indirect Channels**—Indirect channels are able to achieve the lowest out-of-pocket marketing and sales expenses. However, the net price derived from the use of indirect marketing channels is much less than from direct channels because multiple intermediaries capture percentages of the end-user price.

Consider, for example, a manufacturer that sells 200,000 units annually to a market in which it has a 20 percent share. These sales are currently achieved with an indirect marketing channel, as shown in Figure 9-24. After discounting the end-user price of $1,000 per unit to $800 (a 20% discount) and accounting for a 2 percent transaction cost, we see that the pocket price is $784. With a unit cost of $650, the margin is 17.1 percent. Marketing and sales expenses are 5 percent of sales. This results in a net marketing contribution of $18.96 million and a marketing ROS of 12.1 percent. The indirect channel strategy produced a marketing ROI of 242 percent and break-even share of 5.9 percent, well below the current market share of 20 percent. But is there a more profitable channel strategy at this level of market penetration?

To address this question, we might first ask: What level of market share is needed to maintain the current net marketing contribution ($18.96 million) using an alternative channel strategy? Figure 9-24 lists the channel pricing and costs for a direct channel strategy that would use a company-paid sales force. The transaction costs are higher but, as there are no channel discounts, the pocket price is considerably higher ($950). At the same unit cost, this strategy results in an estimated margin of 31.6 percent. The marketing and sales expenses, however, are much higher ($30 million) with this direct channel strategy.

To produce the same net marketing contribution ($18.96 million) would require a 16.3 percent market share, roughly 4 points below the current market share of 20 percent. If the business could hold its 20 percent market share with this channel strategy, it could increase the net marketing contribution to $36 million, almost double the current marketing

FIGURE 9-24 ALTERNATIVE CHANNEL MARKETING PROFITABILITY

Area of Performance	Current	Same Profit	Same Share
Channel Strategy	Indirect Retailer	Direct Sales Force	Direct Sales Force
Market Demand	1,000,000	1,000,000	1,000,000
Market Share	20.0%	16.3%	20.0%
Volume	200,000	163,000	200,000
End-User Price	**$1,000**	**$1,000**	**$1,000**
Retailer Discount	20%		
Wholesale Price	$800	$1,000	$1,000
Distributor Discount			
Sales Agent Commission			
Net Price	$800	$1,000	$1,000
Company Sales Commission	0%	0%	0%
Transaction Costs	2%	5%	2%
Pocket Price	**$784**	**$950**	**$980**
Sales Revenues	**$156,800,000**	**$154,850,000**	**$196,000,000**
Unit Cost	$650	$650	$650
Percent Margin	17.1%	31.6%	33.7%
Marketing & Sales Expenses (%)	5.0%	19.4%	15.3%
Marketing & Sales Expenses ($)	$7,840,000	$30,000,000	$30,000,000
Net Marketing Contribution	**$18,960,000**	**$18,900,000**	**$36,000,000**
Marketing ROS	12.1%	12.2%	18.4%
Marketing ROI	242%	63%	120%
Break-Even Market Share	5.9%	10.0%	9.1%

profits. At a 20 percent market share, this strategy would have a higher marketing ROS (18.4%) but a lower marketing ROI (120%), as the marketing and sales budget is so much greater than that required for the indirect channel strategy. The high level of profit potential makes the investment worthwhile, though. A business that is unwilling to make the investment in marketing and sales would essentially give up $18 million in profits. We will discuss in Chapter 16 how this decision would limit earnings-per-share growth and shareholder value.

The break-even analysis for each marketing channel strategy, also shown in Figure 9-24, provides a way to assess the profitability risk of each channel. The break-even market share is lower for the indirect channel, whether the projected share is 16.3 or 20 percent. Even though margins are lower in the indirect channel, the marketing and sales expenses are much lower and, as a result, the break-even market share is lower. Still, the break-even share of 9.1 percent for the strategy that maintains current share is less than half of the 20 percent current share. The risk is slight when weighed against the profit potential.

■ Summary

Regardless of how attractive a business's products or services may be, if the business cannot reach target customers to provide the desired level of services, it has little chance of marketing success. Customers have product and service requirements, along with preferred points of purchase. Likewise, a business has image requirements and a need for sales effectiveness and cost effectiveness. To be successful, a channel system must meet both customer and business requirements and have a value proposition for both. The channel value proposition for suppliers is a combination of sales growth, profitability, return on capital, and brand leverage.

The biggest decision facing a business is whether to use a direct, indirect, or mixed channel system. In a direct system, the business is responsible for many of the selling, delivery, warehousing, and transaction activities. Direct channel systems include direct selling, direct marketing, telemarketing, and the use of manufacturers' reps and sales agents. An indirect system uses intermediaries who have varying degrees of responsibility for selling, warehousing, delivery, and transaction activities. Indirect systems include different combinations of wholesalers and retailers in the consumer market. In the business-to-business market, indirect systems can also include different combinations of wholesalers and dealers, value-added resellers (VARs), and original equipment manufacturers (OEMs). A mixed channel system uses a combination of direct and indirect channels.

The proliferation of digital marketing channels since the 1990s represents a major change in the way businesses market directly to customers. For virtually all long-established businesses, digital marketing has leveraged their ability to reach customers and capitalize on existing brand awareness, order-entry systems, and operating expenses. For online businesses like eBay, digital marketing is the primary marketing channel and a core element of their approach to serving customers. Many online businesses, however, fail within a few years of their inception because of ineffective digital marketing channels. Managed successfully, digital marketing channels have proved to be an important marketing channel in both B2C and B2B markets.

In many instances, multi-tiered channel systems are more cost-effective than direct systems, as well as more effective in reaching customers. The belief that having more intermediaries in a channel system drives up the cost and, therefore, the price of a product is not true. If a more efficient system were available, marketers would find it. However, rarely is one channel sufficient for reaching all target customers—and the greater a business's market coverage, with a direct, indirect, or mixed channel system, the greater its market share. An important part of a profitable marketing strategy, then, is a well-thought-out and well-managed marketing channel strategy.

■ Market-Based Strategic Thinking

1 Why would HP use more than one marketing channel?
2 Dell relies mostly on direct marketing in the consumer market, so why would Dell use VARs in the business market?
3 Why is the purchase amount for Apple computers different in different marketing channels?

4 Why would the pocket price for commercial printers (large printers sold to businesses) be lower in one market channel than another, even when the end-user list price is the same?

5 Why would Rolex pay higher channel costs and receive a lower pocket price? Wouldn't it always be better for Rolex to use a direct marketing channel?

6 How can a marketing channel with a lower marketing ROI be more profitable?

7 Why would Dell add an indirect marketing channel using Wal-Mart?

8 What factors could cause the rate of online retail sales to rise to 20 percent of all retail sales?

9 What is the difference between a direct and an indirect marketing channel for gift baskets? Why might a business use both?

10 What is a mixed marketing channel? Why would Microsoft Office be marketed with a mixed channel system to large business customers?

11 Are there direct marketing channels in consumer markets? How do they differ from direct channels in business-to-business markets?

12 What role do online marketing channels play in the way individuals buy airline tickets and stocks?

13 How does digital marketing help businesses reach customers, lower costs, and improve customer service?

14 What role do VARs play in the market for computers? How do VARs enhance the customer value of solutions they sell to business customers?

15 How does the use of multiple channels affect the growth of a business that sells flowers?

16 How does the use of a channel system either enhance or detract from customer value in the sale of flowers?

17 What specific factors must a business that sells cheesecakes consider in order to select one channel system over another?

18 How could a channel system be a source of competitive advantage for Lexus?

19 What are some of the ways that a channel system for Kia Motors could contribute to a higher market share?

20 How can improved sales force quality and sales force productivity for a pharmaceutical company like Merck or Pfizer be a source of competitive advantage?

21 How would you determine the profit impact of an alternative channel system for the sales of iPhones?

Marketing Performance Tools and Application Exercises

The three interactive marketing performance tools and the application exercises outlined here will strengthen your understanding of channel mapping and channel profitability. To access the tools, go to **rogerjbest.com.** For the questions in the exercises, you may enter the data presented to obtain the answers. You may also enter other data to see the results, and you may save your work.

9.1 Channel Mapping and Pocket Price (Figures 9-3 and 9-4)

A. How does the overall average pocket price change if the business modifies its sales mix to 30 percent direct sales, 40 percent agent-distributor, and 30 percent distributor-retailer?

B. How does the average pocket price change if the business replaces the direct sales channel with an agent-distributor channel, with a sales mix of 60 percent agent-distributor and 40 percent distributor-retailer?

9.2 Marketing Channel Profitability (Figure 9-5)

A. How does the net marketing contribution and marketing ROI change if the business modifies its sales mix to 30 percent direct sales, 40 percent agent-distributor, and 30 percent distributor-retailer?

B. How does the net marketing contribution and marketing ROI change if the business replaces the direct sales channel with the agent-distributor channel, with a sales mix of 60 percent agent-distributor and 40 percent distributor-retailer?

9.3 Alternative Channel Profitability (Figure 9-24)

A. Using the "Analysis-Profit" column, how much is needed in marketing & sales expenses to maintain a 20 percent market share and same level of net marketing contribution in the alternative channel?

B. Using the "Analysis-Share" column, how much market share is needed to produce the same net marketing contribution if the marketing and sales budget were 20 percent of sales in the alternative channel?

Notes

1. J. Dent, *Distribution Channels: Understanding and Managing Channels to Market* (Philadelphia: Kogan Page, 2008).

2. O. Brooks, "Art of the Deal," *Oregon Business* (April 2006): 18–22.

3. M. Lindstrom and T.F. Andersen, *Brand Building on the Internet* (Dover, NH: Kogan Page Limited, 2000).

4. K. Schnepf, "Customers of Epoxy Resin and Related Products Find E-epoxy.com a Powerful Procurement Channel," news/dow.com/prodbus/2001, retrieved December 2001 (article no longer posted).

5. J. Welch, *Jack: Straight from the Gut* (New York: Warner Books, 2001): 341–51.

6. E. Schonfeld, "Forrester Forecast" (March 8, 2010), http://www.techcrunch.com/2010/03/08/forrester-forecast-online-retail-sales-will-grow-to-250-billion-by-2014/, retrieved February 17, 2011.

7. M. Richtel and B. Tedeschi, "As Some Grow Weary of Web, Online Sales Lose Momentum," *New York Times* (June 17, 2007): 1.

8. K. Rangan, M. Menezes, and E.P. Maier, "Channel Selection for New Industrial Products: A Framework, Method and Application," *Journal of Marketing* (July 1992): 69–82.

9. R. Oliva, "Painting with Business Marketers' Web Palette," *Marketing Management* (Summer 1998): 50–3.

10. F. Cespedes and R. Corey, "Managing Multiple Channels," *Business Horizons* (July–August 1990): 72.

11. R. Haas, *Industrial Marketing Management: Text and Cases*, 4th ed. (Northridge, CA: Kent, 1989): 239; and M. Morris, *Industrial and Organizational Marketing* (Old Tappan, NJ: Macmillan, 1988): 489–523.

12. N. Dawar and P. Parker, "Marketing Universals: Consumers' Use of Brand Name, Price, Physical Appearance, and Retailer Reputation as Signals of Product Quality," *Journal of Marketing* (April 1994): 81–95.

13. J. Anderson and J. Narus, "A Model of Distributor Firm and Manufacturer Firm Working Partnerships," *Journal of Marketing* (January 1990): 42–58.

14. D. Morris, "What's Old Is New in Relationship Marketing," *Marketing News* (February 1994): 4, 8; and R. Robicheaux and J. Coleman, "The Structure of Marketing Channel Relationships," *Academy of Marketing Science* (Winter 1994): 38–51.

15. J.N. DeBonis, E. Balinski, and P. Allen, *Value-Based Marketing for Bottom-Line Success* (New York: McGraw-Hill, 2003).

16. J. Siguaw, G. Brown, and R.E. Widing, "The Influence of Market Orientation of the Firm on Sales Force Behavior and Attitudes," *Journal of Marketing Research* (February 1994): 106–16.

17. R. Ping, "Does Satisfaction Moderate the Association Between Alternative Attractiveness and Exit Intention in a Marketing Channel?" *Academy of Marketing Science* (Fall 1994): 364–71.

18. G. Lilien, P. Kotler, and K. Moorthy, *Marketing Models* (Upper Saddle River, NJ: Prentice Hall, 1992): 434–38; P. Hartung and J. Fisher, "Brand Switching and Mathematical Programming in Market Expansion," *Management Science* (August 1965): 231–43; and G. Lilien and A. Rao, "A Model for Allocating Retail Outlet Building Resources Across Market Areas," *Operations Research* (January–February): 1–14.

Marketing Communications, Social Media, and Customer Response

■ Marketing communications need a measurable customer-response objective in order to be justifiably effective.

Volkswagen's Super Bowl Communications Strategy

• In an effort to generate a pre-advertisement buzz, VW posted *The Force* on YouTube 4 days before Super Bowl XLV. Prior to the game, there were over 10 million views, 10,000 comments, and 62,000 "likes."

• *The Force* television ad aired during the Super Bowl, gaining an estimated 100 million impressions.

• During the week after the Super Bowl, another 18.5 million people viewed *The Force* on YouTube.

• This television ad aired again several months later during the 2011 college football season.

Volkswagen made use of both television and the Internet to gain exposure for the commercial it produced for the 2011 Super Bowl. The commercial aired during the game, and a video of the commercial was posted on YouTube for one week before and one week after the game. During the week before the game, the video accrued 10 million views, 10,000 comments, and 62,000 "likes." It had an estimated 100 million impressions (appearances on users' screens). The week following the game, the YouTube video attracted an additional 18.5 million views. The combination of TV and YouTube was a clever and cost-effective way to build brand awareness for the Volkswagen product among a very large number of consumers.

MARKETING COMMUNICATIONS AND CUSTOMER RESPONSE

The main objective of Volkswagen's Super Bowl marketing communications strategy was to build brand awareness by using a combination of television and the Internet to gain exposure for the company's commercial. The ad was a *brand-image* marketing communication that engaged a mass market. The success of this marketing communications effort can be easily assessed with analytics that track site visits, impressions, and content posted via social media platforms.

The Nike advertisement in Figure 10-1 is a *brand-image* marketing communication that seeks to tie the Nike brand name with an emotional response and form a positive association between the brand and performance. The goal is to produce high recall of the ad and its association with the brand in customers' minds. Tracking these traditional performance metrics requires media market research. The Nike marketing communication has a clear set of objectives on which the company can base performance metrics for gauging the effectiveness of this marketing communication.

Creating effective marketing communications begins with setting objectives for the communications. The next step is to apply customer-response performance metrics to measure the extent to which the objectives have been attained. Businesses seek many different kinds of customer responses with their marketing communications, but most marketing communications can be placed in one of three broad categories according to their objectives—*brand-image*, *brand-information*, or *brand-action* communications.

FIGURE 10-1 NIKE—BRAND-IMAGE COMMUNICATION

Photo by Brian Finke

FIGURE 10-2 COMMUNICATION OBJECTIVES, CUSTOMER RESPONSE, AND PERFORMANCE METRICS

Brand-Image Communications
- **Objective:** Build the brand.
- **Customer Response:** Affective – creates a feeling or emotion tied to the brand.
- **Performance Metrics:** High ad and brand recall, and positive attitude toward the brand.

Brand-Information Communications
- **Objective:** Communicate brand uniqueness and differentiation.
- **Customer Response:** Cognitive – creates interest in the information being presented.
- **Performance Metrics:** High recall of key content and positive brand attitude.

Brand-Action Communications
- **Objective:** Brand engagement and motivation to buy.
- **Customer Response:** Behavioral – creates a sense of urgency and call to action.
- **Performance Metric:** High rate of purchase or response to requested action.

Figure 10-2 uses personal computer ads as examples that profile the three broad categories of communications objectives. Listed for each ad are the desired customer responses and the performance metrics that companies use to measure customer response. Also listed are brief statements of objectives, more fully stated as follows:

- **Brand-Image Communications**—The objective is to trigger an emotional response that builds a strong connection between the brand and the image the company wants to create among its target customers.
- **Brand-Information Communications**—These communications are intended to create interest and offer information in order to achieve high recall among target customers of key product attributes that differentiate the brand.

■ **Brand-Action Communications**—These communications are intended to stimulate potential customers to take action, such as contacting the company, visiting the company's web site, obtaining a free sample, and trying or buying the company's product.

Brand-Image Communications

Brand-image communications are at the heart of marketing efforts for consumer brands like Nike, Lexus, Estée Lauder, Calvin Klein, and Victoria's Secret. These companies have built and strive to maintain a distinct brand-image. Companies like Caterpillar, Cessna, and DuPont use brand-image communications in the business-to-business market. Service businesses like American Express, Waste Management, and FedEx maintain an emotional connection with their brand and its principal benefit, whether it is performance, reliability, status, safety, or another attribute for which the company wants to create an association among its target customers.

Of course, one of the most notable image-building companies is Nike. With the help of the advertising firm Wieden+Kennedy, Nike ads have acquired a reputation for creativity and an ability to inspire. Figure 10-1 is an example of Nike's creative simplicity in using an image and the company's logo to build among target customers an association between Nike and exceptional performance.

Brand-Information Communications

Brand-information marketing communications shape a more complete understanding among target customers of product benefits and stimulate their interest in the brand. The aim is to motivate target customers to include the brand in their "consideration set," a term that refers to the group of brands that a potential customer would consider buying sometime soon. The ultimate goal is to make the company's brand the preferred brand in the customer's consideration set, ultimately resulting in the purchase of the product or service.

The Kyocera advertisement in Figure 10-3 is an example of a brand-information communication. The objective of the print ad is to inform target customers of the cost savings that a Kyocera printer offers over its product life relative to competing printers. Part of the objective is also to encourage readers to go to the Kyocera TCO Tracker Web site. Kyocera has a television commercial with the same core message. When an ad's objectives include motivating potential customers to visit a company's web site, the effectiveness of the ad is highly trackable at a low cost. Kyocera, for example, simply has to track the number of site visitors who use the TCO Tracker (google Kyocera TCO Tracker). A company should also track changes in sales in relation to ad placement, site visits, and total-cost-of-ownership comparisons. Figure 4-14 in Chapter 4 shows an example of Kyocera's customer savings over an average printer life of 3 years.

Brand-Action Communications

The underlying objective of brand-action marketing communications is to motivate interested customers to try or buy the advertised brand.

Figure 10-4 shows a "Deal of the Month" ad, one of a series that focuses on a different Dell computer each month. The originator of the ad is a technical support and software development company that also serves as a value-added reseller of Dell computers.

FIGURE 10-3 KYOCERA—BRAND-INFORMATION COMMUNICATION

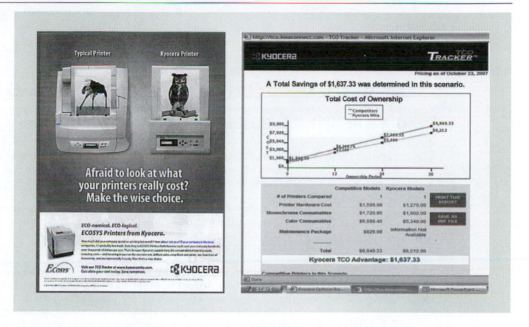

Each month, the software developer e-mails a similar ad to the many individuals and businesses on its client list. The monthly promotions have helped the company become the leading seller of Dell computers in its regional market. Many companies offer similar promotions using traditional and social media platforms for products like clothing, mattresses, cameras, and TVs. Businesses that provide location-based services often use mobile device platforms to advertise promotions that include food specials and happy-hour prices, often based on real-time demand conditions. Using social media, mobile media platforms, and traditional media, businesses can communicate to their target customers a variety of promotions, each with its own objective.

- **Promotional Giveaways**—These promotions offer consumers something for nothing. The classic example is, "Buy one, get one free." Customers perceive the offer as a good value. When they obtain two items for the cost of one, they are likely to also purchase other products. If they find that the product is superior to other brands, they are more likely to buy it again.

- **Promotional Gifts**—The customer has the opportunity to obtain something without having to pay for it. If a customer purchases three bottles of barbecue sauce, for example, a store could offer the customer a free bag of chicken breasts. A company that manufactures colognes may offer its customers sample-sized bottles of new products if they purchase established products. A golf club manufacturer may offer free golf balls to customers who buy new putters. The idea of receiving a free gift for purchasing something that is already desirable appeals to many consumers and will often stimulate additional sales.

- **Minimum Purchase**—Customers who spend a certain amount qualify for promotional gifts. Clinique marketing promotions inform customers that by making a

FIGURE 10-4 BRAND-ACTION MARKETING COMMUNICATION

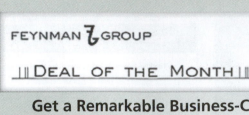

DEAL OF THE MONTH

JANUARY 2011

Get a Remarkable Business-Class Laptop This January

Dell Latitude E5410 Laptop

$1,500

Feynman Group is offering an exclusive **Dell Deal** for the month of January. This business-class laptop offers all the features to keep users happy and productive.

Our custom configuration provides plenty of processing speed along with the Microsoft Productivity Suite. Additionally, this setup offers a professional level widescreen and docking station that will support up to 2 external monitors.

This laptop is ideal for people on the go, and with 3-Year Complete Care Accidental Protection, you'll never need to worry about damages inadvertently caused by your mobile lifestyle. See the complete configuration below, and contact your Feynman Group representative to place your order today!

- Intel Core i3-370 Duel Core 2.40 GHz Processor
- 3 GB RAM
- 180 GB SATA Hard Drive
- 8X DVD+/-RW with Cyberlink Power DVD
- Genuine Windows 7 Professional
- Intel Graphics Media Accelerator 4500MHD Video Card
- Dell Wireless 1501 Mini Card
- 6-Cell Battery

- 65 Watt A/C Adapter
- 14.1" Widescreen Anti-Glare LED Display
- Dell Professional 19" Widescreen External Monitor
- Logitech USB Keyboard/Mouse Combo
- E-Port Plus Docking Station
- Microsoft Office Home and Business 2010 (Word, Excel, Outlook, PowerPoint, OneNote)
- 3-Year Next Business Day On-Site Warranty

purchase at a specified level, they can obtain free samples of lipstick, eyeliner, and moisturizing lotion. Product communications provide ways to build a brand's image and communicate information on the product's benefits, and promotional advertising complements these communications by adding another incentive for trying the products.

DIGITAL MARKETING COMMUNICATIONS

The explosion in digital and social media marketing has been the most significant change in marketing communications since the pretelevision era. Digital marketing communications include e-mail, display advertising, microsites, paid search, mobile messages, blogs, and podcasts. They are designed to provide information and begin a conversation. Social

FIGURE 10-5 BRAND INFORMATION—E-COMMUNICATION AND PERFORMANCE METRICS

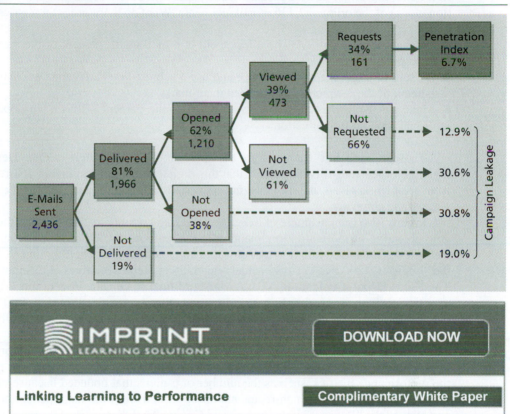

media marketing uses a variety of communication channels, among them Facebook, Twitter, LinkedIn, and YouTube. Social media engagement is much more personal than traditional media advertising and is "viral" in nature, meaning that information carried through social media channels may rapidly spread from one person to another. Social media marketing strives to build individualized and responsive relationships with current and prospective customers.

Let's start with the ways we can use performance metrics to track digital marketing communications. Figure 10-5 shows the results of a brand-information e-mail marketing campaign that was designed to generate leads by targeting 2,436 learning and development managers at Fortune 500 corporations. Imprint Learning Solutions, the organization that conducted the campaign, sent the managers a one-page promotional message about linking learning to performance. The message encouraged them to download a white paper on the subject. As shown in the chart, 19 percent of the e-mails were nondeliverable because of obsolete addresses, at once reducing the number of target customers to 1,966 managers. E-mail tracking metrics showed that 1,210 (62%) of the managers who received the e-mails opened them. Of those who opened the e-mail, 473 (39%) viewed the content; the percentage was determined by the amount of time a message remained opened. Of those who saw the content, 161 (34%) downloaded the white paper. In the end, those who downloaded the white paper accounted for 6.7 percent (the penetration index) of the original 2,436 e-mail recipients. What do these program metrics tell us?

- Use a quality e-mail list. The effort spent in e-mailing 19 percent of the target audience was wasted.
- Be sure to target the right audience and use a subject line that resonates. Thirty-eight percent of the recipients did not open the e-mail.
- Make sure your message is motivating. Sixty-one percent of those who opened the e-mail took no further action.

These three factors accounted for 86.2 percent of the campaign leakage. Despite the high rate of leakage, it is impressive that this digital campaign resulted in 161 responses from recipients, given that they had not requested information and were generally unaware of the company.

Figure 10-6 is an example of a digital marketing communication that had the actionable objective of motivating recipients to participate in a webinar. The organization's web site traffic spiked after the e-mail was sent, resulting in 63 click-throughs (clicks on the "Register" link) that led to 42 actual registrations. Representatives of Eastman Kodak, The Home Depot, Qualcomm, AT&T, Marsh, Mutual of Omaha, Pfizer, Sun Trust, Synergistic Software, TriHealth, Xerox, and several other companies signed up for the webinar. Of the 42 registrants, 35 participated (83%), and several attended a subsequent face-to-face fee-based workshop on the topic.

Inquix Learning, the webinar's sponsor, used Constant Contact to automate the e-mail marketing process. The automated process delivered the messages and provided the performance metrics, such as the number of e-mails that bounced because of nondeliverable addresses and which recipients unsubscribed from the list, opened the e-mail, and clicked the "Register" link. Inquix used Google Analytics to track its web site traffic, as shown in Figure 10-6. A spike in traffic occurred after the e-mails were sent and again when the webinar was delivered. The period of light traffic after the webinar was due to weekend days that followed. GoToWebinar/Meeting handled the webinar registrations and the collection of additional registrant information.

Digital Media Marketing Analytics

One of the great benefits of digital marketing is its ability to track customer engagement. Before-and-after studies for traditional media advertising, such as television, radio, and print, are expensive. Digital marketers have the ability to track results with relative ease and at a fraction of the cost.

As we have just seen, e-mail marketing campaigns can be accurately tracked from deployment through customer action. E-mail marketing services like Constant Contact and Campaign Monitor offer tracking tools that can monitor delivery, opening, and click-through. Recipients of the communications can also be taken to unique microsites or vanity URLs that offer special promotions to track conversion events. By utilizing integrated e-mail tracking and web analytics like those offered by Google, marketers can track recipients of an e-mail campaign all the way to product purchase.

FIGURE 10-6 BRAND-ACTION E-COMMUNICATION AND PERFORMANCE METRICS

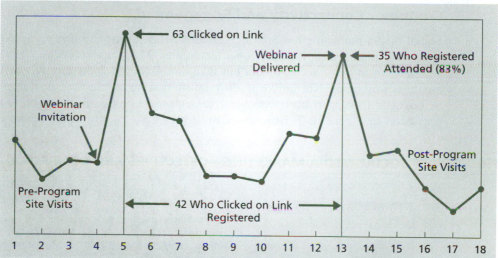

SOCIAL MEDIA MARKETING COMMUNICATIONS

Social media platforms provide a set of marketing communication tools that leverage the use of online platforms to engage current and potential customers in multi-directional conversations. These interactive marketing techniques continue to gain popularity as more marketers explore social media, e-mail marketing, search advertising, and mobile marketing. Within social media marketing, there are a number of broad categories: social networks, content sharing, ratings sites, and location-based services.

New Communications Paradigm

Online communication platforms allow information to spread instantaneously. Consumers now have a powerful means of communicating with one another. The paradigm has fundamentally shifted from a *one-to-many* to a *many-to-many* marketing environment. People can freely share their experiences and opinions (both positive and negative) in a public forum. This is a whole new channel for customer word-of-mouth communications, always the most potent form of marketing communications. With mobile devices, customers now have the ability to capture their customer experience in photos and videos and post them instantly to the web.

Customer use of social media can also pose a problem, as marketers no longer have complete control over their brands. Even potential customers who choose not to participate in online conversations can still see the comments posted by others. One way for companies to reduce possible brand damage is to identify issues early and address them proactively. This potential problem also presents an opportunity: marketers can gain insights into improving operations, customer service, and product offerings by being attentive to the online conversations. The comments that existing and potential customers post can also help marketers improve search engine optimization and determine the best keywords for paid search terms.

Customer Connectivity and Engagement

Social media marketing has provided another set of tools within the marketing mix—not a total replacement for traditional techniques. Many marketers are seduced by the buzz and promise of social media but take an unfocused approach and fail to realize business outcomes. Not unlike traditional marketing techniques, social media must be engaged to support business objectives and must be tied to measurable results, as presented in Figure 10-7. Businesses must take care to ensure that social tactics are

FIGURE 10-7 SOCIAL MEDIA MARKETING—OBJECTIVES AND DESIRED OUTCOMES

- **Brand Building** – Deepen customer relationships and customer conversations with the company and among other customers to strengthen a brand's customer equity.

- **Information Exchange** – Share experiences and exchange information to encourage word-of-mouth communication and a better understanding of product usage and benefits.

- **Problem Solving** – Gather customer feedback, provide customer service, and resolve customer complaints.

Facebook   YouTube   Twitter   LinkedIn   Blogs

driving real outcomes, such as increased traffic to the company's web site, greater capture of qualified leads, or more sales converted. Unless they can demonstrate a measurable return on marketing investment, marketers will be unable to justify their budgets to senior management.

Social Media: New Communications Platforms and Challenges

Engaging in social media marketing was once as easy as setting up Facebook and Twitter accounts, but it has become increasingly more difficult to do this type of marketing effectively. Consumers are suffering from an incredibly complex, crowded, and noisy environment. Marketers are being forced to leverage the tools more creatively and to differentiated audiences in order to cut through the clutter and stand out in these marketing channels. Return on social media marketing is contingent on efficiently using the most appropriate tools to engage the right audiences with conversations that resonate. It is also critical to make the social media marketing strategy an integrated effort across the chosen social platforms and aligned with traditional marketing strategies. There are many different social media tools, and they must be selected and employed strategically to support business objectives and achieve profitable outcomes. We have chosen to focus on the five platforms most frequently used by businesses: Facebook, YouTube, Twitter, LinkedIn, and blogs.

Facebook

The largest and most prominent social network, Facebook claimed a user base of more than 500 million people in early 2011. Of those users, roughly 200 million were actively engaging Facebook on their mobile devices. In early 2011, Facebook users spent over 700 billion minutes a month engaging on the site.[1] The site encourages users to add friends, share thoughts, send messages, and post photos, videos, and links. Users can also indicate that they "like" a particular post or piece of information on another site, thereby signaling an affinity for that content.

   Facebook has become the most popular means of sharing content among people and organizations due to its ease of integration with a variety of web properties. Facebook gives businesses like Cessna in Figure 10-8 a highly effective platform for building relationships with their target customers. Companies are able to create Pages and Groups to build deeper relationships with their communities and to encourage customers to act as brand evangelists. Facebook also offers powerful tools for advertisers and can deliver targeted ads that are based on customers' locations, demographics, and interests. More recently, retailers have leveraged the Facebook platform to create e-tail destinations that allow customers to order their products without leaving the site. Companies can also offer promotions to their fans and track the number of times a particular promotion is liked, shared, commented on, and ultimately converted to a sale.

YouTube

YouTube is the largest and most popular video sharing platform. By affording everyday users the ability to create and post original content for free, YouTube has become a dominant online communication channel. Video content can also be embedded on company-owned

FIGURE 10-8 CESSNA—FACEBOOK INFORMATION EXCHANGE COMMUNICATION

web property or shared on social media platforms. Many companies have turned to YouTube to augment their traditional media spending by creating their own YouTube channels for posting content and videos. Users can share, like, comment on, and post video responses, further deepening the experience.

YouTube also provides a platform for customers to voice their satisfaction or discontent. Consumers can post product reviews and critiques to share with their subscriber bases. This ability, too, presents both an opportunity and a challenge for brands. There is an inherent danger that customer dissatisfaction could become viral and create widespread consumer backlash, but it is also an opportunity for companies to convert dissatisfied customers into loyal ones.

Lenox Tools uses a variety of social media to communicate the use and superior benefits of its products to customers and potential customers. The YouTube video shown in Figure 10-9 is less than 2 minutes long. It shows a Lenox industrial saw being used to cut a double-decker bus in half without the need to replace the blade. The company uses these and other videos as elements of an integrated digital and social media marketing campaign. Lenox also includes links to its YouTube channel and social media platforms in all of its e-mail correspondence, which helps Lenox communicate its product benefits in every e-mail it sends.

FIGURE 10-9 LENOX TOOLS—YOUTUBE BRAND-BUILDING COMMUNICATION

Twitter

Twitter is the largest real-time microblogging service. As of late 2010, Twitter had 175 million registered users who created an average 95 million tweets a day.[2] Users create "tweets"—posts limited to 140 characters in length—that share information of interest with "followers." This information can be thought of as a stream of headlines. Users can provide their followers details about the content of tweets by including a web URL or elaborating in the details pane.

A growing number of businesses have embraced Twitter for its ability to quickly and easily communicate with their customer bases. They use it to announce relevant product information, news, and promotional incentives. Alaska Air, as shown in Figure 10-10, uses Twitter to personalize messages to customers, simultaneously informing them about "great deals" to and from their hometowns. Other companies also tweet about special promotions to their followers and direct them to unique landing pages on their web sites. Customers can then "retweet" the promotion to their followers, thereby increasing the company's reach. By tracking the number of visits and conversation events through the landing page, a company can track the results of its Twitter promotion.

LinkedIn

LinkedIn has established itself as the premier professional social network. With a membership of over 90 million professionals,[3] LinkedIn has become *the* online destination to

FIGURE 10-10 ALASKA AIR—USING TWITTER FOR CUSTOMER PROBLEM-SOLVING COMMUNICATIONS

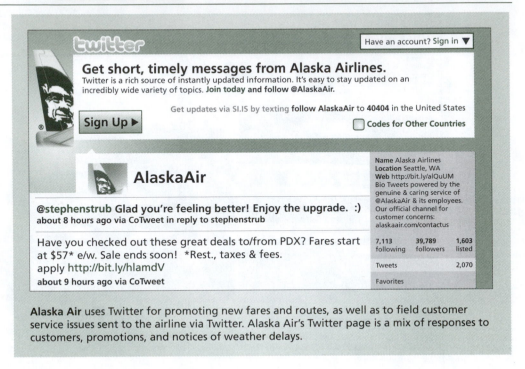

Alaska Air uses Twitter for promoting new fares and routes, as well as to field customer service issues sent to the airline via Twitter. Alaska Air's Twitter page is a mix of responses to customers, promotions, and notices of weather delays.

connect with colleagues, solicit professional advice, and search for jobs. Companies may also create company pages that users can "follow." These pages offer current and prospective employees, customers, and fans a place to track the progress of the business and connect with one another.

LinkedIn has also become the site of choice for business development efforts. The site provides a number of services for soliciting introductions from existing network contacts. LinkedIn also allows users to form and join industry and interest groups—helping companies engage communities in relevant conversations and soft-sell their goods and services.

Blogs

A blog—originally called a web log, a term that led to "we blog"—is a simple, inexpensive mechanism for sharing content online. The platform can be used to post news, opinions, and original work. The advent of blogging platforms has given rise to a new breed of citizen journalists, critics, marketers, and opinion shapers. Blogs are a venue for deepening relationships with subscribers, followers, and passersby. Many bloggers have earned reputations as leaders in their fields by sharing their experiences and knowledge.

Bloggers also have become coveted allies of marketers because of their ability to influence their subscribers. For companies releasing new products, these influencers hold the key to unlocking early market adoption. Companies also leverage blogs to add a human

FIGURE 10-11 HEADBLADE—AN APP FOR CREATING SALES AND AWARENESS

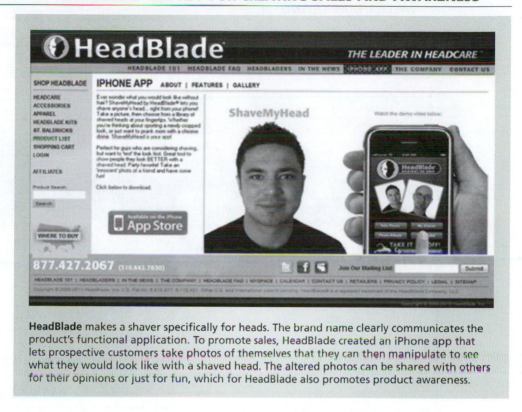

HeadBlade makes a shaver specifically for heads. The brand name clearly communicates the product's functional application. To promote sales, HeadBlade created an iPhone app that lets prospective customers take photos of themselves that they can then manipulate to see what they would look like with a shaved head. The altered photos can be shared with others for their opinions or just for fun, which for HeadBlade also promotes product awareness.

element to an otherwise rigid corporate entity. Blogging provides an easy way to publish and manage content, but unless a blog is updated regularly and carries timely content for subscribers, its value will be diminished.

Leveraging Social Media Tools

Figure 10-11 is the home page for HeadBlade, a company that designs and manufactures shaving products and grooming accessories. The flagship product is the HeadBlade, a razor specifically contoured for shaving heads. In an attempt to lower barriers to purchase and to build brand awareness, HeadBlade created an iPhone app to engage curious prospective customers by letting them see photos of themselves with a shaved head. The iPhone app was also designed to be a fun and interactive buzz generator. It integrates social elements that enable users to share their photos via social networks. The newest update of the app integrates a nonprofit partner, the St. Baldrick's Foundation, which raises funds for life-saving cancer research through head-shaving events nationwide. People can show their support for St. Baldrick's mission by "virtually shaving" in solidarity. HeadBlade has been cited for its innovation before. The shaving device was named a "Best Invention" by *Time* magazine when it was introduced, and the first-generation razor the company sold at retail is in the permanent collection of the Museum of Modern Art in New York.

FIGURE 10-12 OLD SPICE—A CASE STUDY OF THE VIRAL NATURE OF SOCIAL MEDIA MARKETING

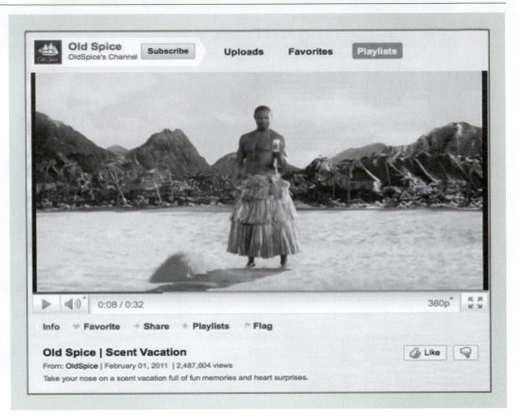

Social Media Marketing Metrics

Measuring the effectiveness of a social media campaign is not always easy. There are many different social media techniques and a large number of metrics to measure effectiveness and ultimately profitability. Engagement metrics can be applied with regard to fans, friends, followers, comments, ratings, likes, clicks, leads generated, buzz, virality, and uploads and downloads. Companies can also monitor macro views, such as share of voice, brand comments, and trending topics, using brand monitoring services or simple mechanisms like search engines and Google Alerts. Social media metrics must then tie related conversion events to profitability or social media ROI.

For the Super Bowl in February 2010, Wieden+Kennedy created a commercial introducing a new brand character, Old Spice Man. Then, in July 2010 as part of the same campaign, the advertising firm shot 180 short comedic YouTube videos. Figure 10-12 shows a scene from one of them. Wieden+Kennedy leveraged Twitter, Facebook, Reddit, and blogs to solicit social media content for the scripts in real time, with some astonishing results: 180 "commercials" aired on YouTube without media distribution costs. The campaign combining the Super Bowl ad with YouTube videos was wildly successful in terms of social media metrics, conversations, and sales.

- Old Spice accounted for 75 percent of conversations in the category during the first 3 months of 2010. Half the conversations were originated by women.
- The YouTube and Twitter social media response campaign was the fastest-growing and most popular interactive campaign in history.
- Total video views reached 40 million in a week. Campaign impressions were 1.4 billion.

Sales of Old Spice Body Wash were up 27 percent following the Super Bowl, up 55 percent in the 3 months following the game, and up 107 percent in July 2010 when the YouTube videos aired.[4]

MARKETING COMMUNICATIONS

As shown in Figure 10-13, worldwide spending on advertising declined by 10.5 percent in 2009 but regained some growth in 2010. As a percentage of sales, spending on nearly all forms of advertising declined somewhat from 2008 to 2010, with digital advertising a notable exception. Some of the growth in the digital category is due to an upsurge in mobile advertising, which constituted 10 percent of digital advertising spending in 2010. When we compare 2010 with 2006, we see that spending on newspaper advertising, as a percentage of total worldwide advertising spending, has declined the most. Magazines and radio have also experienced some slippage.[5] Digital advertising spending is clearly undergoing considerable growth.

Regardless of the communications media channel—digital, social media, print (magazine and newspaper), electronic (TV and radio), outdoor (stationary and moving billboards), or promotional engagements (direct mail, telemarketing, and e-mail)—the fundamentals of marketing communications have the same core objectives of any marketing communications program hierarchy: (1) building a brand's image, (2) creating interest in a product or service, and (3) motivating customers to act. The last section of this chapter looks at the broader issue of the effectiveness of marketing communications, regardless of the marketing venue used.

FIGURE 10-13 GLOBAL MEDIA COMMUNICATIONS SPENDING

Global Media	2006	2007	2008	2009	2010
Worldwide (billions)	$431.6	$458.3	$487.0	$435.8	$451.0
Percentage Change	NA	6.19%	6.26%	−10.51%	3.49%
Television	37.4%	37.5%	36.2%	36.8%	36.1%
Newspapers	28.5%	27.3%	24.8%	22.7%	22.4%
Digital Media	**6.7%**	**8.2%**	**13.5%**	**16.2%**	**18.0%**
Magazines	12.5%	12.1%	11.2%	10.7%	10.2%
Radio	8.3%	8.1%	7.5%	7.0%	6.8%
Outdoor	6.2%	6.3%	6.3%	6.2%	6.0%
Cinema	0.4%	0.4%	0.4%	0.5%	0.5%

FIGURE 10-14 ADVERTISING AWARENESS AND MESSAGE FREQUENCY

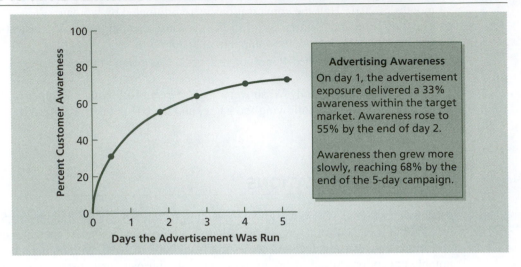

In order for a marketing communication to have any chance of achieving its customer-response objective, it must have some level of message frequency. To better understand how message frequency affects the effectiveness of a marketing communications campaign, let's examine the results of a customer-response study that was conducted by a large nationwide department store. The target market was well defined, the selected media covered 75 percent of the target market, and the campaign featured merchandise that was known to have appeal in this target market. Full-page advertisements ran for 5 consecutive days in two daily newspapers, and radio spots aired during the same 5 days on two stations that ran the ads twice in each of four time slots—early morning, midday, early evening, and late night.

Each evening during the 5-day advertising campaign, target customers were surveyed to determine their level of response. Figure 10-14 shows the level of advertising awareness for each of the 5 days. Although the ad awareness grew to 68 percent by day 5, most of the ad awareness, over 60 percent, was attained by the third day. But of the 68 percent who were aware of the marketing communication, only 43 percent could accurately describe the ad content and recall the store name, as shown in Figure 10-15. Of these respondents, a third stated an intention to act on the marketing communications, and 61 percent of those intending to buy the advertised merchandise actually made the purchase. The net result was that 4.4 percent of the target market took the intended action by purchasing the advertised merchandise.

When buyers were asked how they learned of the advertised merchandise, 46 percent mentioned newspaper A, 23 percent mentioned newspaper B, 18 percent said they heard about it from someone else, and 13 percent mentioned the radio ads. Perhaps a more significant finding was that the average purchase amount was $100, of which the advertised merchandise accounted for only about half. The marketing communications drew 4.4 percent of the target market to the store to buy the advertised merchandise, but these customers bought an almost equal amount of nonadvertised merchandise. The net result was a meaningful gain in sales and net marketing contribution.

FIGURE 10-15 ADVERTISING EFFECTIVENESS AND CUSTOMER RESPONSE INDEX

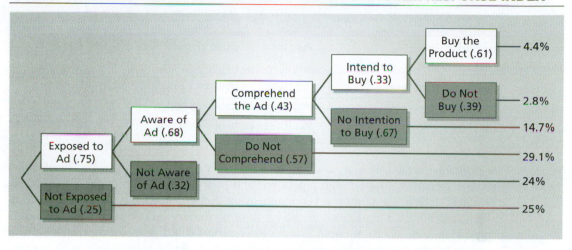

Customer Response Index

An effective marketing communications effort begins with building awareness and understanding of the message among target customers. A successful effort then creates an intent to purchase among a significant number of target customers, a good portion of whom actually make a purchase. Figure 10-15 shows a hierarchical set of customer-response effects from which we can build a customer response index as shown here.

$$\text{CRI (Current)} = 0.75 \times 0.68 \times 0.43 \times 0.33 \times 0.61 = \mathbf{4.4\%}$$

The current customer response index is based on the performance scores along the top of the customer response tree, starting with a 61 percent exposure level. The performance scores at each stage result in a response index of 4.4 percent, but those scores at the different stages also offer an insight as to where we might focus our efforts to improve the customer response for future programs. For example, improving comprehension of the ad content among those who were aware of the ad, from 43 percent to 50 percent, would raise the customer response index to 5.1 percent, a 16 percent increase. The higher response index would have a significant impact on sales, the net marketing contribution, and the ad program's marketing ROI (the net marketing contribution divided by the cost of the ad program).

$$\text{CRI (Improved)} = 0.75 \times 0.68 \times \mathbf{0.50} \times 0.33 \times 0.61 = \mathbf{5.1\%}$$

Improving Customer Response

Possible causes of poor performance in the customer-response hierarchy are listed in Figure 10-16. A low level of target market reach (exposure) usually occurs because the wrong media were chosen or media coverage was too narrow. If appropriate media were used and exposure was broad, then deficiencies in the marketing communication itself

FIGURE 10-16 CAUSES OF LOW LEVELS OF CUSTOMER RESPONSE

Customer Response Deficiency	Marketing Communications Problem
Low Ad Exposure	Poor media selection and/or limited exposure frequency
Low Ad Awareness	Insufficient ad frequency and/or ineffective ad content
Low Ad Content Recall	Insufficient ad frequency and/or ineffective ad content
Low Intentions to Take Action	Insufficient ad frequency and/or weak value proposition
Low Levels of Desired Action	Insufficient ad frequency and/or action not clearly specified

are probably at fault for any low levels of awareness and comprehension. Insufficient message frequency (not enough repetition) and poor ad copy both contribute to target customers' lack of awareness and comprehension. A low percentage rate for the customers who intend to act could also be the result of ineffective ad copy, or of a weak value proposition. Poor ad copy could also be the reason for a disappointing response with regard to taking the desired action, but other factors might be responsible, such as competitor actions or unsatisfactory service during order placement. Identifying the deficiencies in a marketing communication enables a business to correct them.

The importance of customer awareness and response is highlighted in Figure 10-17. For any level of awareness among potential customers, the levels of comprehension, intention, and purchase are successively lower. Perhaps more important, the level of customer loyalty is lower still. Sustained profitability depends on customer retention, and each step in the hierarchy of customer response is a step toward profitability. In the example in this figure, we can see that 30 percent awareness results in a low level of customer loyalty, less than 10 percent.

When awareness is raised to 80 percent, the subsequent customer responses and customer loyalty are higher. Awareness is the first step in new-customer acquisition. The higher the awareness of a product, the higher the customer response and the higher the potential for customer retention. A 5 percent increase in retention produces a 25 percent increase in the average lifetime value of a customer. Raising awareness, then, is a first step in building profits based on brand and customer loyalty.

BUILDING CUSTOMER AWARENESS AND COMPREHENSION

Creating awareness among a large number of people is not the objective of most marketing communications. The objective is to create awareness among and communicate effectively to target customers. Even a memorable advertisement that is well known among the general population is a failure if it does not achieve a high level of awareness and comprehension among target customers.

Media Selection and Customer Awareness

As we saw in Figure 10-16, target-customer awareness and comprehension are affected by media selection, message frequency, and ad copy. To reach target customers effectively, a business has to have a good understanding of the media habits of its target

FIGURE 10-17 ADVERTISING EFFECTIVENESS AND CUSTOMER RESPONSE

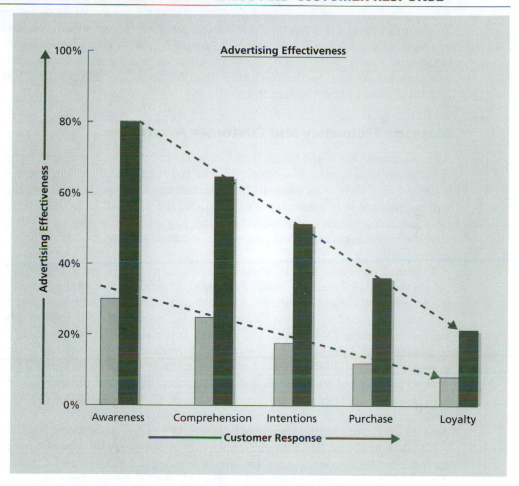

customers. Do they watch television, and, if they do, which programs? Do they listen to the radio, and, if so, which stations and at what times? Which newspapers and which sections of the newspaper do they read? Which magazines do they subscribe to? With respect to exposure to outdoor signage, on which streets and highways are they likely to drive? Do they use the *Yellow Pages*? Are they Internet users or cable TV shoppers? Do they engage in conversations on social media platforms? Do they respond to e-mail marketing campaigns? Do they respond to direct mail advertising? A business must consider all these questions in order to select the right combination of media outlets for cost-effectively reaching its target customers.

A key measure of effective media selection is target market reach. Target market reach is the percentage of target customers who are exposed to the business's message through a certain combination of media. A golf ball manufacturer, for example, wants to reach golfers. The manufacturer might advertise in print media such as *Golf Digest*, *Golf Magazine*, the *Wall Street Journal*, and *Business Week* and on television during broadcasts of golf tournaments. Depending on the subtarget population within golfers, the company may consider utilizing digital and social media tools. Let's assume that using this combination of media the manufacturer reaches 63 percent of its target customers. To obtain a target market reach greater than 63 percent would require the manufacturer to add media that reach target customers who are not exposed to the ads by the current combination of media. If the cost of the incremental reach were more than the incremental economic benefit that was derived from it, then the business would not want to go beyond its current level of target market reach.[6]

Message Frequency and Customer Awareness

After a business has found the right mix of media for effectively reaching target customers, it needs to determine how often to expose target customers to its message in order to achieve a high level of awareness. If it elects infrequent exposure, most target customers will not become fully conscious of the message, and they will have low levels of awareness and comprehension. On the other hand, too many exposures could irritate target customers and negatively affect retained information and perceptions of the ad, product, or company.

Several years ago, AFLAC insurance had a name recognition rating of only 13 percent in the United States. The company decided to undertake a marketing communications campaign to cut through the clutter of mundane insurance ads and raise brand awareness. The company found what it was looking for and spent an initial $35 million on a series of unique, memorable TV commercials. The now-famous AFLAC duck produced more sales leads in the first 2 weeks that the commercials aired than the company had achieved in the previous 2 years, resulting in record revenues. AFLAC's recognition rating skyrocketed to over 90 percent, and revenues grew 30 percent annually over the duration of this advertising campaign. But after several years of hearing the duck screaming "AFLAC!" in various situations, people grew tired of the ads and even found them irritating. At some point, the positive impact of repetition begins to regress into negative perceptions.

Shown in Figure 10-18 are the results of a classic study on message frequency and awareness.[7] In a "concentrated frequency" strategy, 13 consecutive messages were directed to target customers over 13 weeks. As shown, the message awareness steadily increased each week until it reached its highest level in week 13. However, after week 13, no more messages were directed to target customers for the remainder of the year and the message awareness decayed to almost zero. This marketing communications strategy would be appropriate for building awareness and comprehension for seasonal products, political candidates, and special events.

The same message was also sent to a different group of target customers once every 4 weeks throughout the year in a "distributed frequency" strategy. These target customers, like the other group, also received 13 message exposures, but the exposures were spread out over the entire year. During the 4-week period following each exposure, recall of the message decreased, but at the end of each 4-week period, recall was still above the level it had been just prior to the most recent exposure, as Figure 10-18 illustrates. Each additional exposure, then, built from a higher base position. Although this pattern of exposure frequency produced a longer-lasting effect, it never reached the highest level of awareness produced by the concentrated frequency effort. The distributed frequency strategy would be appropriate in building and maintaining target customer awareness and comprehension.

FIGURE 10-18 MESSAGE FREQUENCY AND MESSAGE AWARENESS

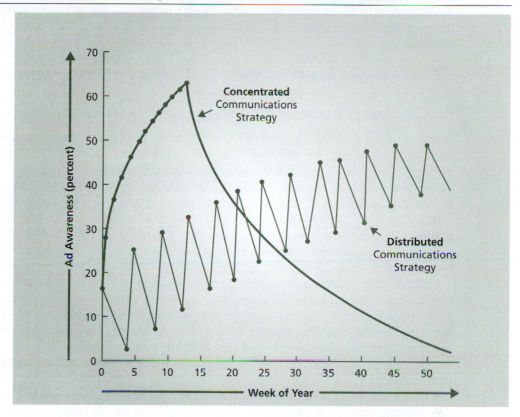

Figure 10-18 assumes that all target customers were exposed to every one of the 13 messages. Typically, however, a target customer is exposed to only a fraction of the total number of messages in an advertising campaign. Nearly all marketing communications send more messages than the target audience receives, as illustrated in the following table.

Ad Recall	0	1	2	3	4	5	6	7	8	Total
Percent Recalling Ad	10%	10%	10%	10%	15%	20%	15%	5%	5%	100%
Weighted Average	0.00	0.10	0.20	0.30	0.60	1.00	0.90	0.35	0.40	3.85

In this example, eight marketing communications were directed to target customers. Ten percent of the customers did not recall seeing any of the ads, whereas 5 percent of them recalled seeing all eight. A weighted average of this recall yields an average message frequency of approximately four. This means that the average target customer was exposed to only about four of the eight marketing communications that the business directed to its target customers during the exposure period.

In television advertising, the combined impact of message frequency and reach produces an index called *gross rating points* (GRPs). A business with a 60 percent reach and a frequency of four produces an impact of 240 GRPs. Because GRPs measure the extent to which an ad reached the target market and how often the ad was seen, they are a far better measure of advertising effectiveness than the dollars spent on advertising.

$$\text{Gross Rating Points} = \text{Reach} \times \text{Frequency} = 60 \times 4 = \mathbf{240}$$

Ad Copy and Customer Response

Because ad copy plays a key role in creating awareness, comprehension, and intentions, a business must be sure that its message is received and accurately interpreted by target customers. For Gardenburger, the stakes were extremely high when it ran an advertisement during the final episode of *Seinfeld*, at a cost of $1.5 million. The cost of this one ad increased the company's advertising expenses by 500 percent. The results, however, were sensational! The ad reached 76 million people, and store sales improved by 328 percent over the same week of the previous year. The ad was expensive, but this marketing communication produced the desired increase in both sales and profits.

But a highly memorable marketing communication that does not communicate the product and its benefits will fail to raise interest in the product and will lower the overall level of customer response. Ad copy can best attract customers when it is based on customer needs and situations that are familiar to customers. It must integrate customer needs and situations with the product's benefits and business's name.[8] If an ad is attractive but fails to create product interest, the ad copy is of limited value to the customer and to the business.

Loctite, as we saw in Chapter 7, at first encountered poor customer response for a new product because of ad copy that was of little value for the company's target audience. The company had introduced a superior metal adhesive under the brand name RC-601 and aimed the ad copy at production managers.[9] The ad was highly technical, which was appropriate for that audience, but it failed to generate any demand for RC-601. Loctite's follow-up customer research revealed that the true target customers were machine maintenance and repair workers, a group that generally was not accustomed to reading highly technical material. After revising the profile of its target customer, Loctite renamed the product Quick Metal and reintroduced it along with new ad copy aimed at the machine maintenance and repair workers. This ad copy, with photographs showing the product's applications, served for both a direct mail piece and a trade-press advertisement. As mentioned in Chapter 7, the results were remarkable: Quick Metal achieved first-year sales at a level higher than any other new product in the company's history.

MESSAGE REINFORCEMENT

Building the awareness, comprehension, and intentions of target customers is critical to achieving a high level of customer response to traditional media advertising. Ads that bring a company a good response rate, however, need to be continuously reinforced to keep the rate high.

FIGURE 10-19 MESSAGE REINFORCEMENT STRATEGIES

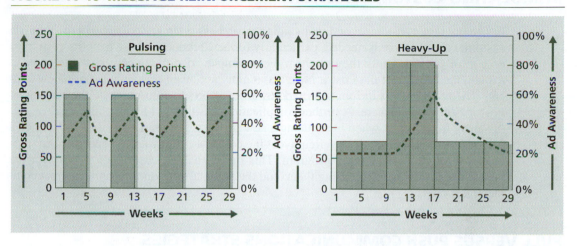

Pulsing

Maintaining a high level of awareness with traditional media is expensive and requires the continual production of new ad copy as the old copy wears out. One cost-effective approach to message reinforcement that maintains awareness and reduces copy wear-out is called *pulsing*.[10] Pulsing involves the use of alternating exposure periods. An example of pulsing is a television advertisement that achieves 150 GRPs over a 4-week exposure period and is run in alternating 4-week periods. As shown in Figure 10-19, a certain level of awareness is built up during a 4-week exposure period; it then diminishes during the following 4-week period of no message exposure, and then awareness is built up again in the next 4-week exposure period.

If a business can maintain a desired level of awareness with pulsing, it can reduce the cost of advertising because it incurs no advertising costs in the alternating 4-week periods of no exposure. A secondary benefit of pulsing is that it reduces copy wear-out due to overexposure to the same messaging. Because the marketing message is not seen on a continual basis, the ad copy's novelty and appeal wear out at a slower rate. Pulsing also reduces the potential for overexposure, which can cause customer irritation and reduce ad effectiveness.

Heavy-Up Message Frequency

Because certain products are purchased more frequently at some times of the year than at others, a business may use a heavy-up exposure pattern to build higher levels of awareness, comprehension, and interest in the advertised product or service. Figure 10-19 illustrates a heavy-up marketing communications program for a well-known brand that has a high level of consumption during the summer. Many other exposure patterns are possible but, in this example, the business elects to maintain a certain level of base awareness throughout most of the year and to heavy-up its message frequency just before and during the prime buying period for its product. The business could also combine a heavy-up strategy for its primary promotion period with a pulsing strategy for the rest of the year.

STIMULATING CUSTOMER ACTION

Informing target customers and maintaining awareness often are not enough to stimulate customer action. More is needed, particularly for new products whose benefits customers do not fully realized until they try them. For example, advertising copy that attempted to explain the benefits of the Post-it Note was simply not taken seriously by target customers.[11] After 18 months in four test markets, 3M's efforts to communicate the benefits of Post-it Notes led nowhere. A further complication was that 3M had a policy against giving away free samples when introducing a new product. The marketing director opened a fifth test market specifically to circumvent the corporate policy and to generate trial purchases through a free-sample program. This move enabled customers to discover the benefits of Post-it Notes by using them, and the product went on to become a great commercial success.

PULL VERSUS PUSH COMMUNICATIONS STRATEGIES

So far we have discussed marketing communications that are aimed directly at target customers, but businesses also use indirect channels to aim marketing communications at their channel intermediaries. Among all U.S. consumer product businesses, about two-thirds of the total marketing communications expense is spent on customer communications and about one-third is spent on intermediary communications.

Customer-directed marketing communications are pull communications. The objectives of a pull marketing communication, as shown in Figure 10-20, are to build awareness, attraction, and loyalty and to reduce search costs. When a pull marketing communication is successful, customers will seek out the product and, in effect, by the

FIGURE 10-20 PUSH-PULL COMMUNICATIONS AND CUSTOMER RESPONSE

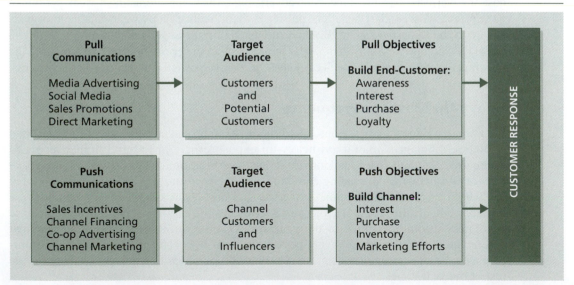

interest they create, pull the product through the channel. A pull strategy must ensure that channel intermediaries carry the product in sufficient quantities.

Push communications are directed at channel intermediaries. The objective in this case is to motivate channel intermediaries to carry a particular product or brand and, in this way, to make it more available to customers. When they are successful, push communications result in wider availability, fewer stock-outs, more-visible merchandising (taking up more shelf space), and a more efficient use of marketing dollars. It is important, however, to understand that it is the combination of both pull and push marketing communications that creates the greatest impact on customer response and therefore produces market share gains.[12]

PULL COMMUNICATIONS AND CUSTOMER RESPONSE

As also shown in Figure 10-20, a wide range of alternative marketing communications can be used to fashion a communications mix designed to create customer pull.[13] To illustrate the power of media advertising, consider the fate of L&M cigarettes. Before cigarette advertising on television was banned, L&M had a 17 percent market share. After the ban, L&M chose to stop advertising altogether, because its management believed that forms of advertising other than television were ineffective. The managers were wrong, and today L&M is no longer on the market. The product had good brand recognition and good customer pull, but without continued reinforcement of the brand name and its positioning, the product faded from customers' minds and, eventually, from the marketplace.

There are many forms of customer-directed sales promotions, such as coupons, rebates, sweepstakes, gifts, and rewards. When United Airlines initiated its Mileage Plus program, it changed how customers selected airlines and flights. Catalogs like those published by L.L. Bean, Eddie Bauer, and Spiegel stimulate customer pull every month by sending mailings to targeted customers. Other forms of direct marketing, including digital and social media marketing, take a similar but even more customized approach to creating customer pull.

Advertising Elasticity

Knowing the responsiveness of consumers to advertising expenditures makes it easier to understand the sales impact of marketing, an important consideration in market-based management. Consumer response to advertising costs is measured as advertising elasticity. It can most easily be measured as the percentage change in sales or volume per 1 percent change in advertising expenses. Although there are considerable variations among products and market situations, short-run advertising elasticities are relatively small compared with price elasticities. A study of 128 advertising elasticities found that the average elasticity was 0.22, and few elasticities were greater than 0.5. An advertising elasticity of 0.22 means that for every 1 percent change in advertising expense, the volume sold will change by 0.22 percent.[14]

Of the several market forces that affect sales, for the apparel company Hart Schaffner Marx the correlation between advertising expenditures and sales is very high, as illustrated in Figure 10-21. The correlation is 0.94. As shown, the percentage of sales devoted to advertising varied over time with an overall average of 3.8 percent. During periods when

FIGURE 10-21 HART SCHAFFNER MARX—SALES-ADVERTISING RELATIONSHIP

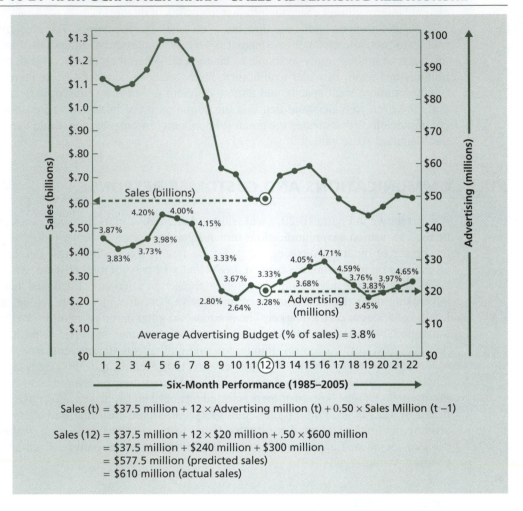

Sales (t) = $37.5 million + 12 × Advertising million (t) + 0.50 × Sales Million (t −1)

Sales (12) = $37.5 million + 12 × $20 million + .50 × $600 million
= $37.5 million + $240 million + $300 million
= $577.5 million (predicted sales)
= $610 million (actual sales)

the percentage of sales devoted to advertising was above this average, the company had increased sales. The advertising elasticity is estimated to be 0.50, using an average of the percentage change in sales per 1 percent change in advertising expenses, as shown here:

Advertising Elasticity = 2.4% change in sales / 4.8 % change in ad expenses = **0.50**

Advertising Carryover Effects

In addition to a short-run advertising impact on sales response, advertising also has been shown to have a long-run carryover effect—that is, the advertising effort made in a given period will produce additional sales response in subsequent sales periods. Advertising carryover coefficients range from 0 to less than 1, with the average carryover coefficient equal to approximately 0.5.[15]

In Figure 10-21 we estimated the advertising carryover effect on sales for Hart Schaffner Marx using regression analysis. The derived equation shows that sales in any given period are based on a constant of $37.5 million, the effect of advertising spending in that period, and the carryover effect of advertising spending in previous periods. The carryover effect is estimated using the lagged sales from the previous period. In this case the carryover effect was estimated to be 0.5.

Let's see how this works for the Hart Schaffner Marx advertising in period 12. The estimated sales impact for period 12 is based on the constant ($37.5 million) plus 12 times the advertising expense in period 12 ($20 million) plus the carryover advertising effect of previous advertising, which was estimated to be 0.5 times the sales from the previous period ($600 million). For period 12, this produced predicted sales of $577.5 million. Actual sales were $610 million, as shown in Figure 10-21.

We can also use the advertising carryover effect to estimate the total sales impact for advertising dollars spent in period 12. As shown in Figure 10-22, in period 12 the advertising produced an estimated sales impact of $240 million in sales. The effect of this advertising with a carryover effect of 0.5 is shown for subsequent periods.

For each period, the carryover coefficient of 0.5 is raised to a power equal to the number of periods since the original advertising. For the period following the advertising impact of $240 million, with a 0.5 carryover effect, the sales impact is $120 million. Two periods after the period-12 advertising effort, the sales impact was 0.25 of $240 million, which is $60 million. Three periods after the period-12 advertising effort, the carryover

FIGURE 10-22 MEDIA ADVERTISING AND SALES CARRYOVER

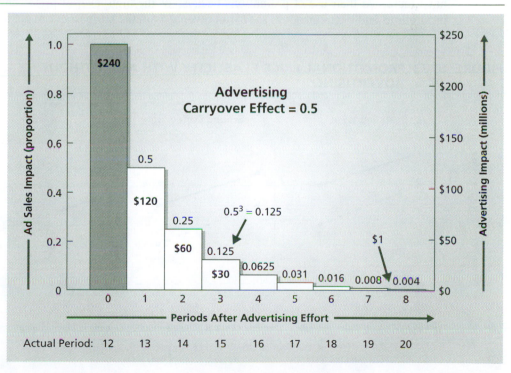

effect is 0.125, which contributes $30 million in sales (period 15). The effect of the advertising in period 12 continues, as shown in Figure 10-22, for a little over 8 periods. The total sales impact of advertising in period 12 can be estimated by using the equation that follows. As shown, the $20 million spent in period 12 had an immediate sales impact of $240 million and overall sales impact of $480 million.

$$\textbf{Sales Effect (period 12)} = 12 \times \text{Advertising Expense}$$
$$= 12 \times \$20\,\text{million} = \textbf{\$240 million}$$

$$\genfrac{}{}{0pt}{}{\textbf{Total Sales Impact}}{\textbf{(advertising in } t = 12)} = \frac{\text{Sales Effect Period 12}}{1 - \text{Carryover Effect}} = \frac{\$240\,\text{million}}{1 - 0.5} = \textbf{\$480 million}$$

Promotional Price Elasticity

The average price elasticity for consumer nondurable products is -1.76, according to a study of 367 brands.[16] For the three product categories shown in Figure 10-23, however, the price elasticities are considerably higher.[17] By combining a price promotion with advertising, the promotional price elasticity can be further increased, as shown in the figure. For example, the promotional price elasticity of sparkling wine increases to approximately 14 with the support of an advertising campaign.

In all three cases shown in Figure 10-23, the promotional price elasticity increased significantly with the use of advertising. For cat litter, this effect was very dramatic, almost doubling the promotional price elasticity. It is also important to note that the promotional price elasticity decreased with the increase in market share. Many businesses have increased their use of promotions because of the high level of price sensitivity to promotions and the tremendous short-run revenue gain the businesses can achieve. But a

FIGURE 10-23 PROMOTIONAL PRICE ELASTICITY WITH AND WITHOUT ADVERTISING

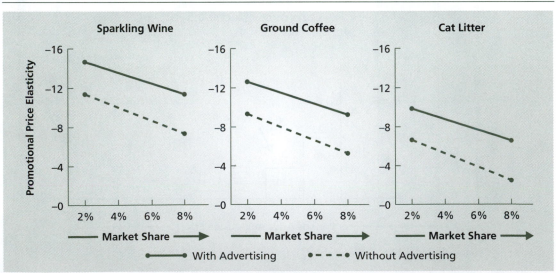

marketing strategy that seeks profitable growth must also produce a higher net marketing contribution. In a market-based business, managers must also assess the profit impact of a marketing communications effort.

PUSH COMMUNICATIONS AND CUSTOMER RESPONSE

As we saw earlier, marketing communications that are directed at channel intermediaries are designed to be push communications; they stimulate intermediaries to engage in aggressive customer promotion efforts. The objective of push communications is to build greater product availability and marketing effort. Businesses that are aggressive in rewarding and supporting channel intermediaries are able to obtain more market coverage (number of desired distributors) than are nonaggressive businesses. This support provides several mechanisms to deliver effective in-store merchandising and marketing efforts of a business's products.

Trade Promotions and Customer Response

Trade promotions that are designed to stimulate purchase are common among businesses that sell products through intermediaries. Quite often, trade promotions involve price reductions to distributors or retailers. The idea is that the price incentive will motivate intermediaries to push the product. In many instances this strategy backfires, as intermediaries run down their inventories before a promotion and then buy more at a lower price during the promotion. The intermediaries then have excessive inventories and buy less following the promotion until inventories return to normal.

For example, in Figure 10-24 the nonpromotion monthly unit sales for a retailer are 10,000 units, resulting in $10,000 in sales at a retail price of $1. The retailer normally keeps a 20 percent inventory, which is enough to cover about 1 week of sales. The product's supplier, however, announced a promotion a few months in advance, giving the retailer time to prepare for it. During the month before the promotion, the retailer bought

FIGURE 10-24 RETAIL PROMOTION PRICE AND SALES

Nonpromotion Performance	Month 1	Month 2	Month 3
Retail Price	$1.00	$1.00	$1.00
Volume Sold	10,000	10,000	10,000
Retailer Cost per Unit	$0.80	$0.80	$0.80
Retailer Inventory	2,000	2,000	2,000
Retailer Sales	$10,000	$10,000	$10,000
Retailer Gross Profit	$2,000	$2,000	$2,000
Supplier Sales	$9,600	$9,600	$9,600
Supplier Gross Profit	$4,800	$4,800	$4,800

Supplier Unit Cost is $0.40

Promotion Performance	Month 1	Month 2	Month 3
Retail Price	$1.00	$0.90	$1.00
Volume Sold	10,000	16,000	7,000
Retailer Cost per Unit	$0.80	$0.70	$0.80
Retailer Inventory	500	4,000	500
Retailer Sales	$10,000	$14,400	$7,000
Retailer Gross Profit	$2,000	$3,200	$1,400
Supplier Sales	$8,400	$14,000	$6,000
Supplier Gross Profit	$4,200	$6,000	$3,000

Supplier Unit Cost is $0.40

less than usual, knowing that the price would be lower the next month. When the promotion began, the retailer offered the product for 1 month at a 10 percent discount. Customers responded and bought 60 percent more than usual. However, the following month retail sales fell because customers had overbought at the promotion price. Even worse for the supplier, the retailer then bought less because of leftover inventory from the promotion month when the retailer purchased more than needed at the lower cost. For the period covering the month before, the month during, and the month after the promotion, the retailer did much better than the supplier. The retailer's sales were $31,400, about 4.7 percent more than the 3-month norm of $30,000, and the retailer's gross profit rose to $6,600 from the $6,000 norm, a 10 percent increase. But the supplier saw a slight decline in sales, from the 3-month norm of $28,800 to $28,400. The supplier's gross profit fell from $14,400 to $13,200, a decline of $1,200—or 8.3 percent less than the gross profit for a normal 3 months.

Push communications are also aimed at "market influencers." These communications are created for those within the market infrastructure who can influence the broader market of both end-user customers and intermediaries.[18] For example, communications that are targeted at industry gurus, consultants, and financial analysts lead to secondary marketing communications that influence trade, business, and general media. These nonmarket sources of influence in turn provide information to channel intermediaries and customers.

■ Summary

Without an effective marketing communications program, a marketing strategy will fail. Marketing communications have many purposes, but they can be placed into three broad categories on the basis of their primary objectives—building brand image, providing brand information, and motivating customer action. Brand-image communications are affective communications that are intended to elicit an emotional and positive association with the brand. They provide little or no information and no call for action. Brand-information communications are cognitive and give customers information that is intended to shape a favorable attitude and brand preference. Brand-action communications are behavioral, summoning customers to take a specific action, often to respond to a promotion or a free trial.

Digital and social media marketing has provided an additional set of tools within the marketing mix, but cannot replace traditional techniques. These tools give consumers a potent means of communicating with one another. The paradigm has fundamentally shifted from a one-to-many to a many-to-many marketing environment. Not unlike traditional marketing techniques, social media must be engaged to support business objectives and must be tied to measurable results. Care must be taken to ensure that the social media tactics are driving real outcomes, such as increasing traffic to the company's web site, capturing qualified leads, and making sales.

Target customers must be made aware of the product and its benefits, continually reminded of them, and stimulated to take action. Building awareness, message comprehension, and interest in a product are essential phases in achieving a high level of customer response. The customer response index is a diagnostic tool that enables a management team to determine the sources of weakness in its marketing communications program. To be effective and cost efficient, a business's marketing communications must reach target customers and have an adequate level of message frequency to maintain desired levels of awareness, comprehension, and interest. Pulsing is a technique in which a business advertises during alternate exposure periods to more economically maintain customer awareness and interest and to reduce the problem of ad copy wear-out. A contrasting technique, heavy-up, is a period of intensive advertising that enables a business to build awareness and interest to higher levels during seasonal buying periods.

To build market share, a business needs both pull and push marketing communications. Pull marketing communications are targeted at customers with the intent of creating enough awareness and interest to motivate them to demand the business's product. This customer demand creates market pull on intermediaries who, in turn, want the business's products on hand to satisfy the customer demand. Push marketing communications are directed at intermediaries, with the intent of creating greater interest in the product, increasing access to it, and pushing it through the channel. Most markets have a marketing communications infrastructure that includes customers, intermediaries, and nonmarket sources of influence. Some push marketing communications are public relations–type communications directed at nonmarket sources that can influence channel intermediaries and customers.

It is difficult to predict the response to a marketing communication in terms of sales, but the customer response index, advertising elasticity, advertising carryover effects, and promotional price elasticity provide a systematic method for estimating the response. Yet, sales response should not be the primary objective of a marketing communication. The primary objective is profit, and so it is important for a company to estimate the profit impact of a communication, especially one related to a promotion. Many sales promotions are not profitable because businesses have been forced into them to minimize losses.

■ Market-Based Strategic Thinking

1 What type of marketing communication is Lexus most likely to create? How could the company measure the effectiveness of its communications effort?

2 What type of marketing communication would be most effective in motivating individuals to donate to a social cause?

3 How would a company such as Apple use a combination of the communication strategies shown in Figure 10-2?

4 Why would a brand-image communication be more effective for a brand with low awareness?

5 How would you evaluate the sales and profit impact of the Kyocera brand-information communication?

6 Why is the Feynman Group's Dell "Deal of the Month" brand-action communication (Figure 10-4) likely to have a high marketing ROI?

7 What role does message exposure play in the success of a marketing communication for General Motors' new Volt?

8 Why are customer awareness and message comprehension critical to the success of a marketing strategy for industrial products?

9 How can interest in ad copy affect interest in a product and subsequently influence customer response?

10 When a business has an excellent marketing communications program and customers indicate high intention to purchase but there is a very low customer response, what kind of a marketing problem does the business face?

11 When should a business use a combination of pulsing and heavy-up marketing communications?

12 Why is the message frequency for a marketing communication considerably lower than the number of messages sent?

13 Why will a business's market share be lower if it is not effective with both pull and push marketing communications?

14 At what stage of a product's life cycle is advertising elasticity likely to be highest?

15 How should the carryover sales effect of an advertising effort be used to evaluate the profit impact of the advertising effort?

16 What behaviors need to be tracked in order to evaluate the profit impact of a trade promotion?

17 How does the promotional price elasticity for a product change with advertising support? What effect does market share have on promotional price elasticity?

18 Why are public relations-type marketing communications important to the overall success of a marketing communications effort?

19 Why are marketing communications directed at a market's infrastructure important?

20 If advertising elasticity is so much smaller than promotional price elasticity, why should a business advertise?

21 How should a business use the advertising carryover effect to evaluate the sales response and profitability of a marketing communication?

22 Why are indirect sales promotions rarely profitable? Why do manufacturers continue to offer indirect sales promotions despite their unprofitability?

23 How does retailer forward-buying affect the profitability of a brand promotion?

Marketing Performance Tools and Application Exercises

The three interactive marketing performance tools and the application exercises outlined here will add to your understanding of customer response to marketing communications, advertising elasticity, and the advertising carryover effect. To access the tools, go to **roger-jbest.com**. For the questions, you can enter the data presented to obtain the answers. You may also enter other data to see the results, and you may save your work. The figure numbers in parentheses are related examples in Chapter 10, but the lettered instructions pertain to the online exercises.

10.1 Marketing Communications and Customer Response (Figure 10-15)

A. Using the data provided, how do the results of this marketing communication change when advertising exposure is only 50 percent?

B. Using the results provided, evaluate the impact of improving ad awareness from 69 to 75 percent.

C. For future advertisements, would it be more effective to work on increasing comprehension by 10 points (from 43% to 53%) or to work on improving intentions to purchase by 10 points (from 33% to 43%)?

10.2 Estimating Advertising Elasticity

A. Using the data provided, how does the advertising elasticity change when the increase in sales after advertising is 10 percent instead of 4 percent?

B. What level of sales is needed to produce an advertising elasticity of .30, given the same increase in the advertising budget as in question A?

10.3 Estimating the Advertising Carryover Effect (Figure 10-22)

A. Using the data provided, how does the carryover effect change when the incremental sales revenue after advertising is $10,000 rather than $5,000?

B. How does the new carryover effect (estimated in the previous question) affect the overall incremental sales of the marketing communications effort?

Notes

1. "Statistics," Facebook (not dated): http://www.facebook.com/press/info.php?statisticsretrieved February 10, 2011.
2. "Twitter Is the Best Way to Discover What's New in Your World," Twitter (September 14, 2010): http://twitter.com/about, retrieved February 10, 2011.
3. "About Us," LinkedIn Corporation (not dated): http://press.linkedin.com/about/, retrieved February 10, 2011.
4. C. Reiss, "Now Look Here, Now Learn from This...," msnbc.com (July 18, 2010): http://www.msnbc.msn.com/id/38282026/ns/business-small_business/, retrieved February 11, 2011.
5. M. James, "Good News, Bad News: Worldwide Advertising Spending Up, U.S. Spending Down," *Los Angeles Times* (June 24, 2010): http://latimesblogs.latimes.com/entertainmentnewsbuzz/2010/06/worldwide-advertising-spending-up.html, retrieved March 15, 2011; S. McClellan, "GroupM Foresees 3.5% Rise in 2010 Global Ad Spending," Adweek (June 24, 2010): http://www.adweek.com/news/television/groupm-foresees-35-rise-2010-global-ad-spend-102683, retrieved March 15, 2011; and R. Wauters, "Advertising Expenditures Dropped 12.3% in 2009, But Digital Grew 7.3%," TechCrunch (March 17, 2010): http://techcrunch.com/2010/03/17/advertising-expenditures-2009/, retrieved March 15, 2011.
6. P. Danaher and R. Rust, "Determining the Optimal Level of Media Spending," *Journal of Advertising Research* (January–February 1994): 28–34.
7. H. Zielske, "The Remembering and Forgetting of Advertising," *Journal of Marketing* (January 1959): 140; and J. Simon, "What Do Zielske's Real Data Really Show About Pulsing," *Journal of Marketing Research* (August 1979): 415–20.
8. B. Wansink and M. Ray, "Advertising Strategies to Increase Usage Frequency," *Journal of Marketing* (January 1996): 31–46.
9. B. Abrams, "Consumer-Product Techniques Help Loctite Sell to Industry," *Wall Street Journal* (April 2, 1981): 29.
10. V. Mahajan, E. Muller, J.E. Little, and H. Zielske, "Advertising Pulsing Policies for Generating Awareness of New Products," *Marketing Science* (Spring 1986): 86–106.
11. C. Havener and M. Thorpe, "Customers Can Tell You What They Want," *Management Review* (December 1994): 42–5.
12. D. Reibstein, "Making the Most of Your Marketing Dollars," *Drive Marketing Excellence* (New York: Institute for International Research, 1994).
13. G. Lilien, P. Kotler, and K. Moorthy, *Marketing Models* (Upper Saddle River, NJ: Prentice Hall, 1992): 329–56.
14. G. Assmus, J. Farley, and D. Lehmann, "How Advertising Affects Sales: Meta Analysis of Econometric Results," *Journal of Marketing Research* (February 1984): 65–74.
15. R. Schultz and M. Block, "Empirical Estimates of Advertising Response Factors," *Journal of Media Planning* (Fall 1986): 17–24.
16. R. Blattberg and S. Neslin, *Sales Promotion Concepts, Methods and Strategies* (Upper Saddle River, NJ: Prentice Hall, 1990): 356.
17. A. Bemmaor and D. Mouchoux, "Measuring the Short-Term Effect of In-Store Promotion and Retail Advertising on Brand Sales," *Journal of Marketing Research* (May 1991): 202–14.
18. R. McKenna, *The Regis Touch: New Marketing Strategies for Uncertain Times* (Reading, MA: Addison-Wesley, 1985).

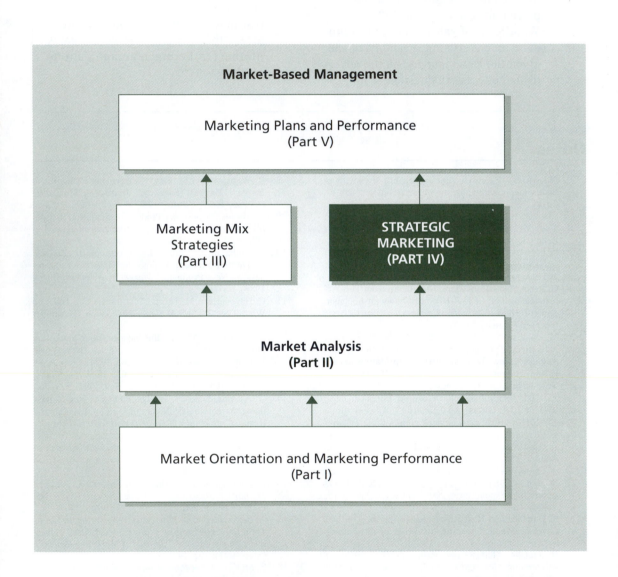

Market-Based Management

Marketing Plans and Performance
(Part V)

Marketing Mix
Strategies
(Part III)

STRATEGIC
MARKETING
(PART IV)

Market Analysis
(Part II)

Market Orientation and Marketing Performance
(Part I)

Strategic Marketing

■ If you come to a fork in the road, take it.
—*Yogi Berra Major League Baseball Hall of Famer*

Just going left or right at a fork in the road is one way for a business to set a strategic direction. A better way, one far more likely to achieve performance objectives, would be for the business to first consider the probable outcomes of its options.

Strategic market planning sets the long-run direction for a business and has a major role in realizing the business's objectives of sales growth, profit performance, and share position over time. Marketing mix strategies, which were covered in Part III, are more tactical but are essential to establishing desired target market positions and generating short-run growth and profits. These target market positioning strategies take a business incrementally toward its long-run goals. Both short-run marketing mix strategies and long-run strategic market plans promote growth, profitability, and share position.

When it undertakes a strategic market planning process, a business assesses each product-market of interest with respect to market attractiveness and the business's competitive position. Using these two dimensions of strategic opportunity and position, Chapter 11 presents a method for building a strategic market planning portfolio that covers a business's existing and potential product-markets.

The strategic market plans generated by the portfolio analysis may be either offensive or defensive. Offensive strategic market plans, presented in Chapter 12, are growth-oriented plans to spur share penetration or market growth or to prepare for entry into new, emerging, or growing markets. Offensive strategic market plans are critical to a business's future growth, market position, and profitability.

Defensive strategic market plans, presented in Chapter 13, are intended to protect market positions and profitability. Defensive plans may be based on holding a market position, reducing the market focus to improve profits, or harvesting or divestment strategies that result in product-market exit. When they are properly executed, defensive strategic market plans can improve profit performance.

Portfolio Analysis and Strategic Market Planning

■ Strategic market planning provides a sales and profit roadmap for the next 3 to 5 years.

Yum Brands' Product Portfolio and Strategic Market Plan

Yum Brands has an impressive portfolio of five well-known brands, which together have almost 37,000 store locations worldwide. In 2011, on the basis of an analysis of the market attractiveness and the competitive position of each of its five store brands, Yum Brands implemented the following portfolio strategy:

■ **Invest to Grow:** KFC, Taco Bell, and Pizza Hut. The company plans much of the growth in these brands to occur outside the United States, with a strong focus on China, where the brands are already in place.

■ **Divest:** Long John Silver's and A&W were sold in late 2011. Long John Silver's had a good market share but in a very small market. A&W was facing tough segment competition from McDonald's, Wendy's, Burger King, and others. Funds from the sale of these brands will be invested in the growth brands.[1]

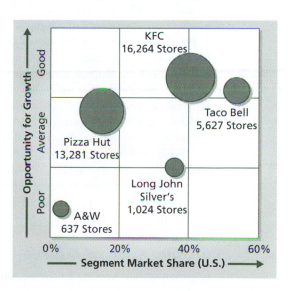

Performance (billions)	2006	2007	2008	2009	2010
Sales Revenues	$9.6	$10.4	$11.3	$10.8	$11.3
Operating Profit	$1.26	$1.36	$1.52	$1.59	$1.77
Operating Profit (% sales)	13.1%	13.1%	13.5%	14.7%	15.7%

Yum Brands had profitable growth from 2006 through 2010 despite a worldwide recession. The company's strategic market plan is to grow sales at a faster rate, improve the average profit margin, and increase Yum Brands' operating profit in dollars and as a percentage of sales.

PORTFOLIO ANALYSIS AND STRATEGIC MARKET PLANNING

The purpose of portfolio analysis is to take a strategic view of *where a business is* and *where it wants to go* with its portfolio of existing and future products. A product portfolio analysis led Yum Brands to divest two of its well-known brands and to focus on the growth of three other brands that are better positioned for profitable growth. A portfolio analysis provides a strategic snapshot of the current situation. Strategic market plans are forward looking and enable a company to make strategic changes to its product portfolio that are in line with the company's strategic vision and performance objectives.

In 1964, Toyota entered the low-price end of the U.S. car market with the Corona, followed in 1966 by the Crown and in 1968 by the Corolla. The Crown was a strong brand in Japan but lasted only a few years in the U.S. market. The Corona lasted almost 10 years. It was the Corolla that established a Toyota product position in the U.S. car market, and that model has prospered to the point where a Corolla is produced every 7 seconds.

But that is only the beginning of the Toyota product portfolio story and the company's pursuit of a grander strategic vision. Starting at the low-price end of the U.S. car market in the 1960s, Toyota adopted a strategic market plan to build its product line by introducing brands at the next quality-price point. The company continued its strategy through the 1970s and 1980s until the Toyota brand reached the limits of its brand status, and then it made an extensive engineering and marketing effort to develop the Lexus. The Lexus was an immediate success and opened a new segment of the market for Toyota.

Toyota then carefully analyzed every market segment on the basis of the price-quality curve and sequentially added new models at different levels of the company's price-quality product portfolio. It introduced new models at the low-price end of the market, as well as at the mid-level price and high-price points, as shown in Toyota's 2010 product portfolio in Figure 11-1.

Portfolio Analysis Models

There is nothing magical about a portfolio analysis model. It typically has two dimensions of performance: a price-quality model and a product life-cycle model. The Toyota price-quality portfolio model in Figure 11-1 may seem simplistic at first glance, but the way it contrasts price against product quality and brand status provides a strategic view of product positioning and the market segments that are served along the price-quality curve. This portfolio model has served Toyota well in managing its strategic growth over the last 50 years.

The product life-cycle model shown in Figure 11-2 is an equally useful portfolio planning model. Portfolio A is an *unbalanced* product portfolio. The business whose products are represented in Portfolio A has not invested in new products, and as the products move through their product life cycles, sales and profits will at some point decline. Portfolio B has been managed more effectively. It is a *balanced* portfolio, one with a high

FIGURE 11-1 TOYOTA PRODUCT PORTFOLIO: 1960s AND 2010

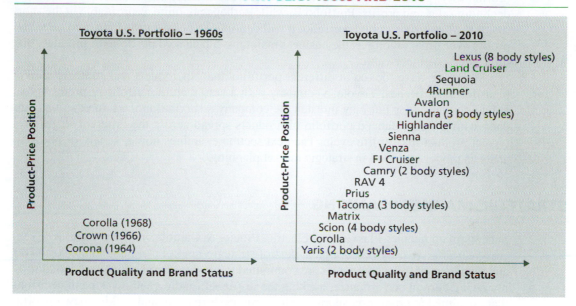

percentage of sales (shown by the sizes of the circles) at the late-growth and mature stages of the product life cycle. The result is good profitability (shown by the dashed line in the graph).

More important, Portfolio B has a great future. Roughly a third of its sales are in the early or growth stages of the product-market life cycle. As product A goes into its decline stage, each of the other products will progress at its market growth rate to the next stage of its product-market life cycle. Although Portfolio A has good short-run

FIGURE 11-2 PRODUCT LIFE CYCLES OF TWO PRODUCT PORTFOLIOS

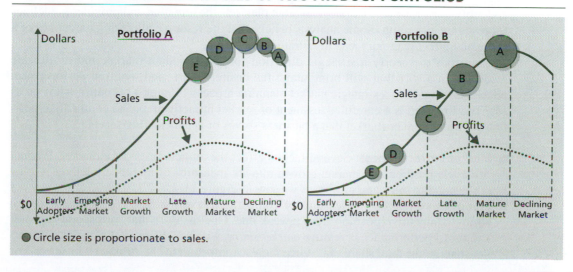

profitability, poor strategic market planning will eventually leave this business with declining sales and profits. Portfolio B, while perhaps not quite as profitable in the short run, is the better-positioned portfolio. It will continue to deliver growth in both sales and profits over time, as long as the business maintains a balanced portfolio of products that offer good customer value.

So far we have looked at different portfolio analysis models and strategic market plans for Yum Brands, Toyota, a company with a very mature portfolio of products that are doing well today but may threaten the company's survival in the future, and a company with a well-balanced portfolio of products spread across the different stages of a typical product-market life cycle. The next section examines how a variety of portfolio analysis models are used in strategic market planning.

STRATEGIC MARKET PLANNING

Successful companies like General Electric, Procter & Gamble, and Toyota achieve success year after year by doing a great deal of strategic market planning.[2] The executives and managers of these companies are committed to serving shareholders by continuously reviewing current performance, tracking the results of funding and investment decisions that are aimed at promoting short- and long-run performance, and seeking new opportunities. An important part of this process is investing for the future and maintaining portfolio diversification to reduce large swings in overall performance.

Each product-market in a business's portfolio in some way affects both the short- and long-run performance of the business, as illustrated in Figure 11-2. The business may want to increase its investment in some product-markets, depending on their current and potential share positions and their performance levels, in order to grow or defend important strategic market positions. In other product-markets, the business may want to reduce its focus in order to achieve a stronger competitive position and profit contribution with available resources. For yet other product-markets, the business may decide to withdraw its resources and divest. Because the resources of any business are limited, a strategic market plan is needed to carefully map a business's future share position, sales growth, and profit performance. A strategic market plan sets the direction and provides guidelines for resource allocation. Some analysts believe that the resource allocation guidelines of a strategic market plan may lead to a strategic advantage.[3]

In order to specify a strategic direction for each product-market and to allocate resources in a way that will bring about the desired short- and long-run performance, businesses engage in a strategic market planning process.[4] Figure 11-3 outlines this process. The first step is a careful assessment of market attractiveness and competitive position for each product-market that a business serves or is considering serving.

- **Market Attractiveness:** Several factors affect the attractiveness of a market. Product life-cycle position and market growth rate are measures of market attractiveness that correspond to sales and profits, as we saw in Figure 11-2.
- **Competitive Position:** Measures of competitive position help a business discern a strong competitive position from a weak one. One measure that corresponds to sales and profit performance is *relative market share*, which is the ratio of a business's market share to the total share of its three largest competitors. The stronger a business's or

FIGURE 11-3 PORTFOLIO ANALYSIS AND STRATEGIC MARKET PLANNING

a product's relative market share, the more profitable it is.[5] Another measure is the share development index, which also relates share growth to sales and profit.

To create the matrix for a portfolio based on the life cycles of a business's products, we begin by building the market attractiveness dimension of the portfolio. Figure 11-4 illustrates how the product's sales and profits vary over the product life cycle. The different levels of performance at different stages of the product life cycle require a business to implement different strategies and allocate different levels of marketing resources as a product moves through its life cycle.

FIGURE 11-4 PRODUCT LIFE-CYCLE PORTFOLIO

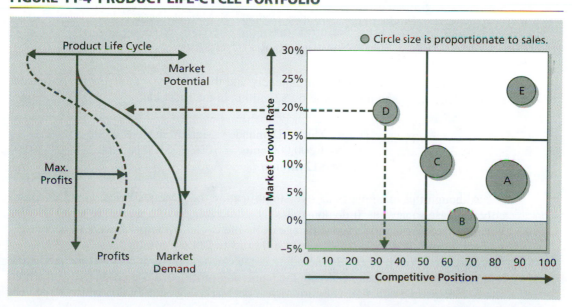

FIGURE 11-5 MARKET SHARE AND POTENTIAL FOR SHARE GROWTH

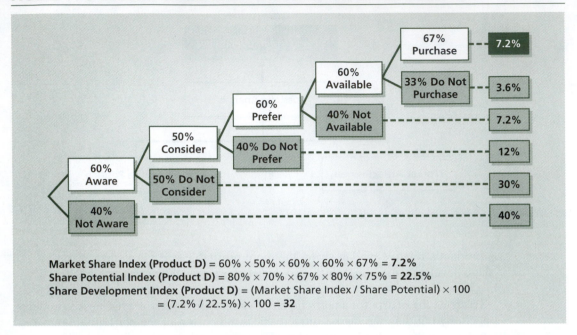

Market Share Index (Product D) = 60% × 50% × 60% × 60% × 67% = **7.2%**
Share Potential Index (Product D) = 80% × 70% × 67% × 80% × 75% = **22.5%**
Share Development Index (Product D) = (Market Share Index / Share Potential) × 100
    = (7.2% / 22.5%) × 100 = **32**

Examining the sales and profits of product D in Figure 11-5 helps us understand the relationship between the stages of the product life cycle and market attractiveness. Assume that the market demand for product D, now in the early growth stage of its product life cycle, is 1 million units annually and the product captures 10 percent of this demand with a price of $100 per unit. The result is $10 million in sales:

$$\text{Sales (current) Product D} = \text{Market Demand} \times \text{Market Share} \times \text{Price}$$
$$= 1{,}000{,}000 \text{ units} \times 10\% \times \$100 \text{ per unit}$$
$$= \mathbf{\$10\,million}$$

If the market grows 20 percent annually and the business maintains its 10 percent market share, sales should increase by $2 million in the first year:

$$\text{Sales (year 1) Product D} = \text{Market Demand} \times \text{Market Share} \times \text{Price}$$
$$= 1{,}200{,}000 \text{ units} \times 10\% \times \$100 \text{ per unit}$$
$$= \mathbf{\$12\,million}$$

Although this example is an oversimplification, because the price would undoubtedly decrease somewhat, it demonstrates the attractiveness of a market in terms of sales when the product is in the growth stage of its life cycle. If the price were to decrease 3 percent, from $100 to $97, sales would still grow to $11.64 million.

But what about profits? By including in the equation the unit cost and the marketing and sales expenses, we can estimate the marketing profits that are produced with a hold share strategy for product D. The current-year net marketing contribution with a 10 percent market share, 40 percent margin, and marketing and sales expenses at 15 percent of sales is $1.5 million.

$$\begin{aligned}
\text{NMC (current)} \atop \text{Product D} &= \frac{\text{Market}}{\text{Demand}} \times \frac{\text{Market}}{\text{Share}} \times \left(\frac{\text{Unit}}{\text{Price}} - \frac{\text{Unit}}{\text{Cost}} \right) - \frac{\text{Marketing and}}{\text{Sales Expenses}} \\
&= 1{,}000{,}000 \text{ units} \times 10\% \times (\$100 - \$60) - \$1.5 \text{ million} \\
&= \$4 \text{ million} - \$1.5 \text{ million} \\
&= \mathbf{\$2.5 \text{ million}}
\end{aligned}$$

The marketing return on sales is 25 percent. If marketing and sales expenses remain at 15 percent of sales, a hold share strategy would produce a $3 million marketing profit in year 1.

$$\begin{aligned}
\text{NMC (year 1)} \atop \text{Product D} &= \frac{\text{Market}}{\text{Demand}} \times \frac{\text{Market}}{\text{Share}} \times \left(\frac{\text{Unit}}{\text{Price}} - \frac{\text{Unit}}{\text{Cost}} \right) - \frac{\text{Marketing and}}{\text{Sales Expenses}} \\
&= 1{,}200{,}000 \text{ units} \times 10\% \times (\$100 - \$60) - \$1.8 \text{ million} \\
&= \$4.8 \text{ million} - \$1.8 \text{ million} \\
&= \mathbf{\$3 \text{ million}}
\end{aligned}$$

We can see, then, that the product life cycle serves as a good indication of market attractiveness not only in terms of share growth and sales, but also with regard to profit.

We still need a way to measure competitive position. There are several different ways to do it, but the one measure that provides a reliable assessment of competitive position is the level of market share. Market share is highly representative of a business's competitive position in the market place, and it can be managed over the product life cycle to provide positive impacts on sales and profit. But, again, a word of caution: a business must manage market share gains to improve profit, not just sales and market share. For this reason, we have selected the share development index (SDI) as the strategic measure of competitive position for the portfolio that is based on product life cycles in Figure 11-6 and Figure 11-7. The SDI also indicates the level of opportunity that exists to improve a product's competitive position: Product D's relatively low SDI of 32 as shown in the two charts means that its potential for greater sales and profit is very high.

Recall that to calculate a product's SDI, we first estimate its market share and share potential indexes. Using the market share performance tree presented in Chapter 3, we can estimate that product D has a market share index of 7.2 percent, as shown in Figure 11-5. The share potential index is the share index that product D would achieve if it could reach all of the performance targets that the company sets for each level of the market share performance tree. In Figure 11-5, these performance targets are represented in the calculation for the share potential index, resulting in a share potential index of 22.5 percent. The ratio of current to potential share multiplied by 100 produces the share development index of 32.

Remember that the market share index is not intended to represent a business's actual market share. Many factors in addition to the ones in the share development tree shape actual market share. However, the market share index is a summary index of the more important share performance metrics—in this case, the five metrics we chose. A

FIGURE 11-6 PORTFOLIO ANALYSIS USING MARKET GROWTH RATE AND SDI

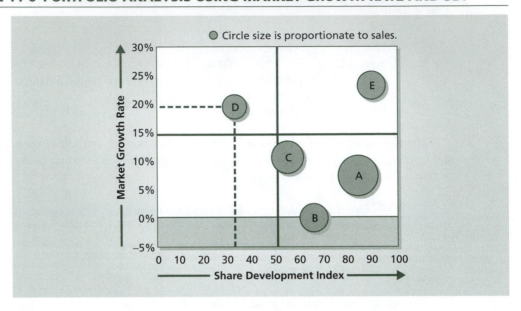

business can expect gains in actual market share to the extent that it improves its market share index.

The example that follows illustrates how an improved market share index can lead to sales and profit growth. A business with sales of $10 million increased its marketing resources to improve its market share index from 7.2 percent to 10 percent during year 1

FIGURE 11-7 PRODUCT-MARKET PORTFOLIO PLAN

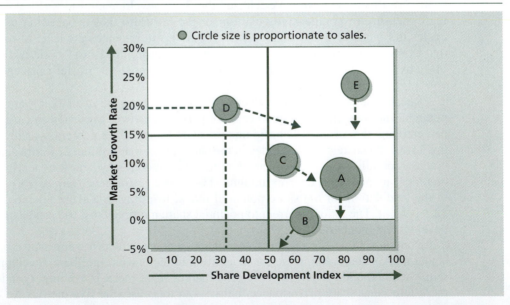

of its strategic market plan, resulting in an estimated 1 percent increase in actual market share—from 10 to 11 percent:

$$
\begin{aligned}
\textbf{Sales (year 1)} \\
\text{Product D} \quad &= \text{Market Demand} \times \text{Market Share} \times \text{Price} \\
&= 1{,}200{,}000 \text{ units} \times 11\% \times \$100 \text{ per unit} \\
&= \textbf{\$13.2 million}
\end{aligned}
$$

The increase in market share resulted in $3.2 million in additional sales revenue. But what about profits? Is this market share strategy profitable? To calculate the net marketing contribution, we take into account that the business increased its marketing and sales budget from $1.8 million to $2 million to support the improvement in the market share performance metrics.

$$
\begin{aligned}
\textbf{NMC (year 1)} \\
\text{Product D} \quad &= \frac{\text{Market}}{\text{Demand}} \times \frac{\text{Market}}{\text{Share}} \times \left(\frac{\text{Unit}}{\text{Price}} - \frac{\text{Unit}}{\text{Cost}} \right) - \frac{\text{Marketing and}}{\text{Sales Expenses}} \\
&= 1{,}200{,}000 \text{ units} \times 11\% \times (\$100 - \$60) - \$1.98 \text{ million} \\
&= \$3.3 \text{ million} - \$2 \text{ million} \\
&= \textbf{\$3.3 million}
\end{aligned}
$$

Had the business pursued a hold share strategy and held marketing and sales expenses at 15 percent of sales, the net marketing contribution would have been $3 million. A grow share strategy in a market that is growing 20 percent per year would produce 10 percent higher marketing profits than a hold share strategy.

But it is equally important to examine a situation in which market share gains result in higher sales and higher market share but a lower marketing profit. Product A in Figures 11-4 and 11-6 is a good example. It is approaching the mature stage of its product life cycle and has achieved 84 percent of its share potential. Given a 5 percent rate of market growth and no price erosion, sales of product A can be expected to increase from $100 million to $105 million with a 20 percent market share:

$$
\begin{aligned}
\textbf{Sales (current)} \\
\text{Product A} \quad &= \text{Market Demand} \times \text{Market Share} \times \text{Price} \\
&= 10{,}000{,}000 \text{ units} \times 20\% \times \$50 \text{ per unit} \\
&= \textbf{\$100 million}
\end{aligned}
$$

$$
\begin{aligned}
\textbf{Sales (year 1)} \\
\text{Product A} \quad &= \text{Market Demand} \times \text{Market Share} \times \text{Price} \\
&= 10{,}500{,}000 \text{ units} \times 20\% \times \$50 \text{ per unit} \\
&= \textbf{\$105 million}
\end{aligned}
$$

With sales of $100 million for the current year, a 20 percent margin, and marketing and sales expenses equal to 10 percent of sales, the marketing profit is $10 million.

$$
\begin{aligned}
\textbf{NMC (current)} \\
\text{Product A} \quad &= \frac{\text{Market}}{\text{Demand}} \times \frac{\text{Market}}{\text{Share}} \times \left(\frac{\text{Unit}}{\text{Price}} - \frac{\text{Unit}}{\text{Cost}} \right) - \frac{\text{Marketing}}{\text{Expenses}} \\
&= 10{,}000{,}000 \text{ units} \times 20\% \times (\$50 - \$40) - \$10 \text{ million} \\
&= \$20 \text{ million} - \$10 \text{ million} \\
&= \textbf{\$10 million}
\end{aligned}
$$

For year 1, a grow share strategy for product A calls for a price reduction of 5 percent. The product's price elasticity is –2, and a 5 percent price decrease would lead to a 10 percent increase in volume sold. The expected outcome would be a 2 percent increase in the business's share of a market that is growing at 5 percent annually, resulting in a significant increase of $9.7 million in sales over the current year:

$$\underset{\text{Product A}}{\textbf{Sales} \text{ (year 1)}} = \text{Market Demand} \times \text{Market Share} \times \text{Price}$$
$$= \textbf{\$109.7 million}$$

But would this grow share strategy be more profitable even when marketing and sales expenses are held at the current-year level of $10 million?

$$\underset{\text{Product A}}{\textbf{NMC} \text{ (year 1)}} = \frac{\text{Market}}{\text{Demand}} \times \frac{\text{Market}}{\text{Share}} \times \left(\frac{\text{Unit}}{\text{Price}} - \frac{\text{Unit}}{\text{Cost}}\right) - \frac{\text{Marketing and}}{\text{Sales Expenses}}$$
$$= 10{,}500{,}000 \text{ units} \times 22\% \times (\$47.5 - \$40) - \$10 \text{ million}$$
$$= \$17.3 \text{ million} - \$10 \text{ million}$$
$$= \textbf{\$7.3 million}$$

Despite the gains in market share, a strategy to grow share with a 5 percent price reduction would reduce profits in year 1 by $2.7 million even with the 5 percent growth in market demand and no increase in the marketing and sales budget. The grow share strategy in this case is a good example of how a blind pursuit of greater market share and sales can lead to lower profits.

Product Life Cycle/Market Share Portfolio

The product-market portfolio plan in Figure 11-7 incorporates all three elements a business uses in the market planning process: business performance, market attractiveness, and competitive position. Performance is represented by the size of each product's circle, which is proportionate to the current-year sales revenue that the product generates. The vertical axis represents the market growth rate, a major factor in determining market attractiveness. The market growth rate corresponds to the stages of the product life cycle presented in Figure 11-2. And the horizontal axis is a scale for the share development index, our measure of competitive position. With this portfolio we can assess the five products with an eye toward selecting the kind of strategic market plan that would be most effective for each one, given the attractiveness of its market, its competitive position, and its present sales performance and potential for improved performance.

- **Product A**—Product A in Figure 11-7 is in the mature stage of its life cycle. Market demand, however, is still growing at 5 percent annually, and the product's share development index of 84 indicates that it has a strong competitive position. The combination of these factors suggests that the product is well worth protecting. This is the time to carefully manage the profit that the product produces; any large investment in marketing and sales expenses would only draw down marketing profits. Product A is a key source of profitability for the business, and it supports the business's other products and the development of new ones.
- **Product B**—Like product A, product B is in the mature stage of its product life cycle, but market demand is no longer growing. There is some room to grow the product's

market share, but a grow share strategy with price cuts is likely to result in lower profits. Product B's future is limited, yet it is still an important part of the business's overall profitability. Eventually margins and marketing profits will fall below performance benchmarks, and then a harvest strategy will be the best approach for product B. But as the business incrementally raises prices during harvesting, it should be on the lookout for the possible formation of a profitable niche market for this product.

■ **Product C**—As product C approaches the late-growth phase of the product life cycle, the company will need to invest in marketing and sales expenses that will enable the product to maintain its market share in a growing market. An even larger marketing and sales budget would be required if the company wished to grow share at this stage of the product life cycle. From both strategic and long-run profit perspectives, it is important to grow share before the product enters the mature stage of its life cycle. Product C will be a major contributor to the portfolio's sales and profits as it moves into late market growth (maximum profits) and eventually the mature stage of the product life cycle.

■ **Product D**—Product D is in the early growth stage of its product life cycle, and the company needs to invest marketing and sales resources to take advantage of the rapid growth in demand for this product. Its low share development index of 32 also suggests that the business needs an effective strategy for achieving more of the product's share potential at this stage of its product life cycle. Strategically, because it is just entering the growth phase of its life cycle, product D will be in a rapidly growing market for some time. Gaining market share now is critical and would make product D a valuable source of profitable growth until market demand reaches its full potential sometime in the future.

■ **Product E**—As product E moves from the emerging market stage of the product life cycle to early growth stage, it is in a very strong competitive position with a share development index of 90. The company needs to make a continued investment to hold product E's excellent share position in a market that is growing 25 percent annually. An inadequate marketing and sales budget at this point would result in share slippage and greatly reduced future profits.

GE/McKinsey Portfolio Analysis

Market attractiveness and competitive position cannot always be fairly represented by a single factor. Many factors can contribute to market attractiveness. The stage of the product life cycle, the market's growth rate, and the market development index are certainly important considerations, but so are the size of the market, its competitive environment, and the ease or difficulty of accessing the market.

Likewise, competitive position could include more than a business's relative market share or its share development index. A strong brand, high product performance, outstanding service quality, high brand awareness, and a cost advantage are also important in shaping competitive position.

For these reasons, General Electric and McKinsey Consulting have developed a portfolio matrix that uses multiple factors to index market attractiveness and competitive position. The multi-factor indexes create a scale that varies from 0 to 100, as shown in Figure 11-8. On the basis of these assessments, the overall portfolio position of product A is average in market attractiveness but very strong in competitive position. A business would likely consider a strategic market plan to protect this product position. But before

FIGURE 11-8 GE/McKINSEY PORTFOLIO MODEL

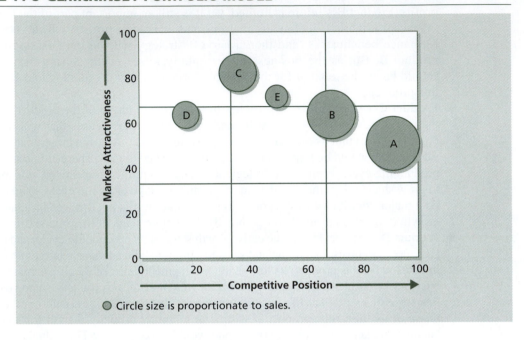

Circle size is proportionate to sales.

we go further into portfolio analysis and strategic market planning, let's take a close look at how market attractiveness and competitive position indexes are constructed.

MARKET ATTRACTIVENESS

A company's long-term objectives serve as the basis for developing performance objectives and a tactical marketing mix strategy. This important step in the strategic market planning process requires an in-depth examination of *market attractiveness*. We need a systematic way to assess market attractiveness, using a common set of criteria against which to compare product-markets.

So what factors make a market attractive or unattractive? Factors that typically shape market attractiveness are market size, market growth, competition, margin potential, market access, and a "good fit" with the company's core capabilities. These factors can be meaningfully grouped into three dimensions of market attractiveness: market forces, competitive environment, and market access, as shown in Figure 11-9.

To create a measure of market attractiveness, each of these three dimensions may be weighted to reflect its importance in relation to the others. In the example presented in Figure 11-10, market forces and market access are both weighted at 30 percent of the total importance, whereas competitive environment is weighted a little more heavily at 40 percent. Each dimension is further broken down into several factors that contribute to that particular dimension of market attractiveness, and each of these factors is also weighted to represent its relative importance within its respective dimension of market attractiveness.

FIGURE 11-9 FACTORS THAT SHAPE MARKET ATTRACTIVENESS

FIGURE 11-10 MARKET ATTRACTIVENESS INDEX

←		Market Attractiveness			→
Very Unattractive	Unattractive	Somewhat Unattractive	Somewhat Attractive	Attractive	Very Attractive
0	20	40	60	80	100

Market Forces Factor Importance: 30%	Relative Importance	Attractiveness Rating	Attractiveness Score
Market Size	40%	80	32
Growth Rate	30%	60	18
Buyer Power	30%	40	12
	100%		62

Competitive Environment Factor Importance: 40%	Relative Importance	Attractiveness Rating	Attractiveness Score
Price Rivalry	50%	40	20
Ease of Competitor Entry	30%	40	12
Number of Competitors	20%	60	12
	100%		44

Market Access Factor Importance: 30%	Relative Importance	Attractiveness Rating	Attractiveness Score
Customer Familiarity	40%	80	32
Channel Access	40%	100	40
Sales/Service Requirements	20%	60	12
	100%		84

$$\text{Market Attractiveness Index} = 30\% \times 62 + 40\% \times 44 + 30\% \times 84$$
$$= 18.6 + 17.6 + 25.2$$
$$= 61$$

By rating the attractiveness of each factor within each dimension, we can calculate an index for overall market attractiveness, as illustrated in Figure 11-10. The industry forces that influence market attractiveness differ from one industry to another, so for a particular business the factors that are appropriate for analysis in each dimension may differ from the ones listed in Figure 11-10. Special care should be taken to ensure that all the factors that shape a particular market's attractiveness are represented on the basis of market and profit performance.[6]

For the product-market in Figure 11-10, each individual market attractiveness factor is rated from "very unattractive" (0) to "very attractive" (100). This rating is multiplied by the relative importance of that factor to obtain a weighted individual factor attractiveness score. The individual factor scores of each dimension are totaled and multiplied by the importance given that dimension.

For example, market size is rated 80 for attractiveness and is assigned a relative importance of 40 percent within the market forces dimension. This method of indexing market attractiveness results in a score of 32 (80×0.4) for the market size factor. The score is added to the scores of the other factors in this dimension to arrive at a total factor-weighted score of 62. The factor-weighted score is then multiplied by 0.3, the relative importance weight assigned to the market forces dimension, to produce a weighted score of 18.6 for market forces. When this process is completed for all the market attractiveness factors and dimensions, the result is an overall market attractiveness index of 61.

COMPETITIVE POSITION

The process of developing a competitive position index is similar to that of computing the market attractiveness index. The first question is, "What makes one business strong with respect to competitive position and another weak?" Many factors determine competitive position. These factors, as we saw in Chapter 6, can be categorized into three dimensions of competitive position: a differentiation position, a cost position, and a marketing position. All three drivers have underlying forces that also shape the business's competitive position,[7] as shown in Figure 11-11.

We assign each of the three dimensions of competitive position a relative weight, just as we did in determining the market attractiveness index, and rate the relative importance

FIGURE 11-11 FACTORS THAT INFLUENCE COMPETITIVE POSITION

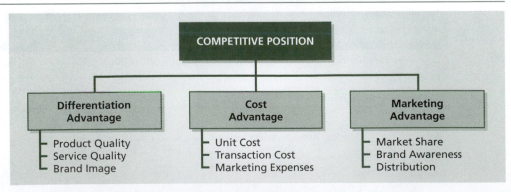

FIGURE 11-12 COMPETITIVE POSITION INDEX

←		Competitive Position			→
Considerably Behind	Clearly Behind	Somewhat Behind	Somewhat Ahead	Clearly Ahead	Considerably Ahead
0	20	40	60	80	100

Differentiation Advantage Factor Importance: 40%	Relative Importance	Attractiveness Rating	Attractiveness Score
Product Quality	40%	80	32
Service Quality	30%	60	18
Brand Image/Reputation	30%	80	24
	100%		**74**

Cost Advantage Factor Importance: 40%	Relative Importance	Attractiveness Rating	Attractiveness Score
Cost of Goods Sold	70%	40	28
Marketing and Sales Expenses	20%	60	12
Overhead Expenses	10%	60	6
	100%		**46**

Marketing Advantage Factor Importance: 20%	Relative Importance	Attractiveness Rating	Attractiveness Score
Market Share	40%	40	16
Brand Awareness	30%	40	12
Distribution	30%	20	6
	100%		**34**

Competitive Position Index = 40% × 74 + 40% × 46 + 20% × 34
= 29.6 + 18.4 + 6.8
= **55**

for each of the underlying factors within the three dimensions, as illustrated in Figure 11-12. Each factor is assessed with respect to the competitive position of the business in its existing market or its potential position in new markets under consideration. When the score for each of the three dimensions of competitive position is weighted by its relative importance, and the three weighted scores are then added, the result is the competitive position index; in this example it is 55 (rounded). The business's index of 55 places its competitive position in the midrange.

The competitive forces that shape the differentiation position for the business shown in Figure 11-12 are relatively strong and make up more than half of the competitive position index. The business's weighted competitive position score with respect to a marketing advantage is a weak 6.8 (20% × 34) due to a lower dimension weighting and generally lower attractiveness ratings for the factors in that dimension.

PORTFOLIO ANALYSIS AND STRATEGIC MARKET PLANS

A *portfolio analysis* is an evaluation of a business, product, or market with respect to market attractiveness and competitive position as an aid in identifying the most appropriate strategic plan. Figure 11-13 shows how this analysis uses the market attractiveness index and the competitive position index in combination with a portfolio of the different types of strategic plans. Product-markets with high indexes for both market attractiveness and competitive position have the strongest portfolio position and the best opportunities for profit performance.[8] Having a product-market in this position usually leads to a strategic market plan to invest to protect the product-market's attractive position. Whenever the

FIGURE 11-13 PORTFOLIO STRATEGIES AND STRATEGIC MARKET PLANS

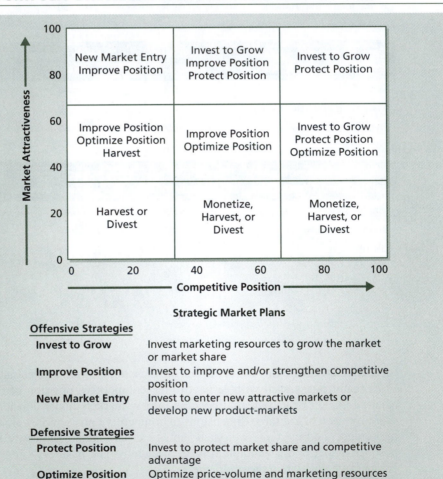

	Strategic Market Plans	
Offensive Strategies		
Invest to Grow	Invest marketing resources to grow the market or market share	
Improve Position	Invest to improve and/or strengthen competitive position	
New Market Entry	Invest to enter new attractive markets or develop new product-markets	
Defensive Strategies		
Protect Position	Invest to protect market share and competitive advantage	
Optimize Position	Optimize price-volume and marketing resources to maximize profits	
Monetize	Manage market position for maximum cash flow with limited marketing resources	
Harvest/Divest	Manage the product for maximum short-run cash flow or minimum losses	

two indexes intersect, there is at least one strategic market plan for the company to consider.[9] The different kinds of strategic plans are listed here according to their objectives:

- **Invest to Grow**—An offensive strategic market plan to invest marketing and sales resources to grow the market or a product's position in a market. Dell, because of a strong portfolio position, has invested heavily over the past 20 years to grow both the personal computer market and its share of the market.

- **Invest to Improve Position** —An offensive strategic market plan that seeks to improve a business's competitive position in an attractive segment of the market. Toyota invested early in hybrid vehicles to strengthen its competitive position in this segment of the automotive market. When Toyota first entered the segment, it was growing in market attractiveness, but few competitors were entering it. As a result, Toyota built an early lead in an attractive market.

- **New Market Entry**—An offensive strategy to enter new attractive markets. Again, Toyota's entry into the hybrid market is an example of this strategy. The company plans to strengthen its competitive position in this market by expanding its line of hybrid cars and stepping up production. New market strategies focus on developing the market and are required for most new products, such as flat-screen televisions, cellular phones, and DVD players when they were introduced. New market development strategies require a large investment in marketing resources, so this segment of the business operates at a loss until market volumes reach break-even levels.

- **Protect Position**—A defensive strategy to protect an attractive market position in which the business dominates with respect to competitive position. Gatorade in the sports drink market and Red Bull in the energy drink market both have market shares of about 80 percent. Although these markets are attractive and growing, these products will come under increasing attack as new competitors enter the market.

- **Optimize Position**—Many businesses implement a defensive strategy in the late-growth stage or the mature stage of the product life cycle. When growth potential is limited and competitive position is set, businesses need to optimize the marketing mix to produce maximum marketing profits. This is the time in the product life cycle when volumes are nearly at full potential and margins are still somewhat attractive. A business can incrementally reduce its investment in marketing resources because the product-market is mature or nearing maturity. A business using this defensive strategy undertakes a conscious effort to reduce its customer base in order to reach a more profitable level of business. Many banks, for example, have redefined their customer base by charging fees for small accounts that cannot be profitably served. As these fees cause many customers to leave, the banks are able to grow profits with a smaller, more focused customer base. When it is managed correctly, a strategy to optimize position at the later stages of the product life cycle allows the product to produce its maximum profits.

- **Monetize Strategy**—A defensive strategy used in less attractive markets in which a business has some level of competitive position. The strategy manages prices and marketing resources in a way that maximizes cash flow without exiting the market. Businesses in the cash flow mode often place limits on payment terms, do not pay for shipping, and offer few customer services. Although the price remains competitive, these businesses minimize investment in their products and strive for maximum cash flow from their market position.

■ **Harvest Strategy**—A defensive strategy for maximizing profits and cash flow as a business slowly exits a product-market. Prices are increased to improve margins as volumes decline. In the short run, the strategy produces a higher gross profit. Reductions in marketing expenses lower the cost of marketing. The business exits the market when no prospect for a short-run profit remains.

■ **Divest Strategy**—A defensive strategy for exiting a market by selling or closing down the business or eliminating the product. Exiting a product-market is simply a way to cut losses quickly and reallocate marketing resources to more productive endeavors.

As shown in Figure 11-13, attractive product-markets usually warrant an offensive strategic market plan. The various kinds of offensive strategic market plans all take advantage in different ways of favorable market conditions and a business's ability to profit in that market. The plan may map out a strategy for growing the market or growing the business's share, or it may present ways to improve the competitive position. An offensive strategic market plan could also guide entry into another existing market or the development of an entirely new product-market.

On the basis of a portfolio analysis and performance objectives, a business selects either an offensive or defensive strategic market plan. Offensive strategic market plans are geared to deliver above-average performance in the areas of sales growth, share position, and long-run profit performance. Defensive strategic market plans, in contrast, are intended to protect important share positions and produce short-run profit performance, while also contributing to long-run profit. Strategic market planning for a business with multiple product-markets often requires a careful balance of offensive and defensive strategic market plans. By doing this, the business can meet short-run profit objectives and investor expectations, invest to protect attractive strategic positions, and simultaneously develop share positions in existing or new markets.

Offensive Portfolio Strategy

Because offensive strategic market plans are more growth oriented than defensive plans, they are more likely to be used in attractive markets.[10] Consider a consumer electronics manufacturer whose sales in the base year of its strategic market plan were $19.38 billion. The business is the market's leader, and its base-year market share was 10.2 percent of a market that was growing at 5 percent to 6 percent annually. Although industry margins were declining, this business maintained above-average margins and produced $3.88 billion in gross profit in the base year. With an efficient marketing strategy, the business produced a net marketing contribution of $2.23 billion in the base year.

Actual Base-Year Performance

$$\text{Sales Revenue} = \text{Market Demand} \times \text{Market Share}$$
$$= \$190 \text{ billion} \times 10.2\%$$
$$= \mathbf{\$19.38\, billion}$$

$$\text{Gross Profit} = \text{Sales Revenue} \times \text{Percent Margin}$$
$$= \$19.38 \text{ billion} \times 20\%$$
$$= \mathbf{\$3.88\, billion}$$

FIGURE 11-14 OFFENSIVE VERSUS DEFENSIVE PORTFOLIO STRATEGIES

3-Year Strategic Market Plan Consumer Electronics Business	Actual Base Year	Offensive Plan Grow Share	Defensive Plan Hold Share	Offensive Plan Year-3 Actual
Market Demand ($ millions)	$190,000	$260,000	$260,000	$280,000
Market Share	10.2%	15.0%	10.0%	14.5%
Sales Revenues ($ millions)	$19,380	$39,000	$26,000	$40,600
Percent Margin	20.0%	17.5%	19.0%	17.5%
Gross Profit ($ millions)	$3,876	$6,825	$4,940	$7,105
Marketing & Sales Expenses (%)	8.5%	9.0%	8.0%	8.8%
Marketing & Sales Expenses ($ millions)	$1,647	$3,510	$2,080	$3,573
Net Marketing Contribution ($ millions)	$2,229	$3,315	$2,860	$3,532
Marketing ROS	11.5%	8.5%	11.0%	8.7%
Marketing ROI	135%	94%	138%	99%

$$\begin{aligned} \textbf{Net Marketing Contribution} &= \text{Gross Profit} - \text{Marketing \& Sales Expenses} \\ &= \$3.88 \text{ billion} - \$1.65 \text{ billion} \\ &= \mathbf{\$2.23\,billion} \end{aligned}$$

The results were a marketing ROS of 11.5 percent and a marketing ROI of 135 percent.

Figure 11-14 shows the actual performance of this consumer electronics company, the estimated results of the company's offensive strategy, the estimated results of a defensive strategy, and the actual outcome of the 3-year offensive plan to grow market share. The offensive strategy to continue growing share in an expanding market, from 10.2 to 15 percent, presented the greater strategic challenge. This strategic market plan would require the company to increase its marketing and sales resources from $1.65 billion in the base year to $3.5 billion in year 3 of the offensive plan. On the basis of market growth and market share assumptions, sales were projected to grow from $19.4 billion to $39 billion.

The business expected that its margins would decrease as it incrementally lowered prices to attract more customers in an effort to grow market share. The year-3 margin was projected to be 17.5 percent, resulting in a gross profit of $6.8 billion. The offensive plan to grow share to 15 percent would produce an increase in net marketing contribution of $1.1 billion. However, decreasing margins and increasing marketing and sales expenses would lead to declines in the year-3 marketing ROS (8.5%) and marketing ROI (94%).

Year 3: Offensive Strategy to Grow Share

$$\begin{aligned} \textbf{Sales Revenue} &= \text{Market Demand} \times \text{Market Share} \\ &= \$260 \text{ billion} \times 15\% \\ &= \mathbf{\$39\,billion} \end{aligned}$$

$$\begin{aligned} \textbf{Gross Profit} &= \text{Sales Revenue} \times \text{Percent Margin} \\ &= \$39 \text{ billion} \times 17.5\% \\ &= \mathbf{\$6.83\,billion} \end{aligned}$$

$$\begin{aligned}
\textbf{Net Marketing Contribution} &= \text{Gross Profit} - \text{Marketing \& Sales Expenses} \\
&= \$6.83 \text{ billion} - \$3.51 \text{ billion} \\
&= \mathbf{\$3.32\,billion}
\end{aligned}$$

Although the business's efficiency in producing marketing profits is projected to diminish, the investment to grow market share will increase marketing profits by approximately $1.1 billion. This investment in market share will also have future benefits as this market approaches maturity and it becomes more difficult to make market share gains.

Defensive Portfolio Strategy

The purpose of defensive strategic market plans is to protect important strategic market positions and to add significantly to short-run cash flow and profit performance. As shown in Figure 11-13, defensive strategic market plans are most commonly implemented in attractive markets by businesses with a strong competitive position or in unattractive markets by businesses with a low competitive position index.

One kind of defensive strategic market plan aims to protect market position within an existing market.[11] Defensive strategic market plans also can involve monetizing for maximum cash flow, harvesting market share positions in existing markets, or divesting.[12] Monetizing and harvesting plans are not likely to generate significant sales revenue growth, and divesting disposes of a losing product-market, but defensive plans to protect (hold) share can greatly improve sales in a fast-growing market. All four types of defensive strategic market plans aim to improve short-run cash flow and profit performance, and in many ways, they define the business's current level of share, sales, and profit performance.

Let's return to Figure 11-14 and estimate this company's 3-year performance using a defensive strategic market plan to protect market share in the growing market. Using the same assumptions we have already made for market growth, margin erosion, and marketing and sales expenses, we find that the business's 3-year performance projections under a defensive strategic market plan are far less impressive than under the offensive plan.

Year 3: Defensive Strategy to Hold Share

$$\begin{aligned}
\textbf{Sales Revenue} &= \text{Market Demand} \times \text{Market Share} \\
&= \$260 \text{ billion} \times 10\% \\
&= \mathbf{\$26\,billion}
\end{aligned}$$

$$\begin{aligned}
\textbf{Gross Profit} &= \text{Sales Revenue} \times \text{Percent Margin} \\
&= \$26 \text{ billion} \times 19\% \\
&= \mathbf{\$4.94\,billion}
\end{aligned}$$

$$\begin{aligned}
\textbf{Net Marketing Contribution} &= \text{Gross Profit} - \text{Marketing \& Sales Expense} \\
&= \$4.94 \text{ billion} - \$2.08 \text{ billion} \\
&= \mathbf{\$2.86\,billion}
\end{aligned}$$

A defensive strategic market plan to protect market share is expected to yield a $6.6 billion increase in sales revenue and a $631 million increase in net marketing contribution. Although many factors could have prevented the business from meeting these goals, if this strategy were successfully implemented it would have protected share position, grown sales revenue, and produced a slightly higher net marketing contribution. But

FIGURE 11-15 OFFENSIVE AND DEFENSIVE STRATEGIC MARKET PLANS

the projections for share, sales, gross profit, and net marketing contribution under a defensive strategy are well below these same projections under the offensive strategic market plan. The business naturally chose to pursue the offensive plan as the better option for profitable growth. The business's actual performance in year 3 was better than the projected performance levels because of higher than expected growth in market demand. The net marketing contribution exceeded the year-3 projection by $200 million. As the market enters the late-growth stage of its product life cycle, the business may need to reconsider a defensive strategy to protect its market leadership position and remain profitable.

Figure 11-15 outlines the kinds of offensive and defensive strategic market plans we have been discussing. As we have seen, a portfolio analysis is a valuable aid in selecting the plan best suited for a particular product-market.

PORTFOLIO DIVERSIFICATION

Diversification across product-markets adds two important advantages to the overall performance of a business. First, it reduces dependence on a single product-market. Second, by diversifying, a business increases the likelihood that its overall performance will be consistent because adverse conditions in one product-market can be offset by favorable conditions in another.

For example, Figure 11-16 illustrates the overall sales of a business that is diversified across different product-markets. In product-market A, the business's core market, sales are growing at an average rate of 1.5 percent annually, but this growth varies from year to year due to economic conditions and competitive forces. Because the business is also positioned in two other product-markets, it is able to take advantage of offsetting product life cycles and competitive forces. Product-market B is growing at 4 percent annually, and product-market C is growing at almost 15 percent. Although sales in each of these two markets are much less than in the business's core market, each contributes to overall sales growth and performance stability.

The unexplained sales variance over the period shown for product-markets A, B, and C is 42 percent, 17 percent, and 57 percent, respectively. When the sales performances of

FIGURE 11-16 PORTFOLIO DIVERSIFICATION AND VARIANCE IN SALES

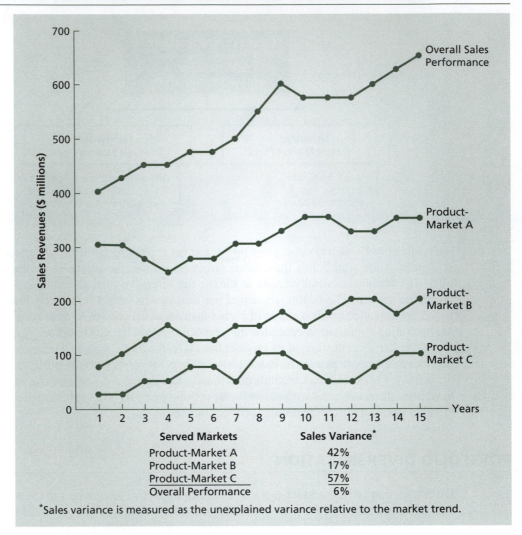

Served Markets	Sales Variance*
Product-Market A	42%
Product-Market B	17%
Product-Market C	57%
Overall Performance	6%

*Sales variance is measured as the unexplained variance relative to the market trend.

all three product-markets are combined, the offsetting effects created by different competitive conditions and product life cycles produce more consistent growth, with only a 6 percent unexplained variance in sales.

Two Levels of Diversification

Product diversification is one of two levels of diversification. Obviously, the less dependent a business is on a single product, the less vulnerable it is to a major change in performance. Coca-Cola, for instance, has a broad line of beverage products that serves virtually all world markets. For Procter & Gamble, product diversification goes further, because it has developed product positions in widely diversified consumer household product-markets.

Market diversification provides another way to achieve growth and reduce risk. DuPont, for example, has diversified across many markets that range from carpets to swimsuits to cookware, using materials such as Nylon, Dacron, Teflon, Lycra, and Kevlar. By serving multiple markets and not being dependent on any one product or market, DuPont has grown to a $50 billion company. In the early 1990s, US West split its company in two to better serve diverse markets: US West Communications, which remained in charge of the more mature core telecommunications businesses, and MediaOne Group, which was created to grow in high-technology markets. In the late 1990s, Hewlett-Packard pursued the same strategy when it split into two companies: an $8 billion test and measurement business named Agilent Technologies, and a $39 billion computer and imaging business that kept the company's original name. This split enabled Hewlett-Packard to move faster in the emerging computer and imaging markets without abandoning its core product-markets in testing and measurement.

Every product-market experiences performance swings, but it is unlikely that all product-markets of a diversified business will experience the same conditions at the same time. This is why participation in several diversified product-markets contributes to performance stability. Product-markets that perform well offset those that do not, whether the poor performance is caused by product life-cycle influences, competitor moves, economic conditions, or some other factor.

MARKETING MIX STRATEGY AND PERFORMANCE PLAN

In order to make a strategic market plan actionable, a business must develop a *marketing mix strategy* in accordance with the strategic market plan and the allocated resources. As the strategic market plan and a corresponding marketing mix strategy are rolled out over a planning horizon of 3 to 5 years, a performance plan outlines the targeted short- and long-run share position, sales growth, and profitability.[13] Examining certain aspects of the strategic market planning process reveals sound approaches to making short-and long-run projections for each area of business performance.

As we have seen, a strategic market plan is a long-term strategy with a 3- to 5-year time horizon and specific performance objectives. A marketing mix strategy is a short-term marketing strategy with a 1-year time horizon. A marketing mix strategy needs to be reviewed each year with respect to changing market conditions and adjusted accordingly to achieve the long-run performance objectives of a strategic market plan. In some instances, market conditions may change so dramatically or so suddenly that the company will need to reassess its strategic market plan to determine whether it remains the best long-run plan to achieve the business's performance objectives in a particular product-market.

Marketing Mix Strategy

A business needs to develop a detailed tactical marketing strategy—or marketing mix strategy—for any strategic market plan with respect to product, price, place, promotion, and service. The degree to which the business is able to achieve the performance objectives of this strategic market plan depends on the effectiveness of the tactical marketing strategy that supports it.

For example, Intel used one tactical marketing strategy to support its strategic market plan to enter the low-end personal computer market, and a different tactical marketing strategy to support a strategic market plan to defend its high-share position in microprocessors. Each plan required different product positioning, pricing approaches, promotions, and sales outlets to achieve a position that would be attractive to target customers relative to competitors' product-price positions.

The strategic market plan sets the strategic direction and provides broad guidelines for resource allocation. However, the marketing mix strategy is the workhorse that has to succeed in order for the strategic market plan to achieve both its short- and long-run performance objectives. The right strategic market plan with the wrong marketing mix strategy normally will not produce the desired levels of performance.

Performance Plan

We saw earlier that a business chooses either an offensive or a defensive strategic market plan on the basis of very different performance objectives and conditions. Offensive strategic market plans are geared to deliver above-average performance in the areas of sales growth, improved share position, and improved long-run profit. Defensive strategic market plans are intended to produce short-run profit performance, protect important share positions, and contribute to long-run profit performance and strategic position.

Offensive strategic market plans require investment in order to produce sales growth and improve share position, which limits short-run profit performance. Defensive strategic market plans promote short-run profit performance but are not particularly effective at growing sales revenue or improving the long-run share position. In the long run, a growth-oriented market strategy will shift from an offensive strategic market plan to a defensive strategic market plan.

Consider Zi-Tech Acoustics, a $250 million business that engineers, manufactures, and markets a variety of acoustic products. Figure 11-17 specifies the market share, sales revenues, and net marketing contribution for each of Zi-Tech's four product lines. A portfolio analysis based on market attractiveness and competitive position produced the product portfolio illustrated in Figure 11-18. Here is a summary of the strategic market plans for each of the company's product lines:

- **Product Line A—Invest to Protect Market Share:** Product line A is in a mature market from which Zi-Tech derives 32 percent of its sales and 41 percent of the business's overall net marketing contribution. The intent of the strategic market plan is to protect share and profits. The company's priority is to hold margins as it invests in marketing and sales at the same rate as the rate of increase for sales. Although growth is nominal (3%), this strategy should produce a modest increase in sales and marketing profits.

- **Product Line B—Optimize Position:** Product line B is in a mature market with no opportunity for growth. Management believes that now is the time to optimize market share to achieve greater profits. The product line is 40 percent of overall sales and 34 percent of overall marketing profits. The strategic intent is to increase prices and decrease marketing and sales expenses as a percentage of sales, which will probably erode market share. The ultimate goal is to find a more profitable combination of margin and market share that will yield greater marketing profits.

FIGURE 11-17 ZI-TECH'S BASE-YEAR PORTFOLIO PERFORMANCE

Base-Year Portfolio Performance	Product Line A	Product Line B	Product Line C	Product Line D	Company Total
Market Growth Rate	3.0%	0.0%	15.0%	–5.0%	5.1%
Market Demand	$400	$400	$500	$200	$1,500
Market Share	20.0%	25.0%	10.0%	10.0%	16.7%
Sales Revenues	$80	$100	$50	$20	$250
Percent Margin	40.0%	30.0%	40.0%	10.0%	33.6%
Gross Profit	$32	$30	$20	$2	$84
Marketing & Sales Expenses (%)	10.0%	10.0%	10.0%	10.0%	10.0%
Marketing & Sales Expenses ($)	$8	$10	$5	$2	$25
Net Marketing Contribution	$24	$20	$15	$0	$59
Marketing ROS	30.0%	20.0%	30.0%	0.0%	23.6%
Marketing ROI	300%	200%	300%	0%	236%

Dollar figures are millions.

■ **Product Line C—Invest to Grow Market Share:** Product line C is in an attractive and growing market. The strategic intent is to invest to grow market share during the growth stage of the product life cycle. This product line is 20 percent of overall sales and 25 percent of overall marketing profits. Implementation of this strategic market plan is likely to reduce prices and margins and require increases in marketing and sales expenses, but market share should grow from 10 to 15 percent in a market that is growing 15 percent annually.

FIGURE 11-18 ZI-TECH'S PORTFOLIO ANALYSIS AND STRATEGIC MARKET PLAN

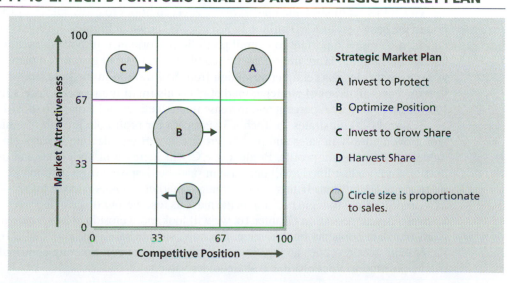

FIGURE 11-19 ZI-TECH'S YEAR-3 PERFORMANCE PLAN

Portfolio Strategy: Product Line:	Hold/Product Share A	Optimize Position B	Invest to Grow C	Harvest Share D	Company Total
Market Growth Rate	3.0%	0.0%	15.0%	−5.0%	6.7%
Market Demand	$437	$400	$760	$171	$1,768
Market Share	20.0%	20.0%	15.0%	5.0%	16.4%
Sales Revenues	$87	$80	$114	$9	$290
Percent Margin	40.0%	37.0%	37.0%	35.0%	37.8%
Gross Profit	$35	$30	$42	$3	$110
Marketing & Sales Expenses (%)	10.0%	8.0%	12.5%	3.0%	10.2%
Marketing & Sales Expenses ($)	$9	$6	$14	$0	$30
Net Marketing Contribution	$26	$23	$28	$3	$80
Marketing ROS	30.0%	29.0%	24.5%	32.0%	27.6%
Marketing ROI	300%	363%	196%	1,067%	270%

Dollar figures are millions.

■ **Product Line D—Harvest Share Position:** Product line D is in an unattractive, declining market with an average competitive position. This product line accounts for less than 10 percent of overall sales. The company wants to adopt a harvest strategy to maximize short-run marketing profits over the next 3 years. The strategy would involve increasing price to improve margins and reducing marketing and sales expenses. Market share and sales are expected to decrease significantly, but profits should increase over the next 3 years.

Given this set of strategic market plans, Zi-Tech hopes to grow sales from $250 million in the base year to $290 million in 3 years. As shown in Figure 11-19, product line C will then be more important to overall portfolio performance in both sales and net marketing contribution. More important, this combination of strategic market plans promises to increase the net marketing contribution from $59 million in the base year to $80 million in year 3. This set of strategic market plans also will improve Zi-Tech's marketing ROS from 23.6 to 27.6 percent and increase its marketing ROI from 236 to 270 percent.

Figure 11-20 illustrates Zi-Tech's 3-year path for profitable growth. Product line A will grow modestly in sales and profits. Product line B will decline in sales but increase modestly in marketing profits. Product line C will increase in both sales and marketing profits. And product line D will decrease in sales but improve from zero marketing profits to about $3 million. If this set of strategic market plans is successful, Zi-Tech will have improved its strategic position in the markets it serves while growing sales and profits over a 3-year period. In Chapter 16, we will look more closely at how strategic market plans translate into shareholder value. For now, we can safely assume that a 16 percent increase in sales revenues and a 35.6 percent increase in net marketing contribution contribute positively to net profit and shareholder value.

FIGURE 11-20 PERFORMANCE PLAN FOR ZI-TECH'S FOUR PRODUCT-MARKETS

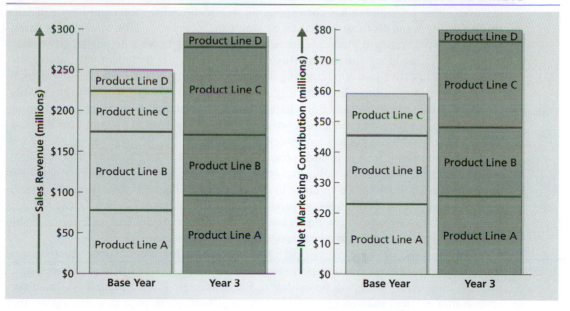

■ Summary

Strategic market planning is a process. It involves assessing business performance with respect to market attractiveness and competitive position. A company makes this assessment for each of its product-markets and any new ones that it may be considering. The product life cycle serves as the basis for an important portfolio analysis in which a business can display its product line over the product life cycle with respect to sales, sales growth, and profitability. A balanced product life-cycle portfolio will include a mix of early, growth, and mature markets.

Several measures of competitive position contribute to a portfolio analysis. One measure that corresponds to sales and profit performance is *relative market share*. Another measure of competitive position, one that also considers sales and profit, is the *share development index*.

The GE/McKinsey portfolio model includes an index of several market attractiveness factors and an index of several competitive position factors. Separate ratings of importance and performance shape the overall performance of these two dimensions. Market attractiveness is indexed with respect to market forces (market size, growth rate, and buyer power), competitive environment (price rivalry, ease of competitor entry, and number of competitors), and market access (customer familiarity, channel access, and sales requirements). Competitive position is indexed with respect to cost advantage (unit cost, transaction costs, and marketing expenses), differentiation advantage (product quality, service quality, and brand image), and marketing advantage (market share, brand awareness, and distribution). The portfolio analysis identifies one or more possible strategic market plans for each product-market the business serves or may enter in the future, on the basis of the product-market's position in the portfolio.

A strategic market plan is a long-run, 3- to 5-year strategic market objective that involves share position but has corresponding implications for short- and long-run sales revenue growth and profit performance. Strategic market plans can be offensive or defensive. Offensive strategic market plans are market penetration strategies to grow share position, sales, and long-run profitability. Offensive strategies include investing to grow, investing to improve position, entering another market, and developing a new market. Defensive strategies include protecting or optimizing position for maximum profits, monetizing for maximum cash flow, harvesting, and divesting. A combination of strategic market plans (one for each product-market) provides an overall view of how the business will grow with respect to share, sales, and profits.

Portfolio diversification in both products and markets is an important aspect of strategic market planning. A portfolio that is too concentrated in one line of products or in one market is subject to more variance in sales and profits than if it were properly diversified. Diversification into unrelated product-markets protects a business's overall performance against downward swings if one product-market should encounter unfavorable conditions. It adds stability to a business's overall performance.

Although the strategic market plan for a given product-market sets short-run and long-run goals with respect to market share, sales revenues, and profits, it does not specify how this performance will be achieved. Each strategic market plan, then, has a corresponding tactical marketing plan. The tactical marketing plan is a marketing mix strategy (product, price, place, promotion, and service) that specifies the tactical details of how the business will achieve the objectives of a given strategic market plan. The plan includes the marketing and sales budget required for implementing the marketing mix strategy. Using these marketing tactics, the marketing and sales budget, and a 3- to 5-year forecast of market share, sales revenues, and net marketing contribution, the business develops a performance plan.

■ Market-Based Strategic Thinking

1 Why would Yum Brands divest such well-known store brands like A&W and Long John Silver's?

2 Why did Toyota enter the U.S. car market at the low-price point of the market instead of the mid-price or high-price point?

3 Why did Toyota add the Lexus and Scion product lines to its product portfolio as separate umbrella brands instead of retaining an all-Toyota product line portfolio?

4 How would Apple use the product life cycle that was used in this chapter to evaluate the current and future sales and profits of a business's portfolio of products?

5 What could be done with regard to Portfolio A in Figure 11-2 to make it a more balanced portfolio over the next 3 to 5 years? How would this change affect short- and long-run sales and profits?

6 Why is it important to use two independent dimensions of performance to build a product portfolio for Kellogg's? Why would these performance dimensions be different for Netflix?

7 For Yum Brands, what is meant by a "strategic market plan"?

8 For General Motors, what is the difference between market attractiveness and competitive position with respect to building a product portfolio?

9 How does a portfolio model based on product life cycle and the market share development index help a growth business like Groupon.com?

10 Why would a business like Coca-Cola opt to use the GE/McKinsey portfolio model over other portfolio models?

11 How would you assess the attractiveness of a new consumer product-market for Procter & Gamble? List the specific factors you would include as you build an index of market attractiveness for a Procter & Gamble consumer market.

12 How would you assess the competitive position of Procter & Gamble in a new consumer product-market? List the specific factors you would include as you build an index of competitive position for a Procter & Gamble consumer market.

13 Using the following information, create a portfolio analysis and specify a strategic market plan for a business that serves the three product-markets A, B, and C.

Product-Market	Share (%)	Sales ($ millions)	Market Attractiveness	Competitive Position
A	10	$20	20	40
B	33	$50	75	80
C	5	$10	85	15

14 Using the information presented in item 13 and the additional information that follows, create a 3-year performance plan with respect to market share and sales revenues for each product-market, given the strategic market plan specified. Also create a projection of overall sales for each year of the 3-year planning horizon.

Product Market	Strategic Market Plan	Share Objective (%)	Market Demand ($ millions)	Market Growth(%)
A	Optimize Position	5	$200	5
B	Protect Share	33	$150	7
C	Grow Share	10	$200	20

15 Under what conditions would Apple use an offensive strategic market plan?

16 Under what conditions would Apple opt to use a defensive strategic market plan?

17 What role do offensive and defensive strategic market plans play in the short- and long-run performance of Apple?

18 How does Apple's level of product-market diversification affect sales growth and performance consistency?

19 Why would the overall variation in sales revenues over a 10-year period be different between General Electric and Dell?

20 How would the sales and profit performance over a 3-year period differ between a business with only defensive strategic market plans and a business with only offensive strategic market plans? Why is it important for Dell to have a balance of offensive and defensive plans?

21 How would an offensive strategic market plan and marketing and sales budget for GE Appliances to grow market share differ from those of a strategic market plan to optimize position and reduce share?

Marketing Performance Tools and Application Exercises

The three interactive marketing performance tools and application exercises outlined here will improve your ability to use portfolio analysis in selecting an effective strategic market plan. To access the tools, go to **rogerjbest. com.** For the questions in the exercises, you may enter the data presented to obtain the answers. You may also enter other data to see the results, and you may save your work. The figure numbers in parentheses are related examples in Chapter 11, but the instructions pertain to the online exercises.

11.1 Product Life Cycle Portfolio (Figure 11-2)
- Using the data provided, adjust the proposed product life-cycle portfolio to the recommended percentage of sales and product life-cycle position. Add product F with 25 percent and product G with 10 percent market penetration.

How will the revised portfolio perform in the future with respect to sales and profit?

11.2 Market Growth Rate–Share Development Portfolio (Figure 11-7)
- Using the data provided (strategy presented in Figure 11-7), adjust the portfolio position based on market growth rate and efforts to improve share performance metrics. What is the potential impact for future sales and profits?

11.3 GE/McKinsey Portfolio (Figure 11-8)
- Using the data provided, alter the market attractiveness and competitive position ratings to create a revised portfolio for product A. How would you expect the revised portfolio to perform with respect to sales and profits?

Notes

1. Yum Brands, Inc., SEC 10-K 2010 Annual Report (February 15, 2011): http://www.yum.com/investors/investor_materials.asp, retrieved March 19, 2011.
2. M. Treacy and F. Wiersama, *The Discipline of Market Leaders* (Reading, MA: Addison-Wesley, 1995).
3. D.A. Garvin, "Leveraging Processes for Strategic Advantage," *Harvard Business Review* (September–October 1995): 77.
4. R.A. Kerin, V. Mahajan, and P.R. Varadarajan, *Strategic Market Planning* (Boston: Allyn and Bacon, 1990).
5. R. Buzzell and B. Gale, *The PIMS Principles: Linking Strategy to Performance* (New York: Free Press, 1987).
6. K. Rangan, M. Menezes, and E.P. Maier, "Channel Selection for New Industrial Products: A Framework, Method and Application," *Journal of Marketing* (July 1992): 69–82.
7. L.W. Phillips, D.R. Chang, and R.D. Bussell, "Product Quality, Cost Position, and Business Performance: A Test of Some Key Hypotheses," *Journal of Marketing* 47 (January 1983): 26–43.
8. M.E. Porter, *Competitive Advantage* (New York: Free Press, 1986).
9. D. Aaker, "Formal Planning System," in *Strategic Market Management* (New York: Wiley, 1995): 341–53.
10. T. Powell, "Strategic Planning as Competitive Advantage," *Strategic Management Journal* 13 (1992): 551–8; S. Armstrong, "The Value of Formal Planning for Strategic Decisions: Reply," *Strategic Management Journal* 7 (1986): 183–5; and D. Sinha, "The Contribution of Formal Planning to Decisions," *Strategic Management Journal* (October 1990): 479–92.
11. W.K. Hall, "Survival Strategies in a Hostile Environment," *Harvard Business Review* (September–October 1980): 75–85.
12. K.R. Harrigan, *Strategies for Declining Businesses* (Lexington, MA: Lexington Books, 1980); K.R. Harrigan and M.E. Porter, "End-Game Strategies for Declining Industries," *Harvard Business Review* (July–August 1983): 111–20; and K.R. Harrigan, *Managing Maturing Businesses* (New York: Lexington Books, 1988).
13. F.V. McCrory and P.G. Gerstberger, "The New Math of Performance Measurements," *Journal of Business Strategy* (March–April 1992): 33–8.

Offensive Strategies

■ You miss 100 percent of the shots you
don't take.
—*Wayne Gretsky*
Former National Hockey League All-Star

The results of Apple's offensive strategies from 2005 to 2010 are stunning. The company's portfolio of differentiated products has created new product-market categories that Apple dominates with a first-to-market advantage.

Apple experienced close to a fivefold growth in sales over the 5-year period, from $13.9 billion in 2005 to $65.2 billion in 2010. Just as impressive is the company's increase in gross margin, from 29 percent in 2005 to 41 percent in 2010. During the same period, Apple was able to cut its sales, general, and administrative expenses from 14.6 to 8.5 percent of sales.

The combination of incredible product innovation, superb marketing, and cost-efficient management allowed the company's operating income to grow from $528 million in 2000 to $18.4 billion in 2010.

Performance	2000	2005	2010
Percent Margin	27.0%	29.0%	41.0%
SGA (% sales)	14.6%	13.4%	8.5%
IBIT (% sales)	6.6%	11.9%	28.2%
Marketing ROI	147%	189%	543%

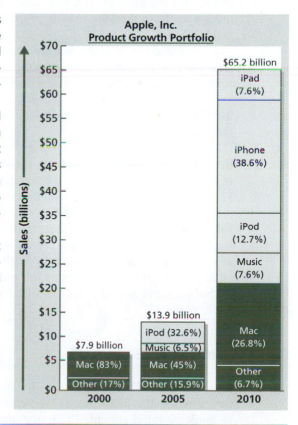

Apple, Inc.
Product Growth Portfolio

$65.2 billion
iPad (7.6%)
iPhone (38.6%)
iPod (12.7%)
Music (7.6%)
Mac (26.8%)
Other (6.7%)

$13.9 billion
iPod (32.6%)
Music (6.5%)
Mac (45%)
Other (15.9%)

$7.9 billion
Mac (83%)
Other (17%)

Sales (billions)

APPLE'S PRODUCT PORTFOLIO AND OFFENSIVE GROWTH

A strategic view of Apple's product portfolio helps us understand how the company grew both sales and margins over a 10-year period and in the process achieved an outstanding average annual rate of sales growth of 23.3 percent. Figure 12-1 presents a product life-cycle portfolio view of the company for 2000, 2005 and 2010. The product life cycles show how each of Apple's product lines was performing at these three points in time. The size of the circle for each product is proportional to its sales: the larger the circle, the greater the sales revenue generated that year by the product. In 2010, for example, the iPhone—represented by the largest circle—was Apple's greatest single source of sales revenue. Sales of software and peripherals are not shown, because the product life cycle for these ancillary products spans all stages of the product life cycle.

The product portfolio for 2000 shows us that at that time Apple was basically a one-product company. With sales of about $8 billion, the Mac represented 83 percent of the company's sales. For Apple, the good news was that this product was strategically only at the mid-point of its product life cycle; there was still plenty of opportunity ahead for additional sales growth. In 2005, however, the portfolio reveals no sales growth for the Mac. In fact, Mac sales fell somewhat, and this happened in a growing market, causing the Mac to lose a fairly significant share of the market between 2000 and 2005.

The launch of the iPod changed everything for Apple. By 2005 the iPod was responsible for 32.6 percent of sales, enabling the company to grow its total sales revenue from $7.9 billion in 2000 to almost $14 billion in 2005, despite the stagnation in Mac sales. Without the iPod, Apple sales would have been only $9.4 billion in 2005. In addition to its considerable contribution to sales, the iPod gave Apple a foothold in a new market that was unrelated to computers.

Apple replicated its offensive growth strategy for the iPod when it introduced the iPhone and then the iPad. By 2010, the iPhone had overtaken the Mac as the sales leader in the Apple product portfolio. The iPad, introduced in 2010, had first-year sales of about $5 billon. Apple also had been significantly upping its effort on the Mac and almost tripled its Mac sales from $6.3 billion in 2005 to $17.5 billion in 2010. The Mac's dramatic sales growth over the 5 years equated to an average annual growth rate of 22.6 percent, which far exceeded the average annual rate of market growth.

Apple exemplifies a company with a great product portfolio and great offensive strategies. Figure 12-1 shows us not only the company's sales growth over a 10-year period but also how it has diversified its products and positioned them on the life-cycle curve.

STRATEGIC MARKET PLANS

Apple, Google, Facebook, and many other well-known businesses experienced substantial growth in the 2000s. Each of these businesses had the benefit of a strategic advantage to guide its rapid growth. Their strategic market plan was market penetration with the development of completely new products for new markets. In every case, however, the strategic market plan addressed three basic performance objectives:

FIGURE 12-1 APPLE—PRODUCT LIFE-CYCLE PORTFOLIO

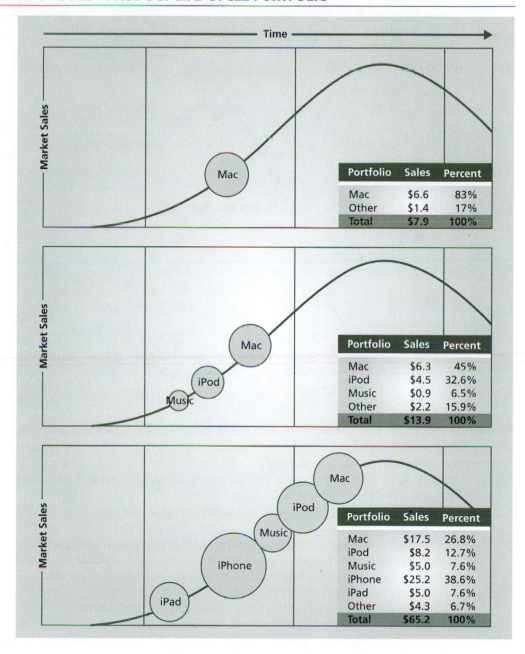

- **Share Position:** How will the strategic market plan contribute to the business's share position in served markets?
- **Sales Growth:** To what degree will the strategic market plan contribute to sales growth?
- **Profit Performance:** How will the strategic market plan affect short- and long-run profit performance?

FIGURE 12-2 MARKET GROWTH AND OFFENSIVE AND DEFENSIVE STRATEGIES

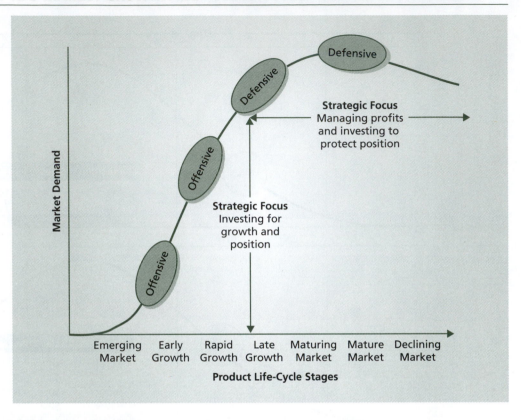

To make the best use of limited resources, a business needs a strategic market plan that carefully maps out future growth and profit performance.[1] Each of the strategic market plans it adopts will in some way affect both its short- and long-run performance in market share, sales, and profit. Depending on the situation, some strategic market plans will be offensive and some will be defensive.

As we saw in Chapter 11, offensive strategic market plans are usually growth oriented and are more appropriate for the growth stage of a product-market life cycle.[2] Their objective is to produce sales growth and improve share position and future profit performance. Defensive strategic market plans are more likely to be implemented in the latter stages of a product-market life cycle. They are often designed to protect important share positions and to be large contributors to short-run sales revenues and profits. Figure 12-2 depicts when each type of strategy is most appropriate. This chapter examines various offensive strategic market plans, and Chapter 13 will present various defensive strategic market plans.

OFFENSIVE STRATEGIC MARKET PLANS

The combination of market attractiveness and competitive advantage creates a portfolio position for any given product-market.[3] As shown in Figure 12-3, attractive markets are most likely to warrant an offensive strategic market plan to improve competitive

FIGURE 12-3 PORTFOLIO ANALYSIS AND STRATEGIC MARKET PLANS

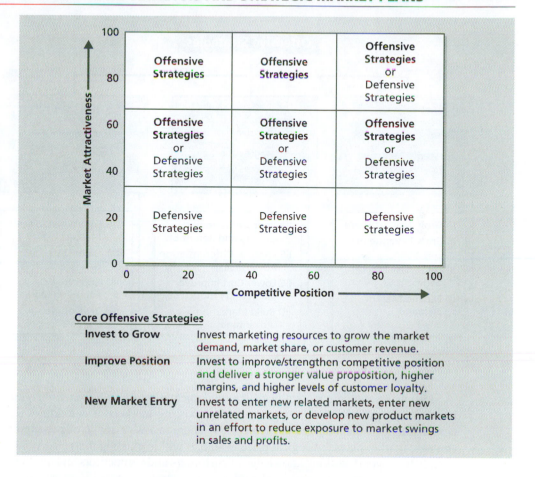

Core Offensive Strategies

Invest to Grow	Invest marketing resources to grow the market demand, market share, or customer revenue.
Improve Position	Invest to improve/strengthen competitive position and deliver a stronger value proposition, higher margins, and higher levels of customer loyalty.
New Market Entry	Invest to enter new related markets, enter new unrelated markets, or develop new product markets in an effort to reduce exposure to market swings in sales and profits.

advantage and share position when the business's competitive advantage is average or below. These offensive strategies can range from improving the competitive advantage and market share in existing product-markets to entering a new market with no established share position. In addition, a business might use an offensive strategic market plan to cultivate an emerging or underdeveloped market where the business would have a strong position of advantage.

There are six portfolio positions in which an offensive strategic market plan could be beneficial. Of these, the three positions with average market attractiveness and the one with highest market attractiveness and highest competitive advantage could instead, under some conditions, be more suitable for a defensive strategic market plan. We would need more information in order to decide between an offensive and a defensive strategic market plan. For example, an offensive strategic market plan may be warranted, given the business's sources of relative advantage. On the other hand, a defensive strategic market plan to protect the current position may be the better alternative for achieving desired performance objectives. A defensive plan could also be appropriate if the business wants to improve profits by optimizing its market focus with minimal investment.

FIGURE 12-4 STRATEGIC MARKET PLANS AND OFFENSIVE STRATEGIES

Offensive strategic market plans are fundamentally geared for growth and inherently involve strategies for penetrating or growing existing markets or entering or developing new markets, as summarized in Figure 12-4. There is a wide range of potential offensive strategic market plans.[4] A logical place to start is within existing markets. A business that already has a good working knowledge of customers and competitors and has the resources in place to serve existing markets should seek to leverage its existing-market position with an offensive strategic market plan to further penetrate and develop its product-markets.

Coca-Cola has been described as "the perfect growth company,"[5] even though it already commands a 50 percent market share of the worldwide carbonated soft drink market. From the company's point of view, Coca-Cola represents only a 2 percent share of stomachs on a worldwide basis. Its annual report pictures 47 empty Coke bottles and one full bottle. Viewing its market in this way has helped Coca-Cola grow its volume at the rate of 7 percent to 8 percent, while PepsiCo, its chief rival, is growing unit volume at the rate of only 1 percent. Clearly, Coca-Cola is challenging its marketing managers to think offensively in finding ways to grow Coca-Cola's share of the nonalcoholic beverage market.

OFFENSIVE CORE STRATEGY I: INVEST TO GROW SALES

Figure 12-4 shows the three offensive core strategies that are used in strategic market planning. The objective of each core strategy may be met using one or more of four fundamental offensive strategic market plans. For example, the objective of the first core strategy is to grow the business in its existing market. The specific strategic market plans for achieving the objective range from market penetration to growing market demand.[6] A business could grow its market share, increase its revenue per customer, enter new market segments, or expand market demand and thereby create a bigger pie, in which its slice is proportionately bigger. The offensive core strategies are numbered I, II, and III, and the four specific offensive strategies are designated A, B, C, and D. This system of numbering and lettering implies no order of importance; it just helps us keep track of the different types of strategies.

Offensive Strategy IA: Grow Market Share

One of the more obvious marketing strategies is to grow market share. But many factors can affect a business's ability to grow share and profitability.[7] Its share potential is one consideration. To what degree has the business achieved its share potential? What factors driving share development need to be managed to grow share in a given product-market? Finally, will share growth actually contribute to profitability? Each of these questions is an important consideration in developing an offensive strategic market plan to grow share.

In Chapter 3, we calculated the share development index (SDI) as the ratio of the market share index to the share potential index. The share potential of a business is the market share that a business believes it can achieve with its tactical marketing strategy, given the strength of its competitive advantage and its marketing effectiveness in a given product-market. The share performance calculation that follows uses a business's estimates that it should perform at 90 percent in product awareness, 50 percent in product preference, 80 percent in intentions to purchase, 80 percent in product availability, and 70 percent in rate of purchase. Performing at these levels results in a share potential index of 20 percent.

$$
\begin{aligned}
\frac{\textbf{Share Potential}}{\textbf{Index}} &= \frac{\text{Product}}{\text{Awareness}} \times \frac{\text{Product}}{\text{Preference}} \times \frac{\text{Purchase}}{\text{Intentions}} \times \frac{\text{Product}}{\text{Availability}} \times \frac{\text{Purchase}}{\text{Rate}} \\
&= 0.90 \times 0.50 \times 0.80 \times 0.80 \times 0.68 \\
&= \textbf{20\%}
\end{aligned}
$$

If a business's market share were 8 percent, the business would be underperforming and, hence, would have an SDI of 40. This would mean that the business has achieved only 40 percent of its share potential index. It would have a good opportunity to grow market share with a market penetration strategy.

$$
\textbf{Share Development Index} = \frac{\text{Market Share Index}}{\text{Share Potential Index}} = \frac{8\%}{20\%} \times 100 = \textbf{40}
$$

To grow share, a business has to examine each area of performance along the share-development path with respect to its expected versus its actual market performance. For instance, the business in the example expects to achieve 90 percent product awareness in its target market. If its actual target-market awareness were only 67 percent, this performance gap would prevent the business from reaching its full market share potential. To grow share, this business would need to examine the key performance gaps in its market share response.

It is also possible that a business has reached its share potential but could still grow its share if it adopted a new strategic market plan. Product improvements that would increase product preference from 50 to 70 percent would raise the market share potential from 20 to 27 percent. Of course, to achieve this level of market penetration, the business would have to adequately communicate and deliver these product improvements to the full satisfaction of target customers.

Perhaps the most important consideration in developing strategies to grow share is to make sure the planned share growth will be profitable. Some methods of growing share can actually reduce the net marketing contribution, as illustrated in the Santa Fe Sportswear example in Chapter 2. Market share is a key competitive metric, but market-based businesses need to resist emphasizing it to the point of ignoring other market-based metrics. It is easy to become caught up in share wars and win the battle for share but lose the war with respect to profits.

Offensive Strategy IB: Grow Revenue per Customer

Harley-Davidson derives 75 percent of its $4.2 billion in sales from the sale of motorcycles. The other 25 percent comes from purchases of clothing, parts, and accessories. Across all product categories, the company's 2010 per customer revenue was $13,630. In clothing alone, Harley-Davidson introduces 1,200 new items annually (excluding riding boots, baby clothes, and clothing for pets). The retail clothes are such an important aspect of communicating the brand that every dealership now has fitting rooms. The incremental sales of related products have much higher margins than the motorcycle sales, and they build customer loyalty. The apparel sales also enhance brand awareness and brand equity, with the wearers of Harley-Davidson clothing communicating the brand name.

As a business approaches 100 percent of its share development index, additional growth based on market share gains becomes increasingly difficult. Up to this point, a business's overall performance could be improved by correcting ineffective tactical marketing strategies, improving competitive position, or increasing a business's marketing effort. Now, with its share potential almost fully realized, the business can improve its overall performance only by growing sales with existing customers, to increase the amount of revenue per customer.

As another example, McDonald's in its early years sold a limited product line of hamburgers, french fries, and drinks. By making product line extensions to add chicken and fish sandwiches, salads, desserts, and a breakfast menu, McDonald's has been able to grow the average amount spent by its existing customers. Of course, these line extensions have also attracted new customers, both those who did not previously patronize fast-food restaurants and those who had been competitors' customers.

For businesses with well-known brand names, such as Kodak, Nike, Honda, IBM, and Disney, it is easy to introduce line extensions by leveraging the high awareness and positive image of the companies' brand names.[8] When Honda entered the lawn mower market in the early 1990s, sales of its mowers were driven by the company's name. Customers immediately perceived the mowers to be reliable, high-quality products. This perception was created by Honda's reputation for quality automobiles, motorcycles, and other motorized products. The high level of name awareness helped the company to quickly penetrate the lawn mower market. When Honda saw that many of its lawn mower customers owned other Honda products, the company then developed a growth strategy that was based on increasing volumes along its entire product line by marketing to existing customers.

Honda's strategy to target existing customers for its other products is aptly expressed in the company's marketing objective: "Our goal is to have five Hondas in every garage." This motto reflects an offensive strategic market plan to get Honda car owners to purchase other Honda products, including lawn mowers, recreational vehicles (motorcycles, snowmobiles, jet skis, all-terrain vehicles, and outboard motors), portable motors, and generators. For Honda, the strategy has been instrumental in growing the company. For any business with a solid brand reputation, the existing customer base offers a considerable opportunity for growing per-customer revenue through sales of other products.

Revenue per customer can also be increased by using price premiums. Businesses that enhance their products with value-added services or those with a reputation for high quality can charge higher prices than competing businesses and still maintain a superior customer value. General Electric's turbine engines, for example, command a price premium because they are high quality, installation services are first rate, and the company has a global reputation for innovative engineering and technical know-how. The price premium enables GE to attain more revenue per customer than many competing turbine manufacturers.

Offensive Strategy IC: Enter New Market Segments

Another offensive growth strategy within existing markets is to enter a new customer segment within an existing market.[9] As the personal computer market grew, the under-$1,000 segment emerged. Soon demand in this segment was growing faster than in any other. Intel, which did not have a product for this segment, saw AMD and other competitors take the lead in this segment. Intel responded by designing a new product for price-sensitive customers. As shown in Figure 12-5, the Celeron chip provided PC manufacturers with a low-cost Intel microprocessor for this market segment. Intel's

FIGURE 12-5 INTEL'S NEW SEGMENT ENTRY STRATEGY

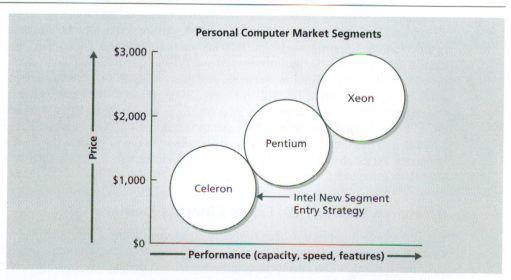

FIGURE 12-6 NEW SEGMENT OFFENSIVE GROWTH STRATEGY IN THE VODKA MARKET

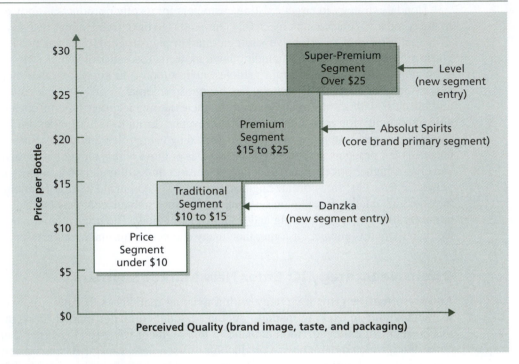

offensive strategic market plan for entering a new market segment gave the company a new source of sales revenue and profitability.

Another illustration of a company successfully entering new segments took place in the vodka market. This market is divided into four segments based on price and differences in taste, brand image, and packaging, as illustrated in Figure 12-6. Absolut Spirits had been successful in the premium vodka market segment and was number two in overall market share, behind market leader Smirnoff. Although Absolut held a strong position in the $15 to $25 premium segment, it lacked market positions in the super-premium segment (over $25) and the traditional segment ($10 to $15). Grey Goose, a competitor's product in the super-premium segment, had seen its U.S. sales increase from 100,000 cases in the late 1990s to 1.4 million cases in 2003. Because the market attractiveness of this segment was clearly improving, Absolut saw a good opportunity for growth. It introduced Level in the super-premium segment to compete with Grey Goose, Belvedere, and Ketel One. The company also positioned Danzka with unique packaging (in a metal container for faster chilling, shaped like a cocktail shaker) in the traditional segment at a suggested price of $13 to $14 per bottle.

Offensive Strategy ID: Expand Market Demand

Because at any point in time the number of customers in any given market is finite, strategies to enlarge a business's customer base include a focus on winning over competitors' customers, but they can also focus on growing market demand by drawing new customers into the market. For example, the market demand for flat-panel TVs was 20 million in 2004. Although Sony and Samsung battle each other for market share, their common offensive strategy is to grow market demand. The worldwide market demand for flat-panel TVs increased from 30 million in 2005 to 217 million in 2011. Clearly the world-wide market is exploding. This type of offensive growth strategy is likely to benefit both companies in the years ahead.

In Chapter 3, we learned to calculate the market development index (MDI). It is sim-ply the ratio of current market demand to maximum market demand (the maximum number of customers possible for a particular geographic market scope). For example, the worldwide MDI for the flat-panel TV is estimated at 62.

$$
\begin{aligned}
\text{Market Development Index} &= \frac{\text{Market Demand for Flat-Panel TVs (2011)}}{\text{Market Potential for Flat-Panel TVs}} \times 100 \\
&= \frac{217 \text{ million (2011)}}{350 \text{ million (worldwide)}} \times 100 \\
&= \mathbf{62}
\end{aligned}
$$

The MDI of 62 indicates that the market has many potential customers who for various reasons have not entered it. As shown in Figure 12-7, five basic forces need to be addressed for the market to reach its full potential. A strategic market plan to grow either the entire market or a specific segment would carefully consider each of these forces.

FIGURE 12-7 GROWING THE MARKET DEMAND FOR FLAT-PANEL TELEVISIONS

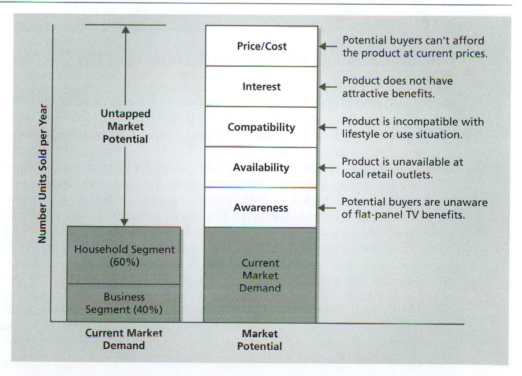

Of these five forces that limit market demand, the three most restrictive are price, availability, and compatibility. Until prices decrease dramatically, many potential customers will not be able to enter the market.

Availability may be addressed by investing in wider distribution networks, recognizing that a flat-panel TV manufacturer may find it economically infeasible to serve customers in some parts of the world. Unless availability is improved, many potential customers will remain outside the market even if prices are lowered.

For the flat-panel TV market, compatibility at first glance does not seem to be a problem. But living environments in many parts of the world are too small for easy viewing of a flat-panel TV. Limited electrical service in some areas also limits product application (compatibility) and slows market development.

Finally, awareness and attraction to benefits best occur from actually seeing a flat-panel TV in operation, but in many worldwide markets, opportunities to view flat-panel TVs are limited by high prices or unavailability. The market for the product will move toward its full potential only when the forces that limit market development diminish.

OFFENSIVE CORE STRATEGY II: IMPROVE COMPETITIVE POSITION

In situations where a business is in an attractive market but has a weak or average competitive position, an investment to improve competitive position may be the best strategy to pursue. The better a business's competitive position, the better its chances of achieving price premiums and a high level of customer retention, which in turn will improve the business's margins and net marketing contribution. This section discusses the four offensive strategies for improving competitive position, as shown in Figure 12-4.

Offensive Strategy IIA: Improve Customer Loyalty and Retention

Businesses spend money to attract new customers in growing markets, but if they do not retain these customers, they will experience higher marketing and sales expenses and lower marketing profits. As we saw in Chapter 1, it costs much more to acquire a new customer than to keep a current one—from 5 to 10 times more. Further, a 2 percent increase in loyal customers has been shown to lower marketing costs by 10 percent. An offensive strategy to increase customer retention and customer loyalty will have an immediate impact on marketing profits (net marketing contribution).

For example, in Figure 12-8 AT&T had an 89.2 percent customer retention rate for a recent year. The company had 65.7 million customers, so this means that AT&T lost 7.1 million customers that year. To hold its customer base at 65.7 million, AT&T had to acquire 7.1 million new customers. Not only is this effort 5 to 10 times more expensive with respect to marketing and sales expenses, but new customers often use less service, resulting in a lower average monthly margin per customer. If AT&T could improve its customer retention rate from 89.2 to 94.2 percent, the company would increase the lifetime value of its customers by 25 percent. For any business, retaining a higher percentage of customers and improving their loyalty is an offensive strategic investment that not only affects short-term profits but also greatly enhances long-run performance.

FIGURE 12-8 CELLULAR PHONE SERVICE CUSTOMER RETENTION

Major Cellular Phone Service Providers (2007)	Customers (millions)	Customer Retention (%)	Lost Customers (millions)
AT&T (AT&T Mobility Ltd.)	65.7	89.2	7.1
Verizon Wireless	61.1	92.8	4.4
Sprint Nextel	53.7	89.2	5.8
T-Mobile USA	28.2	86.8	3.7

Offensive Strategy IIB: Improve Differentiation Advantage

One of the major customer complaints in the wireless communications market is reliability. To address this problem and turn it into a differentiation advantage, Verizon Wireless created a team of 50 "road warriors" who each drove 100,000 miles annually (a total of 5 million miles) in specially equipped cars to test the reliability of Verizon's network against several competitors' phones. An onboard computer system in each car made synchronized inbound and outbound calls that lasted 2.5 minutes each to the home office, with 15 seconds between calls. In addition to connection quality, Verizon checked sound quality by playing recordings of 20 phrases representing all sounds in the English language. Verizon's computer system logged each call and used a global positioning system to note the precise locations where problems occurred. Gridlock produced the most severe test and was the best indicator of how well the system was working. Verizon's efforts to improve reliability resulted in an increase in customer retention from 90 to 92.8 percent over a 3-year period.

To enhance the differentiation advantage achieved through the actual improvement in reliability, Verizon launched an advertising campaign using its "road warrior" testing process as the theme. The often-repeated question in the ads, "Can you hear me *now*?" became a signature line for the company, familiar to almost everyone. The ads' refrain emphasized the importance that customers place on reliability when they choose a phone service. Verizon depends heavily on its source of differentiation because the company is not a low-cost service provider.

Offensive Strategy IIC: Lower Cost/Improve Marketing Productivity

Sony found that its profit margins were shrinking in consumer electronics because prices were eroding faster than manufacturing costs could be lowered. Even though the company was selling higher volumes, gross profits were in decline as margins dropped. To address this problem and restore margins to more acceptable levels, Sony examined its cost structure closely and identified several areas where costs could be cut. To promote standardization, the company pared the number of components used in Sony consumer electronics from 840,000 to just 100,000. To further reduce the cost of materials, it slashed the number of suppliers from 4,700 to just 1,000. Sony also moved more production from Japan to China, where labor costs are much lower, and added more technology to its manufacturing processes. By lowering its costs, Sony improved its profitability and remained a leader in a highly competitive market.

As another example, a 3M business found that many of its distributors who made below-average purchases were frequently late in paying. These distributors were moved to an online purchasing system where they had to provide a credit card number to initiate a purchase. The new procedure left the slow-paying distributors a bit dissatisfied, but the 3M business informed them that they could improve their buying status with on-time payments. In the end, few distributors were lost, and the 3M business greatly reduced its marketing and sales expenses and improved its cash flow. Both of these factors contributed to a higher net marketing contribution and a higher marketing productivity (net marketing contribution per dollar of marketing expense).

Offensive Strategy IID: Build Marketing Advantage

Nautilus was a pioneer brand in the $5 billion home fitness equipment market. The company's direct marketing approach was successful, but Nautilus had not responded to market trends that included more emphasis on cardiovascular equipment and a shift toward in-store purchases. Although Nautilus could retool to produce new products, it was much harder to shift from direct marketing channels, including the company's heavy reliance on infomercials, to selling through retail stores. But because 80 percent of the $5 billion in sales in this market occurred in retail stores, this change was essential. To close this gap and build a marketing advantage, Nautilus not only began selling through specialty sports equipment retailers, but also developed partnerships with Amazon.com, Costco, and Sports Authority. These indirect channel partnerships improved Nautilus's competitive position by giving the company a marketing advantage over its competitors.

OFFENSIVE CORE STRATEGY III: ENTER NEW MARKETS

At some point, every business will need to examine growth opportunities outside its existing markets.[10] Any of three fundamental reasons could lead a business to enter a new market: (1) a limited number of attractive market opportunities within existing markets; (2) attractive opportunities, in terms of meeting the business's overall performance objectives, outside existing markets; and (3) a desire to diversify sources of profitability to reduce variation in performance.[11]

The four basic offensive strategic market plans for entering new markets, as in Figure 12-4, are (IIIA) entry into established related markets, (IIIB) entry into established markets that are unrelated to markets served by the business, (IIIC) entry into new emerging markets, and (IIID) entry into markets with considerable undeveloped market potential. Entry into established markets (related or unrelated) means competing with established competitors for existing market demand, and entry into emerging markets requires significant investment to develop market demand, but often in the absence of strong competition.

Offensive Strategy IIIA: Enter Related New Markets

Not content to rest on its laurels with a 50 percent market share of the worldwide carbonated soft drink market, Coca-Cola has entered the $5 billion energy drinks market, illustrated in Figure 12-9. This is a related new market entry strategy that allows Coca-Cola to develop new sources of sales growth by leveraging its core competencies and competitive advantages.

FIGURE 12-9 NEW MARKET ENTRY OPPORTUNITIES FOR COCA-COLA

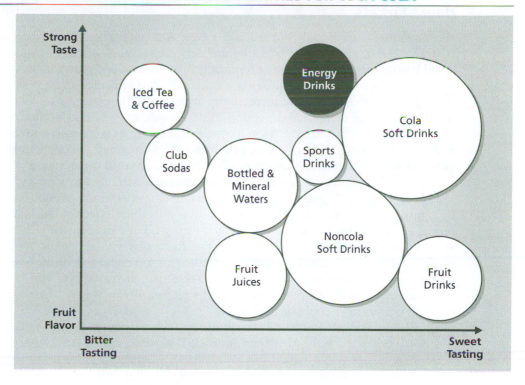

K2 historically was best known as a ski manufacturer. Over a 10-year period beginning in the mid 1980s, K2 steadily increased its share of the American ski market until in the mid 1990s it became the share leader. But the American ski market was by then mature, and opportunities to grow sales by growing the market or increasing market share were limited. This situation led K2 to adopt a related new market entry strategy for the snowboard and inline skate markets. K2 planned to achieve significant sales revenue growth during the subsequent 10 years as a result of this strategy, and in fact the company grew sales dramatically to $1.4 billion by the mid 2000s. The strategy also enabled K2 to leverage its brand awareness, reputation for quality, manufacturing and design expertise, and, in some instances, its marketing channel and sales systems. These factors resulted in a variety of cost and marketing efficiencies, and K2 achieved an impressive gross profit margin of 35.4 percent. In mid 2000s K2's sales were derived from marine and outdoor products (29.2%), action sports (30.2%), team sports (27.5%), and apparel and footwear (13.1%).

Sometimes a business discovers that entry into a new market is blocked by the cost of entry, technology requirements, or a lack of market access. To overcome the barriers to entry, a business can join forces with two or more partner companies that have complementary market expertise and leverage. By blending the strengths of businesses from related markets, the new entities are better equipped to develop and market products that more completely serve and fulfill customer needs. In the telecommunications industry, barriers to new market entry led to many mergers, joint ventures, and strategic alliances among telecommunications, computer, and cable TV companies.

Offensive Strategy IIIB: Enter Unrelated New Markets

Westinghouse acquired CBS in the mid-1990s. A week earlier, Disney had acquired ABC. The Disney acquisition was a *related* new market entry strategy in which Disney could leverage its name, reputation for quality, and creative and production expertise. In contrast, the Westinghouse acquisition was an *unrelated* new market entry strategy that moved Westinghouse into the increasingly attractive communications market. Disney was leveraging its strength in the communications industry, whereas Westinghouse was redefining itself by acquiring CBS in the hope of adapting its competitive advantage to a new, highly inviting market. The two businesses had one thing in common: Both were pursuing new sources of market share, sales growth, and profit performance.

One of the primary advantages of an unrelated new market entry strategy is reduced market dependency. Because most markets go through periods of expansion and contraction, investments in unrelated businesses have a smoothing effect on the revenues and profits of the combined portfolio of product-markets. For example, the residential construction market is a slow-growth market that fluctuates with economic conditions. A manufacturer of earth-moving equipment for this market could reduce the magnitude of swings in performance by entering the mining or agriculture markets or any other market that is unrelated to the residential construction market. In this way, variations in overall business performance could be minimized.

An additional advantage of market diversification is reduced vulnerability. If a business derives the bulk of its performance from one type of market, a permanent downward change in that market would threaten the company's performance and, potentially, its survival. In the mid 1970s, the National Cash Register Corporation (NCR) was focused primarily on the cash register market and had over 80 percent of this market. When competitors entered with a new cash register technology, NCR's market share declined rapidly. In less than 6 years, its share shrank to less than 25 percent, and the company's survival was at stake. A business, then, might pursue an unrelated new market entry strategy for three reasons:

1. **New Source of Growth:** New market diversification offers the potential to add to the business's sales growth and profit performance.
2. **Smoother Performance:** New market diversification offers product diversification, which can reduce the magnitude of swings in sales and profit performance.
3. **Reduced Vulnerability:** New market diversification reduces market dependence and vulnerability, which helps protect the business's performance and, in some instances, its survival.

Although these are important benefits, many businesses have failed to perform effectively in diversified markets and have retreated to their core markets. Mobil's acquisition of Montgomery Ward, Coca-Cola's acquisition of Columbia Pictures, and General Motors' acquisition of Data Information Services were all results of unsuccessful diversified new market entry strategies. The new market ventures were too far removed from the marketing and business expertise of the acquiring company. On the other hand, Phillip Morris's acquisition of the Miller Brewing Company, PepsiCo's merger with Quaker Oats, and Motorola's move into wireless communication products provided the advantages we have listed. These companies, in their new markets, successfully leveraged their marketing and business expertise.

Offensive Strategy IIIC: Enter New Emerging Markets

A business also can grow by entering new emerging markets where the number of current customers is small but market potential is great. Although it is considerably riskier with respect to profit performance, this strategy can enable a business to establish an early leadership position in the market. From this position, a business can influence product positioning and market growth.

High-technology markets have rapidly emerging market demand and relatively short product and market life cycles. Businesses in these markets need to move quickly to capitalize on emerging new market opportunities or they will completely miss this opportunity for growth.[12] A pioneer in these emerging new markets has the potential to achieve a competitive advantage if it can sustain its advantage in these early stages of market development.[13] When pioneers can establish a *dominant design*, they set a standard that other businesses entering the market must follow in order to compete.[14] A good example of establishing a dominant design was the way VHS prevailed over Beta as the design standard in the early evolution of the VCR market.

As an emerging market begins to grow, *early followers* enter the market. Early followers let the pioneer invest in developing the technology, establishing the design standard, and initiating market development. Then they emulate the dominant design and enter the market. Many Japanese companies use an early follower strategy. Comcast and EarthLink both entered the broadband Internet market as early followers. CompuServe, Prodigy, and America Online established dominant positions in the dial-up Internet service market, but as the technology developed and the broadband market emerged, Comcast and EarthLink entered the market, capitalizing on emerging new market demand for high-speed Internet access.

When many customers are attracted to the market, with customer use and experience quickly increasing, the market is in its rapid-growth phase. It is during this phase of market development, as customer needs become more salient and numerous, that segments begin to form. The rapid growth attracts more competitors, many of them focusing on niche markets of customers with unique needs.[15] This is a critical point for a market leader, which must respond by developing multi-segment solutions. If the market leader remains too narrowly focused, it will see its market share erode as new competitors deliver more attractive value propositions for specific segments. A market pioneer that can sustain its market leadership through this phase of a market's development is in the best position to achieve high levels of performance.[16]

Offensive Strategy IIID: Develop New Markets

Apple's initial entry into the personal computer market relied on a strategy that focused on the enormous untapped potential of the personal computer market. Apple's goal was to bring computing power to the masses and thereby grow this new market. The company's original positioning strategy for the Macintosh was: "Only a few have the expertise to operate computers. . . . Introducing Macintosh, for the rest of the world." In the beginning, Apple had few major competitors because it focused on a market that the established computer manufacturers had ignored. Only after Apple's early success revealed the potential of this new market did competitors begin to enter it.

The populations of China, India, and Africa make up over half the world's people, yet many of the products manufactured for the United States and Western Europe have not been formulated for these markets. Constraints due to price, use compatibility, and availability create a large, untapped new market potential for many products.

For example, products that operate with electricity have no market in rural areas of underdeveloped countries where no electrical service is available. General Electric, with its expertise in turbines for jet engines, adapted its technology to enable businesses in areas with no electrical power to produce their own electricity and sell their excess to local utilities. By enabling businesses to "co-generate" electricity on a small scale, GE has created markets for many of its electrical products in remote parts of the world.

A growth strategy to develop an untapped new market involves high risk but offers the potential for high return.[17] The cost of developing a market can be significant even if the product is a good customer solution. On the other hand, there are few if any competitors, so a business has the opportunity to pioneer a market that has so far been largely ignored. With a "first-mover" advantage, the business has the potential to own the market until other competitors venture entry. A notable example is a company called Under Armour, which was launched in 1995 with $40,000 by a college student who maxed out five credit cards developing the market for specialty undergarments for athletes. By 2002, Under Armour had sales of $50 million, and sales continued to increase by a remarkable 72 percent annually to $1.1 billion in 2010, despite market entry by Nike, Adidas, and other large sports apparel companies.

WHEN GROWTH STALLS

Maintaining sales growth is difficult. A comprehensive study of 500 major U.S. and global companies found that, at some point, 87 percent of them over a 50-year period experienced a stall in their sales.[18] Figure 12-10 illustrates the average sales growth before and after the sales stall for these 435 companies. As shown, average sales growth prior to the stall year was somewhat lower than the average for the stall year. The average growth rates for the 15 years following the sales stall were very modest, nothing close to average sales growth for the years prior to the stall year. In the words of the study's authors: "After a burst of energy, growth does not descend gradually; it drops like a stone."

We might assume that companies with a record of strong sales growth could recover after a sales stall and within a few years could once again attain the same levels of sales growth that preceded the stall, but this does not appear to be the case. Let's take a closer look at what happens to companies that experience a stall in sales growth.

Of the 87 percent of the companies that experienced stalled sales, 46 percent were able to rebound fairly quickly with moderate or high growth, but 54 percent continued to see slow or negative growth for several years following the stall. As Figure 12-11 shows, of the 54 percent of companies that continued to experience slow or negative growth, only 7 percent eventually recovered to achieve moderate or high growth, and 26 percent

FIGURE 12-10 WHAT HAPPENS WHEN GROWTH STALLS

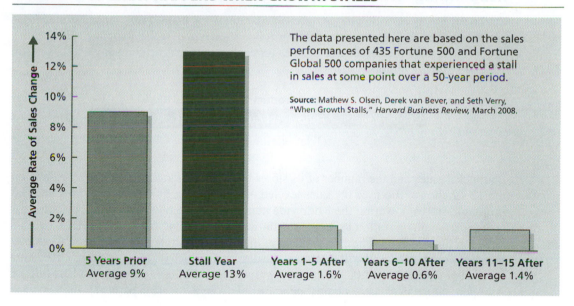

The data presented here are based on the sales performances of 435 Fortune 500 and Fortune Global 500 companies that experienced a stall in sales at some point over a 50-year period.

Source: Mathew S. Olsen, Derek van Bever, and Seth Verry, "When Growth Stalls," *Harvard Business Review*, March 2008.

continued to experience slow or negative growth. The most startling finding of the study was that two-thirds of the companies that experienced a stall ended up being acquired by other companies, filing for bankruptcy, or becoming privately held. The message is clear: Companies that encounter stalled growth—and sooner or later, most do—must immediately develop and implement a strategy to deal with it.

FIGURE 12-11 SALES GROWTH AFTER A SALES STALL

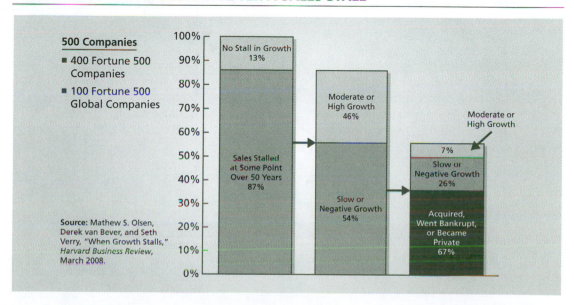

Source: Mathew S. Olsen, Derek van Bever, and Seth Verry, "When Growth Stalls," *Harvard Business Review*, March 2008.

Rebounding with an Offensive Growth Strategy

Starbucks has been following an offensive strategy for many years, opening numerous new stores and adding products to its portfolio. Shown here is the company's 2010 product portfolio with the percentage of sales for each category. The company's total sales in 2010 were $10.7 billion.

Starbucks' Product Portfolio – 2010

Beverages	Food	Equipment	Coffee Beans
75%	19%	4%	2%

Starbucks' sales and the number of its stores have grown quickly over the years, as Figure 12-12 shows. But in 2008, sales leveled off, prompting Starbucks to close some less profitable stores, lowering the worldwide number from 16,690 to 16,635. The company was experiencing a stall in its sales growth, with sales falling from $10.4 billion in 2008 to $9.8 billion in 2009. The effectiveness of the offensive strategies that Starbucks implements to counter the stall will determine the degree to which it can recover. In 2010, store locations increased to 17,009 and profits grew to $1.42 billion on sales of $10.7 billion. As a percentage of sales, operating income grew from 5.7 to 13.3 percent.

FIGURE 12-12 STARBUCKS' SALES GROWTH AND NUMBER OF LOCATIONS

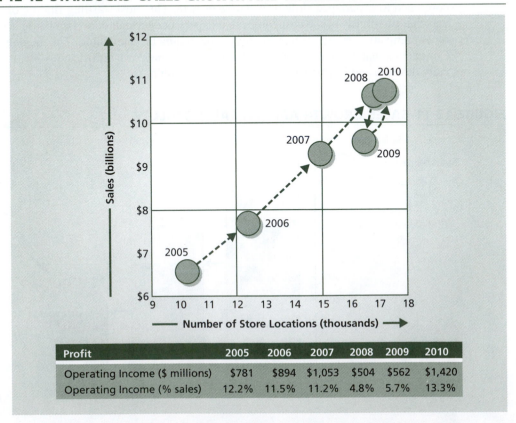

Profit	2005	2006	2007	2008	2009	2010
Operating Income ($ millions)	$781	$894	$1,053	$504	$562	$1,420
Operating Income (% sales)	12.2%	11.5%	11.2%	4.8%	5.7%	13.3%

By late 2010 Starbucks saw that continued growth by adding new stores was becoming more difficult. In early 2011 the company adjusted its offensive strategy and changed its logo.[19] The new logo eliminates the word "coffee" and the Starbucks name from the design, a good indication that Starbucks has developed an offensive strategy to enter new markets—such as noncoffee drinks, fragrances, and apparel—while keeping its three brands of coffee (Starbucks, 15th Avenue, and Seattle's Best).[20] Assuming that this is Starbucks' strategy, its primary objective would be to ensure that the company rebounds from the stalled sales growth it experienced in 2009.

CHOOSING OFFENSIVE STRATEGIC MARKET PLANS

Businesses, especially highly ambitious and aggressive businesses, often pursue multiple offensive strategies. Starbucks' objective has long been to become the world's most recognized and respected brand. To accomplish this, over the years the company has implemented a wide variety of offensive strategic market plans.

A market-based business often has more market opportunities than it has resources to fund. In such cases, the business has to prioritize strategic market opportunities on the basis of its performance objectives. A business with a short-run need for better profit performance would be inclined to select the market penetration strategy shown in Figure 12-13 rather than choosing a long-run market development strategy. The market penetration strategy in this example is expected to produce $14 million in net marketing contribution in 5 years. It offers immediate profit performance and a reasonable level of sales revenue and profit growth.

FIGURE 12-13 ALTERNATIVE OFFENSIVE STRATEGIC MARKET PLANS

Area of Performance	Market Penetration Strategy		Market Development Strategy	
	Base Year	In 5 Years	Base Year	In 5 Years
Market Demand	600,000	600,000	20,000	200,000
Market Share	15%	20%	80%	50%
Market Growth Rate	3%	3%	58%	58%
Target Volume	90,000	120,000	16,000	100,000
Revenue per Customer	$450	$450	$950	$450
Total Revenue (millions)	$40.5	$54.0	$15.2	$45.0
Variable Cost per Customer	$250	$250	$650	$200
Total Variable Cost (millions)	$22.5	$30.0	$10.4	$20.0
Margin per Customer	$200	$200	$300	$250
Gross Profit (millions)	$18.0	$24.0	$4.8	$25.0
Market & Sales Expenses (millions)	$7.0	$10.0	$6.0	$12.0
Net Marketing Contribution (millions)	$11.0	$14.0	−$1.2	$13.0

On the other hand, a business with a good cash position that is facing stagnant growth in maturing markets might pursue the market development strategy shown in Figure 12-13. This offensive strategy would produce a $1.2 million negative net marketing contribution in the first year. However, in 5 years, the strategy would be expected to produce $13 million in net marketing contribution. Although it is riskier, this new market development strategy could provide the business with needed growth and diversification into an attractive market. The selection of one offensive strategic market plan over another depends on the business's short-run profit needs, strategic position and resources, and opportunities for growth.

■ Summary

Businesses have a short-term obligation to investors to meet growth and performance expectations. At the same time, businesses have an obligation to investors, as well as employees, to carve out a set of marketing strategies that will improve the position of the business in the long run. The purpose of strategic market planning is to examine the attractiveness and competitive advantage of each market that is served by a business. On the basis of an assessment of its position, a business develops a strategic market objective and allocates resources accordingly. To accomplish its performance objective, a business generally needs to use a combination of offensive and defensive strategic market plans.

Offensive strategies are more growth oriented and are generally most effective during the growth phase of the product life cycle, whereas defensive strategies are more likely to be used in maturing, mature, and declining markets. Offensive strategies include three core strategies: sales growth, margin improvement, and diversified growth. A company implements these core offensive strategies by using one or more of four specific strategies.

Offensive strategies for pursuing sales growth are focused on existing markets. Sales growth offensive strategies include (IA) increasing market share, (IB) growing customer purchases, (IC) expanding into new-market segments, and (ID) expanding market demand by growing market potential.

Offensive strategies to improve competitive position and ultimately margin are focused on existing markets and strategies that can improve profit margins. They include (IIA) increasing customer loyalty, (IIB) improving a differentiation advantage, (IIC) lowering costs and improving marketing productivity, and (IID) building a stronger marketing advantage.

Offensive strategies with the goal of diversified growth are focused on new markets and strategies that can achieve sales growth outside the current market domain. They include (IIIA) entering new related markets, (IIIB) entering new unrelated markets, (IIIC) entering new emerging markets, and (IIID) developing new markets. A company chooses a good mix of offensive strategic marketing plans by considering the expected impact of each strategy on short-term or long-run growth in revenues and profitability.

A major challenge to any company's offensive strategies is "stalled sales growth." Most companies, even ones that have experienced good sales growth for years, eventually hit an abrupt wall. Sales growth just stops. Although some companies do regain a moderate to high level of sales growth, the majority lingers with low or negative sales growth. Many of these companies are acquired, go bankrupt, or become privately held.

■ Market-Based Strategic Thinking

1 What would Apple's sales and margins have looked like in 2010 if it had the same product portfolio then as it had in 2000?

2 How does the Apple product life cycle portfolio add to the strategic insight into Apple's current and future sales and profit performance?

3 Explain why a business like Ford might shift from an offensive strategy to a defensive strategy over the life cycle of a particular product.

4 How can a business like Campbell's Soup meet short-run growth and profit performance targets and still invest in strategic market plans that are focused on long-run objectives with respect to share position, sales growth, and profit performance?

5 How has Harley-Davidson's offensive strategy to grow revenue per customer affected its sales and profits?

6 How would a Nike offensive strategy to increase market penetration differ from a strategy to grow customer purchases (revenue per customer) in the under-18 female athlete market?

7 Why would Google use an offensive sales growth strategy to expand the Internet search engine market rather than attempting to increase its share of this market?

8 How did Apple's offensive growth strategies affect its percent profit margins?

9 Why would AT&T's efforts to improve customer retention be considered an offensive strategy to improve margins?

10 Absolut Vodka entered two new market segments as part of an offensive strategy to grow sales. Explain the logic of this offensive strategy and why the company elected to create new brand names for each segment shown in Figure 12-6.

11 Microsoft has developed a product called Meeting Pro to help facilitate the running of small business meetings. Although this is a value-added software product, Microsoft offers it at no cost to Windows users. Explain why this is an offensive strategy to grow market share.

12 Why are offensive strategies for General Motors crucial for the long-run success of that company? What kind of offensive strategies could GM use to ensure future growth in sales and profits?

13 Microsoft has embarked on a joint venture with Sony to develop an online alternative to the telephone. What type of offensive marketing strategy best describes this joint venture, and what are the expected short- and long-run performance objectives?

14 How does a market penetration strategy to grow market share differ from a strategy to enter a new segment in the same market for Mac computers?

15 Why would a Starbucks marketing strategy to grow customer purchases (revenue per customer) be potentially more profitable than many other offensive marketing strategies?

16 Why would a business like Marriott first pursue offensive marketing strategies to increase market share or grow revenue per customer, rather than adopting other offensive marketing strategies?

17 What forces limit new-customer growth within the existing market for personal computers? How could a company like Intel grow market demand by addressing these forces?

18 What important considerations should Starbucks evaluate between a related new market entry strategy and an unrelated new market entry strategy?

19 When would a business like Dell pursue an unrelated new market entry strategy?

20 What is the advantage to Apple in growing market demand for a new emerging product-market such as the iPad?

Marketing Performance Tools and Application Exercises

The three interactive marketing performance tools and application exercises outlined here will improve your ability to evaluate the four specific market strategies for each of the three offensive core strategies. To access the tools, go to **rogerjbest.com.** Each of these marketing performance tools is based on Figure 12-4.

12.1 Offensive Strategies—Core Strategy I: Grow in Existing Markets

■ Using the data provided, evaluate the four offensive strategies for growing sales in existing markets.

12.2 Offensive Strategies—Core Strategy II: Improve Margins

■ Using the data provided, evaluate the four offensive strategies for improving margins for sales in existing markets.

12.3 Offensive Strategies—Core Strategy III: Diversify Growth

■ Using the data provided, evaluate the four offensive strategies for growing sales with diversified growth.

Notes

1. D. Aaker, "Portfolio Analysis," *Strategic Market Management* (New York: Wiley, 1995): 155–69.
2. B. Catry and M. Chevalier, "Market Share Strategy and the Product Life Cycle," *Journal of Marketing* (October 1974): 29–34.
3. P. Haspeslagh, "Portfolio Planning: Uses and Limits," *Harvard Business Review* (January–February 1982): 58–73; and S. Robinson, R. Hichens, and D. Wade, "The Directional Policy Matrix Tool for Strategic Planning," *Long-Range Planning* (June 1978): 8–15.
4. D. Aaker, "Growth Strategies," *Strategic Market Management* (New York: Wiley, 1995): 238–59.
5. D. Bogler, "Coca-Cola Goes to War for 'Share of Stomach,'" *Financial Times* (July 5, 1998).
6. C. Lillis, J. Cook, R. Best, and D. Hawkins, "Marketing Strategies to Achieve Market Share Goals," *Strategic Marketing Management*, H. Thomas and D. Gardner, eds. (New York: Wiley, 1985).
7. D. Szymanski, S. Bharadwaj, and R. Varadarajan, "An Analysis of the Market Share-Profitability Relationship," *Journal of Marketing* (July 1993): 1–18; and C.D. Fogg, "Planning Gains in Market Share," *Journal of Marketing* (July 1994): 30–8.
8. D. Sheinen and B. Schmitt, "Extending Brands with New Product Concepts: The Role of Category

Attribute Congruity, Brand Affect and Brand Breadth," *Journal of Business Research* (September 1994): 1–10.
9. G. Hamel and C.K. Prahalad, "Seeing the Future First," *Fortune* (September 5, 1994): 64–70.
10. E. Roberts and C. Berry, "Entering New Business: Selecting Strategies for Success," *Sloan Management Review* (Spring 1985): 3–17.
11. R. Rumelt, "Diversification, Strategy and Profitability," *Strategic Management Journal* 3 (1982): 359–69.
12. G. Stalk, Jr., "Time: The Next Source of Competitive Advantage," *Harvard Business Review* (July–August 1988): 41–51; and T. Robertson, "How to Reduce Market Penetration Cycle Times," *Sloan Management Review* (Fall 1993): 87–96.
12. W. Robinson and C. Fornell, "Sources of Market Pioneer Advantage in Consumer Goods Industries," *Journal of Marketing Research* (August 1985): 305–17; and W. Robinson, "Sources of Market Pioneer Advantages: The Case for Industrial Goods Industries," *Journal of Marketing Research* 25 (1988): 87–94.
14. R. Best and R. Angelmar, "Strategies for Leveraging Technology Advantage," in *Handbook on Business Strategy* (New York: Warren, Gorham and Lamont, 1989): 2.1–2.10.
15. V. Mahajan, S. Sharma, and R. Buzzell, "Assessing the Impact of Competitive Entry on Market Expansion

and Incumbent Sales," *Journal of Marketing* (July 1993): 39–52.

16. G. Urban, T. Carter, S. Gaskin, and Z. Mucha, "Marketing Share Rewards to Pioneering Brands: An Empirical Analysis and Strategic Implications," *Management Science* 32 (1986): 635–59.

17. I. Ayal and J. Zif, "Market Expansion Strategies in Multinational Markets," *Journal of Marketing* (Spring 1979): 84–94.

18. M.S. Olsen, D. van Bever, and S. Verry, "When Growth Stalls," *Harvard Business Review* (March 2008): 51–61.

19. O. Blanchard, "Starbucks: Managing a Brand Expansion, Part 2," The Brand Builder (January 10, 2011): http://thebrandbuilder.wordpress.com/2011/01/10/starbucks-managing-a-brands-expansion-part-2/, retrieved January 11, 2011.

20. Blanchard, *ibid.*

Defensive Strategies

■ The goal of defensive strategies is profit
maximization, not sales or market share growth.

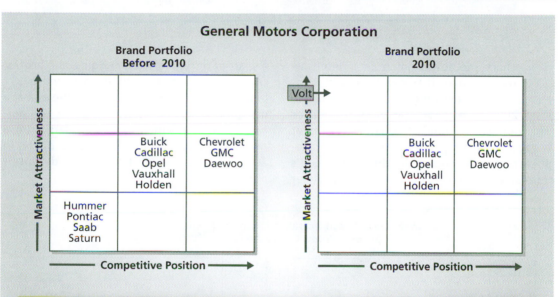

Performance (billions)	2006	2007	2008	2009	2010	Change
Sales Revenues	$207.4	$181.1	$149.0	$104.6	$135.6	Up
Percent Margin	26.4%	12.0%	5.63%	7.04%	12.40%	Up
Sales, Gen., & Admin. Exp.	$33.4	$16.5	$14.3	$12.2	$11.4	Down
Marketing & Sales Exp.*	12.1%	6.8%	7.2%	8.7%	6.3%	Down
Operating Income	$9.3	−$0.4	−$15.9	−$21.0	$7.5	Up
Return on Sales	4.5%	−0.2%	−10.7%	−20.1%	5.5%	Up
Marketing ROI	118%	75%	−22%	−20%	97%	Up

*As a percentage of sales, using 75% of SGA expenses to estimate marketing and sales expenses.

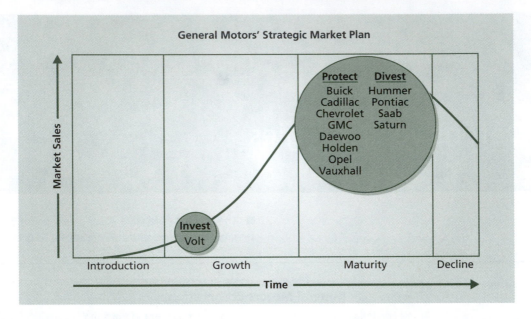

General Motors' Strategic Market Plan

Protect	Divest
Buick	Hummer
Cadillac	Pontiac
Chevrolet	Saab
GMC	Saturn
Daewoo	
Holden	
Opel	
Vauxhall	

Invest
Volt

Introduction   Growth   Maturity   Decline

Market Sales

Time

Perhaps the best example of a defensive strategic plan is General Motors' complete restructuring of its brand portfolio in 2009. That year, GM discontinued or sold four major brands that could not meet its requirements for profitability and strategic growth. As shown in the table, GM's defensive strategy paid off in 2010. After 4 years of declining sales, margins, and profits, GM's performance in 2010 produced a $31 billion gain in sales and increased the average margin from 7.04 percent in 2009 to 12.4 percent. Operating income rebounded from a negative $21 billion in 2009 to $7.5 billion in 2010. GM's defensive strategy was definitely a success.

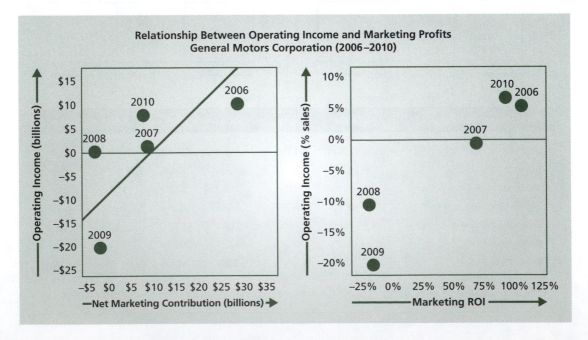

**Relationship Between Operating Income and Marketing Profits
General Motors Corporation (2006–2010)**

GM's strategic market plan also includes the introduction of the Volt. The car is an innovative product for an attractive emerging market, the demand for electric cars, and is expected to add to GM's much-needed growth. The retained brands serve mature markets with relatively slow growth, as shown on the life-cycle curve. By divesting its unprofitable products, GM is in a better position to protect its core brands and invest in the Volt. GM will manage the retained brands for full profit potential while underwriting the Volt to improve overall market share and acquire a significant share of the electric car segment.

DEFENSIVE STRATEGIC MARKET PLANS

Historical share leaders like GM, AT&T, and Kodak have been under attack in their core markets for some time. For each company, a loss of just one share point is considerable in terms of sales revenues, net profit, and cash flow. Relatively new share leaders like Intel, Google and Microsoft face the same challenge. These businesses, like other market share defenders, are engaged in a battle to protect their share positions in the markets they serve.[1]

Businesses in less attractive markets or those with fewer resources are often forced to reduce share to find a more profitable combination of market share and profitability. Others are forced to exit markets slowly with a harvest strategy or quickly with a divest strategy. All defensive strategies are intended to maximize or protect short-run profits or to minimize short-run losses.

A key part of Intel's long-run performance has been its ability to successfully implement a protect-share strategy in the microprocessor market. Any degree of share erosion would lower Intel's unit volume, sales revenues, and net marketing contribution. However, a defensive strategy to protect share is not the same as a hold-resources-constant strategy. To protect share in a market that is growing at 15 to 20 percent a year, Intel will have to continue its rollout of new products and add to its marketing budget. Not doing either would almost guarantee erosion of the company's share position in the microprocessor market.

In general, businesses in high-share positions that are in growing or mature markets use defensive strategic market plans to maintain a level of cash flow that supports short-run profit performance and shareholder value. Without these defensive strategic market plans, the businesses would face a difficult short-run situation in terms of profit performance and would lack the resources to invest in growth-oriented offensive market opportunities.

For example, consider the business situation presented in Figure 13-1. The business serves four markets, one of which is losing money. The first one (M1) is a maturing market in which the business holds a high-share position. The business's strategic market plan for this market is to protect the high-share position. The second (M2) is a slow-growth market in which this business's strategic market plan is to grow share. The third (M3) is a high-growth market in which the business's strategic market plan is to protect its share position. The fourth (M4) is losing money and has been determined to be unattractive. The strategic market plan for this market is to harvest share and maximize short-run profits as the business systematically exits the market. The business also has a fifth strategic market plan: to enter an attractive emerging market (M5) in which the business will lose money initially but which will be a good source of future growth and long-run cash flow.

Using these five market-based management strategies, this business hopes to grow revenue and profits through a series of strategic moves to protect, grow, or harvest market share.[2] Each strategic market plan plays an important role in the business's short- and long-run sales and profitability. For two of these markets (M1 and M3), the company

FIGURE 13-1 STRATEGIC MARKET PLANNING AND PERFORMANCE

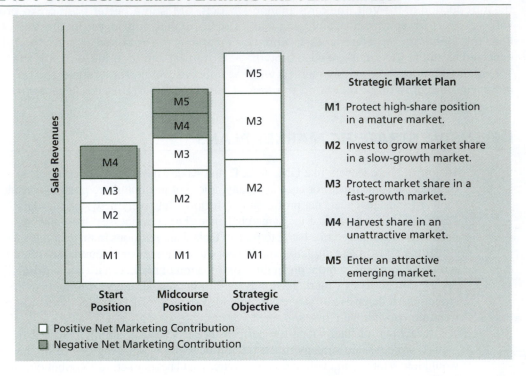

Strategic Market Plan

M1 Protect high-share position in a mature market.

M2 Invest to grow market share in a slow-growth market.

M3 Protect market share in a fast-growth market.

M4 Harvest share in an unattractive market.

M5 Enter an attractive emerging market.

needs to use defensive strategic market plans to protect its share position in different ways. One other market (M4) calls for a defensive strategy to harvest its market share to improve short-run profits and exit the market in the long-run.

The primary goal of a defensive strategy is to protect profitability and key strategic share positions that are worth the investment. A secondary goal of a defensive market strategy is to manage the profitability of businesses that are moving beyond their potential for reasonable sales growth or profitability. With these goals in mind, Figure 13-2 outlines defensive strategic market plans that may be appropriate in different situations.

As shown in Figure 13-3, on the basis of market attractiveness and competitive advantage, certain portfolio positions can lead to more than one defensive strategy. For example, a business with a strong competitive advantage in a fairly attractive market may choose to protect its share position, or it may choose to maximize profits by optimizing or monetizing it. In all cases, defensive strategies are focused on maximizing short-run profits and protecting or improving long-term profits and the strategic position of a business.

DEFENSIVE CORE STRATEGY I: PROTECT POSITION

In many competitive environments, whether in sports or business, the best defense is a good offense. Quite often businesses with a dominant share and a strong competitive position are lulled into the delusion that they are undefeatable, eventually awakening too late to the stark reality that they are about to be overtaken by more aggressive challengers.

FIGURE 13-2 STRATEGIC MARKET PLANS AND DEFENSIVE STRATEGIES

To hold a high-share position in an attractive, growing market, a business must continue investing in a determined effort to sustain its competitive position.

Defensive Strategy IA: Protect Market Share

Market share leaders in many industries have market shares in excess of 50 percent. However, the conditions under which they have to defend their share positions can be drastically different. Campbell's Soup, for example, has a 60 percent share of the mature

FIGURE 13-3 PORTFOLIO POSITIONS AND DEFENSIVE STRATEGIC MARKET PLANS

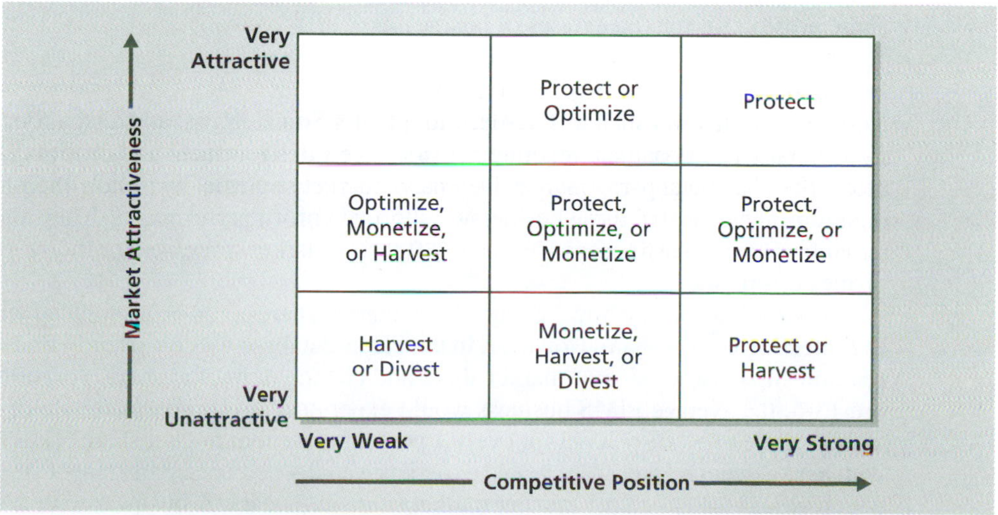

American soup market, Gillette has a 70 percent share of the mature razor and blade market, and Gatorade has a 75 percent share of the U.S. sports drink market. The defensive strategies of these companies are different from those of businesses with high shares in fast-growth markets. Google, with a 65.5 percent share of the fast-growing search engine market, and Microsoft, with a 95 percent share of the rapidly developing desktop operating-system market, must exert greater marketing efforts to protect their high-share positions as their markets continue to experience rapid growth. However, all the share leaders have the same fundamental objective: invest to protect market share. Depending on the nature of the market situation, a defensive strategy to protect market share might take different forms.

Investing to Protect Position in Growth Markets

Protecting a share leadership position in a growth market requires a much greater marketing effort and more investment in new products than would be required in a mature market. The faster a market is growing, the greater investment a company must make in marketing resources to protect share from new and existing competitors. If a business does not invest to protect share in a growth market, its market share is almost certain to decline. Because growing markets are inherently prone to inducing share loss, the resources needed to offset the effects of growth, using a defensive strategic market plan to protect share, must be much greater.

According to the Profit Impact of Marketing Strategies (PIMS) database, the average business will experience approximately a −0.4 percent annual rate of market share change per 1 percent of market growth rate. Thus, a business in a market that is growing at 10 percent annually would encounter a 4 percent rate of share erosion if the effects of market growth are not offset by a defensive strategic market plan. Using this average, a business with a 20 percent market share in a market that is growing 10 percent annually would have an estimated share loss of almost four points in 5 years if it did nothing to offset the negative impact of market growth. Of course, if the market were growing at 15 percent annually, the business would experience a much faster rate of share erosion, as shown in Figure 13-4.

The effects of market growth on market share change differ from industry to industry but are still fairly uniform. Figure 13-4 shows the impact of market growth on market share erosion for four categories of businesses.

Investing to Protect a High-Share Position

Market share leaders such as Clorox, Campbell's Soup, Apple, and Cisco Systems have strong share positions that generate considerable sales revenues and profits that directly affect their financial performance. Defensive market strategies to protect their high-share positions are critical to these businesses' short-run profit performance. They also provide a major source of cash for investment in offensive market strategies for future growth and profit performance.

It is hard to imagine how having a large market share could be a handicap with respect to protecting market share. However, in the PIMS database we consistently find an inverse relationship between size of market share and change in market share. As shown in Figure 13-5, the average PIMS business would experience an approximate rate of change in market share of −0.08 percent for every 1 percent of current market share. Thus a business with a 30 percent market share would experience a −2.4 percent annual rate of share change, which would lead to a 26.7 percent market share in 5 years. A business with a 10 percent

FIGURE 13-4 MARKET GROWTH RATE AND SHARE EROSION

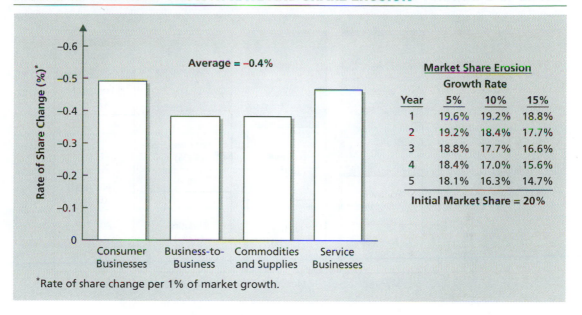

	Market Share Erosion		
	Growth Rate		
Year	5%	10%	15%
1	19.6%	19.2%	18.8%
2	19.2%	18.4%	17.7%
3	18.8%	17.7%	16.6%
4	18.4%	17.0%	15.6%
5	18.1%	16.3%	14.7%
Initial Market Share = 20%			

*Rate of share change per 1% of market growth.

market share would never really feel this effect, because the size of its market share is much smaller, and its share would erode only to an estimated 9.6 percent in 5 years.

High-share businesses, then, have to invest considerably more than do other businesses to protect share, independent of other share-eroding market forces, such as market growth, competitor entry, or competitor strategies. Understanding how the combination

FIGURE 13-5 MARKET SHARE EROSION AND CURRENT SHARE POSITION

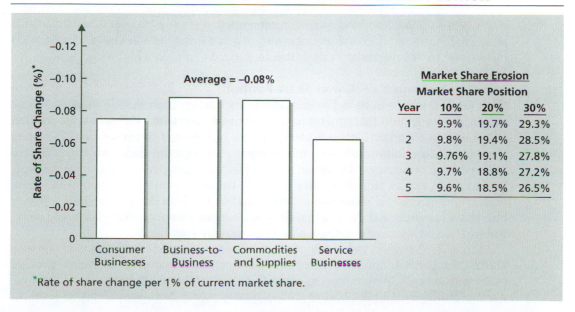

	Market Share Erosion		
	Market Share Position		
Year	10%	20%	30%
1	9.9%	19.7%	29.3%
2	9.8%	19.4%	28.5%
3	9.76%	19.1%	27.8%
4	9.7%	18.8%	27.2%
5	9.6%	18.5%	26.5%

*Rate of share change per 1% of current market share.

FIGURE 13-6 MARKET STRUCTURE AND SHARE POSITION

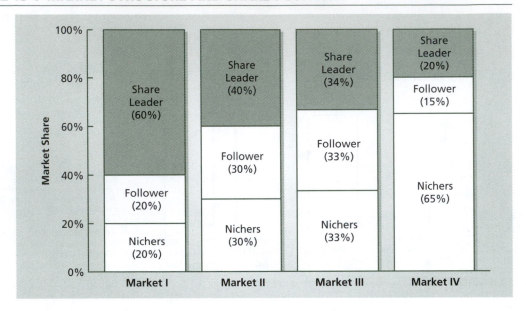

of a high-share position and a high market growth rate erodes market share helps us understand the losses in market share experienced by Eastman Kodak, IBM, AT&T, General Motors, and other high-share businesses. The impact of market share on the rate of market share change is fairly consistent among diverse areas of business in the PIMS database, as illustrated in Figure 13-5.

To successfully defend high-share positions, businesses need to continuously improve their competitive advantage and marketing effort. Share leaders that make temporary cuts in marketing to improve short-run profit only reduce their market share and hurt next year's profits. Share leaders must remain committed to (1) new product development, (2) efforts to improve product and service quality at a rate faster than the competition, and (3) full support for the marketing budgets that are needed to protect a high-share position.[3]

Investing to Protect a Follower Share Position

Not every business can be the share leader in its market. Illustrated in Figure 13-6 are four market structures. Each market has one follower, each with a different share position in its respective market. Let's consider the business in market II that is second in market share but a close follower. Should this follower challenge the leader with an offensive share penetration strategy? Or should it protect its share position and maximize the profits that it can extract from that share position? Depending on the strength of the share leader, the share leader's commitment to defending its share position, and the follower business's resources and short-run profit needs, either strategic market plan would work. But what does a successful defensive follower strategy look like?[4]

Figure 13-7 profiles two average follower businesses in the PIMS database: one with above-average profitability (number-two share position) and one with below-average profit performance. With respect to competitive advantage, share followers with above-average profits have higher relative product quality, which helps support higher levels of

FIGURE 13-7 SUCCESSFUL VERSUS UNSUCCESSFUL SHARE FOLLOWER STRATEGIES

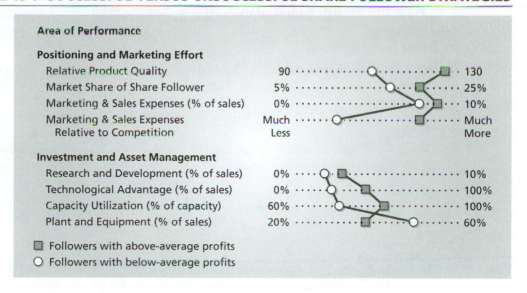

Area of Performance

Positioning and Marketing Effort

Relative Product Quality	90	130
Market Share of Share Follower	5%	25%
Marketing & Sales Expenses (% of sales)	0%	10%
Marketing & Sales Expenses Relative to Competition	Much Less	Much More

Investment and Asset Management

Research and Development (% of sales)	0%	10%
Technological Advantage (% of sales)	0%	100%
Capacity Utilization (% of capacity)	60%	100%
Plant and Equipment (% of sales)	20%	60%

☐ Followers with above-average profits
○ Followers with below-average profits

customer value, price, and unit margin. However, they also invest more aggressively in marketing as a percentage of sales, as well as on a relative basis, in comparison with competitors. These effects produce a slightly higher share, which contributes to a higher level of capacity utilization.

These businesses also invest more in research and development (R&D) as a percentage of sales. This investment translates into a higher level of technological advantage that most likely results in a higher relative product quality. The more profitable followers, then, protect their number-two share positions with investments in both R&D and marketing. As pointed out earlier, without these types of investments, a business could not protect a share position, even in relatively slow-growth markets.

Investing to Protect a Niche Share Position

The strategic decision on whether to engage in a long-run offensive or defensive strategic market plan must also be made by businesses in niche segments of their markets. For example, the niche businesses in Figure 13-6 may elect to pursue offensive strategic market plans to challenge share leaders in the larger market. Or, depending on the market situation, a niche business could pursue a defensive strategy to protect its profitable niche market. In many ways, a niche business is simply the share leader in a more narrowly defined market. Share leaders, followers, and niche businesses, then, can all pursue defensive strategies to protect their market share positions.

A niche business may be a small business with limited resources or a large business that pursues a reduce-market-focus strategy in a larger market while still achieving high levels of profitability.[5] Whether large or small, a niche business could hold the dominant position in its niche market, although the business would have only a small share of the overall market relative to the share held by the market leader. Within its niche market, however, the business is the share leader and has the same need to defend its share position as the leader in the overall market.

FIGURE 13-8 MARKETING STRATEGIES FOR PROFITABLE SHARE LEADERS AND PROFITABLE LOW-SHARE NICHE BUSINESSES

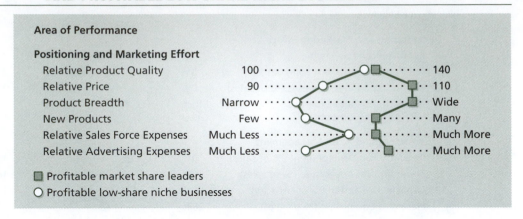

Area of Performance

Positioning and Marketing Effort

Relative Product Quality	100	140
Relative Price	90	110
Product Breadth	Narrow	Wide
New Products	Few	Many
Relative Sales Force Expenses	Much Less	Much More
Relative Advertising Expenses	Much Less	Much More

■ Profitable market share leaders
○ Profitable low-share niche businesses

Shown in Figure 13-8 are average profiles for profitable high-share and profitable low-share niche businesses. A close examination of the two profiles reveals only two areas of commonality: relative product quality and relative sales force expense. Having above-average product quality and above-average customer contact and market coverage are key success factors for profitable niche businesses.

In order to achieve above-average levels of profitability, low-share niche businesses need to focus on their products and keep their expenses low.[6] Their niche focus is most evident in their narrow product line, limited new product development, and limited advertising effort relative to competitors. In addition, a low-share niche business's prices are slightly below the average relative price index of 100. With an average relative price near 96, and relative product quality close to 123, these successful niche businesses create an attractive customer value:

$$
\begin{aligned}
\textbf{Customer Value} &= \text{Relative Benefits} - \text{Relative Price} \\
&= 123 - 96 \\
&= \textbf{27}
\end{aligned}
$$

As shown in Figure 13-9, low-share niche businesses with above-average customer value are more profitable. As a matter of fact, a low-share business with above-average customer value is more profitable than a high-share business with below-average customer value. We can see that an important component of success for niche businesses is above-average customer value and sales coverage with a careful product focus.

Defensive Strategy IB: Build Customer Retention

Protecting a valued share position is a defensive strategy at the core of many successful businesses. The profit impact of holding a 30 percent market share, however, can be quite different depending on whether the business has a high or low level of customer retention.

For example, assume that two businesses each produce $400 of margin per customer the first year and that the margin grows by $25 each year the customer is retained. Assume

FIGURE 13-9 CUSTOMER VALUE, MARKET SHARE, AND PROFITABILITY

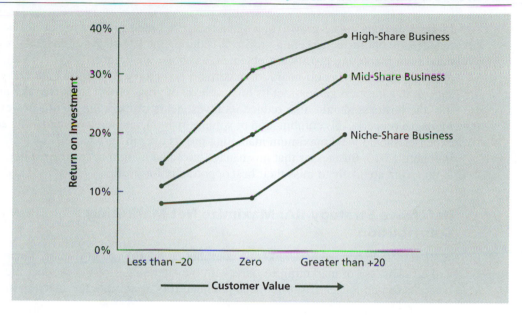

further that each business spends $500 to acquire a new customer and $100 per year to retain a customer. As shown in Figure 13-10, the business with 75 percent customer retention will retain customers for an average of 4 years, whereas an 80 percent customer retention rate will keep customers for an average of 5 years. That's an extra $199 in discounted net cash flow. The analysis demonstrates how a business that can build a higher level of customer retention can be more profitable than a business that maintains the same customer retention rate, even when both have the same market share. Whether a business is a high-share market leader, a share follower, or a low-share niche business, it can build profits with a defensive strategy to protect share while building customer retention.

FIGURE 13-10 PROFIT IMPACT OF A CUSTOMER RETENTION STRATEGY

| 75% Customer Retention* | | | | 80% Customer Retention* | | | |
Year	Net Cash	Discount Factor	Value	Year	Net Cash	Discount Factor	Present Value
0	−$500	$1.000	−$500	0	−$500	1.000	−$500
1	$300	0.870	$261	1	$300	0.870	$261
2	$325	0.756	$246	2	$325	0.756	$246
3	$350	0.658	$230	3	$350	0.658	$230
4	$375	0.572	$215	4	$375	0.572	$215
5	0	0.497	0	5	$400	0.497	$199

Net Present Value at 15% Discount Rate = $452   Net Present Value at 15% Discount Rate = $651

*Customer Life = 1/(1 − Customer Retention)

DEFENSIVE CORE STRATEGY II: OPTIMIZE POSITION

Product-markets in late-growth and mature stages of their product life cycles need to be managed to optimize marketing profits. It is during the late stages of market growth that maximum marketing profits are obtained, as shown in Figure 13-11. As volume produced by market demand nears its maximum potential and margins are not yet fully squeezed, a business can extract its highest level of gross profit. Because sales are slowing, the business should also reduce its investments in marketing and sales expenses. Managed properly, this combination of volume, margin, and reduced marketing and sales expenses should yield maximum marketing profits over the product life cycle, as shown in Figure 13-12. Businesses that mismanage price and margin or overinvest in marketing at this point are likely to miss their best opportunity for profits.

Defensive Strategy IIA: Maximize Net Marketing Contribution

A strategy to maximize net marketing contribution requires careful margin management and efficient use of marketing resources. In the later stages of the product life cycle, a business can no longer afford to make pricing errors or allocate too much to marketing.

FIGURE 13-11 PRODUCT LIFE CYCLE AND MARKETING PROFITABILITY

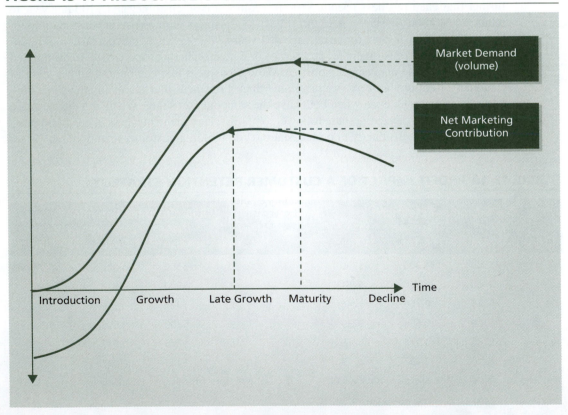

FIGURE 13-12 PROFIT LIFE CYCLE AND COMPONENTS OF MARKETING PROFITABILITY

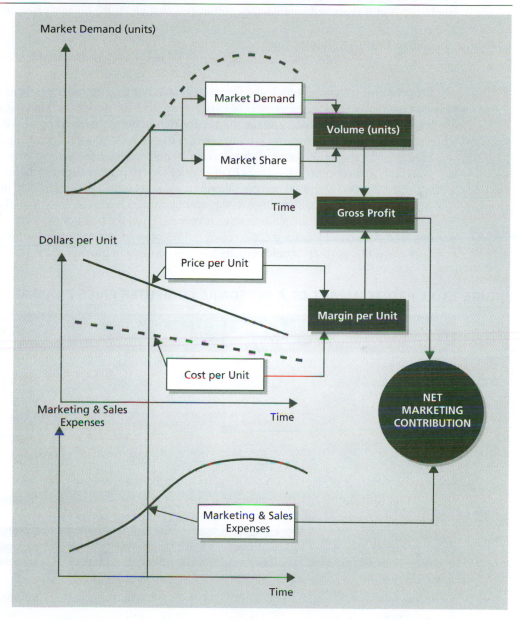

Increases in volume are unlikely to overcome these mistakes, as they might have done in the earlier stages of the product life cycle. The first step in optimizing net marketing contribution is to focus on optimal management of margin-volume rather than price-volume.

Price-volume strategies in the growth phase of the product life cycle are rewarded with higher volumes, sales, and marketing profits. However, in the late-growth and mature stages of the product life cycle, lower prices—which mean lower margins—are not likely to produce higher volumes; market growth is limited, and competitors are likely to step into the gap created by losses in volume. The strategic market planning challenge is to find the right combination of margin and volume, the combination that yields the highest gross profit:

$$\text{Gross Profit} = \text{Volume (units)} \times \text{Margin per Unit}$$
$$= \text{Market Demand} \times \text{Market Share} \times (\text{Price} - \text{Variable Cost})$$

Proper margin management is the first step in achieving an optimized position. In the personal computer market, the price elasticity is close to 2 for most PCs. Margins for PCs are usually 20 percent or lower. As the market for PCs matures and market growth slows, a business may need to rethink its pricing in order to optimize profits.

Figure 13-13 shows (1) the profit impact of a 10 percent price decrease to grow volume and sales and (2) an optimizing strategy to raise prices by 10 percent. Both scenarios are for a PC priced at $1,000 with a 20 percent margin in a market with a price elasticity of −2. As shown, the price decrease will produce a 20 percent volume increase, a 1 point market share increase, and a $80 million increase in sales revenues. From the point of view of sales, this strategy would be considered a great success, but because of lower margins following the price decrease, this business would actually lose $80 million in gross profit.

FIGURE 13-13 PROFIT IMPACT OF A PERSONAL COMPUTER PRICE CHANGE

Area of Performance	Current Performance	10% Price Decrease	Change in Performance
Market Demand	20,000,000	20,000,000	0
Volume Sold	1,000,000	1,200,000	200,000
Market Share	5%	6%	1%
Price	$1,000	$900	−$100
Sales Revenues (millions)	$1,000	$1,080	$80
Unit Cost	$800	$800	$0
Margin per Unit	$200	$100	−$100
Gross Profit (millions)	$200	$120	−$80

Area of Performance	Current Performance	10% Price Increase	Change in Performance
Market Demand	20,000,000	20,000,000	0
Volume Sold	1,000,000	800,000	200,000
Market Share	5%	4%	1%
Price	$1,000	$1,100	$100
Sales Revenues (millions)	$1,000	$880	$80
Unit Cost	$800	$800	$0
Margin per Unit	$200	$300	$100
Gross Profit (millions)	$200	$240	$40

An optimizing strategy to raise prices by 10 percent in a maturing market would reduce volumes, market share, and sales, as shown in Figure 13-13. Although these are not promising results, this defensive strategy would actually yield an $40 million *increase* in gross profit. If the strategic objective is to optimize position in order to maximize profits, then a price increase is the best strategic market plan. Reduced spending on marketing and sales at this stage of the product life cycle could also improve marketing profits, as shown here:

$$\text{Net Marketing Contribution} = \text{Gross Profit} - \text{Marketing and Sales Expenses}$$
$$= \text{Gross Profit} - (\text{Acquisition Costs} + \text{Retention Costs})$$

Because market demand is slowing, investments in marketing to acquire new customers should be reduced, and a greater proportion of the marketing budget should focus on customer retention. Recall that acquiring a new customer costs 5 to 10 times more than retaining an existing customer and, as a market reaches its full potential, fewer customers enter the market. At this point, the business should be able to maintain its market share with a lower level of marketing and sales expenses, assuming customer retention is at a good level of performance. Low retention at this stage of the product life cycle would make it impossible to achieve maximum marketing profits because the business would need to spend heavily on new customer acquisition just to replace lost customers and preserve market share.

Defensive Strategy IIB: Reduce Market Focus

As shown earlier in Figure 13-2, a business may have the choice of more than one defensive strategic market plan. Should it invest in strengthening its competitive position, allocate resources to protect its share position, or reduce its focus position within the market to maximize profitability? All of these can be viable strategic market plans, depending on different market and business conditions.

A decision to pursue a reduce-market-focus defensive strategy is most appropriate when a business does not have the resources to invest in protecting its current share position or when greater levels of profitability can be derived from a narrower, more selective choice of target customers. In either case, the strategy involves narrowing market focus and trimming market share in an effort to improve profit performance. The strategy may lower revenue and entail cuts in the marketing budget, but it will likely lead to higher levels of profitability as a percentage of sales.[7]

The main purpose of a reduce-market-focus strategy is to become more efficient. In Figure 13-14, we see that a mass-market approach is less efficient for this business than a reduce-market-focus strategy in terms of marketing productivity. Although sales and profits diminish, a reduce-market-focus strategy is able to improve marketing productivity from a net marketing contribution of $2 to $3 per budgeted marketing and sales dollar (an increase in marketing ROI from 200% to 300%). This business had to shrink its market share to become more efficient in producing profits.

DEFENSIVE CORE STRATEGY III: MONETIZE, HARVEST, OR DIVEST

At some point in every product-market life cycle, markets will be less attractive and will need to be managed for short-run profits regardless of competitive position. In some mature or declining markets, a monetize defensive strategy can create an attractive cash

FIGURE 13-14 SELECTIVE MARKET FOCUS STRATEGY

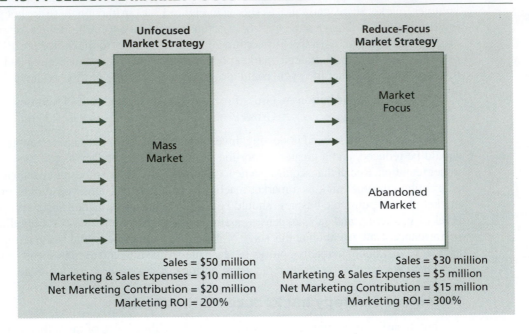

flow for some time. In other situations, the best defensive strategy may be a slow market exit (harvest strategy) or a rapid market exit (divest strategy). In either case, the intent of the defensive strategy would be to maximize immediate cash flow.

Defensive Strategy IIIA: Manage for Cash Flow

In many mature markets, market demand can be expected to remain strong for many years. When an optimize position strategy is not viable, a business may elect to remain in the market with a monetize cash flow strategy. The goal of a monetize strategy is to extract the maximum short-run cash flow from the market. This defensive strategy operates with minimal marketing resources and usually with low pricing levels. Many mature commodity products can be managed with competitive prices and sold with no sales or service. These products are not typically advertised and are often sold on a cash basis. When it is no longer possible to achieve the desired level of cash flow, a business may elect to pursue a harvest or divest strategy.

Defensive Strategy IIIB: Harvest or Divest for Cash Flow

Portfolio positions that warrant a defensive strategy to exit from a market can lead to a harvest market strategy (slow exit) or to a divest strategic market plan (fast exit), as illustrated in the portfolio model in Figure 13-3. When additional profits can be made with a slow exit, a harvest strategy can be a good source of short-run profits. But if a business is losing money in its market, management might be more inclined to pursue a

FIGURE 13-15 HARVEST PRICE STRATEGY

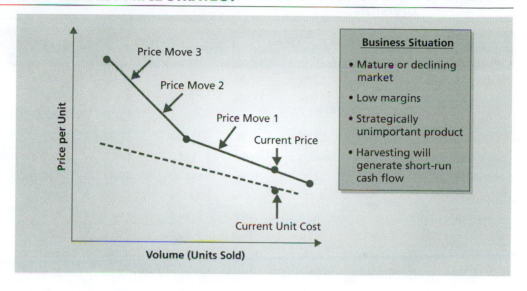

fast market exit strategy and divest the business's share position as quickly as possible. In this case, a divest strategy also improves short-run profits by eliminating a source of negative cash flow.

Harvest Price Strategy

The combination of unattractive markets and weak competitive advantage translates into both a weak strategic position and potentially weak profit performance.[8] When a reduce-focus strategy cannot produce desired levels of performance, an exit strategic market plan warrants consideration. But rather than divest a share position and exit quickly, a business can often significantly improve short-run performance by reducing marketing and sales expenses and systematically raising prices, as illustrated in Figure 13-15.[9]

In a very mature market with below-average profits, a business would use a harvest price strategy to reduce volume. Whereas price increases usually result in lost market share and lower volumes, overall sales often decline only modestly. More important, higher prices produce higher margins. The combination of lower volumes and higher margins results in a higher gross profit.

A harvest price strategy continues to raise prices slowly with expected decreases in volume until the business has exited the market. In many instances, however, a harvest strategy reveals a core of customers who would have paid more all along but, given the lower price, were glad to take it. Price increases in these situations rid a business of price-sensitive buyers. Often at this point, price is not a major issue for the remaining customers, and a business finds that even additional price increases do not seriously reduce demand. Even in commodity markets, some customers value on-time delivery, a reliable supply, and trusted relationships more than a competitive price. When a business sees that it still has a good group of core customers despite the higher prices, it may abandon its harvest-and-exit strategy and focus on maintaining high profits with much smaller

FIGURE 13-16 PRODUCT LINE PERFORMANCE OF A CHEMICAL COMPANY'S DIVISION

Area of Performance (millions)	Silicon Pigments	Primary Products	Specialty Products	Basic Colors	Color Enhancers	Overall Total
Market Demand (pounds)	100	167	154	96	556	1,073
Market Share	10.0%	12.0%	13.0%	26.0%	9.0%	11.7%
Volume Sold (pounds)	10	20.0	20.0	25.0	50.0	125.1
Price per Pound	$4.50	$2.80	$1.60	$0.80	$0.60	$1.46
Sales Revenues	$45.0	$56.1	$32.0	$20.0	$30.0	$183.1
Cost per Pound	$3.90	$2.40	$1.40	$0.80	$0.60	$1.32
Percent Margin	13.3%	14.3%	12.5%	0.0%	0.0%	9.8%
Gross Profit	$6.0	$8.0	$4.0	$0.0	$0.0	$18.0
Marketing & Sales Expenses	$3.0	$5.0	$3.0	$1.5	$2.0	$14.5
Marketing & Sales Exp. (% sales)	6.7%	8.9%	9.4%	7.5%	6.7%	7.9%
Net Marketing Contribution	**$3.0**	**$3.0**	**$1.0**	**−$1.5**	**−$2.0**	**$3.5**
Marketing ROS	6.7%	5.4%	3.1%	−7.5%	−6.7%	1.9%
Marketing ROI	99%	61%	33%	−100%	−100%	24%

volumes. In one large chemical company, this situation occurred, and the company's least profitable product became its most profitable product.

Figure 13-16 depicts the performance of a division within a well-established chemical company.[10] The products manufactured by this division serve very mature markets where market growth is minimal and price competition is fierce. As shown, the division is not highly profitable, with a gross profit of just $18 million on sales of $183.1 million. Two lines of products, basic colors and color enhancers, cannot cover their marketing and sales expenses and produce marketing losses of $1.5 and $2 million, respectively.

The overall net marketing contribution is $3.5 million on sales of $183.1 million, resulting in a marketing ROS of 1.9 percent and a marketing ROI of 24 percent, both well below corporate averages. The company sought to sell this division but could not find a buyer. With nothing to lose, the company's managers then pursued a defensive strategy to reduce share and improve margins with price increases. To further manage these products for cash flow, they reduced marketing and sales expenses. The managers expected to lose market share but were not sure how much. With a lower market share and smaller volumes, they also expected the unit cost per pound to go up because each unit would absorb a greater proportion of the manufacturing overhead. The managers had some concerns that this defensive strategy could lower their already low profit.

As shown in Figure 13-17, however, this strategy greatly improved profits despite significant decreases in market share and volume, as well as increases in the cost per unit. The combination of higher prices and lower volumes produced sales of $170 million, which was $13 million lower than previous sales. But the margins were much higher, with the overall margin increasing from 9.8 to 18.6 percent. The higher margin increased gross profit from $18 million to $31.6 million. The higher gross profit and

FIGURE 13-17 RESULTS OF A DEFENSIVE STRATEGY TO MANAGE FOR CASH FLOW

Area of Performance (millions)	Silicon Pigments	Primary Products	Specialty Products	Basic Colors	Color Enhancers	Overall Total
Market Demand (pounds)	**100**	167	154	96	556	1,073
Market Share	**8.6%**	10.3%	10.7%	17.1%	6.0%	8.6%
Volume Sold (pounds)	8.6	17.2	16.5	16.4	33.4	92.1
Price per Pound	$4.95	$3.20	$1.90	$0.98	$0.75	$1.85
Sales Revenues	$42.6	$55.0	$31.3	$16.1	$25.0	$170.0
Cost per Pound	$4.05	$2.55	$1.50	$0.77	$0.67	$1.50
Percent Margin	18.2%	20.3%	21.1%	21.4%	10.7%	18.6%
Gross Profit	$7.7	$11.2	$6.6	$3.4	$2.7	$31.6
Marketing & Sales Expenses	$ 2.5	$4.5	$3.5	$1.0	$1.5	$13.0
Marketing & Sales Exp. (% sales)	5.9%	8.2%	11.2%	6.2%	6.0%	7.7%
Net Marketing Contribution	**$5.2**	**$6.7**	**$3.1**	**$2.4**	**$1.2**	**$18.6**
Marketing ROS	12.3%	12.1%	9.9%	15.2%	4.7%	11.0%
Marketing ROI	210%	148%	88%	246%	78%	143%

lower marketing and sales expenses resulted in an increase in the overall net marketing contribution from $3.5 million (1.9% of sales) to $18.6 million (11% of sales). The marketing ROIs for all products increased, which contributed to an increase in overall marketing ROI from 24 to 143 percent. The managers' defensive strategy to reduce volume with higher prices and a lower marketing investment thus yielded a significant gain in profit.

Harvest Marketing Resources Strategy

In many instances, a business may not be able to raise prices to harvest share while maximizing short-run profits. It is difficult for a soft drink manufacturer to alter prices in the end market, for instance. In such a case, a business can reduce the marketing resources it devotes to that product and to protecting its market share position. PepsiCo adopted this strategy in the late 1990s for Slice, a product that had less than a 5 percent share of the lemon-lime segment of the soft drink market and was well behind Sprite, which had a 56 percent segment share. Although Pepsi has tried different ways to reposition the brand, including producing Slice with other fruit flavors, the product's market share remained stagnant. In 2010, it was available only at Wal-Mart stores. By not supporting Slice, PepsiCo is maximizing the profits it can take as the product slowly exits the market. Sierra Mist, a product that PepsiCo introduced in 2000, has been far more successful in capturing a significant share of the lemon-lime segment of the soft drink market.

In heavily advertised consumer goods markets, major reductions in the advertising budget can lead to rather dramatic share erosion. The PIMS database tells us that the rate of share change is affected by the rate of change in advertising budget. The calculation that follows gives us the rate of share loss for a consumer product that experienced a

25 percent reduction in its advertising budget for each of 3 consecutive years. In this case, a 10 percent market share eroded to 9.6 percent in 3 years:

$$
\begin{aligned}
\textbf{Market Share (3 years)} &= \text{Market Share} \left[1.00 + (0.05 \times \text{Change in Advertising Budget}) \right]^3 \\
&= 10\% \times \left[1.00 + (0.05 \times -0.25) \right]^3 \\
&= 10\% \times (1.00 - 0.0125)^3 \\
&= 10\% \times 0.96 \\
&= \textbf{9.6\%}
\end{aligned}
$$

When advertising budgets are large, reductions of 25 percent for three successive years result in substantial savings. As long as the product has an adequate profit margin, a business could improve short-run profits as it reduces marketing and sales expenses and slowly loses market share. The profits taken in the short run from the harvested product would normally be reallocated to a more attractive product-market in which the business hopes to build a stronger share position and achieve its desired level of profit.

Divest Market Strategy

One of the most difficult decisions any business faces is whether it should quickly sell off (divest) an unattractive product. In some instances, the product is one on which the company was built, and it is difficult to let it go. In other cases, the product represents a major investment, and a business resists abandoning it because of the money already spent to make it a successful venture. As a result, businesses often hang on to unattractive market positions for far too long despite a weak or average competitive position.

Figure 13-18 shows the portfolio of General Electric's clock and timer products as it existed in the late 1970s. Many of the products were in unattractive markets, had a weak competitive position, or both. GE divested the businesses shown in the blue portion of the

FIGURE 13-18 GE'S DIVESTMENT STRATEGY

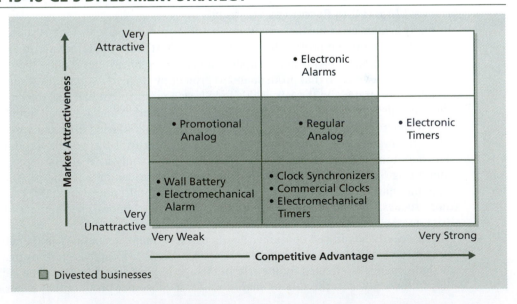

figure and invested in the two that were in more attractive markets. Eventually, it also divested these products because they no longer matched the overall performance objectives of the company.

To divest a share position, a business can either find a buyer for the business or simply close down the operation and sell its assets. In most cases, the desired choice is to find a buyer. Selling usually yields a greater return and preserves the employment of those working in the business.

Sometimes a divest strategy, although it is desired, is not feasible. For example, a business that has a 25-year commitment to produce a critical component for a government missile cannot easily exit the product-market; it has a responsibility to supply that product for the duration of the contract. Likewise, producers of pharmaceuticals or other life-supporting products may have a difficult time divesting a share position for either legal or ethical reasons.

CHOOSING DEFENSIVE STRATEGIC MARKET PLANS

Consider a business that is making $25 million in net marketing contribution with an average competitive position in a market with below-average attractiveness. The business is performing reasonably well, but an average competitive position in an unattractive market does not warrant an offensive strategic market plan to grow share. The share position is profitable enough to keep, so a harvest defensive strategy may not be appropriate either. The remaining choices are a protect-share strategy and a reduce-market-focus strategy.

As shown in Figure 13-19, if the business were to pursue a protect-share strategy, it would need to invest in marketing and other activities, such as R&D, to maintain its 30 percent share. By doing so, the business estimates that it could produce sales revenues of

FIGURE 13-19 SELECTING A DEFENSIVE STRATEGY

Area of Performance	Estimated Performance in 3 Years	
	Protect-Share Strategy	Reduce-Focus Strategy
Market Demand (millions)	2,000	2,000
Market Share	30%	20%
Unit Volume	600,000	400,000
Unit Price	$400	$450
Sales Revenues (millions)	$240	$180
Unit Cost	$300	$300
Unit Margin	$100	$150
Gross Profit (millions)	$60	$60
Marketing & Sales Expenses (millions)	$30	$20
Net Marketing Contribution (millions)	$30	$40

$240 million over the next 3 years. A protect-share strategy would produce $30 million in net marketing contribution. With marketing and sales expenses also equal to $30 million, a protect-share strategy would yield a marketing ROI of 100 percent.

The alternative defensive market plan would be to reduce market focus. This strategy would intentionally reduce market share from 30 to 20 percent. But the selective focus of the strategy would yield a higher average price and unit margin and would require a smaller investment in marketing and sales expenses. The result would be a $60 million reduction in sales revenue but an increase in net marketing contribution from $30 million to $40 million. With marketing and sales expenses of $20 million, this strategy would result in a marketing ROI of 200 percent, twice that of the protect-share strategy.

A business will encounter many market situations and must maintain a well-defined set of performance objectives, including both short-run and long-run objectives. After recognizing its objectives and its positioning in each of its markets, the business needs to develop a set of strategic market plans that will meet its objectives. Businesses generally need a combination of offensive and defensive strategic market plans. The offensive plans are geared for growth and improving share position, and the defensive plans are important sources of short-run profits and essential in defending strategic share positions. Both kinds of market plans play key roles in meeting a business's performance objectives.

■ Summary

Businesses have a short-term obligation to investors to fulfill promises of growth and profit performance. At the same time, they have an obligation to investors and employees to carve out a set of strategic market plans that will improve the position of the business in the long run. The primary purpose of a defensive strategic market plan is to protect a key strategic share position while managing the business's competitive position to produce the short-run growth and profit that meet the business's performance objectives.

Defensive strategic market plans are critical to the short-run profit performance of a business and to protect key strategic share positions that will support future profit performance. Strategically, important share positions need to be protected with a defensive strategic market plan. A defensive strategy to protect market position can include improved customer retention, which can dramatically improve profits with little or no change in sales revenue. A business may also use a reduce-market-focus strategy to more narrowly allocate its resources in an effort to better defend a desired share position and improve the profits derived from this market.

Protecting market share requires much more than a business-as-usual marketing effort. Market forces such as market growth rate, market share size, and competitor entry all create share-eroding forces that can cause share to decrease if it is not offset by improved competitive position or increased marketing effort. Declines in relative competitive position in the areas of new product sales, product quality, and service quality can also contribute to market share erosion—and decreases in marketing effort in the areas of sales force and marketing communications will adversely affect defensive strategic market plans that are designed to protect an important share position.

In unattractive markets or in mature markets where growth is limited and margins are low, a business may shift from an invest-to-protect a protect-share defensive strategy to an optimize defensive strategy. An optimize position strategy could involve price increases to improve profits while sacrificing volume, share, and sales revenues, as well as reductions in marketing and sales expenses to a level that is focused primarily on customer retention. A reduce-market-focus strategy goes one step further by raising prices to drastically reduce market volume and focus on certain customers in order to optimize profits.

If a business either is in an unattractive market or has a weak competitive position, it may elect to use an exit strategic market plan. If the business is profitable and capable of producing good short-run profits, it should use a harvest strategy. This type of strategy could involve raising prices, reducing marketing resources, or both. It enables a business to exit a market slowly while maximizing short-run profits.

On the other hand, if a business is losing money or would like to free up resources at a faster rate, it could choose a divest strategy. A divest strategy normally seeks to sell the business in order to maximize the value derived from its assets and goodwill. If there are no buyers, a business may have to use an accelerated harvest strategy. In some instances, a business may be prevented from exiting a share position because of legal or ethical considerations.

Companies tend to hold on too long to products that should be divested. Holding on to them ties up resources that the company could redirect to offensive market strategies designed to improve the performance of one of its other products.

■ Market-Based Strategic Thinking

1 Why did General Motors' 2009 defensive strategic market plan produce improved performance in 2010?

2 Why was it important for General Motors to develop the Volt?

3 How do defensive market strategies contribute to a business's performance objectives (sales growth, share position, and profit performance)?

4 What are the differences between defensive market strategies and offensive market strategies?

5 Why is it more difficult to protect Apple's iPhone market share in a high-growth market than Apple's Mac in a slow-growth market?

6 Why do share leaders like Microsoft, Google, and Intel have to work harder than share followers to protect share?

7 What are some of the key aspects of performance that would enable a share follower like Yahoo to achieve the same level of profit as a share leader?

8 What aspects of positioning and marketing effort may be managed to achieve a high profit with a reduce-market-focus strategy for Dr. Pepper?

9 Why should a reduce-market-focus strategy with above-average customer value deliver above-average profits for Ben & Jerry's Ice Cream?

10 How do defensive market strategies contribute to the long-run share position and profit performance for a company like General Motors?

11 Compare defensive market strategies to protect a share position with strategies to exit a share position in terms of their contributions to short-run profit performance and the overall share position of the business.

12 Why would a mature paint company pursue a reduce-market-focus strategic market plan?

13 What is the primary objective of a monetize strategic market plan?

14 Under what conditions would a business select an exit market strategy over a strategy to protect share position?

15 When should a business pursue a harvest market strategy, and how could that strategy affect short-run profit performance?

16 When should a business pursue a divest market strategy, and how could that strategy affect short-run profit performance?

17 Why might a company continue to support one of its products in a harvest- or divest-share portfolio position rather than harvesting or divesting it?

Marketing Performance Tools and Application Exercises

The three interactive marketing performance tools and application exercises outlined here allow you to evaluate the two relevant market strategies for each of the three defensive core strategies. To access the tools, go to **roger-jbest.com.** Each of these marketing performance tools is based on Figure 13-2.

13.1 Defensive Strategies—Core Strategy I: Protect Position

■ Using the data provided, evaluate the two strategies for protecting profits.

13.2 Defensive Strategies—Core Strategy II: Optimize Position

■ Using the data provided, evaluate the two strategies for maximizing profits without exiting markets.

13.3 Defensive Strategies—Core Strategy III: Monetize, Harvest, or Divest

■ Using the data provided, evaluate the two strategies for maximizing short-run cash flow.

Notes

1. D. Potter, "Strategy to Succeed in Hostile Markets," *California Management Review* (Fall 1994): 65–82.
2. S. Schoeffer, "Market Position: Build, Hold or Harvest," *PIMS Letter No. 3* (1978): 1–10.
3. P. Bloom and P. Kotler, "Strategies for High Market-Share Companies," *Harvard Business Review* (November–December 1975): 63–72.
4. D. Clifford and R. Cavanagh, *The Winning Performance: How America's High and Mid-Size Growth Companies Succeed* (New York: Bantam Books, 1985).
5. C. Woo and A. Cooper, "The Surprising Case for Low Market Share," *Harvard Business Review* (November–December 1982): 106–13.
6. R. Linneman and J. Stanton, Jr., "Mining for Niches," *Business Horizons* (May–June 1992): 43–51.
7. R. Hamermesh and S. Silk, "How to Compete in Stagnant Industries," *Harvard Business Review* (September–October 1979): 161–8.
8. V. Cook and R. Rothberg, "The Harvesting of USAUTO?" *Journal of Product Innovation Management* (1980): 310–22.
9. K.R. Harrigan, "Strategies for Declining Businesses," *Journal of Business Strategy* (Fall 1980): 27.
10. G. Seiler, "Colorful Chemicals Cuts Its Losses," *Planning Review* (January–February 1987): 16–22.

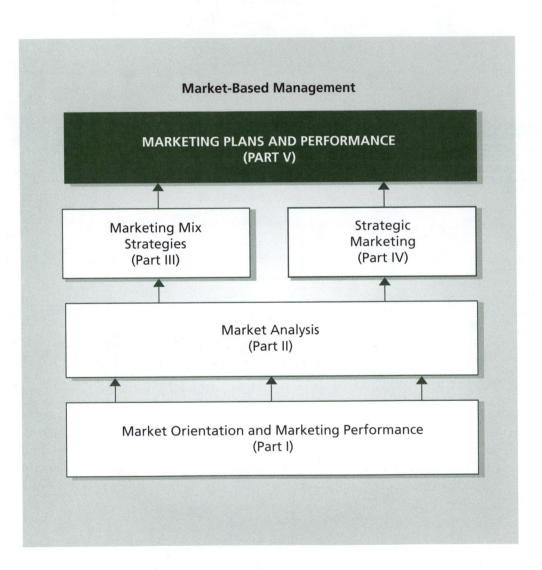

Market-Based Management

MARKETING PLANS AND PERFORMANCE
(PART V)

Marketing Mix
Strategies
(Part III)

Strategic
Marketing
(Part IV)

Market Analysis
(Part II)

Market Orientation and Marketing Performance
(Part I)

Marketing Plans and Performance

■ It is better to be prepared for an opportunity and not have one than to have an opportunity and not be prepared.
—*Whitney Young, Jr., 1960s Civil Rights Leader, Executive Director of the Urban League, and Dean of the School of Social Work, Atlanta University*

Given a set of specific performance objectives, a market-based business will develop and implement a proactive marketing plan for moving the business toward those performance objectives.

Chapter 14 presents a process and structure for *developing* a market-based marketing plan, one that encompasses an analysis of a business's current situation and results in a marketing strategy, supporting marketing mix strategies, a performance plan, and a performance review.

Chapter 15 addresses the *implementation* of a market-based marketing plan and the various forces that affect success. Plan ownership, management's commitment to the plan, performance measurements, adaptation, and an adequate allocation of resources all contribute to successful implementation. A company should track forward-looking marketing performance metrics, such as customer awareness, customer

perceptions of performance, trial usage, and customer satisfaction, along with backward-looking metrics such as sales, market share, customer retention, and measures of profit performance.

Finally, it is important for those in responsible marketing positions to understand how a marketing strategy and its supporting marketing mix strategies individually and collectively affect *financial performance*, including net profit, earnings per share, financial metrics, and ultimately, shareholder value. Chapter 16 demonstrates how each aspect of a market-based marketing plan—with its focus on customer value and customer satisfaction—ripples through the organizational maze of financial accounting to affect each aspect of profitability. The final chapter of *Market-Based Management* affirms that, regardless of a business's assets, technology, and financial leverage, there is only one source of positive cash flow, and that is the customer; everything else is expense.

Building a Marketing Plan

■ Chance favors the prepared mind.
—*Louis Pasteur*

Stericycle Marketing Plans
MBM Plan versus Actual

S tericycle, Inc., serves health care facilities and providers with a cost-effective and environmentally safe method for disposing of medical waste. Sales have grown from $22 million in 1995 to $1.18 billion in 2009, as shown in the bar chart.[1] In 2010, Stericycle was the leader in the global medical waste disposal market, holding a 14 percent market share and producing sales of $1.44 billion.

In the first edition of *Market-Based Management*, we made a 3-year forecast of $59 million in sales for Stericycle in 1998. Actual sales were $64 million. In the second edition, we projected $208 million in sales for 2000, and actual sales were $324 million. Our 3-year marketing plan in the third edition produced a forecast of $486 million for 2003, and actual sales were $454 million. In the fourth edition, our marketing plan projected sales of $619 million for 2006, and actual sales were $789 million. In the fifth edition, our marketing plan projected $1 billion in sales for 2009, and actual sales were $1.18 billion. In this sixth edition, the 3-year Stericycle Sample Marketing Plan projects that sales will reach $2.01 billion in 2013. As the bar chart shows, we also projected marketing profits for each planning period, and our projections were close to actual results.

This chapter presents the process of building a marketing plan by applying the same process in developing the 2011–2013 Stericycle Sample Marketing Plan.

CREATIVITY VERSUS STRUCTURE

The process of building a proactive marketing plan takes a delicate balance of creativity and structure. It is a process in which the opportunity to think creatively—to explore market issues outside the realm of day-to-day business—is a prerequisite. Yet, as shown in Figure 14-1, a marketing plan must be structured to ensure accuracy and comprehensiveness, and it must credibly link marketing strategies, resources, and performance objectives to the market situation.

Developing a marketing plan is similar to creating a painting. The imaginative use of light and color can make a painting interesting and appealing, but without some degree of form to add meaning to the composition, the painting may be intriguing but confusing. On the other hand, all form and no creative expression yields a sterile picture without much emotion. The same is true for a marketing plan: both creative insight and analytical structure are necessary to paint a meaningful picture of a marketing strategy and a logic-based path that connects the plan to desired performance objectives within the context of a well-portrayed market situation.

A well-developed marketing plan helps a business systematically understand its market and provides a marketing strategy and supporting marketing mix strategies to help the business achieve its predetermined set of performance objectives. A business with no

FIGURE 14-1 BUILDING A MARKETING PLAN—CREATIVITY VERSUS STRUCTURE

CREATIVITY	STRUCTURE
• Challenge current thinking with respect to market definition, competition, channels, solutions, communications, etc. • Attempt to understand what customers want but can't get, why customers leave, and what noncustomers seek. • Look outside your industry for other approaches and best practices applied successfully to marketing challenges.	• All relevant factors that affect performance are accounted for in the plan. • The Marketing strategy is credibly linked to the external factors and performance objectives. • All the dots are connected in a way that reconciles the marketing strategy and marketing and sales budget with performance objectives.

marketing plan obviously forgoes the opportunity to uncover key market insights that are a direct result of strategic market planning. At the other extreme, a highly formalized marketing plan, paradoxically, can be little better than no marketing plan at all.[2] A business using a highly formalized process to develop its marketing plan can regress to a level of filling out forms to serve as the basis for the plan.[3] An overly rigid process might bring to light a few market insights, but many important ones will remain undetected.

What is needed is an open system that encourages exploration and creative insight and, at the same time, provides a structure that ensures thoroughness and accuracy. With an open system, marketing planners should act as facilitators in the planning process rather than as developers of the marketing plan.[4] As facilitators, they coordinate the acquisition of information, set schedules, manage progress, and ensure that the business's mission, customers, and goals remain focal points in the planning process. Although there are recognizable organizational hurdles in this process, businesses that use a formal planning process are more likely to achieve improved performance than businesses that do not use a formal process.[5]

BENEFITS OF BUILDING A MARKETING PLAN

A sound marketing plan is indispensable to a proactive market orientation. Businesses with a strong market orientation are in continuous pursuit of customer, competitor, and market intelligence and work cross-functionally to create value-added customer solutions. Although these activities are ongoing, important additional benefits result from the process of developing a marketing plan.

Identifying Opportunities

It is not the *plan* itself, but the *process*, that helps a business uncover new opportunities and recognize important threats. A systematic evaluation of the market and the business's internal capabilities provides an opportunity to step back from day-to-day tactical marketing decision making and take a broader, more comprehensive view of the market and the business situation.[6] K2, for example, has become the share leader in the U.S. market for snow skis. K2's systematic evaluation of the U.S. ski market revealed that it was a mature market, which made additional share penetration difficult. However, in the process of performing this situation analysis, K2 realized that there were emerging markets in snowboards and inline skates. This discovery, in turn, led to new market entry strategies that have provided significant growth, a more diversified strategic position, and new sources of profit.

New opportunities also include all-new product-markets that offer distinctly different value propositions. Toyota introduced the Prius hybrid as the first environmentally friendly car. For target customers, the Prius made all other cars irrelevant. The authors of *Blue Ocean Strategy* report that true innovations such as Toyota's lead to better sales and profits than do incremental innovations.[7]

Leveraging Core Capabilities

As K2 aggressively entered the snowboard and inline skate markets, it was able to leverage its brand name and awareness in closely related markets. K2 was also able to leverage existing manufacturing and engineering expertise, as well as sales and distribution systems that served the ski market. One important benefit to a carefully thought-out market plan, then, is the greater utilization of production capabilities and business and marketing systems that are already in place. Likewise, Clif Bar, Inc., introduced the Luna nutritional energy bar for women, leveraging the company's knowledge of its product and market into an unserved segment of the market. Bayer did the same when it expanded the use of its aspirin product to heart attack prevention.[8]

Adopting a Reduce-Market-Focus Strategy

Most markets are complex aggregates of many smaller markets and market segments. These segments can be broken down further into market niches. Without a good marketing plan, a business could find itself vaguely positioned in a variety of market segments—a situation that could lead it in all directions in the search for customers without really being able to fully satisfy any of them.

A good marketing plan will profile target customers to the extent that the positioning strategy can be customized around the needs of the target segment and that the marketing effort can be directed at these target customers. The process of developing the marketing plan brings target customers into sharp focus, separating them from everyone else. The quote in Chapter 1 by Charles M. Lillis, former CEO of MediaOne Group, is relevant here also: "I will know when our businesses have done a good job of market segmentation and planning when they can tell me to whom we should *not* sell."

Resource Allocation

A company that focuses on a well-defined target market is also cost efficient. If a business's managers do not accurately identify their target customers, they will spend much time and money marketing to people who are not likely to buy from the business. Or if nontarget customers do buy, they will be difficult to retain because the value proposition will not deliver the customer satisfaction they desire. A well-focused marketing plan leads the business in more productive directions, allowing it to spend fewer dollars to accomplish performance objectives because it does not misspend resources on nontarget customers.

Building a Performance Roadmap

A marketing plan also serves as a roadmap for both the marketing strategy and expected performance. An effective plan includes projections for market share, sales revenue, and profits over a specified planning horizon. Mapping the future in this way may seem like a fairly easy task, but the business world is so complex that many circumstances influence a given market, a business's marketing strategy, and the resources that are needed. Constantly changing conditions within a business's market include those related to customer needs, competitors' moves, and the economy. In addition, market information is often incomplete or inaccurate or both.

The environment *within* a business can also contribute to difficulties in developing a marketing plan. Marketing strategies often are driven internally by short-run profit objectives rather than by market-based performance objectives. Furthermore, resources are not always allocated on the basis of strategy needs and performance objectives but are dictated by organizational needs, political motives, or a desire to improve short-run profits. These and other factors make it challenging to develop meaningful marketing plans and impede their successful implementation.

BUILDING A MARKETING PLAN

An effective marketing plan is the result of a systematic, creative, and yet structured process that uncovers market opportunities and threats that a business can then address in order to achieve its performance objectives. As illustrated in Figure 14-2, the development of a marketing plan is a *process*, and each step in the process has a *structure* that enables the marketing plan to evolve from abstract ideas and a compilation of information into a comprehensive document. The final document should be easy to understand and logical in its conclusions and should demonstrate the high probability of success for its proposed strategies. This section is devoted to an in-depth discussion of each step in the process by which a marketing plan is developed.

PART I: SITUATION ANALYSIS—WHERE ARE WE NOW?

The process for building a marketing plan as outlined in Figure 14-2 starts with a detailed situation analysis of the market and business with respect to current market forces, the business's competitive position, and the business's current performance. The primary purpose of a situation analysis is to uncover key performance issues that usually go unnoticed in day-to-day business operations. First, we need to go deeper into the market and the business's operations to fully understand customer needs, competition, and channel systems, as well as business positioning, margins, and profitability.

A thorough situation analysis is required for a business to understand current performance and market conditions and to uncover the key issues that affect performance. As shown in Figure 14-3, the output of the situation analysis is used to build the marketing strategy. The marketing strategy must reconcile current performance and market conditions with desired performance objectives. The combination of the situation analysis and marketing strategy drives the performance objectives of the marketing plan with respect to market share, sales, margins, and marketing profitability.

To better understand this process, let's apply it to an example. As in the previous five editions of *Market-Based Management*, we will develop a 3-year marketing plan for Stericycle, the company whose sales revenues and marketing profits are profiled in the bar chart on this chapter's opening page. The 3-year plan that we will develop is only an example—not the company's actual marketing plan. The purpose is to demonstrate the process of building a performance-driven market-based plan. This sample marketing plan will use publicly available data, but it also will use some data improvised by the author to illustrate certain parts of the marketing plan.

In Figure 14-5, the first page of the Stericycle Sample Marketing Plan summarizes the company's market position and the purpose of the marketing plan. The next page of the sample plan, page 1.0, is an introduction to the situation analysis section (Part I of the plan).

We will explore the process of building a market-based marketing plan by following the steps in Figure 14-2. We will begin with the two components of the situation analysis:

FIGURE 14-2 BUILDING A MARKETING PLAN—PROCESS

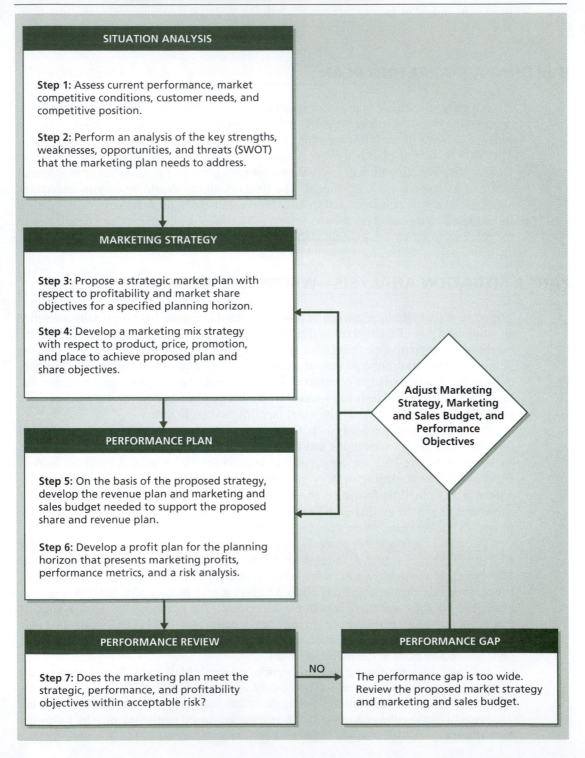

SITUATION ANALYSIS

Step 1: Assess current performance, market competitive conditions, customer needs, and competitive position.

Step 2: Perform an analysis of the key strengths, weaknesses, opportunities, and threats (SWOT) that the marketing plan needs to address.

MARKETING STRATEGY

Step 3: Propose a strategic market plan with respect to profitability and market share objectives for a specified planning horizon.

Step 4: Develop a marketing mix strategy with respect to product, price, promotion, and place to achieve proposed plan and share objectives.

PERFORMANCE PLAN

Step 5: On the basis of the proposed strategy, develop the revenue plan and marketing and sales budget needed to support the proposed share and revenue plan.

Step 6: Develop a profit plan for the planning horizon that presents marketing profits, performance metrics, and a risk analysis.

Adjust Marketing Strategy, Marketing and Sales Budget, and Performance Objectives

PERFORMANCE REVIEW

Step 7: Does the marketing plan meet the strategic, performance, and profitability objectives within acceptable risk?

NO

PERFORMANCE GAP

The performance gap is too wide. Review the proposed market strategy and marketing and sales budget.

FIGURE 14-3 BUILDING A MARKETING PLAN—CORE BUILDING BLOCKS

(1) an assessment of a business's current situation and (2) an analysis of strengths, weaknesses, opportunities, and threats (SWOT). Later, we will apply the situation analysis to create a marketing strategy (Part II of the sample plan) and a performance plan (Part III).

Step 1: Assess Current Situation

A fact-based analysis of the current situation is the first requirement in building a successful market-based marketing plan. But acquiring accurate information on "where we are now" with respect to performance, market conditions, and competitive position is often the most challenging aspect of building a market-based performance plan. When specific information is not readily available, managers may be tempted to work around it, as though it were not relevant to appraising their business's current situation. Unfortunately, this is not an acceptable approach. In some cases, the information may truly be unavailable, and then managers will have to make estimates based on their experience and knowledge of the market. Where estimates are vulnerable to error, this should be noted so that the estimates may be reconsidered as the plan evolves. The marketing plan is not an event; it is the product of an ongoing process to improve a business's understanding of its market and its position and performance in that market.

For managers who are new to the process of building a market-based performance plan, conducting an analysis of the current situation is particularly challenging. Our development of the Stericycle Sample Marketing Plan should help clarify the process. But when you are applying the process to your own marketing plan, the realities of achieving performance objectives within a specific timeline will hit you right between the eyes. For managers who are experienced with performance-driven situation analyses, the Stericycle Sample Marketing Plan will likely offer new information and add to their

FIGURE 14-4 COMPONENTS OF CURRENT SITUATION

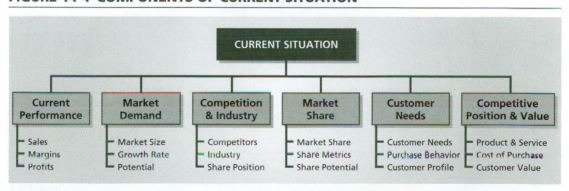

FIGURE 14-5 STERICYCLE SAMPLE MARKETING PLAN: SITUATION ANALYSIS

SAMPLE MARKETING PLAN: 2011–2013

=== **STERICYCLE** =======

Stericycle is the market leader in the worldwide medical waste disposal market. The purpose of this marketing plan is to review the current situation and propose a marketing plan for the next 3 years.

The marketing plan has three sections:

- Situation Analysis: Where We Are Now. . . . . .Pages 1.0–1.8
- Marketing Strategy: Where We Want to Go. . . . . .Pages 2.0–2.5
- Performance Plan: What We Expect to Achieve. . .Pages 3.0–3.4

*The purpose of this sample marketing plan is purely instructional. All information it contains has been taken from published sources or created by the author for educational purposes. All assumptions, estimates, and strategies are those of the author and not those of **Stericycle, Inc.***

—Roger J. Best
Market-Based Management
Sixth Edition (2011)

SAMPLE MARKETING PLAN: 2011–2013　　　　　　　　　　　　　　　　　　　　**[STERICYCLE]**

PART I
SITUATION ANALYSIS

The situation analysis is the bedrock of a performance-based marketing plan. It provides a meaningful summary of sales, profits, market share, competition, competitive position, and market demand, as well as a SWOT analysis of strengths, opportunities, weakness, and threats.

Page 1.0

RECENT PERFORMANCE   [STERICYCLE]

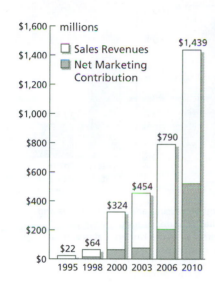

Performance (millions)	2008	2009	2010
Market Demand	$9,200	$9,600	$10,300
Market Share	11.8%	12.3%	14.0%
Sales Revenues	**$1,086**	**$1,178**	**$1,439**
Percent Margin	47.9%	50.3%	49.4%
Gross Profit	$520.0	$592.5	$710.9
Marketing & Sales Expenses*	$153.1	$171.2	$201.5
Marketing & Sales Exp. (% sales)	14.1%	14.5%	14.0%
Net Marketing Contribution	**$366.9**	**$421.7**	**$509.4**
Marketing ROS	33.8%	35.8%	35.4%
Marketing ROI	240%	247%	253%

*Estimated as 75% of Sales, General, & Administrative Expenses

- The market is growing at roughly 6.3%, and market share is increasing, while percent margins are holding at close to 50%.

- Marketing and sales expenses vary from 14% to 14.5% of sales. Marketing profits have increased, as have marketing ROI and marketing ROS

Page 1.1

WORLDWIDE MARKET DEMAND   [STERICYCLE]

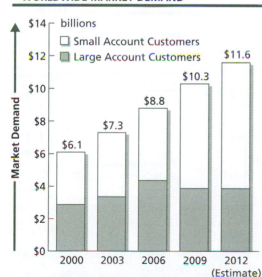

Stericycle serves about 460,000 customers worldwide.

Small Account Segment: About 448,700 are small-quantity waste generators, such as outpatient clinics, medical and dental offices, long-term and sub-acute care facilities, veterinary offices, municipalities, and retail pharmacies.
Steri-Safe® is our core product for this segment.

Large Account Segment: About 11,300 are large-quantity waste generators, such as hospitals, blood banks, and pharmaceutical manufacturers. They are served with our **Bio Systems®** programs and management services.

The worldwide medical waste disposal market is growing at 6.3% annually and is impervious to economic downturns. People are living longer and the world population is growing; as a result, the volume of medical waste is increasing.

Page 1.2

WORLDWIDE PRESENCE AND GLOBAL SALES MIX   [STERICYCLE]

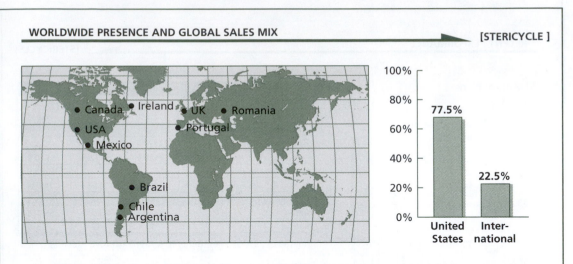

- Stericycle networks include a total of 113 processing and combined processing and collection sites and 135 additional transfer, collection, and combined transfer and collection sites around the world.
- Stericycle completed 180 acquisitions from 1993 through 2009, with 130 in the United States and 50 internationally. The map shows countries in which Stericycle has a presence.
- During 2009, Stericycle completed 23 acquisitions, of which 16 were regulated waste businesses in the U.S. and 7 were regulated waste businesses in Canada, Latin America, and Europe.

Page 1.3

CUSTOMER RETENTION AND LIFETIME VALUE   [STERICYCLE]

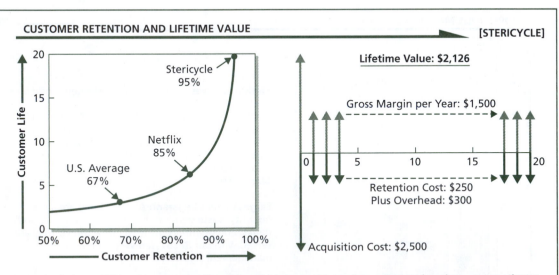

- Stericycle has a 95% customer retention rate, which is very high when compared to the average of 67%.
- The average customer produces an estimated $1,500 per year in gross margin.
- The high retention rate translates into an average customer life and cash flow of 20 years. Using a 20% discount rate, the net present value of the average customer's 20-year cash flow is $2,126.
- The cost of acquiring a new customer is estimated at $2,500. Retention cost is estimated at $250 per customer, plus an allocated company overhead expense of $300.

Page 1.4

INDUSTRY ATTRACTIVENESS AND COMPETITION

[STERICYCLE]

Industry Forces	Relative Imp.	Small Account Segment	Large Account Segment
Competitor Entry	15%	60	75
Competitor Exit	15%	90	50
Substitutes	20%	80	50
Buyer Power	25%	70	25
Supplier Power	5%	90	90
Price Rivalry	20%	70	30
Attractiveness Index		**74.5**	**45.5**

The higher the score (0 to 100) for each industry force, the more favorable it is for potential profits.

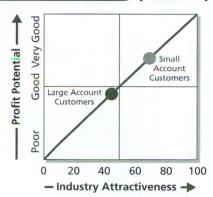

Competition (2009)	Sales (millions)	Gross Margin	Market Share
Stericycle	**$1,178**	**50.3%**	**12.3%**
US Ecology Inc.	$132	35.3%	1.3%
Waste Management	$118	37.1%	1.1%
All Others Worldwide	$9,092	N/A	86.4%

- The large account segment offers good profit potential, and the profit potential in the small account segment is very good.

- Stericycle is the market share leader in a very fragmented market. Our margins are much higher than competitors'.

Page 1.5

SHARE PERFORMANCE METRICS

[STERICYCLE]

Share Metrics	2010	Potential
Served Market	45%	60%
Company Awareness	70%	80%
Consideration	75%	80%
Preference	67%	75%
Purchase	80%	90%
Market Share Index	**12.7%**	**25.9%**
Share Dev. Index	**49**	**100**

- Restricted market reach is the main factor limiting market share growth.
- Low awareness is the second-largest cause of share leakage.
- Moving potential customers from awareness to consideration offers another opportunity to grow share.
- We estimate our share potential at 25.9%. This is based on achieving the target levels in the above table.
- An SDI of 49 means only about half of our share potential has been realized. There is still room for considerable market share growth.

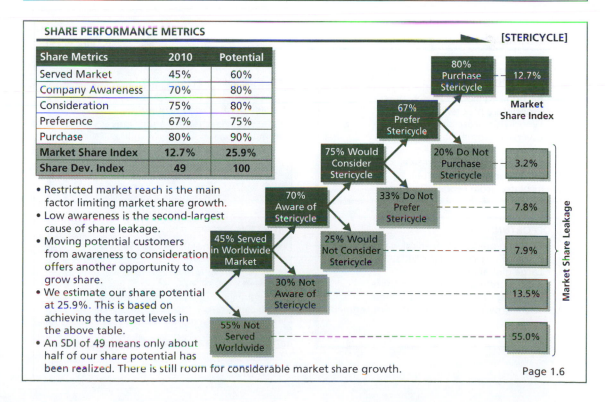

Page 1.6

COMPETITIVE POSITION AND CUSTOMER VALUE → [STERICYCLE]

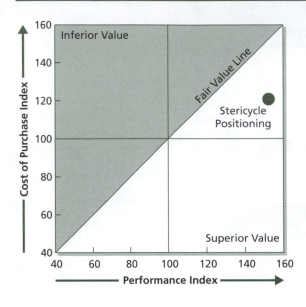

- Stericycle's **performance index** of 155 is based on product performance, service quality, and company reputation. (An index of 100 is used as the competitor average.)

- Superior **product performance** is built on product reliability, safety, and ease of use.

- **Service quality** is built on consistency, response to problems, and competency.

- **Brand reputation** is built on being well known and having a reputation for competence.

- The **cost of purchase index** of 120 is based on relative price and cost of usage.

- The **customer value index** of 35 is the difference between the performance index and cost of purchase index.

Page 1.7

SWOT ANALYSIS → [STERICYCLE]

STRENGTHS
- Recognized market leader.
- Proprietary process technology.
- Worldwide processing locations.
- Diverse customer base with a 95% customer retention rate.
- Branded products (Steri-Safe, Bio Systems, and Steri Tub).
- Insulated from economic swings.

WEAKNESSES
- Exchange rate fluctuations.
- Fewer high-quality acquisitions.
- Heavy governmental regulation.
- International political instability.
- Environmental regulations.

OPPORTUNITIES
- Growing market for medical waste disposal services and products.
- Large global market.
- Opportunity to grow market share.
- Licensing of international partners.
- Share growth in the small account segment.

THREATS
- Anti-American sentiment in some regions of operation.
- Pressure to reduce health care costs.
- Patent expirations.
- Lawsuits and compliance violations.
- Big competitors entering the market.
- Low barriers to market entry.

Page 1.8

confidence. The sample plan focuses on accurately assessing the company's current situation to build an effective marketing strategy and performance plan. So let's get started with the hard part.

Figure 14-4 summarizes the data that are needed to fully capture the current situation. As mentioned, marketing managers may have to use estimates or assumptions in place of actual data, especially when they are new to the process of developing a market-based analysis of a business's current situation. Over time, however, any estimates or assumptions should be replaced with market data. Managers may feel a bit uneasy about making estimates or assumptions, but almost every marketing manager needs to make them in order to develop a business's initial assessment of its current situation. The assessment will give a business's marketing managers a better knowledge of their market, leading them to discover new data sources.

The real enemy is a completely blank piece of paper. Even a good guess or rough estimate is better than doing nothing. Estimates and assumptions at least can be modified as the actual data emerge, but a blank piece of paper provides no guidelines at all for thinking about and arriving at an understanding of a business's current situation.

The remaining portion of this section discusses each aspect of the current situation presented in Figure 14-4. To help us understand the assessment process, we will examine each aspect in turn to develop the situation analysis for the Stericycle Sample Marketing Plan.

Current Performance

The best place to begin an analysis of the current situation is with an accurate appraisal of the business's performance. The appraisal might include only the most recent year of sales, margins, and profits, or it could include the previous 2, 3, or more years. In our Stericycle Sample Marketing Plan, we present on page 1.1 a summary of sales and marketing profits from 1995 to 2010, as well as a more detailed summary over the past 3 years, from 2008 to 2010. It is vital to use the company's performance for previous years as the beginning point in a marketing plan, as it presents a historical perspective. Assessing previous performance is essential to planning future performance.

Market Demand

An important element of a situation analysis is an appraisal of the market with respect to demand. What is the market's present size, and where is the market heading in terms of its growth rate and price trends? What is the upper limit on market demand, the point at which the market will reach its full potential? Each of these considerations has strategy implications. A market in early development, far from its market potential and growing rapidly, will require a different strategy than does a fully developed and very slow-growing market.

For Stericycle, the sample plan reports worldwide market demand for every 3 years starting in 2000, when demand was $6.1 billion, and going to 2012, when the sample plan projects demand at $11.6 billion. As stated on page 1.2 of the plan, worldwide demand is growing at 6.3 percent annually. Also of significance is the division of the market into two distinct segments: (1) small account customers who generate relatively small amounts of waste, and (2) large account customers who generate large amounts. The two segments have different needs, demographics, and behaviors with respect to medical waste. The small account customers include physicians, dentists, veterinarians, small clinics, and small labs. The large account customers include hospitals, blood banks, research labs, and pharmaceutical companies.

As page 1.2 of the sample plan shows, the small account segment, because it has a great many more customers, has in recent years produced more sales revenue than the large account segment. It also has been growing at a faster rate. Again, the overall market growth rate, the sizes of the two market segments, and the growth rate of each segment all have implications for determining a marketing strategy and achieving performance objectives.

Page 1.3 of the sample plan shows Stericycle's current locations around the world, as well as a graph showing the percentages for the company's U.S. and international sales. In 2010, over three-quarters of the company's sales were in the U.S. market.

Customer Performance

Around the world, Stericycle has about 460,000 customers, most of them in the small account segment. The company's customer retention rate of 95 percent is driven by customer satisfaction and loyalty. High customer retention is an important part of Stericycle's success, as the company's average customer life is 20 years. This long customer life allows Stericycle to capture customer sales and profits over a long period of time before having to replace a customer. As page 1.4 of the sample plan shows, the lifetime value of the average Stericycle customer is $2,126, calculated on the basis of a 20 percent discount rate and the estimates provided. The actual rate of return on this 20-year cash flow is 38 percent, well above the 20 percent discount rate that is used. Maintaining its high customer retention is a priority in the marketing strategy of this sample marketing plan.

Industry Attractiveness and Competition

Page 1.5 of the situation analysis section presents a summary of the industry and competition forces that influence profit potential, either favorably or unfavorably. The industry forces for both market segments are favorable. For the small account customers, an overall industry attractiveness index of 74.5 suggests that this segment has the potential to earn profits well above average. The industry attractiveness index for the large account customers is 45.5, indicating that this segment has average profit potential.

The medical waste industry consists of many, mostly small, businesses. As page 1.5 shows, Stericycle's market share is about 10 times larger than those of its two closest competitors. Because of the many small competitors worldwide, this market is highly fragmented, with a very low level of market concentration. This situation should favor Stericycle's ability to continue its growth through the acquisition of other medical waste management companies around the world. Consolidation of the industry is many years away.

Share Performance Metrics

To help us understand Stericycle's opportunities to grow its market share and achieve its share potential, page 1.6 of the sample plan presents the company's share performance metrics. The page includes a market share development performance tree, which, as we saw in Chapter 3, is a sequence of share performance metrics that shape market share. At each level of the share development performance tree, a particular performance metric measures share performance. By multiplying Stericycle's positive share metrics, we arrive at a market share index of 12.7 percent. Stericycle's market share index, then, is somewhat lower than its actual 2010 market share of 14 percent, as shown in the recent performance table on page 1.1 of the sample plan. Most businesses have a market share index that is at least slightly different than their actual market shares, but the market share index should approximate actual market share if all the input data for the performance metrics are accurate.

The share potential index is an estimate of the share performance index if the business were to achieve maximum levels of performance for each share metric. When we divide Stericycle's market share index of 12.7 percent by the share potential index of 25.9 percent and multiply by 100, we obtain a share development index of 49. This means that Stericycle has attained 49 percent of its share potential. The share potential and share development indexes are explained in Chapter 3.

In order for the company to continue building market share, it must address the largest areas of share leakage. As page 1.6 shows, the company loses 55 percent of its share potential due to the 55 percent of the worldwide market that is unserved. Another significant source of share leakage is the 30 percent of potential customers who are unaware of Stericycle, resulting in a share leakage of 13.5 percent. To improve the served market performance metric, Stericycle must expand its market reach. A greater reach will likely require acquisitions and more transfer centers. To improve awareness, Stericycle needs more effective marketing communications, particularly in the small account segment, which is highly fragmented and spread around the world. Addressing these issues, particularly in a market where the competition is relatively weak, should allow Stericycle to grow market share over the next 3 years.

Competitive Position and Customer Value

As the market leader, Stericycle is ahead of all its competitors in product performance, service quality, and company reputation. When each of these factors is rated and weighted by its relative importance, the sample plan estimates that Stericycle has a 55 percent overall performance advantage, as shown in the fair value map on page 1.7 of the plan. The company's cost of purchase index, which is based on customer perceptions of the total cost of purchase, is 20 percent above the industry average, due to Stericycle's slightly higher prices and the fact that customers are not fully aware of the savings Stericycle offers in usage costs. The company's customer value index of 35 is the difference in its performance index (155) and its cost of purchase index (120). Stericycle's high customer value is a major reason for the company's 95 percent customer retention rate and strong customer loyalty (an average customer life of 20 years). This is why businesses with high levels of customer value produce high levels of profitability.

Step 2: Perform SWOT Analysis

To complete the situation analysis phase in the development of a marketing strategy, we must now comprehensively examine the situational forces that were uncovered by the analysis of the current situation, along with other forces that the analysis may not have captured. For example, trends in governmental regulation, health costs, and waste disposal could be significant influences on future performance. The role of a SWOT analysis is to document all present and possible future influences on performance, negative or positive.

As Figure 14-6 shows, a SWOT analysis is a summary of situational influences, categorized as *strengths, weaknesses, opportunities,* and *threats.* This organizational structure is used to identify the most important issues and address them in the marketing strategy section of the marketing plan.

FIGURE 14-6 SWOT ANALYSIS

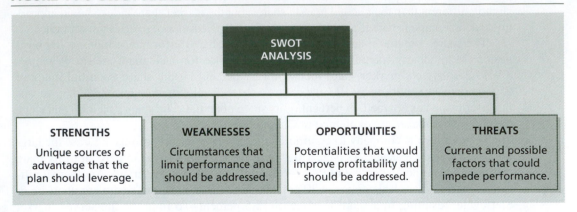

In the Stericycle Sample Marketing Plan, the SWOT analysis is derived from the analysis of the medical waste recycling market and Stericycle's current position and performance in that market. Page 1.8 shows several strengths, weaknesses, opportunities, and threats that Stericycle needs to address in order to build its marketing plan. The SWOT analysis can help the business understand the degree to which each of these key issues affects the results of its performance metrics.

Because the key issues serve as the primary guideline in developing the marketing strategy, they must be carefully specified and articulated. This step in the planning process will have a major part in determining the marketing strategy and its impact on future performance.

PART II: MARKETING STRATEGY—WHERE DO WE WANT TO GO?

As a business's managers prepare to develop a marketing strategy, they must carry forward into their strategic thinking each issue identified in the situation analysis, including those articulated in the SWOT analysis. The first box in Figure 14-7 lists the components of the situation analysis, around which the issues are organized. These components affect the strategy the managers will develop for taking the business to the desired level of performance. Developing a marketing strategy for a marketing plan encompasses two steps in the overall process of building a marketing plan, as presented in Figure 14-2. The Stericycle Sample Marketing Plan includes both steps.

Step 3: Develop a Strategic Market Plan

On the basis of the insights brought to light by the situation analysis, a business's managers develop a strategic market plan that will guide the development of specific marketing mix strategies. The primary purpose of a strategic market plan is to give a business a *strategic direction* by creating a set of performance objectives and to guide the development of marketing mix strategies.[9] To facilitate this process, managers use a strategic market planning portfolio.

FIGURE 14-7 BASING THE MARKETING STRATEGY ON THE SITUATION ANALYSIS

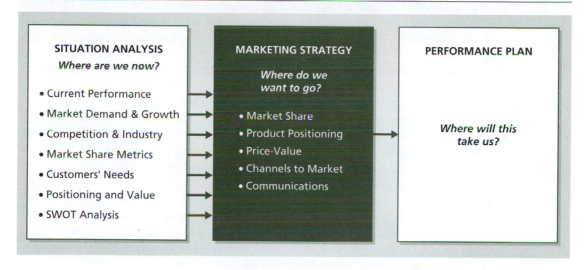

The portfolio could be based on any of the models presented in Chapter 11. In most cases, the vertical axis of the portfolio represents the attractiveness of a market. Product life-cycle position, market growth rate, market development opportunity, or an index of several forces are commonly used to represent market attractiveness. The horizontal axis is typically a measure or multi-factor index of the business's or product's competitive position. Market share, relative market share, market share index, customer value, or a multi-factor competitive position index are commonly used to represent competitive position.

Using the product's or market's portfolio position and the influences that the situation analysis uncovered, a business's managers specify a strategic market plan for each product or market in the portfolio.[10] These strategic market plans provide the direction for achieving strategic objectives, future positioning, and investment, as illustrated under the box for "Strategic Market Plan" in Figure 14-8.

FIGURE 14-8 COMPONENTS OF A MARKETING STRATEGY

Recall from earlier chapters that strategic market plans may be offensive or defensive. Examples of an offensive strategic market plan are presented in Chapter 12. These include investment strategies to grow market share, improve competitive position, keep pace with fast-growing markets, and invest selectively in attracting customers within a market. A variety of defensive strategic market plans are presented in Chapter 13. These plans include hold strategies to protect an important strategic position, optimizing strategies, and harvest and divestment strategies.

For our Stericycle Sample Marketing Plan, we use the multi-factor GE/McKinsey portfolio model presented on page 2.1 of Figure 14-9. The small account segment is positioned in a highly attractive market with a strong competitive position. On the basis of this portfolio position and the opportunities to grow share in this segment, an invest-to-grow-market-share strategy is recommended. This establishes the strategic direction for this segment's market plan.

The large account segment is positioned in the portfolio as average in overall market attractiveness and slightly above average in competitive position. This market segment has growth potential but, due to strong competitive forces in the segment, making a profit is a bit more difficult. A selective investment strategy is recommended. This strategy would invest in customers who are deemed to be good investments because of their high customer lifetime value. The strategic roadmap for this segment is different than for the small account segment and will require a different marketing mix strategy to achieve the segment's performance objectives.

Key Issues

Given the strategic market plan to grow share in the small account segment and the plan to grow profit in the large account segment, the next step is to identify the key issues from the situation analysis that need to be addressed by the marketing strategy over the next 3 years. Page 2.2 of Figure 14-9 summarizes the issues that the strategy must address in order to achieve the goal of each segment's strategic market plan. The remainder of the marketing strategy section addresses those issues.

Step 4: Develop a Marketing Strategy

The next step is to develop a marketing strategy that recognizes the strategic market plan and addresses key issues. Figure 14-8 includes the major elements of the marketing strategy: the strategic market plan, market share and share performance metrics, a competitive positioning strategy, a channel strategy, and a communications strategy. Not every category shown in Figure 14-8 requires its own page. In the Stericycle Sample Marketing Plan, pricing strategy is included as part of the Customer Value and Customer Retention page, as pricing is not changing. If a marketing strategy included a major shift in pricing, a separate page in the marketing plan would be warranted.

Market Share and Share Performance Metrics

Each of the two Stericycle strategic market plans needs to have very specific market share objectives and share performance metrics for the planning horizon. The marketing strategy section could simply state how share is expected to play out over the planning period, but a more comprehensive approach would be to specify objectives for share development during the plan's time horizon, along with the changes that are necessary in the share performance metrics to realize these objectives.

FIGURE 14-9 STERICYCLE SAMPLE MARKETING PLAN: MARKETING STRATEGY

STERICYCLE SAMPLE MARKETING PLAN: 2011–2013   ▶   [STERICYCLE]

PART II
MARKETING STRATEGY

This section addresses the key issues cited in the Situation Analysis section. It presents marketing strategies to grow market share, protect competitive position, and improve Stericycle's positioning in the worldwide medical waste disposal market.

Page 2.0

PORTFOLIO ANALYSIS AND STRATEGIC MARKET PLANS   ▶   [STERICYCLE]

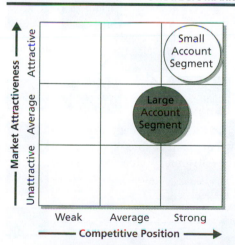

Market Attractiveness

- On the basis of market size, the market growth rate, and price competition, the small account segment is very attractive.
- The large account segment is attractive but to a slightly lesser degree.

Competitive Position

- On the basis of market share, margins, and the positioning of our competitors, our competitive position in the small account segment is strong.
- Our competitive position in the large account segment is not as strong as our position in the small account segment, but it is still above average.

Strategic Market Plans
Small Account Segment: Invest to grow market share.
Large Account Segment: Selectively invest to grow profits.

Page 2.1

KEY ISSUES [STERICYCLE]

- **Market Growth:** Invest to keep pace with the worldwide market growth rate of roughly 6.3% annually. We expect worldwide market demand to increase from $10.3 billion in 2010 to $11.6 billion in 2012.

- **Market Share:** Invest to grow market share from 14% in 2010 to 15.4 percent in 2012, with focused efforts to grow share in the international market.

- **Customer Retention:** Invest in customer retention. Retaining a higher percentage of our customer base of 460,000 customers means more profit, as fewer marketing and sales dollars need to be spent to replace lost customers. The cost of customer replacement is 5 to 10 times more than the cost of retention.

- **Product Positioning:** Continue to improve and support our core brands (Steri-Safe and Bio Systems), as well as our various marketing programs, such as our "mail-back program" for customers outside our served market reach.

- **Marketing and Sales Communications:** Build awareness, consideration, and preference in the international markets where we are not well known.

- **Environmental Attention:** Closely monitor regulatory trends and compliance, while paying close attention to trade and economic conditions in the international markets we serve.

Page 2.2

MARKET SHARE AND PERFORMANCE METRICS [STERICYCLE]

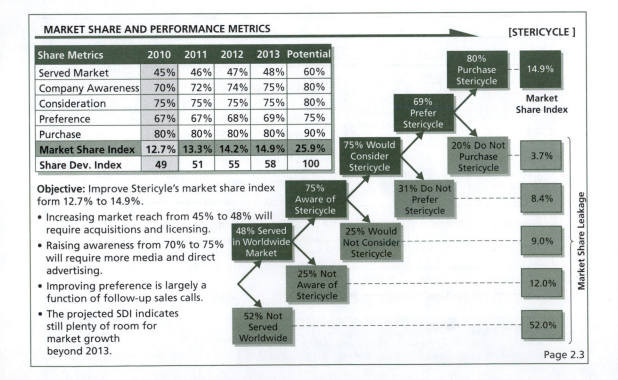

Share Metrics	2010	2011	2012	2013	Potential
Served Market	45%	46%	47%	48%	60%
Company Awareness	70%	72%	74%	75%	80%
Consideration	75%	75%	75%	75%	80%
Preference	67%	67%	68%	69%	75%
Purchase	80%	80%	80%	80%	90%
Market Share Index	12.7%	13.3%	14.2%	14.9%	25.9%
Share Dev. Index	49	51	55	58	100

Objective: Improve Stericyle's market share index form 12.7% to 14.9%.

- Increasing market reach from 45% to 48% will require acquisitions and licensing.
- Raising awareness from 70% to 75% will require more media and direct advertising.
- Improving preference is largely a function of follow-up sales calls.
- The projected SDI indicates still plenty of room for market growth beyond 2013.

Page 2.3

CUSTOMER VALUE AND CUSTOMER RETENTION

[STERICYCLE]

Area of Performance	Imp.	Performance Attributes	Advantage	Index
Product Performance	70%	Product Reliability, Safety, Ease of Use, Training	50%	150
Service Quality	30%	Consistency, Response to Problems, Competency	30%	130
Company Reputation	10%	Well Known, Reliable, Experienced	10%	110
Performance Index	**100%**			**155**

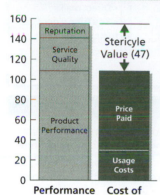

Area of Performance	Rel. Imp.	Cost of Purchase Attributes	Advantage	Index
Purchase Price	70%	Price paid	20%	120
Usage Cost	30%	Lower operating costs	−20%	80
Purchase Index	**100%**			**108**

- We must strive to improve all performance attributes in each of the three key areas of performance.
- Communicating our story is important. Being number one in the key areas of performance means nothing if customers do not understand how our high performance lowers their operating costs.
- We have a usage cost advantage relative to competitors. The advantage needs to be communicated to customers, with information on how it lowers the total cost of purchase.

Page 2.4

MARKET SHARE AND PERFORMANCE METRICS

[STERICYCLE]

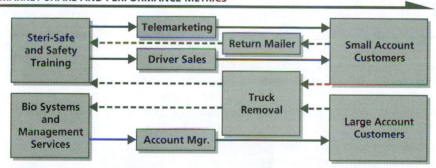

- Two separate channel strategies are needed for the small and large account customers, as shown above.
- Large account customers require more management services and a higher level of technical knowledge because of the complexity of their medical waste environment. Efficiency, service and low cost are key value drivers in the large account channel.
- Small account customers can be served in a variety of ways and require fewer on-site management services. Consistent performance, good customer communication, and a fast response to problems are key value drivers in this channel.

Page 2.5

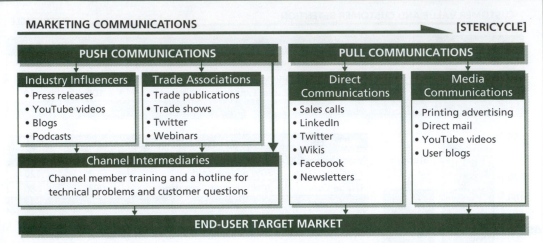

MARKETING COMMUNICATIONS   [STERICYCLE]

PUSH COMMUNICATIONS

Industry Influencers
• Press releases
• YouTube videos
• Blogs
• Podcasts

Trade Associations
• Trade publications
• Trade shows
• Twitter
• Webinars

Channel Intermediaries
Channel member training and a hotline for technical problems and customer questions

PULL COMMUNICATIONS

Direct Communications
• Sales calls
• LinkedIn
• Twitter
• Wikis
• Facebook
• Newsletters

Media Communications
• Printing advertising
• Direct mail
• YouTube videos
• User blogs

END-USER TARGET MARKET

• Not all parts of the world are engaged in social media and social media marketing communications, but for those that are, social media represent an important marketing communications channel for both providing and receiving information.

• Where social media marketing communications are not utilized, more traditional one-on-one and media communications are needed.

• Push communications targeted at channel intermediaries and channel influencers are a necessary part of our worldwide communications effort.

Page 2.6

In the Stericycle Sample Marketing Plan, we elected to use a separate page for share objectives. Page 2.3 of Figure 14-9 presents the share performance metrics and the market share index projected for 2013. The objective is to increase Stericycle's market share index from 12.7 percent in 2010 to 14.9 percent in 2013. Also shown on page 2.3 are the projected results of the share performance metrics for each year of the marketing plan. Performance gains in "served market," "awareness," and "preference" are critical to growing Stericycle's market share index to 14.9 percent. If the company is successful, it will still be well short of its share potential index of 25.9 percent. By 2013, projections would increase the company's share development index to 58.

Competitive Positioning Strategy

The purpose of the positioning strategy page is to make explicit the current and proposed product positioning with respect to product, service, and brand benefits. What specifically is going to change with respect to benefits as a result of this marketing strategy? How are prices going to be managed given changes in delivered benefits? How are the nonprice costs of purchase expected to change with the proposed positioning strategy? Finally, what will be the impact on customer value and how will these changes affect the proposed value proposition? All these considerations must be clearly addressed if the plan is to achieve the desired impact with respect to product positioning.

In the Stericycle Sample Marketing Plan, the company intends to hold its competitive edge in overall performance with a performance index of 155, while improving efforts to communicate the savings in usage costs that customers derive from Stericycle's products and services. The goal is to lower the company's cost of purchase index from

120 to 108 by making customers more aware of the ways that Stericycle reduces their total cost of purchase compared with other medical waste management companies. If successful, Stericycle would improve customer retention and loyalty, and it would also add another dimension to attracting new customers. Chapter 4 explains how customer value is computed and how a superior value contributes to above-average profits.

Channel Strategy

A business's channel strategy is a roadmap that the business follows in selling and delivering its products and services to target customers. For each channel that links the business with customers, the business should know the average revenues, margins, and marketing and sales expenses. Managers can then compute the marketing ROI for each channel and take into account the profitability of their various channels when they are making distribution decisions. Channel mapping and channel strategies are presented in Chapter 9.

The Stericycle Sample Marketing Plan presents a channel map that shows the channels for both segments. The channels are different, as the two segments have different needs that require different products and services. As shown on page 2.5 of the sample plan, Steri-Safe is the primary service offered to small account customers, and the sales effort relies on driver presentations. The collection of medical waste from customers in this segment is by truck and waste-return mailers. In some geographical markets, the trucks move waste to transfer centers that in turn move it to Stericycle waste treatment sites.

Sales in the large account segment are the function of customer account managers. The process promotes good service, problem solving, and the discovery of opportunities to improve products and services. Removal is by truck. Revenue per customer in this segment is high, but margins are lower and the percentage of marketing and sales expenses is higher.

Communications Strategy

The marketing strategy section of a marketing plan should also include a page on "Marketing Communications." This page is a concise but all-inclusive presentation of the kinds of communications that are needed to affect customer awareness, consideration, trial, and preference. The material includes both push and pull communications. As we saw in Chapter 10, push communications are directed at channel intermediaries and channel influencers, and their objective is to create a market push from within the channel system. Pull communications are directed at target customers and are equally important. Their objective is to create interest among customers, motivating them to acquire more information or to evaluate products. The page describing a marketing plan's communications strategy does not include the cost and other details about the strategy, as these specifics are part of a business's marketing and sales budget and media plan.

Page 2.6 of the sample plan presents the overall intent of Stericycle's communications strategy. The push communications strategies are focused on trade associations and industry influencers. In some international markets, Stericycle may find it more cost effective to contract with third-party channel intermediaries that would pick up medical waste. As shown on page 2.6, Stericycle will use a mix of traditional push communications—trade publications, trade shows, press releases, channel training, and hotlines—along with digital marketing communications that include YouTube videos, blogs, podcasts, Twitter, and webinars. The goal of these push communications is to indirectly influence customers with respect to medical waste management best practices, safety, and Stericycle as an industry leader in medical waste management and removal.

Pull communications are aimed directly at target customers, both current and potential, and include a combination of traditional direct communications and digital communications. The right communications mix will vary greatly according to the part of the world market that is served. In some markets where target customers generally do not have access to computers, digital marketing is not feasible. In most of Stericycle's geographical markets, however, digital media offer a new channel of marketing communications that in most instances has a much lower cost. The goal of Stericycle's pull communications program is to provide information and services to existing customers and to reach potential customers who may not be aware of the company or the customer value it offers.

PART III: PERFORMANCE PLAN—WHAT IS THE EXPECTED IMPACT?

The marketing plan's section on marketing strategies leads us to the performance plan, covered in the third and last section of a marketing plan. In the plan's first section, the situation analysis helped us understand where the business is now and what the key issues were. The marketing strategy in turn addresses these issues and gives the business an overall strategic direction. It serves as a general guideline in developing the marketing mix strategies for carrying out the marketing strategy.

As shown in Figure 14-10, each aspect of the marketing strategy, including the tactical marketing mix components, will affect the performance plan, as will certain elements of the situation analysis. For example, let's assume that in the situation analysis section the market was projected to grow at 8 percent annually. If the objective is to grow share from 14 to 16.2 percent, we know that sales projections also need to be increased. Similarly, if we had found that the overall market was going to grow at 10 percent annually,

FIGURE 14-10 DEVELOPING A PERFORMANCE PLAN

FIGURE 14-11 COMPONENTS OF A PERFORMANCE PLAN

this also would affect sales projections and the marketing and sales budget needed to keep pace with faster-than-expected sales growth.

Recognizing the effects of a marketing strategy and situation analysis on the elements of a performance plan, as listed in Figure 14-11, we will address each of these elements by using Stericycle's performance plan for illustration. Figure 14-12 presents a sample marketing and sales budget for the company, and Figure 14-13 presents the company's performance plan.

Step 5: Develop a Revenue Plan and Marketing and Sales Budget

Revenue Plan

In order to develop a performance plan, a business first translates the objectives of the market share strategy into a *revenue plan*. One important part of a growth plan is information on the market demand page in the situation analysis section (Figure 14-5, page 1.2).

FIGURE 14-12 SAMPLE BOTTOM-UP MARKETING AND SALES BUDGET

Marketing Expenses – 2010 (millions)		Sales Expenses (millions)	
Marketing Management	$5.0	Sales Management	$9.0
Marketing Professionals	$6.0	Sales Professionals	$40.0
Marketing Support	$6.0	Sales Support	$20.0
Advertising Expenses	$29.5	Customer Service	$30.0
Sales Promotion Expenses	$20.0	Customer Training	$25.0
Market Research	$1.0	Sales Literature	$10.0
Total Marketing Expenses	**$67.5**	**Total Sales Expenses**	**$134.0**
Percentage of Sales	4.7%	**Percentage of Sales**	9.3%
		Marketing & Sales Budget	**$201.5**
		Budget: Percentage of Sales	14.0%

Current demand and the estimated market growth rate are used to create an estimate for future demand. Sales are a function of this demand and the market share objectives.

For example, in the Stericycle Sample Marketing Plan, market demand is projected to grow from $10.3 billion in 2010 to $12.4 billion in 2013, as shown on page 3.1 of Figure 14-13. Because Stericycle's objective is to grow market share from 14 percent in 2010 to 16.2 percent in 2013, sales revenues should grow from $1.44 billion in 2010 to $2.01 billion in 2013. The revenue plan also presents expected growth in market demand, market share, served customers, and revenue per customer for each year.

Marketing and Sales Budget

Market share gains are not free. Even a strategic market plan to hold share in a growing market needs an increased marketing and sales budget. A business needs to allocate resources in the form of a *marketing and sales budget* based on the strategic market plan and the marketing strategies. Without adequate resources, the marketing strategies cannot succeed and performance objectives will not be achieved.

Determining the marketing and sales budget is one of the more difficult challenges in developing a marketing plan. Specifying the budget does not need to be a precise process, but allocations must represent a logical connection with the marketing strategy and performance objectives. A business builds its marketing and sales budget on one of three models, using its specific strategic market plan and the marketing mix strategies that are designed to achieve the target level of performance. Stericycle could elect to use any of the three kinds of budgets described in the following paragraphs.

Percent-of-Sales Marketing and Sales Budget. The percentage of sales that a business uses is often based on previous experience, but it could vary from past experience depending on the nature of the strategic market plan that will be implemented. An aggressive growth strategy might require more than the normal percentage of sales to achieve share and sales objectives. On the other hand, a harvest strategy may slowly reduce marketing and sales expenses as a percentage of sales while market share is harvested over time.

A typical hold strategy may keep marketing and sales expenses as a percentage of sales at the same level. But the marketing and sales budget's dollar amount will still change as a constant percentage of increasing sales. The Stericycle Sample Marketing Plan uses the percent-of-sales budget methodology. As illustrated on page 3.2 of the plan, the marketing and sales budget as a percentage of sales will increase from $201.5 million in 2010 (14 percent of sales) to $281.5 million in 2013 (still 14 percent of sales). The same percentage of sales is used to establish each the budget in dollars for all years. Also on page 3.2 is the marketing ROI for each year. Because percent margins and the percentage of sales allocated for marketing and sales stayed the same for the 3 years of the marketing plan, the marketing ROI is 257 percent for each year.

Customer-Mix Marketing and Sales Budget. The cost of customer acquisition and retention and the combination of new and retained customers are used to establish a customer-mix marketing and sales budget. Because the rate of new-customer acquisition can change the budget that is required, many market-based businesses see the customer-mix approach to funding the marketing and sales budget as the best approach.

Assuming the acquisition cost per customer is about 10 times the retention cost per customer, and assuming the acquisition cost of a new customer is $2,500 and the cost to retain an existing customer is $250, as presented on page 1.4 of Figure 14-5, we can determine the marketing and sales budget for 2010 as follows:

$$
\begin{aligned}
\text{Marketing \& Sales} \\
\text{Budget for 2010}
\end{aligned}
=
\begin{aligned}
\text{Marketing} \\
\text{Administration} \\
\text{Cost}
\end{aligned}
+
\begin{aligned}
\text{Acquisition} \\
\text{Cost per} \\
\text{Customer}
\end{aligned}
\times
\begin{aligned}
\text{Number} \\
\text{of New} \\
\text{Customers}
\end{aligned}
+
\begin{aligned}
\text{Retention} \\
\text{Cost per} \\
\text{Customer}
\end{aligned}
\times
\begin{aligned}
\text{Number of} \\
\text{Retained} \\
\text{Customers}
\end{aligned}
$$

$$= \$15.8 \text{ million} + \$2,500 \times 31,400 + \$250 \times 438,600$$

$$= \$15.8 \text{ million} + \$78.5 \text{ million} + \$107.15 \text{ million}$$

$$= \mathbf{\$201.5\ million}$$

In this example, we estimated that the fixed marketing administrative expense was $15.8 million. The estimate is for illustration purposes only and should not be interpreted as Stericycle's actual administrative expense. Because Stericycle's customer retention rate is 95 percent and its overall customer base grows at the same rate as the market growth rate (6.3%), we can estimate that the company attracted 31,400 new customers in 2010. With this information, we can determine the total acquisition and retention costs, as shown in the equation. The sum of the acquisition cost, retention cost, and marketing administration cost comprise the marketing and sales budget. The challenge in this approach is determining how much of the marketing administrative costs should be considered customer acquisition costs and how much should be customer retention costs.

Bottom-Up Marketing and Sales Budget. A bottom-up approach to developing a marketing and sales budget specifies each marketing task and the amount needed to accomplish it, given a particular strategic market plan and the task-related marketing mix strategies. For example, Figure 14-12 is a hypothetical representation of the marketing and sales budget that Stericycle needed to produce sales of $1.44 billion in 2010. The sample budget is for the purpose of illustration only. The figures for the various allocations are the author's and are based on estimates of the amounts that a business of this type would spend on the different aspects of its marketing and sales effort.

As shown, marketing and sales expenses were 67.5 million (33% of overall marketing and sales expenses). About 75 percent of the marketing expense budget was for advertising and sales promotions. Sales expenses in 2010 (in this example) were $134 million. Most of the sales expenses (67 percent of the total sales expenses) were for sales professionals, sales support (internal sales personnel), and customer service. Given the worldwide market served, the differences in the geographical markets, and the company's growth objectives, these marketing and sales expenses are quite reasonable.

Step 6: Marketing Profit Plan

In the profit plan, all elements of a marketing plan merge into a forecast of percent margins and marketing profitability. Sales revenues are brought forward from the revenue plan, and the marketing and sales budget allocations needed to support these sales forecasts are also brought into the profit plan. When the numbers are combined, as shown on page 3.3 of Figure 14-13, we can estimate the net marketing contributions for each year of the planning horizon. In this case, a significant increase in marketing profits is projected over the 3 years—from $509 million in 2010 to $724 million in 2013. Both marketing ROS and marketing ROI are projected to improve slightly over the 3-year plan.

FIGURE 14-13 STERICYCLE SAMPLE MARKETING PLAN: PERFORMANCE PLAN

PART III
PERFORMANCE PLAN

This section is based on the situation analysis and the proposed marketing strategy. It presents a performance plan with respect to sales, margins, the marketing and sales budget, and profitability.

Page 3.0

REVENUE PLAN: 2011–2013 ➤ [STERICYCLE]

Stericycle, Inc. ($ billions)	2009	2010	2011	2012	2013
Market Demand (worldwide)	$9.6	$10.3	$10.9	$11.6	$12.4
Market Growth Rate	6.3%	6.3%	6.3%	6.3%	6.3%
Market Share (worldwide)	12.3%	14.0%	14.6%	15.4%	16.2%
Sales Revenues	$1.178	$1.439	$1.602	$1.791	$2.011
Sales Growth Rate	8.7%	22.1%	11.3%	11.8%	12.2%
Customers Served (worldwide)	431,020	460,000	488,980	519,786	552,532
Revenue per Customer ($ actual)	$2,733	$3,128	$3,276	$3,446	$3,640

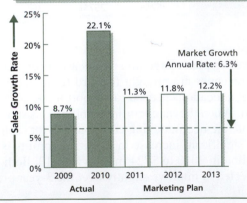

- Worldwide medical waste market demand is projected to grow at 6.3% annually.

- The annual rate of Stericycle's sales growth is projected to increase from 11.3% to 12.2%. The increase requires growth in market share, which is projected to reach 16.2% in 2013.

- Customer growth is a function of growing our served market and increasing market share. The average revenue per customer equals total sales divided by the number of customers served.

Page 3.1

MARKETING AND SALES BUDGET AND MARKETING ROI: 2011–2013

[STERICYCLE]

Stericycle, Inc. (millions)	2009	2010	2011	2012	2013
Sales Revenues	$1,178	$1,439	$1,602	$1,791	$2,011
Percent Margin	50.3%	49.4%	50.0%	50.0%	50.0%
Gross Profit	$592.5	$710.9	$801.0	$895.5	$1,005.5
Mrktg. & Sales Exp. (% sales)	14.5%	14.0%	14.0%	14.0%	14.0%
Marketing & Sales Exp.*	$170.8	$201.5	$224.3	$250.7	$281.5
Net Marketing Contribution	$421.7	$509.4	$576.7	$644.8	$724.0
Marketing ROI	247%	253%	257%	257%	257%

* 75% of sales, general, & administrative expenses.

- It is critical that spending on marketing and sales keep pace with sales growth. A budget of 14% of sales has worked effectively in the past and should be continued.
- Our marketing ROI is well above the average for Fortune 500 companies, as shown below.

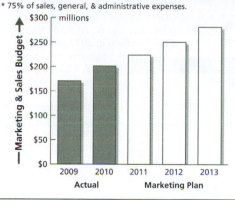

Performance Metric	Average	Median
Marketing ROI	163%	135%
Operating Income (%)	10.4%	11.1%

Page 3.2

MARKETING PROFIT PLAN: 2011–2013

[STERICYCLE]

Stericycle, Inc. ($ billions)	2009	2010	2011	2012	2013
Market Demand	$9.6	$10.3	$10.9	$11.6	$12.4
Market Share	12.3%	14.0%	14.6%	15.4%	16.2%
Sales Revenues	$1.178	$1.439	$1.602	$1.791	$2.011
Percent Margin	50.3%	49.4%	50.0%	50.0%	50.0%
Gross Profit	$0.593	$0.711	$0.801	$0.896	$1.006
Marketing & Sales Expenses (% sales)	14.5%	14.0%	14.0%	14.0%	14.0%
Marketing & Sales Expenses*	$0.171	$0.202	$0.224	$0.251	$0.282
Net Marketing Contribution	$0.422	$0.509	$0.577	$0.645	$0.724
Marketing ROS	35.8%	35.4%	36.0%	36.0%	36.0%
Marketing ROI	247%	253%	257%	257%	257%

*75% of sales, general, and administrative expenses.

- The marketing plan is expected to significantly increase the net marketing contribution and keep marketing ROS and ROI well above their averages for major companies.
- Net marketing contribution is projected to grow from $509.4 million in 2010 to $724 million in 2013, a 42% increase.
- The growth requires an increase in marketing and sales expenses from $201.5 million in 2010 to $281.5 million in 2013, a 39% increase.
- Marketing ROS and marketing ROI are both projected to increase slightly over the next 3 years and remain well above most other Fortune 500 companies

Page 3.3

BREAK-EVEN ANALYSIS AND RISK ASSESSMENT [STERICYCLE]

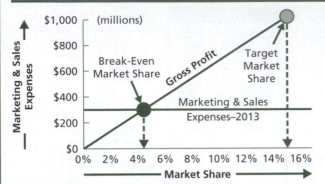

Break-Even Analysis–2013

- Break-even analysis is a form of risk assessment. The closer a company's break-even point to target, the riskier the investment.
- Break-even market share is the market share needed to recover a company's investment in marketing and sales. At this point the net marketing contribution is zero.
- Our investment in marketing and sales expenses is projected to be $281.5 million in 2013, and our company would need only a 4.5% market share to break even on this investment.
- The target share for 2013 is 16.2%. This is almost four times the break-even share of 4.5%.

Performance (millions)	2010	2011	2012	2013
Market Demand	$10,300	$10,900	$11,600	$12,400
Share Objective	14.0%	14.6%	15.2%	16.2%
Sales Revenues	$1,439	$1,602	$1,791	$2,011
Percent Margin	49.4%	50.0%	50.0%	50.0%
Gross Profit	$710.9	$801.0	$895.5	$1,005.5
Marketing & Sales Expenses	$201.5	$224.3	$250.7	$281.5
Break-Even Sales	$409	$448	$502	$564
Break-Even Share	4.0%	4.1%	4.3%	4.5%

Page 3.4

PROJECTED INCOME STATEMENT: 2011–2013 [STERICYCLE]

Stericycle, Inc. (millions)	2009	2010	2011	2012	2013
Sales Revenues	$1,178	$1,439	$1,602	$1,791	$2,011
Percent Margin	50.3%	49.4%	50.0%	50.0%	50.0%
Gross Profit	$592.5	$710.9	$801.0	$895.5	$1,005.5
Marketing & Sales Expenses[1]	$170.8	$201.5	$224.3	$250.7	$281.5
Net Marketing Contribution	$421.7	$509.4	$576.7	$644.8	$724.0
Other Operating Expenses (10% sales)	$149.5	$138.7	$160.2	$179.1	$201.1
Operating Income	$272.2	$370.7	$416.5	$465.7	$522.9
Operating Income (% sales)	23.1%	25.8%	26.0%	26.0%	26.0%
Interest & Taxes[2]	$95.8	$162.8	$166.6	$186.3	$209.2
Net Profit	$176.4	$207.9	$249.9	$279.4	$313.7
Earnings per Share[3] ($ actual)	$2.03	$2.38	$2.86	$3.20	$3.59

1. Estimated as 75% of sales, general, and administrative expenses.
2. Years 2009–2010 are actual, and 2011–2013 are estimated using 40% of operating income.
3. 87.4 million shares.

The marketing plan is expected to deliver the following results:
- Grow sales from $1.4 billion in 2010 to just over $2 billion in 2013, with an increase of $80 million in marketing and sales expenses over the same period.
- Increase operating income from $371 million in 2010 to $523 million in 2013.
- Drive earnings per share to new highs each year.

Page 3.5

Break-Even Analysis

Understanding the concept of break-even sales helps us evaluate the effort that is needed to recover a business's investment in a marketing and sales budget. In 2010, Stericycle invested $201.5 million in marketing and sales. Break-even sales in 2010 were $409 million. After a business goes beyond the break-even level of sales, it starts making a profit.

However, as we saw in Chapter 8, a more desirable measure is break-even market share, because it provides a better framework for judging profit potential and risk. Recognizing that market share can vary only between zero and 100 percent, we pose the question, How much market share is needed to break even? For Stericycle, break-even market share was 4 percent in 2010. By 2013, the break-even share is expected to increase to 4.5 percent, as the marketing and sales expenses will increase $80 million over this 3-year period. Stericycle's market share was 14 percent in 2010, so the company's actual share is considerably ahead of its present break-even share and even ahead of the somewhat higher break-even share projected for 2013. We know from Chapter 8 that a business that implements a strategy to grow share when it has only a small difference between its actual market share and its break-even share faces a greater risk of loss than a business with a large difference.

Income Statement

Although it is not a necessity, a performance plan could include an income statement. Preparing the statement requires a good knowledge of the nonmarketing overhead expenses and some method of projecting the changes that the expenses will undergo with changes in sales. Using a percentage-of-sales approach can be a safe way to estimate these expenses. On the income statement in the Stericycle Sample Marketing Plan, the overhead expenses, or "other operating expenses," are estimated at 10 percent of sales, as shown on page 3.5 of Figure 14-13.

Using this information, we can estimate the operating income and pre-tax return on sales. As shown in the sample plan, the operating income as a percentage of sales is projected to remain high, at around 26 percent. To compute each year's projected expense for interest and taxes, the sample plan uses 40 percent of the year's projected operating income. The percentage is based on the operating income and the percentages of this income that Stericycle paid in interest and taxes in 2009 and 2010. In 2009, Stericycle paid a little more than 40 percent, and in 2010 it paid a little less. We can now estimate the projected net profit for each year. The projections on page 3.5 of Figure 14-13 suggest that net profit will grow from $207.9 million in 2010 to $313.7 million in 2013. As investors hold 87.4 million shares, earnings per share are estimated to grow from $2.38 in 2010 to $3.59 in 2013.

Step 7: Performance Review

Step 7, the *performance review*, involves the ongoing monitoring of marketing and profit performance in light of the marketing plan's timeline. If the business fails to meet the desired performance objectives that are stated in the strategic market plan, then it must reevaluate the market plan with respect to all the inputs that were used to build it, as shown in Figure 14-3.

These performance gaps require the business to consider several options. One is to reexamine its pricing, customer and channel discounts, unit costs, and the marketing and sales budget to determine whether there are opportunities to improve performance.

A second alternative is to reexamine the entire marketing plan. A review of the situation analysis and the key performance issues might suggest that other tactical marketing mix strategies would more effectively achieve the desired performance objectives. Whichever the case, credible marketing mix strategies must be linked to the market situation, key performance issues, and available resources and then linked to the projections of external marketing metrics and internal profit metrics.

The Stericycle Sample Marketing Plan represents a map for strategically navigating the business toward greater profitability over a 3-year period. As shown in Figure 14-2, after the marketing plan is implemented, performance gaps are likely to emerge because of changing market conditions and the effectiveness of the proposed marketing mix tactics. Addressing these performance gaps as they occur is a critical part of the process for developing and implementing a marketing plan. The business may need to modify, adapt, or even abandon the marketing strategy and adopt a new one in order to achieve its performance objectives. We will learn more about successfully implementing a marketing plan in the next chapter.

■ Summary

A marketing plan serves as a roadmap. It carefully outlines a business's current situation, the desired destination (objectives), and the conditions that the business will face on the way to its destination. Assessing the market situation reveals a set of key issues that need to be addressed in order to reach the destination. A situation analysis and an identification of key performance issues are the major inputs to any marketing plan and are essential for accomplishing the business's performance objectives.

The marketing strategy and supporting marketing mix strategies presented in a marketing plan will not succeed just because they have been laid out. Resources in the form of people and money need to be allocated to implement the strategies. If adequate resources are not available, a business may not be able to attain its objectives, and it will have to revise or abandon its strategies.

The benefits of a good marketing plan are many. The planning process leads a business to discover new market opportunities, make better use of assets and capabilities, better define its market focus, improve marketing productivity, and establish an effective process for evaluating progress toward goals. There is a planning paradox, however. It goes without saying that a business with no marketing plan is severely restricted, but it is also true that one with a highly formalized marketing plan is not much better off. The business with no marketing plan will not see the market around it, and it will therefore be largely unaware of the opportunities and threats that need to be addressed in order to meet its objectives. But a business that develops a highly formalized plan may in the process regress to merely filling out forms and miss the subtler aspects of the market that a structured approach balanced with creativity would reveal.

Developing a marketing plan involves both structure and creativity. The process begins with a broad view of market opportunities, a view that encourages consideration of all market opportunities. For each market opportunity, the business sets a strategic market objective on the basis of market attractiveness and competitive position attained or attainable in the market. For each market the business pursues, it needs a separate situation analysis and marketing plan. The situation analysis enables the business to uncover factors that may limit performance. These key performance issues are the basic materials from which marketing strategies are built. Each aspect of the strategy must be scrutinized with respect to the market situation, key issues, marketing mix strategies to address those issues, and the resources needed to achieve specific performance objectives. With the marketing strategy and budget set, the business must estimate market and financial performance metrics, projected over a specified time frame. If the marketing plan fails to produce desired levels of performance, the marketing strategy and its supporting marketing mix strategies need to be reexamined.

■ Market-Based Strategic Thinking

1 How would the process of developing a marketing plan help Stericycle achieve a higher level of sales growth and profitability?

2 Why would a business like Coca-Cola with a strong market orientation do a better job of preparing a situation analysis than a business with a poor market orientation?

3 How could a business that does no strategic market planning and one that engages in highly formalized strategic market planning both miss meaningful market insights?

4 How would a company like Apple with a sound marketing planning process differ from a business with no marketing plan in the following?

Discovering opportunities

Leveraging existing systems, assets, and core capabilities

Implementing a market-focused strategy

Allocating resources

Planning performance

5 Why does the first step in the strategic market planning process involve a situation analysis?

6 What is the role of a SWOT analysis in the strategic market planning process? What is the role of key issues in the SWOT analysis?

7 For each product-market opportunity, how is a strategic market plan determined?

8 How does the strategic market plan for a given product-market influence the marketing mix strategies for that product-market?

9 How are key performance issues identified in the SWOT analysis used in selecting a strategic market plan and building marketing mix strategies?

10 Why is the development of a marketing and sales budget so important to the success of the marketing plan?

11 What are the various ways that a business could develop a marketing and sales budget for a given strategic market plan and the supporting marketing mix strategies?

12 How should the resources needed to support a marketing plan be logically linked to the key issues, the marketing strategy, the marketing mix strategies, and expected performance?

13 What is the purpose of the performance plan? What role should it play in the successful implementation of a marketing plan?

Marketing Performance Tools and Application Exercises

The three interactive marketing performance tools and application exercises outlined here may be accessed online at **rogerjbest.com.** They will add to your understanding of developing and implementing a sound, performance-driven, market-based marketing plan that will have a positive impact on profits.

14.1 Market Demand and Market Share

A. What would be the changes in the net marketing contribution if the market growth rate varied by plus 1 percent to 7.3 percent or by minus 1 percent to 5.3 percent?

B. What would be the changes in the net marketing contribution as the result of a 1-point drop in market share to 15.2 percent or a 1-point increase to 17.2 percent?

14.2 Customer Revenue and Percent Margin

A. How much does customer volume need to change to achieve the planned net marketing contribution for 2013 if the average customer revenue decreases by $500 in 2013?

B. How would the net marketing contribution, marketing ROS, and marketing ROI change by increasing the percent margin 2 points to 52 percent in 2013?

14.3 Marketing and Sales Expenses

A. What would be the affect on the net marketing contribution, marketing ROS and marketing ROI if the marketing and sales expenses as a percent of sales were 15 percent of sales in 2013?

B. What would be the affect on net marketing contribution, marketing ROS and marketing ROI if marketing and sales expenses were 13 percent of sales in 2013?

Notes

1. *Stericycle, Inc., 2009 Annual Report*, "Selected Consolidated Financial Data," 20.

2. D. Aaker, "Formal Planning System," *Strategic Market Management* (New York: Wiley, 1995): 341–53.

3. A. Rijvnis and G. Sharman, "New Life for Formal Planning Systems," *Journal of Business Strategy* (Spring 1982): 103.

4. H. Mintzberg, "The Fall and Rise of Strategic Planning," *Harvard Business Review* (January–February 1994): 107–14; and B. Tregoe and P. Tobia, "Strategy versus Planning: Bridging the Gap," *Journal of Business Strategy* (December 1991): 14–9.

5. T. Powell, "Strategic Planning as Competitive Advantage," *Strategic Management Journal* 13 (1992): 551–8; S. Armstrong, "The Value of Formal Planning for Strategic Decisions: Reply," *Strategic Management Journal* 7 (1986): 183–5; and D. Sinha, "The Contribution of Formal Planning to Decisions," *Strategic Management Journal* (October 1990): 479–92.

6. P. Kotler, *Marketing Management: Analysis, Planning, Implementation and Control*, 7th ed. (Upper Saddle River, NJ: Prentice Hall, 1991): 62–72.

7. W.C. Kim and R. Mauborgne, *Blue Ocean Strategy: How to Compete in Uncontested Market Space and Make Competition Irrelevant* (Boston: Harvard Business School Press, 2005).

8. D. Aaker, "Think Big," *The Wall Street Journal* (September 15–16, 2007): R10.

9. G. Hamel and C.K. Prahalad, "Strategic Intent," *Harvard Business Review* (May–June 1989): 63–75; and M. Treacy and F. Wiersema, "Customer Intimacy and Other Value Disciplines," *Harvard Business Review* (January–February 1993): 84–93.

10. R. Varadarajan, "Product Portfolio Analysis and Market Share Objectives: An Exposition of Certain Underlying Assumptions," *Journal of the Academy of Marketing Science* (Winter 1990): 17–29.

Marketing Metrics, Performance, and Strategy Implementation

■ **If you can't measure it, you can't manage it.**
—*from* **The Balanced Scorecard**
by Robert Kaplan and David Norton,
Harvard Business School Press, 1996

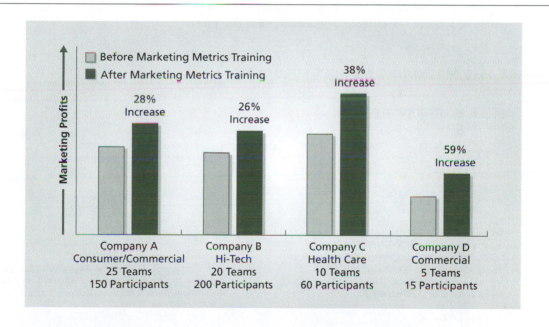

The four companies in the graph are Fortune 500 companies that participated in a marketing metrics training. Each of the companies formed several teams of three to six members who participated in an instructor-led webinar. The teams applied the marketing metrics that were presented during the webinar sessions to their areas of product-market

responsibility. The webinar involved approximately 1 hour of instruction, after which team members spent 2 hours applying the metrics, using their companies' actual data. The instructor then reviewed the performance tables and other materials that the teams produced.

The graph shows the improvement in marketing profitability (net marketing contribution) the companies could achieve if they successfully implemented the marketing metrics that the teams applied. Performance would improve an average of 32 percent. Because these are large companies, the average gain in marketing profits would be over $5 million.

The marketing metrics training webinar conducted for the four companies used marketing metrics discussed at http://marketingmetricssolutions.com/, as shown in Figure 15-1. The same site also offers a free white paper, *Getting Started Using Marketing Metrics*.

MARKETING METRICS AND PERFORMANCE

Businesses are obsessed with *financial results* because they tell what has happened. But rarely do businesses fully understand all the reasons for their financial results. *Marketing performance metrics* measure the factors that are actually driving profits in the market.

Many marketing performance metrics lead financial performance. A business might see that its sales and profits are steady, but when the business's managers also see that forward-looking marketing metrics, such as customer satisfaction and customer retention, are falling, that signals a coming problem. If the company fails to address poor levels of performance for these metrics, customers may soon start exiting faster than they can be replaced, leading to a decline in sales and profit.

FIGURE 15-1 MARKETING METRICS SOLUTIONS

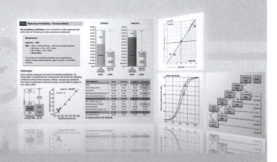

Marketing Metrics Resources

- **White Paper** – *Getting Started Using Marketing Metrics*, available at the above Web site: MarketingMetricsSolutions.com.

- **Marketing Metrics Blogs** – Available at MarketingMetricsSolutions.com.

FIGURE 15-2 MARKETING PERFORMANCE METRICS

Figure 15-2 lists five categories of marketing performance metrics. We know from earlier chapters that *market metrics*, the first category, measure market conditions and a business's performance in that market, expressing the measurements as indexes or scores. A high index or score in one market, however, may be a poor one in another. Because the standards for the different levels of performance vary across industries, a business normally sets its own performance benchmark for each market metric or for any marketing metric in general.

The four other categories of marketing performance metrics are *customer metrics, competitiveness metrics, marketing profitability metrics*, and *digital media metrics*. The chapters listed in Figure 15-2 offer more detailed discussion of each category. The figure does not include price-value metrics, which are presented in Chapters 4 and 8. Price-value metrics are more advanced product-market metrics for companies that are dealing with pricing issues.

BARRIERS TO GETTING STARTED IN USING MARKETING METRICS

Despite the demonstrated link of marketing metrics to profitability, many companies are not using them. A survey of CEOs found that 51 percent of them believed a lack of credible performance metrics was their biggest concern with regard to marketing effectiveness, as illustrated in Figure 15-3.[1] Although we have considerable evidence that managing marketing metrics can be linked to improved market performance and profitability, as Figure 15-3 shows, most marketing managers and other marketing professionals have not adopted the discipline of measuring and managing marketing metrics. Let's take a look at the barriers to using marketing metrics and how they can be overcome.

Most companies recognize the need for marketing metrics and the benefits they provide. But they struggle in getting started for a variety of reasons. A 2009 survey of 400 companies found that 75 percent of them saw the need for marketing metrics, but only 25 percent had implemented a marketing metrics program.[2] Here are the five barriers to using marketing metrics that companies most commonly cite:

- They are too complex and too difficult to use.
- They do not solve my business's problems.
- There are too many; I don't know where to start.
- I do not have the data nor the budget to gather the data.
- I do not have the time for this type of work.

FIGURE 15-3 THE NEED FOR MARKETING METRICS AND LINKS TO PERFORMANCE

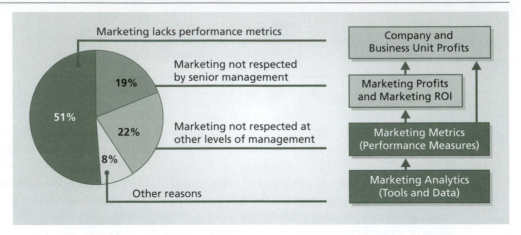

We offer the following recommendations for overcoming these barriers, clearing the way to the many valuable benefits that a business can obtain by applying marketing performance metrics.

Usage Barrier I: "They are too complex and too difficult to use."

If a marketing metric is truly too hard to use, it is not worth using. To get started, a company should adopt marketing metrics that are intuitive and make sense for its business operations. Some marketing metrics are complex, but if these are important for a company's marketing operations, they can be added later, after the company has had some success in using the marketing metrics it first selects.

For example, the marketing managers of one large chemical company decided to start with the three metrics that had the most meaning for the company's business operations and that would be easy to present to senior management as credible measurements. We will consider this example in greater detail when discussing Figure 15-4. This company found that it is better to start with a few marketing metrics that everyone will understand than a long laundry list that senior managers might find confusing.

FIGURE 15-4 DIVISION A—MARKETING METRICS SCORECARD

Marketing Performance Metrics	Marketing Metric Insight	Performance Current	Objective
Market Development Index	Market potential and future market growth	65	75
Share Development Index	Opportunity to grow market share	43	60
Customer Retention (annual)	Opportunity to grow customer profits	75%	80%
Net Marketing Contribution (millions)	Marketing's contribution to company profits	$350	$375
Marketing Return on Investment	Return on investment in marketing & sales	133%	150%

Usage Barrier II: "They do not solve my business's problems."

What are the biggest business or marketing challenges the company faces? This is the place to start when selecting the appropriate marketing metrics. After this question has been carefully answered, then the next question is, "Which marketing analytics and marketing metrics would help us better manage solutions to these challenges?"

This is the approach that a major Dow Jones company took. The company needed a strategy to compete profitably in a price-sensitive segment, a segment that was much larger than the premium and value segments in which the company was already well positioned. Given this business challenge, the company selected five marketing analytics and applied them to this segment in five international markets. The strategy for each of the five countries was somewhat different, but the collective strategies projected a 59 percent profit improvement following application of the five marketing metrics.

Usage Barrier III: "There are too many; I don't know where to start."

We will address this issue in more detail in the next section. Our recommendation is to start with marketing profitability metrics, because they are the ones that best demonstrate a marketing program's contribution to a company's profits. Booz-Allen Consulting offers the following observation:

> The reason for marketing's low level of credibility is largely because marketing lacks disciplined financial-return measures to assess the value of its contribution to the enterprise.[3]

Marketing needs credible, finance-based marketing profitability metrics that hold up under the scrutiny of CFOs and senior management. Chapter 2 presented three marketing profitability metrics that any company can apply today: net marketing contribution, marketing ROS, and marketing ROI. These metrics, particularly marketing ROI, immediately enable marketing managers to demonstrate the contribution of their marketing and sales strategies to the company, showing that an investment in marketing is efficient. After the marketing profitability metrics are in place, a company's marketing program can begin exploring other marketing metrics that would help address the major business and marketing challenges facing the company. Two resources a company can use to search for the marketing metrics that will address those challenges are listed under "Notes" at the end of this chapter.[4]

Usage Barrier IV: "I do not have the data nor the budget to gather the data."

Manager insights, experience, and intuitions are a good place to start[5] and require no budget. As shown in Figure 15-5, manager insights and "best estimates" are a satisfactory beginning. Marketing managers need to overcome their fear of using imperfect data. They should feel comfortable estimating the data needed for any marketing analytic. The data can easily be revised with team consensus or if market research uncovers more accurate information. Marketing analytics provide a way to capture the collective thinking of a marketing team. Data validation can follow if needed and important.

FIGURE 15-5 MARKETING PERFORMANCE SCORECARD

THE EFFECTS

Financial Results

- Financial Metrics
- Profitability Metrics
- Productivity Metrics
- Cost Metrics

THE CAUSES

Marketing Performance

- Market Metrics
- Customer Metrics
- Competitiveness Metrics
- Marketing Profitability Metrics
- Digital Marketing Metrics

Marketing Performance Metrics	Performance	
	Current	Objective
Market Metrics		
Product Awareness	60%	75%
Share Development Index	35	50
Customer Metrics		
Customer Satisfaction (% very satisfied)	15%	25%
Customer Retention (annual)	75%	80%
Competitiveness Metrics		
Performance Advantage Index	15%	20%
Customer Value Index	12	25
Marketing Profitability Metrics		
Marketing Return on Sales	18%	25%
Marketing Return on Investment	150%	200%
Digital Marketing Metrics		
Web Site Unique Visits (monthly)	325	500
Requests for information (percent)	15.3%	20.0%

Usage Barrier V: "I do not have the time for this type of work."

Applying marketing metrics should not be extra work, but a part of work. Managing marketing performance and profitability is in fact an important part of a manager's responsibility. After attending a presentation on how to use pricing metrics to manage for profitable growth, not just sales growth, a company's product manager offered this comment:

> Had we launched at a market-based price we could have increased our gross margin by $14 million. This block of instruction has really highlighted the importance of doing a price-volume analysis prior to launching a new product.

Marketing metrics are too important to be simply an add-on to the marketing or product manager's responsibilities. Metrics should be at the core of their management efforts. As the web site screen print in Figure 15-1 says, "If you don't measure it, you can't manage it." If marketing managers are paid to manage marketing performance, it seems obvious that they should be measuring it.

GETTING STARTED WITH MARKETING METRICS

Given the barriers to initiating a metrics approach for measuring marketing performance, the best starting point is identifying five areas of marketing performance that are believed to have a significant impact on sales and profit. Assuming the marketing team can make good estimates for the data needed or can obtain them without great expense, this is the place to start.

There is nothing magical about selecting the right marketing metrics for getting started. Figure 15-4 lists five metrics that a Fortune 500 company chose. The mangers selected them because the insights they would offer could be directly or indirectly linked to profit and because they were easy to understand, so could be clearly communicated to senior management and across the organization. With company-wide adoption, the metrics would also provide a much-needed means for assessing across the company's diverse divisions those aspects of marketing performance that were most significant.

It is important that the selected marketing metrics are accepted by everyone in the marketing program and by senior managers. After they have been adopted and after a period of regular use, the marketing team may want to expand its dashboard of marketing performance metrics to track performance with regard to investments in specific marketing and sales strategies.

Figure 15-5 presents a more balanced view of marketing performance based on a broader use of marketing metrics. Again in this example, the company has a list of metrics that it considers manageable and relevant to its operations. As shown in the figure, the company used a graphic to communicate the positive financial impact of managing marketing performance on the basis of metric results. Efforts to convey the significance of marketing metrics add to their meaningfulness and credibility across the organization.

FORWARD-LOOKING VERSUS BACKWARD-LOOKING METRICS

Primarily, marketing metrics are ongoing measures of marketing performance. Because many marketing performance metrics precede financial performance, using them is especially critical to successfully developing and implementing a marketing plan and achieving the desired financial performance.

Chapter 2 introduced the two broad categories of marketing performance metrics: *forward-looking* marketing performance metrics and *backward-looking* marketing performance metrics (see Figure 2-8).[6] Both are important, but forward-looking marketing metrics are particularly important because they are the indicators of future financial performance.[7] Backward-looking marketing metrics correspond more closely to internal financial metrics that measure past performance.

Forward-Looking Marketing Performance Metrics

Customer awareness, customer interest, product trial, and customer satisfaction, along with perceptions of relative product quality, service quality, and customer value, are all forward-looking marketing performance metrics. Changes in each, positive or negative, precede actual changes in customer behavior. As a result, these in-process measures of customer thinking and attitudes are important leading indicators of a business's future performance.

For example, customers may be satisfied, but their perceptions of the value they derive from the product, relative to competing alternatives, are steadily diminishing. The business may have done nothing wrong to dissatisfy its customers; competitors may simply have improved their delivery of customer value on the basis of a combination of total

FIGURE 15-6 CUSTOMER SATISFACTION—A KEY FORWARD-LOOKING MARKETING METRIC

Previous Year Customer Satisfaction	Percent	Annual Revenue	Percent Margin	Customer Retention	Customer Profit
Very Satisfied	15%	$4,500	50%	−$700	$1,550
Satisfied	70%	$3,000	40%	−$500	$700
Somewhat Dissatisfied	10%	$1,500	35%	−$300	$225
Dissatisfied	5%	$1,500	35%	−$300	$225
Average	100%	$3,000	40.80%	−$500	$756

Current Year Customer Satisfaction	Percent	Annual Revenue	Percent Margin	Customer Retention	Customer Profit
Very Satisfied	10%	$4,500	50%	−$700	$1,550
Satisfied	65%	$3,000	40%	−$500	$700
Somewhat Dissatisfied	20%	$1,500	35%	−$300	$225
Dissatisfied	5%	$1,500	35%	−$300	$225
Average	100%	$2,775	39.8%	−$470	$666

benefits and total cost. However, the net effect is that customer perceptions of the value created by the business's product have diminished, making the customers vulnerable to competitors.

The whole purpose of forward-looking marketing metrics is to track customer perceptions and attitudes that precede actual changes in customer behavior and a business's financial performance. Customer satisfaction is an important metric that measures several levels of satisfaction.[8] Very satisfied customers are loyal and buy in relatively large amounts and often buy higher margin products and extra services.[9] Satisfied customers are less loyal and usually switch back and forth with competitors' products. Dissatisfied customers, of course, are likely to leave. Those who complain can usually be retained, but if the cause of their dissatisfaction is not addressed, they will remain vulnerable to competitors. As pointed out in Chapter 1, however, fewer than 10 percent of dissatisfied customers ever complain,[10] and of the over 90 percent who do not, most stop buying from the business.

To appreciate the value and importance of customer satisfaction as a forward-looking metric, let's review the results presented in Figure 15-6. In the previous year the company had 15 percent "very satisfied" customers, 70 percent "satisfied," 10 percent "somewhat dissatisfied," and 5 percent "dissatisfied." Due to customer purchase behavior and considering the customer retention expenses allocated to each level of customer satisfaction, the company produced average annual sales per customer of $3,000 and an average annual customer profit of $756. However, a current-year customer survey shows a decline in "very satisfied" and "satisfied" customers. If this situation were allowed to play out, customer defections would cause average annual sales to drop by $225 per customer and average customer profit to fall by $90. If the company had 10,000 customers, that would be a decrease of $900,000. Businesses that effectively use measures of customer satisfaction have a forward-looking metric that enables them to take corrective action in time to avoid a negative impact on financial performance.

A market-based business with several forward-looking marketing metrics can quickly detect any changes in customer perceptions and attitudes. With an early warning signal, the business can take corrective action before customers alter their purchase behavior. If the company did not use forward-looking marketing metrics, a customer-dissatisfaction problem would likely go undetected until a decline in financial performance became a reality.

Backward-Looking Marketing Performance Metrics

Backward-looking marketing metrics include the metrics that measure market share, customer retention, and revenue per customer. These metrics are applied simultaneously with financial performance metrics, normally at the end of a reporting period, but they provide a different set of diagnostic insights into a business's performance. Let's assume that sales revenues are increasing and ahead of forecast, and financial performance is also better than expected. Most businesses would feel pretty good about this improving performance. However, if backward-looking marketing performance metrics show that the business is losing market share in a growing market, and poor customer retention is masked by new customer growth, the business should be concerned. Without backward-looking marketing metrics, a business has only internal measures of performance, which give us only part of the picture.

Even for a business that is maintaining its market share, poor customer retention has a serious impact on financial performance, as illustrated in Figure 15-7. In this example, the business's 20 percent market share and 75 percent customer retention rate produces an average customer lifetime value of $88 using a discount rate of 20 percent. The actual rate of return on this level of customer cash flow over 4 years is 21.9 percent. Increasing customer retention to 80 percent extends the average customer life from 4 years to 5 years and adds 1 more year of profitability to the average customer life. As shown in Figure 15-7, the average customer lifetime value with an 80 percent customer retention increases to a remarkable $490, five and a half times more with the same 20 percent market share. Of course, the average customer lifetime value would likely be even greater because customers usually buy more the longer they stay with a company.

SUCCESSFUL STRATEGY IMPLEMENTATION

Nike is famous for innovation and its *Just Do It* marketing campaign—but the company's marketing success did not happen by accident. Nike has a company culture that motivates management behaviors which are conducive to the successful implementation of strategies. Nike's Eleven Maxims foster an awareness and understanding of the company's approach to marketing among all managers and other employees:

1. It Is Our Nature to Innovate.	6. Be a Sponge.
2. Nike Is a Company.	7. Evolve Immediately.
3. Nike Is a Brand.	8. Do the Right Thing.
4. Simplify and Go.	9. Master the Fundamentals.
5. The Consumer Decides.	10. We Are on the Offense. Always.

And Number 11: Remember the Man (Nike Co-Founder Bill Bowerman).[11]

FIGURE 15-7 CUSTOMER RETENTION—A KEY BACKWARD-LOOKING MARKETING METRIC

75% Customer Retention and 4-Year Customer Life Period	0	1	2	3	4	5
Sales		$3,000	$3,000	$3,000	$3,000	$0
Gross Margin		$1,500	$1,500	$1,500	$1,500	$0
Retention Cost		−$500	−$500	−$500	−$500	$0
Acquisition Cost	−$2,500	$1,000	$1,000	$1,000	$1,000	$0
Discount Rate	20%					
Present Value Factor	1.00	0.833	0.694	0.579	0.482	0.402
Net Present Value	−$2,500	$833	$694	$579	$482	$0
Average Lifetime Value	**$88**					

80% Customer Retention and 5-Year Customer Life Period	0	1	2	3	4	5
Sales		$3,000	$3,000	$3,000	$3,000	$3,000
Gross Margin		$1,500	$1,500	$1,500	$1,500	$1,500
Retention Cost		−$500	−$500	−$500	−$500	−$500
Acquisition Cost	−$2,500	$1,000	$1,000	$1,000	$1,000	$1,000
Discount Rate	20%					
Present Value Factor	1.00	0.833	0.694	0.579	0.482	0.402
Net Present Value	−$2,500	$833	$694	$579	$482	$402
Average Lifetime Value	**$490**					

We have seen that a sound marketing plan provides a business with the roadmap it needs to pursue a set of performance objectives. However, even the best marketing plan does not guarantee that the company will reach its performance objectives, any more than having a roadmap guarantees that someone planning a cross-country car trip will arrive at the desired destination. A marketing plan must be successfully implemented. Successful implementation is directly related to the structure of a business's marketing effort.

For example, a manufacturer of electric utility equipment engaged in an extensive market segmentation project in an effort to revitalize its sales and profitability. The effort revealed several new market segments, all reachable and judged as attractive. The manufacturer then developed a multi-segment marketing strategy with a separate strategy for each market segment. But the sales force was structured into three geographical regions and had not participated in the segmentation study and strategy development. The marketing manager knew that without the support of the sales reps, the marketing strategy would fail.

To implement this strategy successfully, the marketing manager had to sell it to the three regional vice presidents for sales. Two regional sales VPs agreed to implement the strategy, but the third chose not to participate. The results, shown in Figure 15-8, illustrate the importance of effective strategy implementation. In the two regions (A and B)

FIGURE 15-8 SALES IMPACT OF A SUCCESSFUL STRATEGY IMPLEMENTATION

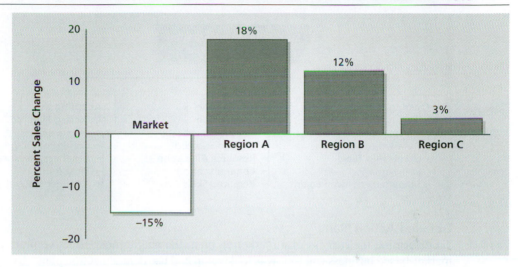

where the marketing strategy was implemented, sales increased by 18 and 12 percent, even though total demand in the market declined by 15 percent. By contrast, the region (C) that did not implement the marketing strategy had only a 3 percent sales gain.[12]

To achieve marketing success and reach its performance objectives, a business needs to develop a good marketing plan and to execute it well. A good marketing plan without a dedicated implementation effort will fail. The next two sections cover the forces that affect the implementation of a marketing plan and the mechanics of a marketing plan variance analysis.

MANAGING SUCCESSFUL STRATEGY IMPLEMENTATION

It is next to impossible to implement a poor plan and obtain good results, but implementing a superb plan can also fail to deliver the desired performance. Figure 15-9 shows three major forces that contribute to success or failure in implementing a marketing plan. Each of these forces is influenced by underlying factors that can cause the force to have a positive or negative impact on successful implementation. Collectively, these factors will shape the behavior and organizational structure in a way that either facilitates or impedes successful implementation.[13]

Owning the Marketing Plan

Perhaps the most common reason a marketing plan fails is a lack of ownership. If a business's senior managers, marketing and sales managers, and other key employees do not have an ownership stake in the plan, with responsibility for its success, it will be business as usual for all but a frustrated few. As shown in Figure 15-9, ownership of a marketing plan can be enhanced with detailed action plans, a plan champion or ownership team, compensation based on performance metrics, and top management involvement.

FIGURE 15-9 SUCCESSFUL IMPLEMENTATION OF A MARKETING PLAN

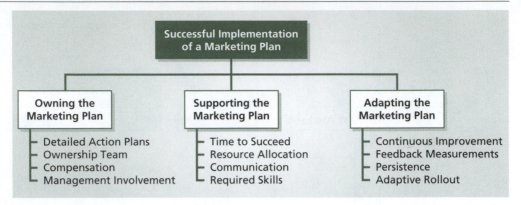

Detailed Action Plans

To determine the success of a marketing plan, the single most effective practice that a market-based business can follow is to develop and use detailed action plans. Every aspect of the marketing strategy and its supporting marketing mix strategies is supported with a detailed plan that specifies the actions that need to occur during implementation. Figure 15-10 outlines how a particular tactical marketing mix strategy within a marketing plan would be implemented. In this case, the strategy is broken into five important action items, each of which must occur for that aspect of the marketing plan to succeed. As shown, for each of the five action items the plan assigns an individual a specific responsibility, delineates a measure or goal, and sets a time frame for completion of the action item.

Any number of action items could be added to this action plan, but the important point is that significant elements of this strategy have specific ownership. Individuals take personal responsibility and become accountable for implementing a portion of the marketing plan. When individuals take ownership of particular aspects of the process, a business breaks the business-as-usual routine, creating an environment that fosters successful implementation of the plan.

FIGURE 15-10 DETAILED ACTION PLAN FOR A CHANNEL STRATEGY

Channel Strategy—To create adequate end-user product availability, 80 manufacturers' representatives and 5 missionary salespeople will be used to sell and distribute our product to 5,000 industrial supply houses in the United States and Canada.

No.	Action Item	Responsibility	Measure	Time Frame*
1.	Identify target supply houses and establish contracts.	P. Eliot	5,000 Dealers	12 months
2.	Contact manufacturers' reps.	T. Garcia	80 Reps	6 months
3.	Hire missionary sales force.**	P. Wilson	5 People	3 months
4.	Develop rep training program.	S. Bradley	Program Pilot	6 months
5.	Develop dealer training program.	R. Otto	Program Pilot	6 months

*From time of implementation
**A missionary sales force provides customers with information but does not engage in sales.

Champion or Ownership Team

Assigning responsibilities for detailed action plans means that a wide range of people will be involved in implementing the plan, but every successful marketing plan has a champion or an ownership team—one person or a group of people who are highly devoted to the plan and lead its successful implementation. Although there is nothing wrong with choosing a single owner or champion, the creation of an ownership team can leverage the unique talents of many people and exert more organizational leverage than can a single individual.[14] Using an ownership team keeps the implementation process on track even when some members of the team are away for extended periods because of business trips, training programs, illness, or vacations.

Compensation

Most people respond to financial rewards. Tying the compensation of those who are principally responsible for implementing the marketing plan to performance metrics increases their incentive to achieve success. Compensation can be tied to both external marketing metrics and internal financial metrics. Marketing metrics are most important in the early stages of implementing a marketing plan. Measurements of end-customer awareness and interest, product availability, and trial can occur well before the results of financial metrics, such as sales revenue and net profit, are reported. The purpose of tying compensation to the results of marketing metrics is to immediately create motivation and responsibility.

Management Involvement

Senior managers must stay committed to an ongoing review of a marketing plan's development and performance. When top managers lessen the time they spend reviewing the development of a plan and its performance after implementation, they implicitly signal a lack of interest and support. This signal weakens the motivation of the ownership team and the plan's chances for success.

Supporting the Marketing Plan

Many factors affect a business's level of commitment to a marketing plan, but the most important ones are time to succeed, resource allocation, communication, and skills to succeed.[15]

Time to Succeed

In many instances, commitment to a marketing plan weakens when financial performance is not on track. If meaningful marketing metrics are not employed, a business may pull support for a marketing plan without knowing why the plan is not working. Perhaps the marketing plan is good but implementation has been poor. Or perhaps the marketing metrics are on target but the financial metrics need more time to achieve the desired levels of performance.

The length of time it will take to succeed depends in part on the type of strategic market plan that the business is pursuing and the nature of the market opportunity. A share-penetration strategy in an existing market generally takes less time to succeed than a strategy to enter a new, undeveloped market. In either case, the time to succeed, along with marketing metrics that measure progress, are important aspects of the marketing plan and its successful implementation.

Resource Allocation

If the process and structure of developing a marketing plan are followed as described in Chapter 14, the marketing plan will have sufficient resources with respect to personnel and funding. If the required resources are not reserved for implementing the plan, the chances for success are greatly reduced. Of course, if the resources needed are not systematically determined during the plan's development phase, it is even more likely that the plan will lack the needed resources. (It is rare that marketing plans receive more resources than they need.) An important step in the successful implementation of a plan is to ensure that the business has committed the necessary resources.

Communication

It is difficult to obtain support either internally (within the company) or externally (from the market) if the marketing plan and its strategic intent are not aggressively communicated. Although senior management and the marketing management team are likely to fully understand the logic and tactics of the marketing plan, others in sales, customer support, manufacturing, and finance may not be entirely aware of the plan's objectives and the strategies for achieving them. As a result, these employees, who often have key roles in successful implementation, will continue in a business-as-usual mode of operation. To facilitate communication and understanding, some businesses create videos that describe the performance objectives and strategies of their marketing plans and then have their employees attend viewing sessions. Internal communication of a marketing plan, including the specific roles that individuals within the business play with respect to implementation, is critical. As much as possible, these job functions should be integrated into the detailed action plans. Key individuals will then understand their roles and responsibilities in the successful implementation of the plan.

Skills to Succeed

Do those implementing the plan have the skills to *effectively* implement it?[16] For example, a bank that wishes to improve customer satisfaction and retention may need to do some training to strengthen customer-focused attitudes among employees. Two of the five action items detailed in Figure 15-10 involve training. In order for the strategy in Figure 15-10 to succeed, it is essential to train manufacturers' reps and distributors with respect to the product's features, its service requirements, how to sell the product, and how to explain the value it delivers. If they do not receive training, the strategy is unlikely to be successful.

In many instances, even members of the management team need additional training. A business with an objective to increase sales by introducing a product that offers new customer benefits may need to provide some management training on the new product's benefits. Without the necessary skills, the management team might produce a meaningful objective but have no way of accomplishing it.

Adapting the Marketing Plan

The planning process does not stop when implementation of the marketing plan begins; planning continues over the plan's time horizon. Like all systems, a marketing plan needs to adapt to unanticipated changes. To survive, as well as to succeed, the marketing plan needs built-in adaptability. Four factors that contribute to the adaptive nature of a marketing plan are continuous improvement, feedback measurements, persistence, and an incremental, adaptive rollout of the plan.

Continuous Improvement

A marketing plan that does not adapt to changing market conditions will fail. Because market conditions are complex and almost always in flux, a business must modify its marketing plan in response to the changing conditions. In many instances, the modifications are minor fine-tuning of the business's marketing plan and value proposition. However, in some cases, a whole new strategy may be required.

The term *adaptive persistence* has been used to describe the success of many Japanese marketing plans. One of Japanese management's greatest assets is the ability to adapt when a marketing plan is not working and to stick with the plan—*to persist*. The whole concept of continuous improvement is implicit in Japanese marketing plan implementation. Although the marketing plan sets the direction and provides the initial roadmap, after it is in place the flexibility to adapt is an important aspect of continuous improvement.

Feedback Measurements

An essential element of any adaptive system, whether it is mechanical, electrical, or human, is feedback. Mechanical, electrical, and human systems have internal sensors and feedback mechanisms. Management systems also require measurements to provide a mechanism for feedback. Forward-looking marketing performance metrics are the internal sensors for a marketing plan feedback system. These measurements signal the marketing plan's progress toward achieving its performance objectives in sales, market share, net profit, and net marketing contribution.

Key forward-looking marketing metrics that provide leading signals of the marketing plan's success include

- Customer awareness, interest, intentions to buy, trial, and repeat purchase;
- Channel intermediary market coverage, interest, support, and motivation; and
- Business responsiveness to customer inquiries and problems.

Each of these marketing metrics has to reach an effective level of performance before the financial metrics will show improved results. The marketing metrics provide an early indication of the progress of the marketing plan. If the results of the marketing metrics are behind the target performance levels specified in the marketing plan, improved performance as measured by financial metrics will materialize more slowly than projected.

The forward-looking marketing metrics also signal aspects of the marketing plan that may be failing. Is it the channel system, the communications strategy, or the product-price positioning strategy that is the cause of the plan's slow progress toward its objectives? Knowing the source of the problem enables a business to devise effective new strategies for improving the plan in light of market conditions.

Persistence

Japanese companies provide insight on the need for persistence as well. They often are cited as exemplars of successful marketing, but rarely have Japanese marketing strategies worked initially. As mentioned, two great traits of Japanese managers are adaptation and persistence during the implementation phase of their marketing plans. Japanese marketing managers remain committed to their objectives and persist by adapting their marketing plans. Their determination to make their marketing plans work is one of the secrets of their marketing success.

In comparison, American managers often are quick to drop a marketing plan when it meets the first bit of resistance. Perhaps expectations of performance have been overstated, or the time needed to succeed has been underestimated. Because marketing plans that were developed in a corporate office may lack the realism of the marketplace, they may need to be adapted during implementation. Without a high degree of management persistence, there is little chance of successful implementation, particularly when aspects of the marketing plan need to be modified.

Adaptive Rollout

An adaptive rollout is an incremental implementation of a marketing plan that allows for feedback and corrective adjustments early in the implementation process. The rollout starts in one region of a broader market—the southwestern states, for example. After the regional rollout, strategies are refined and then rolled out in another region. This process of fine-tuning strategies continues until all regions of the market are served. One disadvantage of a regional rollout is that it sends a signal to competitors about a company's intent for the entire market.

There are many advantages, however. First, fewer resources are required for a small-scale regional implementation of a marketing plan than for a market-wide effort. Second, the company can correct problems with distributors, marketing communications, and product positioning more readily on a small scale. Third, if the marketing plan is more effective than planned, the company can add to production capacity to avoid stockout (depletion of inventory caused by a rise in demand) and lose opportunities to capture customers when they want to buy. Fourth, even if the marketing plan is tracking as planned on a regional basis, a regional rollout will provide additional marketing insights that can be advantageously integrated into the plan during full implementation. Fifth, the revenue generated from a successful regional rollout can be used to help fund a wider or full rollout. Because of these benefits, many foreign competitors use regional rollouts when they enter the U.S. market.

Many U.S. businesses are reluctant to spend the time that adaptive rollouts require, however. But rarely does a marketing plan proceed exactly as conceived on paper. A full rollout risks the loss of customers and distributors if the business's value proposition is ineffectively presented. In addition, the cost of a full rollout when things go wrong is enormous, even if the company is able to retain all its customers and distributors through the repositioning period.

Assessing the Implementation of a Marketing Plan

Figure 15-11 lists the main ingredients for success in implementing a marketing plan and shows a profile of a business that worked to improve its plan implementation. No single factor presented in Figure 15-11 will make or break the successful implementation of a marketing plan. However, when all of these factors are adequately addressed, the chances for successful implementation are greatly improved. Although this business did not perform well for every factor, its overall performance was much better than in the past. A good marketing plan with this level of implementation effort will enable a business to achieve its desired level of performance within the timeframe allotted.

At the heart of the successful implementation of a marketing plan is a business's market orientation. The greater the degree to which the business has created a market orientation, the better its chances for successful implementation.[17] A market-based

FIGURE 15-11 ASSESSING THE IMPLEMENTATION OF A MARKETING PLAN

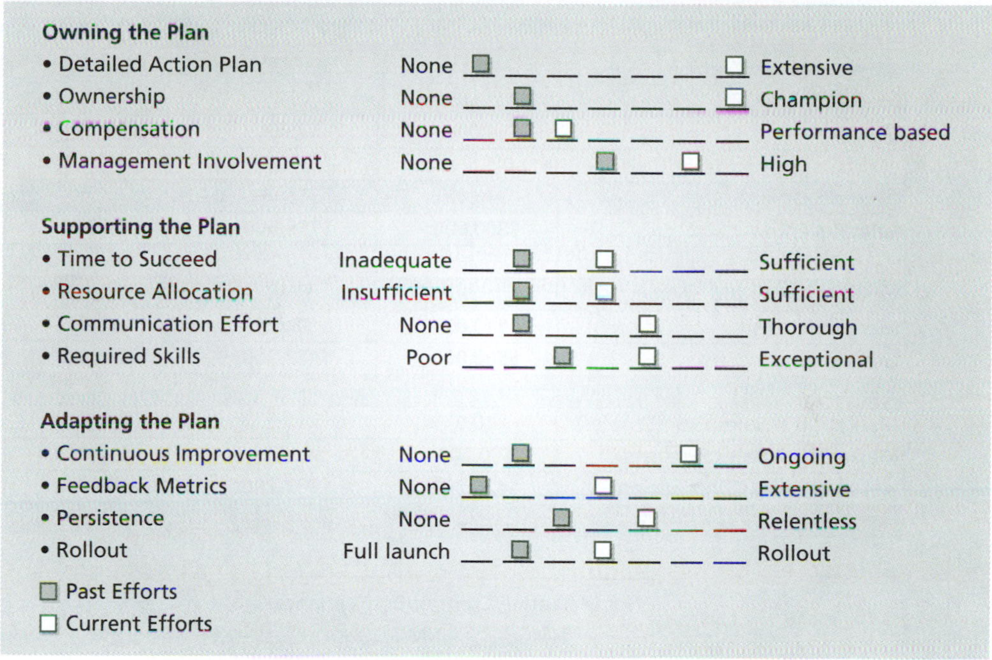

Owning the Plan
- Detailed Action Plan   None ▣ _ _ _ _ _ _ ▢ Extensive
- Ownership   None _ ▣ _ _ _ _ _ ▢ Champion
- Compensation   None _ ▣ ▢ _ _ _ _ Performance based
- Management Involvement   None _ _ _ ▣ _ ▢ _ High

Supporting the Plan
- Time to Succeed   Inadequate _ ▣ _ ▢ _ _ _ Sufficient
- Resource Allocation   Insufficient _ ▣ _ ▢ _ _ _ Sufficient
- Communication Effort   None _ ▣ _ _ ▢ _ _ Thorough
- Required Skills   Poor _ _ ▣ _ ▢ _ _ Exceptional

Adapting the Plan
- Continuous Improvement   None _ ▣ _ _ _ ▢ _ Ongoing
- Feedback Metrics   None ▣ _ _ ▢ _ _ _ Extensive
- Persistence   None _ _ ▣ _ ▢ _ _ Relentless
- Rollout   Full launch _ ▣ _ ▢ _ _ _ Rollout

▣ Past Efforts
▢ Current Efforts

business with a strong customer focus and competitor orientation across job functions has a greater level of market sensitivity and urgency from which to develop and implement its plan.

VARIANCE ANALYSIS

After implementing a marketing plan, marketing managers need to compare the planned results with the actual results at periodic intervals in the plan's time horizon to determine which variables are contributing to the plan's performance. If a business achieves the first-year net marketing contribution performance objective, it might be because all the strategic variables performed as planned. Or the same result could be due to an underperformance in some variables of the NMC equation, combined with an overperformance in others. Variance analysis allows a business to isolate the components of marketing performance to understand better how each is contributing to the NMC:

$$\text{NMC} = \text{Volume} \times \text{Margin per Unit} - \text{Marketing \& Sales Expenses}$$
$$= (\text{Demand} \times \text{Share}) \times (\text{Price} - \text{Variable Unit Cost}) - \text{Marketing \& Sales Exp.}$$

Consider the business in Figure 15-12, which has a marketing plan that projected $420,000 for the net marketing contribution for year 1 of the plan. The actual NMC at the end of year 1 was $86,800 less than estimated in the plan, as calculated in the first tier of the diagram. What was the primary cause of this shortfall in performance?

FIGURE 15-12 VARIANCE ANALYSIS—PLAN VERSUS ACTUAL PERFORMANCE

Area of Performance	Plan	Actual	Variance
Market Demand (units)	200,000	230,000	30,000
Market Share (%)	25.0	23.0	–2.0
Volume	50,000	52,900	2,900
Price per Unit	$16.00	$15.00	–$1.00
Sales Revenues	$800,000	$793,500	–$6,500
Variable Cost per Customer	$6.00	$7.00	$1.00
Margin per Unit	$10.00	$8.00	–$2.00
Gross Profit	$500,000	$423,200	–$76,800
Marketing & Sales Exp. (% sales)	10.0	11.3	1.3
Marketing & Sales Expenses	$80,000	$90,000	$10,000
Net Marketing Contribution	$420,000	$333,200	–$86,800

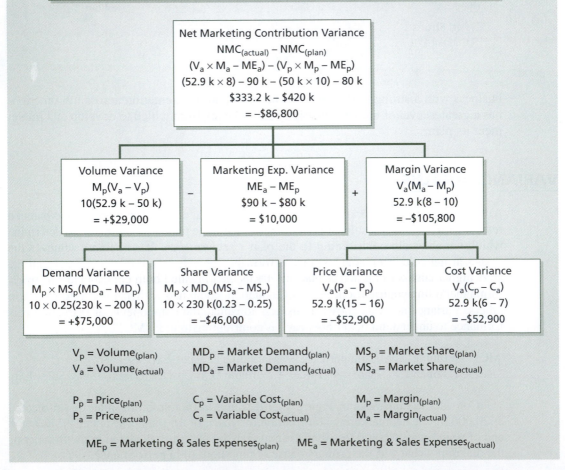

Net Marketing Contribution Variance
$$NMC_{(actual)} - NMC_{(plan)}$$
$$(V_a \times M_a - ME_a) - (V_p \times M_p - ME_p)$$
$$(52.9\,k \times 8) - 90\,k - (50\,k \times 10) - 80\,k$$
$$\$333.2\,k - \$420\,k$$
$$= -\$86,800$$

Volume Variance
$$M_p(V_a - V_p)$$
$$10(52.9\,k - 50\,k)$$
$$= +\$29,000$$

Marketing Exp. Variance
$$ME_a - ME_p$$
$$\$90\,k - \$80\,k$$
$$= \$10,000$$

Margin Variance
$$V_a(M_a - M_p)$$
$$52.9\,k(8 - 10)$$
$$= -\$105,800$$

Demand Variance
$$M_p \times MS_p(MD_a - MD_p)$$
$$10 \times 0.25(230\,k - 200\,k)$$
$$= +\$75,000$$

Share Variance
$$M_p \times MD_a(MS_a - MS_p)$$
$$10 \times 230\,k(0.23 - 0.25)$$
$$= -\$46,000$$

Price Variance
$$V_a(P_a - P_p)$$
$$52.9\,k(15 - 16)$$
$$= -\$52,900$$

Cost Variance
$$V_a(C_p - C_a)$$
$$52.9\,k(6 - 7)$$
$$= -\$52,900$$

V_p = Volume$_{(plan)}$ $\qquad$ MD_p = Market Demand$_{(plan)}$ $\qquad$ MS_p = Market Share$_{(plan)}$

V_a = Volume$_{(actual)}$ $\qquad$ MD_a = Market Demand$_{(actual)}$ $\qquad$ MS_a = Market Share$_{(actual)}$

P_p = Price$_{(plan)}$ $\qquad$ C_p = Variable Cost$_{(plan)}$ $\qquad$ M_p = Margin$_{(plan)}$

P_a = Price$_{(actual)}$ $\qquad$ C_a = Variable Cost$_{(actual)}$ $\qquad$ M_a = Margin$_{(actual)}$

ME_p = Marketing & Sales Expenses$_{(plan)}$ $\qquad$ ME_a = Marketing & Sales Expenses$_{(actual)}$

The second tier in the diagram shows the calculation of the variances between actual and planned volume (V_a minus V_p), actual and planned marketing and sales expenses (ME_a minus ME_p), and actual and planned margin per unit (M_a minus M_p). The volume sold was higher than planned, the unit margin was lower, and marketing and sales expenses were higher. Of the $86,800 negative variance in the NMC, $10,000 is attributable to the difference between actual and planned marketing and sales expenses. However, performance variances in volume and margin can be broken down further.

As illustrated in Figure 15-12, a variance in volume reflects any difference in actual versus planned market demand, plus any difference in actual versus planned market share. In this example, a positive variance in market demand was responsible for an increase in the net marketing contribution of $75,000, and a negative variance in market share was responsible for a decrease by $46,000. Taken together, the greater-than-planned market demand and the smaller-than-planned market share were responsible for the positive variance of $29,000 in volume ($75,000 minus $46,000). The volume variance in turn contributed the same amount to the NMC ($10 in planned margin times 2,900 more units sold equals $29,000).

The margin variance in this example is also derived from more than one source of performance. Actual prices were lower than planned and actual costs were higher than planned. In this case, the price variance and unit cost variance each had a negative impact of $52,900 on the net marketing contribution, for a combined negative variance of $105,800 in total margin.

The fundamental marketing profitability metric for planning purposes is the net marketing contribution equation. Examining the sources of the net marketing contribution in terms of their underlying performance variances allows us to see which aspects of the plan worked and which did not. With this information, a marketing manager is better equipped to make adjustments in the marketing plan and to project future performance more accurately. The insights a marketing manager could gain from the variance analysis in Figure 15-12 include the following:

- If market demand had not been greater than expected, the performance gap in the net marketing contribution would have been much wider. In other words, a little good luck was involved.
- If the business had achieved its planned market share, the net marketing contribution shortfall would have been less than it was.
- A higher cost per unit and lower unit prices than planned both contributed to a lower net marketing contribution.
- The higher-than-planned marketing and sales expenses will have to be addressed in future profit planning.

A situation in which actual marketing profits are lower than expected is likely to draw the attention of senior management. But what about a situation in which no differences occur between actual and planned net marketing contribution, actual and planned volume sold, and actual and planned marketing and sales expenses? Such a situation is illustrated in Figure 15-13. The marketing plan is obviously on track. A finance-oriented business would note that price per unit is $10 higher than in the marketing plan but would also investigate the higher variable cost per unit. A finance-oriented

FIGURE 15-13 VARIANCE ANALYSIS SHOWING "HIDDEN" CONCERNS

Area of Performance	Plan	Actual	Variance
Market Demand (units)	1,000,000	1,250,000	250,000
Market Share (%)	25.0	20.0	−5.0
Volume	250,000	250,000	0
Price per Unit	$450.00	$460.00	$10.00
Sales Revenues	$112,500,000	$115,000,000	$2,500,000
Variable Cost per Unit	$200.00	$210.00	$10.00
Margin per Customer	$250.00	$250.00	$0.00
Gross Profit	$62,500,000	$62,500,000	$0
Marketing & Sales Exp. (% sales)	13.3	13.0	−0.3
Marketing & Sales Expenses	$15,000,000	$15,000,000	$0
Net Marketing Contribution	$47,500,000	$47,500,000	$0

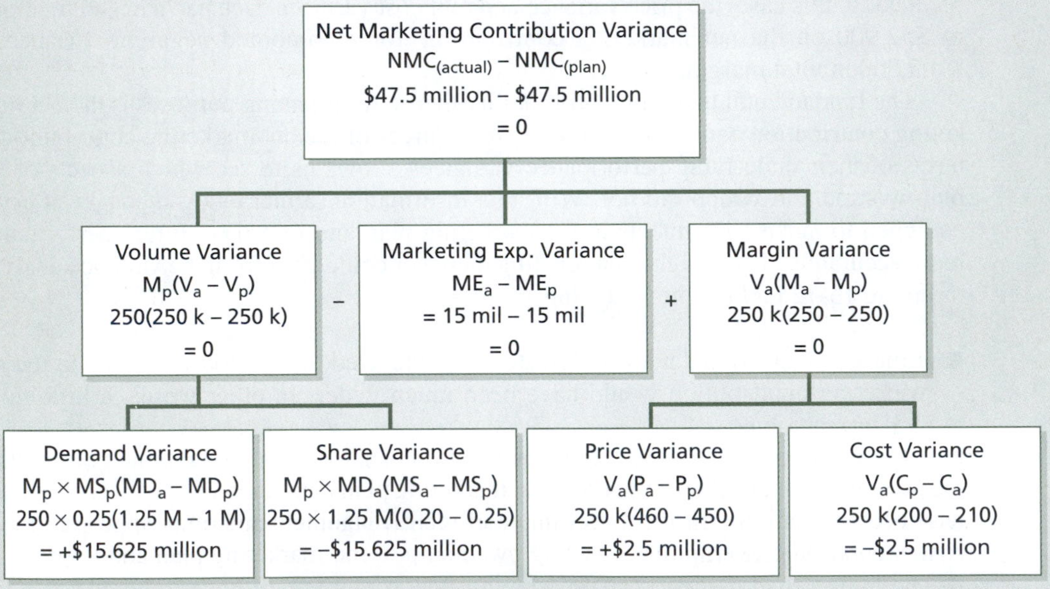

Net Marketing Contribution Variance
$$NMC_{(actual)} - NMC_{(plan)}$$
$47.5 \text{ million} - \$47.5 \text{ million}$
$= 0$

Volume Variance
$$M_p(V_a - V_p)$$
$250(250\,k - 250\,k)$
$= 0$

$-$

Marketing Exp. Variance
$$ME_a - ME_p$$
$= 15\,mil - 15\,mil$
$= 0$

$+$

Margin Variance
$$V_a(M_a - M_p)$$
$250\,k(250 - 250)$
$= 0$

Demand Variance
$$M_p \times MS_p(MD_a - MD_p)$$
$250 \times 0.25(1.25\,M - 1\,M)$
$= +\$15.625 \text{ million}$

Share Variance
$$M_p \times MD_a(MS_a - MS_p)$$
$250 \times 1.25\,M(0.20 - 0.25)$
$= -\$15.625 \text{ million}$

Price Variance
$$V_a(P_a - P_p)$$
$250\,k(460 - 450)$
$= +\$2.5 \text{ million}$

Cost Variance
$$V_a(C_p - C_a)$$
$250\,k(200 - 210)$
$= -\$2.5 \text{ million}$

business, however, would rarely look beyond volume and would probably fail to recognize performance variances in market demand and market share.

A business that does not track market share, market demand, and other marketing performance metrics will usually discover too late that its marketing plan is not working. In contrast, a market-based business that tracks performance metrics and conducts an annual variance analysis over the life of the plan will know whether its actual marketing performance matches the planned performance and where any shortcomings in the plan are.

The variance analysis in Figure 15-13, for instance, shows the independent effects of variances in market demand and market share on the net marketing contribution. This information would alert the business to a disturbing performance gap in market share. As the market is growing faster than expected, the business may have underresourced its marketing and sales expenses, which is causing the business to fall short of its intended share goal. With this variance analysis, a market-based business would recognize the higher-than-expected market demand and would be able to take steps to achieve the target market share of 25 percent. Although the analysis shows that performance variances in price and variable cost had a smaller impact on the net marketing contribution for that particular year, the price and variable-cost variances are nevertheless important in modifying the marketing plan or in developing an effective future plan.

The examples presented in Figures 15-12 and 15-13 show us why the implementation of a marketing plan is more likely to succeed when a business's managers track performance metrics and conduct periodic variance analyses to determine how well the plan is performing over time.

■ Summary

Marketing metrics are an important part of responsible market-based management. It is critical that marketing managers and marketing professionals establish a credible set of marketing metrics that link marketing performance to company sales and profits. The use of marketing metrics has been demonstrated to benefit financial performance, yet many companies resist adopting them. This chapter identified five common barriers to usage and recommended solutions for overcoming them.

Most businesses, especially at first, cannot apply all of the many marketing metrics that have been developed. It is best to start with a small set of marketing metrics, chosen with the organization's needs, capabilities, and budget in mind, that can be tied to business objectives. Some of these may be forward-looking marketing metrics (e.g., customer retention) and others may be backward looking (e.g., market share). Likewise, some marketing metrics could be external (e.g., customer satisfaction) and others internal (e.g., marketing ROI).

Developing a proactive, market-based marketing plan is only half of the work. The plan must also be effectively implemented. Without ownership, support, and adaptation, the plan will fail. Detailed action plans, a marketing plan champion or team, performance-based compensation, and the involvement of top management and other appropriate personnel contribute to employees feeling ownership of the marketing plan and improve its chances of successful implementation.

Successful implementation also requires time to succeed, sufficient resources, a comprehensive communications effort, and skills on the part of those involved. The business must show a readiness to respond to any unanticipated obstacles, such as swings in market conditions, that will likely arise during implementation. The probability of unexpected impediments requires that marketing plans be adaptive. Continuous efforts to improve the plan, on the basis of feedback measures, are an important part of successful implementation. Businesses that are persistent in adapting their marketing plans have a greater chance for success. A regional rollout provides a less expensive venue than a full-scale rollout, and one that entails fewer risks, in which to adapt the marketing plan.

Performance metrics, including marketing and financial metrics, play a key role in implementing a marketing plan. Marketing performance metrics are external measures of marketing performance, such as awareness, customer satisfaction, and market share. Financial performance metrics are internal measures of performance, such as unit margin, net profit, and return on investment. Marketing performance metrics consist of both forward-looking metrics and backward-looking metrics. Customer awareness, customer satisfaction, and perceived product performance are examples of forward-looking marketing performance metrics. Backward-looking marketing performance metrics include market share, revenue per customer, and customer retention. Forward-looking marketing metrics can forecast the success or failure of a marketing plan and its implementation effort, and they are also indicators of future financial performance.

Finally, an important part of assessing the implementation of a marketing plan is determining which parts of the plan are performing as expected and which are not. Variance analysis is a periodic, systematic assessment of each area of performance. The technique holds the effects of all variables except one constant to allow this single variance between planned and actual performance to be assessed with respect to its impact on profits. The analysis allows a manager to fully understand the reasons behind a marketing plan's performance for any year of the plan and to take corrective action. In some situations, managers may discover large negative variances hidden behind many smaller positive variances. After a marketing plan ends its last year of implementation, a final variance analysis is used to assess the plan's success during the entire course of its timeframe, giving managers the information they need to develop more effective marketing plans in the future.

■ Market-Based Strategic Thinking

1 Why would training in the area of marketing metrics for Campbell Soup Company help improve marketing performance and company profits?

2 How would a company like General Motors use marketing metrics to improve company profits?

3 How would you recommend a company like United Airlines get started using marketing metrics to better manage its marketing performance and profitability?

4 Why are forward-looking marketing metrics important to a business like Starbucks?

5 How do backward-looking marketing metrics help a business like McDonald's better understand its marketing performance?

6 Why is implementation of a marketing plan as important as plan development in achieving marketing success?

7 How do detailed action plans contribute to individual ownership of a marketing plan?

8 Why does a marketing plan need a champion or an ownership team?

9 How should a business tie compensation to successful implementation of a marketing plan?

10 Why is "time to succeed" an important part of implementing a marketing plan?

11 What signal is senior management sending when it does not take the time to review the marketing planning process and the performance of the plan after implementation?

12 What is meant by *persistence* in terms of commitment? What is meant by the term *adaptive persistence* as it is used to describe the Japanese style of marketing plan implementation?

13 Why are continuous improvement and feedback measures important aspects of the successful implementation of a marketing plan?

14 What are the advantages and disadvantages of a regional rollout of a marketing plan?

15 What roles do resources, organizational communications, and training play in the successful implementation of a marketing plan?

16 Why are performance metrics important to the implementation process?

Marketing Performance Tools and Application Exercises

The three interactive marketing performance tools and application exercises outlined here will add to your understanding of the use of variance analysis in assessing the performance of a marketing plan. To access the tools, go to **rogerjbest.com.** Enter the data in each exercise to see the results. You may also enter your own data to see the results, and you may save your work. The three tools are based on Figure 15-13.

15.1 Variance Analysis—Market Demand and Market Share
■ Change the actual market demand to 1,250,000 and actual market share to 23 percent, separately, to first evaluate the impact of each change on sales and profits. Then change both actual values to evaluate the combined effect of both variances on sales and profits.

Finally, return both values to the plan values.

15.2 Variance Analysis—Revenue and Cost per Customer
■ Change the actual price to $460 and the variable cost per unit to $210, separately, to evaluate the impact of each change on sales and profits. Then change both actual values to evaluate the combined effect of both variances on sales and profits. Finally, return both values to the plan values.

15.3 Variance Analysis—Marketing and Sales Expenses
■ Change the actual marketing and sales expenses as a percentage of sales to 14 percent to evaluate the impact on profits.

Notes

1. P. Hyde, E. Landry, and A. Tipping, "Making the Perfect Marketer," *Strategy + Business* (Winter 2004).
2. J.M. Carr, B. Blake, and K. Gustafson, "The Marketing Performance Advantage," http://cmgpartners.com/ (Chadwick Martin Bailey Inc.), retrieved January 2011.
3. Hyde, *op. cit.*
4. P. Farris, N. Bendle, P. Pfeifer, and D. Reibstein, *Marketing Metrics* (Wharton School Publishing, 2007); http://marketingnpv.com/; *Marketing Metrics Handbook,* http://www.marketingmetricssolutions.com/introduction.cfm.
5. J. Pfeffer and R. Sutton, "Why Managing by Facts Works," *Strategy+Business* (Spring 2006).
6. D. Gensch, "Targeting the Switchable Industrial Customer," *Marketing Science* (Winter 1984): 41–54.
7. G. Cressman, "Choosing the Right Metric," *Drive Marketing Excellence* (November 1994), New York: Institute for International Research.
8. R. Kaplan and D. Norton, "The Balanced Scorecard—Measures That Drive Performance," *Harvard Business Review* (January–February 1982): 71–9.
9. R. Peterson and W. Wilson, "Measuring Customer Satisfaction: Fact or Artifact," *Journal of the Academy of Marketing Science* 20 (1992): 61–71.
10. T. Jones and E. Sasser, Jr., "Why Satisfied Customers Defect," *Harvard Business Review* (November–December 1995): 88–99; F.F. Reichheld and W.E. Sasser, Jr., "Zero Defections: Quality Comes to Services," *Harvard Business Review* (September–October 1990): 106–11; and F.F. Reichheld, "Loyalty Based Management," *Harvard Business Review* (March–April 1993): 64–73.

11. Jacob Tyler Creative Group, "Nike's 11 Maxims" (August 5, 2010): http://optimize4you.articlealley.com/nike-11-maxims-1680142.html, retrieved October 10, 2011.

12. P. Byrne, "Global Logistics: Only 10 Percent of Companies Satisfy Customers," *Transportation and Distribution* (December 1993); and T. Eck, "Are Customers Happy? Don't Assume," *Positive Impact* (July 1992): 3.

13. N. Piercy and N. Morgan, "The Marketing Planning Process: Behavioral Problems Compared to Analytical Techniques in Explaining Marketing Plan Credibility," *Journal of Business Research* 29 (1994): 167–78; and N. Piercy, *Marketing Organization: An Analysis of Information Processing, Power and Politics* (Chicago: George Allen & Urwin, 1985).

14. R. Ruekert and O. Walker, Jr., "Marketing's Interaction with Other Functional Units: A Conceptual Framework and Empirical Evidence," *Journal of Marketing* (January 1987): 1–19.

15. W. Egelhoff, "Great Strategies or Great Strategy Implementation—Two Ways of Competing in Global Markets," *Sloan Management Review* (Winter 1993): 37–50.

16. T. Bonoma, *The Marketing Edge: Making Strategies Work* (New York: Free Press, 1985).

17. G. Day, "Building a Market-Driven Organization," *Market-Driven Strategy* (New York: Free Press, 1990): 356–76.

Market-Based Management and Financial Performance

■ Customers are the only source of cash flow. Everything else is expense.

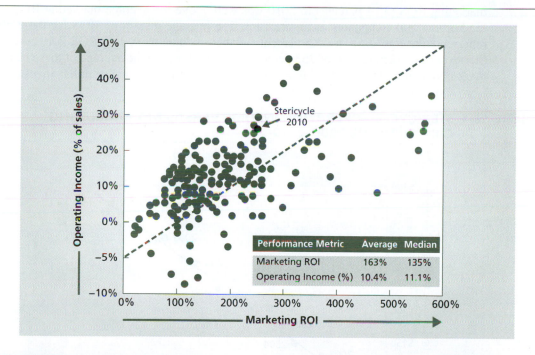

OPERATING INCOME VERSUS MARKETING ROI

In Chapter 14 we presented a sample marketing plan for Stericycle, Inc., the market leader in worldwide medical waste management. In 2010, the company had sales of $1.44 billion and an operating income of $371 million, which was 25.8 percent of sales.[1] Stericycle's net marketing contribution that year was $509 million (35.4 percent of sales), and its investment in marketing and sales expenses was $201.5 million, resulting in a marketing ROI of 253 percent. As shown in the figure above, the marketing ROI and operating income as a percentage of sales were well above the average for the Fortune 500 companies in the graph. The Chapter 2 appendix lists these companies.

FINANCIAL IMPACT OF MARKETING PROFITABILITY

Over a period of 10 years, Stericycle grew its net marketing contribution from under $100 million in 2000 to slightly over $500 million in 2010. As shown in Figure 16-1, this growth in marketing profits corresponds with growth in operating income, which increased from about $75 million in 2000 to $370.7 million in 2010. The correlation shown is over 0.9 and helps illustrate the usefulness of measuring, managing, and reporting net marketing contribution as a measure of the impact of a company's investment in marketing and sales on financial performance.

Figure 16-2 shows how net marketing contribution is derived from sales, percent margin, and marketing and sales expenses. As shown, operating income is the amount that is left over after deducting all other business expenses but before deducting interest and taxes. For Stericycle, other expenses run around 10 percent of sales, but they can vary from year to year, which makes the correlation shown in Figure 16-1 less than perfect.

Figure 16-2 also shows two other important marketing metrics, marketing return on sales (marketing ROS) and marketing return on investment (marketing ROI). Stericycle's marketing ROS (35.4 percent) in 2010 was well above the average marketing ROS for the Fortune 500 companies in Figure 16-3. The average marketing ROS for these 200 representative companies is 23.5 percent and their median marketing ROS is 19 percent. Stericycle's marketing ROI of 253 percent is also well above the average of these benchmark companies. This level of marketing ROI means that for every dollar invested in

FIGURE 16-1 STERICYCLE—OPERATING INCOME VERSUS NET MARKETING CONTRIBUTION, 2000–2010

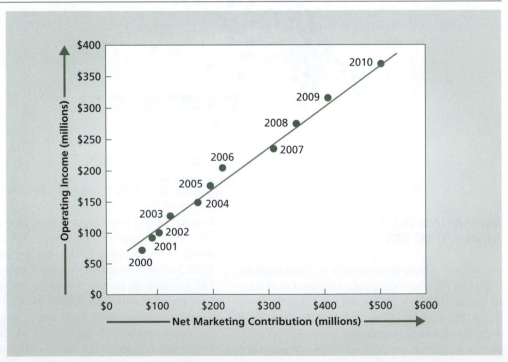

FIGURE 16-2 STERICYCLE—ADDING MARKETING METRICS TO 2010 FINANCIAL PERFORMANCE

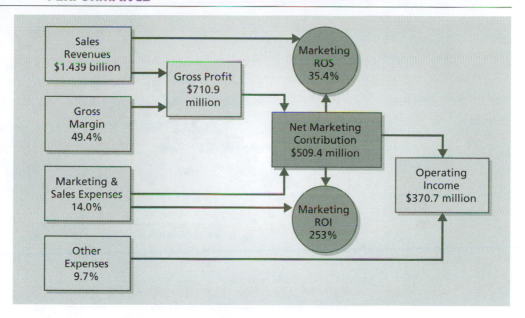

marketing and sales expenses in 2010, Stericycle produced $2.53 in net marketing contribution. Every company could benefit by adding these three marketing metrics, summarized as follows, to its financial reporting.

■ **Net Marketing Contribution**—Provides a measure of marketing profits that demonstrates how much the company's investment in marketing and sales contributes to company profits.

■ **Marketing ROS**—The net marketing contribution as a percentage of sales. A company's operating income as a percentage of sales is equal to the marketing ROS minus other expenses as a percentage of sales.

■ **Marketing ROI**—The ratio of net marketing contribution to a company's investment in marketing and sales expenses. The higher the ratio (expressed as a percentage), the more productive the company's marketing and sales strategies.

Marketing ROS and marketing ROI offer another advantage that helps us fully understand and manage marketing profitability. Because they are percentage metrics, they may be calculated separately for a company's regions, divisions, markets, and product lines, and then the separate measurements may be compared with the company's average marketing ROS and marketing ROI. These percentage marketing performance metrics also may be used to benchmark the company with publicly traded competitor companies and with companies outside the industry, as in the graph on the chapter's first page.

Figure 16-2 illustrates how the three marketing profitability metrics may be included in normal financial analysis and reporting. Including the metrics to the company's financial reporting helps to justify a company's investments in marketing and sales, and it adds to an understanding of how that investment affects company profits.

FIGURE 16-3 OPERATING INCOME (% SALES) VERSUS MARKETING ROS

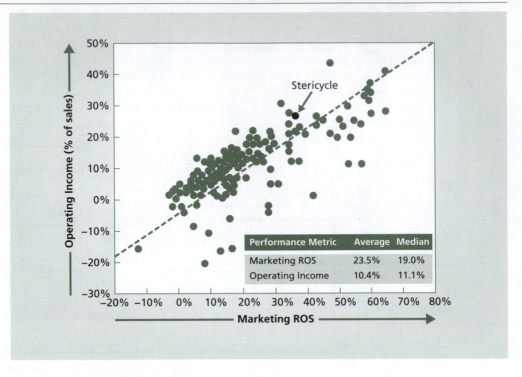

Performance Metric	Average	Median
Marketing ROS	23.5%	19.0%
Operating Income	10.4%	11.1%

BASIC INPUTS TO MARKETING PROFITS AND PROFITABLE GROWTH

Figure 16-2 offers a good understanding from a financial perspective of how a company's net marketing contribution, marketing ROS, and marketing ROI fit into the company's basic profitability model. We can expand this model to include the basic marketing inputs that drive these three marketing performance metrics, as illustrated in Figure 16-4. This section examines the ways that these basic marketing inputs influence Stericycle's current and future marketing performance metrics and operating income.

Market Demand

The size of a market and its market potential and growth rate have a significant impact on any company's ability to grow its sales and profits. For Stericycle, in 2010 the worldwide market demand for medical waste recycling was estimated to be $10.3 billion. This level of market demand is in itself significant, and adding to it is the market's ongoing growth, estimated at 6.3 percent annually.

As shown in Figure 16-5, the market's estimated growth rate translates into a projected worldwide demand of $12.4 billion in 3 years, a 22 percent increase. If Stericycle were satisfied to simply hold its 2010 market share of 14 percent, over the next 3 years sales would grow to $1.76 billion, and the net marketing contribution would increase from $509.4 million to $615 million. The increase takes into account greater spending on marketing and sales, with the annual marketing investment set at a constant 14 percent of annual sales.

FIGURE 16-4 STERICYCLE—MARKETING INPUTS TO PROFITABLE GROWTH

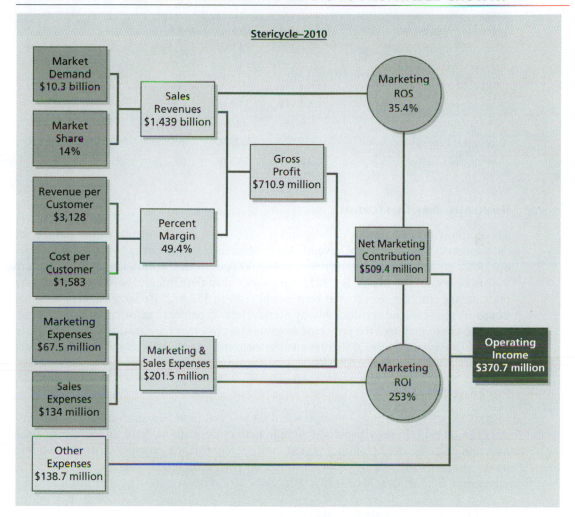

Market Share

Every year since Stericycle's beginning in the early 1990s it has grown market share in a growing market. Companies in a similar situation—competing in a fast-growing market— often find that simultaneously growing their share of that market can be a challenge. However, in our assessment of market share presented in the Chapter 14 sample marketing plan, we estimated that Stericycle's upside market potential was 25.9 percent, almost double its current market share of 14 percent. The sample marketing plan projected the company's market share to grow from 14 percent in 2010 to 16.2 percent in 2013, as shown in Figure 16-5.

If we were to hold market demand at the 2010 level ($10.3 billion) and Stericycle's market share increased as planned, sales would grow to $1.67 billion in 2013, and the net marketing contribution would grow from $509.4 million to $601 million. Over this same period, the marketing and sales budget would increase from $201.5 million to $234 million.

FIGURE 16-5 THE IMPACT OF STERICYCLE MARKET INPUTS

Stericycle, Inc. ($ billions)	2009	2010	2011	2012	2013
Market Demand (worldwide)	$9.6	$10.3	$10.9	$11.6	$12.4
Market Growth Rate	6.3%	6.3%	6.3%	6.3%	6.3%
Market Share (worldwide)	12.3%	14.0%	14.6%	15.4%	16.2%
Sales Revenue	$1.178	$1.439	$1.602	$1.791	$2.011
Sales Growth Rate	8.7%	22.1%	11.3%	11.8%	12.2%
Customers Served Worldwide	431,020	460,000	488,980	519,786	552,532
Revenue per Customer ($ actual)	$2,733	$3,128	$3,276	$3,446	$3,640

Revenue per Customer

The combination of market growth and market share growth increases the number of customers and the amount of revenue per customer as the amount of medical waste per customer grows. In 2010, Stericycle had 460,000 customers worldwide, most of them in the small-account segment. By 2013 we projected in the Chapter 14 sample marketing plan that the company's customer base would grow to 552,532. An increase in the number of customers is helped considerably by Stericycle's 95 percent rate of customer retention.

The combination of the projected revenue and customer base results in an increase in revenue per customer. In 2010, revenue per customer was $3,128. By 2013, revenue per customer is estimated to be $3,640.

Percent Margin

In 2010, Stericycle's percent margin was 49.4 percent, based on an average cost per customer of $1,545. In the Chapter 14 sample marketing plan, we held the percent margin over the 2011 to 2013 planning period at 50 percent. If the cost per customer were to increase at half the rate of growth in revenue per customer, the percent margin could increase to 52.5 percent by 2013.

Marketing and Sales Expenses

Stericycle's success is in part due to its continued investment in marketing and sales expenses. This is not easy, as it is a significant investment. In the sample marketing plan we proposed to continue to invest in marketing and sales expenses as a percentage of sales, in this case 14 percent. This decision would increase spending from $201.5 million in 2010 to $281.5 million in 2013. In Figure 16-4, we estimated that roughly 33 percent of this investment was in marketing expenses and 67 percent in sales expenses, a subjective estimate that could be far from Stericycle's actual allocations.

CUSTOMER PERFORMANCE METRICS AND PROFITABILITY

When a company is focusing on profitability and financial performance metrics, it is easy to lose sight of the customer, the only asset which is not accounted for in most financial discussions. Yet, we have considerable evidence that customer performance metrics like customer satisfaction and customer retention are related to profitability. In this section we want to revisit these two customer performance metrics, examining how good and bad performance with regard to these metrics can affect the profitability of a business unit or company. The customer is the one source of positive cash flow, so it is the responsibility of those in marketing to understand how customers affect a business and its profitability.[2] This section attempts to bring into focus the important role of customers in making a business profitable.

Customer Satisfaction

The American Customer Satisfaction Index (ACSI) was developed by Claus Fornell at the University of Michigan Business School to measure customer satisfaction with respect to the goods and services that are available to household consumers in the United States. Research using this measure of customer satisfaction revealed that businesses scoring in the top 25 percent in customer satisfaction produced an average shareholder value three times greater than businesses in the bottom 25 percent.

Higher levels of customer satisfaction correspond with higher levels of profitability. In general, satisfied customers buy more and are often much more profitable than customers who are less satisfied or dissatisfied. To illustrate the profit impact of customer satisfaction, consider the previous-year customer satisfaction data presented in the top table in Figure 16-6. In this example, the overall customer satisfaction index (0 to 100) is 82, with 25 percent of the customers "very satisfied." In this year, 97 percent of the customers were satisfied and 3 percent were dissatisfied. Satisfied customers also produced roughly double the revenue per customer and three times the gross profit of "somewhat dissatisfied" and "dissatisfied" customers.

The bottom table presents a declining situation, with the customer satisfaction index slipping from 82 to 73. Many businesses would not view this decline as highly

FIGURE 16-6 CUSTOMER SATISFACTION AND CUSTOMER PROFITABILITY

Current Situation	Customer Satisfaction Score	Percent	Avg. Customer Revenue	Percent Margin	Gross Profit
Very Satisfied	100	25%	$3,500	53%	$1,855
Satisfied	80	70%	$3,000	50%	$1,500
Somewhat Satisfied	60	2%	$2,500	50%	$1,250
Somewhat Dissatisfied	40	2%	$1,500	35%	$525
Dissatisfied	20	1%	$1,200	35%	$420
Very Dissatisfied	0	0%	$1,000	35%	$0
Average	82	100%	$3,067	50.3%	$1,543

Declining Situation	Customer Satisfaction Score	Percent	Avg. Customer Revenue	Percent Margin	Gross Profit
Very Satisfied	100	15%	$3,500	53%	$1,855
Satisfied	80	60%	$3,000	50%	$1,500
Somewhat Satisfied	60	14%	$2,500	50%	$1,250
Somewhat Dissatisfied	40	9%	$1,500	35%	$525
Dissatisfied	20	2%	$1,200	35%	$420
Very Dissatisfied	0	0%	$1,000	35%	$0
Average	73	100%	$2,834	48.8%	$1,383

significant. But the percentage of satisfied customers decreased from 97 to 89 percent, and "very satisfied" customers dropped from 25 to 15 percent. These declines result in a drop in the annual revenue per customer from $3,067 to $2,834. Gross profit per customer drops from $1,543 to $1,383, more than 10 percent.

Because customer satisfaction is a forward-looking marketing metric, a company that regularly applies it and detects declining customer satisfaction can take corrective action before profit losses actually occur. When customer satisfaction begins to decline, a company's sales and profits usually remain constant for some period of time, as it is often hard for customers to switch immediately to an alternative supplier. In the case of car purchases, it would be a couple of years before an automotive company saw the effect of diminishing customer satisfaction on sales and profits. When captive customers have no alternative but to remain with a company, sales and profits may not go down at all, even though customer satisfaction is extremely low. But if viable choices become available, the company's sales and profits will drop like a stone.

The ACSI[3] provides a broader insight into the impact of customer satisfaction on profits and shareholder value.[4] For the 10 years covered in Figure 16-7, companies in the ACSI database with high levels of customer satisfaction had a higher stock price index than the S&P 500 index. In contrast, companies with a low customer satisfaction index had an average stock price below the S&P 500 index. In fact, the companies with low customer satisfaction had the same stock price index after 10 years as in year 1.

Customer Retention

High levels of customer satisfaction generally correspond to high levels of customer retention. However, in situations where choice is limited or switching costs are very high, we have seen that companies can enjoy high levels of customer retention even though they have relatively poor levels of customer satisfaction. Whether satisfaction is high or

FIGURE 16-7 STOCK PRICE INDEX AND CUSTOMER SATISFACTION

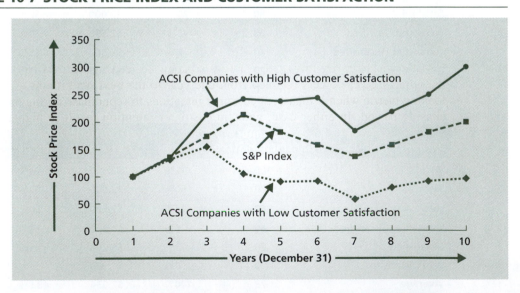

FIGURE 16-8 CUSTOMER RETENTION AND CUSTOMER PROFITABILITY

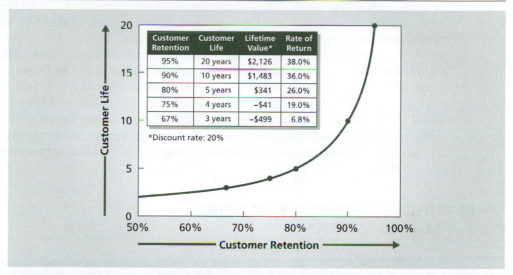

Customer Retention	Customer Life	Lifetime Value*	Rate of Return
95%	20 years	$2,126	38.0%
90%	10 years	$1,483	36.0%
80%	5 years	$341	26.0%
75%	4 years	–$41	19.0%
67%	3 years	–$499	6.8%

*Discount rate: 20%

Period:	0	1	2	3	18	19	20
Customer Revenue		$3,000	$3,000	$3,000	$3,000	$3,000	$3,000
Gross Margin (50%)		$1,500	$1,500	$1,500	$1,500	$1,500	$1,500
Customer Retention Cost		–$250	–$250	–$250	–$250	–$250	–$250
Overhead (10%)		–$300	–$300	–$300	–$300	–$300	–$300
Acquisition Cost	–$2,500	$950	$950	$950	$950	$950	$950
Discount Rate	20%						
Net Present Value Factor	1.000	0.833	0.694	0.579	0.038	0.031	0.026
Net Present Value	–$2,500	$792	$660	$550	$36	$30	$25
Customer Lifetime Value	$2,126						

low, the customer retention metric acts as a backward-looking metric when it measures the number of customers retained from one year to the next, and it acts as a forward-looking metric when it measures customer intentions to repurchase during the next purchasing period. In either case, gains in customer retention result in higher customer profitability, and declines in customer retention result in lower customer profitability.

For the example in Figure 16-8, the company's customer revenue per year is $3,000 and its margin is 50 percent. The annual customer retention cost $250, with an allocated overhead expense of 10 percent of sales. The acquisition cost for a new customer is $2,500. The company uses a 20 percent discount rate to estimate the average customer lifetime value for different levels of customer retention. For the customer base we used a 95 percent retention rate and an average customer life of 20 years, as estimated in the Chapter 14 sample marketing plan. As shown, the result is an average customer lifetime value of $2,126. The rate of return for this cash flow is 38 percent. At 38 percent, the average customer lifetime value is approximately equal to zero. If customer retention were to drop from 95 to 90 percent, the customer life would shorten from 20 years to 10 years, and the customer lifetime value would decrease from $2,126 to $1,483. The rate of return is not drastically affected because the net present values of the cash flows from years 11 to 20 have a limited impact.

When customer retention drops to 80 percent there is a notable decrease in both the average customer lifetime value ($341) and rate of return (26%). Both results are still acceptable with a discount rate of 20 percent. If customer retention were to drop to 75 percent, the average customer lifetime value would be negative and the rate of return would be lower than the discount rate of 20 percent. Although customer metrics like customer satisfaction and customer retention are not reported in any financial statement, they are nevertheless critically important external metrics for measuring a company's performance.

MARKETING PROFITS AND FINANCIAL PERFORMANCE METRICS

Net profit is the driving factor in assessing the profitability of a company. There are several key financial metrics that tie net profit to other aspects of the company's financial structure. These financial metrics are percentage or ratio metrics, which makes it easy to compare one year's results with another's, as well as one company's results with those of competitors and benchmark companies outside the industry.

Figure 16-9 shows six financial metrics that are routinely included in company annual reports and used by financial analysts to track the performance of companies. They are return on sales, return on assets, return on equity, return on capital, economic profit, and earnings per share. The purpose of this section is to review these financial metrics and understand how a company's net marketing contribution affects net profit and the company's financial metrics.

Return on Sales

Return on sales indexes net profit as a percentage of sales. Because it is a percentage metric, we can compare a company's financial performance with that of any other publicly traded company. Shown in Figure 16-9 is Stericycle's 2010 performance and its performance relative to three key marketing profitability metrics. The company's 2010 return on sales was 14.4 percent, higher than US Ecology, one of its direct competitors, which had a return on sales of 10.5 percent. Another competitor, Waste Management, had sales of $12.5 billion in 2010 and a return on sales of 7.6 percent. Return on sales is one of the most commonly used financial metrics.

From a marketing profitability standpoint, the net marketing contribution (NMC) lies at the heart of return on sales:

$$\textbf{Return on Sales} = \text{Net Profit/Sales} \times 100\%$$
$$= \$207.9 \text{ million}/\$1.439 \text{ billion} \times 100\%$$
$$= \textbf{14.4\%}$$
$$\textbf{Return on Sales} = (\textbf{NMC} - \text{Other Expenses} - \text{Interest \& Taxes})/\text{Sales} \times 100\%$$
$$= (\$509.4 \text{ million} - \$140 \text{ million} - \$163 \text{ million})/\$1.439 \text{ billion} \times 100\%$$
$$= \textbf{14.4\%}$$

FIGURE 16-9 STERICYCLE—MARKETING PROFITS AND FINANCIAL METRICS, 2010

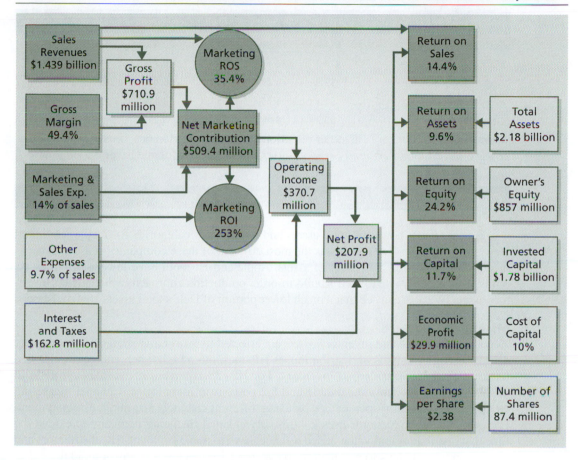

If the net marketing contribution drops, the company would need to reduce other expenses, interest, and taxes in order to maintain a 14.4 percent return on sales. Of course, if the net marketing contribution grows faster than other expenses, there is potential for a higher return on sales.

Return on Assets

Most businesses do not realize the impact of marketing strategies on a business's investment in assets. As we will see, the assets of a business are indirectly affected by marketing strategies. We will limit our discussion to accounts receivable, inventory, and fixed assets, as they are the assets that normally account for most of a business's investment in assets.

$$\textbf{Return on Assets} = \text{Net Profit}/\text{Assets} \times 100\%$$
$$= \$207.9 \text{ million}/\$2.182 \text{ billion} \times 100\%$$
$$= \textbf{9.6}\%$$
$$\textbf{Return on Assets} = (\text{NMC} - \text{Other Expenses} - \text{Interest \& Taxes})/\text{Assets} \times 100\%$$
$$= (\$509.4 \text{ million} - \$140 \text{ million} - \$163 \text{ million})/\$2.182 \text{ billion} \times 100\%$$
$$= \textbf{9.6}\%$$

FIGURE 16-10 MARKETING ASSETS AS A PERCENTAGE OF TOTAL ASSETS

Balance Sheet (billions)	Apple	% Sales	Dell	% Sales	HP	% Sales
Cash & Equivalents	$11.2	17.2%	$13.9	22.6%	$10.9	8.7%
Marketable Securities	$14.4	22.1%	$0.5	0.7%	$1.0	0.8%
Accounts Receivable	$9.9	15.2%	$10.1	16.4%	$27.6	21.9%
Inventory	$1.1	1.7%	$1.3	2.1%	$6.5	5.2%
Other Current	$5.2	8.0%	$3.2	5.1%	$8.2	6.5%
Fixed Assets	$33.5	51.4%	$9.6	15.6%	$70.2	55.7%
Total Assets	$75.3	115%	$38.5	63%	$124.4	99%
Company Sales	$65.2		$61.5		$126.0	
Sales to Assets Ratio	0.87		1.60		1.01	

Figure 16-10 shows the total assets and major asset categories for Apple, Dell, and Hewlett-Packard. In 2010, Dell was the most efficient of these companies at asset management, with sales of $1.59 per $1 of assets. Apple and HP both have lower sales to assets ratios. This is partly due to Dell's build-to-order production approach, which lowers inventory assets. We also can see that a much lower portion of Dell's total assets are fixed assets.

Marketing Assets

Accounts receivable and inventory assets are affected by marketing strategies. A company selling through channels of distribution, as HP does, has a higher percentage of sales tied up in accounts receivable and inventory. For HP, 27.1 percent of its sales are tied up: 21.9 percent in accounts receivable and 5.2 percent in inventories. Channel marketing strategies can lower this percentage by using different channels and methods of payment. For example, Cisco Systems uses a third-party channel financing company to extend the time that distributors and value-added resellers have to make payment. The distributors and VARs can take 60 days to pay their accounts, but Cisco receives payment in 30 days. The channel financing program has allowed Cisco to lower its accounts receivable while increasing sales by providing more liquidity to channel partners. In this case, both the numerator and denominator for the return-on-assets equation are increased.

Service quality also can affect accounts receivable because it often makes a difference in how fast customers pay their bills. Eight out of 10 Fortune 500 companies report that the level of customer service they receive affects their decision to pay a bill on time. More than half of Fortune 500 companies withhold payment from suppliers when they are dissatisfied with the service they receive.[5] Businesses with a strong customer focus and a commitment to service quality and customer satisfaction are in general paid faster than businesses that deliver poor service. Service quality affects customer retention and profit in the numerator and accounts receivable in the denominator of the return on assets equation.

Return on Equity

Stockholders invest money in a company that in turn creates a source of funds for the company to invest in its operations. For Stericycle, with total assets of $2.18 billion and liabilities of $1.323 billion, the owner's equity of $857 million is the difference. Owner's equity serves as the basis for another financial metric, known as return on equity. It tells us how much profit a company makes with the shareholders' investment. For 2010, Stericycle's return on equity was 24.2 percent.

$$\text{Return on Equity} = \text{Net Profit}/\text{Owner's Equity} \times 100\%$$
$$= \$207.9 \text{ million}/\$857 \text{ million} \times 100\%$$
$$= \mathbf{24.2\%}$$

As with other financial return metrics, the net marketing contribution is the all-important element:

$$\text{Return on Equity} = (\mathbf{NMC} - \text{Other Expenses} - \text{Interest \& Taxes})/\text{Equity} \times 100\%$$
$$= (\$509.4 \text{ million} - \$140 \text{ million} - \$163 \text{ million})/\$857 \text{ million} \times 100\%$$
$$= \mathbf{24.2\%}$$

Return on Capital

The shareholders' investment in a company in the form of owner's equity is one source of capital for the company. Companies also can borrow in the form of a long-term debt to obtain additional funds for investment. Stericycle's invested capital of $1.78 billion shown in Figure 16-11 includes long-term debt of $923 million and owner's equity of $857 million. Investors and financial management companies pay close attention to these investments of capital and a company's return on capital. Stericycle's return on capital is 11.7 percent, slightly higher than the company's estimated cost of capital:

$$\text{Return on Capital} = \text{Net Profit}/\text{Invested Capital} \times 100\%$$
$$= \$207.9 \text{ million}/\$1.78 \text{ billion} \times 100\%$$
$$= \mathbf{11.7\%}$$

FIGURE 16-11 STERICYCLE—OWNER'S EQUITY AND INVESTED CAPITAL

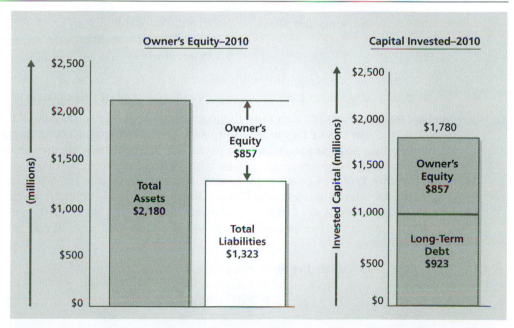

As with other financial return metrics, it is important to keep in mind the importance of the net marketing contribution. As shown in the following equation, the net marketing contribution is a key factor in achieving a return on capital of 11.7 percent:

$$
\begin{aligned}
\textbf{Return on Capital} &= \textbf{(NMC} - \text{Other Expenses} - \text{Interest \& Taxes)}/\text{Capital} \times 100\% \\
&= (\$509.4 \text{ million} - \$140 \text{ million} - \$163 \text{ million})/\$1.78 \text{ billion} \times 100\% \\
&= \textbf{11.7\%}
\end{aligned}
$$

SHAREHOLDER METRICS

Recognizing the importance of the customer satisfaction management and generally all aspects of market-based management with respect to net profit, assets, and return measures of profit performance, we can now broaden our discussion of the ways that market-based management affects shareholder value.[6]

As we examine the impact of market-based management on shareholder value, we will keep in mind that return measures of performance, such as return on sales, return on assets, and return on equity, are valid indicators of a business's financial well-being. They are excellent measures of financial performance. Shareholder value metrics, however, are especially important because they measure earnings per share, economic profit,[7] and the price-earnings ratio. All of these metrics, as summarized here, start with market demand and the efficiency of a business's effort to capture market share.

Earnings per Share—Net profit divided by the number of shares equals earnings per share. For Stericycle, a net profit of $207.9 million in 2010 and 87.4 million shares translates to $2.38 per share. This is up from $2.03 per share in 2009, as shown in Figure 16-12.

$$
\begin{aligned}
\textbf{Earnings per Share} &= \text{Net Profit}/\text{Number of Shares} \\
&= \$207.9 \text{ million}/87.4 \text{ million shares} \\
&= \textbf{\$2.38 per share}
\end{aligned}
$$

As with other financial return metrics, we can see in the next calculation the importance of the net marketing contribution, as it is a key part of net profit.

$$
\begin{aligned}
\textbf{Earnings per Share} &= \textbf{(NMC} - \text{Other Expenses} - \text{Interest \& Taxes)}/\text{Number of Shares} \\
&= (\$509.4 \text{ million} - \$140 \text{ million} - \$163 \text{ million})/87.4 \text{ million shares} \\
&= \textbf{\$2.38 per share}
\end{aligned}
$$

Economic Profit—Economic profit tells us the amount that is left over after the cost of capital is taken into account. This dollar metric is equal to net profit minus invested capital times the cost of capital, as shown here for Stericycle in 2010. In the computation, we set the cost of capital at 10 percent. Stericycle's actual cost of capital is probably less.

$$
\begin{aligned}
\textbf{Economic Profit} &= \text{Net Profit} - \text{Capital} \times \text{Cost of Capital} \\
&= \$207.9 \text{ million} - \$1.78 \text{ billion} \times 10\% \\
&= \$207.9 \text{ million} - \$178 \text{ million} \\
&= \textbf{\$29.9 million}
\end{aligned}
$$

FIGURE 16-12 HOW MARKETING PROFITS CONTRIBUTE TO FINANCIAL PERFORMANCE

Stericycle, Inc. (millions)	2009	2010	2011	2012	2013
Sales Revenues	$1,178	$1,439	$1,602	$1,791	$2,011
Percent Margin	50.3%	49.4%	50.0%	50.0%	50.0%
Gross Profit	$592.5	$710.9	$801.0	$895.5	$1,005.5
Marketing & Sales Expenses (% sales)	14.5%	14.0%	14.0%	14.0%	14.0%
Marketing & Sales Expenses[1]	$170.8	$201.5	$224.3	$250.7	$281.5
Net Marketing Contribution	**$421.7**	**$509.4**	**$576.7**	**$644.8**	**$724.0**
Marketing ROI	247%	253%	257%	257%	257%
Other Expenses (10% sales)	$149.5	$138.7	$160.2	$179.1	$201.1
Operating Income	$272.2	$370.7	$416.5	$465.7	$522.9
Operating Income (% sales)	23.1%	25.8%	26.0%	26.0%	26.0%
Interest & Taxes[2]	$95.8	$162.8	$166.6	$186.3	$209.2
Net Profit	**$176.4**	**$207.9**	**$249.9**	**$279.4**	**$313.7**
Earnings per Share[3]	**$2.03**	**$2.38**	**$2.86**	**$3.20**	**$3.59**

1. 75% of sales, general, and administrative expenses.

2. 2009–2010 are actual; 2011–2013 are estimated using 40% of operating income.

3. 87.4 million shares.

On the basis of Stericycle's 2010 financial results and an assumed cost of capital of 10 percent, the economic profit is $29.9 million. If we break down net profit to include the net marketing contribution, other expenses, interest and taxes, we can see the role of the net marketing contribution in determining the economic profit:

$$
\begin{aligned}
\textbf{Economic Profit} &= (\textbf{NMC} - \text{Other Expenses} - \text{Interest \& Taxes}) - \text{Capital} \times \text{Cost of Capital} \\
&= (\$509.4 \text{ million} - \$140 \text{ million} - \$163 \text{ million}) - \$1.78 \text{ billion} \times 10\% \\
&= \$207.9 \text{ million} - \$1.78 \text{ billion} \times 10\% \\
&= \$207.9 \text{ million} - \$178 \text{ million} \\
&= \textbf{\$29.9 million}
\end{aligned}
$$

Price-Earnings (PE) Ratio—A company's PE ratio is the ratio of the company's stock price to its earnings per share. The higher the PE ratio, the greater the risk to investment. For Stericycle, the PE ratio varied from 38.4 in 2009 to 36.5 in 2010, on the basis of the actual stock price and earnings per share at the end of each year. Figure 16-13 shows that Stericycle's stock price increased by 280 percent from 2005 to 2010. During the same period, the S&P 500 started with a stock price index of 100 and ended 2010 with the same index of 100. Dow Jones U.S. Waste & Disposal peers increased from an index of 100 in 2005 to an index of 142 in 2010, about half of Stericycle's 2010 stock price index.

Although a company's PE ratio changes over time, as do many other factors affecting stock price, we used a PE ratio of 37 to estimate earnings per share and to project the stock price for Stericycle in years 2011 to 2013. The company's future

FIGURE 16-13 STERICYCLE STOCK PRICE PERFORMANCE, 2005–2010

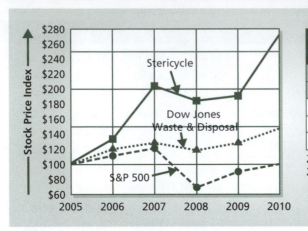

Year	Earnings per Share	PE Ratio	Stock Price
2009	$2.03	38.4	$78
2010	$2.38	36.5	$87
2011	$2.86	37.0	$106
2012	$3.20	37.0	$118
2013	$3.59	37.0	$133

2009–2010: Actual Results
2011–2013: MBM Forecast

net profit and earnings per share depend a great deal on whether Stericycle achieves its planned net marketing contribution as presented in Figure 16-12 and in the Stericycle Sample Marketing Plan in Chapter 14.

MARKET-BASED MANAGEMENT

To be profitable, a business needs to achieve above-average marketing and operational performance.[8] In fact, marketing and operational performance are interrelated. A business with a low level of customer satisfaction can expect sales to decline and customers to take longer to pay their invoices. These businesses have to spend more marketing dollars in an effort to keep sales at their present level. The combination of falling sales among current customers, higher accounts receivable, and more money spent on marketing influences the results of all the marketing and financial metrics that are used to measure a business's performance.

The central theme of this and the previous editions of *Market-Based Management* has been that businesses with strong market orientations empower themselves to develop marketing strategies that

■ Deliver high levels of customer satisfaction and superior customer value;
■ Improve market position, sales, and profitability; and
■ Improve earnings and shareholder value.

Market-based management, as shown in Figure 16-14, creates a climate within a business that gives rise to a strong market orientation. A strong market orientation translates into a strong customer and competitor focus and a team approach that cuts across organizational functions. The result is a business that is in a highly favorable position to develop and deliver market-based strategies designed to attract, satisfy, and retain customers. Implemented successfully across a wide range of market situations, a market-based approach will deliver higher levels of profitability, cash flow, and shareholder value than will a cost-based approach.

We must always remember that the only source of positive cash flow is the customer. Technology, assets, and management are of little value without customers. The job of a

FIGURE 16-14 MARKET-BASED MANAGEMENT AND SHAREHOLDER VALUE

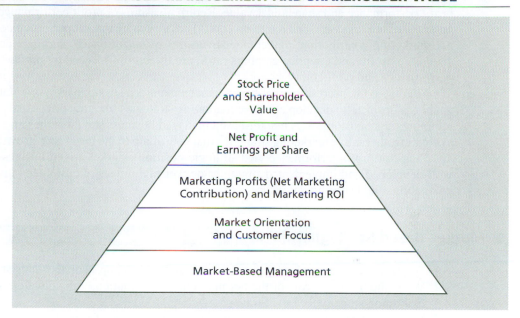

market-based business is to understand customers, the competition, and the market environment within the context of the business's technology, assets, and management capabilities and to render a market-based strategy that delivers superior levels of customer satisfaction, profitability, and shareholder value.

■ Summary

A marketing strategy and its supporting marketing mix strategies directly affect customers and sales revenues. They also affect margins, net profit, and marketing and sales expenses. These factors in turn lead to a net marketing contribution. Because operating and overhead expenses are beyond the control of marketing managers, the net marketing contribution plays an important role in evaluating the profit impact of marketing strategies. Throughout this book we have sought to determine the profit impact of a marketing strategy based on the net marketing contribution it produces. Marketing ROS—net marketing contribution divided by sales—is a percentage metric of marketing profitability based on sales. Marketing ROI—net marketing contribution divided by marketing and sales expenses—provides a measure of efficiency with respect to money invested in marketing and sales. Because these are percentage metrics, performance may be measured across a company and compared with publicly traded competitors and noncompeting benchmark companies in other markets.

Marketing strategies also directly affect assets. Changes in sales produce corresponding changes in accounts receivable and inventory. Likewise, a major increase in volume based on a particular marketing strategy may require additional operating expenses and investment in fixed assets. Marketing strategies affect both the numerator and denominator of the return on assets equation. This awareness gives us a much broader view of the impact of a marketing strategy on a business's profitability.

The net marketing contribution for each product-market strategy contributes to both profit performance and shareholder value. Return measures of profit performance (return on sales, return on assets, and return on equity) are driven by market performance and the net marketing contribution. Shareholder measures of performance (earnings per share, economic profit, and the price-earnings ratio) are directly influenced by product-market performance and profitability.

Finally, at the heart of market-based management is a strong market orientation that enables a business to develop effective marketing strategies for attracting, satisfying, and retaining target customers. A market-based managed business should at the same time be evaluating alternative marketing strategies that contribute to the business's growth, short- and long-run profit performance, and strategic position. Market-driven businesses with well-developed and implemented strategies deliver high levels of customer satisfaction, profitability, and shareholder value.

■ Market-Based Strategic Thinking

1 Why is it important for Stericycle to understand the profit impact of marketing strategies?

2 What should be the role of the net marketing contribution in the development of a marketing strategy for Levi Strauss?

3 Why is net profit often a misleading indicator of the profit impact of a marketing strategy for a company like General Motors?

4 Why are percentage metrics such as marketing ROS and marketing ROI important in explaining a company's marketing profitability?

5 How would you use the graphic on this chapter's first page and Figure 16-4 to assess Apple's 2010 marketing ROS (27.5 percent) and marketing ROI (323 percent)?

6 How does market demand for a company like Netflix affect its net marketing contribution and operating income?

7 Explain how Stericycle's market share gain affected its net marketing contribution, net profit, and return measures of performance.

8 How will Netflix's net marketing contribution and marketing ROI change if it succeeds with a plan to increase revenue per customer?

9 Why would companies with higher levels of customer satisfaction produce higher stock price indexes than those with low levels of customer satisfaction, as shown in Figure 16-7?

10 Why would a company with declining customer satisfaction not notice any immediate change in sales or profit?

11 How do investments in customer retention contribute to higher levels of profit performance?

12 Why should shareholders and Wall Street analysts be interested in a business's customer retention?

13 Explain how the net marketing contribution of a marketing strategy affects return measures of profit performance.

14 How do changes in customer retention affect shareholder measures of performance, such as earnings per share?

15 How does a marketing strategy affect the assets of a business? Why should a change in marketing strategy change the accounts receivable and inventory? When will the fixed assets change?

16 How would you use the net marketing contribution for a company like Clorox to forecast net profit and earnings per share?

17 Why should a market-oriented business with a passion for customer satisfaction produce higher levels of earnings per share and, therefore, have greater shareholder value than a business that is not market oriented?

Marketing Performance Tools and Application Exercises

The three interactive marketing performance tools and the application exercises outlined here will add to your understanding of the positive impact of market-based management on financial performance. To access the tools, go to **rogerjbest.com**. For the questions, you may enter the data presented to obtain the answers. You may also enter other data to see the results, and you may save your work.

16.1 Market Demand and Market Share
- Change market demand from $4,000 to $3,800, change market share from 25 percent to 22.6 percent, and evaluate how sales, profits, and financial performance change.

16.2 Percent Margin and Marketing Expenses
- Lower the revenue per customer to $1,480 and increase market share to

26 percent. Then return revenue per customer to $1,500 and increase marketing expenses from 17 percent to 18 percent. Which change has the greatest impact on performance?

16.3 Asset Management and Invested Capital
- Increase assets from $1,500 to $1,550 (which lowers the assets to sales ratio from 0.67 to 0.65) and evaluate the impact on financial performance. Then return assets to $1,500, decrease the long-term debt from $500 to $400, and evaluate the effects of this change on financial performance.

Notes

1. Stericycle, Inc., Form 10-K Annual Report for 2010 (February 28, 2011): http://www.stericycle.com/ ("Information for Shareholders and Analysts"), retrieved March 2011.
2. R. Kaplan and D. Norton, "The Balanced Scorecard—Measures that Drive Performance," *Harvard Business Review* (January–February 1992): 71–9.
3. E. Anderson, C. Fornell, and S. Mazvancheryl, "Customer Satisfaction and Stock Valuation," *Journal of Marketing* (October 2004): 172–85.
4. L. Aksoy, B. Cooil, C. Groening, T.L. Keiningham, and A. Yalcin, "The Long-Term Stock Market Valuation of Customer Satisfaction," *Journal of Marketing* (July 2008): 105–22.
5. "Customer Service Impacts Cash Flow," *Positive Impact* (August 1993): 5–6.
6. S. Schoeffler, "Impacts of Business Strategy on Stock Prices," *PIMS Letter No. 20* (1980): 1–9.
7. "Valuing Companies," *Economist* (August 2, 1997): 53–5; E. Olsen and T. Rawley, "Stock Prices Performance: Corporate Agenda for the 1980s," *Journal of Accounting and Corporate Finance* (Spring 1987): 3–15; B. Birchard, "Mastering the New Metrics," *CFO: The Magazine for Senior Financial Executives* (October 1994); B. Barmhardt, "Chicago's Top 100 Companies," *Chicago Tribune* (May 15, 1995); T. Rawley and L. Edwards, "How Holt Methods Work for Good Decisions, Determine Business Value More Accurately," *Corporate Cashflow Magazine* (September 1993); and B. Reimann, "Stock Price and Business Success: What Is the Relationship?" *Journal of Business Strategy* (Summer 1987): 38–50.
8. R. Hayes, "Strategic Planning: Forward in Reverse," *Harvard Business Review* (November–December 1985): 111–9.

GLOSSARY

acquisition cost The marketing expense to acquire one new customer.

adjacent segment strategy Strategy that targets a segment of customers who have slightly different needs than current customers.

advertising carryover effect Sales that occurs in periods after which an advertisement was run.

advertising elasticity The percentage change in volume per 1 percent change in advertising expenditures.

advocates Customers classified as "top performers" who buy nearly everything a company has to sell.

agents, brokers, and reps Salespeople who work for a business on a commission basis.

American Customer Satisfaction Index (ACSI) A company customer satisfaction index that varies from 0 to 100, calculated every year for companies in many industry sectors.

articulated market demand Current market demand, calculated on the basis of articulated customer needs.

assets Cash, accounts receivable, inventory, plant and equipment, and other assets.

backward-looking metrics Metrics that track performance over a previous period (such as a month or a year).

bottom-up marketing budget A budget based on the cost of each specific marketing task needed to implement a tactical marketing strategy.

bottom-up price presentation Presentation of the lowest priced product in a product line first, followed by the next lowest priced product, and so on until the highest priced product in the product line is presented.

brand assets Assets that a brand can attain, considering factors such as market leadership, awareness, brand relevance, reputation for quality, and brand loyalty.

brand encoding The process of branding products within a business using a combination of company name, name, sub-brand name, number, letter, product name, or key benefit.

brand equity The attractiveness of a brand due entirely to its name and brand image. Also can be measured as brand assets minus brand liabilities.

brand image The perceived image represented by a brand in the mind of a target customer.

brand interaction (information exchange) A communications strategy designed to create a customer dialogue and information exchange.

brand-action communications Marketing communications intended to prompt some type of customer action.

brand-image communications Marketing communications designed to build a brand image and create an emotional response.

brand-information communications Marketing communications designed to communicate specific information about the brand.

brand liabilities Liabilities a brand can incur as the result of customer dissatisfaction, environmental problems, product failures and recalls, lawsuits, consumer boycotts, and questionable business practices.

brand management The process of naming products and managing brands and brand-line extensions to attain maximum brand equity and a brand's full profit potential.

brand personality The personality a brand takes on based on human personality characteristics.

break-even market share The market share needed to reach a break-even volume.

break-even volume The number of units that a business needs to sell to produce an operating income equal to zero.

build brand (pure brand) A communications strategy that is designed to create an emotional customer response in an attempt to build an emotional connection between the target customer and the product.

capital The sum of the owner's equity and the long-term debt the company had incurred; the amount obtained from investors and lenders that the company has invested in its business.

captive customers Customers who want to switch to another brand but cannot because of the cost, difficulty in switching, or lack of options.

channel mapping The process of mapping all relevant channels from a pocket price to target customer prices or from target customer prices to the company's pocket price.

channel margin The margin required by a channel intermediary.

channel marketing expenses Marketing and sales expenses associated with a marketing channel.

channel partners Companies within a business's marketing channels that distribute, resell, or add value to a business's products and participate in the process of connecting businesses with end users.

channel system A particular combination of distribution and sales channels.

cluster analysis A statistical method that is used to group customers on the basis of similar needs into needs-based market segments.

cobranding Combining two brand names to create a new brand.

company benefits The level of perceived benefit that a customer attaches to a company or brand name.

competitive advantage A relative advantage of one business over another that is sustainable and that translates into a benefit that is important to target customers.

competitive benchmarking Comparing a company with another company outside the first company's industry (the benchmark company) with regard to a business practice in which the benchmark company is known for excellence.

competitive bid pricing Pricing a bid using the historical success of past price-to-cost bid ratios and the competitive bid situation.

competitive performance metrics Marketing metrics that gauge the competitive position of a product or business.

competitive position A business's position relative to a benchmark competitor's position with regard to price, product quality, delivery, new product sales, and so on.

competitor analysis Benchmarking a key competitor with respect to important areas of performance.

competitor orientation The degree to which a business tracks competitors' strategies and benchmarks its performance relative to competitors.

competitor reactive pricing Setting price on the basis of competitors' prices without knowing what customers need or would be willing to pay for the business's product or service.

competitor response price elasticity The percentage change in a competitor's price per 1 percent change in the price of a business's product.

complementary product A product that is sold along with another product.

conjoint analysis (measurement) A statistical method for deriving the customer preferences for different levels of price and product performance.

continuous innovation Incremental improvement of products along the same technology curve.

cost advantage A sustainable lower cost relative to competition.

cost of capital The percentage paid (like interest) for capital.

cost of purchase index A measurement of a product's relative advantage against competing products with regard to price and other customer cost considerations.

cost-based pricing Pricing that is determined by a business's cost and margin requirements.

cost-plus pricing Pricing based on the cost of the product plus a desired profit margin.

cross price elasticity The percentage change in volume in one product when the price is changed 1 percent in another product.

crowd sourcing Obtaining ideas from consumers on-line and through other social media for product improvements or new products.

customer focus The degree to which a business seeks to understand customer needs and use situations and tracks customer satisfaction.

customer life The number of purchase periods a customer is retained by a business.

customer lifetime value The net present value of cash flows produced over a customer's purchase life of a company's product or service.

customer loyalty Allegiance on the part of customers to a particular business or product.

customer loyalty index A measurement of a business's level of customer satisfaction, customer retention, and customer recommendation.

customer metrics Marketing performance metrics that track customer satisfaction, customer retention, customer loyalty, and customer value.

customer mix marketing budget A marketing budget based on the cost of new customer acquisition and retention.

customer profitability Gross margin per customer, minus the marketing and sales expenses needed to serve a customer.

customer reactive pricing Setting price by reacting to customer demands for price and product features but without taking into account competitors' prices and product positioning.

customer relationship management A process of developing and managing one-on-one relationships with target customers.

customer relationship marketing Marketing programs that are designed to personalize or customize a business's offerings to selected customers.

customer retention rate The percentage of customers retained from one purchase period to another.

customer satisfaction The degree to which customers are satisfied or dissatisfied with a business, product, or specific aspect of a product or service provided by a business.

customer satisfaction index An overall index of a business's customer satisfaction.

customer surveys Marketing surveys that track customer purchases, intentions to repurchase, and performance perceptions.

customer terrorists Dissatisfied customers who share with others the bad experiences they have had with a product, brand, or company.

customer touch points The opportunities that a business has to interact with customers and thereby improve the customer's experience.

customer value Total benefits minus the cost of acquiring those benefits.

customerization value pricing A pricing process in which customers build their own product and price.

database marketing A database of customer purchases, preferences, needs, and demographics that is used in customized marketing communications, product offerings, and extra services.

day in the life of a customer A market-research approach that involves observing from the customer's point of view the process of acquiring, using, and disposing of a product.

defensive strategy (defensive strategic market plan) A long-run plan to protect or exit a market position.

demographic trap Segmenting customers on the basis of demographics alone without considering customer needs.

differentiation advantage A sustainable product or service advantage that translates into a benefit that is important to target customers.

digital marketing The use of web sites, blogs, e-mail, podcasts, mobile, and social media platforms in marketing.

direct channel system A channel system that retains ownership of the product and requires management of its sales, distribution, and customer service.

discontinuous innovation Product improvement that occurs when the current dominant technology is abandoned for a new technology (e.g., the switch from vacuum tubes to solid state electronics).

discount factor The net present value of $1 when discounted from a particular point in time and at a particular discount rate.

discount rate A business's cost of capital.

discriminant analysis A statistical method that helps identify demographic characteristics that differentiate one needs-based segment from another.

disruptive innovation Product improvement that occurs when the current technology is altered over time (e.g., gradually making a product smaller, less expensive, or easier to use).

distributors Intermediaries who take title (ownership) of a product and are responsible for its sale and distribution and for customer service.

divest market strategy A defensive strategic market plan to exit a market by selling or closing down a business.

early adopters Customers who follow innovators in adopting a new product or technology (13.5 percent of the total).

early majority Customers who follow innovators and early adopters in adopting a new product or technology (34 percent of the total).

earnings per share Net profits (after taxes) divided by the number of shares held by shareholders.

economic profit Net income after taxes minus capital times the cost of capital.

economic value The customer value created by a product, as determined by the difference in the total cost of purchase of a competing product.

economic value-added Net profit (after taxes) minus the product of a business's investment in capital assets times its cost of capital.

empathic design process An observational approach to discovering the problems, frustrations, and inconveniences that customers experience when they use a company's product.

evocative brand names Brand names that are designed to evoke a feeling or perception.

exit market strategies Defensive strategic market plans that specify a market exit strategy, ranging from immediate exit with a divestment strategy to slow exit with a harvest strategy.

experiential brand names Brand names that communicate the experience provided by the product, such as the experience of discovery conveyed by the brand name Navigator.

external performance metrics Marketing performance metrics that track external performance with respect to market penetration, competitive position, and customer satisfaction.

fighter brands Low-priced, lower performance brands that are designed to fight low-price competitors while protecting the price-performance position of higher priced brands in a product line.

flagship brand The highest priced and highest quality brand in a business's product line.

flanker brand A product extension of a business's core brand.

floor pricing Setting a price using a financial requirement, such as gross margin or return on investment.

focus groups A discovery method in which target customers answer questions about a product or customer use situation.

forward buying The practice of buying a greater volume of a product when it is on sale.

forward-looking metrics Performance metrics that are leading indicators of future performance.

founder/owner brand names Brand names that are derived from the founder or owner of a business.

frontal attack strategies Competitive strategies that directly attack a competitor's market share.

functional brand names Brand names that are derived from the basic function of a product.

GE/McKinsey Portfolio A portfolio matrix that uses multiple factors to index market attractiveness (on the vertical axis) and competitive position (on the horizontal axis).

generic product life cycle The product life cycle for a product category, or "generic product market," such as cereal or cars.

gross profit Total sales minus total variable costs.

grow market share strategy A long-run offensive strategic market plan to grow market share.

harvest market strategy A defensive strategic market plan to slowly exit a market while maximizing profits.

harvest pricing Raising price in a series of steps in an effort to improve margins and maximize gross profit until the product exits the market.

heavy-up message frequency A period during which a business increases its advertising effort.

high potentials Profitable customers who are not yet loyal to a product or business.

horizontal brand-line extension Extending the brand to a line of related products.

horizontal market opportunity A market with closely related substitute products.

indirect channel systems Channels in which intermediaries take ownership of a business's product and take the responsibility for its sale and distribution and for customer service.

industry analysis A structural analysis of a competitive environment that is based on competitor entry/exit, buyer/supplier power, substitutes, and competitive rivalry.

ingredient cobranding Adding a brand name to another product's brand (e.g., "Intel inside" on Dell and Compaq computers).

internal performance metrics Performance metrics that are internal measures of a business's operations.

innovators The very first customers to adopt a new product or technology (2.5 percent of the total).

in-the-box strategy Internal strategy that lacks both customer and competitor intelligence.

invented brand names Brand names that are created from root words, partial words, or names that are poetic constructions on the basis of the rhythm or the experience of saying the name.

inventory turnover The number of times an inventory is sold per year.

knowledge advantage An advantage in both customer and competitor intelligence that a business has over its competitors.

laggards The last customers to adopt a new product or technology (16 percent of the total).

large-segment strategy A segment strategy that is focused on the largest market segment in a market.

late majority The customers who adopt a new product or technology after 50 percent of the market has already adopted it (34 percent of the total).

lead-user analysis An examination of the ways in which innovators and highly involved early adopters use a new product, which can offer insights into how a product can be improved or a new product developed.

life-cycle cost analysis A method for discovering the total amount that a product costs a customer over the usage life of the product.

low-cost leader pricing Setting price on the basis of cost of production, in an effort to have the lowest price in the market.

loyal customers Customers under the broader classification of "top performers" who always repurchase a business's products or services.

margin per unit The selling price of a product minus all the variable costs associated with producing, distributing, and selling the product.

market adoption forces Market forces that affect the rate of new-product adoption.

market analysis An external analysis of market demand, customer needs, competition, distributors, and environmental forces that influence market demand and customer behavior.

market attractiveness The relative attractiveness of a market on the basis of market forces, competitive environment, and market access.

market-based management Delivering superior customer value and company profitability by having a strong market orientation and managing the markets.

market-based organization A business that is organized around markets and that uses market units as profit centers.

market-based pricing Pricing on the basis of the needs of target customers, competitors' product positions, and the strength of a business's product, service, or brand advantage.

market definition A specification of market scope that makes clear who the current and potential customers are.

market development index The ratio of current market demand to market potential (maximum market demand).

market focus A business orientation that is focused on customers and competitors.

market infrastructure Channel intermediaries and channel influencers who shape opinions and communicate information about a business and its products.

market orientation The degree to which a business has a strong customer focus and competitor orientation and works as a team across functions to develop and deliver a market-based strategy.

market penetration strategies Offensive strategic market plans that are designed to further penetrate existing markets or enter new markets.

market performance metrics Marketing metrics that track the attractiveness of a market.

market potential The maximum market demand that should occur when all potential customers have entered a market.

market segmentation View of a market that groups customers into segments on the basis of similar needs and differentiating demographic characteristics.

market share The percentage of current market demand obtained by a business.

market share index A hierarchy of market share factors (such as awareness, availability, interest, intention to buy, and purchase) that results in an estimate of market share.

market vision A broad view of the market based on a fundamental customer need that goes beyond existing product solutions.

marketing advantage A sustainable advantage over competitors in channels of distribution, sales force, or marketing communications.

marketing analytics Analytical concepts and tools that allow a company to conduct performance measurements that create specific marketing metrics.

marketing earnings per share (EPS) The net marketing contribution of a business or product divided by the number of shares, which provides a metric on the extent to which the marketing effort contributes to earnings per share.

marketing expenses All fixed expenses associated with selling, marketing, and managing a marketing strategy that is targeted at a particular market.

marketing mix A combination of the four Ps (product, price, promotion, and place) designed for a specific target market.

marketing performance metrics Metrics that track how a product or business is performing with respect to market performance, customer performance, competitive performance, and marketing profitability.

marketing planning process A process that starts with a situation analysis; continues with a specific strategic market plan, a tactical marketing strategy, and a marketing budget; and which results in a performance plan.

marketing productivity The amount of the net marketing contribution that is produced by a strategy per dollar of fixed marketing expenses.

marketing profitability The net marketing contribution for a product, business, or company.

marketing profitability metrics Net marketing contribution, marketing ROS, and marketing ROI.

marketing profitability portfolio A portfolio matrix that shows the positions of products or markets relative to marketing ROS on one axis and marketing ROI on the other.

marketing return on investment (marketing ROI) The net marketing contribution divided by marketing expenses for a product, business, or company.

marketing return on sales (marketing ROS) The net marketing contribution divided by sales for a product, business, or company.

marketing strategy The year-to-year marketing mix plan that will guide an overall strategic market plan to a desired marketing and profitability objective.

mass collaboration A web-based methodology that is designed to allow customers, professionals, suppliers, and employees to share their ideas with respect to improving existing products or developing new ones.

mass customization An individualized marketing mix in which products, prices, promotion, and place are customized to the individual needs of a niche market or individual customers.

mass market A market that is not segmented; all customers and potential customers are treated as one group.

mass personalization Individualized marketing communications that recognize individual customers by name, purchase behavior, needs, and demographics.

message frequency The average number of times a target customer recalls seeing or hearing an advertisement in a given period of time.

Millennials The generation that has been entering the consumer market since about 2000.

misfits Customers classified as "nonprofits" who will not remain customers due to a poor fit with the business's product; as a result the business will never recover the cost of acquiring these customers.

mixed channel system A combination of direct and indirect channels whereby a business reaches, sells to, and serves some customers, but intermediaries reach, sell to, and serve others, or a business and intermediaries interact with the same customers at different customer touch points.

monetizing strategies Strategies that minimize marketing and sales investment and seek to maximize cash flow.

morphemes   Parts of words that are used to create brand names.

multi-dimensional scaling   A statistical method that helps a business understand customer perceptions of competitors and their preferences for products.

multi-segment strategy   The combination of two or more separate and distinct marketing mix strategies (the four Ps: product, price, promotion, and place) that were created for different needs-based market segments.

needs-based segmentation   Market segmentation on the basis of customer needs and/or the benefits they seek in a particular buying situation or to solve a particular problem.

net marketing contribution (NMC)   Gross profit (sales times percent margin) minus the marketing and sales expenses incurred to produce it.

net present value   The value in today's dollars of a cash flow that occurs over time, using a discount rate.

net profit   Sales revenues minus all expenses including taxes and interest.

new-market entry strategies   Offensive strategic market plans that are designed to enter new markets.

new opportunities   A business's first-time customers ("new potentials") or returning customers ("win-back customers") who are not yet profitable but who, if well managed, may become loyal and profitable.

niche market (segment) strategy   A strategy that targets a small segment of a market often overlooked or ignored by large competitors.

oblique strategies   Indirect, noncombative competitive strategies that lead competitors to follow a business's competitive moves.

offensive strategies (offensive strategic market plans)   Long-run plans (intended to span 3 to 5 years) to penetrate markets or enter new markets.

one-on-one marketing   Building one-on-one relationships with the key customers whom a business wants to retain.

operating expenses   Overhead expenses that are not the direct result of marketing activities.

operating income   Sales minus all expenses before taxes and interest.

optimizing strategies   Strategies that seek to optimize the marketing mix and marketing investment needed to maximize profits.

original equipment manufacturers (OEMs)   Businesses that manufacture new products from component products they buy from other manufacturers and suppliers.

penetration pricing   A strategy of setting low prices to achieve a high market share or high-volume position.

perceived value pricing   Pricing to create a greater customer value based on customer perceptions of product, service, and company benefits, and the perceived cost of acquiring those benefits.

perceptual mapping   A display of competing products that considers their relative substitutability and includes customers' ideal products as determined by the strength of the customer preference for each competing product.

performance-based value pricing   Selecting a price that when combined with other performance features yields a total score (value) greater than competing total scores derived from a conjoint analysis.

performance plan   A summary of strategic thinking, given a particular market situation, that results in a sales plan, marketing and sales budget, and marketing profit plan.

performance scorecard   A summary of a business's marketing performance using selected marketing performance metrics.

performance timeline   A forecast of market and profit performance metrics that spans the next 3 to 5 years.

plus-one pricing   Adding at least one differentiating feature that allows a product to price slightly above competing products that lack this product or service feature.

pocket price   The actual price paid to a company for a product after all discounts, sales commissions, shipping charges, and other transaction costs are deducted.

pocket-price bandwidth   The percentage difference between the lowest pocket price and the highest (a business's different channels or regional markets produce different pocket prices).

portfolio analysis   An evaluation of a product, market, or business with respect to market attractiveness and competitive advantage.

price elasticity   The percentage change in unit volume for a product per 1 percent change in price.

price per unit   The selling price of a product or service.

price premium   The dollar amount, or percentage, by which the price of a product exceeds competing products.

price-earnings ratio   The price of a share of stock in a business divided by the business's earnings per share.

prisoner's dilemma   A price situation in which businesses are forced to follow downward price moves by competitors in order to remain competitive.

product adoption forces   Product forces that affect the rate of new-product adoption.

product benefits   The overall benefit that a customer derives from the product performance and features.

product bundling   Combining for sale two or more products at a total price that is lower than the price a consumer would pay to purchase each product separately.

product differentiation   The degree to which a business's product is meaningfully different from and superior to competing products, as perceived by customers.

product life cycle   The life of a product as it progresses from introduction through growth, maturity, and decline.

product life-cycle portfolio   A product portfolio positioned along the product life cycle on the basis of percentage of total sales.

product life-cycle profit index   A profit index that is based on the percentage of a business's sales at different stages of the product life cycle.

product life-cycle/share development portfolio   A strategic market-planning portfolio that uses the product life cycle on the vertical axis and the share development index on the horizontal axis to depict a combination of profitability and growth.

product line advantage   A competitive advantage due to a broader product line that offers customers more choices and that contributes to a higher level of profits.

product line extensions   Products that are added to a product line under an umbrella brand that is well known and has an established reputation for quality.

product line positioning   A planned sequence of alternative product offerings that differ in product performance and price.

product line scale   The effect of product line extensions or deletions on the cost of producing and marketing a line of products.

product line substitution   The degree to which the sales of products are cannibalized with the addition of substitute products to the product line.

product positioning The relative value of a business's product features and price in comparison with competitors' product features and prices, from customers' perspective.

product quality differentiators Unique aspects of a product that differentiate a company or brand from its competitors.

product quality enhancements Features that a business offers in its product that are not offered in competitors' products.

product quality emotional enhancements Factors, such as a business's reputation for high quality, that foster a special bond with customers.

product unbundling Offering for sale an individual product that is normally sold as part of a product bundle.

product-focused A business that is focused internally on product development and that utilizes marketing primarily as an advertising and sales function.

product-market A market definition that defines the specific intended market of a product.

product-market diversification The degree to which a business has different products across different markets.

promotional price elasticity The percent volume increase per 1 percent price decrease during a price promotion.

protect strategy A defensive strategic market plan in which a business develops a marketing strategy to protect its competitive position and market share.

pull communications Marketing communications that are directed at end-user customers in an attempt to motivate target customers to seek a business's products (i.e., pull the products through the channel).

pure promotion (stimulate action) A communications strategy designed to stimulate action, often to motivate purchase.

push communications Marketing communications that are directed at intermediaries in an attempt to motivate them to sell a business's products to target customers (i.e., push the products through the channel).

quality aesthetics Product and service attributes that affect the perceived quality of a product.

quality drivers The critical product and service attributes that drive customer perceptions of performance.

quality enhancers Extra product and service attributes that enhance customer satisfaction.

quality killers Product and service attributes that do not meet customer expectations of performance at a high level all the time.

reactive strategies Strategies that are based on either customer intelligence or competitor intelligence.

reduce-focus pricing strategy A defensive market strategy that uses a planned reduction in market share (by reducing the focus to a smaller number of customers) to improve profitability.

reference price The price customers would pay for the full-featured product offered in the customerization value pricing process.

relative cost A business's cost per unit relative to a competitor's cost per unit.

relative market share A business's market share divided by the share of the market share leader competitor or next largest share competitor.

relative price A business's price divided by the price of a competitor or the average price of several competitors.

relative product quality An overall relative index that is based on customer perceptions of each aspect of product

quality of a business's product compared with a competitor's product.

relative service quality An overall relative index that is based on customer perceptions of each aspect of a business's customer service compared with a competitor's service.

repeat customers Customers who demonstrate a high level of repeat purchase but who are not loyal and also buy other brands.

retention cost The cost of retaining one customer over a given period of time.

return on assets The net profit produced by a business divided by its total assets.

return on capital The net income after taxes produced by a business divided by its investment in capital.

return on equity The net profit produced by a business divided by its owner's equity.

return on sales (ROS) The net profit produced by a business divided by its total sales.

reverse innovation/invent to order A process that starts by listening to lead users articulate "what they want but cannot get" from present products, followed by an effort to create value with a new product that addresses these unfulfilled needs.

sales revenue The price times the volume sold for each of the products sold by a company.

segment attractiveness The attractiveness of a segment on the basis of market forces, competitive intensity, and marketing access to the segment.

segment identification The demographic characteristics that distinguish one needs-based segment from other needs-based segments.

segment marketing mix strategy A marketing mix that is developed specifically for a target market segment.

segment marketing profitability The net marketing contribution that a business derives from a particular market segment.

segment positioning The product–price position and value proposition developed specifically for customers in a given market segment.

segment pricing Pricing that is based on segment price sensitivity and customer need for additional product features or services.

segment strategy acid test A test of the segment product positioning strategy and value proposition that involves the proposed strategy and two competing alternatives.

served market demand The size of the target market to be served by the business.

service benefits The overall benefit a customer derives from the various components of service that a business provides.

service differentiation The degree to which a business's service is meaningfully different from and superior to competing products from customers' perspective.

service quality differentiators Those unique aspects of service that differentiate a company or brand from its competitors.

service quality enhancements Enhancements that competitors do not offer.

service quality emotional enhancements Service-related factors, such as a business's record for prompt and courteous service, that foster a special bond with customers.

share development index The percentage of current market demand obtained by a business.

share performance metrics Marketing performance metrics that are related to a product's market share, such as metrics for customer awareness, product availability, customer preference and interest, intent to buy, purchasing, and service quality, which work in a hierarchy to collectively produce a market share index.

situation analysis   An external analysis of market forces and an internal analysis of business performance that are used to identify key performance issues and guide strategic market planning and the development of tactical marketing strategies.

skim pricing   A high-price position that attracts a limited number of customers but is sustainable because competitors cannot match the business's competitive advantage and value proposition.

social media marketing   Marketing efforts that use online social marketing media, such as Twitter, Facebook, YouTube, and blogs.

social media marketing analytics   Specific marketing analytics that track online social media marketing efforts (e.g., the number of YouTube views).

social media marketing communications   Marketing communications that are designed specifically for online social media.

spinners   Customers under the broader classification of "unprofitable customers" who buy only when a promotion is offered and as a result are not profitable and not loyal.

strategic market definition   A broad definition of market demand that includes the business's served market and relevant substitute product-markets.

strategic market planning   The process of developing of a long-run (3 to 5 years) strategic market plan that includes specific performance objectives with respect to market share, sales revenues, and profitability over the planning horizon.

strategy implementation   The actions taken to implement, track, and adapt a tactical marketing plan derived from a specific strategic market plan.

subsegment strategy   A further delineation of customers within a segment on the basis of demographics or product usage.

substitute products   Products that can be substituted for one another.

supply chain management   The management of the flow of physical materials, information, and money to and from a business and its suppliers and channel partners.

strengths, weaknesses, opportunities, and threats (SWOT) analysis   A summary of these factors uncovered in a situation analysis.

tactical marketing strategy   A 1-year marketing mix strategy (the four Ps: product, price, promotion, and place) for a particular target market and specific strategic market plan.

target market   A collection of customers on whom the business has decided to focus in building a marketing mix strategy.

team approach   The degree to which a business works across functions as a team to create and deliver market-based customer solutions and implementation strategies.

test market   A test of a product in an isolated market in which sales can be tracked and evaluated to determine the impact of a new product or a variation in the marketing mix.

tipping point   The inflection point in the product life cycle curve where market demand shifts from slow market growth to an exponential rate of growth.

top-down marketing budget   A marketing budget that is based on a certain percentage of sales.

top-down price presentation   Presentation of the highest priced product in a product line first, followed by the next highest price product, and so on until the lowest priced product in the product line is presented.

total customer experience   The satisfactions and challenges that customers encounter during all aspects of acquiring, owning, using, and replacing a product or service.

trade-off analysis   A research technique that uses customer preferences for different combinations of price, product, service, and company benefits, the results of which guide a business in its product development, service offerings, and pricing decisions.

two-tier marketing channel   A channel and sales system that involves two or more intermediaries.

umbrella brand   A core brand that is well known and under which brand extensions can be easily introduced.

unarticulated market demand   Market demand that has not occurred because customers have not recognized a need for a product or product feature.

underachievers   Customers under the broader classification of "high potentials" who are loyal (they buy often) but who are not profitable or are minimally profitable (they buy in small amounts).

unprofitable customers   Customers whose purchases are too small or too few to cover the business's cost of acquiring them.

untapped market opportunities   The gap between current market demand and market potential, also called the "untapped market potential."

value in-use pricing (value pricing)   Pricing to create a dollar savings for a customer on the basis of a lower total life-cycle cost compared with a competitor's total life-cycle cost.

value map   A graph of relative performance and relative price.

value proposition   A short statement that communicates how a product or business creates value for target customers.

value-added resellers (VARs)   Businesses that buy a variety of components from several manufacturers and package them as a system for certain market applications.

variable cost per unit   All of the variable costs associated with the sale of one unit.

variance analysis   A breakdown of net marketing contribution that is based on actual and planned performance and that enables a better understanding of how a marketing plan achieved its results.

vertical brand-line extensions   Variations in the brand that add more variety and options for customers.

vertical market opportunities   Integration along the supply chain that starts with raw materials and moves vertically through different stages of production, distribution, sales, and service.

volume   The number of units sold of a particular product in a given period of time.

win-back customers   Customers under the broader classification of "new opportunities" whom a business previously lost to a competitor but who are buying again from the business and, if well managed, can become loyal and profitable customers.